AF836168

THE CURRENCIES OF CHINA

AN INVESTIGATION OF
GOLD & SILVER TRANSACTIONS AFFECTING CHINA

WITH A SECTION ON COPPER

BY

EDUARD KANN
Member, Shanghai Exchange Brokers' Association

FOREWORD BY

JULEAN ARNOLD
American Commercial Attaché, Peking

SANFORD J. DURST
Numismatic Publications
New York, N.Y.

Copyright
©
1978

Sanford J. Durst
133 E. 58th Street
New York, N.Y. 10022

Library of Congress Number 78-56484

ISBN 0-915262-22-3

Originally Published by

Kelly and Walsh Ltd.
Shanghai, China
1926

All rights reserved. May not be reproduced without the permission of the publisher in writing.

This book has been produced with an attractive, durable cover. It is the opinion of the publisher that paper dust jackets are ecologically wasteful, and for that reason are not provided.

FOREWORD.

A knowledge of the intricacies of silver exchange and silver currency in their relations to gold and gold transactions in China is essential to success in import and export trading with this country. The success of many a foreign trade transaction hinges upon exchange. The essentials in the China currency situation and Chinese banking and the instruments of credit in China are a necessary factor in the equipment of the foreign trader. Fortunately, Chinese bankers and Chinese business men are realizing the importance of currency reform, particularly the necessity of a uniform currency for China. Foreign business interests will benefit greatly through this much needed reform. However, in order to make their influence felt, the foreign business men in China will find it necessary to secure for themselves a clear understanding of the essentials in the Chinese currency situation. They will not only help themselves in their trade relations with China through such an understanding but will place themselves in a position to be helpful toward effecting the necessary reforms.

Mr. Kann's compilation on the currencies of China offers the material necessary to an adequate knowledge of this important factor in Chinese commercial and financial life. Thus, as one interested in foreign trade with China, I am pleased to recommend the careful perusal of this publication as outlined by Mr. Kann.

JULEAN ARNOLD,
American Commercial Attaché, Peking.

JUNE 19, 1925.

FOREWORD TO THE REPRINT EDITION

Understanding the intricacies of Chinese currency from the standpoint of the student of the late 1970's is difficult, so difficult that today's numismatist is severely handicapped in his pursuit of knowledge.

The complex inter-relationships of China's gold and silver currencies, whether in ingot or bar form or coined into convenient money form, are almost beyond comprehension today. Since the heyday of the gold and silver standards in China in the last two decades of the 19th century and first two decades of this, almost three generations have passed.

Numismatics 50 years ago was not the exacting discipline of learning it has become today, especially in backward China. Yet men were at work even then recording for posterity the nuggets of wisdom which we need so much to look back on the pages of that era in the Far East.

Towering head and shoulders above other researchers into the numismatic byways of pre-Communist China was one man—Eduard Kann.

In 1926 Kann wrote his first great masterwork on Chinese numismatics and economics, "The Currencies of China," the book which lies open before you. It records in minute detail the history and background of metallic currencies in the Middle Kingdom—gold, silver and copper—and examines their relationships with each other and with the currencies of other lands.

Twenty-seven years later, in 1953, he published his second great lifework, "Illustrated Catalog of Chinese Coins." Either work would have assured him a niche in the shrine of China's Numismatic Hall of Fame (were there such a place), but both works—combined with hundreds of lesser literary efforts—leaves him standing alone at the pinnacle of that shrine.

In 1966, when the Second Revised Edition of Kann's "Illustrated Catalog" was published by the late Sidney Frey, I felt honored to write its introduction. I feel even more honored to pen these few words of introduction to Sanford Durst's publication of the 1926 opus, because, in the ensuing dozen years, Eduard Kann has come to exert an even more awesome influence on Chinese numismatics, and his name is now better known.

"The Currencies of China" has been long out of print, and it is needed today for a more complete understanding of China's metallic moneys. Kann even delves into such fascinating areas as regional gold mining, the Chinese mints, efforts to introduce a true gold standard, and the use of foreign trade dollars in China.

As a young man, Kann left his native Vienna in 1901 to work for a London banking firm, and the following year the bank transferred him to his first post in China, the bank's Shanghai branch.

The young Austrian liked China and things Chinese. China and its people liked him. For 47 years he was to consider the country his home.

During the Chinese Revolution of 1911-1912 he was associated with the Russo-Asiatic Bank in Shanghai and later in Japan. Still later he became manager of the Russo-Asiatic Bank branch in Changchun, Manchuria. Married in 1913, he moved often in the bank's employ, serving in the branches in Vladivostok, Hangchow and Chefoo.

As World War I opened Kann found himself, an Austrian, working for a bank of his country's enemies, the Russians. His widow, Margaret, recalls that at one point her husband's life was endangered by a Cossack detachment in Changchun.

Leaving the Russo-Asiatic Bank, he resided in Peking 1915 to 1917, and later joined the Banque Industrielle de Chine, a French institution, 1917 to 1919. In the 1920's he was associated with the Chinese American Bank of Commerce and finally, in the 1930's, undertook to operate on his own as a bullion broker. In this he was successful, having achieved an enviable reputation through publication of this volume.

He remained a bullion broker in Shanghai until just before the fall of that city to the Communists in June, 1949. He made his home in Hollywood, Calif. from then until his death in 1962 at age 82.

Untiring and methodical in its treatment of the subject matter, "Currencies" became the pattern for all Kann's precise later works in numismatics, and in philately, archeology, history and other subjects.

It is my hope, as well as that of the publisher Sanford J. Durst that you come to know the author as well as the book as you use this volume. He was a warm and wonderful human being.

Russell Rulau
Iola, Wisconsin
July, 1978

PREFACE.

China, for centuries past, has been a most interesting field for research in every branch of science. By virtue of its enormous size, the high degree of its civilisation—dating from prehistoric times—its attainments in the fine arts and the characteristic industry and culture of its people, the country has been made the subject of close investigation. There is scarcely a branch of science which has not been minutely examined and described by the investigator of things Chinese. Reference works have been written in almost all foreign tongues, on the literature, the language and the arts of China. Publications setting forth the country's mineral resources, its means of communications and its trade, are numerous and often of a high standard of merit. But there is a noticeable lack of authoritative literature on China's currency—a subject which is equally important to the country and to the world at large, and which compensates for its many intricacies by the very great interest and practical value attaching to so fascinating a topic.

In A.D. 1868, Baron F. von Richthofen set out on a journey of investigation which took him through the entire length and breadth of China and her outlying dependencies. The results of his discoveries, extending over years, have been laid down in a book which has since become a standard reference work on China. Although the purpose of his journey was mainly one of geological investigation, von Richthofen has availed himself of the opportunity to record his impressions of every phase of the life of the Chinese people. There is probably no single aspect of China and her enormous population which has not been treated except the one which plays so important a rôle, viz., money. In fact there would appear to be a tendency on the part of most of the writers on subjects concerning China, to avoid the discussion of the country's currencies.

Authoritative literature on China's monetary system is not altogether wanting. H. B. Morse's writings on Chinese currency are of the highest standard and have become dictum. But they are too much condensed and are intended principally to serve historical purposes. The changes in China's monetary system, consequent upon the establishment of the Republic, are of a far-reaching nature and have not yet found a place in Mr. H. B. Morse's standard work. The various foreign publications on the world's monetary systems have reserved but little space for that of China, in spite of its genuine interest and importance to the commerce of the entire world.

It is therefore with the firm conviction of an existing want, and the sincere attempt of filling the need, that I have undertaken the task of writing a book on the currencies of China. It is a work intended, above all, to serve the requirements of the practical banker and merchant, and, incidentally, to answer the requirements of the historian, the statistician and the general student of matters relating to China. The book is the result of my twenty-five years of experience with practical banking in many parts of China. It discusses solely the metallic currencies of the country, not only for the reason that these are the backbone of China's monetary system, but also because of the fact that metallic currencies alone lend themselves to direct international arbitrage transactions. The history of banknotes in China is a long one and could not possibly have been embodied in this volume.

My book is divided into three sections: gold, silver, and copper currency. Undoubtedly the question of silver as currency is of paramount importance to the country's foreign trade. Yet gold for currency purposes has begun to play a rôle in China, the importance of which is not yet generally recognised; its connection with international arbitrage is a most intimate one. It is my belief that this endeavor is the first attempt to coherently describe the functions of gold in China as a medium of international arbitrage.

I have thought it useful to include in my work a chapter on the currency system of Hongkong, owing to the latter port's proximity to China, and on account of the intimate relations of the respective monetary systems.

My sources of information have been clearly mentioned, mostly in the text itself. Regulations, proclamations, historical items, etc., are often quoted verbatim, so as to make my study more composite and authoritative. I have purposely refrained from tendering advice and from suggesting how things ought to be; instead, I have endeavored to present a description of China's metallic currencies as they have been in the past, and especially how I found them at the present time. I have not had the good fortune of personal consultations with experts during the compilation of my book, which in consequence is likely to be open to the charge of omissions and errors, such as are probably inherent in most first editions of works of a technical nature. Friendly criticism will therefore be highly appreciated and turned to good account.

E. KANN.

SHANGHAI, *February, 1926.*

TABLE OF CONTENTS.

SECTION 1.

GOLD AND GOLD TRANSACTIONS.

SECTION 2.

SILVER AND SILVER TRANSACTIONS.

SECTION 3.

COPPER AND COPPER COINAGE.

APPENDICES

INDEX OF FORMULÆ

THE CURRENCIES OF CHINA

CHAPTER I

GOLD AS CURRENCY IN CHINA

IN ANCIENT TIMES

GOLD was never legal tender in China and is not likely to be chosen as the standard of currency for a long time to come. On the other hand there is undoubted authority for the assertion that gold, unminted, was recognised in China as early as 1100 B.C. as a measure of values and subsequently as a suitable medium for circulation. Its use as such did not influence copper cash from remaining the principal currency; but gold was occasionally employed in settlement of large payments, which otherwise might have presented difficulties of transport.

According to the well-known orientalist Terrien de Lacouperie, who bases his statement on the Annals of the former Han Dynasty, gold was first legalised as a medium of circulation in 1091 B.C. In the 13th year of Tcheng, second King of Tchou, his minister established the nine treasury offices.

The currency, metal and silk, was then regulated. Gold in the shape of a square *tsun* (inch) was decreed to weigh one *kin* (catty).

In 221 B.C. the King of Ts'in assumes the title of She Hwang-Ti, "the first universal emperor." The use of pearls, gems, tortoise-shells, cowries, and tin was henceforth forbidden for currency. Issue of new currency, more convenient and smaller than that of 336, also inscribed P'an Liang, in round pieces with a square hole for bronze, and for gold in small cubes called Yh. These Yh's were similar to the ones issued during the Tchou dynasty and weighed also one *kin*.

In A.D. 10 Wang Mang established new sorts of currency in gold, silver, tortoise-shells, cowries and copper, in order to replace his coinage of knife money. The gold currency unit was called *kin* and had the value of 10,000 cash. No specimen of these gold pieces have survived to this day.

In A.D. 558–565 Sassian gold and silver coins circulated under the Northern Tchou dynasty in Shensi.

In his article on *A Gold Coin of the Ming Dynasty,*[1] Mr. A. M. Tracey Woodward refers to sources proving the use of gold as currency in remote times of China's history. He writes:

In the *Stewart Lockhart Collection of Chinese Copper Coins,* published in 1915, reference is made to gold. Of several thousand years ago, it quotes the Historical Records of Ssu-ma Ch'ien (司馬遷), or 史記 *Shih Chi,* for the statement that the media of barter under the Emperor Shun (舜), 2255 B.C., and during the Hsia dynasty, 2205–1818 B.C., were of three kinds of metal, described as yellow (gold); white (silver); and red (copper). Ma Tuan-lin (馬端臨) avers that at the commencement of the Han dynasty, 206 B.C., the place of pearls, jade, tortoise-shells and gems as currency, was substituted by gold and copper. Some Chinese authorities have declared that the casting of metallic money was done to tide over a temporary emergency, and that this casting ceased as soon as the stress of the times relented. A more extensive reference is made to gold on pages X–XI which is worth quoting in full. "The metals used for media of exchange have been gold, silver, copper, iron, white metal and lead. No gold coins have been cast, but in the Chou dynasty there were gold pieces an inch square and weighing one Chin 斤 or 16 Liang or ounces, from which they were called either 一斤 1 Chin, (one Chin), or 一金 1 Chin,—(one gold piece). In the Ch'in dynasty the gold unit was one 鎰 I or 20 Liang or ounces and was called (上幣) Shang Pi, money of higher value, copper being designated Hsia Pi (下幣), money of lower value. The Han dynasty reverted to the Chin or gold unit of the Chow dynasty and in the year 95 B.C. the Emperor Hsiao Wu Ti (孝武帝) had gold pieces made into the shape of the foot of the unicorn and the hoof of a horse to celebrate the auspicious appearance in that year of a white unicorn, of a famous horse and of gold in the Mountain of T'ai Shan. It appears, therefore, that during the Chou, Ch'in and Han dynasties there was a gold standard of value represented by a certain weight, as well as copper currency. As time went on the gold standard was replaced by a silver standard . . . " In

[1] Published in the *New China Review* for August, 1921.

Chuan 369, page 6, Kuan Tzu (管子) states that when Liu Kuang-shih (劉光世) was governor of Hupeh, *circa* A.D. 1130-1131, he cast gold, silver and copper coins, but Stewart Lockhart regards them as tokens, mentioning as reason therefore, that they were not strictly a regular Government issue.

"A curious passage in the *Su-chow-fu chih,* a book on Soochow topography, throws some light on old Chinese gold coins. It states that during A.D. 1175, one Han Yen-ku, then a brigadier stationed at Soochow, ordered the execution in that city of a Shupan, for acts of bribery. As a result of carrying into effect the extreme penalty, the culprit's property was confiscated, and an enormous amount of gold was found in his possession, given as—gold shoes, 15,720 taels; gold wine cups weighing 6,730 taels, five pecks of small gold lumps; gold coins, 60 strings, and other gold articles. Brigadier Han shortly afterwards lost his life in the Nu-chen Tartar War. The above statement, if correct, would lead to the inference that during the 12th century gold generally, and gold coins in particular, must have been immensely in circulation. Possibly this gold was the same as the coins mentioned by Kuan Tzu.

With regard to the use of gold in China we quote J. Edkins' work entitled *Chinese Currency:*

In the Han dynasty gold was cheap, because Buddhist image-worship had not then created a demand for this metal. Consequently it was in use for paying salaries and for market purchases. Gold is mentioned in A.D. 1375 as ten times the value of silver. A few years later ten piculs of rice were purchased with one tael of gold. This quantity was doubled in 1397 by a special enactment of the Emperor. In 1413, 30 piculs of rice were ordered by authority to be the equivalent of one tael of gold.

Gold leaf was profusely employed in the palaces of the golden dynasty. When the Mongols conquered this dynasty, very much gold was used in Buddhist temples. Kublai built the Wan-an-si (萬安寺) and ordered it to be richly ornamented with gold leaf, both on the images and on the windows and walls.

Buddhist liturgical books were written out with gold leaf.

An ancient writer (草木子) says that when gold is made into gold leaf it cannot be restored to its original condition. The beating out of gold leaf is highly wasteful. The Emperor about A.D. 490 forbade the manufacture on this account. A similar edict was promulgated in A.D. 1008. Neither gold nor silver were allowed to be in this form wasted. In A.D. 1040 a special edict made it criminal to glue gold leaf on Buddhist images.

In the year 1167 an edict forbade gold thread to be used on clothing. Those who wove and sold such clothing were treated as criminals and prosecuted.

In the year 1311 the Mongol Emperor published an edict forbidding the manufacture of gold leaf, of liquid gold to use in washing various articles, and gold thread woven into ornaments of dress.

The Chinese, when gold is beaten very thin, attach it to Buddhist images by means of gum. When gold is used as money it is in the form of bars or ingots.

In the Tang dynasty, gold leaf was used to paste laudatory sentences and titles on sacrificial tablets.

The same writer, in *Banking and Prices in China,* refers repeatedly to gold as a medium of circulation in China's early history:

In A.D. 977 the treasurer of Kiangsi stated in a memorial that in his province silk worms and mulberry trees were scarce, while gold was exceptionally cheap. The people suffered loss if silk fabrics were appraised at a low rate, while the revenue was insufficient if the value of gold was rated too high. According to the old system the best gold was priced at 10,000 cash a tael or ounce. There were three qualities of gold: best, second best and inferior.

In A.D. 1142 Cheng Kang Chung was acting as governor of the provinces of Szechuan and Shensi. He sent to the Emperor 10,000 taels of gold of Szechuan origin, the gold having been collected in payment of grain tribute.

According to historical records the Mongol Emperor Wu Tsung, at the beginning of the 14th century, issued banknotes, which were supposed to be redeemable against silver in denominations of from two silver taels down to two copper cash. One paper tael of silver was equivalent to 5,000 cash in the paper notes. One mace of gold was equivalent to one tael of silver.

This statement indicates clearly that in those times the ratio in China between silver and gold was 10 : 1 .

As regards the relation of gold to prices of silver in China towards the close of the 18th century, we find the following interesting statement in J. Edkins' *Currency in China:*

The Tung-hua-hsü-lu says that in A.D. 1782 a quantity of gold was confiscated in Chekiang province. It was 4,748 taels in weight. The Viceroy sent silver to Peking instead of gold, and it amounted to taels 73,594. This is a proof that exchange was then at 15½. This fact is noteworthy, because this was the gold value of silver in Europe in the last century. Foreign trade accounts for the ratio being the same in Europe and Asia during the latter half of the last century.

Of considerable interest is a find of an old Chinese gold coin at Shanghai. On 6th April, 1921, Chinese labourers, excavating the new site for the City Water works, dug up a number of jute bags containing coins inscribed "Hung Wu" (洪武) A.D. 1368-1398, "Hsuan Te" (宣德) A.D. 1426–1435, and "Chia Ching" (嘉靖) A.D. 1522–1566, all of the Ming Dynasty. The workmen lost no time in offering part of the coins for sale to passers-by, but soon policemen were attracted to the scene and carried off the money bags to headquarters. As soon as the Peking government heard of the find it telegraphed to Shanghai, ordering that the coins be promptly forwarded to the Capital. Mr. A. M. Tracey Woodward has kindly shown to the writer a gold coin originating from this particular episode. In a highly interesting essay, entitled *A Gold Coin of the Ming Dynasty* he has been endeavouring to solve the question as to its origin, notably regarding its right to be considered a coin or merely a charm. Mr. Woodward, in his modesty, does not venture to force upon the public his apparent conviction that the object referred to is a coin. After having referred to the despatch of the coins to Peking, Mr. Woodward writes *inter alia:*

Two weeks later, I was approached by a native money dealer who showed me the three-quarters of a gold coin inscribed 正德通寶, "Chen Te T'ung Pao" or Currency of the Cheng Te period. After purchasing the gold piece, although the dealer refused to explain the circumstances which led to its having been brought to me, he admitted that it came from the above find, adding in typical Chinese fashion: "more better no talkee other man how fashion have catchee this curio money, my belong only sell man."

Expert opinion was sought. One authority, whilst admitting its age, considered it more in the nature of an amulet; this latter, is, however, an ornament generally inscribed with mystic characters, not Currency of the Cheng Te period. Should we then consider it a charm coin? In its present state, the weight is 125.74 grams; diameter 48.5 mm.; thickness slightly irregular, from 7.5 to 8 mm.; cast in red gold, but altered on the surface into dull yellow by long contact with water filtered through alluvial soil; it is a little corroded. Exactly 15 millimetres are missing from the right angle diameter, we are thus able to determine the weight, when in its original entirety, at about 179.77 grams or say 4.75 taels. Allowing a quarter tael for corrosion and graft, for the officials under the Ming dynasty were no exception to their predecessors or successors. We have then a coin ostensibly made to represent five taels in gold, or the equivalent of 50 taels in silver, the ratio of these two metals being, in former times, 10 to 1. I have before me several 50-tael gold pieces minted during the T'ung Chih period, A.D. 1862–1874, *id est,* representing the nominal value of 50 taels of silver, the pieces themselves weighing about five taels of gold; this fact would apparently corroborate the above deduction, notwithstanding that the minted pieces were made at a considerably later period. Should we then, in view of the facts *ut supra* of a specific and standard weight having been given to the piece, designate it a charm coin?

In bringing these arguments to a close, it may be added that this gold coin was not excavated from a grave, but dug up within the ex-walls of the Shanghai City. Investigation into the annals of the locality where it was found, disclosed the important fact that a few hundred years ago, the Ground Tax Office of the City of Shanghai stood over the spot. What prompted the bags containing coins generally to be secreted underground, should not remain a mystery. Also, why in the city itself, beneath the very floor of that tax office and by whom, may be ascribed to a person connected with officialdom whose scruples were not immaculate, but who reaped as reward only the preservation of his secret unto eternal oblivion. Should we then conclude that this daily handler of currency of the realm was unconscious of the fact that this gold piece was only a charm coin? or must we grant him the benefit of the doubt, and assume that his power of discrimination between a gold coin as currency, was perspicuous enough to realize its complete impotency, were it only a charm coin? Further, if the solution of the mystery of this treasure trove is correctly ascribed to an employee of the Ground Tax Office, even if the piece was intended as a charm coin, was it tendered and accepted in payment of taxes? Circumstantial evidence and logical deductions reply affirmatively, and hence it follows that the charm coin nature of the gold piece *de facto* ceases, retaining its "charm" only where its power of purchase is concerned, much the same as the charm which money in our day possesses. It may be remarked incidentally, that not only did the coin occupy less space underneath the floor in the earth, but entailed less labour in burying it, probably precipitately done,—than its equivalent of 5,000 copper coins would have involved.

How then should this gold piece be classified? I have endeavoured to advance the pros and cons but the answer to the question remains indefinite.

IN MODERN TIMES

INTRODUCTORY

The foregoing essay on the recognition during China's early history of gold as a measure of value, affords convincing proof that the yellow metal has always been held in high esteem amongst China's commercial community, as an indisputable basis for the liquidation of financial obligations. But this assertion is not meant to imply that gold had at any time been selected as the pivot for China's currency system.

On the other hand it is on record that in A.D. 220 metallic currency was abolished, in order to be substituted as circulating media by commodities like grain, rolls of silk, etc. The new measure failed, of course, due to the unpreventable deterioration of commodities through frequent use.

It is not our intention to discuss at this stage the advantages which would be accruing to China if she had adopted the gold-standard. The merits of the case may conveniently be left over for another occasion. What we are concerned with is the fact that, at least until the close of the first quarter of the twentieth century, China has not been able to adopt the gold-standard for her national currency. As long as this is the case the metals composing China's monetary standards are practically merchandise to other countries trading with her. A common measure of values is thus eliminated, unless the respective prices of the metals concerned is comparatively stable. Notwithstanding the genuine interest attaching to this important topic we shall not enlarge on it at this stage.

Chinese Gold Coins.

While gold coins were never actually issued for circulation throughout the entire domain of China, they have temporarily circulated as recognised medium of exchange within certain provinces or dependencies of the vast country. Apparently there is no classified list available regarding the existence of Chinese modern gold coins. As the subject certainly is deserving of close investigation and attention, the writer is venturing to compile such a list which, though incomplete, may serve as an incentive to bring it up to date.

Since 1850 the following gold coins have been struck for circulation:

(1) Taiping tael gold coin.
(2) Turkestan gold tilla.
(3) Tibetan gold coin.
(4) The Yuan Shi Kai 10 and 20 dollars gold coins.
(5) The Yunnan 5 and 10 dollars gold coins.

Apart from these isolated instances, which denote a circulation, limited either as to space or to time, China has been devoid of gold coins meant to act as legalised medium of circulation.

Gold coins were struck in China in celebration of memorable events; but these undoubtedly bear the character of medallions,—of souvenirs. They were to prevent the world from forgetting the rule of three Presidents of the Republic and of one of China's provincial military governors.

These medallions have nothing to do with the currency question; even their numismatic value remains doubtful. It is solely with the idea of preventing students from confounding these issues with legalised coins that mention is made here of their existence.

Sun Yat Sen Commemorative Coins.

In commemoration of the Revolution various coins were struck with the bust of Sun Yat Sen, probably in 1912.

Amongst these were the one dollar and the 20-cents piece in silver. Both coins were also minted in gold and bear distinctly the character of medallions. The coins are described[1] as follows:

DOLLAR.—Same as the silver dollar, but struck in gold. Diameter 39.3 mm.; edge, milled.

Obverse.—Portrait of Dr. Sun Yat Sen in profile to the left, within a linear and beaded circle. Above 中華民國 "The Republic of China"; below 開國紀念幣 "Coin commemorative of the change of regime"; right and left a branch of peach blossom.

Reverse.—Within a linear and beaded circle an open wreath of rice and bean, enclosing the characters 壹圓 "One Dollar." Around the circle the legend * MEMENTO * BIRTH OF REPUBLIC OF CHINA.

Chinese legend in *ku-t'i* character. The character 民 appears on this, as well as on many other republican coins, in the form which became fashionable after the establishment of the Republic, viz. with the last stroke projecting (民). This is explained as symbolising the triumph of democracy (the people raising their heads) through the overthrow of the Manchu dynasty and the proclamation of a popular form of government.

TWENTY CENTS. Same as the silver 20-cents piece, but struck in gold. Diameter 23 mm.; edge, milled.

Obverse.—Head of Dr. Sun Yat Sen taken from the obverse of the One Dollar just described. Around, the legend * MEMENTO * BIRTH OF REPUBLIC OF CHINA.

Reverse.—The military and national flags of the Republic, within a beaded circle. Around the circle, Chinese legend (in *k'ai-shu* characters) as on the observe of the One Dollar.

The size of this piece, which does not bear any indication of value, is that of a 20-cents coin. There is no doubt that it was issued as a coin, as the Chinese legend on the reverse shows; but apparently very few specimens were struck, these being distributed amongst officials, and never put in circulation.

The Nyi Tsye Ch'ung Medallions.

When the Military Governor of Anhui Province, Nyi Tsye Ch'ung, retired in 1920 from the Tuchunship of Anhui, various medals were struck by the provincial Mint

[1] Dr. Giuseppe Ros in the *Journal of the North China Branch of the Royal Asiatic Society*, Vol. XLVIII, 1917.

at Anking as a souvenir of his rule.[1] The medallions were made in bronze, silver and gold in two types.

Type I of the gold coin weighs 17.63 grams, size 28¼ mm., thickness 2¼ mm., the rim is unmilled. It bears the legend meaning, "Souvenir of the Military Officer of Anhui" (安武軍紀念).

Type II measures 31½ mm., in diameter, weighs 21.84 grams, rim ungrained. The obverse reads: "made at the Anking Mint," with the characters meaning "Souvenir." "The Ninth Year of the Chinese Republic" (中華民國九年安慶造幣廠造紀念).

The Tsao Kung Medallions.

Immediately upon being "elected" by parliament to the presidency of China, Tsao Kung caused the constitution of the country to be promulgated without delay. In commemoration of this event a gold coin was issued in 1923 by the provincial Mint at Tientsin. The said coin is intended to serve merely as a souvenir and bears distinctly the character of a medallion. It weighs one Tientsin tael, is 1½ inches in diameter and contains about 60% pure gold. The obverse shows the bust of Tsao Kung, without inscription, while the reverse is adorned by two crossed Republican flags, above which the following inscription in Chinese appears in a half-circle (憲法成立紀念), meaning, "In remembrance of the promulgation of the constitution."

Yuan Shi Kai Medallions.

What might possibly have been intended as coins destined for circulation were turned, by force of circumstances, into gold medallions.

Mr. A. M. Tracey Woodward, who has made a close study of Chinese coins, has the following to tell in his essay entitled: *The Influence of Yuan Shi Kai on Chinese*

---

[1] Mr. A. M. Tracey Woodward in the *New China Review*, February, 1923.

Coins:—

The fruitless endeavours of Yuan Shi Kai to establish his Chinese Empire, did not react on silver coins only, but became visible on gold and copper coins as well. In gold a ten dollar piece was made. It was minted at Tientsin, and besides the legends, it bore the characters (Shih Yuan) reading "Ten Dollars." There is no doubt that the coin was made with the deliberate intention that it should be placed in circulation, for which purpose the dies were kept by the mint for future use; in November 1920, when I visited the mint, these dies were placed before my view. However, after the first lot (which was distributed to various officials as souvenirs) was minted, the political horizon became gloomy for Yuan Shi Kai and no more were made, at least during the life of the late President. Edges, milled; Average weight, 112.442 grains; Diameter, 21.5 mm.; Gold, 730 fine; Thickness, 1.5 mm. The weight given of 112.442 grains represents a very fair average, although it is evident that little care was exercised in preparing the planchets, as a uniformity in weight was not adhered to strictly, the size being the principal consideration; I have met with the two weight extremes of 126.782, and 93.369 grains, certainly revealing gross irregularity. The coins are found in the two different colours of Chinese yellow gold, and American red gold.

A second coin was struck under the very close observation of the mint governor, and only very few pieces were made; they were all sent to Peking accompanied by the dies, which I am informed were destroyed there. Each piece was put up in a neat native satin-lined specially-prepared case of Imperial yellow, being that hue with a tendency to orange, measuring $4\frac{1}{16}$ by $4\frac{1}{16}$ by $1\frac{9}{16}$ inches. The few pieces thus encased were presented only to a privileged few of Yuan Shi Kai's immediate entourage.

Both the obverse and reverse dies differ from Type I, even the cords of the epaulets are in the case more minutely detailed than in the subsequent copy. Edges, milled; Average weight, 694.871 grains; Diameter, 39 mm.; Gold, 850 fine; Thickness, 2.75 mm. In connection with the unsuccessful attempt above referred to, I have been informed that Yuan Shi Kai had also had prepared another gold piece depicting him in the garb of an Emperor in native dress, with the hat the Chinese Emperors wore centuries ago; but in the absence of more concise information, this rumour is only given here for what it is worth.

Apparently there was a third attempt made to produce a ten dollar gold coin with the portrait of Yuan Shi Kai; same was struck in Tientsin in 1916. It is unlikely that the coin referred to is synonymous with one of the pieces described by Mr. Woodward, as it differs in most details from the same.

Under the heading of *Coins of the Republic of China* Dr. Giuseppe Ros has published an illuminating article in the *Journal of the North China Branch of the Royal Asiatic Society* (1917). Referring to the gold coin under discussion Dr. Ros writes *inter alia:*

At the Tientsin Mint a die for a gold coin of the value of ten dollars, dated "the beginning of the Hung-hsien (period)" had been engraved, and from it only a limited number of pieces was struck under the strict watch of the mint director, for presentation to "His Majesty." I am told that the die was afterwards sent to Peking, without even a sample piece having been kept at the mint.

Continuing Dr. Giuseppe Ros describes the ten dollar coin as follows:

TEN DOLLARS. Gold (gr. 8.009, 850 fine) diameter 21; edge, milled.

Obverse.—Head of Yuan Shi Kai, same as on the silver series of the third year of the Republic.

Reverse.—A winged dragon grasping a bunch of arrows in the left fore claw, and a scepter in the right. Legend, above: 中華帝國 "The Empire of China"; below: 洪憲紀元 "The beginning of the Hung-hsien (period)," with the characters 拾圓 "Ten dollars," right and left.

The article on *Coins of the Republic of China* is well illustrated and contains also a photograph of the ten dollar piece described by Dr. Giuseppe Ros. Therefore it would appear that altogether three distinct Yuan Shi Kai ten dollar coins were minted, in order to be turned into medallions, though against the original intention of the designers.

Apart from the coins already referred to, the writer has seen the ordinary Yuan Shi Kai one dollar coin in gold. He has likewise been shown the Tientsin one tael coin (which has never been put into circulation) made of gold. It requires but little investigation to assert that those and similar productions are unauthorised and illogical. They have no legalised value, are merely the result of the whims of an undisciplined Mint director and represent for the collector of coins a curiosity without numismatic value.

After having made mention of these side issues, which are quite unconnected with any currency system, we may revert to the legalised issues of gold coins in China.

(1) *Taiping Tael Gold Coin.*

In A.D. 1849 an anti-dynastic movement was started by Hung Hsiu-Tsh'uan, who, after having adopted the Christian religion, proclaimed himself the brother of Christ. The movement originated in the province of Kuangsi, spread from there into Hunan and then along the Yangtze river to Nanking, which city was proclaimed the capital of the "Empire of Eternal Peace," the T'aiping Tien Kuo (太平天國). Therefore the name of "T'aiping Rebellion." The movement, which had become organised in 1850, found its end only in 1864.

During the rule of the T'aipings in Nanking a gold coin was issued there. As was the case with ancient Chinese coins the denomination was not inscribed on the coin, but was supposed to represent 25 taels of silver according to the ancient parities.

(2) *Turkestan Gold Tilla.*

In 1862, at a time when China was still engaged in wars against the foreigners and the T'aiping rebels, the Mohammedan tribe of "Tung Kang" rose in arms against the government.

The rebellion, originating in Kansu province, spread quickly amongst the Mohammedan population of Aksu, Harasher and Kutsh. A military leader, Yakub Beg by name, who had conquered Kashgaria, defeated the Mohammedan tribes in 1870, forcing these to submit to his rule. Yakub Beg then made Aksu the capital of his new empire, which was recognised as an independent state by Great Britain and Russia.

Until his death in 1877 Yakub Beg ruled over Eastern Turkestan, holding the territory against the Chinese from whom he had taken it.

He introduced a new currency into his domain, amongst which was a gold coin, very well engraved. It was made after the pattern of the Khanates of Khokand and Burhara and bore the name of Abdul Asiz, the then Sultan of Turkey.

The gold tilla weighed 58 grains and equalled in value 20 of the small silver coins named tanga, which exchanged nominally for 50 small Chinese copper cash, called *pul.* The tilla bears the Mohammedan year 1292 on both sides, which means A.D. 1874. On the obverse its inscription reads: "Darb dares—Sultanah Kaishgar" (struck in the capital city Kashgar). On the reverse it is inscribed: "Sultan Abd—ei—Asiz Khan."

During the reign of Kwang Hsu (1889-1908) gold coins of one and two mace denomination were current in Chinese Turkestan (Hsinkiang).

(3) *Tibetan Gold Coin.*

A gold coin was in circulation in Tibet during the reign of Hsuan Tung (1909-1911). The inscription, inclusive of the denomination, are in Tibetan, for which idiom the writer has not yet found a translator.

(4) *The Yuan Shi Kai Gold Dollars.*

Two gold coins were minted in 1919 in Tientsin, which were intended to serve as medium of currency. With the collapse of the ambitious scheme of Yuan Shi Kai the proposed plan of issuing gold coins was buried. About these coins Mr. Tracey Woodward writes in the *New China Review* as follows:

There are two more gold coins bearing the effigy of Yuan Shi Kai that remain to be mentioned, but these are legitimate productions from the Tientsin mint. I refer to the 8th year $10 and $20 pieces. These two pieces were the net residue of a trial to create a gold currency, which, due to a premature issue, resulted abortively. In the first instance the questions affecting a gold issue were not sufficiently deliberated upon, although the weights of the coins are harmonious as representing an unvarying intrinsic value, and furthermore, a sufficiently appreciable quantity of coins was not made, so that those which appeared were quickly absorbed by numismatists, bankers, curio hunters and others with similar tendencies, which quickly caused their disappearance from public hands. The legend (Chung Hwa Min Kuo Pa Nien Tsao) read: "Made in the 8th year (of the) Chinese Republic." Yuan Shi Kai's influence on present Chinese coins is well featured here, as the sole reason of his effigy on the pieces was that this would lend a greatly enhanced prestige to them. $20, Edges, milled; Weight, 128.865 grains; Diameter, 22 mm.; Thickness, 1.75 mm.; Gold, 850 fine. $10 Edges, milled; Weight, 257.963 grains; Diameter, 26 mm.; Thickness, 2 mm.; Gold, 850 fine."

(5) *Yunnan Gold Dollar Coins.*

To the military governor of Yunnan province, Tang Chi Yao, belongs the distinction of having placed into actual circulation large amounts of locally minted gold coins.

The writer, early in 1920, obtained a fair quantity of those coins from Yunnanfu for Mr. Tracey Woodward, who dealt authoritatively with *Tang Chi Yao Coins* in the *New China Review* for June, 1921:

There are two coins in gold, $5 and $10 respectively. The reverse shows the face of Tang Chi Yao rather plainly. Above the head, in a half circle, the following characters are inscribed: (Tang, Governor-General [of the] Military Government) 軍 務 院 撫 軍 長 唐.

On the obverse, we find the usual two republican flags with the star between the flag-poles. The legend in the upper half of the circle is 擁護共和紀念金幣 (Gold coin commemorating the defence of the Republic); and in the lower half 當 銀 幣 伍 元 (equivalent to 5 silver dollars). Size, 18.75 mm.; weight, 4.516 grams average; milled edges. The coins are in red gold.

The inscriptions of the $10 piece are identical with those found on the $5 coin, except the Chinese character for 10, in place of 5. The size of the $10 coin is 23.75 mm.; average weight, 8.510 grams; edges milled; exists in red and yellow gold.

There are sundry dies for each of the two coins and a corresponding number of different types is traceable.

So far goes the authority of Mr. Woodward. He does not state what the fineness of these gold coins is. The writer understands that it is 750/1000 on an average. The coins referred to deviate one from the other to a considerable extent, so that one can only speak in the "average."

The motives of Tang to produce gold coins are interesting. His independence from the Central Government at Peking as well as his effigy were documented and made immemorial on the silver coins and copper coins issued under his regime. The cause of adding gold to his enterprise was the fact that in 1919 the price of silver went so high, that gold cost only 18 taels an ounce. At this stage Tang's treasurer bought gold and turned it into coins at a large profit. When the price of silver dropped 50% from its high level, those gold coins gained considerably in value, though not quite to the same extent as bar gold, as they contained a more than fair margin for their creators. But their value increased rapidly and sufficiently to cause their disappearance from circulation. In other words Yunnan's gold coins have become merchandise. There was never an attempt on the part of the authorities to create a gold currency, but merely circulation. The Governor's Treasury gained by the issue and the people by the cessation of circulation.

The report on the trade of Mengtze for 1919, written by acting Customs Commissioner A. Pichon, contains the following passage relating to the Tang Chi Yao gold coins:

> To make up for the stringency of the money market the provincial Mint issued gold. Something had to be done to prevent a rush on the local government official *Futien* Bank, whose notes were becoming practically the only currency, so the authorities imported gold bars, gold leaves, British sovereigns, and American gold dollars, and these were turned into a $10 gold coin, which has been put on the market to relieve the uneasiness that was growing. These came out towards the end of October. As the value of silver had reached an exceptionally high price, gold as coin was cheaper and by issuing them the Mint Authorities hoped that it would remain in the province because the melting of these coins to take out the pure gold would not be a profitable operation.

Assays of these \$10 gold coins have been made and their value comes to about 8 silver dollars. The coin is reported officially to contain 25 cents of a K'up'ing tael weight of pure gold. In all it is said that \$9,000,000 worth of these coins have been placed in the market, but they have not as yet been accepted by the peasants, who believe them to be of brass, and they therefore would for choice rather take a banknote. This prejudice will certainly not last when they have realised that the coins really contain gold and that they are worth nearly as much as the silver piece. Other gold coins of the value of \$5, weighing 12½ cents of the K'up'ing tael weight, have been promised but have not yet put in an appearance.

The Chinese Maritime Customs, in their *Decennial Reports 1912–1921* (Vol. II, pages 352/353) deal with the unique subject in a detailed manner, which is here quoted *verbatim:*

In reviewing Yunnan currency for the last decade the two most prominent features that present themselves are the downfall of Yunnan money on other markets and the introduction of bimetallism. Nothing much of note happened in the money market during the years 1912-1918, but towards the end of the decade the local scarcity of silver, which has ever been pronounced in the history of Yunnan, eventually had the inevitable effect of depreciating local currency to such an extent as to render difficult, and sometimes impossible, all financial dealings with the outside world. So long as exports remained greatly in excess of imports and merchants could bring into Yunnan the silver obtained in payment thereof, so long was the premium on Yunnan currency in Hongkong maintained. Towards the end of the decade, however, the state of trade underwent a change, and merchants, encouraged by the unprecedented rise in silver, making purchases in gold-standard countries extremely profitable, and by the premium on local currency in Hongkong, turned their attention to imports to the disadvantage of exports. After the Armistice came the slump in tin, on which the province depends chiefly for its purchasing power; and, as huge quantities of this metal had been exported to Hongkong, where it remained unsold, the consequence was that silver was not forthcoming to replace that which had gone to pay for the imports. Mexican and new Republican dollars disappeared from the market, the embargo in 1917 on the export of all treasure from both Hongkong and Tonkin having cut off those sources of supply, and in consequence Yunnan was left to its own financial resources. Melting the good dollars and re-minting bad dollars, half-dollars, and subsidiary coins was the consequent outcome, causing matters to go from bad to worse.

The exchange on Hongkong, which had stood at a premium of from anything between 1 and 10 per cent. during the first 7 years of the decade, reversed completely, and towards the end of 1919 as many as 140 Yunnan dollars were required to purchase $100 Hongkong currency; the average discount on Yunnan currency, however, during 1919, 1920, and 1921 was about 27 per cent. The scarcity of silver led to a further issue of notes by the government bank, and a certain uneasiness amongst the natives became manifest, in consequence of which the provincial government, fearing a run on the bank and encouraged by the cheapness of gold, endeavoured to stem the tide by the introduction of bimetallism. Gold bars, gold leaf, British sovereigns, and American gold dollars were imported in large quantities, melted and re-minted into gold coins. A $10 gold coin made its first appearance in October 1919. This coin, which was struck in red gold, bore the effigy of the Military Governor T'ang Chi-yao (唐繼堯). Its size was 23.75 mm., and its average weight 8.510 grams, containing 0.25 K'up'ing tael weight of pure gold. $9,000,000 of these coins were reputed to have been put into circulation. They were followed shortly after by a $5 coin of similar design; the size of the $5 coin being 18.75 mm. and its average weight 4.516 grams, containing 0.125 K'up'ing tael weight of pure gold. There was considerable hesitation on the part of the peasants before they could be induced to accept these coins, but this prejudice was overcome finally, and they circulated freely, easing the situation to a considerable extent. The life of this currency, however, was short; the silver dollars in circulation were of such poor quality, and exchange rates on Tonkin, Hongkong, and Shanghai were so unfavourable, that "Gresham's law" had full play and "the bad currency drove out the good." Merchants realised that they saved considerable on remittances by melting the gold coins and exporting them in the form of gold leaf, gold bars, and even gold articles for personal adornment, and the exodus of General T'ang Chi-yao in February 1921 appeared to be the signal for the wholesale melting and exportation, in a different form, of these coins. They rose to a premium of 30 per cent. and shortly after became unobtainable.

Gold Bars.

Gold bars, in the shape of small oblong bricks, are plentiful within the borders of China. Since their fineness is determined and their weight fixed, they undoubtedly do form an ideal medium of circulating currency. In the North of China gold is met with in the shape of small shoes as nearly as possible 1000 fine. No means are available to the writer by which he could determine when gold in the shape of bars has first appeared on the market. Probably the period is a recent one, apparently dating back only one or two centuries.

Gold in the shape of bars has reached such importance that the subject demands discussion in a special chapter.

IMPORTS INTO AND EXPORTS FROM CHINA OF GOLD.

The following table, covering movements of gold to and from China from 1890–1924 inclusive, has been compiled from official Chinese Maritime Customs publications. The latter are noted for their accuracy and reliability. Yet in the case under review there are many factors which call for comment. First of all the value of gold imported and exported is in conformity with old established usage, given in the Customs currency, in Haikwan taels, *i.e.*, in silver. Though perfectly justified on the part of the Customs authorities, the statistical material represents perforce a fallacious picture, as it is seemingly an anomaly to indicate the value of gold in terms of the ever-fluctuating silver. In order to supply a partial remedy and enable students to form a correct view, we shall indicate, at a later stage, the average sterling rates for each of the 35 years under review.

Secondly, it stands to reason that in course of years appreciable quantities of gold are brought, or smuggled, into the country without Customs inspection. This remark relates not only to foreign gold coins brought in by travellers, but also to organised secret imports in passengers' baggage of gold and gold coins. The embargo on the export of gold, which existed in Japan since 1917, was repeatedly ignored by people who, in contravention of the law, smuggled Japanese gold yen coins out of the country and into China. Such transactions were not notified to the Customs authorities of either country. Furthermore, considerable quantities of alluvial gold, washed from the sands of the Amur river, were often brought across from the Russian river bank without incommoding the customs authorities of either one of the two nations concerned. These factors will account for a portion of the "invisible" imports of gold into China.

Mention ought to be made here of certain imports of gold coins which have entered China from Siberia between the years of 1917 and 1922. That particular flow of gold came principally as a result of the upheaval there and was an exceptional feature. We cannot do better than supplement our prefatory remarks with the more authoritative comment supplied by the Statistical Secretary of the Chinese Maritime Customs, which is quoted here *in extenso.* But first of all we should like to record the figures as supplied by the Customs authorities:

	Haikwan Taels
Total imports of gold, 1892 to 1924 . . .	264,933,000
Total exports of gold, 1892 to 1924 . . .	350,865,000
Difference	85,932,000

	Haikwan Taels
Net total imports of gold, 1890 to 1924 . .	98,047,000
Net total exports of gold, 1890 to 1924 . .	189,455,000
Excess of exports over imports 1890 to 1924 .	91,408,000

From the Chinese Maritime Customs Reports: Returns of Trade and Trade Reports, 1919.

TREASURE: According to the tables that follow this report there were imported into China, in bars and coin, gold of the value of 51 million Haikwan taels and silver 62 million Haikwan taels. These figures may be taken as fairly correct for silver, but do not include the considerable amounts of gold which reach this country from America by parcel post and are not declared at the Customs. A return for 1919, published by the American authorities and quoted in the *North China Daily News* of the 25th March 1920 gives the total shipments to the Far East as follows:

	Gold	*Silver*
Japan	G.$94,114,189	G.$ —
China	79,295,738	87,828,718
India	—	109,180,051

Converted at the average exchange rate for the year—Haikwan taels 1 = G.$1.39—these figures make the importation of gold, from America alone, 57 million Haikwan taels, and of silver 63 million Haikwan taels. The imports and exports of gold and silver for the past 10 years are shown overleaf, Hongkong and Macao being treated as domestic ports in the case of exports and as foreign in that of imports.

These figures leave out of account the very considerable sums brought into the country by returned emigrants and are probably otherwise defective. They show clearly, however, that up to 1913 China was a steady importer of silver, although the balance of trade as shown in the Customs Returns was as steadily against her. During the period 1914 to 1917, however, she parted with large sums to India, and the fact that the void then created had sooner or later to be filled, combined with the activity of the export trade and the universal collapse of paper as currency, is probably enough to account for the country's large absorption of silver during 1918 and 1919. The assumption, so freely advanced and adopted, that the Chinese of the interior have suddenly taken to "hoarding" in defiance to habits of centuries, would seem to be somewhat premature, to say the least. Exception made of the recent issue of $10 gold pieces by the Yunnan government—to the value, it is reported, of 9 million dollars—as a substitute for silver, gold does not yet enter into the monetary system of China, and the movements of this metal, as recorded in the above table, would appear to be mainly speculative. Large quantities were exported abroad during the first years of the war and brought back in the early part of 1917. When the embargo imposed by America and Japan in that year was removed by the former—in June 1918—China hastened to help herself freely, but there is no reason to suppose that she is going to be a large competitor for the world's supplies.

The Returns of Trade and Trade Reports for 1920 contain the following interesting remarks regarding the movements of gold to and from China.

Gold, as is known, does not in China perform the functions of currency. That it had, nevertheless, to be imported in such growing quantities in recent years may be explained by the fact that the abnormal high value of silver created a keen desire amongst the populace, extending even to the lower classes, to turn into gold whatever savings in silver they possessed, the favorite form being to purchase gold articles for adornment. This forced up the importation of gold in 1919 and at the beginning of 1920. Since silver has fallen in price the gold thus bought is reconverted into silver, with substantial profit to the owner, thus accounting for an ample margin of gold available for export during the latter half of 1920.

MOVEMENTS OF GOLD TO AND FROM CHINA.

(*Figures in Haikwan taels.*)

Compiled from statistics published by the Chinese Maritime Customs for the period from 1890 to 1924 inclusive.

Imports.

Year	In Bars & Dust	In Coin	Total	Net Imports
1890	—	—	—	
1891	—	—	—	
1892	100,727	244,990	345,717	
1893	210,181	250,902	461,083	
1894	23,465	16,012	39,477	
1895	263,342	41,432	304,774	
1896	761,452	6,714	768,166	
1897	1,045,794	80,508	1,126,302	
1898	859,621	9,004	868,625	
1899	693,388	2,648	696,036	
1900	863,059	5,350,562	6,193,621	1,202,315
1901	141,014	768,771	909,785	
1902	5,900	187,377	193,277	
1903	1,045,611	2,958,369	4,003,980	104,715
1904	5,669	9,925,181	9,930,850	8,446,415
1905	6,107	11,103,501	11,109,608	7,059,064
1906	7,633	6,998,883	7,006,516	3,840,123
1907	1,172,773	7,101,248	8,274,021	2,450,247
1908	106,500	1,407,925	1,514,425	
1909	45,802	967,995	1,013,797	
1910	5,906	3,553,518	3,559,424	
1911	40,823	3,982,707	4,023,530	1,532,882
1912	284,437	9,012,091	9,296,528	7,458,105
1913	84,143	2,981,147	3,065,290	
1914	11,106	850,061	861,167	
1915	47,485	771,342	818,827	
1916	8,447,997	11,455,120	19,903,117	11,800,849
1917	711,036	13,160,742	13,871,778	8,847,203
1918	408,955	819,367	1,228,342	
1919	32,910,493	18,168,150	51,078,643	41,182,214
1920	23,022,152	27,944,728	50,966,880	
1921	3,079,857	26,419,375	29,499,232	
1922	1,548,623	8,259,157	9,807,780	4,122,911
1923	998,590	9,147,308	10,145,898	
1924	259,512	1,787,249	2,046,761	
		Total in Haikwan taels	264,933,257	98,047,043

MOVEMENTS OF GOLD TO AND FROM CHINA.

(*Figures in Haikwan taels.*)

Compiled from statistics published by the Chinese Maritime Customs for the period from 1890 to 1924 inclusive.

Exports.

In Bars & Dust	In Coin	Total	Net Exports	Year
—	—	—	1,783,228	1890
—	—	—	3,693,246	1891
6,937,128	748,203	7,685,331	7,339,614	1892
7,919,125	1,893	7,921,018	7,459,935	1893
12,810,548	1,791	12,812,339	12,772,862	1894
7,133,832	48,590	7,182,422	6,877,648	1895
8,882,755	—	8,882,735	8,114,569	1896
9,634,950	3,094	9,638,044	8,511,742	1897
8,566,304	6,164	8,572,468	7,703,843	1898
8,327,543	8,272	8,335,815	7,639,779	1899
4,543,447	447,859	4,991,306		1900
5,510,378	2,034,720	7,545,098	6,635,313	1901
9,331,594	271,904	9,603,498	9,410,221	1902
3,666,166	233,099	3,899,265		1903
1,379,714	104,721	1,484,435		1904
2,439,105	1,611,439	4,050,544		1905
2,264,053	902,340	3,166,393		1906
5,350,352	473,422	5,823,774		1907
10,588,270	2,443,740	13,032,010	11,517,585	1908
7,218,014	617,153	7,835,167	6,821,370	1909
4,068,610	467,642	4,536,252	976,828	1910
2,103,515	387,133	2,490,648		1911
1,827,267	11,156	1,838,423		1912
2,730,748	1,720,142	4,450,890	1,385,600	1913
12,757,741	1,104,176	13,861,917	13,000,750	1914
17,959,904	251,136	18,211,040	17,392,213	1915
7,977,982	124,286	8,102,268		1916
4,700,424	324,151	5,024,575		1917
2,264,081	17,578	2,281,659	1,053,317	1918
4,966,276	4,930,153	9,896,429		1919
35,228,151	33,241,209	68,469,360	17,502,480	1920
35,997,523	9,962,104	45,959,627	16,460,395	1921
1,432,832	4,252,037	5,684,869		1922
8,181,329	7,631,782	15,813,111	5,667,213	1923
7,857,852	3,924,372	11,782,224	9,735,463	1924
Total in Haikwan taels		350,864,954	189,455,214	

Official average £ value of Haikwan tael: *(sight draft).*

1890	**5*s.*/2¼*d.***	**1908**	**2*s.*/8*d.***
1891	**4*s.*/11*d.***	**1909**	**2*s.*/7³/₁₆*d.***
1892	**4*s.*/4¼*d.***	**1910**	**2*s.*/8⁵/₁₆*d.***
1893	**3*s.*/11¼*d.***	**1911**	**2*s.*/8¼*d.***
1894	**3*s.*/2⅜*d.***	**1912**	**3*s.*/0⅝*d.***
1895	**3*s.*/3¼*d.***	**1913**	**3*s.*/0¼*d.***
1896	**3*s.*/4*d.***	**1914**	**2*s.*/8¾*d.***
1897	**2*s.*/11¾*d.***	**1915**	**2*s.*/7⅛*d.***
1898	**2*s.*/10⅝*d.***	**1916**	**3*s.*/3¹³/₁₆*d.***
1899	**3*s.*/0⅛*d.***	**1917**	**4*s.*/3¹³/₁₆*d.***
1900	**3*s.*/1¼*d.***	**1918**	**5*s.*/3⁷/₁₆*d.***
1901	**2*s.*/11⁹/₁₆*d.***	**1919**	**6*s.*/4*d.***
1902	**2*s.*/7⅕*d.***	**1920**	**6*s.*/9½*d.***
1903	**2*s.*/7⅝*d.***	**1921**	**3*s.*/11⁷/₁₆*d.***
1904	**2*s.*/10⅖*d.***	**1922**	**3*s.*/9*d.***
1905	**3*s.*/0¹/₁₀*d.***	**1923**	**3*s.*/5¾*d.***
1906	**3*s.*/3½*d.***	**1924**	**3*s.*/7⅞*d.***
1907	**3*s.*/3*d.***		

CHAPTER II

THE VARIOUS SHAPES IN WHICH GOLD IS USED IN CHINA

GOLD is a convenient object for a certain portion of the Chinese population to trade with. It is a favored form of investment for the people, because it does not deteriorate in substance, it never loses value through change of fashion, it is easily hidden or hoarded in case of danger and it offers the possibility of a chance to sell at a profit. The idea of using gold as a standard of currency in China has been no more than hinted at by some foreign economists.

The bulk of China's population does not know that gold is a commodity which has a fixed value and standard attached to it. People here have been accustomed all their lives to think and count in terms of copper and silver. It is quite natural therefore, that they should consider silver as "the golden calf" round which the universe is revolving.

Foreigners are convinced that gold is the pivot in the circle of metals and standards. And the Chinese are equally convinced that silver holds the place of honor. After all, both are right within their sphere.

In the absence of any definition emanating from the Chinese Government as to a legal monetary standard pertaining to the country, probably it will be admissible to style copper the currency of the poor and silver the currency of the rich people. In China gold is distinctly an article of trade, subject to wide fluctuations in price, notwithstanding the fact that the yellow metal is placed in a different category abroad.

The following are the principal shapes in which gold is usually met with in China:

(*a*) Chinese gold coins,
(*b*) Foreign gold coins,
(*c*) Jewellery,
(*d*) Gold dust,
(*e*) Gold leaves,
(*f*) Gold bars.

Chinese Gold Coins.

Chinese gold coins, having been fully described in the previous chapter, need not be referred to again here.

Foreign Gold Coins.

These are imported from countries where there is a free circulation of gold; which means that banknotes can be cashed against gold coins at par and that there is no export prohibition in force relative to the yellow metal.

The bank in China very rarely imports the coin for its own account. In almost every instance it acts on behalf of a Chinese client, who has agreed to pay a certain price either in taels or in telegraphic transfer of the same gold currency, plus charges and commission. The Chinese buyer, upon receipt, will turn the coin almost invariably into gold bars or gold leaves.

For the importing bank the matter resolves itself into a simple exchange transaction. If a Chinese buyer desires to place an order for the import into Shanghai of 100,000 gold dollars from San Francisco and pay in taels upon arrival of the shipment here, the importing bank will first ascertain at what rate of exchange it can cover itself locally, by buying in the open market 100,000 U.S. dollars, telegraphic transfer for ready delivery. Say the rate is 75 U.S. dollars equal to 100 Shanghai taels; consequently the tael equivalent will be

Shanghai taels	133,333.33
add 1% for freight, charges, interest, commissions, etc.	1,333.33
Total Shanghai Tls.	134,666.66

This is the sum which the importing bank will receive from its Chinese client upon arrival of the gold coin at Shanghai. The charges, which are variable, have been indicated here at 1% and are supposed to cover interest and commissions.

The Chinese buyer would also have the option to remit cover by cable through another bank. In such an event the importing bank will add its actual charges, interest, and a commission for its services. In short, the operation for the importing bank is merely on a commission basis and touches hardly the domain of arbitrage.

It is different with the Chinese buyer, who has entered into the transaction, because he sees a profit, or has good reasons for expecting certain benefits. The coins, upon arrival in Shanghai almost certainly will be melted down, in order to be converted into Shanghai gold bars and sold as such in the local market.

Technicalities:

The Chinese importer should know that:

(*a*) 1 U.S. 10 dollars gold piece is 900/1000 fine and weighs 0.5375 ounces troy.

(*b*) Gold, 1000 fine, is valued by the U.S. Mint at $20.6718 per ounce troy.

(*c*) 1 Shanghai gold bar weighs 10 Chauping taels and is 978/1000 fine.

(*d*) 100 ounces troy (1000 fine) are equal to 82.7815 Canton taels weight.

(*e*) 100 ounces troy (0.978 fine) are equal to 84.64366 Canton taels weight.

(*f*) 84.64366 Canton taels weight, at 102.50, are equal to 86.75933 Shanghai (Chauping) taels.

The first problem is to find the weight in Shanghai (Chauping) taels of U.S. $100,000 fine gold.

U.S.$100,000 ÷ 20.6718 = 4837.5081 ounces troy (1000 fine)
4837.5081 ounces × 86.75933 = 4196.98976 Shanghai taels weight, 978/1000 fine.

The same problem can be solved by means of a

Formula:

? Shanghai taels weight, 0.978 fine.	:	100,000 U.S. $ (1000 fine)
20.6718 U.S. $ (1000 fine)	:	1 troy ounce
100 troy ounces	:	86.75933 Shanghai taels weight, 0.978 fine

$$\frac{100{,}000 \times 86.75933 \times 0.978}{0.978 \times 20.6718 \times 100} = 4196.98976 \text{ Shanghai taels weight.}$$

The next problem will be to determine the value in U.S.A. currency of 1 gold bar of 10 Shanghai taels weight and of the usual fineness of 0.978. By U.S.A. currency is meant the gold dollar of the legal fineness of 0.900.

Formula I.

? U.S. dollars	:	1 gold bar of 10 Shanghai taels weight, 0.978 fine
1 gold bar of 10 Shanghai taels weight, 0.978 fine	:	11.78542 ounces troy, 0.978 fine
0.5375 ounces troy, 0.900 fine	:	10 U.S. dollars

$$\frac{10 \times 0.978 \times 11.78542 \times 0.978 \times 10}{10 \times 0.978 \times 0.5375 \times 0.900} = \text{U.S. \$238.267}$$

Formula II.

? U.S. dollars	:	1 Shanghai tael weight of gold bar, 0.978 fine
1 Shanghai tael, 0.978 fine	:	565.70 grains troy, 0.978 fine
25.8 grains troy, 0.900 fine	:	1 U.S. dollar

$$\frac{0.978 \times 565.70 \times 0.978}{0.978 \times 25.8 \times 0.900} = \text{U.S. \$23.8267}$$

Therefore the amount of 238.267 U.S. $ (gold 900/1000 fine) will be required to turn out 1 gold bar of 10 Shanghai Chauping taels weight and of a fineness of 0.978. Add charges and interest (variable), say 1%, and the real cost per bar would be 240.649 dollars.

Say the market rate for U.S. Currency, T.T., is G.$75 for 100 taels.

240.649 ÷ 75 = 320.865 Shanghai taels (currency) for each gold bar, ready delivery.

Should gold bars be quoted in the Shanghai market lower than 320.90 taels (for effective spot delivery), then it would not pay to import gold coin from America.

Only if the quotation is above 320.90 taels the transaction would turn out remunerative.

There is another method of calculation. The example given for the cost of U.S. $100,000 at 75, plus 1% charges, resulted in a total of Shanghai taels 134,666.66

$$134{,}666.66 \div 4196.98976 = 320.865$$

The figure of 4196.98976 is *a constant* and represents the taels weight equivalent (0.978 fine) of 100,000 U.S. dollars.

Charges vary but were, in 1925, as follows:

Freight San Francisco-Shanghai on $100,001	—1/8%	$125.00
Insurance	„ 1/8%	125.00
5% Interest for 25 days	„	340.00
Landing charges, petties, etc.		60.00
Compradore's brokerage		100.00
Boxes, San Francisco commissions		100.00
Total		$850.00

N.B.—In April, 1925, a premium of 2 per mille was asked at Shanghai for insurance on gold shipments to San Francisco. Such premium was to cover all risks, including theft and pilferage, as well as war risk.

Gold Yen Coins.

The principles underlying the problem of arbitrage with Shanghai gold bars and U.S. gold coin apply equally to the Japanese gold yen. In fact, these two were the only gold coins which were ever imported into China in noteworthy quantities, if we overlook the temporary and accidental inflow of Russian gold coins to Shanghai during the prolonged upheaval in Siberia, between 1918 and 1920.

Since 1917 there has been an embargo on the export from Japan of gold coin. Towards the close of 1924 the value of Japan's currency had declined about 25%. By April of 1925 the yen had appreciated in price, but was then still about 20% below parity. It is generally expected that in course of time the yen will steadily gain in value, until brought to gold parity once more.

Be this as it may; we are here primarily concerned with the principle, which we propose to elucidate.

The Japanese gold yen is of a fineness of 900/1000 and weighs 12.86 grains. This means that the contents of gold, 1000 fine, are 11.574 grains.

The Shanghai tael weight is 565.70 grains.

The charges for shipping gold coin from Japan to Shanghai are:

Freight about 1/8%	.125
Insurance 3/4°/₀₀	.075
Landing charges, boxes, etc.	.050
Total	.25

Interest is not included. Neither has Japan correspondent's commission or compradore's brokerage yet been considered.

Formula.

? yen	:	1 Gold bar of 10 Shanghai taels weight
1 Shanghai tael	:	565.70 grains troy
1000 grains troy	:	978 grains pure
11.574 grains, 1000 fine	:	1 yen
100.25 with charges	:	100 yen

$$\frac{10\times 565.70\times 978\times 100}{1000\times 11.574\times 100.25} = 4.76822976$$

Divide the price of gold bars at Shanghai by the constant of 4.768. The result will be the tael rate at which telegraphic transfer on Japan can be bought in order to pay for the shipment of coin.

Say gold bars are quoted at Shanghai at 321 Shanghai taels:

$$321 \div 4.768 = 67.32 \text{ taels.}$$

		Sh. Tls.
100 yen are		67.32
Less interest 7 days at 7%	.08	
„ compradore's commission 1 °/₀₀	.06	
„ Japan correspondent's commission ½ °/₀₀	.03	
„ ¼% profit	.15	
		.32
Net . .		Sh. Tls. 67.00

Therefore, unless one can buy cable transfer on Japan in Shanghai at the rate of 67 taels for 100 yen, it will not pay to import coin from Japan.

Jewellery.

Chinese jewellery made from gold is as nearly as possible 1000 fine and very soft. No importance is attached to the artistic finish of the average object, as is witnessed by the goldsmith's fee amounting to one dollar for every tael's weight of gold. Like gold bars and gold leaves, gold ornaments (rings, bangles, bracelets, etc.) bear the inscription *Dzu Tsu* (足赤) meaning pure gold, and have the name of the goldsmith's shop embossed.

The ornaments referred to are studded very rarely with precious stones, are seldom presented as souvenirs, and have practically no artistic features. They are acquired with the knowledge of their intrinsic value and because they are easily hoarded in case of danger and quickly pawned or sold in the hour of need. The usual gold ornaments in China are purchased and sold by weight, the fineness being uniform and known.

The foregoing remarks do not mean to imply that the country is entirely without gold ornaments of high artistic value. The Museum in Peking contains numerous golden objects, originating from the past glories of former Imperial Courts. Those articles are of great value and are remarkable for their artistic splendour.

But these are rare exceptions. In China, jades, pearls, porcelains and ivories are sought for as presents or as adornment, much more than golden objects. In short, golden jewellery in China is merchandise.

It is difficult to estimate the proportion of the quantity of gold used in the Occident annually for industrial purposes (jewellery, watches, ornaments, plating, etc.), and coinage. Probably 50% of the total is a conservative estimate regarding the former employment.

In China gold entering the country is nearly in its entirety converted into bars and leaves, and scarcely 5% is handled by the jeweller.

Yet this is no case against China and no argument against gold.

Gold Dust.

The quantity of alluvial gold found in the shape of dust in China is very small indeed. Gold dust is sold by the gold washers either to smelting shops direct, or oftener through middlemen. Gold in the form of dust is unimportant in the gold trade of China.

Gold Leaves.

At Canton—It is principally at Canton where gold leaves are produced, though Hongkong is the trading center. In North China, as well as at Shanghai, gold leaves are little known and little used.

The manufacture of gold leaves from either gold bars or gold coin (chiefly American double eagles) has been for many years an established industry in Canton. Gold in this shape is refined in such a manner, as to be as near as possible 1000 fine. The manufacturer's seal, as well as the year, are embossed on each leaf, also the notation of *Dzu Tsu* (足赤), "sufficient red."

The leaves (which are made in various sizes) are inserted in a sort of book and then placed in a box, holding from 50 to 100 Canton taels weight of gold leaves.

The purpose for which gold in this shape is produced is chiefly to enable people with small means to acquire gold in moderate quantities and to be able to hide it conveniently or to carry it unnoticed on the person.

It is especially the American double eagle which is used for the manufacture of gold leaves. United States gold coins are 900/1000 fine. The $10 piece weighs 516 grains troy, so that it contains 464.4 grains of fine gold. It will produce 0.801 Canton taels weight of gold leaves, 1000 fine.

The charge for converting coins into leaves (including the refining of the gold) is Small Coin $0.80 for one tael weight of leaf gold, which works out at Small Coin $0.64 for each double eagle. This charge is subject to change.

The quotations at Canton refer to one Canton tael weight of gold leaves against so many Canton taels weight of Small Coin dollar. Say 715 pieces of 20-cents pieces weigh 100 Canton taels, which means $1.43 (Small Coin) for one tael. If, for example, the quotation should be 42.25, it would mean that one has to pay 42.25 Canton taels weight in 20-cents pieces for one tael weight of gold leaves.

To find the parity rate, use the following:

Formula.

? Canton taels weight in Small Coin $	:	1 tael weight of gold leaves
0.801 tael weight of gold leaves	:	1 Double Eagle
1 Double Eagle	:	Cost in Small Coin $, plus $0.64 charges
1.43 Small Coin $	:	1 Canton tael weight in Small Coin

$$X = \frac{\text{Cost of 1 Double Eagle, plus \$0.64 Small Coin}}{0.801 \times 1.43}$$

The figure of 1.43 is variable, because the weight and fineness of the 20-cents pieces have varied considerably in course of the past few years.

At Hongkong—Gold leaves manufactured at Canton are retained in part within the country and the balance is exported to Calcutta, Singapore or Saigon. The export takes place from Hongkong in boxes, containing from 50 to 100 Canton taels weight of gold leaves in folders. One Canton tael weight is 579.84 grains troy.

The following used to be the procedure in connection with export of gold leaves from Hongkong. The exporter weighed the contents in the presence of a representative of the bank which had agreed to discount the drafts drawn against the particular shipment, usually at seven days after sight. The bank itself delivers the parcels on board the steamer.

At destination the bank will, immediately upon arrival of the steamer, take delivery of the shipment through one of its representatives, in order to avoid paying heavy storage charges.

According to a tariff issued in July, 1924, by Fung Mamter & Co., gold and silver refiners of Hongkong, charges there were as follows:

Melting charge for gold bullion — U.S. $1 for the first 1000 ounces, and $0.10 for each 100 ounces in excess of 1000 ounces.

Refining charge per gross ounce:

Gold 400 to 949¾ fine	U.S. $0.04
„ 950 to 1000 „	„ 0.02
With an additional charge for base content above 100/1000	„ 0.01

Between Hongkong and India—In connection with gold leaves exported to Calcutta from Hongkong the following problems may arise:

Formula 1.

? pence	:	1 rupee
X rupees (Calcutta price)	:	1 tolah
48.32 tolahs	:	15 taels weight
1 tael weight	:	Buying price in Hongkong $
1 Hongkong $	:	T.T. rate on India in pence

X = 0.31043 as constant

(Add charges and interest).

Formula 2.

? rupees	:	100 Hongkong $
X Hongkong $ (buying price)	:	1 Canton tael
15 Canton taels	:	48.32 tolahs
1 tolah	:	rupees price in India

X = 3.2213 as constant

(Without charges and interest).

Formula 3.

? Hongkong $	:	1 Canton tael weight (gold leaves)
100 Canton taels weight	:	322.133 tolahs
1 tolah (leaf gold)	:	Calcutta price in rupees
1 rupee	:	X Hongkong $

Constant 322.133

(Without charges and interest).

Multiply the constant by price of gold in India and divide by Hongkong price for pure gold.

---

1 tolah = 180 grains or 11.664 grams.

Between Shanghai and Hongkong—

Formula 4.

? Shanghai taels (currency)	:	1 Hongkong $
Price in Hongkong $	:	for 1 Canton tael weight
1 Canton tael weight	:	579.84 grains
553.2516 grains pure (weight of 10 taels gold, 0.978 fine)	:	price in Shanghai taels.

Constant 1.04806

In order to find the parity between the Shanghai tael and the Hongkong dollar multiply the constant by the Shanghai gold bar price and divide by the Hongkong gold leaves price.

Between Hongkong and London—

Formula 5.

? pence	:	1 Hongkong $
Hongkong price in $ for pure gold	:	per 1 Canton tael weight
1 Canton tael weight	:	1.208 ounces troy
1 ounce of pure gold	:	84.95 shillings
1 shilling	:	12 pence

Constant 1231.435

To be divided by the Hongkong price for pure gold.
Charges and interest to be considered yet.

Between Hongkong and Japan—

Formula 6.

? Hongkong $	:	100 Gold yen
1 yen	:	0.75 grams pure gold
31.1 grams	:	480 grains
579.84 grains	:	1 Canton tael weight
1 Canton tael weight	:	Hongkong $ price for pure gold

$$X = \frac{0.75 \times 480}{31.1 \times 579.84} = \mathit{1.996337\ as\ constant}$$

Charges and interest to be considered yet.

Multiply this constant by the Hongkong price for pure gold, in order to obtain the parity between yen and Hongkong dollar.

Between Hongkong and New York—

Formula 7.

? Hongkong $	:	1 U.S. $
800 U.S.$ is the price paid for	:	43 ounces gold, 0.900 fine
1.208 ounces troy	:	1 Canton tael weight of pure gold
1 Canton tael weight of pure gold	:	Price in Hongkong $

$$X = \frac{43 \times 0.900}{800 \times 1.208} = 0.04 \textit{ as constant}$$

Multiply the constant by the price of pure gold in Hongkong in order to obtain the Hongkong and the U.S. dollar parity.

For actual transactions consider charges and interest.

Gold Bars.

Gold bars are undoubtedly the most interesting and the most important link in the chain. It has therefore been decided to discuss this subject exhaustively in a separate chapter.

Industrial Uses.

About the extraction of gold in China by the native methods, about the manufacture of gold bars and gold leaf, Sir Alexander Hosie writes as follows in his book:[1]

> The usual native method of extracting the gold from the ore is as follows: The quartz is crushed, carried to the nearest running water, and washed in a basket lined at the bottom with a mixture of wood-oil and lime. The stone is washed away, and the gold sinking to the bottom is collected and placed in a bowl of quicksilver, which is then squeezed through a piece of cloth. The gold remaining in the cloth is then melted up and cast into ingots, which are sold to the goldsmiths at from Tls. 27 to Tls. 31 per Chinese ounce according to quality. It has now to be refined. The crucibles, which are bowl-shaped, are made of clay, coal-ashes, and sand, and are manufactured at Chungking, Lu Chou, and Chiung Chou. The crucible is first made red-hot in a charcoal furnace, described fully under "Silver," and the gold placed therein. As soon as the latter melts certain small proportions of saltpetre, borax, and arsenic are added to the molten metal, according to the amount of impurities it is seen by the operator to contain. The

[1] *Szechwan, Its Products, Industries and Resources.* By Sir Alexander Hosie. Shanghai, Kelly & Walsh, Limited.

saltpetre causes the gold to spread and allow the impurities to rise to the surface; the borax and arsenic mix with and attract these impurities to the side of the crucible, whence they are removed by means of an iron rod having a tooth-shaped hook at the end. When the impurities have all been eliminated, the crucible is seized by a pair of tongs and the molten metal poured into an iron bar-mould, whence the bar of gold is, on solidifying, removed again by tongs and plunged into cold water. It now appears as a yellow bar weighing about 10 or 12 Chinese ounces worth some Tls. 38 an ounce. I was told that the price in Shanghai was Tls. 42 an ounce but as Ch'engtu Tls. 95 are equal to Shanghai Tls. 100, the margin of profit cannot be very great. The gold is brought to the furnace by the owner, and the operator charges 100 cash for casting each bar, and hands over the crucible with its dregs, along with the bar, to the owner. The dregs are, I understand, further treated for any remaining metal. The moulds, as already stated, are of two sizes. The smaller bars measure 3½ by $\frac{9}{10}$ by ½ Chinese inches, and weigh about 10 Chinese ounces. These are stored as treasure or exported. The larger bars measure some 8 Chinese inches long, weigh about 12 Chinese ozs., and are mostly used for the manufacture of gold-leaf. One of these latter bars is beaten out on an iron anvil by hammer, the sheet during the process of hammering being heated from time to time in a charcoal fire to render the metal more ductile. When completed the sheet is cut up by scissors into 96 leaves, which are usually known as gold-leaf. These leaves are then placed in a charcoal fire in a stove with a sprinkling of a mixture of ground salt and dust between the leaves, and the whole covered with live charcoal. When the fire has burned itself out the gold leaves, each measuring $3\frac{9}{10}$ by $3\frac{1}{10}$ to 3½ Chinese inches, are removed, brushed, and washed clean in cold water. They are now ready to be manufactured into gold ornaments, circular gold leaves, and "Fo Chin," or "Joss Gold."

To manufacture circular gold leaf, known as "Hoyeh Chin," $\frac{8}{10}$ Chinese ounce of gold-leaf is taken and cut up into 1,000 small pieces, each of which is placed between two small sheets of black paper "Wu Chin Chih" made in Hang-chou Fu, in the province of Che-kiang, and the whole packed tightly in many layers of the tough paper called "P'i Chih" the bark paper of Kweichow, made from the inner fibrous peel of *Broussonetia papyrifera.* The packet is gummed firmly and beaten on a flat smooth stone by one man for two days, when the thin sheets of gold are removed more or less round in shape and about 2½ Chinese inches in diameter. The sheets are used for gold-plating.

To make "Fo Chin," or "Joss Gold" the circular sheets of the above are placed each between two square (nearly 7½ inches) sheets of the same black paper, and the whole enclosed as before in many layers of bark paper. The packet is now hammered on a smooth oval stone by two men seated opposite to each other for two days, one of the men holding the packet by one of its corners. The thin sheets are then removed, taken separately and spread on a slightly curved leather (horse) pad with a centre of cotton wool and a wooden handle attached to the centre underneath. Before the gold sheet is laid on the pad, however, the latter has a thin dusting of charcoal ash sprinkled on it to prevent the gold adhering to the leather. The edges to the sheet of gold are then squared by a long knife set in a narrow wooden frame and the parings are utilized for filling any holes or imperfections in the sheet itself, which is then cut up into small squares ¾ Chinese inch from six to twelve in number. Each of these tiny square sheets of gold is raised by knife, usually with the assistance of the breath, and placed between a fold of fine paper. In this form each sheet is valued at from two to three cash. They are done up in tiny bundles and used for gilding images, signboards, carved characters, and woodwork generally.

The black paper above referred to is universally used by the medicine shops for dispensing powders. The surface, being smooth and glossy, does not admit of the powder adhering to it—annoyance to which patients and nurses are frequently subjected in more civilized countries.

I may mention that a primitive blow-pipe is in common use among the gold- and silversmiths in Ch'engtu.

Left: A Gold Bar, 1000 Fine, Used by Goldsmiths. (Side view).
Right: Shanghai Gold Bar, 0.978 Fine. (Side view).
Each bar is equal to 10 taels weight. Nearly actual size.

Left: SHANGHAI GOLD BAR, 0.978 FINE.
Right: A GOLD BAR, 1000 FINE, USED BY GOLDSMITHS. 10 CHAUPING TAELS WEIGHT.

CHAPTER III

GOLD BARS

Description.

GOLD in the shape of bars plays a most important rôle in China. Gold bars are derived partly from golden articles, and to a larger extent from coins, melted down and refined to the degree required. In shape gold bars are small oblong bricks with rounded off corners. They weigh as nearly as possible 10 Shanghai taels.

In North China still may be found gold bars, weighing from 5 to 10 taels, having the shape of sycee and being as nearly as possible 1000 fine. However, bars of this shape which are used to hoard savings, are seldom encountered nowadays. They are of very little account to international trade or even to transactions within China.

Gold bars handled at Shanghai are in shape and size similar to those produced in modern times at Peking and Tientsin, namely oblong slabs weighing about 10 Chauping taels. Gold bars destined for export from Shanghai are often cast into bricks of 70 Chauping taels weight, as these are more convenient for handling. The cost of turning gold coin into gold bars has, in 1925, been about three Shanghai taels for every 10 Chauping taels weight. The following figures indicate the standard fineness of gold bars produced at Shanghai, Tientsin and Peking:

Shanghai bars	978	1000ths
Tientsin ,, ...	980	1000ths
Peking ,, ...	985	1000ths

Each bar is embossed with the firm name of the smelter, besides the year in which it was manufactured and the characters (金標), meaning "surface gold," *i.e.,* gold containing alloy.

The origin of gold bars has already been discussed when treating the import of gold coins, and therefore does not need to be referred to again.

The weight of gold bars is as follows:

Shanghai: 10 Chauping taels (366.71 grams).

Tientsin bars are 1.35% lighter in weight, which means that one Shanghai gold bar equals 1.0135 Tientsin gold bars in weight (361.325 grams).

Peking bars: one Shanghai gold bar weighs 1.0183 Peking bars (360.118 grams).

Legitimate Transactions in Gold Bars.

Gold bars have become of enormous importance to the financial markets in China, notably for Shanghai. They are sold for actual delivery by Chinese holders to banks, who will buy, whenever the parity permits it, for export abroad.

But the bulk of transactions in gold bars is made for delivery on settlement day (which at Shanghai is the sixteenth day of each month). Contracts for delivery exceeding two months are not permissible. There is a Gold Exchange, to which members send their representatives.

The full name in English of the said institution is "Shanghai Gold Stock Exchange, Ltd." Henceforth, when referring to it, we shall, for the sake of brevity, speak about it as the "Gold Exchange."

The dealings on the Gold Exchange influence the currency market all over China and reflect to a considerable extent the price of silver throughout the world.

Probably the question will arise in the mind of the reader why the Chinese have selected the gold bar as the basis of their financial operations.

The reasons are manifold. China is a country using silver for her internal commercial transactions. She receives, however, gold from abroad for her exports and

SHANGHAI GOLD STOCK EXCHANGE, LIMITED,
KIUKIANG ROAD, SHANGHAI, CHINA.

pays gold to foreign countries for her imports. Thereby the element of gold exchange is created.

The argument will arise to the observer why the Chinese operator does not deal in legally recognised gold coins of any foreign country, instead of in gold bars, whose organism is of much more complicated nature than that of the American Gold dollar or the Japanese Gold yen?

The answer is that his faith in foreign gold standards has been shaken by considerable depreciation of almost all countries' currencies and by a subsequent prohibition of export from those countries of gold in any shape, except jewellery. The gold bar is an object which anyone in China can acquire if he pays the price for it. It is merchandise and consequently not subjected to government restrictions. Finally, it is an object appreciated in spite of its complicated mechanism (or because of it), seeing that it has always been thus, since grandfather's time.

Transactions in gold bars on the part of Chinese operators date back some decades. Before the advent of the Great War gold bars were produced from imported coin, whenever the parity permitted this. And they were sold for the purpose of being exported abroad,—again when the parity permitted it; this means whenever there was a profit. In other words, originally operations in gold bars were arbitrage transactions.

Already in the beginning of the present century there existed an Association of gold dealers in Shanghai. The members dealt in gold with parties who had direct use for it, be it for adornment or for the more prosaic export abroad.

But there was no Gold Exchange. Such an institution had began already to take roots before the advent of the European war, and developed fully during that memorable period. To-day it commands the attention of the world, by means of its huge transactions and through its powerful influence on the price of silver. The Chinese operator will correct the last sentence and say instead "on the price of gold"; and he is right from his point of view.

Speculative Transactions in Gold Bars.

Gold bars at Shanghai are the object *par excellence* in which to speculate. The gold bar market at Shanghai does not immediately influence the markets of other places in China, which cannot follow the numerous and rapid changes. These are occurring every few minutes and keep on varying from 9 a.m. till 5 p.m.; business is interrupted for about one hour and a half for lunch. Even on Sunday mornings there are quotations on the Gold Exchange, though very limited business only is transacted on holidays.

Gold bars contracted for forward delivery against taels are bought and sold in Shanghai daily for huge amounts, with the idea of reversing the transaction before due date, and receiving or paying differences.

The Gold Exchange guarantees payment of differences to the winner and protects itself by asking for adequate margin deposits on contracts for forward delivery. As soon as there is a difference of five taels on the price of a gold bar (compared with the original contract price) the Exchange demands payment of the requisite difference.

A second "immoral" aspect of the gold bar market is the following: Chinese gold dealers, who are openly termed "the speculators" often see, or desire to see, silver prices lower or, at other times, higher.

They will therefore acquire an oversold position in any gold currency (U.S.$, £, yen) if they believe in higher silver prices. In the event of the speculators foreseeing a downward tendency of the silver market they will go overbought in gold currency.

As soon as the banks feel that there is a sudden heavy demand for gold currency (banks' sale of telegraphic transfer) they will, in self-defence, lower their selling rates for gold currency. The contrary will take place if "the speculators" suddenly desire to sell large amounts of gold currency to banks.

In order to obviate this drawback, the speculator will, if parity permits it, operate on the Exchange instead, by either selling or buying the requisite amount of gold bars.

Or he will begin to operate on the Gold Exchange without attempting to sell to or buy from banks. In other words, "the speculators" will attempt to influence the silver market by either buying or selling considerable quantities of gold bars. As the exchange market at Shanghai is very sensitive, the gold dealers will succeed probably in influencing the silver market.

In order to illustrate the power which the operators on the Gold Exchange have acquired,—and moreover the influence which they are wielding through the magnitude of their transactions,—the following statements of fact are here recorded. There is a certain difficulty as to classification; the subject matter has certainly its legitimate aspects, beside its speculative sides. So it is left to the judgement of the unbiased reader to determine which of the two is paramount.

As a consequence of the daily transactions at the Gold Exchange the market price of bar silver in London and in New York is often directly influenced. But the gold dealers' ambitions are not satisfied with this achievement.

Knowingly, though for purposes of their own, "the speculators" of Shanghai have at times directed the stability of currency of a powerful neighbouring country; and when it suited their book they caused the dislocation of foreign exchanges. The following may be a bold statement to make. But nevertheless it is an assertion for which the writer assumes full responsibility, after having had the opportunity to closely watch the happenings in the Gold Exchange. In the spring of 1924 the Japanese yen began to decline considerably in value. After having passed through violent fluctuations the Yokohama–New

York quotation fell in the early autumn of 1924 to 38 U.S. dollars. This represents a depreciation of nearly 25% on the original par value of Japan's currency. It is beyond doubt that one of the factors responsible for the instability and depreciation of the yen was the Chinese speculators at Shanghai, who had decided to sell Japanese currency for forward delivery. Some of the operators from Kiukiang Road, Shanghai, covered their transactions by simultaneous purchases of U.S. currency, for the same delivery. Others bought £, some covered themselves by buying gold bars for delivery on settlement day, while many remained uncovered. But they were all unanimous in selling yen in very large amounts. Those sales of yen in Shanghai called for cover in Japan or in New York. The immediate consequence thereof was a continual fall in the value of Japan's currency. It is true that after the great earthquake catastrophe, economic conditions in Japan were not brilliant. But just at a time when the trade balance began to turn in favor of that country, the value of the yen had been forced down to its lowest level, chiefly because the Shanghai gold dealers wanted it thus.

As "the speculators" could not go on selling yen *ad infinitum,* they started to liquidate and subsequently to square their oversold yen position. This they succeeded in accomplishing with handsome profits to themselves.

In the early spring of 1925 "the speculators" at Shanghai commenced to buy Japanese currency, for the purpose of creating an overbought position in yen. By the end of March, 1925, they were reliably estimated to be overbought about 85 million of yen, a good portion of which had its counterpart in other gold currencies. A position of 85 million yen, created within the short space of about six weeks, had a considerable influence on the stability of Japanese currency which, in consequence, had rapidly risen to the level of 42 U.S. dollars for 100 yen. The perseverance on the part of the Shanghai gold dealers in continuously buying yen in very large amounts was the principal factor to cause a marked improvement in another country's currency. The persistent purchases of yen at Shanghai called for cover of large sums in Japan and in the United States. The immediate result was that Japan's currency gained in value, chiefly through the enterprise of the members of the Gold Exchange.

The appreciation in the value of the yen was not due to any noteworthy improvement in Japan's general economic position, to her budgetary situation or to a more favorable trade balance. As a matter of fact, the latter had turned more unfavorable to Japan when "the speculators" undertook their spring offensive, which ended in a victory for themselves and incidentally also for the yen.

Within two weeks the Shanghai gold dealers' overbought position of 85 million yen was liquidated by its creators without visibly disturbing the market and without impairing the current value of the yen.

This authentic incident proves not only the courage and skill of the Shanghai gold dealers, but also their great influence on the economic destinies of other nations.

The operations of "the speculators" had, as already described, grown in magnitude of amounts to such an extent, that the Exchange Banks had to look for means to prevent the reckless speculations and manipulations of the gold dealers. The opportunity presented itself after the Gold Exchange had temporarily closed its doors, as an expression of sympathy with the general strike movement which was inaugurated at Shanghai on June 2nd, 1925. After its re-opening for business, on the 26th day of the same month, there was a general abstention from new business. At the beginning of July, 1925, the foreign Exchange Banks, with a view of restricting speculative exchange contracts, issued regulations which were similar to those practised already in 1920, but which were then tacitly abandoned after they had been in use for a few months. The new regulations provide for a margin of 4% on the amount sold or bought on behalf of "the speculators," banks retaining the right to call for a further deposit of 4% in case of need. These regulations had an excellent effect, preventing irresponsible parties from operating.

Terms Relating to the Gold Bar Market.

Quotations for gold bars are based on the Japanese yen for parity. The reason for this fact is that Japan is situated in the immediate vicinity of Shanghai. Until the end of the European war Japan was a country with free gold circulation. Furthermore, gold coins from Japan could be obtained within a few days after having been ordered from there; on the other hand gold bars shipped from China to the Mint at Osaka could reach destination in six days. In comparison with other countries gold transactions with Japan meant a considerable saving of interest and freight charges.

Before going into further details it will be advisable to get acquainted with the principal features connected with the gold bar market at Shanghai.

At a later stage[1] will be found a complete transaction of the statutes of the Gold Exchange. At this time it is only intended to briefly refer to the contents of the principal rules in connection with the scope of the said institution.

Transactions on the Gold Exchange are limited to the following four commodities:

(1) Gold mined in China. This means gold in the shape of sand or small nuggets.

(2) Gold bullion and coin of all countries. This refers to the import and export of foreign gold coins and/or gold bars, respectively, to the sale and purchase of these commodities, in their original shape.

(3) "Red" gold. This means gold as nearly as possible 1000 fine, for use in goldsmiths' workshops. Transactions are concluded per "Ping," or in multiples of "Pings."

---

[1] See Appendix I.

Each "Ping" is 50 Chauping (Shanghai) taels in weight, but the price quoted for "red" gold is per 10 Chauping taels.

(4) Shanghai gold bars. These are supposed to be of a fineness of 0.978 and of a weight of 10 Chauping (Shanghai) taels per bar. Transactions are concluded per "Ping," or by multiples thereof. One "Ping" consists of seven gold bars, weighing 70 Chauping taels. Therefore one can buy, for instance, 49 bars, or 105 bars, or 700 bars, but not 100 or 500 gold bars.

Quotations for these four commodities are in Shanghai taels (currency). According to the original regulations prices of gold at the Exchange are in taels and its subdivisions, up to five tael cents. In practice gold bars are never quoted at fractions lower than one-tenth of one tael. For example, Shanghai taels 271.40 per gold bar.

Of the four articles described above Shanghai gold bars are by far the most important commodity. These are dealt in for cash delivery, which is interpreted as delivery on the same day. It is often arranged that delivery takes place one day before the departure of the steamer carrying the gold,—if intended for export. "Cash bars" command a premium over (fictitious) gold bars sold for forward delivery; such premium fluctuates between 1 and 10 taels per bar, according to the abundance or otherwise of local stocks. All that has been said in this paragraph refers to rates of exchange for foreign gold currencies with free circulation and not to "gold currency" which has been depreciated.

As will be shown later on the mint par of one Shanghai gold bar of 10 Chauping taels weight and of a fineness of 0.978 is yen 476.823, or U.S. dollars 238.267. When, in April of 1925, for example, the yen was at a discount of about 20% and gold bars at Shanghai were being quoted say taels 275 per bar, it goes without saying that one could not have then obtained an actual gold bar for the price of 275 Shanghai taels, but merely fictitious bars, for delivery on settlement day. Real "cash bars" could have been bought only at the equivalent in Shanghai taels of U.S. dollars 238.267, plus a market premium of say 3%.

The seller of "cash bars" has the right to deliver on settlement day, in place of actual gold bars, foreign gold coins, but only gold yen or gold dollars. Each bar is to equal either gold dollars 240 or gold yen 480. In such an event the seller has to pay to the buyer 50 tael cents per bar to cover mint expenses.

'In case gold coins from abroad are contracted for through the Gold Exchange and such coins, through unforeseen circumstances, not arriving in time for settlement, the buyer is entitled to have the contract fulfilled on the basis of the Hongkong and Shanghai Banking Corporation's opening rate for telegraphic transfers on Japan. Yen 480 are equal to one gold bar. The amount of three taels is to be paid for freight on each bar or its equivalent.

The bulk of the transactions taking place on the Gold Exchange consists of fictitious gold bars, bought or sold with the idea of setting off on due date, which means receiving or paying differences. According to existing regulations forward contracts are limited to two months, but it should be borne in mind that this term is the maximum time granted. The sixteenth day of every month is settlement day on the Gold Exchange, so that one can buy or sell for forward delivery, but not further ahead than the second settlement day.

Gold bars can also be dealt in at the Gold Exchange for delivery within a month. Although the official regulations are silent on the subject, it is according to previous usage that on the coming settlement day (which is the coming sixteenth day of the month) the seller has the right either to deliver the actual gold bars or to cancel his contract at three taels over the parity with the Japanese yen, based on the Hongkong and Shanghai Banking Corporation's official opening rate for telegraphic transfer on Japan on the day of settlement. Needless to say, the seller has also the option to set off his previous sale of gold bars, by buying through the Gold Exchange an identical amount of gold bars for the same delivery. In such an event he will either pay or receive the difference (if any) from the Gold Exchange on settlement day.

Brokerage is charged by the Gold Exchange to both buyer and seller, at the rate of taels 0.06 for each bar. Out of this charge nine tael cents are handed to the brokers and three tael cents to the Gold Exchange. The latter refunds 25% of the brokerage collected to the brokers as a bonus.

There is a second *bourse* in existence at Shanghai, where gold bar transactions are being concluded daily on lines similar to those in vogue at the Shanghai Gold Stock Exchange, Ltd. The second institution referred to forms a department of the Chartered Stock & Produce Exchange (Shanghai), Ltd. Transactions in gold bars there are carried on on a much smaller scale; the turnover is estimated to approximate about 10% of the turnover reached by the Shanghai Gold Stock Exchange, Ltd., of Kiukiang Road.

Transactions in Gold Bars.

To summarize what has been described so far under the heading of "gold bars" it may be briefly stated that transactions in that commodity are taking place with one of the following objects:

(*a*) Speculation pure and simple, with the idea of either receiving or paying differences on due date.

(*b*) As a hedge against the fluctuations of foreign currencies contracted for forward delivery.

(*c*) As a hedge against goods to be imported or exported in gold currency, for which exchange has not been fixed with a bank.

(*d*) To deliver actually the gold bars contracted for, with the idea of having these shipped abroad.

Having already discussed speculation in gold bars, it is unnecessary to enlarge upon the subject.

The purposes mentioned under (*b*) and (*c*) are somewhat identical in nature and resolve themselves into questions of parities. Every transaction at the Gold Exchange is registered and quickly heralded by telephone and by runners to all it may concern. As business is very brisk, there is not only a large variety of rates quoted, but considerable differences and ups and downs do occur daily.

Quotations on the Gold Exchange are composed of facts and hopes and fancies, spiced with the vagaries of cross-rates, inspired by the monsoon in India, deeply concerned with the political and seismic situation in Japan, enlivened by the war-like preparations of some Chinese general, depressed by the pacific assurances given by his rival, influenced by the stocks of silver funds at Shanghai, interested in the daily offtake of silver bars in Bombay and ruled by the "overbought" or "oversold" position of the members of the Gold Exchange.

The gold bar market can also be influenced by the price of cotton yarn at Shanghai; the reasoning for the motives is based on a somewhat peculiar logic.

The principal center in the Far East for the cotton industry is at Osaka, Japan. The quotations at the Cotton Goods Exchange there are cabled daily to Shanghai and resolve themselves into one item, styled *Sanpin* (品三), which means "Three goods."

As a matter of fact the *Sanpin* quotation at Osaka is the official price for a bale of standard cotton yarn of 20 counts, weighing three piculs, or 400 pounds. If the *Sanpin* quotation in Osaka declines it is more than likely that Shanghai prices for cotton yarn will follow suit.

A fall in the price of *Sanpin* might mean reduced purchases of Indian raw cotton on the part of spinners; —at least in theory. If exports from India are being curtailed, silver is liable to come down in price; again, at least in theory. In such an event the quotations for gold bars in Shanghai are liable to rise.

The *Sanpin* quotations at Osaka, until the Great War, had a direct influence on the Shanghai market, and especially so on gold bar quotations. Since about 1920 that influence has been on the wane, but it still asserts itself at occasions to this day.

Shanghai official rates of exchange not unfrequently remain unaltered at the same level for a week or more. Actual market rates are livelier in temperament, but they are slow when compared with gold bar quotations. And they would be more stagnant still, if they were not influenced by quotations emanating from the Gold Exchange.

It is for these reasons that the average Chinese operator prefers to settle the bulk of his gold currency transactions, genuine and imaginary, at the Gold Exchange and share its favors and sorrows alike.

In order to show how an operator can hedge by means of gold bar transactions, the following examples are cited:

> On September 17, 1924, a "speculator" buys £10,000 T.T. from the X Bank, for October delivery, at the rate of 3*s.*/5*d.* for one tael. At the same time he hedges by selling at the Gold Exchange 224 gold bars at 259.50 taels, for delivery October settlement.
>
> He will have to pay for £10,000 @ 3*s.*/5*d.* taels 58,536.58.
>
> He will receive for 224 gold bars, sold @ 259.50, taels 58,128.
>
> In order to liquidate his position he will have to reverse it by selling £10,000 T.T. for October delivery and by buying 224 gold bars for delivery October settlement.
>
> This he does on 6th October, 1924, with the following result:

He receives for £10,000 at 3*s.*/5¾*d.* taels 57,458.03.

He pays for 224 gold bars at 249.30 taels 55,843.20.

He loses therefore on the £10,000, taels 1,078.55 and gains on the 224 gold bars taels 2,284.80. Net result is a profit of taels 1,206.25.

As losses are just as likely to occur to the operator as gains, and as results depend largely on changing cross-rates and other circumstances, the operation is in the nature of a speculation. But it is not a speculation with wide risks, because the transaction is one of gold against gold currency and not subjected to the wild fluctuations of silver prices.

One often hears that "Chinese speculators have an oversold position of about £1,500,000" or "they are overbought about £800,000." Such estimates are usually correct; but it is difficult to know how much of the position referred to is covered by gold bars, *i.e.*, how much has been "hedged." And it must be stated to the credit of "the speculators" that the bulk of their overbought or oversold position is covered usually by gold bars and that therefore the smaller part remains uncovered.

It makes an enormous difference whether the speculators are oversold say £1,000,000 (all currencies combined, as U.S.$, £ and yen) against taels, or whether they have a counterpart in the shape of gold bars. In the former case they would have to cover by buying £1,000,000 against taels, thus influencing and probably upsetting the silver markets of the world. In the latter case they have operated with gold against gold currencies, and thus they have had to contend with changes in cross-rates, but not with silver prices.

In this way gold bars do form a convenient hedge for operations in foreign gold currencies.

As the whole structure of the gold bars market at Shanghai is based on the Japanese gold yen, it is only logical that a large part of speculative operations in gold bars is being covered by counter-transactions in yen currency. It has become a favorite occupation of the more conservative class of speculators to cover transactions in gold bars by simultaneous operations in Japanese yen, with the object of reversing the transactions as soon as the parity will permit it. This procedure offers good opportunities, because the daily market quotations for gold bars at Shanghai are unusually numerous and wide in variation. In order to become successful the operator has to remain in constant touch with the gold bars market and to be satisfied with moderate margins of profit.

The following example is meant to illustrate the assertions contained in the foregoing paragraph. For the purpose of rapid calculation yen 480 are considered to be the parity of one Shanghai gold bar of 10 Chauping taels weight and of a fineness of 0.978.

Say on a certain day of April, 1925, Shanghai banks have been selling yen at the rate of 56½ Shanghai taels for 100 yen, for delivery in June, 1925. At a certain minute of the same day gold bars have been quoted at the Gold Exchange at the rate of 276.40 Shanghai taels per bar

$$56.5 \times 480 = 271.20 \text{ (parity)}.$$

Consequently there was a deviation from the theoretical parity, amounting to Shanghai taels 5.20 for every gold bar. It would apparently have become remunerative to sell gold bars at the price of 276.40 taels per bar and to purchase simultaneously yen at the rate of 56½ taels, both for delivery two months hence. In the interval the operator would have to watch the market with a view of reversing the original transaction, as soon as the disparity between gold bars and yen has been reduced or disappeared altogether. Transactions in this particular branch of arbitrage are very extensive at the Gold Exchange.

The hedging by means of gold bars on the part of merchants (referred to under (*c*) page 49) is somewhat similar in tendency to the example just cited, though the motives differ.

In the following instance a Chinese merchant is supposed to have contracted for the importation of cotton piecegoods from England at a cost of £10,000, which becomes due for payment within one month.

> Say the Bank is willing to sell to him £10,000 T.T. at 3*s.*/3*d.* On the same day gold bars at Shanghai are quoted at 276. The London-Japan cross rate is 1*s.*/10*d.* per yen. Official yen rate at Shanghai is 57 Shanghai taels equal to 100 yen.
>
> The Chinese merchant buys £10,000 T.T. from the Bank at 3*s.*/3*d.* for delivery within a month at his option.
>
> The Chinese merchant sells gold bars on the Exchange at Shanghai taels 276, plus mint charges of taels three per bar, making Shanghai taels 279. Divide this figure by the constant of 4.768, in order to obtain the taels equivalent of yen. Then divide the Japan-London cross rate by the official yen rate at Shanghai, thus:
>
> $$\frac{279}{4.768} = 58.50 \text{ taels for 100 yen,}$$
>
> $$\frac{22}{58.50} = 37.60d.$$
>
> or 3*s.*/1⅝*d.* per Shanghai tael.
>
> The difference is 1.40 penny per tael or 3½%, which he is liable to gain, by hedging with gold bars.
>
> In this way he stands to make a profit of about 3½%, always provided that the Japan-London cross-rate (of 1*s.*/10*d.* per yen) has not altered on the day of settlement.

Gold Bars from Peking and Tientsin.

Peking gold bars are of a fineness of 0.985, but they are below the weight of Shanghai bars. One Shanghai bar equals 1.0183 Peking bars.

In order to buy large amounts of gold, Peking will probably have to either draw on Shanghai or demand shipment of sycee. In the former case the actual drawing rate (T.T. selling for Shanghai taels) will have to be considered, in the latter instance the out-turn of sycee actually shipped. This would mean 107 Shanghai taels = 100 Peking taels.

Formula:

$$\frac{\text{Shanghai price for gold bars} \times 0.985}{1.0183 \times 0.978 \times \text{drawing rate on Shanghai.}}$$

Gold bars in Tientsin are 0.980 fine and weigh 1.0135 for every Shanghai tael weight. If Tientsin buys large quantities of gold bars for account of Shanghai, such purchases will be paid for by drawing T.T. on Shanghai (market rate) or by ordering shipment of sycee from Shanghai; the latter will turn out at a cross-rate of 1,064 Shanghai taels to 1,000 Tientsin taels.

Formula:

$$\frac{\text{Shanghai gold bar price} \times 0.980}{1.0135 \times 0.978 \times \text{drawing rate}}$$

It has to be borne in mind that charges and interest for shipments from Peking and Tientsin to foreign countries will be higher, on almost every item, when compared with Shanghai. The gold has to be transhipped at Shanghai and is therefore subject to extra freight, additional insurance and interest.

Relation Between Gold Bar and T.T. Quotations.

To the arbitragist, who witnesses the frequent fluctuations in the price of gold bars, the question must arise: which is the relation between the difference of two gold bar quotations and the market price of the yen, the U.S.$ or the pound sterling? If, for instance, gold bars are quoted at 270 Shanghai taels per bar and yen T.T. is obtainable at 55½ taels per 100 yen and, thirty minutes later, the gold bar quotation has risen to 271 Shanghai taels per bar; which should be the corresponding quotation in taels for 100 yen?

Refer to the constant of 4.76822976 which, with charges, etc., is taken as 480 (yen per bar of 10 Shanghai taels weight.)

Divide the gold bar quotation by 480, in order to obtain the yen parity. The difference between two gold bar quotations which vary from each other by one tael is 0.209 taels or, in round figures, 21 candareens.

For example:

Price of 1 gold bar

(*a*)	410 ÷ 480 = 85.416	taels
or	411 ÷ 480 = 85.625	„
	difference 0.209	taels
(*b*)	262 ÷ 480 = 54.583	taels
or	263 ÷ 480 = 54.792	„
	difference 0.209	taels

This means that ⅛ (of a tael) in the Shanghai yen quotation represents as nearly as possible *60 candareens in the price of gold bars.*

The identical principle is applicable to Shanghai quotations for T.T. on New York, on the basis of the difference between two quotations for gold bars. Refer to the constant of $238,267 which, for our purposes, is taken here at 238.

Example:

Price of gold bars.

262 × 238 = 62.356	taels
263 × 238 = 62.594	„
difference 0.238	taels

Therefore, if two gold bar quotations vary by one tael, the corresponding difference in the U.S. dollars quotation will be 0.238. This means that a difference of about 50 candareens in gold bar prices is about equivalent to ⅛ in the U.S.$ T.T. quotation in Shanghai.

The relation between £ T.T. quotations in Shanghai and a difference between two rates for gold bars is determined similarly.

Multiply the constant of 11644 by the quotation of gold bars.

For example:

Price of gold bars

$$410 \times 0.11644 = 47.74040$$

$$\text{or} \quad 411 \times 0.11644 = 47.85684$$

$$\text{difference} \quad 0.11644$$

This difference corresponds to nearly ⅛ of a penny for one Shanghai tael; or 1/16 of a penny for each variation in the gold bar price of 50 candareens.

CHAPTER IV

EXPORT OF GOLD BARS

IF there should be any misgivings with regard to the existence of the gold bar, it is hoped that this chapter will explain its *raison d'être* and prove its usefulness. Under the above heading it will be shown that gold bars are merchandise, or may be treated as such when parities permit.

When exported, gold bars, wrapped in soft paper and wadding, are packed either into bamboo tubes, usually ten small bars into each tube, or they are placed into small, but strong wooden boxes. The parcels are then wrapped with hessian cloth, sown up and secured by thin steel-wire; finally they are provided with a number of seals.

The export of gold bars is made possible if the parity permits it. The parity is based on yen. Multiply the constant of 4.7682 by the market rate for T. T. on Japan and add charges and interest to the result. If gold bars for spot delivery (actual bars) are obtainable below the parity, it will be possible to export gold and obtain a profit. The theoretical as well as the practical aspect of the question will be demonstrated presently.

In principle gold bars may be exported to any country willing to buy them at the seller's price. There are no restrictions placed in the way by the Chinese Government, and there is no duty imposed on gold shipments, inward or outward, by the Customs.

As Japan has been chosen as the country on whose currency gold bar quotations are based, it is only fair that the export of gold bars from China to the land of the Rising Sun should be treated first.

Export to Japan:

To Mr. H. O. White, of Shanghai, credit is due for having created the following:—

Formula:

How many Shanghai taels	: 1 gold bar
Gold bar 1	: 10 Shanghai taels (weight)
Shanghai tael 1	: 565.7 grains
Grains troy 1,000	: 978 grains pure
Pure grains 11.574	: 1 yen
With charges every 100.25	: 1,000 yen
Yen 100	: Ruling rate in Shanghai for yen

$$\frac{10\times 565.7\times 978\times 1{,}000}{1{,}000\times 11.574\times 100.25\times 100} = 4.76822976$$

This is *the constant.* If multiplied by the market rate for yen T.T. ruling at Shanghai, it will give the parity for gold bars.

For example:—On a certain day yen T.T. can be sold in the market at 54 taels for 100 yen. Say gold bars are quoted (for cash delivery) at 256.30 Shanghai taels per bar:

$$54\times 4.76822 = 257.49$$

Say 210 bars are consigned from Shanghai to the Mint in Osaka. These 210 bars, at 256.30 taels, have cost here altogether . .	Tls. 53,823.00
Add: Charges and interest 0.30%	„ 161.47
Total Shanghai	Tls. 53,984.47
210 bars, at 476.8229 yen per bar of 10 taels each, will realise in Osaka.	Yen 100,132.80
These have been sold at Shanghai at the rate of 54, making	Tls. 54,071.71
Less: ⅛% brokerage	„ 67.59
Net proceeds	Tls. 54,004.12

There remains a small profit of taels 19.65 on the transaction.

Mintage charges in Japan amount to about 0.16, but these are in abeyance probably to encourage the import of gold into Japan.

Export to Germany:

During the decade preceding the Great War the bulk of the gold bars on the market at Shanghai were shipped to Germany. The Reichsbank did everything in its power to encourage the influx of gold into the country. It paid at times a little above mint par and, in the case of China banks, granted advances against gold consigned to its coffers, without charging interest on such advances.

During the Great War and for many years after, paper currency ruled supreme in Germany, and considering the enormous burden which that country is to carry, it would appear that Germany was keener to reconstruct everything that had been destroyed, before rebuilding its old currency system.

Yet Germany's vitality is well known, and it is quite possible that she may start again to import gold from China. As a matter of fact, Germany has decided, in the early autumn of 1924, to re-introduce the gold-standard and to mint gold coins. Subsequent upon the conclusion of a huge international gold loan in favor of Germany, under the provisions of the Dawes scheme, gold in appreciable quantities began to be exported from the United States to Germany in the early part of 1925. In view of of these new circumstances the following particulars may once more be destined to serve practical purposes. If, however, it should be their fate to remain mere theory, —then let them be a souvenir of byegone times.

Formula:

? Gold marks	: 1 gold bar of 10 Shanghai taels weight
1 Shanghai tael weight	: 366.5 grams, 0.978 fine
1,000 grams	: 2784 Gold marks

$$X = \frac{10 \times 366.5 \times 0.978 \times 2784}{1,000} = \textit{Mks. 997.8886} \text{ for each gold bar.}$$

Shipping charges, insurance, cost of minting and interest are not included in the above calculation.

German gold coins are 0.900 fine.

Out of 1 kilogram gold, 1,000 fine, 279 coins of 10 marks each were coined under the old laws; or 139½ coins of 20 marks each.

The gross weight of a 20 marks gold piece is 7.9649 grams; its fine weight 7.1684 grams.

Out of 1 kilogram gross (alloy 0.900 fine) 125.55 gold coins of 20 marks each are coined.

The mint par of the gold mark and the pound sterling is 20.43 marks.

Although the government Mint used to coin 2,790 gold marks out of 1 kilogram fine gold, it paid only 2,784 marks for the same quantity, deducting 6 marks for coinage fee.

Export to France:

To the best of our knowledge export of Shanghai gold bars (except by way of experiment) to France has never taken place, for reasons of parities. In order to supplement the chain of possibilities the following details are supplied.

The French standard for gold coins is 0.900. The weight of French gold coins is as follows:

20 francs piece (6.45161 grams, or 99.563 grains) contains pure gold 89.607 grains.

10 francs piece (3.2258 grams or 49.781 grains) contains pure gold 44.803 grains.

155 coins of 20 francs each weigh 1 kilogram.

The mint par of the 20 francs piece is shillings 15.1032.

The theoretical mint par of £1 = frs. 25.223, the practical mint par frs. 25.148.

The French Mint buys gold 0.900 fine at the price of	Frs. 3,100.00
per kilogram, but deducts for seigniorage	„ 6.70
Mint tariff per kilogram standard gold.	Frs. 3,093.30

Divide this figure by the fineness of 0.900 in order to obtain the price of pure gold (1000 fine), viz., *Frs. 3,437.00.*

Some of the conditions under which the Banque de France will purchase gold bars are:

Fineness is not to be below 0.996 and bars are to be free from impurities injurious to the process of coining (like iridium, arsenic, etc.) The weight of gold bars must not be less than 6 kilograms, and should not exceed 13 kilograms. Each bar must be accompanied by two certificates from approved assayers. After acceptance of the bar gold the Bank makes an advance of 95% to the seller, charging interest at a very low rate, until the gold has been turned into coin; then the remaining 5% is delivered over.

To find the tariff rate for gold other than 1000 fine, multiply 3,437 by the fineness and divide by 1000. For example: 1 kilogram gold of English standard would be worth in France

$$\frac{3{,}437 \times 916.2/3}{1000} = \textit{Frs. } 3{,}150.58$$

The out-turn of Shanghai gold bars, shipped to France, can be measured by the following:—

Formula:

? francs	: 1 gold bar of 10 Chauping taels weight
1 Chauping tael	: weighs 0.3665 kilogram
1 kilogram gross	: contains 0.978 kilogram pure gold
1 kilogram pure gold	: is paid with Frs. 3.437

$$10 \times 0.3665 \times 0.978 \times 3{,}437 = \textit{1,231.95 francs.}$$

Deduct all charges, interest *en route* and melting and assay fees. Consider also interest for 36 days, at the rate of 1% per annum, charged by the Banque de France on its advance, making just 1 per mille on the amount. In addition brokerage and/or Paris Correspondent's charges must be considered.

The countries, members of the Latin Coin Convention, whose gold coinage was based on the standard prevailing in France, were as follows: Spain, Italy, Belgium, Rumania, Switzerland, Bulgaria, Finland and Servia.

Export to British India:

During recent years India has figured as importer of large amounts of gold. The gold coins current in India being:

	Weight	*Weight*	*Contents of pure gold*
15 rupees (mohur)	180 grains	or 11.66 grams,	165 grains
10 „	120 „	„ 7.76 „	110 „
5 „	60 „	„ 3.88 „	55 „

The fineness of India's gold coin is 11/12ths, which means 165 grains fine gold to 15 grains alloy.

1,000 mohurs weigh 11.664 kilograms (375 ozs.), and their contents of pure gold equals 10.692 kilograms (343.75 ozs.).

The mint parity between England and British India is 15 rupees equal to £1, which means 1 rupee = 1*s.*/4*d.*

Weights: 1 tolah = 180 grains or 11.66 grams.

Export of Shanghai gold bars to British India are quite feasible. In order to ascertain its rentability refer to the following:—

Formula:

? rupees	: 100 Shanghai taels currency
Price in Shanghai taels	: for 1 gold bar 10 taels weight
10 Chauping taels weight	: 565.70 grains
180 grains	: 1 tolah
1,000 tolahs gross	: 978 tolahs fine
1 tolah fine	: Price in India in rupees

$$\frac{10 \times 100 \times 565.70 \times 978}{10 \times 180 \times 1{,}000} = \textit{30.73636 as constant}$$

Multiply the constant by the price in India of bar gold for 1 tolah and divide by the price of gold bars (for actual delivery) at Shanghai.

Consider all charges and interest, which have not yet been taken into consideration.

Although not in direct relation with gold bars shipped from Shanghai, the following formulæ (supplied by Messrs. Kracht & Murphy, Far Eastern Exchange and Bullion Brokers of New York) are interesting and may serve for purposes of arbitrage initiated at Shanghai:

Formulae.

Gold Shipments Between New York and India.

U.S. Government Mints buy GOLD at	$20.67	per troy oz. fine.
" " " sell " "	$20.67183462	" " " "
plus a bar charge of ½°/₀₀ making	$20.68217054	" " " "

Examples of Gold Parities.

Between NEW YORK and INDIA		Between INDIA and NEW YORK	
? rupees	: 1 tola fine	? $	: 1 oz. fine
1 tola fine	: 180 grains fine	1 oz. fine	: 480 grains
480 grains fine	: $20.6821	180 grains	: 1 tola
$1.00	: 100 cents	1 tola	: rupees 25-4-3
30.90 cents	: 1 rupee	1 rupee	: 30.90 cents
		100 cents	: $1.00
rupees 25-0-7.1	excluding charges		*$20.8175*

? rupees	: 1 tola fine	? $	: 1 oz. fine
1 tola	: 180 grains	1 oz. fine	: 480 grains
480 grains	: 1 oz. fine	180 grains	: 1 tola
1 oz. fine	: $20.6821	1 tola	: rupees 25-4-3
$4.60	: 240 *d.*	1 rupee	: 16 *d.*
16 *d.*	: 1 rupee	240 *d.*	: $4.60
rupees 25-4-8	excluding charges		*$20.6603*

? rupees	: 1 tola fine	? $	: 1 oz. fine
1 tola	: 180 grains	1 oz. fine	: 480 grains
180 grains	: 1 oz. fine	180 grains	: 1 tola
1 oz. fine	: $20.6821	1 tola	: rupees 25-4-3
$48.80	: 100 yen	rupees 158.50	: 100 yen
100 yen	: 158.50 rupees	100 yen	: $48.80
rupees 25-3-0.6	excluding charges		*$20.744*

We arrange shipping as follows:

Minimum $100,000.00 { *@ $20.82 per troy oz. fine costs, postage, insurance Bombay,* excluding interest and your bank's charges.

(a) BY REGISTERED MAIL:

Cartage, packing, containers, postage, our banks handling commission and our brokerage .	0.50%	
Insurance against all risks, actual value plus 5%	0.16%	0.66%
In addition you have to calculate interest for 28 days transit time from New York via France-Marseilles to Bombay, which at say 5% (under your Letter of Credit) would be . . .		0.37%
Total cost		1.03%

Plus Bombay bank charges.

(b) BY FREIGHT by DIRECT STEAMER from NEW YORK to BOMBAY:

@ $20.8373 per oz. fine CIF BOMBAY, excluding interest.

Freight	0.50%	
Insurance against all risks, plus 5% value . .	0.16%	
Packing including kegs, cartage, B/L, customs, our bank's handling and shipping commission and including our brokerage . . .	0.08%	0.74%
You calculate interest under your L/C for average transit time, say 36 days @ 5%		0.50%
Total cost to you		1.24%

Plus your landing and bank charges.

(c) BY FREIGHT via LONDON to BOMBAY on through B/L, Cunard or White Star Liner and P. & O. boat:

@ $20.9407 per oz. fine CIF BOMBAY, excluding interest.

Freight	1.00%	
Insurance against all risks, plus 5% value . .	0.16%	
Packing including kegs, cartage, B/L, customs, our bank's handling and shipping commission and including our brokerage . . .	0.08%	1.24%
You calculate interest under your L/C for transit time, 36 days @ say 5%		0.50%
Total cost to you		1.74%

Plus your landing and bank charges.

Export to England:

Weight of Sovereign	123.2750 grains troy.
Fineness	22 carat or 0.916.2/3.
Pure gold	113.0021 grains.
Shanghai tael weight	565.7 grains.
Gold bars	10 Chauping taels weight and 0.978 fine.
Price per oz.	£3/17*s.*/9*d.*
1869 Sovereigns	are coined out of 40 lbs. troy weight of gold, 11/12ths fine.
40 lbs. troy	equal to 230,400 grains of 11/12ths gold or 211,200 grains of pure gold.

Formula.[1]

? Shanghai taels	:	1 gold bar
1 gold bar	:	10 Shanghai taels weight
1 Shanghai tael	:	565.7 grains troy
1,000 grains troy	:	978 grains pure
916-2/3 grains	:	1,000 grains
480 grains	:	1 ounce
Every ounce with charges 100.75	:	100 ounces
1 ounce	:	£3/17*s.*/9*d.*

$$X = 11644.18$$

Divide the constant by the sterling T.T. market rate at Shanghai in order to obtain the equivalent price for gold bars in Shanghai taels.

For example: If T.T. on London can be sold at 3*s.*/3*d.* for 1 Shanghai tael, the parity of Shanghai gold bars will be taels 298.57 per bar (provided the sterling remains at mint par).

If the full weight of gold is known, multiply it by the fineness, then multiply the product by 12 and divide by 11. The result will be the standard weight.

For example: 120 oz. of gold 0.980 fine = 128.29 oz.

Formula:

$$\frac{\text{Full weight} \times \text{fineness} \times 12}{1{,}000 \times 11}$$

[1]From *Exchange Calculations.* By Harry Owen White, Shanghai, 1899.

In order to find the mint value of gold, the full weight and fineness of which are known, convert first into standard ounces and multiply by the price at which the mint buys standard gold.

The present system of gold coinage was adopted by Great Britain in 1816. According to the Coinage Act of 1870 the weight of the sovereign is to be 123.27447 grains (equalling 7.98805 grams). Its fineness has been fixed at 11/12ths pure gold and 1/12th alloy.

The standard fineness of Great Britain's gold coins dates back to the times of Henry VIII, who reigned from A.D. 1509 till 1547. It had then been prescribed by law that out of a mixture of 24 parts, 22 parts had to be pure gold and the remaining two parts alloy. Therefore the standard of Great Britain's gold coinage is based on:

$$\frac{24 \text{ carats}}{22 \text{ carats}} = \frac{11}{12} = 916.2/3$$

The troy pound is not to be confounded with the pound avoirdupois. The troy pound is divided into 12 ounces troy, @ 20 pennyweights, @ 24 grains. Therefore 1 pound troy equals 5760 grains,—as compared with 7000 grains contained in one pound avoirdupois.

Out of 40 troy pounds of gold (which means 480 ounces troy) 1869 sovereigns (equal to 37,380 shillings) are coined. Therefore out of one ounce troy standard gold

$$\frac{37.380}{480} = 77.875 \text{ (or 77 shillings } 10\tfrac{1}{2} \text{ pence)},$$

which is the fixed mint price for 1 ounce troy of standard gold.

As already said, the weight of one sovereign is 123.27447 grains. This figure is based on the following calculation:

$$\frac{40 \text{(pounds troy)} \times 5760 \text{(grains)}}{1869 \text{ (sovereigns)}} = 123.27447 \text{ grains}$$

The Bank of England offers £3/17*s.*/9*d.* for a standard ounce of gold, although the mint price is 1½*d.* higher. The reason for this reduction lies in the fact that, although the British Mint makes no charges for coinage, it returns gold coins only two weeks after receipt of the gold. The Bank of England, on the other hand, pays for its gold purchases at once, deducting merely interest for 14 days at the rate of 4% per annum, which is 1½ pence.

The value of 1 ounce troy of pure gold (1,000 fine) would be one-eleventh more, *i.e.,* 84 shillings and 11½ pence.

Some of the reasons why gold bars from China are rarely, if ever, consigned to Great Britain, may be traced to the regulations in force in connection with the purchase of gold.

The Royal Mint is forced by law to conduct the coinage of gold free of charge for the public. The Bank of England is acting as purchasing agent for the Mint and is, according to the law of 1844, obliged to buy gold of British standard fineness at the rate of £3/17*s.*/9*d.* an ounce troy. The Bank has imposed the following regulations in connection with the acquisition of gold:

> The bars are being assayed at the cost of ¼*d.* per ounce. They must weigh 400 ounces, which is the minimum quantity bought by the Bank. There is really no limit to the fineness of the gold offered, though bars below the English standard of 0.916.2/3 are rarely tendered. The gold acquired by the Bank is weighed in ounces and decimals of ounces (not grains), the smallest fraction being 0.025.

The following is a practical example of how Shanghai gold bars would be treated by the English Mint: Melted into bars of 400 ounces and being 0.978 fine, each bar would fetch £1,658/16*s.*/1*d.*, as per following calculation:

400 oz., 0.978 fine, equal 391.20 oz. pure gold.

In order to convert the gold into the English standard of 11/12th, 1/12th of alloy will have to be added. 1/12th of the gross weight means 1/11th of the fine gold contents, because 1/12th is 1/11th of 11/12ths. Consequently 1 ounce of pure gold is equal to one 1/11th ounce of standard gold. . . . . 391.20 oz.

	plus 1/11th . .	35.56 „
		426.76 oz.

Therefore 400 oz. of Shanghai gold bar 0.978 fine are 426.76 standard ounces @ £3/17*s.*/9*d.* = £1,659/ 0*s.*/7*d.*

Less	4*s.*/6*d.*	for assay.
	£1,658/16*s.*/1*d.*	net proceeds.

Shortly after the outbreak of the World War, in 1914, the payment of gold against banknotes was stopped and the free circulation and export of gold suspended in England. In course of the next ten years the value of the sterling fluctuated violently. So, for example, was the value of the pound sterling, on a certain day of November, 1920, only U.S.$ 3.37. In the beginning of May, 1925, its value had risen practically to parity.

The British Government decided then to re-introduce the gold-standard, though with certain restrictions only. On 29th April, 1925, an Act on the resumption of the gold-standard system was passed by the British Parliament (first reading). About the new and modified scheme Reuter reported at the time as follows:

"The Gold-Standard Bill repeals the subsection of the previous Act under which the holder of a currency note was entitled to obtain gold payment at face value. It also repeals the previous regulations under which any person was entitled to have gold bullion minted, but makes an exception in the case of the Bank of England. Nevertheless, it enforces on the Bank of England the responsibility for redeeming legal tender on request in the form of bars of gold bullion of approximately 400 ounces. Finally, it empowers the Treasury on any condition it thinks fit to raise any money necessary to exchange operations providing such loans and credits are redeemable within two years."

Export to America:

Since 1920 very large quantities of gold bars have been shipped from Shanghai to the United States of America.

There was a total interruption of export in 1922, when the parity did not allow gold bars being shipped from China to the States, but shipments were continued again in 1923 and 1924.

During the first eight months of 1925 gold bars to the value of only U.S.$ 100,000 were shipped from China to America. Prospects for exporting large quantities of gold bars were very poor in the late summer of 1925, if one may judge by the fact that it was impossible to find in August a single gold bar of 0.978 touch in Shanghai. The few gold bars which were then procurable were of the so-called "red gold," with a fineness of about 0.996, for use in the goldsmiths' arts.

Before dealing with the relationship of Chinese gold bars and United States gold coin, it will be advisable to devote some remarks to the latter.

According to the Act of 12th February, 1873, the public has the right to demand free coinage from standard gold, 0.900 fine. The mint price of standard gold is fixed at $18.60465 per ounce troy.

This means that 10 ounces of standard gold are valued at	$186.0465
Consequently 9 ounces of pure gold at . .	$186.0465 and
„ 1 ounce „ „ „ „ . .	$ 20.6718

The gold coins of the United States are all 0.900 fine:

	Gross weight Grains	*Fine weight Grains*	*Fine weight Grams*
$20.00 (Double Eagle)	516	464.4	30.0926
$10.00 (Eagle)	258	232.2	15.0463
$ 5.00 (Half Eagle)	129	116.1	7.5231
$ 2.50 (Quarter Eagle)	64.5	58.05	3.7615

The mint parity of the United States currency is as follows:

				One U.S.$ equals:
Great Britain . . .	1 pound	$4.86656	:	49.316 pence
France and the Latin coin convention .	1 franc	$0.19295	:	5.1826 francs
Germany	1 mark	$0.23821	:	4.1979 marks
Netherlands . . .	1 florin	$0.40195	:	2.4878 florins
Russia	1 ruble	$0.51456	:	1.9433 rubles
Japan	1 yen	$0.49845	:	2.0061 yen

The law provides that 25.8 grains of standard gold shall constitute $1; this figure provides for 10% copper alloy, *i.e.*, 2.58 grains of copper and 23.22 grains of fine gold. As 1 ounce troy equals 480 grains, 480 ÷ 25.8 = $18.60465 per ounce standard gold.

This means exactly $800 for 43 ounces troy (20,640 grains) of gold, 0.900 fine.

1 kilogram standard gold (0.900 fine) is valued at U.S. $664.6144.

It has already been explained that gold 1,000 fine is valued by the Mint at $20.67183 per ounce and the reason therefor.

There are, however, some mint charges to be deducted, namely, a refining and parting charge of ½ cent to 4 cents per ounce, according to the fineness of the bullion.

A melting charge of $1.00 for 1,000 ounces of bullion.

A charge of 2 cents per ounce of copper, but only for bullion above 0.900 fine, *i.e.*, when copper has to be added to bring the bullion to standard.

Finally a charge for extracting such elements as iridium, arsenic, etc. (provided they are present), which must be removed, in order to make the bullion suitable for coinage. Charges are at actual cost to the Government.

These terms, applied to an example of Shanghai gold bars, would give the following illustration:

> Say 4,200 Shanghai gold bars are shipped to America, weighing 49,500 ozs. and being 0.978 fine. These are equal to 53,790 ozs. of American standard of 0.900, or to 48,411 ozs. of pure gold.

Basic price is 48,411 × 20.67183	$1,000,743.96
Charge for copper alloy, 2 cents per ounce on 6,206 ounces	124.12
Melting charge	49.50
Refining charge of ¾ cts. per oz. on gross weight	376.25
Net proceeds	$1,000,194.09

Here a note of warning may be sounded as to the handling of gold bars from Shanghai. The fineness of gold shipped from China is guaranteed by the sellers. If it exceeds 0.978 a refund is made by the buyer at Shanghai, but if it is below this standard, a refund is claimed from the seller. A bank at Shanghai often makes a large shipment of gold bars to the States; such consists frequently of bars contracted for with sundry sellers.

It is true that the bars are numbered, but if they are melted together and then found at the assay to be deviating from the fineness of 0.978, it will be impossible to ascertain whose bars had been deficient. In such an event it will be impossible to allocate the claim to the party concerned. Therefore it is advisable to have a clearly stipulated lot of gold bars melted separately.

Claims at Shanghai are settled according to the actual fineness on the strength of the Mint's assay certificate. For instance, a bank at Shanghai buys 70 gold bars with a guaranteed fineness of 0.978. This would mean 68,460 units of fine contents. After assay at the U.S. Mint it was ascertained that some bars were only 0.960, others 0.945 fine. The total difference was certified to amount to 1,220 units of fine contents. The bars were originally purchased at Shanghai taels 282.50 per bar, so that the seller will have to refund to the bank here taels 344.65.

After these preliminary remarks it may be appropriate to turn to the consideration of actual shipments of gold bars to America. These are, for reasons of proximity, consigned to San Francisco, but may just as well be directed to any other of the four remaining Mints at Carson, Denver, Philadelphia and New Orleans. Or they may be addressed to one of the following government assay offices at New York, Boise, Charlotte, Deadwood, Helena, Seattle and St. Louis.

The question of packing the bars has already been discussed previously.

Charges and interest fluctuate and would at present amount to:

Packing and postage	0.030%
Brokerage at Shanghai	0.050%
Insurance	0.015%
Mint charges	0.040%
Correspondent's commission and other incidentals in America	0.250%
Total charges	0.385%
Interest, 30 days at 5%	0.415%
Total . . .	0.80 %

Regarding cost of shipping of gold bars the following rates were in force in April, 1925, as quoted by the Pacific Mail Steamship Co.

From Shanghai to San Francisco on a value of

Under U.S.	$ 25,000	⅜%
From	$ 25,001 to $100,000 . .	¼%
Over	$100,000	⅛%

Inquiries made at the Chinese Post Office at Shanghai, regarding the cost of shipping gold bars to America, resulted in the receipt of the following official information:

"POST OFFICE,
Shanghai, March 19th, 1925.

Dear Sir,

In reply to your letter of the 17th instant regarding shipment of gold bars to U.S.A., I have to inform you that parcels containing bullion, sent per direct steamers to U.S.A., are accepted at senders' risk.

The rate of postage is $0.24 per lb. plus the usual registration fee of $0.10 per parcel, and the limit of weight is 50 lbs.

Kindly note that these parcels should be packed in such a manner as to easily admit of Customs examination on arrival at the office of destination in nailed or screwed cases, but that is, not in soldered tins nor outwardly sealed with lead or wax.

Yours faithfully,
(Signed) Deputy Commissioner,
B.O. Commissioner."

Formula I.

? U.S.$	: 1 Shanghai gold bar of 10 taels weight
10 taels weight	: 11.78542 oz. troy, 0.978 fine
1 ounce troy	: 480 grains
258 grains, 0.900 fine	: 10, U.S.$

$$\frac{10\times 11.78542\times 0.978\times 480\times 10}{10\times 258\times 0.900} = \mathit{238.267}$$

Formula II.

? U.S.$	: 1 Shanghai gold bar
1 Shanghai gold bar	: 565.70 grains weight, 0.978 fine
480 grains	: 1 ounce
43 ounces, 0.900 fine	: 800 U.S.$

$$\frac{565.70\times 0.978\times 800}{480\times 43\times 0.900} = \mathit{238.267}$$

Formula III.

? U.S.$	: 1 Shanghai gold bar
1 Shanghai gold bar	: 11.78542 oz. weight, 0.978 fine
1 oz. gold, 1.000 fine	: 20.6718 U.S.$

$$11.78542\times 0.978\times 20.6718 = \mathit{238.267}$$

Or finally, the following reasoning: Gold, 1,000 fine, is valued by the U.S. Mint at $20.6718 per ounce. The question will be: How does this compare with the Shanghai (Chauping) tael weight?

Formula:

? Shanghai tael (Chauping) of gold in weight	: 100 ounces troy, 1000 fine
1 ounce troy, 1000 fine	: 480 grains, 1000 fine
565.70 grains, 0.978 fine	: 1 Shanghai (Chauping) tael of gold in weight.

$$\frac{100\times 480}{565.70\times 0.978} = \mathit{86.75933}\text{ Shanghai (Chauping) taels weight.}$$

4196.98976 Shanghai taels weight (0.978 fine) ÷ 86.75933 = 4837.5081 ounces troy, 1000 fine.

4837.5081 ounces troy (1000 fine) × 20.6718 = U.S.$100,000

$100,000 are equal to Shanghai (Chauping) taels weight of gold bars 0.978 fine	4196.98976
Consequently the value of one gold bar of 10 Shanghai (Chauping) taels weight, 0.978 fine, is . . .	$238.267
The constant is	U.S.$238.267
Deduct charges and interest (variable)	„ 0.800
	U.S.$237.467

In order to find the mint parity between Shanghai gold bars and U.S. dollars divide the constant of 238.267 by the bank's buying rate for telegraphic transfer on America, and deduct expenses and interest.

Example:

Market rate for T.T. on America is 78.

238.267 ÷ 78 =	305.47	
Less	2.47	charges, interest.
Mint par	303.00	Shanghai taels.

If gold bars are obtainable in Shanghai below this figure, it will be feasible to ship gold from Shanghai to the United States at a profit.

CHAPTER V

A GOLD-STANDARD FOR CHINA

THE attempts to introduce gold coins into China's currency system,—be it as one of the measures of value or as a preliminary step towards the final adoption of gold as the basis of China's currency,—have already been referred to in the chapter "Gold as Currency in China." It has been shown there that occasionally either the Central Government, or some of the provincial governors, have minted gold coins for circulation in China. Those attempts were bound to end in failure, because the essentials for the introduction of an effective gold currency were lacking. Numerous have been the endeavors to reform the currency system of China and coincidently to introduce the gold-standard there. But many of the proposals presented showed complete lack of understanding of basic conditions connected with the subject and an absolute ignorance of monetary principles.

The schemes relative to the introduction of a gold-currency for China, as presented to the Chinese Government by experts, had to remain unfulfilled, partly owing to the opposition by certain influential officials, principally, however, because the Peking Government was lacking the authority and the means which are essential for the carrying into effect of those schemes.

It is beyond the scope of this essay to add to the already considerable number of Chinese currency reform projects. The following review is intended to be a historical record of proposals in connection with the introduction of the gold-standard in China. Only reform schemes presented by official and semi-official parties have been taken account of here and are presented in chronological order.

The first official proposal for a Gold-standard Currency.

To Hu Chu-fen, the then mayor of Peking, belongs the distinction of having first advocated currency reform for China. In 1895 Hu submitted a memorial to the throne which contained various suggestions with regard to reforms in general, including reforms of government finance in particular. He urged the adoption of a uniform coinage system in gold, silver and copper and the foundation of a government bank under the control of the Board of Revenue, with the right to issue notes.

The proposals as submitted by Hu Chu-fen were not capable of realisation, because, even had the country then been ripe for the change, the author himself would not have been conversant with the mechanism which his scheme entailed. The proposals, as far as they were related to the adoption of a gold currency in China, had been doomed to failure right from their inception. But they are recorded here as the first official attempt to even suggest gold as the metal which might be employed for the coinage of a portion of Chinese national money.

Sheng Kung-pao's Scheme.

Towards the end of 1896 Sheng Hsuan-huai—popularly known as Sheng Kung-pao — who was then a junior Secretary in the Tsung-li Yamen, submitted an extensive programme relative to currency reform. Sheng was a man of great personality and gifted with many talents. His scheme with regard to the reform of China's coinage system aroused a good deal of interest. It was based on the Chingping tael (0.900 fine) as the monetary unit. A Central Mint was to be erected at Peking and branch Mints at Tientsin, Shanghai, Canton and Wuchang. The use of sycee or silver bullion was to be prohibited. A national bank, with a capital of five million taels, all shares to be held by Chinese only, was to be established. Gold coins were to form part of the new currency system.

In spite of Sheng's forceful character and resourceful mind his project could not be carried into effect. Apart from the fact that as an official of the Ministry of Foreign Affairs he was not conversant with the intricacies of a far-reaching financial system, conditions within China were then very difficult ones, as the lost war with Japan had taxed China's resources to the utmost. Notwithstanding Imperial sanction, which was granted in February of 1897, Sheng's scheme remained merely a project. This was the second official attempt to propose the introduction of gold coins in China.

The English Monetary System for China.

In the early part of 1897 Yang Yi-chi, who was then a junior official in one of the Ministries, moved by the embarrassments of his Government in finding the means for the payment of interest and principal for its foreign gold loans, proposed officially the introduction of the English monetary system into China, with the gold pound as the unit. In order to prevent gold from leaving the country he suggested that its export through the port of Shanghai should be made illegal. The only good point in connection with this scheme was the motive. The project itself was rather naive and supplied further proof that it is not sufficient to be an official in order to suggest a workable reform plan for the improvement of a currency system.

1900 and After.

The Boxer War of 1900 and its consequences for China are well known. One of the results was that China's statesmen recognised the necessity of introducing reforms, especially in the country's currency system. Noteworthy achievements have to be recorded, for in 1901 and 1902 China's silver and copper currencies underwent radical changes which, had they been efficiently controlled, would have been of enormous benefit to the country. But it is gold with which we are concerned at the moment.

The war indemnity which China had to pay to Japan was fixed at £38,082,884; this supply of gold was used by Japan for the introduction there of the gold-standard. In 1894 China, commanding no credit amongst her own citizens, had contracted foreign loans for a total sum of £6,635,000. In order to enable her to hand over to Japan the indemnity, three larger gold loans had to be raised by China abroad, between the years of 1895 and 1898. These loans were the Franco-Russian Loan of 1895 for £15,800,000 (face amount frs. 400 millions at 4% interest), the Anglo-German loan of 1895 for £16,000,000 at 5% and another 4½% loan for the same amount and from the identical source, granted in 1898. Then, in 1901, the Boxer indemnity was added to China's gold obligations. Originally settled at 450 million taels, the said indemnity was payable within 39 years. At the then ruling rate of exchange of three shillings per tael the debt represented £67,500,000 in gold. Interest at the rate of 4% per annum was to be added to the debt, which thus would amount to nearly one milliard of taels.

It will be seen that by 1901 China was already saddled with a very heavy debt, the principal and interest of which were payable in gold currency. As misfortune would have it the price of silver began just then to decline further from its already low level, thereby adding to China's serious embarrassment. The price of silver, measured in terms of gold, has been as follows during those critical years:

	Lowest. Pence	*Average for year.* Pence
1900	27	28¼
1901	24 15/16	27 3/16
1902	21 11/16	24 1/16
1903	22⅛	24¾
1904	24 7/16	26⅞

This meant that China's obligations grew heavier in 1902; a remedy was sought and the possibility of introducing an effective gold-standard was then reconsidered.

A series of international engagements gave added emphasis to the urgency of the reform of China's currency.[1] Article 2 of the Treaty of Commerce and Navigation (Mackay Treaty) entered into with Great Britain on September 5, 1902, states that "China agrees to take the necessary steps to provide for a uniform national coinage which shall be legal tender in payment of duties, taxes, and other obligations throughout the Empire by British as well as Chinese subjects." China made a similar pledge in the treaty of commerce with the United States, signed on October 8, 1902.

The Example given by other Countries.

Urged by treaty obligations, which China had recently undertaken to carry into effect, persuaded by the example set by the few remaining countries, which just at that time had undertaken to replace the silver currency standard by the gold-standard, China, in 1902, had the earnest intention to adopt gold as the material best suited for her standard of values.

India, the greatest silver using country, had already in 1893 joined the ranks of nations enjoying the benefits conferred by a gold-standard. This India has accomplished in spite of the fact that she had then but little use for gold coins as a medium of circulation, seeing that the bulk of her population consisted of people with very modest means. Yet as a basis for international commercial relations the gold-standard has rendered incalculable service to India.

During 1902 the American authorities decided to reform currency conditions in the Philippine Islands, where the financial state of affairs was represented as having been chaotic. On March 2, 1903, the gold-standard was officially introduced for use in the Philippine Islands.

[1] *The Currency Problem in China.* By Wen Pin Wei. (1914).

On November 25, 1902, the gold exchange standard was adopted by Siam. (Replaced in 1908 by an effective gold standard).

A Currency Committee had been appointed already in 1893 to suggest improvement in the currency system of the Straits Settlements and the Malay States. The said committee mentioned tentatively the desirability of a gold standard for the Straits Settlements. But the project had to be shelved owing to serious opposition against its realisation on the part of the local British community. In 1902 came the remarkably large decline in the sterling price of silver, which incident was forming such an obstacle to trade that in June of that year the Singapore Chamber of Commerce appealed to the Home Government for the introduction of a fixed exchange standard. It will be noticed that the havoc caused by the continuous depreciation of the gold value of silver induced the Straits Settlements to clamour for a speedy remedy simultaneously with, though independently from, China.

The result of the appeal for assistance was the appointment of the Straits Currency Committee, whose deliberations culminated in the decision to introduce the gold exchange standard. The new system was to be based on the one then in vogue in British India. It took some years before experiments were finally concluded and before the value of the Straits dollar (0.900 fine and weighing 312 grains) was definitely fixed at 2*s.*/4*d.* This happened in January of 1906.

After those districts had decided to adopt the gold exchange standard there remained only two countries as involuntary abstainers, namely Mexico and China. It is notorious that since Mexico has also adopted the gold standard system, China of all the countries in the world, has not yet been enabled, at the close of the first quarter of the twentieth century, to acquire the gold-standard for her currency system.

Conjointly with Mexico, China in 1902 requested the United States of America to institute an official inquiry into the silver situation. The principal object of the inquiry was the search for ways and means, whereby the ratio between gold-using and silver-using countries could be established, without impairing the use and usefulness of silver for coinage purposes.

The Chinese Memorandum.

The step taken by the Chinese Government was full of sincerity. The memorandum, dated January 22, 1903, was handed to the Washington Government by the Chinese Chargé d'Affaires, Shen Tung, and may now claim historical value. It is reproduced here *in extenso.*

NOTE FROM THE CHINESE CHARGE D'AFFAIRES TO THE SECRETARY OF STATE OF THE UNITED STATES OF AMERICA.

Mr. Shen to Mr. Hay.

No. 277.] CHINESE LEGATION,
Washington, January 22, 1903

SIR: Referring to my note No. 276, of the 19th instant, in which I informed you that I had received instructions from the Imperial Government relative to a proposed plan looking toward an international concert of action bearing upon the monetary question, I have the honor to submit to you the accompanying memorandum containing the views of my Government relating to the abovementioned subject.

It is the confident hope of the Imperial Government that the subject-matter of its memorandum may receive the careful consideration of the Government of the United States, and that such steps may be taken as it may deem proper toward bringing about the desired end, to the mutual benefit of all concerned.

Accept, sir, etc., SHEN TUNG.

(Inclosure.)

MEMORANDUM.

The serious results which are threatened by the recent fluctuations in the value of silver bullion to the commerce, both of gold-

and silver-standard countries, have induced the Chinese Imperial Government, acting in concert with the Mexican Government, to ask the co-operation of the United States in seeking a remedy for these conditions for the mutual benefit of all concerned. Safe and profitable trade between any two countries is dependent to a considerable degree upon relative stability in the value of their currencies. This stability is destroyed in the trade between a gold-standard country, like the United States, and a silver country, like China, when the variations in the gold value of silver, as was the case during the year 1902, reached nearly 10 cents an ounce in gold in a single year, or nearly 20 per cent upon the price of silver bullion.

The problem of securing relative stability of exchange between the gold and silver countries is one whose importance is not limited to silver countries, but comes home with force to all those gold-standard countries which are seeking markets for their products in silver countries and are seeking the extension of their trade in the Orient. The importance of this trade is indicated in some measure by the following table of the imports into certain silver-using countries for the latest year for which data is obtainable, based in some cases upon official figures, and in others upon those presented in the *Statesman's Year-book* for the year 1902, reduced to round figures in American gold coin:

Imports of certain silver-using countries.

China	$196,934,342
Mexico	65,083,451
Philippine Islands	32,141,842
The Straits Settlements	150,000,000
Federated Malay States	18,000,000
Indo-China	35,750,000
Cochin China	24,000,000
Tonking	12,300,000
Siam	12,600,000
Korea	5,500,000
Bolivia	3,300,000
Colombia	11,083,028
Guatemala	1,521,900
Honduras	1,074,050
Nicaragua	3,500,000
Paraguay	1,838,710
Total	$574,627,323

This large volume of imports into the silver countries, exceeding the entire annual import trade of the United States, as recently as 1879, comes almost exclusively from the gold-standard countries which are engaged in the manufacture of finished goods for the world's markets and are profoundly interested in the extension of those markets. The table given does not include British India and several silver countries in South America which might become parties to an engagement for giving stability to the relative value of the money of gold and silver countries.

It will be noted that the largest amount of imports in the table given above is credited to the Chinese Empire. This large volume of trade is threatened in the present state of the Chinese fiscal and currency systems with a decline, the limit of which no one could foresee. The heavy indemnity imposed by certain of the powers upon the Chinese Government has led to large offerings of silver on the Chinese market and has diminished the power of that country to purchase foreign goods to a point which threatens to materially reduce the existing export trade to China from the United States, Great Britain, France, Germany, and other countries.

The foreign trade of China, while standing at the head of the above table in the order of magnitude, is small at present in proportion to the population and resources of the Chinese Empire. The exports from the United States to China have multiplied many fold within twelve years, and now exceed 24 million dollars. The present volume of imports of merchandise into China, however, amounts to only about 50 cents per capita in gold, and affords but a slight measure of what the trade of China might become if expanded in the future as rapidly as even that of Japan, which has advanced in ten years from about $1.25 to nearly $3 per capita. An import trade of $3 per capita for the Empire of China, with its nearly 400 million people, would represent the enormous sum of $1,200,000,000, or one-third more than the largest amount ever attained by the import trade of the United States. The encouragement of a commerce so important as this seems to the Chinese Imperial Government to be worthy of the most serious consideration of the Western powers. It would afford an outlet for the produce of the labor of many thousands of workers of Europe and America, and employment for many millions of the capital of those nations, and would dot the Pacific and Indian oceans with the flags of a carrying trade as large as that now required in the entire commerce between Europe and the United States.

While a readjustment of the currency of China upon a stable relationship with that of the gold-standard countries would not in itself, perhaps, accomplish so tremendous a revolution as would be involved in the creation of a trade of more than a thousand millions, yet it would be one of several steps in that direction which would contribute greatly to accelerate an event of such paramount importance to the capitalists and the producing masses of the Old and New Worlds. The necessity is becoming more and more keenly felt by American and European manufacturers for the opening of new and the extension of already existing markets in every direction for the absorption of their goods, in order that means may be found for relieving overproduction and affording profitable returns to the investment of capital. China, with her immense population and consequently large potential capacity for absorbing foreign products, offers a most important field for American and European manufactures, the ready absorption of which would tend to relieve overproduction and contribute materially to the prosperity of the manufacturing nations.

If results such as these are within the range of the influence of a reorganization of the monetary system of China, in harmony with the system of other powers where silver is the principal money in use, it is evident that the Chinese Imperial Government acts from no narrow and selfish motive in asking the United States and the Republic of Mexico to join her in seeking an international arrangement for securing greater fixity of relationship between the moneys of the gold and silver countries.

Questions of finance and economics should be considered in all their bearings, with due attention to their far-reaching effects, and not merely upon results which bring immediate benefit. Important as are the indemnity payments to the several powers, and ready a China is to meet them to the best of her ability, they represent but a trifling proportion of the benefits which may be derived by the Western powers from a policy which would give to China a permanent uniform monetary system, and make her a wide market for the products of American and European factories and workshops.

It is with a view to finding a remedy for the monetary causes which threaten to retard this development, and to preserve the export and carrying trade of the leading manufacturing nations to the silver countries, so that trade may not lose its healthy activity, and confidence may be restored to investors and manufacturers, that the co-operation of the United States is asked in representations to other leading powers in favor of international concert of action on this subject. The Government of China does not seek the restoration of the free coinage of silver by either the gold or silver using nations. It is recognized by this Government that bimetallism in the sense of the free coinage of both metals is a policy which has been definitely discarded by leading powers of Europe and by the United States, and that it would be futile to propose its restoration.

It is, therefore, not the expectation nor the wish of this Government that the gold-standard countries should take any action tending to impair their monetary standard or to make material changes in their monetary systems. It is desired that the governments of gold countries having dependencies where silver is used and the governments of silver countries shall co-operate in formulating some plan for establishing a definite relationship between their gold and silver moneys, and shall take proper measures to maintain such relationship. One such plan, it is reported, has already been proposed in both Houses of the Congress of the United States with reference to the Philippine Islands. It is this and other plans designed to accomplish the same end which the Government of China would be glad to have considered by the United States and other governments, with the view to the adoption of the best attainable monetary arrangement by those countries which are not prepared under existing conditions to adopt a currency system involving the general use of gold coins.

The co-operation of the United States with the Chinese Imperial Government and with the Republic of Mexico in presenting this subject to other governments would, in the opinion of this Government, aid greatly in securing a prompt and satisfactory solution of an economic problem which threatens the ruin of the silver-using countries on the one hand, in the vain effort to meet increasing gold obligations abroad, and which threatens also the commercial prosperity of the gold-using countries by destroying the purchasing power of their customers. It would, we believe, contribute materially to the permanent satisfactory settlement of this problem if Great Britain and France, with their important colonial possessions in Asia, and if Germany and Russia and other countries having large commercial and territorial interests there, would unite with the United States and China in the adoption of a common standard for a new coinage system in the silver countries; in recommendations for the readjustment of the fiscal and monetary relations of China with the other powers which would permit that country to continue to be a user of silver and a purchaser of the products of the manufacturing nations; and in such provision for their own subsidiary currencies as would tend to promote stability of relationship between their gold and silver money. The Chinese Imperial Government will welcome the co-operation of the United States in this matter in any form which may be acceptable to that power, and earnestly pray that the subject may receive the prompt and serious consideration which, in the opinion of this Government, it merits.

The request of the Chinese Government was complied with by an Act of Congress of March 3, 1903. The said Act authorised the creation of a Commission on International Exchange. The Commissioners nominated were Jeremiah W. Jenks, H. Hanna and Charles A. Conant. The members were requested to confer with the Governments of China and Mexico, as well as with the authorities in the principal European countries, with the object of formulating and submitting some feasible policy with regard to currency questions.

Long before the Commission on International Exchange could have functioned in China, an imperial edict was issued at Peking (on 22nd of April, 1903), appointing Prince Ch'ing and Ch'u Hung Chi conjointly to adjust the country's finances, to employ competent persons and to study the fiscal policy of the country. Or in the words of the edict. ". . . to consider carefully all necessary steps to make improvements in that direction and carry them out with diligence." The proclamation ends up thus:

"You, a Prince and a Minister of State, are required to carry this out with undaunted courage, unflinching energy, and strong determination, in order that our currency may be improved, and the benefit therefrom will be so widespread as to gratify our earnest desire to benefit our people by adopting necessary reforms. Respect this."

The practical results of the investigations and studies carried out by those two high dignitaries, and extending over two years, were practically nil, apart from the establishment of a Government Mint at Tientsin. Prince Ch'ing was then occupying a position with functions somewhat similar to those of a Prime Minister, while Ch'u Hung Chi was Minister of Foreign Affairs. Both functionaries were not versed in questions of high finance and, moreover, were severely handicapped by the selfish actions of the provincial governments, especially in regard to the latter's independent coinage policy.

In the spring of 1903 the great Osaka Exhibition was opened. The Chinese Government availed itself of that opportunity to delegate Prince Tsai Chen and Grand Councillor Na Tung to visit Japan in their official capacity. Na Tung was specially charged to investigate the working of the gold-standard system in Japan with the object of having it introduced into China.

It will have been noted that in course of 1902 and 1903 there was feverish activity in China regarding currency reform in general and the gold-standard system in particular.

Sir Robert Hart's Scheme.

Under date of April 10, 1903, Sir Robert Hart, then Inspector-General of Chinese Maritime Customs, proposed the adoption of a gold-exchange standard for China. The principle contents of his plan were as follows:[1]

(1) Foreign countries all have a gold standard, and their silver coins do not fluctuate in value. The market price for gold in China changes from day to day. Silver in China circulates usually in the shape of sycee, and only to a small extent as coins. Owing to a considerable increase in the world's output of silver the price of the white metal is continually declining.

On account of the frequent fluctuations in the price of silver traders suffer much inconvenience, and as besides China is bound to pay the Boxer indemnity in gold currency, it would be advisable to adopt the gold-standard. It is essential for China to have a silver coinage, but the value of her silver coins should be regulated by their gold price; and that price must be fixed.

(2) If China had gold in abundance it would be easy to introduce a gold currency and to assign a fixed value to her silver coins. Silver coins can only secure a fixed gold value by uniform purity and uniform mode of manufacture, obtained by the establishment of a Central Mint. All provincial Mints have to discontinue operations.

(3) The value of Chinese silver currency should be fixed permanently in gold. Eight taels should always be equal to one English pound sterling. There ought to be four Chinese silver coins and two copper coins in use, viz., the 1 tael, (liang) half a tael, one-quarter of a tael and one tenth of a tael. In copper there ought to be the 100th and 1000th part of a tael. A period should be fixed, at the expiry of which the circulation of all other coins should be prohibited.

(4) The machinery belonging to the provincial Mints should all be sent to the Central Mint to be retained there for use. A foreign mint expert should be employed. The silver tael and half taels should contain nine parts silver and one part copper. The quarter tael and the tenth of a tael should be 0.800 fine. The use of alloy removes the temptation to melt the coins for profit. Previous to the issue of the new coins the provinces should be ordered to transfer all the silver stocks from the official treasuries to the Central Mint to be transformed into coin. The new Mint should be open to the public for free coinage of silver.

---

[1] See *Banking and Prices in China.* By J. Edkins.

(5) After the Central Mint has commenced working the circulation of foreign coins should be prohibited. The use of sycee should also be made an illegal practice, but the Mint should always be authorised to exchange silver against newly made coins.

Foreign merchants established in China are bound to use the silver money of the country. They can obtain silver by paying for it in gold or gold currency. The gold thus obtained can be used for either the payment of China's war indemnity, or as a gold currency reserve, respectively for the manufacture of gold coins. In this way the new Chinese silver coins may have given to them a fixed gold price both in China and abroad.

(6) Deals with the advisability of establishing a government bank and describes the functions of such an institution.

It seems that this memorial was one of the many suggestions presented at that period to the Peking Government, without being acted upon.

Hu Wei-tê's Proposal.

The U.S. Commission on International Exchange carried on its conferences at the principal European capitals, passing through St. Petersburg last. From there Professor Jeremiah W. Jenks was ordered by the United States Government to proceed to China in order to investigate monetary conditions in that country and to subsequently propose the American plan for financial reforms. At that time Hu Wei-tê was Chinese Minister at the Russian capital. As he had been instructed by his Government to report on the deliberations carried on at St. Petersburg, Hu submitted a lengthy memorial to Peking, strongly favoring the adoption of a gold-standard for China. The plan submitted by Hu was well intentioned, but as the author was not versed in the intricacies connected with currency questions, many of his suggestions were impracticable and not capable of realisation. For this reason, and for many additional causes besides, the memorial was added to many others and placed on record, where it remains to this day.

Space will not permit the reproduction here of Hu Wei-tê's memorial in its entirety. Therefore we quote merely some passages from its introductory remarks, but as much as possible from the contents of the plan itself:[1]

If the monetary systems of the countries do not agree, it is impossible to prevent loss. To have a good monetary system a country must have a definitely fixed coinage, using gold, silver, and copper at a definite fixed ratio. The coins must be of the same pattern, value, and fineness throughout the country, if the best interest of the people is to be considered and it is desired to secure the faith of foreign nations. Those who have a gold standard do not, for that reason, suffer any loss in exchange, and international intercourse is easily arranged.

Financial experts have estimated the year's yearly output of gold, and there is no cause for concern lest it be not enough for the supply of the people of every country. As to the output of silver, there is no end to it. The greater the supply of silver the cheaper it gets, so that the present high price of gold is not in reality that gold is dear, but rather that silver is cheap. China has made a practice of using silver, and consequently, using this as a standard, the Chinese consider that gold has daily gotten dearer. Other countries have made a practice of using gold, on the other hand, and hence, using this as a standard, they consider that silver has daily gotten cheaper. A gold-standard country is like a man who has accumulated riches to buy grain—if the grain is cheap, he reaps the benefit. A silver-standard country is like a farmer who has accumulated his grain and holds it for a rise in price—if the price goes down, he suffers. So silver-using countries and gold-using countries are in the same case as two people making a barter, in which one man's daily increase of loss (on account of his waiting each day for a higher price) is only the other man's daily increase of gain. Therefore, if we use uncoined silver for money we are in just such a case of barterers with those countries which have a gold coinage, and it is needless to say which country is the loser. To use uncoined silver for money is like using uncooked rice for food or uncut cloth for clothing, for uncoined silver is nothing more than a product of the earth. Other nations consider silver merely as a commodity and not as money.

Your servant now begs to suggest a new plan for China. In this plan there will be six points considered, and the first of these is: We must adopt a fixed name and weight for our coins. All countries having a national coinage system have a special name for their coins, *e.g.*, the English pound, American dollar, Russian rouble, German mark, and French franc. With the exception of the pound, which is only in gold, they all use silver and gold together, using two metals, but a single nomenclature. One gold

[1] *Gold-Standard in International Trade.* (1904).

piece is worth 5 or 10 or 20 pieces, as the case may be, and one silver piece is worth so many copper ones, and each piece has its own particular name. Having established the relative value for the coins for the whole country, no other coins will be allowed circulation, nor will there be the slightest difference in weight.

The reason for such measures will be to prevent all chances for corrupt practice. In China we use taels (ounces) of silver. These taels are merely the signification of the weight and are not the name of any coin. A piece of silver is now merely so many ounces, whereas if we had a standard coinage it would have a special name. And besides the ounce itself differs greatly in different parts of China, which only increase the chances for tricky reckoning among the Chinese themselves, and has long caused our system to be rejected by the foreigners. Once dispense entirely with the name "tael" and introduce a national uniform coinage for the whole country, and our financial relations at home and abroad will have stability. The American commissioner at the time of the conference called our prospective new coin a "tael," but that was only because there was no new name for it and he used the old one temporarily; it was not that he thought the new coin must of necessity be called a "tael." We call our copper coins by the name of "wen" and our silver ones by the name of "yuan." We call our silver pieces "yuan" because they are round, and "yuan" means round.

As to the weight of the new coin, the Government should take into consideration the weight which the people are in the habit of using as well as the general standard of other countries, and then make regulation by law. After a thorough investigation of the state of affairs both at home and abroad, it is my opinion that we should decide upon the now generally used weight of 0.72 ounce (as in the Mexican dollar) as the standard to be adopted and adhered to, and not retain the useless and uneven tael system. According to the new system 1 yuan would be worth 1000 small cash, which would be a very simple system in exchange. Your servant discussed this matter with Mr. Jenks, of the United States Monetary Commission, and he also thought this plan the best, because a dollar weighing an ounce would be too heavy and too large, and, besides, no country has such coin in use, nor for that matter, is there any such coin in use in the Chinese market. If China really adopts a coin of the weight of 0.72 of an ounce, it will be more convenient and bring much better results. Mexico is now considering the adoption of a coin worth just half of an American gold dollar. The new coin is to be of the same weight as the Mexican dollar, which has long been in use in China.

If we adopt such a coin as this, having a definite value with relation to the American dollar, then it will have a definite value with relation to the coins of every other country, because the American dollar itself has a definite relative value with the coins of other countries. The matter of exchange then will be perfectly simple and also definite, which will be most beneficial. If our coin then has a definite name and weight, we can arrange a table of values relative to gold. For example, 10 silver yuan can be worth 1 large gold coin and 5 silver yuan can be worth 1 small gold coin. We can also coin fractions of the unit and have coins of one, two, and five tenths of that value. Then we can divide these up into copper coins and have the small silver 10 cent piece worth 100 cash. We can continue to use the copper coins now in circulation and will not need to coin new ones. We can add new ones, however, of 5, 10, 20 and 50 cash value for convenience and to accord with the system.

After deciding upon the name and weight, we must consider, secondly, the amount of money to be coined. Every nation must have a certain amount of money in circulation. This depends upon the number of inhabitants and their standard of living. Statistics show that on a conservative average Americans spend in one month $15 per man, Frenchmen spend 100 francs, and Germans spend 28 marks. The Chinese, according to the experts, are an economical people, and an average of $2 per man is enough. That being the case, the coinage for the whole country should be limited to 800 million dollars, and we could at first coin only a quarter of that amount, or 200 million dollars. Of this 200 million dollars 15 per cent. should be made into gold coins and the rest into silver pieces. In every $100 there should be one gold coin of $10 value and one of $5 value. The remaining $85 out of the $100 should be made into silver coins.

The third thing to be considered is this, when the old silver coins are called in and the new silver coinage decided upon, all coining of the old kind must be stopped and the old money be taken in by degrees for recoining. The output of the new coinage will then increase daily and its use also be extended day by day. For the first few years, in taking back the old coins, the Government can not but give the full market value of the same, in order to give the people assurance in the matter; but after ten or more years the coins can be bought at the rate of ordinary silver and it will not be necessary to consider them at their coin value. Moreover, the new coins will be 92 per cent. pure silver, and the remaining 8 per cent., which will be alloy, will be the nation's just seigniorage, so that the more money we coin the more of this surplus will we obtain. With this surplus the Government can not only pay its debts and the cost of coinage, but it can also store up its gold reserve. If all the 800 million dollars are coined, the surplus will amount to 64 million dollars. Such a system must prevent, as it does in other countries, the importation of foreign coins for domestic use, and the deserved seigniorage will then revert to the country making the coins and can not be taken away by foreigners. As China heretofore had no fixed coinage system, she was forced to make use of the Mexican dollar and the seigniorage went into foreign pockets and became an excessive drain upon China's wealth, although there are but few people in the country who realize the extent of the injury. Then, too, China is now in close connection with other nations by railroad and steamship, and if we do not soon take measures to prevent it, it will not be Mexico alone who is lying in wait to encroach upon our sovereign rights. For this reason the adoption of a new system should be pressed the more vigorously.

Fourthly, we must consider from whence is the capital coming with which we are to start the new coinage. When a nation starts a new monetary system, it first decides upon the amount of money to be coined, then it decides upon the time of putting the new coins into use. In the meantime while the amount of money coined is insufficient and the time for beginning its use has not arrived, it i evident that the old silver still in circulation and the gold and silver in use in trade can not be included in the capital for the new coinage. Where, then, have we all the necessary money stored away? When a nation starts a new system of coinage, do they not always count upon borrowing the money first? With two indemnities on her hands already, it is assuredly not easy for China to speak of borrowing money; but to borrow money for a coinage, when the money will stay right within the country, is a transaction which will benefit the country; it is not in any way like borrowing money to pay debts, where the money goes into the hands of another. Now the coins for such a great system as this can not all be made in a day, and we should first decide how large a loan we wish to make and then borrow a certain portion each year, borrowing only as much as we can coin, and thereby reducing the amount of interest we must pay. So, if we decided to coin 200 million dollars, we can divide it up and first borrow 15 million dollars gold, and with this amount buy 30 million ounces of silver bullion.

With this we can coin more than 30 million dollars, and with the new coins buy silver bullion again. Thus we can buy and coin, buy again and coin again, and so on in an endless circle, gradually making up the whole amount decided upon to be coined. But in making this loan we should consult with the prominent business men of the various nations, and not drag the nations themselves into the affair, for merchants are always solicitous for the security of their interests, and will necessarily desire that China have no setbacks, but be at peace. The Governments themselves, however, secretly wish us to have trouble and to become involved.

Fifthly, let us consider the matter of putting the new coins into circulation. This is a matter which rests entirely with the Government. When the Government has decided upon the date upon which to put the new coins into circulation, they should pay all the officials' salaries and soldiers' remunerations, etc., in the new coins. If, at first, the usage in the general market is not extensive, then the Government can make regulations requiring that the new coins be used in making payments due the Government. When the provinces send in their returns they should be required to send them in the new currency. The customs offices should accept no duties unless paid according to the new system. Thus it can be pressed upon the people gradually until in each province it can be made a rule that all collections, etc., above a certain sum must all be paid in the new coins. When the populace sees the great advantage of the new system, how easily it is reckoned, and how it puts a stop to the "squeeze" of the various kinds of money sharks, will they not realize what a nuisance the old system was and gladly adopt the new one? The eastern and southern provinces favored the use of the Mexican dollar for these very reasons, and the longer they used it the further its use spread. Suppose some one says that the new coin is not really worth its face value and hence it is not to be expected that the people will take any stock ir it. Just let such a person know that the old silver, though full weight, will not purchase goods in the market, whereas the new coins, although they are only 92 per cent. pure, are current everywhere and that this is the case because the authority to put a new coin into circulation and to put a stop to an old one, rests with the Government alone.

Lastly, we must make the people have faith in the new system; the people of China as well as the people of foreign nations must have confidence in it. Your servant has already discussed the subject of how we should give our own people confidence, and now as to the people of other countries. When the new system is put into operation, we should take the gold we have borrowed and deposit it among the various foreign banks, thereby letting all nations know that we have some gold in reserve. A statement should be made of the money taken in and the output of the Mint each year, and this statement should be forwarded to the foreign ministers in Peking. This is also in harmony with the general method in other countries. It is evidence of the way in which things are being done, it clears away all suspicion of fraud, and it insures trust in us throughout all the world. If the reports of the Chinese imperial Customs were not published in this way each year and distributed at home and abroad, who would put any faith in that system? As the day of Mr. Jenks's arrival is near, I have used that little ability I possess in composing this memorial, displaying as little ignorance as possible, in the hope that the official who shall receive such appointment may find some matters that may be useful. I humbly beg that the Throne will decide whether or not my suggestions are practicable, but I greatly fear lest they prove to be of no use.

In view of the fact that the United States Monetary Commissioner will shortly arrive in China to investigate the coinage question, your humble servant has with all due respect prepared this very slight contribution in the form of a memorial, which he craves may be given the favor of the Imperial glance."

Nothing can afford a clearer proof of the lack of understanding as to what was really proposed, than the memorial submitted to the throne by the Board of Revenue in reply to Minister Hu Wei-tê's suggestions. The Board apparently thought that a gold-standard could be introduced into China through contributions from "expectant" officials. Those citizens who desired to purchase official rank were commanded to pay half of the amount due in gold.

And the results? China is no nearer the coveted reforms now, in 1925, than where she was when those memorable memorials were drafted in 1903.

The rescript to Hu Wei-tê's suggestions is so remarkable in its composition and way of reasoning that it is deemed worthy of being preserved for posterity. We quote in full:[1]

MEMORIAL OF THE BOARD OF REVENUE IN RE SALE OF OFFICE TO RAISE FUNDS FOR A GOLD RESERVE.

We have made further investigation of the suggestions submitted by Hu Wei-tê, the minister to Russia, in his memorial on the reform of the currency, in which he asks that gold coins may be issued in addition (to silver). His report as to the advantages and disadvantages is very thorough. Recently there have been numerous discussions of the financial administration which have suggested that China ought to coin gold to relieve the situation caused by the depreciation of silver. We, your ministers, have taken pains to investigate the subject very carefully, and find that at present all the nations on the globe, except China, have a gold coinage; that gold is dear and silver cheap, and that on this account trade suffers much injury, and that without the coinage of gold it will be impossible to prevent it; but a supply of gold must first be obtained before there can be a gold coinage. When Japan was about to adopt a gold coinage, she first collected gold

[1] *Gold-Standard in International Trade.* (1904).

for ten years before proceeding to mint it. A great deal of gold is hoarded by the Chinese people, and simply because the government does not use it, it is unnecessarily wasted in the manufacture of gold vessels and ornaments; besides not a little in recent years has been exported to other countries. It becomes very necessary, therefore, to adopt some method to secure a reserve of gold which may meet the demand for minting purposes.

As to this matter we find that the memorial of the bureau of national administration has already received the sanction of the Throne, and is to the effect that they propose that persons who wish to purchase restoration to lost rank and those who desire to purchase promotion, as well as those who want to be advanced on the list of expectants by making subscriptions and thus secure the right to an earlier appointment to fill a vacancy, shall be required to pay one-half of the sums respectively required in gold, Treasury standard, at the rate of 1 ounce of gold for 32 ounces of silver; that, as to the application of the rule, as those who are to purchase restoration to rank are to be permitted to purchase only the former rank and nothing above it, they still more ought not to be allowed to purchase the right to return to the particular post formerly held, and that the privileges accorded under this rule are not to be allowed in cases in which removal has been for comparatively serious offences; that in the case of those who have never had official appointments and desire to send in large sums of money, they ought first to report at the board of revenue, which should take the matter into consideration and fix the amount to be paid (for the rank), all to be paid in gold, after which the board should request an edict, and if the Imperial sanction should be given the board of revenue should then receive the gold.

It seems to us that by agreeing to the proposal under these restrictions it may perhaps be possible to accumulate the gold.

As in duty bound we have prepared this supplementary report and respectfully submit it, humbly praying the favor of the Imperial glance.

Imperial rescript received: "Let it be as proposed."

"Respect this."

Professor Jenks's Gold-Exchange Standard Scheme.

We have already referred to the official mission of Professor Jeremiah W. Jenks, who in the beginning of 1904, presented his proposals on currency reform to the Chinese Government. Those proposals, setting forth the main points of his plan as worked out in discussions with the European government experts, were embodied in a pamphlet, printed in both English and Chinese. The pamphlet was widely circulated among Chinese officials, foreign dignitaries and the most important business concerns of China. Before beginning his conferences with the Imperial Government Professor Jenks asked permission to visit the most important treaty ports as well as some of the large cities in the interior of China, with a view of investigating business conditions on the spot.

Professor Jenks left China on August 27, 1904. Before his departure he had found it necessary to issue a second pamphlet in English and Chinese, because as he explains, "owing to the brevity of the first pamphlet several parts of it were misunderstood, especially by Chinese officials and business men, and very many inquiries have been made for a more detailed discussion of many of the points therein raised."

Apart from Dr. G. Vissering's proposal, which followed ten years later, Professor Jenks's reform scheme is the only scientific plan with regard to currency reform in general and to the introduction of the gold-standard in particular. It is impossible to discuss here at length the proposals and arguments of Professor Jenks, owing to the limited space which is at our disposal. Students are referred to the valuable work published officially by the Commission on International Exchange, consisting of Messrs. Hugh H. Hanna, Charles A. Conant and Jeremiah W. Jenks. (Washington, 1904). The book is entitled *Gold-Standard in International Trade: Report on the Introduction of the Gold-Exchange Standard.*

The short excerpts which follow here are quotations from the book just referred to. With regard to his travels for investigating local conditions in various parts of China, Professor Jenks writes as follows:

First.—To secure a general view of monetary conditions in China and of the methods of doing business under the various conditions found in different provinces. In the interior many days were passed in localities where no money is employed excepting copper cash and chunks of silver (sycee) which have to be weighed out by scales which each dealer or traveler keeps for the purpose. As opportunity offered, conversations were held not merely with officials of all ranks, but also with bankers, merchants, and even with day laborers, local travelling peddlers, roadside workmen, etc. In this way a reasonably accurate idea was secured of the methods of conducting business without any generally recognized currency and of the probable ability of the people of all classes to deal with a new and uniform money.

Second.—Conferences with the officials from day to day, both those of high rank, such as viceroys and governors, and those of lesser rank, such as local district magistrates, gave an opportunity to estimate the qualifications of those in whose hands would need to be placed to a greater or less extent the administration of the new system when it should be adopted.

Third.—The attitude of the people of various classes, officials, business men, and common people, toward a change in the system and toward the new monetary system suggested, was ascertained.

Fourth.—Opportunity was offered to explain in part the main points of the system proposed to the viceroys and other leading men, officials, bankers, merchants, etc., so that thus valuable criticism of the plans from the point of view of those familiar with local conditions was secured, and in many cases opportunity was offered to remove from the minds of those who did not understand the purpose of the invitation of the Chinese Government or its attitude toward the United States in this matter the natural suspicion regarding the motive of the United States in undertaking this work; and, furthermore, objections which would naturally occur to those not familiar with the administration of currency systems, were overcome.

Regarding Professor Jenks's plan for the adoption of a gold-exchange standard we quote herewith his own summary:

Suggestions Regarding a New Monetary System for China.

1. The Chinese Imperial Government promptly to take effective steps, satisfactory to a majority of the indemnity treaty powers, to establish a general monetary system consisting chiefly of silver coins with a fixed gold value.

2. In the establishment and management of this system China to invite and employ acceptable foreign assistance.

3. In pursuance of his plan, the Chinese Government to appoint a foreign controller of the currency, who shall have general charge of the system for China; he to have acceptable associates in charge of the mint or of such work as he may prescribe.

4. The controller to make monthly reports in detail of the condition of the currency, including amounts in circulation, loans, drafts on foreign credits, etc. His accounts (but not those of the general Government) to be open at reasonable times to inspection by accredited representatives of the powers interested in the indemnity, provided the Chinese Government judges that such a provision would be wise in order to secure confidence in the system. Such representatives, as also the associate controllers, to have the right of suggestion and recommendation.

5. The Chinese Government to adopt a standard unit of value. The unit to consist of—grains of gold, and to be worth presumably, approximately, the gold value of a tael, or somewhat more than a Mexican dollar. Provision to be made for the free coinage of suitable pieces, multiples of this unit 5, 10, and 20, on demand, for a reasonable coinage charge. Eventually some to be coined on Government account.

6. China to coin as rapidly as possible—silver coins, with an appropriate device, about the size of a Mexican dollar, for circulation in the country. These to be maintained at par with the standard gold unit at a ratio of about 32 to 1. More to be coined thereafter, according to needs, as indicated by provisions following. Subsidiary and minor coins, silver, nickel, and copper, of suitable weight and value to be provided.

7. Both the gold and silver coins to be receivable at par in payment of all obligations due to the Chinese Imperial Government in any of the provinces. When such obligations have been made in silver, the new coins may be tendered instead at their coin value.

8. The Government at its discretion, in conjunction with the viceroys, from time to time to declare, by proclamation, in the various provinces the new coins legal tender for debts incurred after a date fixed in the proclamation. Previous debts to be paid as contracted.

9. For the maintenance of the parity of the silver coins, the Chinese Government to open credit accounts in London and other leading commercial centers against which it may draw gold bills at a fixed rate, somewhat above the usual banking rates. For example, if the usual banking rate on London, under the system, were about 1 of the new coins for 2*s*., the Government might sell if the rate rose to 1.02 for 2*s*. Such drafts to be made only under the direction of the controller of the currency, but to be made on demand for all depositors of the new silver coins in sums of not less than, say, 10,000 taels.

10. Should it be necessary to make a loan for the establishment of a general monetary system with adequate exchange funds, it to be secured by sources of revenue sufficient to yield an amount which will provide for the needed interest and sinking fund, such revenues to be managed in a way satisfactory to the parties interested.

11. The seigniorage profit from coinage to be kept as a separate fund. Whenever 500,000 taels worth shall have been accumulated, it to be placed as a gold deposit with the several foreign depositaries in proportion to drafts made upon them. This process to be continued till at least   taels worth shall be in the gold fund on deposit.

12. For replenishing the gold fund after its reduction by drafts, the controller to honor silver drafts drawn by the foreign agents of the treasury in exchange for gold, at rates fixed by the controller.

13. Provision to be made for a banking law under which bank notes kept at par with the legal-tender currency may be issued by an imperial bank or by other responsible banks under the supervision of the controller.

14. As rapidly as is practicable the new currency to be introduced into the various provinces, the controller making use of the local government, banks, business houses, and such other agencies as are best suited to the purpose.

15. Within five years the new system to be introduced into all the treaty ports, and as possible elsewhere, and all customs duties to be collected in terms of the new currency. Local taxes to be collected in new currency as fast as it is adopted in provinces, and provision also to be made for the keeping of the tax accounts under the new system.

16. The new system to be put into effect when   of the new coins are ready for circulation.

17. The controller and the representatives of the powers to be authorized to recommend economic reforms to the Imperial Government.

We have already referred to the second pamphlet, the issue of which was necessitated by adverse criticism and misunderstanding of the scheme. In that pamphlet Professor Jenks gives another summary of his plan under the heading of "Outline of the American Plan":

It is perhaps wise to indicate in outline at the beginning the main points of the plan which has been advocated by the American Commission in order that the papers that follow may take their places as a more detailed explanation of a system already outlined. The following is therefore submitted:

(*a*) The Chinese Government to assume supervision or control of the various provincial mints, so that the entire coinage system of the Empire will be managed in harmony.

(*b*) The establishment of one uniform system of imperial coins, consisting of silver coins, nickel coins, and copper coins, which shall be uniform throughout the Empire, and in due time a legal tender for all obligations, public and private; the minting of all other coins to be stopped.

(*c*) These silver, nickel, and copper coins to be established on a decimal system and to be maintained at proportionate values one to the other.

(*d*) A gold unit consisting of a fixed number of grams or decigrams of gold to be established as the basis of the currency. The silver and copper coins to be issued at fixed values proportional to this unit, and to be maintained thereafter at this fixed gold value. It is understood that gold will not be used in general circulation within the country itself, although a small amount may be coined, but that the currency shall be the silver and copper coins above mentioned and bank notes based upon them.

(*e*) The establishment of a gold reserve sufficient to maintain these coins at the fixed gold value, but not necessarily to furnish a gold circulation for the country itself.

(*f*) The Chinese Government to manage this system in accordance with the principles established elsewhere by successful experience; and, therefore, in order to secure the necessary confidence of Chinese and foreign business men, to employ to assist in the establishment of the system foreign expert advisers of the highest standing whose reputation and work will secure confidence.

(*g*) The establishment of a national bank, of subordinate treasury agencies, and of other means that may be recommended by the experts and that may prove essential for the successful carrying out of the system.

It is well known that the plan, as submitted by Professor Jenks, has never been carried out. As a matter of fact, no earnest attempt has been made in that direction. Opposition was raised by high officials on various grounds, not the least important amongst which was the proposed employment of a foreign comptroller.

The principal objections came from Chang Chi-tung, Viceroy of Hupeh province. Chang, one of China's foremost statemen, opposed the introduction of the gold-standard system as unsuitable for the needs of China; what she needed was a new and uniform silver currency.

Making use of the opportunity Chang Chi-tung suggested that China should have a silver currency with a tael coin as the unit. Chang was supported by the then Viceroy of Chili province, Yuan Shih Kai, and as a result of their joint plea the Government agreed to adopt the K'uping tael as the unit of the new currency. A special edict was issued on November 19, 1905, embodying the regulations for the new coinage.

About 600,000 taels coins have been minted at Wuchang as an experiment. But with this trial the scheme died calmly and was laid to rest beside the currency reform plans submitted by Professor Jeremiah W. Jenks.

New Reform Plans of 1905.

Already before the arrival of Professor Jenks in China the Board of Revenue, in co-operation with the ministers of the Financial Commission, tried to find a home-made formula, on the basis of which China's currency system was to be successfully remodelled. Subsequently the endeavors of the official organs were promoted by Viceroy Chang Chi-tung's opposition to the plans of Professor Jenks. Furthermore, the provinces had inaugurated a piratical money-raising policy by flooding the country with newly minted copper coins. This unnecessarily large addition to the circulation was responsible for a considerable depreciation of the copper cent. The total production of 10-cash copper coins in 1904 was estimated at 1,693,700,000 pieces. During the following year a further quantity of 5,806,300,000 pieces was minted by the 16 copper Mints. The 846 coinage presses, which were installed there by the end of 1905, had a capacity of producing annually 16,000,000,000 copper coins. It will readily be understood what a curse those modern coinage machines threatened to become to the country. No apology is therefore needed for referring to the justification of new and persistent wishes on the part of the Government to institute further currency reforms. As these included gold as one of the metals for coinage, the proposals are here briefly recorded.

On August 22nd, 1905, Imperial sanction was given to a proposal regarding the reform of China's national currency. The plans then submitted consisted of ten regulations regarding the newly proposed currency and of eight rules concerning the Government Mint at Tientsin. The said regulations were the result of deliberations, extending over two years, between the Board of Revenue and a specially selected group of dignitaries.

The ten regulations constituting the memorial did not mention the standard for the newly proposed national currency. But in the mint regulations were embodied the following general declarations:[1]

> (1) The coinage of the three metals will be known as the "Ta-ch'ing gold coinage," "the Ta-ch'ing silver coinage," and "the Ta-ch'ing copper coinage." All three are designed for general circulation throughout the empire.
>
> (2) The original intention in the establishment of the central mint was the reform of the currency, by issuing a currency in three metals, gold, silver and copper, but the establishment of a currency system is a matter of serious importance and we cannot avoid a careful investigation to determine the proper weight and fineness of the gold and silver coins, and this problem has yet to be thoroughly considered and decided.
>
> The question of the coinage unit was left an open one.

The same author, after referring to the details of the mint regulations, continues:

> Three months after the above memorials and regulations had been published, the Ministers of the Financial Commission and of the Board of Revenue submitted further and more definite regulations. In rejecting the proposal for introducing the new system on the gold standard the Ministers, in the memorial submitting the new regulations, declared that China's accumulations of gold were not large and that hitherto both in public and private transactions it had been customary to use silver and copper. Hence they deemed it unwise to accept the gold standard. In another place they stated that after the silver coinage had been successfully introduced into circulation, then they would consider the matter of accumulating bullion for the minting of gold coins.

The Gold-Standard Scheme of 1907.

China had been carefully watching developments in the gold-currency schemes of India, the Straits, Siam, the

[1] *The Currency Problem in China.* By Wen Pin Wei. 1914.

Philippine Islands and Mexico. By force of circumstances she was prevented from following the example set by those countries; but the unintentional delay taught China valuable lessons. Had she been enabled to carry the gold-currency scheme into effect, she would have saved herself the cost and trouble of modifying the system, as most of those countries were forced to do.

The continual postponement of the currency-reform project caused much disappointment amongst many of the government officials. In the commencement of 1907 the Chinese Minister to Great Britain, Wang Ta-hsie, presented a memorial to the throne, suggesting the immediate adoption of the gold-standard for China. The memorial, however, only called forth severe criticism on the part of the Board of Revenue. Making use of that opportunity the Board announced its policy with regard to its own gold-currency scheme. According to Wen Pin Wei[1] the following were the chief characteristics of the project:

> The Board of Finance recognised the necessity of establishing the currency on the gold basis as early as possible. It declared that the pure gold system, such as is found in countries where the gold-standard coin is the only legal-tender coin among all the coins in circulation, the silver and copper coins being subsidiary and limited in legal-tender quality, was impracticable. Nor was the limping gold-standard, such as is found in countries (the United States, France, etc.) where some silver coins minted at a fixed ratio with gold enjoy unlimited legal-tender privileges, practicable in China. The Board found that China had not such a stock of gold as the adoption of the former system would require, and that the latter was not suitable because it is the result of historical circumstances not found in China. The gold-exchange standard was found to be the only feasible system. It must therefore be the aim of the reform. To attain this aim the Board found four possible courses to follow:
>
> (1) To introduce the uniform national coinage based on silver; and subsequently to give the silver currency a fixed parity with gold; the course by which British India adopted her gold-standard.
>
> (2) To introduce the silver coins at a fixed value in gold at the very beginning, and to maintain them thereafter at their gold value; this being the Philippine currency system.

[1] *The Currency Problem in China.* By Wen Pin Wei. 1914.

(3) To introduce the system in a manner similar to (2); but at the same time to introduce a partial note circulation as a substitute for token silver coins.

(4) To introduce the new national silver coins in the silver basis to replace the old coins and bullion currency. Subsequently to extend the note circulation to replace the new standard coins; the coins so withdrawn to be held as a trust fund or sold for gold. When the note circulation becomes universal, to declare for free coinage of gold at the market ratio of a given time and convert the silver notes into gold notes. If the gold reserves prove insufficient at any time the notes may be redeemable in silver bullion at its market value in gold.

The last procedure the Board attributed to a suggestion said to have originated with Samuel Ingham, Secretary of the Treasury of the United States under President Jackson. Ingham had recommended that gold certificates should be issued in exchange for silver which was to be kept in stock. These certificates should be issued at the mints and the Treasury on demand. When they were presented for redemption the Government should give silver bullion at the gold value in the market. In this way it was expected to establish the single gold standard without serious difficulty.

The Board compared these four courses and found the fourth preferable because it combined the advantages of the others while free from the objections against them. In adopting this course the necessary steps to take would be (a) to prepare the necessary administrative machinery, (b) to put into circulation the silver coins, (c) to replace the coins by substituting a note circulation, (d) to recoin the standard pieces into subsidiary coins, and finally to declare for gold coinage at the market ratio of the day and maintain the circulation at that ratio thereafter. The essential thing as a preparation, the Board declared, would be to prepare a sufficient gold stock, to accomplish which would require six or seven years of strenuous effort.

This State paper is in striking contrast with the memorials and edicts that had been issued up to date. It indicates that the Board of Finance was no longer constituted of men without experience and knowledge as had generally been the case in the past. The course of action it announced as best, however, was not intended to be put into immediate effect. On political and financial grounds a bank-note circulation should be preferable to Government currency notes. Yet without a sound and strong banking system to extend and maintain it, such a course was indeed a mere theoretical possibility. For many years a metallic currency must be the only suitable one for the bulk of transactions in China, and the masses could not be expected to acquire the habit of using credit money in a short while. It, however, opened a new way of passing from a silver to a gold basis, differing from the procedure of British India.

Commenting on the policy thus outlined, the Ministers of State subsequently declared that the reform must be undertaken step by step, and dwelt at considerable length upon the difficulties of introducing this plan of reform. But nothing further was heard about their scheme, and the Government continued its policy of inaction.

Dr. G. Vissering's Scheme.

In the beginning of 1911 Sheng Kung-pao was appointed Minister of Communications. Through his instrumentality a loan was signed on April 15, 1911, between the representatives of American, British, French and German banking groups on the one part, and Duke Tsai Tze, the Minister of Finance, on the second part. The aggregate amount of the loan was 10,000,000 sterling, the rate of interest 5 per cent, and the price of issue 95 per cent. The loan was contracted for the purpose of reforming China's currency system, but it was agreed to permit 30% of the proceeds to be used for the development of Manchuria. Of the £1,000,000 which were to be disbursed immediately for that purpose only £400,000 were actually handed over. The balance of the loan, 70% of the net total, was to be used for currency reform and was to be handed over to the Chinese Government, as soon as the representatives of the Four Power syndicate were satisfied with the reform project to be proposed by China. Meanwhile meetings took place in London and Berlin between representatives of the Four Power group and the Chinese Government with a view of finding a suitable scheme for the reform of China's currency system. It was agreed to invite Dr. G. Vissering, late President of the "Javasche Bank" to act as monetary adviser to the Chinese Government under the terms of the currency loan agreement. Dr. Vissering's appointment was made just on the eve of the Revolution, which broke out on October 10, 1911, and which resulted in the overthrow of the Manchu dynasty. All projects for reform had to be postponed *sine die.* Dr. G. Vissering carried on his investigations for one year, when he was succeeded by Dr. E. A. Roest; the latter died at Mukden in January, 1913. After his death the Chinese Government invited Dr. G. Vissering again to act temporarily as its honorary adviser.

The results of Dr. G. Vissering's investigations, carried on with the assistance of his collaborator, Dr. Roest, were laid down in two volumes, entitled *On Chinese Currency,* published in 1912 and 1914 by J. H. Bussy, Amsterdam. Our aim, to give an outline of China's attempts to introduce the gold-standard, permits merely brief reference to the passages connected with gold as standard for China's currency. Before doing so, it should be mentioned that the £10,000,000 currency loan has never materialised, nor has the currency of China been reformed on the basis of Dr. Vissering's recommendations, or those of anybody else—at least not at the time when these lines were written, autumn 1925.

The conclusions arrived at by Dr. G. Vissering may be summarised in his conviction that the only feasible system for China is the gold-exchange standard. But he does not overlook the fact that primarily China must be able to induce the provinces to accept token coins at their face value, furthermore to prevent counterfeiting within her territory, as well as the importation of counterfeit money from abroad. Unless these basic conditions are complied with, the gold-exchange standard would become a dismal failure. As a practical expedient Dr. G. Vissering proposes two independent standards: a gold-exchange standard side by side with the partly already existing silver standard, with the ulterior view of gradually supplanting the latter by the gold-exchange standard. The author recognises the necessity of having the copper cash, the silver coins, as well as sycee, circulate without disturbing financial conditions, until the population had been educated to freely accept token coins at their face value. Dr. Vissering is fully aware of the difficulties which are bound to arise in such a vast country as China, when it is intended to introduce radical reforms into her financial system. He therefore counsels to go step by step.

During the first period of transition the following measures should be taken:

(*a*) A gold unit for future use must be created as a foundation for the new standard system. Not an actual gold coin, but a fictitious gold unit, or a theoretical bank unit.

(*b*) A central bank to be organised with the exclusive right of issue. The said bank is to issue notes in the new gold unit. But these banknotes are to be made redeemable in gold values abroad only on presentation of amounts exceeding 50,000 units. The gold reserve held in foreign countries is to be accumulated from the equivalent received against the issue of those gold banknotes and must be employed exclusively for the purpose of maintaining their full value. At least a portion of the reserve held abroad should be brought to China as soon as circumstances will permit.

(*c*) The new gold unit should be introduced as book currency and as money of account. The foreign as well as the Chinese banks are to give their full support to this scheme. This means that the bank should introduce the new gold unit alongside of the already existing silver units, the tael and the dollar. The working of the new system would surely cause complications in the beginning, but the ultimate object is the retention of the new gold unit and the abolition of silver as a standard of currency.

(*d*) The banknotes, issued in the new theoretical gold unit, should eventually be proclaimed legal tender.

These measures are a short summary of the proposals destined for realisation during the first period. By way of comment it may be stated that Dr. Vissering saw the principal advantage in the adoption of the theoretical gold unit in the certainty about the figure at which the future final gold unit will be fixed; this would prevent the speculation on the price of silver and on the gold par. China is advised to closely study the conditions relating to the balance of trade. It is also pointed out that a fictitious currency unit is not new in the monetary history of foreign nations. As a matter of fact China herself has fictitious currency units in the K'uping tael and also in the Haikwan tael. Dr. Vissering lays stress on the advisability of not permitting the issue of banknotes to be made a Government issue, because former governments have often abused that privilege and there remains the temptation of repeating previous bad examples. He also advises to keep the percentage of gold reserve as high as possible in the beginning, but thinks it feasible to reduce the percentage of gold held in reserve against banknotes issued to 50% in course of about ten years.

The second period of transition should be inaugurated (*e*) by the fixing of the fineness and the weight of the subsidiary coinage and the token silver coins. This can be ventured as soon as the Chinese Government feels that it is capable of maintaining the gold value of the token coins. Dr. Vissering suggests that the coinage ratio should be similar to the ratio in vogue in Japan, in British India or in the Philippine Islands, namely 21 parts silver are equal to 1 part of gold.

Dr. Vissering considers the monetary unit as fixed by law of May, 1911,—the silver dollar of 0.72 K'uping taels weight, too large and suggests therefore a coin one-third of the K'uping tael. Estimated at a silver value of 28 pence per standard ounce (444 grains fine) the equivalent of one-third of a K'uping tael (575.8 grains, 0.987 fine, or 568.3146 grains if 1000 fine) would contain 189.4382 grains of fine silver.

The value in gold currency of such a silver coin, at the price of 28 pence per standard ounce, would be 11.946553 pence. As the gold sovereign contains 7.32238 grams of pure gold, the newly proposed unit will have a gold value of 0.3644883 grams of fine gold, *viz.*, 7.322238 ÷ 240 × 11.946553. At the ratio of 21 to 1 the contents of the silver unit would be 7.6542543 grams of silver 1000 fine, or gross 8.504727 grams, 0.900 fine.

Gold coins of 10 and 20 units should ultimately be coined, the first one with contents of 3.644883 grams of fine gold and the latter with double that weight, namely 7.289766 grams.

(*f*) The token coins should be issued simultaneously with the subsidiary coins. The latter were to be 0.800 fine, consisting of the half unit and the one-fifth unit coins.

Besides two nickel and three copper coins were proposed.

(*g*) A gold reserve should be built up against the token coins.

(*h*) After all these coins have been circulated, the one and two unit silver coins should be proclaimed legal tender to an unlimited extent; then the 10 and 20 unit gold coins should be decreed unlimited legal tender, and finally the gold certificates. From now on steps should be taken to demonetize and withdraw from circulation the old copper cash coins, the silver dollars as well as sycee. This last measure has been grouped by Dr. G. Vissering under the third and final period.

It is a matter of regret that lack of space does not permit discussion of details of Dr. Vissering's gold-exchange scheme. Under the circumstances a skeleton outline is all that can be given here.

Tsao Ju-lin's Gold-Standard Scheme of 1918.

The outbreak of the European war and the latter's protraction may serve as an explanation why China could not obtain for some years advice and funds from the Occident. The question of introducing the gold-standard system into China lay dormant until August, 1918, when another official move was made to procure for China a stabilised currency system based upon a gold reserve. The then Minister of Finance, Tsao Ju-lin, petitioned the President to authorise the issue of gold currency notes in preparation for the introduction of an effective gold standard, based on a gold dollar containing 0.0752318 grains of pure gold.

He referred to the arguments, which had already often been employed in support of a gold standard for China, namely (1) that China's foreign loans and indemnities, representing one-third of her annual budget, were in gold currency; (2) that the fluctuations in the price of silver were a serious obstacle to China's trade with foreign countries; (3) that practically all the nations used gold as standard of their currency system.

On August 10, 1918, a Presidential mandate was issued, promulgating the rules and regulations required by the Minister of Finance.

The regulations in question were the following:—

REGULATIONS FOR THE ISSUE OF GOLD CURRENCY NOTES.

1. With a view to facilitating international trade and preparing for the adoption of a currency system with a gold basis the bank or banks appointed by the Currency Bureau shall be allowed to issue gold currency notes.

2. The unit of the gold currency shall be one gold dollar which shall contain 0.725.318 Kungfun of pure gold, that is, 2.01688 candareens of K'uping tael.

One-tenth part of a gold dollar shall be called a "cho," one hundredth a "fun," one thousandth a "li," etc.

3. The denominations of the gold currency notes shall be: one dollar, five dollars, ten dollars, twenty dollars, fifty dollars, and one hundred dollars.

The Government may order the bank or banks appointed by the Bureau to issue gold currency notes of small denominations, such as five-cho (half a dollar), two-cho (one-fifth of a dollar), and one-cho (one-tenth of a dollar), and the Government Mint may be ordered to mint copper coins of one "fun" denomination.

4. Before the coinage of such gold dollars the holder of the gold currency notes may remit the money to other cities in this country or to foreign countries through the specified banks and after the coinage of such gold dollars, the holder of such gold currency notes may exchange them for gold coins as well as remit them to any city in the country or to any foreign country.

The gold currency notes may be exchanged at the specified banks for foreign gold coins or string gold. All ornaments made of pure gold shall be considered equivalent to sterling gold and they shall be valued according to the quantity of pure gold they contain.

5. The proportionate value of the gold currency notes and the national currency now in circulation will necessarily not always be the same. But it shall be made known to the public by notifications issued by the specified banks from time to time, and gold currency notes and current silver coins in circulation may be exchanged at the said banks at the notified value.

6. The specified banks shall have an adequate gold reserve against the amount of notes issued. This gold reserve shall either be in our national gold dollars, or gold bullion, or foreign gold coins deposited with the exchange banks in both Chinese and foreign commercial ports. The public shall be notified by the specified banks once every ten days about the amount of the gold reserve and the places where this reserve is deposited.

This gold reserve shall be subject to the inspection of the special delegates of the Currency Bureau at any time.

7. The gold currency notes may be used in public and private dealings at the proportionate value as notified from time to time by the specified banks.

The use of the gold currency notes shall not be restricted.

8. The specified banks may deposit and carry on other forms of business with the gold currency notes.

9. These regulations shall be enforced from the date of promulgation.

With his memorial to the President, the Minister of Finance sent in a review on the history of China's currency, in which certain passages relate to the gold-standard question. The contents of those passages show clearly the influence left on China's statesmen by the doctrines of Dr. G. Vissering. We quote *verbatim* from the *China Year Book* (1921–1922):

In the winter of the first year of the Republic (1912) Dr. Vissering, of Holland, brought his book on China Currency Reform to Peking, recommending the simultaneous adoption of a gold exchange standard and a silver standard; the new unit to contain 0.3644883 gram of pure gold; all books of the State Bank to be written in gold currency; gold notes to be issued to represent the new gold unit inconvertible into gold in China but convertible into foreign gold coins in foreign countries where a Chinese reserve is available; existing Chinese and foreign silver and copper coins to be allowed to circulate according to their intrinsic value, until several tens of years afterwards when China would be strong and able to prohibit counterfeiting; the ratio then to be fixed at 21:1 and silver dollars to represent the gold unit to be minted, thus introducing in its entirety the gold exchange standard. The book produced a good deal of discussion among officials and people.

Why a Gold Note is necessary (preliminary to a gold-standard). —Although it is imperative for China to adopt a gold-standard, we have to take into consideration the difficulties of carrying out such a measure. In the first place, China does not produce much gold, and does not hold much gold. It would be difficult, therefore, to mint gold coins at once. Secondly, the normal ratio between gold and silver is disturbed by the European war, and it is not advisable at present to fix the legal ratio. In the circumstances it is necessary to make some modifications in methods in carrying out our programme. We will adopt the suggestions made by a former Secretary of State for Finance of the United States, and the suggestions of Dr. Vissering, modified to suit present conditions in China, and fix a gold unit called the Chin-yuan (gold dollar) to contain 0.752318 gram, equal to 2.01688 candareens, K'uping weight. One-tenth of a gold yuan should be called a gold dime; 1/100th should be called a *feng;* 1/1000th should be called a *li:* all in decimal progression. The Government will permit the Bank of China and the Bank of Communications to issue gold notes. These two banks will keep a separate set of books in gold currency. The notes will be used in deposits, loans, and other transactions, to gather together the people's surplus gold and to make people accustomed to the use of gold. On the other hand, the Government will foster the growth of China's international trade and increase the circulation of gold notes so as to secure a big gold reserve, and at the proper moment the Government will declare the ratio between gold and silver and enforce the gold standard. Then the gold note or the gold dollar will take the place of the silver dollar, and the silver dollar may be gradually recalled or used as a token coin of the gold yuan, and the token coins provided in the National Coinage Law will continue to be used as token coins of the gold yuan. In this way no disturbance or panic will be experienced by the market and the gold standard will come into force automatically.

Under Tsao Ju-lin's plan Japan was to give a loan for currency regulation purposes to China. The proceeds of the loan were to be deposited in Government banks in Japan and gold-currency notes were to be issued against this reserve, to be used as official Government currency within China. At that time a serious boycott against everything Japanese broke out throughout China and an outcry was raised against the idea that China's currency reserve should be held in a foreign country.

Although the plan was feasible, containing many sound features, it had to be abandoned under the circumstances just described. It is more than probable that the Yuan Shih Kai 10 and 20 gold dollars pieces, which have already been described in detail, were coined in anticipation of Tsao Ju-lin's attempt, to introduce the gold-standard system into China, becoming law.

The non-realisation of the plan just mentioned has not precluded certain provinces of China from introducing gold coins as temporary media of circulation.

CHAPTER VI

THE PRODUCTION OF GOLD IN CHINA

AMONGST the many sayings by the sage Mencius is the maxim "In order to increase wealth the producers must be numerous, the consumers few." Economists have proved to the world that wealth is the product of labour. Labour is the original purchase price that is paid for every thing. It would be fallacious to pretend that the wealth of the world has originally been purchased by means of gold and silver. It was acquired in the first place by toil of the human body. The result was not influenced by the alternative as to whether it was our own body that had to toil, or whether we could save ourselves the hardships of severe manual labour by imposing it upon others.

Physical labour seldom makes a man wealthy. The acquisition of riches depends chiefly on the quantity of labour which one can command or which one can procure at a low cost. In other words, it remains an undeniable truth that almost all wealth is acquired from the labour of other people and, therefore, if one is unable to command other people's labour one will remain poor.

While labour undoubtedly remains the creator of wealth, the laws of economics demand that it should be wisely directed in order to prevent the production of barren results. During the past 2,000 years labour in China has been proverbially cheap. Indeed, it was common practice amongst the sundry dynasties, which governed the country during the Middle Ages, to often compel the poor classes to form labour battalions for the purpose of toiling on the Government's behalf, against a remuneration which was barely sufficient to keep soul and body of the slaving masses together. One of the monuments from those times is the Great Wall of China, the result of forced labour, a gigantic landmark of an unproductive age and of ill-directed energy and human strength.

Numerous were the attempts on the part of provincial governments to herd a large number of poor families together with a view of forcing them to work mines, trusting to be able to extract from the sand of rivers large quantities of the precious metals. The results were invariably poor, as the deposits of gold proved to be a disillusionment. But the risks were not large, as labour then cost almost nothing and lives were considered worth just as much. China at no time was rich in gold deposits, unless they are still deeply embedded in the bowels of the earth, unnoticed by searching eyes and elusive to modern technical skill.

The population of China, from times immemorial, understood to appreciate the majestic glory of gold: to men, it meant power; to woman, soul's delight. Indefatigable have been the endeavors to extract the radiant metal from Chinese soil. Yet all attempts to find appreciable quantities have resolved themselves merely into false ambitions and unfulfilled hopes.

Regarding gold mining in China in olden times, J. Edkins in *Banking and Prices in China* writes as follows:

> Gold was first looked for with serious purpose under Kublai in the prefecture of T'sing-chow about 1268. An order was given that Yu-t'sung-kang and Kau-hing-tsung should employ four thousand people, who were not registered farmers, to dig for gold at Tsi-hia in Teng-chow prefecture. In 1278 two thousand gold washers were appointed under the magistrates of T'sing-chow and Lui-chow to dig for gold. Gold washing in Manchuria was under the management of Li-te-jen at Hu-pe-yu valley in the district of Lung-shan. Each year three ounces of gold were contributed to the revenue. In 1276 gold was washed at Shwang-ch'eng and Ho-chow on the east of the Liau river.

In 1287 a manager of gold mines near Nanking was appointed. He had under him 7,365 families at various points in the province of Kiang-che, who conducted their operations at seventy localities. No gold was forthcoming at Nanking. The manager and the men in his employ were dismissed. In Anhwei gold washing in the districts of Hwei-chow, Jan-chow, Ch'i-chow, and Sin-chow was under the control of the magistrates of these cities, and they received the government share from the mines. Kiangsi contributed Taels 100 of gold in the year 1286 from the prefecture of Fu-chow. The locality was Siau-t'sau-chow (小曹周) in Lo-an-hien. In Hu-kwang gold was worked at Chang-te, Feng-chow, Yuen-chow, and T'sing-chow. Ten thousand families were employed in washing for gold under the treasurer. In Si-chwen, on account of its being too heavy a strain on the people, in 1295 washing for gold was stopped by order. In Yunnan the annual contribution of gold was, in 1277, in all 105 ingots of 50 Taels each.

The adoption of scientific mining methods, combined with an intensified craving for the acquisition of glittering gold, was not capable of altering the disappointing results experienced in connection with the incessant hunt for the precious metal. Reliable statistics, regarding the production of gold within China's borders, are conspicuous by their absence. Yet it is an unquestioned fact that the result of gold mining in China has, for millenia of years, grotesquely been out of proportions to the intensity with which searches have been carried on,—to the multitude of toilers employed and to the vastness of human energy wasted.

William F. Collins, in *Mineral Enterprise In China*, often refers to gold mined in China. The conclusions he arrives at generally corroborate the views set forth here. *Inter alia* he writes:

The working and closing down of gold "mines" is so frequently recorded in old Chinese writings that many have believed China's gold deposits to be extraordinarily rich.

The actual position is well presented by Baron Richthofen. Writing in 1872 he says:

From my own experience on the subject, I have arrived at the conviction that the great number of places in which gold is washed from river sand, in China, at the present day, far from furnishing a proof of the wealth of the country, is, on the contrary, clear evidence of the superabundance of human labour, the general prevalence of relatively low wages, and the poverty, individually, of those engaged in the search for gold. It is not at all unlikely that the early settlers in China had better returns from the same occupation, because the gold had accumulated in the river sands through countless ages before their arrival. The gold-washers of to-day, with probably very few local exceptions, earn less than the lowest wages which they can get for ordinary labour, and take to that occupation in those seasons only when there is the least demand for field work. We can, therefore, safely conclude that (with those few exceptions) the greater the yield in gold, the greater will be the poverty of any one Province. The sum total is, in some over-populated countries, not inconsiderable, and has quite misled the judgment of even those who have witnessed the miserable condition of the gold-diggers. It appears, indeed, that Yunnan, together with the rest of the metalliferous country, is the only portion of China where the gain which gold has brought to those who have been engaged either in mining for it or in washing it from the sand of rivers, has been such as to compare favourably with that obtained from other industrial enterprises. The number of places in which gold occurs in the various hilly countries of Europe is probably greater, on an average, than in equal areas of China. But no notice is taken of them, because nobody could be induced there to wash gold with such little return as is generally obtained in China, if Yunnan is excepted.

The *Encyclopædia Sinica* has the following to say about gold mining in China:

Little gold is mined in China; the most promising localities appear to be the Mo-ho mines on the river of that name, (an affluent of the Amur), and the neighbourhood, where prospectors have worked since 1866. Attempts to mine gold have also been made in many parts of Central and South Manchuria, especially near Hingking and on the upper waters of the Hun River. There are also mines near Jehol (Kouliang, etc.), and at Chaoyang, Lanping, etc., further east in Chihli. On the Russian frontier, near Urga, and in E. Mongolia, gold is collected, and in Sining prefecture, etc., Kansu, as well as in Ili.

In S. China gold exists in Chao-ching fu and there is placer gold in Lienchow (near Pakhoi); in Kuangsi it occurs in four districts, especially in Pinglo; there is a little in Hunan and in Tsun-i district of Kuichou.

Another source of supply is the mines and river beds of the Tibetan borderland of Ssuch'uan. Here Viceroy Chao Erh-feng initiated the policy of official working, but a mining engineer reported adversely on the prospects, even with the use of modern machinery, and the venture came to an end. However, private enterprise is still carried on in the Tachienlu, Litang, Derge, and other districts. A rough official estimate of the annual yield is 12,000 Chinese ounces, worth £45,000. Non-continuous veins are said to exist, but the Government proposes to resume operation when funds are available. In Yunnan the most notable mines are those at Talang where there is a considerable yield annually. T. T. Read, in his article on the Mineral Resources of China, comes to the conclusion that with the exception of Manchuria and the Yunnan-Ssuch'uan region the gold mining industry gives little promise of growth.

In the Amur region there are estimated to be 5 million tons of high-grade ore *(Far Eastern Review,* October 1913) but how much of this is in Chinese soil is not stated.

But little space is devoted to gold mining in China in the issue of 1925 of the *China Year Book:*

The gold production in China exclusive of Outer Mongolia was estimated at 108,000 taels or Chinese ounces in 1916. No complete statistics are yet available for a later period. It has considerably decreased since then because of the great fall of gold prices in terms of silver during the last period of the World War and the resulting disorganization in many mines.

North Manchuria (including Heilungkiang and Northern Kirin) is the biggest producer of gold; the following are the productions of the principal mines in that region.

Mine	*1918*	*1919*	*1920*	*1921*	*1922*
Yuchin (Amur)	10,601	3,554	3,057	2,124	—
Kwantu (Amur)	16,000	4,500	4,100	7,814	2,890
Kumar (Amur)	9,001	7,535	1,056	1,714	3,076
Sansing (Kirin) . . .	531	275	142	132	127
Kwang Sing Co (Amur) .	—	—	—	703	1,606
Total (taels) .	36,133	15,864	8,355	12,487	7,699

All these mines are working alluvial deposits.

In Shantung some gold is produced from placers in Yishui and from quartz veins in Chaoyuan. Quartz veins are also worked in Yenyuan, Szechwan, and in Pingkiang, Hunan; the production is very small. In Western Kansu gold is washed from alluvial sands and gravels near Sining and Tatung; about 10,000 ounces per year are produced.

Many other auriferous regions are known to exist in Western China, among which is the Altai Region; no data are available of the exact amount of gold produced. The von Grote concession in Outer Mongolia has had a considerable output reaching 50,922 taels in 1910. But since then it steadily declined. The gold was first obtained from alluvial deposits but auriferous rocks are also worked afterwards. The Russians have been considering the transfer of the mining right to some other foreign concern, which has not yet been approved by the Peking Government.

An attempt is being made by the writer to indicate the principal places where gold has been traced in China. The list following does not claim to be complete in any way. But all eventual omissions are pardonable *in anticipando,* because none of the places which have eventually been omitted in the list are of sufficient importance to be passed on to posterity.

Classified according to provinces the following are some of the chief centers, known or suspected to contain traces of gold.

Gold Mining in Shantung Province:

In its issue of 3rd June, 1922, the *Weekly Review of the Far East* publishes a detailed list of places in Shantung Province, where gold has been traced. The article gives the following particulars:

Occurrence: Penglai (蓬萊縣).

Wenteng (文登縣).—Longhushan (猳虎山), Shushan (庶山).

Longhushan and Shushan are both located 20 *li* southeast of Wei-hai-wei. They were first exploited in the Ming Dynasty, and again mined in 1900 by the Wei-hai-wei Mining Company, a British concern, but operations ceased in 1906.

Fushan (福山縣). Gold placers occur between 20 and 30 *li* southwest of the city, the important localities being Mashanchai (馬山寨) and Laotzeshan (老子山).

Ninghai (甯海縣).—Miaoshan (茅山), Kwenshan (桂山). Kinniushan (金牛山).

Forty *li* southwest of Ninghai, now named Mowping (牟平) and 60 *li* southeast of Chefoo, there is a river flowing from the Kweishan, and in it is found gold placer. The productive point is named Kowtow (溝頭). The placer has been mined since the Ming Dynasty, and was most prosperous during 1894; working has now ceased.

The Kinniushan auriferous veins:

The quartz of the granite among the granite gneiss occurring 60 *li* south of Ninghai bears gold which was not worked until 1894, and now operations are at a standstill. The gold content in the mineral is estimated at about 0.0015 per cent.

Chaoyuan (招遠縣), Loshan (羅山).—Loshan (洛山), Mapuling (馬步嶺), Kinhwashan (金華山) and Chungyehtsi (中葉集).

The Loshan (羅山) auriferous veins:

The Loshan is also named the Kinshan (金山), and is located 30 *li* northeast of Chaoyuan, and 20 or 30 *li* south of Hwanghsien. The Kinshan of Chao yuan, in fact, is comprised in two hills, the Loshan and the Linglungshan (玲瓏山). The gold deposit is one of the most important in the province. It is only a distance of 70 *li* from Lungkowkang (龍口港), but the journey offers considerable obstacles to travellers.

Along the large quartz veins in the gneiss of this hill there are rock veins which appear to be basalt, varying in depth and extending to several *li*. The trend of this rock is slightly in the direction of west and east. These veins are called the Talinglungshan (大玲瓏山) veins. Besides, there are over ten small quartz veins in the Siaolinglungshan (小玲瓏山) which are slightly goldbearing. In Chengwan (井灣) the iron pyrite also bears gold to the amount of 3 per 100,000. It is slightly commingled with chalcopyrite and galena, but cannot be mined by the amalgam process. The ore of best quality yields gold in 2 per 10,000, and the out-crops also yield the same amount.

This auriferous deposit has been mined for over forty years, and about 300,000 tons have been excavated yielding gold to the value of more than $2,000,000.

The Mapuling (馬步嶺) and the Kinhwashan (金華山) auriferous veins.

Located 50 *li* northwest of Chaoyuan.

Tsisia (棲霞山).

Pingtu (平度山).—Pingtu auriferous veins.

The Pingtu auriferous veins.

These are also known as Kiutien (舊店) auriferous veins, located 70 *li* southeast of Yehhsien (掖縣), on the south-eastern foot-hill of Shwangshan (雙山), Santsoshan (三座山), 95 *li* northeast of Pingtu, and 180 *li* of Lungkowkang (龍口港). The deposit has been mined since the Ming Dynasty, and operations were continued until 1891. The quality of the ore is rather poor.

Biotite-granite and diorite are found in gneiss, and the quartz veins in the gneiss are auriferous. The ore excavated is over 200 *chih* above the water level, below is iron pyrite yielding mostly poor auriferous ore, and therefore working ceased before operations were carried deeper. The gold produced amounted to more than $1,000,000 in value. Although the Pingtu auriferous veins are inferior to the Chaoyuan auriferous veins, nevertheless, they are an important gold deposit.

Yehhsien.—Hunglwanfow (洪巒埠) and Siakiufu (夏邱輔).

Mowping (牟平縣).—Gold placer is found in the Sinliho (辛里河). Kowtowtsun (溝頭村), belonging to Lungwoshe (龍窩社) of the Putsi sub-district (普濟區).

Tsimo (卽墨縣).—Mashan (馬山), located 20 *li* north.

Linchu (臨朐縣).—Hulushan (胡盧山).

Ankiu (安邱縣).—Tingtzekow (丁子溝).

Poshan (博山縣).—Omishan (娥眉山) and Twanshan (團山).

Ishui (沂水縣).—Hungshihkiao (紅石橋) also named Isui.

Chuhsien (莒縣).—Yehchwan (野泉) and Chipaoshan (七寶山).

Licheng (歷城縣).—Gold is produced in the Kinhsiuchwan (錦繡川) which rises from Taishan and is a tributary to the Yellow River.

Pingyinshan (平陰山).—Antzeshan (安子山).

Mr. William F. Collins, in his work *Mineral Enterprise in China,* says the following about gold deposits within the province of Shantung:

The result of geological and prospecting research by the Germans proved the Province to be far poorer in mineral resources than was expected. The Wei-hai-wei gold deposits, after being worked for a short period by a strong British Company, were abandoned in 1906. The ancient Chao Yuan Mine, forty miles south-west of Chefoo, was worked for a time under foreign supervision and 200,000 tons of ten dollar ore developed, but proved disappointing in depth. Efforts have also been made to work gold mines at Ping-tu, Tengchou and T'ung Tsing, but without success. At the Ping-tu mine, equipped with a 20-stamp mill and rock-drills under an American staff, a quartz-vein 4–12 feet thick was worked from 1886 to 1889. In two years 1500 tons of concentrates were raised, but at a depth of 300 feet the ore-body was found to be too poor for profitable working. A stamp mill and plant were erected by a German firm at Maoshan, thirty miles from Chefoo, but operations resulted in considerable loss to the capitalists concerned.

Rea's *Far Eastern Manual (1923)* gives the following particulars regarding gold mines in Shantung province:

Chuyuan Gold Mine.—Location: On the Chuyuan Ho, 40 miles SW of Chefoo; Shantung Province.

Remarks: A quartz vein from 40 to 90 feet wide has been uncovered for more than a mile in length; 200,000 tons of ore, worth $10 per ton, has been developed. The ore is about 40 per cent. free milling; years ago a chlorination-plant was in operation upon the tailings from the stamps. The mine has been operated unprofitably by several different foreign companies. When the Germans established Tsingtau they formed a company to operate this mine and installed considerable machinery. Their efforts were unsuccessful and the machinery was removed in 1907.

Ishui Gold Mining Bureau.—Office: Ishui, Shantung Province. Mine: Hung Shih Bridge, 60 *li* S.W. of Ishui. Annual Output: (average) 2,700 taels. Remarks: The mine formerly was operated by a Sino-German Company, and was taken over by the Chinese government after the outbreak of the European war.

Laiwu Gold Mine.—Location: Shu Chia Ling, Tung Shen, Laiwu, Shantung Province. Area: Over 10,000 sq. ft. Capital: Over $20,000.

The *Encyclopædia Sinica* says:

The best known mine in China is that of Chou-yuen, about 40 miles S.W. of Chefoo, where a quartz vein from 40 to 90 feet wide has been uncovered for more than a mile in length; 200,000 tons of ore have been developed here, but the mine has been closed for some time. At P'ingtu, near by, are other mines probably of considerable value.

The following remarks with reference to gold deposits in Shantung province are contained in the Chinese Maritime Customs Decennial Reports 1912–1921:

The Chaoyuan (招遠) gold mine, in the district of Chaoyuan, is said in former times to have produced a considerable output, but at present the yield is only 20 to 30 ounces a day. The P'ingtu (平度) gold mine was first opened during the reign of T'ien Ch'i (天啟), of the Ming (明) dynasty, and in its palmy days the daily output reached 600 ounces. It is now under the management of a native concern. The mine is said to have been nearly worked out and the present output can hardly cover expenses. Though there are many other gold mines scattered over the province, none deserves particular notice.

Gold Mining in Hupeh Province:

On the exposed sandflats between Sunday Island, 35 miles below Shasi, and Tungshih, 40 miles above, a miserable pittance is earned by thousands during the winter months (for centuries) by alluvial gold washing. The dust is distributed equally through the sand, and a net gain of 200 cash per day is reckoned good—a poor wage even for Shasi. The gold is of fine quality and enjoys a local value higher than its sterling one, due to its portability. It has, for this reason alone, in recent months realised £6 per ounce. —*(Chinese Maritime Customs Decennial Reports 1902–1911)*.

Gold Mining in Hunan Province:

Pingkiang Gold Mining Bureau.—Location: Pingkiang, Hunan Province. The bureau is managed by the Hunan Provincial Government. Officer: Director, Peng Chi. The operation of the mine was suspended for several years, owing to bad management and civil war. Work was recently resumed with 400 laborers; to be increased to 1,000.

Present Daily Output: 80 piculs of ore from two mines, the Peishiho and Tahpaolung. Beginning with an output of 1,934 taels in 1912, the yield gradually decreased to 766 taels in 1917. In 1918, operations were suspended until 1922.

Mines: There are a number of mines, scattered over a mountainous district. The formation consists of gray slatey schist, carrying veins of quartz. There are numerous small workings dotted about the hillsides, most of which have been abandoned as either profitless or on account of the inability to cope with the water. In most cases the adits on the creek banks were driven down hill, with the inevitable result that the working became flooded.

Ching Tang Gold Mine.—Location: Pingsiang, District of Hunan Province, near the Kiangsi border. Operated by the Hunan Mining Bureau.

Output: About 1,500 taels, or Chinese ounces, of pure gold per year. The mine has been worked to a depth of 650 ft. Miners are paid about 225 cash per eight hour shift. The Bureau furnishes the tools and explosives.—(Rea's *Far Eastern Manual, 1923)*.

The gold mine in the Pingkiang district (平江) of the Yochow prefecture is now said to produce some 400 to 500 ounces troy of gold per month, and the number of men employed is said to be 2,000. In 1906 foreign machinery was imported and four foreign engineers were engaged. This machinery was never used, and the foreigners left the mine after a short stay. The mine is now being exploited by Chinese methods.—*(Chinese Maritime Customs Decennial Reports 1902–1911)*.

Gold Mining in Szechuen Province:

Maha Gold Mine.—Location: 50 miles NW of Ningyuan, Szechuen Province. The mine is operated jointly by the Central government, the Szechuen provincial government and the merchants. The mine has been worked for hundreds of years by native methods. In recent years there has been an effort to introduce modern methods. Some machinery was purchased in America with funds supplied by the Central government, but only part of it actually reached the mine. Revolutionary disturbances and disagreements between the government and private interests have retarded the development of the property.

Lode: The mine contains a wide lode varying from 10-ft. to 50-ft. and 100-ft. The richer ore-shoots average 12 or 14 dwt. of gold per ton, and carry considerable silver, copper and lead, and the lode from end to end averages 6 dwt. The ore has only been washed from time immemorial by sometimes as many as 15,000 men at a time, both in the valley in which the mine is situated, and in the sands and gravel bars of the Yalung river, 4,000-ft. below the present workings. The ore selected for crushing is carried by hand over the summit of the ridge to the Kolodo creek 400-ft. below, where there are 80 stamps worked by 40 overshot water-wheels. Each stamp weighs about 40-lbs. and crushes 600-lbs. of ore daily in a stone mortar. About 50 per cent. of the gold content of the ore is saved by means of quicksilver, which is obtained from a cinnabar mine situated at Hangcho to the south of Kwa Pit. The amalgam is taken to the Mining Bureau at Shaaba, where the miners are paid half its value, as they work on a 50 per cent. royalty. The workings are quite free from water, and as the lode dips with the slope of the mountain, the mine can be worked by adits to a great depth. The workings on the Mala mine extend for 550-ft. along the strike of the vein and to a depth of 400 ft. on its dip, which is 35° from the vertical. For the most part, the lode has been worked in a primitive way by the Lolos, an aboriginal tribe, under the supervision of Chinese.

Yu Hua Mining Co., Ltd.—Tientsin, Chihli Province. Established: April, 1914. Registered: October, 1916. Capital: $100,000.

Remarks: The Company was formed to mine for gold in Erhkai, Wutun, Mowkung, Szechuen Province.— (Rea's *Far Eastern Manual, 1923)*.

Gold mines in the district of Tatsienlu (打箭鑪) are plentiful. One is found at Mienning (冕甯), in the Kienchang district; and one at Tuihoshih (對河石), opposite the river in Sungpan (松潘), to the north of Chengtu. But these mines, owing to the non-existence of individual mining rights, are not worked.—*(Chinese Maritime Customs Decennial Reports 1912–1921)*.

A section of the Fowkiang (涪江), a tributary to the Yangtse, between Mienyang (綿陽) and Tungchwan (潼川), Szechwan province, yields placer gold. Over 100 washers' camps have been erected. The total daily output of these camps is estimated at a little more than one tael (weight) in the low water season in winter.—*(Chinese Economic Bulletin, No. 208, of 1925)*.

A remarkable piece of news comes from Peking. There, in Autumn of 1924, the Pao Hwa Co., Ltd. (寶華有限公司) has applied to the Ministry of Agriculture and Commerce for registration. The company was formed by Szechuenese merchants residing in Peking, with the object of exploiting gold in the Kinshakiang (金沙江) in Szechuen, meaning literally "Gold Sand-River." The plan for raising the requisite capital includes the issue of premium bonds, the drawn numbers of which are exchangeable at par value for the shares of the company. This unique method of raising capital seems to indicate that the investment of funds in the gold-sand-river-mine is a sporting chance in the full meaning of the word.

Regarding gold mining in Szechuen province Sir Alexander Hosie, in his book,[1] says the following:

The traveller who enters Szechwan by the Yangtsze in winter cannot fail to be struck by the rude placer mining which is carried on the numerous shingle banks exposed in the bed of the river during that season, but, so far as I have been able to ascertain from personal inquiry and observation, the amount of gold annually won from the bed of the Yangtsze does little more than compensate the unemployed peasantry for their labour, and cannot be other than insignificant. There is a mistaken idea that all this gold is washed down from its source in Tibet during the annual rise in the river, but this is disproved by the fact that placer mining is also carried on in the Szechwan tributaries of the main river, and the traveller to Ch'engtu by the Min River sees the same busy search for gold in its exposed bed. Every prefecture ("Fu") is credited with the precious metal; but careful inquiry goes to show that the important gold-bearing quartz is found only in the west and north-west of the province. The district of An Hsien, in the Department of Mien Chou, to the north of Ch'engtu, yields small nuggets of gold, reputed to be the finest, and is closely followed in quality by the product of Litang in the far west. There is a large number of quartz mines in the Ta-chien-lu district but the fact that the gold-bearing strata lie principally within the area occupied by the Tibetans and other tribesmen where Chinese are unable to work without protection accounts for the backward condition of the gold-mining industry. There is, however, a Government mine supplied with foreign plant in the district of Mien-ning Hsien, in the range of mountains between the An-ning River in the Chien-ch'ang Valley and the Ya-lung River. This is the Maha mine, to operate which a grant of T. 100,000 was made by the Provincial Treasury. It had not been worked lately, but another attempt was about to be made to run it. There were

[1] *Szechwan, Its Products, Industries and Resources.* By Sir Alexander Hosie. Shanghai, Kelly & Walsh, Ltd.

others interested in it besides the Government. One native bank contributed T. 20,000 and held 200 Chinese ounces of gold worth about T. 37 an ounce, or a value of T. 7,400, against its contribution. The Provincial Government had, however, forbidden the bank to dispose of these bars, probably the total output up to that time, as it and other investors were interested creditors, and no arrangement for the division of the spoil had yet been arrived at. Most of the gold that finds its way into the province comes from Tibet.

Gold Mining in Chihli Province:

Numerous deposits of gold and silver exist at points in the Jehol (Chengteh) district, the gold being derived for the most part from the alluvium and silver from argentiferous galena. The best known gold mine is that of Ching Ch'ang Kou Liang, forty miles north-west of Ch'ao Yang in Chihli, which in six years yielded 43,000 ounces of gold from 39,000 tons of fissure-vein quartz. A few small gold mines were being worked with British capital in this district in 1913.—*(William F. Collins).*

Gold Mining in Kwangtung Province:

Tung Fong Siao Ta Tze Kow Gold Mining Co., Ltd.—Location: Siao Ta Tze Kow, Chaoyang, Kwangtung Province. Established: July, 1904; Registered: January, 1905. Capital Tls. 40,000.—(Rea's *Far Eastern Manual, 1923).*

Gold Mining in Yunnan Province:

Gold is found and worked in the sub-prefecture of Talang(他郎), 40 *li* from the town of the same name. A mine was there once opened, in the reign of Tao Kuang (道光) of the Ching dynasty, about A.D. 1821. It is the only important gold mine in this district, and is fairly productive, in spite of the very primitive machinery used. A yearly tax of Tls. 50 is levied on this mine by the Chinese officials.—*(Chinese Maritime Customs Decennial Reports 1902–1911).*

Gold Mining in Shansi Province:

The principal places in Shansi Province, where gold has been traced:

Yuhsien (盂縣).—Gold placer.

Wensi (聞喜).—Gold placer.

Yuanku (垣曲).—Gold placers occur in the west of Tanshan (潭山) and Kinghungsze (金中寺).

Yangcheng (陽城).—Gold placer.

Taning (大寧).—Gold placer.

Taichow (代州).—Gold placers occur in Shetowchu Hwaputungshan (化不動山), Mayashih (馬牙石), and

Yaiti (崖底).—*(Weekly Review of the Far East, June 3, 1922).*

Gold Mining in Kwangtung Leased Territory:

Alluvial gold is found at 15 places in the Dairen Territory. Those which may be looked on with some hope of profit are only four—Meikiatun (梅家屯), Ikiatun (衣家屯), Pochekow (破車溝) and Shengshuisze (勝水寺). Some of them were first mined by natives, and then by Russians, but now none of them are worked. —*(Chinese Maritime Customs Decennial Reports 1902–1911).*

Gold Mining in Manchuria:

The alluvial gold of Northern Manchuria, found along the banks of the Amur, the Yalu, the Tumen, and the Liao Rivers, is derived from alluvials believed to be of recent age; some at least of these have an average gold content of 1.07 dwt. per ton. In 1915 the Manchurian production was about 120,000 ounces. The gold districts (Ch'ang) of Manchuria are about twenty in number. The most important mines are Moho, situated about the junction of the Argun and Silka Rivers, Chiap'ikou about 100 miles south-east of Kirin, and Tumentzu on the Korean frontier. The Moho alluvials are said to have produced as much as 100,000 ounces of gold monthly within recent times.—*(William F. Collins).*

In Manchuria placer gold has been worked, but nowhere on a large scale, and at no time was there any promise of great strikes of gold. The best-known places for these deposits are Chiap'ikow (夾皮溝), in the Sungari Valley, belts at Tunghwa (通化) and Hwaijen (懷仁), in the valley of the Hun, a tributary of the Yalu River, Wufenglow (舞鳳樓) and Wantientze (萬店子), on the Upper Hun River, flowing north of Fushun, belts in the Huifa River (輝發河) valley and the valley of the Chai River (柴河), flowing immediately north of Tiehling (鐵嶺). At each of these places a considerable amount of placer gold has been gained in the past. Gold veins at Chiap'ikow, Paomachuan (跑馬圈) 38 miles south of Tunghwa,—Siangluwantze (香爐灣子) about 12 miles south-east of North Shanchengtze (山城子),—were at one time vigorously operated, but now all of them lie utterly neglected. At other places much prospecting and experimental working has been conducted, but nowhere for any length of time, and not a single mine of any magnitude would appear to have been struck. —*(Chinese Maritime Customs Decennial Reports 1912–1921).*

Regarding gold mining at Mo-ho, in Heilungkiang province, the following remarks are taken from J. Edkins' work, entitled *Chinese Currency* (Shanghai, 1901):

In the *Chung-wai-pao* of August 3rd, 1899, there is mention of the output of the Mo-ho mines. From June, 1898, to January, 1899, the amount of gold was 6,806 gold taels. At Kwan-yin-shan it was 9,125 gold taels. Changed for silver the amount realised was taels 426,600. The gold diggers receive six-tenths. Gold is changed on the Mo-ho mines at the rate of 268 taels of silver to one tael gold, if we can trust the correctness of this account.

In 1866 gold was not yet found at the Mo-ho river. By an edict in November the searchers for gold were allowed to receive land without payment for two years. In the third year of occupation they would pay a tax of 110 cash a mow.

The *Chung-wai* of December 24th, 1900, says the output of gold at the Mo-ho river was in 1888 and 1889 each 9,000 taels; in 1890 and 1892 was 85,000 taels; in 1891, 12,000 taels; in 1894, it was 108,000 taels; in 1895, 100,000 taels; in 1896, 300,000 taels. After that time the rule was that the government appropriated six-tenths of the output.

Sansing Gold Mining Bureau.—Mines: Sansing, Kirin Province. Output: 142,055 taels in 1920. Remarks: in the neighborhood of Sansing, gold is found in 30 different places in a ravine about 100 *li* in length, called Tatungkow. The mining industry here, originally in control of the merchants, was taken over by the provincial government and placed in charge of the Sansing Bureau in 1907.—(Rea's *Far Eastern Manual, 1923)*.

Gold mining has long been carried on in the neighbourhood of Sansing (三姓), where the precious metal is found distributed over 30 different places in a ravine about 100 *li* in length, called Tatungkow (大東溝). The industry, which was originally in the hands of a mercantile company, was taken over by the provincial government and placed under the control of the Sansing Gold Mining Office in 1907. The present annual output is about 2,000 ounces; of this total, seven-tenths are given to the miners as payment; of the remaining three-tenths, half is appropriated for office expenses and half, *i.e.*, 300 ounces of gold, is handed over to the provincial treasury. The gold mines at Wanlukow (萬鹿溝), Wuhulin (五虎林) and Liangshuichüan (涼水泉), situated in the midst of dense forests alongside the Russian frontier, north of Suifenho (綏芬河) district, were taken over, as a protective measure, by an official company styled the Tung Lu Kung Wu Tiao Ch'a Chü at the same time as the Sansing mines. The company has been dissolved since then, but a Weyüan still resides in the locality, issuing licenses to miners at the rate of 4 *fen* of gold a month. The total amount of gold received as license fees is at present about 50 ounces per annum, so that it would appear that more than 100 miners are employed there. A vein of gold, reported to be rich, has also been discovered recently by the Wuhulin (五虎林), Weiyüan at Hsinglungkow (興龍溝), in the Mishan

(密山府) prefecture, and a small sum has been appropriated for experimental working.

During the past two years prospecting licenses have also been issued to various mercantile companies for gold mining at two places in Tayenkow (大沿溝), situated in the Hwachwan district (樺川縣) and at Chienshuikow (淺水溝), in the Ningan prefecture.

These remarks are taken from the Chinese Maritime Customs Decennial Reports 1902–1911. From the same source we learn the following particulars about gold deposits in the Hunchun district in Manchuria, near the Corean border:

Gold is stated to be found at the following places, viz., Shachinkow (沙金溝), Kankowtze (干溝子), Ertaokow (二道溝), Santaokow (三道溝), Szetaokow (四道溝), Wutaokow (五道溝), Liutaokow (六道溝), Siangfangtzekow (香房子溝), Siaoliutaokow (小六道溝), Liushuhotze (柳樹河子), Sipehchakow (西北岔溝), and probably at other places, if investigations were made by experts. These places are all situated at distances varying from 35 to 260 *li* in an east-north-easterly direction from Hunchun along the range of hills on the northern bank of the Hungch'i-ho (紅旗河).

The most important gold mine is at Santaokow. The superintendant introduced the license system, which is now generally followed there as elsewhere. For the payment of 2½ *fen* weight in gold anybody can obtain a license, which gives the holder permission to dig for gold: at the present rate this license fee is equal to about Mexican $1. At present there are about 3,000 men working at the gold mines; of these 2,000 are engaged at Santaokow. During 1911 the total gain of gold from the mines has averaged, roughly, from 4,500 to 4,600 *liang*. The average value of 1 *liang* of gold is 160 *tiao,* or, say, Mexican $40. The work is conducted in a very primitive manner; but such as it is, it pays well and is of great importance to the inhabitants of this town and district.

Wu Tung Ho Gold Mine.—Location: Wutungho, Heilungkiang Province. Capital: $300,000, in 60 shares of $5,000 each.

Particulars: This mine originally was operated by the officials but now has been taken over by the merchants. Under the officials the mine was worked at a heavy loss.

Yuchingkow Gold Mine Bureau.—Location: Huma, Heilungkiang Province. Operated by the Chinese Government.

Output: 3,001 taels in 1920. This is one of several gold mines in the district controlled by the government since 1915. The alluvial gold of this field is derived from alluvials believed to be of recent age. Some of these deposits have an average gold content of 1.07 dwt. per ton.

Kuma Gold Mining Bureau.—Location: Hsing Lung Kow, Huma, Heilungkiang Province.

Operators: Chinese Government Gold Mining Department.

Established: 1915.

Area: 28,080,000 mow.

Annual Output: 30,000 taels (average for a term of years).

Mines: The principal mines operated by the Kuma bureau are Kuchanghsinkow, Hsinglungkow, Wanhsingkow, Hsingkiangkow, Kosungkow, Tehsungkow, Pehsihlikow and Washihilkow.

History: The first gold mine in the field was discovered by a Russian who operated it secretly for a time. When the Chinese authorities became aware of its existence, an official administration was appointed. Previous to the forming of the government bureau, the Ministry of Finance reported: "Now we have found that gold ore in the province of Heilungkiang is exceedingly rich. All the regions along the river from Chichienho on the north-west to Taipingkou on the south-east for a distance of several thousand *li* are auriferous. There have been five gold mining enterprises, the Muho, Kuma, Kwantu and Chichienho, which are official concerns and the Chingkou a semi-official undertaking." In 1914, 1915, and 1916, 10,000 to 20,000 miners were employed and the annual production was more than 40,000 taels. A period of depression followed, when only about 1,000 taels were yielded annually. The losses from 1917 to 1921 are estimated at $400,000. After the re-organization of the administration in May, 1921, the mines made a profit of $2,000 in seven months.

Kwantu Gold Mining Bureau.—Location: Lopeh, Heilungkiang Province. Operated by the Chinese Government Gold Mining Department since 1915. This is one of the five leading gold mining enterprises in the province, which are under official management.

Annual Output: From 5,000 taels to 20,000 taels in the last ten years.—(Rea's *Far Eastern Manual, 1923).*

"It is fully realised that the prosperity of Heilungkiang province depends mainly on the development of its gold-fields," says Mr. R. F. C. Hedgeland, Commissioner of Customs for Aigun in his annual report for 1924, "and during the past two years the country in the center of the Aigun, Nenchiang, and Lopei districts has been the scene of much activity on the part of gold seekers. The total gold exported through this office during 1924 was valued at Hk. Tls. 2,763,507, as against Hk. Tls. 3,235,900 in 1923, and, on the basis of 0.822857 tael being the equivalent of 1 ounce troy, amounted to roughly 115,850 ounces troy, as compared with 136,169 ounces for the preceding 12 months. If current rumour is to be believed, the amount of gold actually won during the year was a little under 300 poods (106,642 ounces), as compared with, roughly, 250 poods (88,869 ounces) in 1923. That still better results were not obtainable is said to be attributable in part to the exhaustion of some of the richer and more easily worked deposits and to higher operating costs having made it unprofitable to treat lower-grade ore, from which wealth could be obtained if costs were on a more reasonable scale. It is understood that the output of the Feng Yuan Gold Mining Company (逢源商辦金廠) reached approximately 200 poods (71,095 ounces), as against 170 poods (60,431 ounces) in 1923, but the net result of the work accomplished by its subsidiary, the Taiping Gold Mining Company (太平商辦金廠), is said to have been a loss of, roughly, $150,000. Progress made by the Te Yuan (德源金廠) and Ku Ma Erh (庫瑪爾金鑛局) Companies, whose properties were thought to hold ore of considerable promise, has proved very disappointing, and neither company produced more than about 20 poods (7,110 ounces). Three of the other companies who have undertaken development and exploratory work during the year appear to be on the verge of bankruptcy, and, generally, results have been so disappointing that it is unlikely that further capital will be obtained to continue the search for payable zones until such time as a considerable drop in mining costs has come about."

The *Chinese Economic Monthly,* in its issue No. 2 of November 1923, gives the following particulars about gold mines in Kirin Province:

District	*Location*	*Area*	*Remarks*
Hwachwan (樺川)	Tungkow (東溝)	over 1,200 sq. *li*	Taken over by the Ministry of Finance.
Han (依蘭)	Heipeishan (黑嘴山)	" 700 " "	Do.
Panshih (磐石)	Maoerhshan (帽兒山)	1,080 mow	1918, Tung Hsing Gold Mining Co. (東興金礦公司)
Do.	Tachwanyen (大泉眼)	1,368 "	1918, Liu Chih-pu (劉芝圃)
Yenki (延吉)	Pokoshihtze (鵓鴿哨子)	2,560 "	1917, Sun Tu-nan (孫圖南)
Tungning (東甯)	Siaosuifenho (小綏芬河)	2,800 "	1914, Li Kia-ao (李家鰲)
Hwachwan (樺川)	Shwanglungho (雙龍河)	2,700 "	1916, Chen Hsing Mining Co. (振興金礦公司)
Itung (依通)	Shaotiaopei (籬條背)	2,655 "	1918, Ning Hsi-wei (甯西圍)
Panshih (磐石)	Towtaokow (頭道溝)		1917, Hsu Kioh yuan (徐覺園) License cancelled because ore unworkable.

District	*Location*	*Area*	*Remarks*
Mishan (密山)	Nantienmen (南天門)		1913, Hsiao Hwei Liang (蕭惠良) Prospection expired.
Hwatien (樺甸)	Litzekow (栗子溝)		1914, Chieh Shin (解鑫) Prospection expired.
Holung (和龍)	Erhtaokow (二道溝)		1917, Sun Shen-shu (孫星樞) Prospection expired.
Ningan (寧安)	Chiensuikow (淺水溝)		1910, Ku Pei-lan (顧佩蘭) Prospection expired.
Muling (穆稜)	Chiupikow (楸皮溝)		1913, Hsiao Hwei Liang (蕭惠良) Prospection expired.
Hwatien (樺甸)	Litzekow (栗子溝)	430 mow	1917, Tang Pao-kwei (唐寶珪)
Do.	Do.	2,651 „	1917, Chieh Shin (解鑫)
Do.	Pichowling (皮州嶺)	2,090 „	1918, Kung Chi-chin (孔季璡)
Do.	Chiapikow (夾皮溝)	520 „	1917, Chiang Chia-chen (蔣嘉深)
Holung (和龍)	Santaokow (三道溝)	549 „	1917, Tu Chen-chu (屠振初)
Wangtsing (汪清)	Topenkow (托盤溝)	1,629 „	1917, Chang Wei-cheng (張維城)
Muling (穆稜)	Changshowshan (長壽山)		1918, Chang Kin-men (張金門) and Shan Hsi (單錫)
Kirin (吉林)	Futaiho (富太河)		Applications were made prior to the establishment of the Kirin Industrial Commissioner's Office and are still awaiting Government sanction.
Do.	Erhtaokow (二道溝)		Do.
Do.	Chepeitzekow (車貝子溝)		Do.
Do.	Yangmukow (楊木溝)		Do.
Do.	Wukiashao (五家哨)		Do.
Itung (伊通)	Tsingtuitze (青堆子)		Do.
Mengkiang (濛江)	Tungpeicha (東北岔)		Do.

District	*Location*	*Area*	*Remarks*
Mengkiang (濛江)	Nwanmutiaotzekow (煖木條子溝)		Applications were made prior to the establishment of the Kirin Industrial Commissioner's Office and are still awaiting Government sanction.
Do.	Hsinkaiho (新開河)		Do.
Do.	Lowho 漏河)		Do.
Do.	Tungpeicha (東北岔)		Do.
Do.	Liuho (溜河)		Do.
Do.	Liutaotangho (六道湯河)		Do.
Do.	Hwangnikangtze (黃泥崗子)		Do.
Panshih (磐石)	Hwangkwachiakow (黃瓜架溝)		Do.
Hwatien (樺甸)	Hankiakow (乾家溝)		Do.
Do.	Muchiho (木奇河)		Do.
Do.	Erhtaoho (二道河)		Do.
Do.	Hanyachow (汗窰溝)		Do.
Do.	Wanliangho (萬兩河)		Do.
Do.	Shahotze (沙河子)		Do.
Do.	Towtaoho (頭道河)		Do.
Do.	Pataoho (八道河)		Do.
Shulan (舒蘭)	Sanchaho (三岔河)		Do.
Yenki (延吉)	Erhsantaokow (二三道溝)		Do.
Ningan (甯安)	Shalanchan (沙蘭站)		Do.
Do.	Peikow (北溝)		Do.
Do.	Nanhutow (南湖頭)		Do.
Do.	Weitzekow (葦子溝)		Do.
Do.	Kinkeng (金坑)		Do.
Do.	Yentungshihtze (煙筒硝子)		Do.

District	*Location*	*Area*	*Remarks*
Ningan (甯安)	Laoyehkow (老爺溝)		Applications were made prior to the establishment of the Kirin Industrial Commissioner's Office and are still awaiting Government sanction.
Do.	Chiensuikow (淺水溝)		Do.
Do.	Tungchienmiao (東淺毛)		Do.
Do.	Szejenkow (四人溝)		Do.
Do.	Liushuho (柳樹河)		Do.
Do.	Paichaikow (白柴溝)		Do.
Do.	Tutowtzekow (土豆子溝)		Do.
Do.	Wuhulin (五虎林)		Do.
Hunchun (琿春)	Santaokow (三道溝)		Do.
Do.	Liushuho (柳樹河)		Do.
Do.	Tsoshukow (柞樹溝)		Do.
Do.	Siangfangtzekow (香房子溝)		Do.
Hunchow	Liutaokow (六道溝)		Do.
Do.	Shakinkow (沙金溝)		Do.
Do.	Erhkweitzeku (二鬼子谷)		Do.
Do.	Wakangchai (瓦剛寨)		Do.
Do.	Matita (馬滴塔)		Do.
Do.	Szetaokow (四道溝)		Do.
Do.	Wutaokow (五道溝)		Do.
Do.	Hsipeichakow (西北岔溝)		Do.
Do.	Hulupieh (苛蘆別)		Do.
Tungning (東甯)	Wanlukow (萬鹿溝)		Do.
Do.	Kutzekow (脖子溝)		Do.
Do.	Kiaochiehtingtze (交界頂子)		Do.

District	*Location*	*Area*	*Remarks*
Tungning (東寧)	Kanglanho (缸闌河)		Applications were made prior to the establishment of the Kirin Industrial Commissioner's Office and are still awaiting Government sanction.
Holung (和龍)	Shihmentze (石門子)		Do.
Do.	Wangpeipotze (旺白脖子)		Do.
Do.	Szetunfushentung (四屯福深峝)		Do.
Do.	Chengtzekow (城子溝)		Do.
Do.	Erhtaokow (二道溝)		Do.
Do.	Chiapikow (夾皮溝)		Do.
Do.	Hsiaoliutaokow (小六道溝)		Do.
Do.	Hweichingchieh (恆慶街)		Do.
Do.	Wulungtung (五龍洞)		Do.
Do.	Chaisuiling (彩水嶺)		Do.
Do.	Shakinkow (砂金溝)		Do.
Do.	Chungchenweitze (鐘城崴子)		Do.
Do.	Shasungpei (杉松背)		Do.
Do.	Pataoho (八道河)		Do.
Do.	Hwochihtung (火已洞)		Do.
Omu (額穆)	Tangkiawei (唐家崴)		Do.
Do.	Hukiatien (胡家店)		Do.
Do.	Peitayang (北大洋)		Do.
Wangtsing (汪清)	Tawangtsingkow (大旺清溝)		Do.
Do.	Hsiaowangtsingkow (小旺清溝)		Do.
Do.	Shakinkow (砂金溝)		Do.
Do.	Lishukow (梨樹溝)		Do.
Do.	Erhkengta (二根塔)		Do.

District	*Location*	*Area*	*Remarks*
Wangtsing (汪清)	Wangpapotze (王八脖子)		Applications were made prior to the establishment of the Kirin Industrial Commissioner's Office and are still awaiting Government sanction.
Do.	Hwoshaopu (火燒舖)		Do.
Do.	Pinghulukow (冰葫蘆溝)		Do.
Do.	Hsitapo (西大坡)		Do.
Llan	Kishengho (吉星河)		Do.
Do.	Miaoling (廟嶺)		Do.
Do.	Limukow (梨木溝)		Do.
Do.	Hsinkow (新溝)		Do.
Do.	Tangketaying (唐疙瘩營)		Do.
Do.	Mafenpao (馬糞包)		Do.
Do.	Erhtaohotze (二道河子)		Do.
Do.	Yanganchang (永安廠)		Do.
Hwachwan (樺川)	Tatsingpei (大青背)		Do.
Do.	Hsiaotsingpei (小青背)		Do.
Do.	Liushuho (柳樹河)		Do.
Do.	Tsingtsuitze (青咀子)		Do.
Do.	Hwapikow (樺皮溝)		Do.
Do.	Hsiaochengshunho (小正身河)		Do.
Do.	Shwangchatow (雙岔頭)		Do.
Do.	Lannikow (亂泥溝)		Do.
Do.	Szechienfang (四間房)		Do.
Do.	Yungtzekow (甬子溝)		Do.
Do.	Shihtowkow (石頭溝)		Do.
Do.	Hsiaonankow (小南溝)		Do.

District	*Location*	*Area*	*Remarks*
Mishan (密山)	Hsinglungkow (興龍溝)		Applications were made prior to the establishment of the Kirin Industrial Commissioner's Office and are still awaiting Government sanction.
Do.	Tsingshantzekow (青山子溝)		Do.
Suiyuan	Chinwangyukow (秦皇漁溝)		Do.
Muling (穆稜)	Liangsuichwan (涼水泉)		Do.
Do.	Chiupikow (秋皮溝)		Do.
Do.	Yangmuchuntze (楊木椿子)		Do.
Do.	Sankotingtze (三棵頂子)		Do.
Do.	Talishukow (大梨樹溝)		Do.
Tungkiang (同江)	Yangnukang (楊牛崗)		Do.
Do.	Hanchungkow (寒溝)		Do.
Yaoho (澆河)	Tataiho (大帶河)		Do.
Do.	Hsiaochiehhokow (小佳河溝)		Do.
Nungan (農安)	Bank of Itung River (伊通河)		Do.

Gold Mining in Mongolia:

A fifty-year mining concession was obtained in 1899 by a Mr. G. V. von Grote over an area in Northern Mongolia bounded on the west by the great road from Urga to Kiachta, on the east by the Onon River, on the south by the Great Road from Onon River to Urga, and on the north by the Russian frontier. Of the profits six per cent. was first to be paid to the shareholders, and from the remainder three-tenths was to go to the Board of Revenue, two to the Mongol nobles and the remaining five to the shareholders. A Russian company called the Societe Mongolor was formed and American machinery imported. Operations were at first unsuccessful, but since 1910 dividends of from 150 per cent. to 300 per cent. have been earned.

In 1913 the Company was working eight mines in the Iro basin and active prospecting was in progress. The Company employed upwards of 7,000 Chinese coolies, from whose foremen the gold was bought, and sold in Belgium and France.—(W. F. Collins, in *Mineral Enterprise in China).*

Mongolyor Mining Company:

The Company works the following fields in the Iro River basin: Iro, Tologoika, Mogi, Harganate, Narin-Harganati, Yalbik, Ulentoi and Nikho, while outside the Iro basin, work is carried on in the valleys of the Kudara, a tributary of the Chikoi in Mongolia, Tereltzi, tributary to the upper Kerulen, and Hera Gol at Tzo Modo.

History: This Russian company was organized by Baron von Grote, who secured from the Chinese government a concession to prospect for and mine all the gold found in the two aimaks, or districts, of Tuschetu-khan and Tsetsen-khan. The early directing of the work in Mongolia was in the hands of I.V. Pokrovski. Some of the early development work was done by American engineers. The original proposal to use dredges and similar large scale work proved impracticable.

Mining Methods: The company uses 3 methods for obtaining its gold. There are: (1) Work by the company itself by means of laborers hired by the day; (2) The lease of whole areas to capitalised organizations who find all the necessary capital for exploitation, pay no rent, but are bound to sell all gold obtained to the Mongolyor Company; (3) Lease of small areas to minor combinations of laborers who are provided by the company with the necessary equipment and are bound to sell all gold to the company.—(Rea's *Far Eastern Manual, 1923).*

Speaking of the von Grote gold mining concession in Mongolia the *Chinese Economic Bulletin* (1923) has the following to say:

At the close of the last century the possibility of developing gold mines in Mongolia began to attract the attention of foreigners. In 1896 a Mr. V. von Grote obtained a concession from the Mongolian authorities to work gold mines in certain localities under the jurisdiction of Tushetu Khan (圖什圖汗) and Tsetsen Khan (車臣汗).

The mining area was later on extended to the whole territory of Tsetsen Khan and Tushetu Khan and under the auspices of Mr. von Grote's Russian-financed company which was generally known as the Mongolian Company, was founded in 1900. In 1915, the Urga government declared its independence of the Chinese Government and granted to the company additional rights to prospect and develop all the gold mines in the whole territory of Tushetu Khan and Tsetsen Khan for a period of sixteen years, with the option of renewing the contract on its expiration in 1931.

In 1921, by a sixty years' lease, the Russian company conceded its mining rights to the Mongolian Trading Company, an American firm, which later on transferred the same mining rights to the

Peking Mongolian Mining Company, which is financed by both Chinese and American capital. The last-named company was recently floated with the aid of an American merchant with a capital of $600,000, one third of which is represented by Chinese interests.

The total mining area in which the company has the right to operate and prospect covers 263,000 square miles and over twenty-one gold mines have already been worked. The following list shows the names of the mines and the total output of each during the years between 1902 and 1920:

Name of Mine	*Quantity of Gold Produced between 1902 and 1920, in Ounces.*
Iro	10,376,770
Burlo	15,367,010
Adjir	4,592,550
Tirildja	4,291,837
Vereya	276,511
Khaganatui	34,670,796
Buguntai (Tolgol)	109,598,955
Yalbik	5,657,328
Kudara	13,827,673
Kuitun	1,148,325
Tzurkhudzun	440,613
Arkingol	9,254
Ulentui	2,938,880
Ulan-Tologol	43,615
Mogol	18,510,786
Narin Khaganatui	39,448,397
Ikhe Henguchi	578,265
Nelkha	1,827,910
Kozulika	230,584
Dzoun-Modo	17,796,740
Name Unknown	27,444,894
Total	309,347,693

(Apparently the last three figures are meant to be decimals of ounces).

Gold Mining in Chinese Turkestan:

Among the mineral resources, *gold* occurs in the Altai mountains at Yu-tien (于闐), Ho-tien (禾闐), Ta-chen (塔城), Wu-su-hsien (烏蘇縣), Sui-lai-hsien (綏來縣) and near Karashar, the rivers at Yu-tien and Ta-chen being the heaviest producer. The metal is usually exported to India. — *(Chinese Economic Monthly, 1925, No. 12).*

SECTION 2

SILVER AND SILVER TRANSACTIONS

CHAPTER VII

SILVER PRODUCTION AND DISTRIBUTION

Where Silver is Found.

THE world's annual production of silver during the first quarter of the twentieth century has averaged, in round figures, 192 million ounces.

The two largest silver-producing countries are the United States of America and Mexico. Both sources have been responsible for an almost equal supply of silver during the past twenty-five years, each to the extent of about 32% of the total world's production. These two countries are therefore supplying practically two-thirds of the silver reaching the market, namely 64%

Canada's output is about	10%
South America's output is about . . .	8%
Total American output .	82%
Australia's output is about	6%
Other countries output is about. . . .	12%
Total . .	100%

As will be seen from an itemised table appearing on pages 153–154, the production of silver since the discovery of America, *i.e.*, between A.D. 1493 and 1900,

was	8,828,531,000	ounces
Between 1901 and 1924 (inclusive) .	4,622,414,541	„
Total world production . .	13,450,945,541	„

This means that the output during the last 24 years has been nearly 56% of the total production of the preceding 408 years, a highly significant fact.

The following table shows the world production (in thousands of fine ounces) of silver since 1910, classified according to countries of origin. It will be observed that, apart from the United States where the output has been fairly steady, there are wide fluctuations in the size of the production. Mexico, the largest producer, has had an output of only 22,800,000 ounces in 1916, as compared with 92,000,000 ounces in 1924. Canada produced 32,869,000 ounces in 1910, and only 12,794,000 ounces in 1921.

The production of bar silver of the two principal countries, the United States and Mexico, for the period from 1901 to 1909 inclusive, is shown in detail in the following list. Reliable figures, giving particulars of yearly production of the remaining producing countries, are not available.

Table showing the production of Silver of the United States and Mexico for the years 1901 to 1909 inclusive.

(Figures are in thousands of fine ounces).

Calendar year	*United States*	*Mexico*
1901	55,214	57,416
1902	55,500	65,071
1903	54,300	64,718
1904	57,683	62,114
1905	56,101	59,467
1906	56,518	56,477
1907	56,515	69,154
1908	52,441	63,655
1909	54,722	62,563

The following brings the table, showing silver production of the world, up to the end of 1924.

(Figures are in thousands of fine ounces).[1]

Calendar Year	*United States.*	*Mexico.*	*Canada.*	*South America.*	*Austral-asia.*	*Others.*	*Total.*
1910 . .	57,138	71,372	32,869	14,477	21,546	24,314	221,716
1911 . .	60,399	79,032	32,741	14,434	16,578	23,009	226,193
1912 . .	63,767	81,234	31,625	16,825	14,738	22,715	230,904
1913 . .	66,601	70,704	31,525	13,126	18,129	23,623	223,908
1914 . .	72,455	27,547	28,407	10,449	3,573	26,021	168,452
1915 . .	74,961	39,570	26,626	13,687	10,108	19,253	184,205
1916 . .	74,415	22,838	25,460	15,580	8,478	22,072	168,843
1917 . .	71,740	35,000	22,221	15,451	6,512	23,264	174,188
1918 . .	67,810	62,517	21,285	15,561	6,872	24,123	198,168
1919 . .	56,682	65,904	16,021	14,753	7,188	15,912	176,460
1920 . .	55,362	66,662	12,794	13,763	7,469	18,163	174,213
1921 . .	53,052	64,500	13,100	—	—	40,669	171,286
1922 . .	56,240	81,077	17,612	12,000	9,000	37,613	213,542
1923 . .	73,296	90,859	17,755	29,855	10,868	19,785	242,418
1924 . .	65,407	92,000	19,736	29,000	10,800	20,100	237,043

The statistical material quoted so far would be incomplete without a *resumé* showing the division of the world's production since the discovery of America, according to countries of origin. The following table purports to do this in a manner as correct as possible. In the absence of accurate statistics relative to the early production of some districts, reliable figures are not available for our purpose; such items have been grouped together under the caption "Other countries." All figures quoted are approximate and represent thousands of fine ounces of silver.

World's production of silver from 1493 to 1924, arranged according to countries of origin.

(In thousands of fine ounces).

Period.	Mexico.	U.S.A.	South America.	Canada.	Australia.	Other Countries.
1493-1900..	3,320,000	1,438,870	2,440,000		186,000	1,440,060
1901-1910..	630,000	556,130	164,800			200,000
1911-1924..	872,000	911,155	212,000	443,372	295,200	335,000
	4,822,000	2,906,155	2,816,800	443,372	481,200	1,975,060

[1] The figures are taken from the "*Bankers' Economic Service*", New York, Special Bulletin, and differ somewhat from the totals as published by the Director of the Mint.

This table is very instructive indeed. It shows that during the 431 years, for which statistical material is available, the Americas have been responsible for a supply of nearly 11 billion ounces of silver as compared with slightly over 2½ billion ounces relating to the rest of the world. Expressed in round figures the table shows that of the world's entire production of silver the Americas have supplied 80%, while the four other continents have been responsible for only 20% of the sum total.

Besides, there are other facts to be noted from the above table especially with regard to the countries of origin.

By far the largest output of silver, since the discovery of America, has been derived from *Mexico.* That country was responsible for a yield of 4,822,000,000 fine ounces of silver, which means nearly 36% of the world's total production till the end of 1924.

Before the landing of the Spanish expeditionary force under *Cortes* (in 1519) the *Aztecs,* one of the Indian tribes inhabiting Mexico, were using silver for adornment and in the decorative arts. Enormous quantities of silver were mined by the Spaniards during their rule over Mexico, which extended over 300 years. The principal silver mining district was the State of *Zacatecas,* to which were added, in the course of years, the silver-producing states of *Guanajuato, Durango, Sonora, Melico, Hidalgo, Chihuahua, San Luis Potosi, Sinaloa, Jalisco* and *Oaxaca.*

To this day Mexico has remained the largest silver-producing country. It is reliably reported that the bulk of the silver-bearing deposits are still unexplored, partly owing to the lack of communications, and partly owing to the unstable form of government there. These factors are responsible for the wide fluctuations of the Mexican silver output.

The second largest producer of silver is the *United States of America;* the total output there, up to the end of 1924, aggregates 2,906,155,600 fine ounces of silver, which represents 21.60% of the world's total production. The title of the United States to rank as a silver-producing country is of recent origin, namely from 1860. Before that time the country's output was insignificant.

Counting from the discovery of America until 1860 a total production of	928,500	ounces
only is recorded for the United States.		
From 1861 until 1880 (inclusive) the production totalled	356,687,600	„
From 1881 to 1900 inclusive . . .	1,081,260,300	„
	1,438,876,400	„
From 1901 to 1910 inclusive . . .	556,130,200	„
From 1911 to 1924 inclusive . . .	911,155,000	„
Grand total . .	2,906,155,600	„

Regarding the location of the chief United States silver mines the following table, showing recent production (in fine ounces), will give particulars:

State	*1917*	*1924*
Alaska	1,207,200	666,200
Arizona	6,962,300	6,349,300
California	2,107,100	3,367,000
Colorado	7,291,500	3,287,000
Idaho	11,402,500	8,035,200
Michigan	684,200	153,200
Missouri	63,300	97,400
Montana	14,555,000	13,154,900
Nevada	11,217,700	9,523,800
New Mexico	1,535,800	783,300
Oregon	172,100	47,500
South Dakota	190,400	90,800
Tennesee	107,000	93,000
Texas	587,900	719,500
Utah	13,361,000	18,178,800
Washington	266,100	194,300
Sundries	29,300	51,000
Total ounces	71,740,400	64,792,200[1]

[1] Since re-adjusted to 65,407,000 ounces.

The beginning of organised silver mining in the United States of America dates back to 1860. During the first 10 years the annual production was only 7,800,000 ounces, as compared with an annual average of 64,897,000 ounces for the last 10 years of our review.

The next largest producer of silver is *South America*, whose total output amounts to 2,816,800,000 ounces, which represents nearly 20.9% of the world's production of silver. The term *South America* includes also districts situated in *Central America*.

The principal South American silver-producing country is *Peru*. The Spaniards landed there first in A.D. 1527, and continued as rulers of the country until 1820.

One of the richest *Peruvian* mining districts was found in *Cerro de Pasco* in the *Andes*.

Other South American producing centers are *Chile* and *Bolivia*, both of which yielded large quantities of silver in olden times, but are now of but minor importance to world production. The principal silver-mining districts in Chile are situated within the province of *Atacama* and at *Caracoles*. In Bolivia the *Potosi Mine* was famous for its great riches in silver-ore. At present the *Huanchaca* Mine is by far the most lucrative silver mine.

The silver-mining districts of Central America (notably in *Colombia)* and South America have lost much of their old glory. They rank third in place in regard to world production, but have been relegated to fourth place since the beginning of the twentieth century. The following reliable figures will give an idea of the recent state of affairs. Between the years 1912 and 1924 the output of Central and South America has been as follows: (in ounces, 1000 fine).

	1912	*1915*	*1918*	*1923*	*1924*
South America:	13,981,000	13,687,000	15,561,000	27,355,000	26,500,000
Central America:	2,846,000	2,920,000	2,900,000	2,500,000	2,500,000

The country taking fourth place as a silver-producer is *Australasia.* The history of silver mining there resembles that of Canada in its comparative recency (1882) and in the fact that the bulk of the silver output is derived from one mining district only, the *Broken Hill,* situated near the western border of *New South Wales.* The production of the Broken Hill Proprietory Mine for certain years, since its discovery, was as follows:

1885	35,600	ounces
1890	7,727,900	,,
1893	12,505,400	,,
1894	14,054,400	,,
1899	4,720,700	,,
1904	5,602,500	,,
1909	1,301,300	,,
1914	3,137,300	,,

These figures refer to one mining enterprise only,—though by far the most important one. The total production for Australasia may be put at 781,200,000 ounces, which represents about 3.6% of the entire world output of silver.

During recent years Australia has been supplying about 10 million ounces of silver per annum.

Fifth place in regard to participation in the total of the world's production is held by *Canada,* whose production of silver is given at 443,372,000 ounces; the bulk of this output was mined in the course of the twenty years ended in 1924. Canada has so far contributed only 3.2% to the entire world's production.

Silver in very small quantities was obtained in Canada many years ago as a bye-product from lead-ores. As recently as 1904, silver mines of phenomenal wealth have been discovered at *Cobalt* (Ontario). On page 145 are shown particulars relative to the world's production of silver for the period 1910 to 1924. If some of the items concerning Canada are compared with the following figures it will be seen that the districts containing the Cobalt mines are responsible for more than 90% of Canada's total production of silver.

Output of Cobalt Mines.

1904	207,000 ounces
1907	10,023,000 „
1910	30,645,000 „
1911	31,508,000 „
1914	25,162,000 „
1917	19,402,000 „
1924	11,273,000 „

The balance of the world's silver production (since A.D. 1493) is represented by 1,975,062,000 ounces. This figure includes the united outputs of Europe, Asia and Africa and amounts to 14.7% of the total world production.

Silver mining was well advanced in Europe during the Middle Ages. The chief producing districts were situated in *Bohemia* (Joachimsthal, Pribram), in the Austrian *Tyrol* (near Innsbruck); in *Hungary* (Schemnitz); in *Saxony* (Schneeberg); and in *Spain* (near Sevilla); and also at Herrerias. Nearly every country on the European Continent did or does produce silver, mostly as a bye-product from other ores, but quantities are so small that they do not call for comment. The whole of Europe is nowadays responsible for annual quantities of five to seven million ounces of silver.

Amongst the Asiatic countries *Japan* is the largest producer of silver; her output is about equal in size to that of the entire European production. Silver is also being mined in *Burma* (India) to the extent of about two million ounces a year.

Africa produces only a little over one million ounces of silver as a bye-product from other ores.

The production during recent years of the three Continents, grouped under "Other Countries" may be put at between 20 and 24 million ounces a year.

To summarise: The entire world's production of silver from A.D. 1493 to 1924 (inclusive), expressed in percentages, has been as follows:

Mexico	36. %
U.S.A.	21.60%
South America	20.90%
Canada	3.20%
Total for the Americas	81.70%
Australasia	3.60%
Europe, Asia, Africa	14.70%
Total	100. %

Silver production in China is infinitesimal. Under the heading of *Production of Silver in China* will be found a list of mines situated within the borders of that country. The said list is more in the nature of a register of disappointed hopes, for silver has to this day not yet been found in China in paying quantities.

It is difficult to state what may be the cost of production of silver. The bulk of the white metal is obtained as a bye-product from other ores. Though the number of silver mines is considerable, it must be borne in mind that the cost of production varies according to local working conditions and the richness of the ore.

Until quite recently London was the only market for the world's surplus production of silver. The sale and purchase there is to this day in the hands of four firms of brokers who meet daily and fix the price of silver according to the tenor and the amount of orders on hand. But since the outbreak of the Great War, New York has taken a large share in the disposal of bar silver. Its influence has been steadily on the increase and is now, in 1925, strong enough to threaten the supremacy of London as the principal factor influencing silver prices.

The uses for silver are manifold. Its main employment is for coinage purposes. Silver has a wide use as a material in the industrial arts, notably in the Orient, where silver adornments are very popular amongst the poorer classes, who invest their savings in silver bracelets, rings, hair pins, etc. In Europe and America silver serves, chiefly, the practical art industries, such as cutlery, plate, watches, and vessels. But it has in recent years also found extended use in the chemical and film industries.

A considerable part of silver is eventually lost to the world. This remark refers chiefly to the industry of silver-plating, from which the silver cannot again be recovered. The wear from circulating silver coins is considerable. Hoarding silver by burying it in the ground is a common practice in India and China, and it stands to reason that the secret of the hiding place remains often unrevealed after the death of the owner of the treasure.

World's Consumption of Silver.[1]

(In thousands of fine ounces)

	1924	*1923*
Shipments—		
To India from U.S.	81,200	36,700
To India from England. . .	27,000	64,000
To China from U.S. and Canada	39,100	62,000
To China from England . .	2,600	15,000
Arts and Manufactures—		
In the U.S.	28,000	29,200
In England	4,500	4,000
Coinage—		
U.S. Mint under Pittman Act .	1,100	50,000
U.S. Mint—Dore bullion for subsidiary coinage	3,300	—
Mexican Government . . .	11,300	11,500
European Countries. . . .	50,000	—
Other Buyers—		
Origin and destination unknown	7,900	15,000
Total .	256,000	287,400

[1] Compiled by Handy & Harmon.

World's Production of Silver since the Discovery of America.[1]

Period.	*Annual average for period. Fine ounces.*	*Total for period. Fine ounces.*
1493–1520	1,511,050	42,309,400
1521–1544	2,899,930	69,598,320
1545–1560	10,017,940	160,287,040
1561–1580	9,628,925	192,578,500
1581–1600	13,467,635	269,352,700
1601–1620	13,596,235	271,924,700
1621–1640	12,654,240	253,084,800
1641–1660	11,776,545	235,530,900
1661–1680	10,834,550	216,691,000
1681–1700	10,992,085	219,841,700
1701–1720	11,432,540	228,650,800
1721–1740	13,863,080	277,261,600
1741–1760	17,140,612	342,812,235
1761–1780	20,985,591	419,711,820
1781–1800	28,261,779	565,235,580
1801–1810	28,746,922	287,469,225
1811–1820	17,385,755	173,857,555
1821–1830	14,807,004	148,070,040
1831–1840	19,175,867	191,758,675
1841–1850	25,090,342	250,903,422
1851–1855	28,488,597	142,442,986
1856–1860	29,095,428	145,477,142
1861–1865	35,401,972	177,009,862
1866–1870	43,051,583	215,257,914
1871–1875	63,317,014	316,585,069
1876		67,753,125
1877		62,679,916
1878		73,385,451
1879		74,383,495
1880		74,795,273
1881		79,020,872
1882		86,472,091
1883		89,175,023
1884		81,567,801
1885		91,609,959
1886		93,297,290
1887		96,123,586
1888		108,827,606
1889		120,213,611
1890		126,095,062

[*continued overleaf*]

[1] The figures contained in this table are taken from the "*Annual Report of the Director of the Mint*" (Washington).

World's Production of Silver since the Discovery of America.—continued.

Period.	*Total for period. Fine ounces.*
1891	137,170,000
1892	153,151,762
1893	165,472,621
1894	164,610,394
1895	167,500,960
1896	157,061,370
1897	160,421,082
1898	169,055,253
1899	168,337,452
1900	173,591,364
1901	173,011,283
1902	162,763,483
1903	167,689,322
1904	164,195,266
1905	172,317,688
1906	165,054,497
1907	184,206,984
1908	203,131,404
1909	212,149,023
1910	221,715,763
1911	226,192,923
1912	230,904,241
1913	210,013,423
1914	172,273,596
1915	173,000,507
1916	180,801,919
1917	186,125,017
1918	203,159,431
1919	179,849,940
1920	173,296,382
1921	171,285,542
1922	209,815,448
1923	242,418,410
1924	237,043,000
Total production of silver from the discovery of America to the end of 1924, fine ounces,	13,450,945,541

Silver Prices during the Middle Ages.

In attempting to glean price quotations during the Middle Ages, we find frequent references to the fall of silver values subsequent upon the discovery of abundant silver mines in America. The effects of an ever-increasing silver output there were distinctly felt in Europe about 1570, when the price of grain and other commodities, measured in terms of silver, rose considerably.

Reliable statistics regarding price levels of silver are not available for the term preceding the beginning of the nineteenth century. To obtain an idea of conditions prevailing about 1750, we refer to Meggens' *Postscript to the Universal Merchant,* (1756), wherein it is stated that "the annual importation of precious metals into Spain, at an average of six years, viz., from 1748 to 1753, both inclusive; and into Portugal at an average of seven years, viz., from 1747 to 1753, both inclusive; amounted in silver to 1,101,107 pounds weight.

"The silver, at 62 shillings per pound Troy, amounts to £3,413,431/10*s.*/0*d.*"

This corresponds to a quotation of 62 pence per ounce Troy. The fineness is not indicated, but nevertheless the statement provides a basis for the then ruling price levels.

The Depreciation in Value of Silver.

For forty years, beginning with 1833, the average price of bar silver remained at about 60 pence per standard ounce. Then followed a steady decline which, for the following 20 years, brought silver to the average level of 50 pence. From then onward, until after the outbreak of the World War in 1915, quotations for the white metal fell to the record figure of $23\frac{11}{16}$ pence, which was the yearly average silver price in 1907 and again in 1915. Even the influences of the European war, combined with the provisions of the Pittman Act, could not revive the old glory of silver. Its temporary elevation gave way to a relapse about two years after the conclusion of the armistice, and the opinion was justified that the good old days for silver were over.

The first collapse set in during the memorable year of 1893, the impetus coming from America. There the

Sherman Act had been in force for some time. According to its provisions the Government was obliged to purchase 4,500,000 ounces of silver each month. When this law was repealed in 1893, a collapse of great magnitude began. At the same time the Mints in British India, which had been open to the public for the free coinage of silver, discontinued the privilege. Before the close of the last century various countries had decided to change from the limping standard (Russia, Austria), and others from their silver to a gold-standard (Mexico, Siam, Indo-China, Straits Settlements). These changes came but gradually and remained in some instances merely on paper; yet they had a sentimental effect on the already declining silver prices.

During the first three years of the World War prices showed moderate rises, but as soon as America had entered the war, in 1917, quotations took a sharp upward turn. At that time China had an enormous demand for her export produce and consequently became a large buyer of bar silver. India was then faced with a peculiar problem. It became a paying proposition to melt the rupee and sell the silver thus procured. In order to prevent this illegal practice, the Indian Government placed an embargo on the export of silver. But all this could not prevent a further rise in the price of silver, which on September 21, 1917, had reached 55 pence per ounce. This represents a rise of about 40% within two months.

The following two years saw silver prices fluctuating, but moving continually upward, the average quotation being $57\frac{1}{16}$ pence per ounce for the year 1919, and $61\frac{1}{2}$ pence for 1920. Until 1919 the allied countries continued to make purchases of enormous quantities of silver for coinage. Exports for bar silver from Great Britain, or through India, to China were forbidden in 1917 and 1918. From America they were permitted by license only. As China was in want of great quantities of silver, which could scarcely be procured, prices were maintained at high levels.

The Pittman Act.

On March 21, 1918, it was officially announced from Washington that the Government would be empowered by Congress to melt and dispose of 200 million silver dollars out of a total of 460 million dollars, which the Government then held against its issue of silver certificates. The premature publication of this news caused prices to soar, before the Government had an opportunity to realise its project with regard to the control of silver prices.

On April 10, 1918, a bill was introduced into the Senate by Senator Pittman, becoming law on April 25. It was officially defined as:

> An Act to conserve the gold supply of the United States; to permit the settlement in silver of trade balances adverse to the United States; to provide silver for subsidiary coinage and for commercial use; to assist foreign governments at war with the enemies of the United States; and for the above purposes to stabilise the price and encourage the production of silver.

That Senator Pittman was the spokesman for the American silver interests is of secondary importance. His bill empowered the Government to melt and sell 350 million U.S. dollars held in the U.S. Treasury. The condition was that no sale could be effected below one dollar per ounce. The Government was forced to repurchase in the open market the total amount it had sold during the war. There was no limit as to time in which the original stocks (207 million ounces) had to be replaced. The final purchase was accomplished in 1923. One of the conditions provided that the silver offered to the U.S. Treasury at $1 an ounce under the terms of the Pittman Act be American mined and refined.

After-war Effects.

In common with almost all commodities, silver declined sharply as soon as the world realised that there was to be peace again. Nothing can better illustrate what the change really meant than the following comparison of figures:

(in pence, per standard ounce).

	1921	*1920*	*1919*	*1918*	*1917*	*1916*
Highest silver price	43⅜	89½	79⅛	49½	55	37⅛
Lowest silver price	30⅝	38⅞	47¾	42½	35 11/16	26 11/16
Range of silver prices	12¾	50⅝	31⅜	7	19 5/16	10 7/16
Average silver price	36⅞	61½	57 1/16	47 9/16	40⅞	31 5/16

The critical year was 1920, when silver reached the record price of 89½ pence per ounce, falling subsequently to 38⅞ pence, a difference of 50⅝ pence within the same year. Apart from the conclusion of the war activities, 1920 saw many radical changes in the financial policy of almost all Continental countries. Such policies were necessitated by dire need. Most of the parties concerned, having been taught by bitter experience to do without many a luxury, arrived at the conclusion that silver was not a necessity.

It was in 1920 that continental countries shipped to England silver, in coins or in bullion, to the extent of £3,300,000. During the same year France made considerable direct shipments of bar silver to China, resultant from the melting of five franc pieces. It was also in 1920 that France abandoned the Latin Convention, in terms of which a considerable number of countries had issued gold and silver coins of a uniform weight and fineness. From then onward the signatories were no more bound by restrictions for minting their coins. In fact, most of the participants ceased coinage altogether and covered expenditure by means of the printing press. Towards the close of 1920 Great Britain decided to reduce the fineness of her silver coins from 0.925 to 0.500. This plan was carried out in the following years with the result that quantities, variously estimated at from 50 million to 95 million ounces, became available to the market.

In 1921 silver recovered somewhat after its rapid fall towards the close of the previous years. The output of the United States was readily absorbed by the Treasury in accordance with the stipulations of the Pittman Act. India had an excellent monsoon and became a large buyer of bar silver, taking £6,368,000 worth from Great Britain alone, who also shipped silver to the value of £3,558,000 to China in 1921. At the same time the latter country bought altogether 38 million ounces from the U.S.A.

The following three years were less eventful for silver, quotations for which remained fairly steady:

	1922	*1923*	*1924*
	pence.	*pence.*	*pence.*
Highest silver price	37⅝	33 11/16	36
Lowest silver price	30⅜	30	31½
Range of silver prices	7¼	3 11/16	4½
Average silver price	34 7/16	31 15/16	34

The supplies derived by continental countries from demonetised coins had ceased by 1923, but the effect thereof had been offset by the fulfilment of the provisions of the Pittman Act.

The year 1924 opened with rather low silver quotations. But towards the end of spring it became apparent that most of the European countries had found it inconvenient to get along with a paper currency. Various countries suddenly decided that they must introduce silver coins once more. These were Russia, Poland, Yugo-Slavia, Austria and Germany. Constant and rather heavy purchases, notably in America, were instrumental in keeping prices fairly high during the summer and autumn of 1924, roughly at a level of 35 pence per standard ounce.

Owing to the very heavy stocks of silver in Shanghai the price of bar silver began to decline in November and continued on its downward move during the closing month of the year. On December 30, 1924, bar silver stood at 31½ pence per standard ounce, the lowest rate for the year. The average quotation for 1924 was 34 pence.

During the first half year of 1925 the price of bar silver remained remarkably steady, at a level of roughly 31¾ pence per standard ounce.

Due to political difficulties which have presented themselves in China, that country became a buyer for reduced quantities only. By the end of the first semester of 1925 silver stocks in China were still excessively heavy, which must be taken as a significant indication of the acute inactivity of the country's trade and consequent requirement of silver supplies.

India, on the other hand, has been experiencing, since the summer of 1923, a series of excellent crops and of general prosperity. In settlement of her favorable trade balances India is continually importing silver, the volume of which is estimated at 108,200,000 ounces for 1924 and 100,700,000 ounces for 1923. Towards the end of 1924 India began to import large quantities of gold, but it is thought that this was a temporary measure only and that India would continue to be the mainstay of the world's silver markets.

NET IMPORTS OF SILVER COIN AND BULLION INTO BRITISH INDIA SINCE 1890.

(Figures are in British standard ounces and are taken from *Financial and Commercial Statistics of British India).*

Fiscal year ended March 31	*Net Imports Standard ounces*	*Fiscal year ended March 31*	*Net Imports Standard ounces*
1890	38,644,000	1908	97,915,000
1891	51,529,000	1909	73,740,000
1892	32,348,000	1910	61,015,000
1893	45,524,000	1911	54,876,000
1894	54,329,000	1912	32,229,000
1895	27,040,000	1913	91,077,000
1896	27,018,000	1914	71,107,000
1897	25,929,000	1915	55,766,000
1898	44,285,000	1916	32,932,000
1899	23,165,000	1917	92,194,000
1900	18,646,000	1918	74,531,000
1901	40,435,000	1919	237,029,000
1902	39,005,000	1920	96,942,000
1903	42,274,000	1921	22,230,000
1904	70,182,000	1922	64,134,000
1905	74,349,000	1923	86,057,000
1906	84,318,000	1924	100,000,000[1]
1907	118,199,000	1925	106,000,000[1]

[1] Estimated.

HIGHEST, LOWEST, AND AVERAGE PRICE OF BAR SILVER IN LONDON, PER OUNCE BRITISH STANDARD (0.925), SINCE 1833, AND THE EQUIVALENT IN UNITED STATES GOLD COIN OF AN OUNCE 1,000 FINE, TAKEN AT THE AVERAGE PRICE.

Calendar years.	Highest Quotation.	Lowest Quotation.	Average Quotation.	Value of a fine ounce at average Quotation.	Calendar years.	Highest Quotation.	Lowest Quotation.	Average Quotation.	Value of a fine ounce at average Quotation.
	d.	*d.*	*d.*			*d.*	*d.*	*d.*	
1833....	59⅞	58¾	59 9/16	$1.297	1879....	53¾	48⅞	51¼	$1.12392
1834....	60¾	59¾	59 15/16	1.313	1880....	52 13/16	51½	52¼	1.14507
1835....	60	59¼	59 11/16	1.308	1881....	52⅞	50⅞	51⅝	1.13229
1836....	60⅜	59⅝	60	1.315	1882....	52⅜	50	51 13/16	1.13562
1837....	60⅜	59	59 9/16	1.305	1883....	51 3/16	50 1/16	50 9/16	1.10874
1838....	60⅛	59½	59½	1.304	1884....	51⅜	49½	50 11/16	1.11068
1839....	60⅝	60	60⅜	1.323	1885....	50	46⅞	48 9/16	1.06510
1840....	60¾	60⅛	60⅜	1.323	1886....	47	42	45⅜	.99467
1841....	60⅜	59¾	60 1/16	1.316	1887....	47⅛	43¼	44 11/16	.97946
1842....	60	59¼	59 7/16	1.303	1888....	44 9/16	41⅝	42⅞	.93974
1843....	59⅝	59	59 3/16	1.297	1889....	44⅜	41 15/16	42 11/16	.93511
1844....	59¾	59¼	59½	1.304	1890....	54⅝	43⅝	47¾	1.04634
1845....	59⅞	58⅞	59¼	1.298	1891....	48¾	43½	45 1/16	.98800
1846....	60⅛	59	59 5/16	1.300	1892....	43¾	37⅞	39¾	.87145
1847....	60⅜	58⅞	59 11/16	1.308	1893....	38¾	30½	35 9/16	.78030
1848....	60	58½	59½	1.304	1894....	31¾	27	28 15/16	.63479
1849....	60	59½	59¾	1.309	1895....	31⅜	27 3/16	29 13/16	.65406
1850....	61½	59½	61 1/16	1.316	1896....	31 15/16	29¾	30 13/16	.67565
1851....	61⅝	60	61	1.337	1897....	29 13/16	23⅝	27 9/16	.60438
1852....	61⅞	59⅞	60½	1.326	1898....	28⅜	25	26 15/16	.59010
1853....	61⅞	60⅝	61½	1.348	1899....	29	26⅝	27 7/16	.60154
1854....	61⅞	60⅞	61½	1.348	1900....	30¼	27	28 5/16	.62007
1855....	61⅝	60	61 5/16	1.344	1901....	29 9/16	24 15/16	27 3/16	.59595
1856....	62¼	60½	61 5/16	1.344	1902....	26 1/16	21 11/16	24 1/16	.52795
1857....	62⅜	61	61¾	1.353	1903....	28½	21 11/16	24¾	.54257
1858....	61⅞	60¾	61 5/16	1.344	1904....	28 9/16	24 7/16	26⅜	.57876
1859....	62¾	61¾	62 1/16	1.360	1905....	30 5/16	25 13/16	27 13/16	.61027
1860....	62⅜	61¼	61 11/16	1.352	1906....	33⅛	29	30⅞	.67689
1861....	61⅜	60⅛	60 13/16	1.333	1907....	32 7/16	24 3/16	30 3/16	.66152
1862....	62⅛	61	61 7/16	1.346	1908....	27	22	24⅜	.53490
1863....	61¾	61	61⅜	1.345	1909....	24⅞	23 1/16	23 11/16	.52016
1864....	62½	60⅝	61⅜	1.345	1910....	26¼	23 3/16	24⅝	.54077
1865....	61⅝	60½	61 1/16	1.338	1911....	26⅛	23 11/16	24 9/16	.53304
1866....	62¼	60⅜	61⅛	1.339	1912....	29 11/16	25⅛	28 1/32	.60835
1867....	61¼	60⅜	60 9/16	1.328	1913....	29⅜	26 1/16	27 9/16	.59791
1868....	61⅛	60⅛	60½	1.326	1914....	27¾	22⅛	25 5/16	.56300
1869....	61	60	60 7/16	1.325	1915....	27¼	22 5/16	23 11/16	.51100
1870....	60¾	60¼	60 9/16	1.328	1916....	37⅛	26 11/16	31 5/16	.67200
1871....	61	60 3/16	60½	1.326	1917....	55	35 11/16	40⅞	.84000
1872....	61⅛	59¼	60 5/16	1.322	1918....	49½	42½	47 9/16	.98400
1873....	59 15/16	57⅞	59 3/16	1.29769	1919....	79⅛	47¾	57 1/16	1.12100
1874....	59½	57¼	58 5/16	1.27883	1920....	89½	38⅞	61½	1.01900
1875....	57⅝	55½	56 11/16	1.24233	1921....	43⅜	30⅝	36⅞	.63100
1876....	58½	46¾	53⅛	1.16414	1922....	37⅝	30⅜	34 7/16	.67900
1877....	58¼	53¼	54 13/16	1.20189	1923....	33 11/16	30	31 15/16	.65300
1878....	55¼	49½	52⅝	1.15358	1924....	36	31½	34	.67900

N.B.—The figures contained in the above table, up to 1903, are from *Gold Standard in International Trade;* thereafter from Messrs. Pixley & Abel's compilations and other financial publications.

About Silver in China.

Silver as a medium of currency within China is of such great importance, that many chapters must be devoted to the treatment of this interesting subject. Silver in Chinese arts plays a considerable rôle, especially in the South. The Chinese silversmiths' products include vases, utensils for the dining room table, ornaments of many kinds, hair bangles, bracelets, rings and many other articles. During recent years it has become fashionable to present to friends congratulatory messages engraved on silver sheets, instead of written on scrolls. A new branch of artisanship has lately been developed in China; photographs are sometimes reproduced on plates of silver and enamel. Altogether it can be asserted that the use of the white metal in China's art industries is noteworthy and growing considerably.

But the chief use of silver in China is for currency purposes. As China does not produce silver in quantity, the white metal must be imported from abroad. The following table, compiled from Chinese Maritime Customs publications, contains particulars relative to the import of silver into China and to the export, or rather re-export, from that country. The figures cover a period of 34 years, beginning from 1890. For that and the following year only the net balance is available.

Between the years 1892 to 1924 inclusive China imported silver in bars and sycee, value Haikwan taels	782,879,000
silver in coin . . . " " "	493,711,000
Total imports Haikwan taels .	1,276,590,000
During the same period China exported silver in bars and sycee, value Haikwan taels	256,305,000
silver in coin . . . " " "	662,965,000
Total exports Haikwan taels .	919,270,000
There remains a balance in favor of imports, amounting to Haikwan taels . . .	357,320,000
Deduct net exports 1890 & 1891, Haikwan taels	6,689,000
Net imports Haikwan taels .	350,631,000

Assuming that the figures contained in the tables are complete, there is a net balance of Haikwan taels 350,631,000 worth of silver imported into China.

The net import of silver into China during the last ten years, ending 1924, alone amounts to 266,420,000 Haikwan taels in value, representing an annual average excess of imports over exports of 26,642,000 taels in value. In view of the fact that the balance of trade has always been unfavorable to China, this apparent anomaly requires elucidation.

The accuracy of the material supplied by the Chinese Maritime Customs has become proverbial. Yet that body can only deal with objects that come actually under its cognisance. The authorities in China had often been compelled to prohibit the movement of light weight coins; but the manufacturers, being determined to reap profits, found ways and means to smuggle their depreciated coins into various parts of the country.

Furthermore, there often exists an embargo on the export from certain provinces of silver coins and sycee. Such restrictions are circumvented whenever possible. These deceptions are rarely brought to the direct notice of the Customs authorities, with the result that at least statistics suffer. It may be justificatory to offset the net exports of gold from China, during the period of time under review, namely 91 million Haikwan taels in value. Even then there remains the respectable sum of about 260 million taels worth of imported silver to be accounted for. The import of specie generally is tantamount to the payment for goods bought from a given country, in excess of goods sold during the same span of time to the identical country. The excess of imports into China over exports varied during recent years between 100 million and 300 million Haikwan taels. How then can the steady import of silver into China be logically explained?

Although it may sound somewhat strange, we venture to state that the import of precious metals into a country, which does not produce those metals from its own mines, is synonymous in principle with the importation of cotton piece goods, of steel, of wheat,—of merchandise in general. China's continuous import of silver has to be viewed from this standpoint.

It now remains to be explained how China's unfavorable trade balance is compensated for by her numerous branches of invisible exports.

Chinese emigrants domiciled in the United States, in the South Sea Islands, the Straits Settlements, etc., have acquired considerable wealth, which is remitted to the home country for investment there. There is a continuous stream of savings from overseas to China, estimated to amount to at least 200 million dollars each year. Then there are huge sums flowing into China intended for the upkeep of Christian Missions, their schools and their hospitals. Diplomatic and Consular officials' expenditure also account for a respectable sum. Travellers from foreign lands likewise contribute towards the funds which are destined to transform China's apparent debit into a credit balance.

Movements of Bar Silver in China.

The following table gives values of silver in bars and sycee combined. By far the bulk of the silver entering China arrives in shape of bars, each weighing approximately 1050 ounces troy. We have compiled the following table (covering the three years 1922 to 1924 and the first eight months of 1925) with a view of showing the origin, the destination and the employment of the bar silver entering Shanghai. Apart from this commercial center considerable shipments are at times consigned to Hongkong direct, for use by the provincial Mint at Canton. Such direct shipments, which were large in volume during 1922–1923, are not included in our list which is meant to refer to Shanghai only.

Import of Bar Silver into Shanghai:

Year	*From U.S.A.*	*London*	*Re-shipments from Eastern ports*
1922	23,107 bars	17,541 bars	167 bars
1923	50,204 „	14,750 „	6,394 „
1924	31,796 „	10,642 „	2,316 „
1925 (8 months)	27,106 „	6,338 „	236 „
	132,213 bars	49,271 bars	9,113 bars

Export of Bar Silver from Shanghai:

Year	*Mints Nanking and Hangchow*	*Other provincial Mints*	*Re-shipments to London & India*
1922	12,571 bars	4,826 bars	2,037 bars
1923	48,830 „	1,373 „	1,890 „
1924	8,871 „	1,423 „	1,860 „
1925 (8 months)	16,186 „	915 „	888 „
	86,458 bars	8,537 bars	6,675 bars

From these figures it appears that out of a total number of 190,597 bars imported during the three years and eight months

88,927 bars have been converted into sycee,
94,995 „ have been converted into silver dollars and subsidiary coins,
6,675 „ have been re-shipped abroad.

[*Table showing movement of Silver to and from China—Imports and Exports—appears overleaf*].

MOVEMENT OF SILVER FROM AND TO CHINA.

(Figures in Haikwan taels.)

Compiled from statistics published by the Chinese Maritime Customs for the period from 1890 to 1924 inclusive.

Imports

Year	In Bars & Sycee	In Coin	Total	Net Imports
1890	—	—	—	
1891	—	—	—	
1892	1,101,699	9,224,013	10,325,712	
1893	8,227,286	11,711,452	19,938,738	9,721,231
1894	24,124,516	12,281,184	36,405,700	25,751,309
1895	22,321,287	24,614,922	46,936,209	35,916,772
1896	2,948,951	14,703,640	17,652,591	1,720,407
1897	5,350,671	15,054,487	20,405,158	1,809,564
1898	16,372,222	14,985,138	31,357,360	4,985,219
1899	10,643,303	14,058,562	24,701,865	1,349,797
1900	20,453,545	18,705,221	39,158,766	15,445,012
1901	6,712,803	7,649,693	14,362,496	
1902	4,788,569	13,648,910	18,437,479	
1903	6,822,720	16,178,445	23,001,165	
1904	4,718,460	18,800,178	23,518,638	
1905	7,815,888	23,612,846	31,428,734	
1906	5,558,060	13,774,678	19,332,738	
1907	445,450	6,624,170	7,069,620	
1908	10,543,774	9,572,828	20,116,602	
1909	22,055,008	8,809,300	30,864,308	6,840,637
1910	30,644,728	13,953,806	44,598,534	21,794,647
1911	35,149,081	25,933,876	61,082,957	38,306,002
1912	28,407,775	16,690,522	45,098,297	19,248,652
1913	46,608,824	9,102,666	55,711,490	35,968,364
1914	7,661,852	8,836,892	16,498,744	
1915	11,564,126	9,153,380	20,717,506	
1916	13,300,691	23,787,629	37,088,320	
1917	16,197,966	11,309,326	27,507,292	
1918	22,629,175	13,495,054	36,124,229	23,494,927
1919	49,014,547	13,079,160	62,093,707	53,125,289
1920	100,602,785	25,751,603	126,354,388	92,638,978
1921	75,471,368	14,073,239	89,544,607	32,430,713
1922	59,488,790	16,197,718	75,686,508	39,572,012
1923	70,831,435	23,109,369	93,940,804	67,196,227
1924	34,301,912	15,227,196	49,529,108	26,002,538
	782,879,267	493,711,103	1,276,590,370	553,318,297

MOVEMENT OF SILVER TO AND FROM CHINA.

(Figures in Haikwan taels.)

Compiled from statistics published by the Chinese Maritime Customs for the period from 1890 to 1924 inclusive.

EXPORTS

IN BARS & SYCEE	IN COIN	TOTAL	NET EXPORTS	YEAR
—	—	—	3,557,772	1890
—	—	—	3,131,886	1891
3,761,112	11,949,332	15,710,444	5,384,732	1892
669,394	9,548,113	10,217,507		1893
916,501	9,737,890	10,654,391		1894
3,538,188	7,481,249	11,019,437		1895
2,321,389	13,610,795	15,932,184		1896
1,485,543	17,109,951	18,595,594		1897
6,084,769	20,287,372	26,372,141		1898
3,284,368	20,067,700	23,352,068		1899
4,456,494	19,257,260	23,713,754		1900
344,549	20,115,749	20,460,298	6,097,802	1901
5,821,571	26,460,562	32,282,133	13,844,654	1902
4,152,880	24,893,652	29,046,532	6,045,367	1903
9,186,564	27,941,804	37,128,368	13,609,730	1904
4,819,489	33,805,422	38,624,911	7,196,177	1905
7,494,445	30,516,161	38,010,606	18,677,868	1906
13,474,492	24,803,258	38,277,750	31,208,130	1907
3,689,226	28,694,292	32,383,518	12,266,916	1908
3,712,340	20,311,331	24,023,671		1909
6,885,132	15,918,755	22,803,887		1910
3,529,479	19,247,476	22,776,955		1911
11,144,499	14,705,146	25,849,645		1912
6,132,474	13,610,652	19,743,126		1913
5,746,143	24,375,550	30,121,693	13,622,949	1914
10,969,860	28,129,960	39,099,820	18,382,314	1915
42,753,869	23,012,577	65,766,446	28,678,126	1916
33,080,586	15,409,804	48,490,390	20,983,098	1917
5,457,452	7,171,850	12,629,302		1918
1,990,592	6,977,826	8,968,418		1919
10,015,836	23,699,574	33,715,410		1920
23,607,383	33,506,511	57,113,894		1921
6,639,865	29,474,631	36,114,496		1922
3,651,833	23,092,744	26,744,577		1923
5,486,967	18,039,603	23,526,570		1924
256,305,284	662,964,552	919,269,936	202,687,521	

CHAPTER VIII

SILVER AS CURRENCY

In the Occident.

ALTHOUGH gold was used in olden times as money and as coin, the fact must not be lost sight of that since the beginning of modern civilisation silver has been the standard of currency, retaining that position for a very long span of time.

As will be seen from the table of average silver prices, reproduced in the previous chapter (page 161), it happened in the early seventies of the last century that the value of silver began to recede steadily. The chief reason for the decline in the value of the white metal is to be found in the determination of almost all of the European countries to replace silver by gold as the basis of currency. The fluctuations in the price of silver, up to 1872, had been so small, that it was not difficult to fix a ratio between the value of gold and silver.

Before the discovery of the silver mines in America, until about 1540, the proportion of fine gold to fine silver was regulated in all European Mints at 1 to 10 and later at 1 to 12. About the middle of the nineteenth century the proportion was raised to 1 to 15, some years later to 1 to 16. The beginning of the twentieth century saw the removal of all officially fixed proportions between silver and gold. Measured by the amount of labor which gold and silver could purchase, both metals had lost considerably in value, but silver much more than gold. Many countries adhered to the bimetallic standard for a long time. So, for example, a purely gold standard was introduced by Russia as late as 1895. The Latin Union, having adopted a uniform currency, with the franc as unit, had discontinued the free coinage of silver in 1874. Yet France was amongst the last of the European countries to abandon silver as the standard of her currency.

Opinions of economists differed considerably as to the benefits which the change of standards from silver to gold involved. It took many years before most of the countries concerned became resigned to the necessity of adhering to the gold standard. While Europe had turned from the white to the yellow metal, the United States of America, being a large producer of silver, fought hard to retain silver and to extend its use as a medium of circulation.

According to a law passed by Congress in February of 1878, the Government was to make monthly purchases of 2 million dollars worth of silver. In 1890 the famous Sherman Act was passed by Congress, providing that the United States Treasury was to acquire every month 4,500,000 troy ounces of silver for coinage purposes. Those coins were to be put into circulation at the ratio of 16 to 1. The disastrous effects, which the repeal, in 1893, of the Sherman Act had on the price of silver, are too well known to require elucidation. The origin and effects of the Pittman Act of 1918 have been discussed on page 157 *et seq.*

The Great World War has not only robbed all Europe of the bulk of gold reserves, but necessity has taught all the Occident to consider silver coins as a luxury. With remarkable rapidity silver coins disappeared from circulation. While a moderate percentage was hoarded, the bulk of the silver coins on which the majority of the European Treasuries could lay their hands went into the melting pot, in order to wander in the shape of bullion into the wide world. For a number of years many countries were living on the printing press.

In the same measure as the reconstruction of Europe began to take shape, the tendency became discernible to reintroduce silver there as token currency and replace therewith a part of the depreciated banknotes. It was in the summer of 1924 that considerable purchases for coinage purposes were initiated by Russia and Austria (both buying on the London market), Germany, Poland, Yugo-Slavia and others (purchases being made principally in the United States).

On April 24, 1925, the Government Banks of the following European countries held bullion reserves as per list herewith:

Banks of—	*April 24, 1925.*			*April 25, 1924.*		
	Gold.	*Silver.*	*Total.*	*Gold.*	*Silver.*	*Total.*
	£	£	£	£	£	£
England ..	128,733,163	....	128,733,163	128,122,914	....	128,122,914
France **a** ..	147,277,550	12,640,000	159,917,550	147,120,357	11,920,000	159,040,357
Germany ..	42,468,550	**d**994,600	43,463,150	23,244,150	3,475,040	26,719,190
Aus.-Hun .	**b**2,000,000	**b**	**b**2,000,000	**b**2,000,000	**b**	**b**2,000,000
Spain.....	101,441,000	25,761,000	127,202,000	101,155,000	26,179,000	127,334,000
Italy......	35,587,000	3,361,000	38,948,000	35,322,000	3,423,000	38,745,000
Netherl'ds.	42,040,000	1,700,000	43,740,000	46,380,000	739,000	47,119,000
Nat. Belg .	10,891,000	3,010,000	13,901,000	10,819,000	2,785.000	13,604,000
Switzerl'd.	19,300,000	3,582,000	22,882,000	21,451,000	3,856,000	25,307,000
Sweden ...	12,982,000	....	12,982,000	15,043,000	....	15,043,000
Denmark .	11,637,000	989,000	12,626,000	11,643,000	741,000	12,384,000
Norway ..	8,180,000	....	8,180,000	8,182,000	....	8,182,000
Total week	562,537,263	52,037,600	614,574,863	550,482,421	53,118,040	603,600,461

a Gold holdings of the Bank of France this year are exclusive of £74,572,836 held abroad. **b** No recent figures. **c** Gold holdings of the Bank of Germany this year are exclusive of £ 7,718,200 held abroad. **d** As of Oct. 7, 1924.

In the autumn of 1914 the Secretary for the Treasury in Washington issued an appeal to the banks and the general public to make the widest use of U.S. silver coins and circulate these in preference to small bills. The waste of $1 banknotes, and subsequently their replacing cost, was so enormous that the Government would benefit to a great extent if silver coins were used by the American public in place of $1 bills.

Thus silver in the Occident has gained back a portion of its old glory, but not its old value. Whether or not the demand for new coinage will be proportionate to the output remains to be seen.

The following figures, showing the total silver fine ounces consumed in coinage by the United States and the World during the years 1914–1923, are taken from the *Year Book of the American Bureau of Metal Statistics:*

	United States	*World*
1914	4,400,885	179,593,224
1915	2,976,024	225,116,911
1916	6,424,149	292,148,559
1917	21,276,122	286,596,805
1918	18,425,915	238,692,502
1919	8,560,716	298,300,518
1920	18,125,805	220,318,663
1921	68,814,302	155,168,399
1922	65,217,584	227,210,117
1923	50,781,282	192,237,682

The above amounts do not consist alone of newly produced metal, but include a certain quantity of silver derived from demonetized coin. For example, in the 1923 world's total an amount of 11,512,040 fine ounces is included for U.K. coinage, but no purchases were made for mintage by the Royal Mint during that year.

In the Orient.

Silver as currency plays a paramount rôle in the Orient. Now, in 1925, China is the only country in Asia without a gold currency. Some of the other Asiatic countries, while not adhering to the gold standard in the full sense of the word, have adopted the gold exchange standard. These are British India, the Philippine Islands, the Straits Settlements and the Dutch East Indies. In order to maintain the value of their silver coins they draw, in case of need, on gold reserves abroad or they remit gold bullion.

India has during the past few decades been the most important factor regarding consumption of silver; she has retained that reputation to this day. In 1870, in terms of the Indian Coinage Act, the Government was obliged to exchange rupee coins against silver bullion, weight for weight. As India's trade was principally with Great Britain, the former's silver standard, with its ever fluctuating rates for gold exchange, became very inconvenient to the mother country. Various commissions were appointed to study the problem. After years of close investigation the following proposals were made by Lord Herschel and accepted by the Government on May 31, 1893. Firstly, to close the government Mints to the public for free coinage, and secondly, to fix the official rate, at which rupees in coin or banknotes were to be supplied in exchange for gold currency, at one shilling and four pence.

The carrying into effect of those far-reaching measures happened to coincide with the passing of the Sherman Act in November of 1893. That year was a very critical one for trade all over the world. Large supplies of silver became available in America and threatened to flood the world.

In order to protect itself and to nurse its newly-adopted child the Indian Government, in 1894, imposed a 5% *ad valorem* duty on all silver entering the country. In spite of the adoption of these measures the market quotation for the rupee did not exceed 1 shilling and 2½ pence, at which price it stood at the opening of 1898.

It was therefore resolved to borrow abroad for the purpose of creating a gold reserve in England. This measure, combined with the withdrawal of silver rupees from the market, had the desired effect of lifting the exchange up to one shilling and four pence.

The following years saw further highly important reforms with regard to Indian currency, which by now was based on gold as legal tender. As we are merely concerned with the aspect of silver it would be beyond the scope of this essay were an attempt made to wade deeper into the developments of India's currency system.

The United States, in 1903, introduced a similar system into the Philippine Islands. Japan made use of the war indemnity obtained from China to change, in 1897, from the silver to the gold currency standard. The Netherlands

Indies, which had previously suffered through an over-issue of copper coins, adopted the pure silver standard in May of 1854. But in 1877 it was considered imperative to adopt the gold standard, by introducing the Dutch 10 florins gold piece as standard coin. Silver, though token coins only, remains legal tender.

In China.

Silver was known to exist in China as a medium of payment nearly five thousand years ago. But it was not regulated currency until comparatively recently, and its legalised use as coin dates back a few short decades only.

Silver to this day is by no means legalised standard currency in China, and consequently not legal tender. It is merely one of the currencies in use within this huge country.

The import as well as the export of the white metal is not prohibited by the laws of China, and no customs barriers or duties restrict its movements. On the other hand it must be admitted that, since about 1920, sundry provincial governors have placed an embargo, often temporarily, on the export of silver in the shape of sycee or coin. This measure was deemed expedient in order to maintain inter-provincial rates of exchange, thus preventing quotations from falling, owing to the province becoming denuded of its silver reserves.

The years 1923 and 1924 have witnessed a procedure which runs contrary to the one just described. Many provinces have had cause to issue orders against the import into their domain of the output of some of the provincial Mints, notably the Mints at Canton, Fukien and Anking. These establishments have been flooding the country with coins of inferior fineness, thereby causing great hardships to economic life. It will therefore be understood that the embargo was justified as a measure of defense.

Apart from the attempts made by some of the provincial Mints to circulate coins of an inferior fineness, there have always been counterfeiters at work who have put into circulation imitation or low grade silver coins.

In March of 1925 large quantities of new 20-cent coins, supposed to have been turned out by the Canton Mint, made their appearance on the Shanghai market. Upon analysis these were found to contain only 30 per cent. of silver. Some of the more unscrupulous exchange shops at Shanghai bought those 20-cent pieces at a discount of 40 per cent., putting them into circulation over the counter as genuine coins. Considerable loss was caused to the public and to trade. It is feared that not only Shanghai was victimised, but that many parts of China were flooded with these spurious coins.

In the opening paragraph of this chapter it has been asserted that silver was not used in the shape of legalised coins until quite recently. This statement is correct if we overlook two attempts to introduce silver coins.

Silver, alloyed with tin, was coined in B.C. 119 by Yuen Shou (元狩) in three denominations: (1) 3000 cash, round in shape and with a round hole in the center. As emblem it bore a dragon; its name was Tchuan (撰) and its weight eight liang or ounces: (2) 500 cash, square in shape, weighing six liang, and its device a horse: (3) 300 cash, oblong, adorned with a tortoise and weighing four liang.

As the face value of these coins by far exceeded their intrinsic value, they were soon counterfeited by the people. The purchasing power of these coins diminished rapidly and one year after their issue they were no more accepted in circulation. No specimen appears to have survived.

Preceding the reign of the Hsia and Shang dynasties (B.C. 1990–1050) three kinds of money were in existence, namely gold, silver and copper. But, higher in value than these were pearls and jade.

According to *Terrien de Lacouperie (Catalogue of Chinese Coins,* 1892), Wang Mang, who had dethroned the infant emperor, assuming in his own name the supreme power, in A.D. 10 brought about radical changes in the empire's currency. He suppressed by decree the Wu Tchu cash, the standard currency of the Han dynasty, and replaced it by new moneys in gold, silver, tortoise-shells, cowries and copper.

Wang Mang's mind was engrossed with the idea of suppressing all memories of the eclipsed dynasty by a return to the old practices of the Tchou dynasty still cherished by the people. The unit of the silver currency was one liu (流), weighing eight taels; only the weight was fixed, while the value varied according to the purity of the metal. Those found in the region of Tchu She (朱提) of Kien Wei (犍爲), in Szechuen province, were worth 1580 cash, while those made of inferior silver, found in other parts of the empire, were valued at only 1000 cash. No specimens of this silver money have been preserved, and no precise description of their design has been transmitted.

During the reign of Hsiao Tsung of the Southern Sung dynasty, in 1183, silver coins were minted in weights of 1, 2, 3, 5 and 10 taels; the value of each tael was fixed at 2000 cash. These coins were intended as a circulating medium for the settlement of commercial transactions, as official government currency, as well as metallic reserve for paper notes in circulation. After three years trial the coinage of silver in China was abandoned, and it remained dormant for about eight centuries.

The main cause for the speedy withdrawal of silver coins was forgery; already in those remote times some people produced imitation coins.

In one of China's dominions, namely, Tibet, silver coins were minted in 1793, by order of the Chinese government representative. The minting was under the supervision of four officials, jointly appointed by the Chinese resident and the Dalai Lama.—(Dr. S. W. Bushell in Volume XXXII of the *Journal of the North China Branch of the Royal Asiatic*

Society). According to the rules detailed in the official Regulations of the Board of Revenue these coins are directed to be cast of pure sycee silver in two denominations: 1 *ch'ien* and 5 *fen, i.e.,* 10 and 5 tael cents. However, one tael of silver exchanged for only 9 of the 1 *ch'ien* coins and 18 of the 5 *fen* pieces, which means that the mint's profit amounted to 10%. The inscription on the obverse was ordered to be in Tibetan, and the date was to be engraved on the rim. In the subsequent reigns it was decreed that on the silver coinage of Tibet one-fifth of the issues should still be inscribed with the reign of Ch'ien Lung, in memory of the great emperor's conquests.

With regard to silver coinage in Turkestan, Dr. S. W. Bushell writes:

> Yakub Beg made Kashgar his capital and ruled Eastern Turkistan till his death on 17th May, 1877, during the Chinese campaign for the reconquest of the territory.
>
> His coinage was modelled after that of the Khanate of Burhara and Khokand, but he did not, strangely, put his own name upon the new money, inscribing instead that of Abdul Aziz, and thus acknowledging the suzerainty of the Sultan of Turkey. The coins are well engraved, with borders and ornamental details borrowed from central Asian coinages. The gold tilla, weighing 58 grams was equivalent to twenty of the small silver coins called tanga which exchanged nominally for fifty of the small Chinese copper cash known there as pu.
>
> The tilla is dated 1292 on both sides, which is equivalent to A.D. 1874, the tanga is dated 1291 of the Hijrah era (A.D. 1873).
>
> The re-conquest of Kashgaria by the Chinese was carried out by Tso Ts'ung-t'ang when he was viceroy of the provinces of Shensi and Kansu. Preparations were made on an extensive scale, cloth mills with foreign machinery were erected at Lan-chou-fu, the capital of Kansu, and a mint was also started there to coin silver money perforated in the middle with a square hole after the pattern of the ordinary Chinese cash. This was issued in 1876, with a Chinese inscription on the obverse, Turki on the reverse. It had, however, a very limited circulation, being replaced by new money struck at Kashgar and Yarkand as soon as these cities had surrendered to the Chinese.
>
> This Lan-chou-fu silver money is inscribed on the obverse, Tsui yin ch'ien, "one mace of pure silver;" on the reverse, "Bir miskal Kamush," which is the equivalent of the above in Turki,

kamush, according to Ney Elias, being the name given to small pieces of sycee silver in everyday parlance at Yarkand and Kashgar.

The Chinese had re-occupied Eastern Turkistan before the close of the year 1877, and in 1878 new silver money was in circulation, roughly struck in four designs after the Chinese pattern, but not perforated in the middle. The Chinese inscription on the obverse is identical in all, being Kuang-hsu yin ch'ien "Silver money of the period Kuang-hsu," which is the title of the reigning Emperor of China.

The 1 mace coin has a trilingual inscription on reverse: (1) Chinese, yi ch'ien, "one mace;" (2) Manchu (on the left), Kashigar; (3) Turki (on the right) Kashgar 1295 (*i.e.,* 1878).

The 5 fen coin is also trilingual: (1) Chinese, wu fen, "five-tenths of a mace;" (2) Manchu, Kashigar; (3) Turki, Kashgar.

The third design is also trilingual: (1) Chinese, wu fen; (2) Manchu (on the right), Yerkiyang; (3) Turki (on the left) Yarkand.

The fourth pattern is trilingual: (1) Chinese, wu fen; (2) Turki Yarkand 1295 (equivalent to A.D. 1878).

Silver as Currency in Modern China.

Having discussed the use of silver as currency in China in ancient times, as well as its employment for identical purposes in her outlying domains, it merely remains to refer to the rôle which the white metal plays as a medium of circulation in modern times.

Mention has already been made of sycee taels, the introduction of which as currency is variously estimated to date back 700 to 1000 years. *Sycee* is derived from the Cantonese pronunciation of *Hsi Ssu* (細絲), meaning fine silk. It is current in ingots or shoes which are called *Yuan Pao* (元寶). Sycee silver is often styled *Wen Yin* 紋銀), denoting pure silver. The term of *Tael* is probably derived from the Indian weight "tola," or from the Malayan "tahil."

The term *sycee* is thus explained in Giles's *Glossary of Reference:*

The term *Sycee* (fine silk) originated in the five Northern provinces (Chihli, Shantung, Shansi, Shensi and Honan). When the Shansi Bankers melt silver into ingots, after it has been liquified and poured into the mould, and before it has again solidified, the mould is lightly tapped, when there appear on the surface of the silver fine, silklike, circular lines. The higher the "touch" of the metal, the more like fine silk are these "circlings" on the surface of the silver. Hence ingots of full quality are classified as sycee.

Apart from sycee the white metal has served extensively for centuries in the shape of dollar coins. These had originally been imported into China, principally from Mexico, U.S.A. and Japan. Since A.D. 1890, dollars have been minted within the country; this resulted in the gradual disappearance from circulation of foreign coins. China has also produced a very large quantity of subsidiary silver coins.

The genesis, the composition and the uses of sycee and dollars as media of circulation in China are of such vital interest that special chapters will be devoted to their discussion.

Silver as Tribute in China.

Emperor Tai Tsung, in A.D. 1236, created a law according to which tribute was to be paid in silk. But it soon became a general practice to tender silver in place of, or in addition to, silk. Originally the farmer had to pay, as annual tribute, six taels of silver. In 1255, under emperor Mangu, the amount of the yearly tribute was reduced to four taels, of which one-half was payable in silver and the other half in silk. Mangu was followed, in 1260, by Kublai Khan, who divided the country into ten provinces. Detailed regulations were then enforced with regard to the payment of tribute, and special tax offices were entrusted with its collection. Taxes, payable in silk and silver, in accordance with a minutely worked out scale, were levied according to the income, the standing, and the wealth of the taxpayer.

Under Kublai Khan's rule, the intention was clearly discernible to show the ideal features of democracy. As already has been said the taxpayers, most of whom were farmers, were divided into many classes, who were then called upon to provide revenue. The poorest class was exempted from paying taxes during the first year of the new era; in the following year half of the dues were demanded, to be followed in the third year by the collection of the full amount according to schedule.

The next higher class was required to pay its dues in the first year in banknotes,—which were then depreciated,—to the face amount of one tael five mace. At the close of each successive year the taxpayer was required to increase his contribution by five mace, until the total tax reached four taels.

Apart from the tribute levied in silk and in silver, farmers were required to contribute further sums in the shape of banknotes. The rich man's quota was one tael; the poor farmer's contribution amounted to half a tael only, payable in banknotes. Priests, scholars and soldiers were exempt.

Kublai Khan's regulations were so detailed, that even the time for the payment of tribute was fixed beforehand. While taxes in silk were due in September, contributions in silver were payable in August, November and December of every year. The wealthy were expected to make payment first, with the poorer population following.

CHAPTER IX

BAR SILVER AND CHINA

THERE is no fixed standard of currency in the broad sense of the world within China. The masses in the interior use, practically all through their lives, the copper cash and the copper cent, and although no law has defined hitherto the term of "currency" as applicable to China, it is beyond doubt that, by reason of its wide scope, the copper coin is the real currency of the country.

For international trade and exchange, silver is employed, and although China is the second largest silver-using country in the world, it would be erroneous to assume that she has a silver-currency standard.

Silver as a medium of currency circulates in China in the shape of taels, dollars, or small coin (the theoretical decimal of the dollar). As silver in quantity is not mined in China, it has to be imported from the world's silver markets, New York and London. Until recently London was the principal market for silver, but since the World War New York has become the chief center of distribution. Practically all the taels, the dollars and the small coin circulating in China have had their origin, directly or indirectly, in imported bar silver, to which the following remarks are devoted.

Import of Bar Silver from America.

The United States are producing from 60,000,000 to 70,000,000 ounces of silver each year, which is about one-third of the world's output. The consumption within the country for industrial purposes is estimated at 20,000,000 to 30,000,000 ounces annually, and the balance is exported abroad. In addition to the surplus production of the United States, New York and San Francisco have become trading centers for the silver produced in Mexico and Canada. New York is gaining fast on London in importance as the world's market for bar silver, many factors being in favor of the former place.

Since 1923 China and India have bought the bulk of their requirements in U.S.A. instead of, as formerly, in London. The importance of the United States of America as a silver-producing country has already been discussed in the chapter "About Silver Production and Distribution." The following figures relate to the movements of bar silver to and from the United States and are meant to show the latter's importance as a distributor of the white metal.

Year	*Total imports*	*Total exports*
1921	$63,242,000	$ 51,575,000
1922	$70,806,000	$ 64,607,000
1923	$74,454,000	$ 72,459,000
1924	$73,945,000	$109,891,000

The following table shows particulars regarding the principal sources of imports and the principal destination of U.S.A. exports of bar silver for the period of 1910 to 1924 inclusive:

Imports *(In thousands of dollars)* *Exports*

Calendar Years	*From Mexico*	*Total*	*To India*	*To China and Hongkong*	*Total*
1910	27,040	45,878	—	5,619	57,361
1911	24,860	43,746	1,424	7,959	65,665
1912	29,697	48,401	1,840	9,580	71,962
1913	22,033	35,868	1,419	11,422	62,777
1914	14,871	25,959	121	6,039	51,603
1915	20,488	34,484	—	8,372	53,599
1916	15,629	32,263	2,384	9,470	70,595
1917	31,986	53,340	24,392	20,624	84,131
1918	51,017	71,376	163,154	43,108	252,846
1919	63,303	89,410	109,181	87,828	239,021
1920	53,197	88,060	642	86,221	113,616
1921	41,250	63,243	3,233	23,191	51,575
1922	48,453	70,806	11,971	33,079	62,807
1923	50,049	74,454	23,721	38,311	72,469
1924	45,828	73,945	54,119	24,233	109,891

In comparing the figures relating to the U.S. exports of silver, the tendency becomes at once apparent to increase direct shipments to consuming countries, instead of using other places as intermediaries. Allowance should be made for the unit employed in the above table, where the dollar has been used and not the fine ounce, but nevertheless the trend toward direct shipments is manifest. It is especially India that calls for comment. After the conclusion of peace, in 1920, she took only $642,000 worth of silver from America. In 1924 the total value of her direct imports from the States had reached $54,119,000 in value.

San Francisco in 1924 shipped, mainly to China, 41,711,624 ounces of silver, against 58,520,926 in 1923. New York in 1924 exported 114,161,880 ounces of silver, against 41,711,624 ounces in 1923, with the Pittman Act in operation during the first half of the year. Of the 1924 shipments 30,701,803 ounces went to England, 81,180,176 ounces to India and 2,279,901 ounces to other countries.

The ratio between the total U.S.A. exports of silver, for the years 1921 to 1924 inclusive, and the shipments directed to India and China, is as follows:—

1921	51%	to the Orient.
1922	82%	
1923	86%	
1924	71%	

Procedure in dealings in silver in the United States differs considerably from the methods in vogue in Great Britain. Conditions prevailing in the United States silver markets have been described with rare precision by Mr. E. D. Kracht (of the firm of Kracht & Murphy, silver bullion and exchange brokers of New York). The terms cited in the report were substantially unchanged in November, 1925. The following is a *verbatim* reproduction of the report referred to. Only a few passages have been deleted on account of their having become obsolete in the meantime.

The American Silver Market.

The following outline is believed to be of interest to foreign operators and intended to provide a better understanding of conditions and advantages of the New York silver market:

Yearly New Production:

U.S.A.	about	60,000,000	ozs.	fine
Mexico	„	80,000,000	„	„
Canada	„	15,000,000	„	„
	about	155,000,000	ozs.	fine

Volume of the New York Market.—With negligible exceptions, all of the above silver produced in Mexico, Canada, and the United States is sold in New York for delivery either in New York, San Francisco or London. This combined new production together with improved shipping facilities provide jointly an excellent, sound basis on which a considerably larger silver and silver exchange business is transacted for any desired delivery. The scope of the New York silver market has broadened lately considerably, the volume has increased and will undoubtedly continue to do so in the future. It may be safely assumed that the total volume of the silver business transacted in New York may approximate anywhere between three hundred million to five hundred million ounces annually.

Shipping Ports.—The two principal ports for export of the entire production of Mexico, Canada and United States are New York and San Francisco. Vancouver shipments originate either from New York or from Canadian Cobalt district. New York and San Francisco receive the silver by water and by rail. The larger or smaller volume coming to either of these ports is determined by the factor whether China or India is the main buyer for the time being. When London and/or India is the buyer, most of the silver from Mexico and Canada comes to New York, and when China enters the market as the deciding buyer, most of the silver will go to San Francisco. Practically no silver reaches Indian ports at the present time directly from San Francisco (although silver may be shipped from there to China to be reshipped to India via Hongkong or possibly by Manila or Singapore).

Silver Storage Facilities: in New York.—All banks, silver dealers and mining companies holding a silver stock in New York, store same in the vaults of the United States Safe Deposit Company, 32 Liberty Street, in the heart of the New York financial district. This company does not buy nor sell silver for its own account, but specializes in silver storage and has the finest vaults and best facilities for handling in and out by electric elevator. The storage charge is 1 cent per bar per day, minimum charge 5 cent per bar. All silver in New York stored in the same vaults, delivery charges from vault to vault which would result otherwise, are eliminated. Delivery between banks is made "over the counter" by presenting a non-negotiable silver storage certificate of the U.S. Safe Deposit Company with the corresponding bar-list from the seller. Silver stored in these vaults often changes hands four, five times or even more often before it is moved out.

In San Francisco conditions are different. There, various banks use their own vaults, so that when delivery is made, it may entail the removal of silver from the vaults of one bank to the vaults of another with transfer expenses. The market rule is that the seller has to deliver to the order of the buyer, free of charge, from vault to vault. In addition to foregoing facilities, there are in New York, San Francisco and Cobalt large refiners or mining companies that agree to store the silver sold to customers for a few days, (that is to say, until the time the buyer desires to ship the silver) in their vaults at the risk of the buyer. Where this storage is extended for any length of time a small charge is made. Leaving the silver in the vaults of these refiners or miners has the advantage that same can be delivered from there directly to steamer or express connection saving drayage.

Assays.—There is no assay obligation or charge for the seller in New York, neither in San Francisco. All silver is purchased from large and reputable mining companies, banks or refiners, and delivered from refining companies which represent an absolute guarantee. Each bar bears marks of origin as well as bar number, and as the entire business is practically in the hands of the banks, refining and mining companies, there is no possibility that claims should arise in regard to unsatisfactory assays. To the writer's knowledge, no claim has ever been presented in New York in this regard. Silver shipped from Mexico to the United States after leaving the refinery, has to pass for assays through the Mexican Mint which issues the corresponding certification of assay; then it goes directly into the vault of the bank and does not leave same until shipped abroad or used domestically.

New York Silver Quotations.—Unlike London there is no official quotation for New York on which orders can be automatically executed. Around noon time there is given out by a New York silver-dealing house of old standing a so-called "official" quotation for New York silver delivery. This quotation is never on the basis of the actual market price for silver in New York. It has therefore absolutely no value for the silver trader, except that silver mining companies have contracts running with silver refineries for liquidation on the basis of this so-called New York official price. As a rule this price is about ½% below the actual silver price in New York, and, when China is buying, about 1¾% below San Francisco. The New York silver market is therefore an open market from morning to evening with price fluctuations according to demand and supply.

Silver Prices in New York.—Are quoted for New York, San Francisco or London delivery from spot up to six months forward. New York and San Francisco deliveries are quoted in dollars per troy ounce 999 fine, while London deliveries are invariably quoted in sterling 925 fine. New York and San Francisco transactions are either for immediate delivery, for delivery within a week or for delivery for the first half or second half of each month forward, the seller having the privilege to deliver at his option during the course of the delivery contracted. London deliveries are in accordance with London custom either for prompt delivery in London, for two months forward delivery in London according to date, or for prompt shipment from New York. Any other London delivery may also be contracted according to the market requirements. Silver dealers, miners, refiners and banks sell for various deliveries, so that there is a rather wide market for all deliveries.

Far Eastern silver buyers or sellers may have their silver business for London delivery executed in New York on a sterling basis without New York having to touch the London market at all. New York has the advantage of being the producer, and in case of need there is always the possibility of obtaining and shipping silver from New York to London within ten days. As a result at times considerable savings could be effected by covering London short sales in the New York market, and making delivery in London either by the outright purchase of silver that New York banks or mining companies may be long in London or by shipping the silver from New York to London.

Shanghai, Hongkong, Bombay and London silver quotations reach New York about 10 a.m. At the same time whoever interested in London deliveries, either the London or the New York dealer, will make firm bids or offers always on a sterling basis and for London delivery, prompt as well as forward. At times quite extensive trading takes place. As a rule, however, after the London official price has been established, London tries to buy below the official quotation or to sell above same. Cable service between New York and London requires about fifteen minutes for a reply.

New York enjoys the advantage of being the principal market of supply, and being able at the same time to trade with London in the morning, and with San Francisco in the afternoon, the large mining and refining companies that maintain offices in New York await usually market development before taking any action. Their business starts around 11 a.m. They may sell before that time, provided they find the price attractive enough. By far the larger part of the transactions is for 50,000 ounce lots. There are few refining or mining companies that feel inclined to sell silver in larger quantities on the same price basis. Therefore, where silver is to be bought in 100,000 ounce lots or more, it may be to advantage to buy from various sources instead of trying to execute the order with one and the same seller. Since the buyer has always the privilege of having his silver delivered to vaults as specified by him, the procedure of buying from several sources does not entail any extra expenses nor any extra handling, except for making payments to different sellers.

Payments for Silver: are made in New York funds for New York as well as for San Francisco delivery. These New York and San Francisco deliveries may also be paid for in bankers check on London if transacted in sterling. Deliveries in London are against payment in London. Silver may also be bought in New York against Yen, Rupee or Tael cable transfer.

Mexican Mining Companies, before shipping their silver, find out whether the highest price is obtained in New York or San Francisco. They will then ship and consign to a banking correspondent, and when selling directly through a broker, the banking correspondent will deliver the silver against payment and transfer the funds at minimum charge.

Foreign banks may do business by cabling their buying and selling orders directly to a New York broker. After the order is executed arrangement may be made through New York banking correspondents to either receive or deliver the silver against payment, and/or arrange for shipment at a minimum of expense; or credit may be opened directly in favor of the "silver seller," which will either be a bank, a mining or refining company or silver dealer, with a minimum capitalization of one million dollars, payment against original bill of sale, bar-lists and delivery of the silver to the vaults or to steamer.

Silver Brokerage in New York amounts to $\frac{1}{16}$ cent per troy ounce 999 fine, and is always payable by the seller. While in the distant past there were no *Brokers* specializing in silver and Far Eastern exchange exclusively—there being only silver *Dealers* and silver dealing banking institutions—the broker's service is now to the distinct advantage of *all* buyers and sellers alike, bringing the most favorable quotations into direct contact at a minimum of expense.

Banks' Shipping Commission on Silver varies according to the size and value of shipments between ½ per mil and ⅛%.

Delivery to Steamer is made by responsible express companies who also supply the armed guard; the corresponding charge for New York is 25 cents per bar and has been included in the enclosed schedule of shipping charges. This charge can be saved if refining companies can deliver directly to steamer.

Shipping Charges.—See separate schedule.

Shipments New York–London. — Shipping charges are 1.05% including interest at 5% and ½ per mil assay and adjustment of weight charged in London. Shipments go forward every Saturday by regular fast passenger boats, taking seven days to Southampton, the silver arriving in London over-next Monday, after nine days transit time. These Saturday boats of the White Star Line and others sail regularly throughout the year. In summer time regularly, in winter time irregularly, the Cunard Line has sailings from New York to Southampton on Tuesdays. These steamers are six to seven days boats, and the silver should reach London not later than over-next Wednesday. Both Saturday and Tuesday boats have ample time to make the over-next Friday's connections of the P & O boats from London to Bombay with a total transit time New York–Bombay of five weeks.

While silver from New York is in transit to London for reshipment to either Bombay, Hongkong or Shanghai at the thru freight rate of 1%, instructions may be given to the steamship companies before the silver arrives in London, not to make a shipment as originally intended to Bombay, Hongkong or Shanghai, but instead to have the silver delivered in London. This privilege ought to be of considerable advantage to any Bombay, Hongkong or Shanghai silver operator who purchases forward silver in New York. He can decide a day or two before arrival in London in regard to final destination. Where the silver is not transhipped in London to a Far Eastern port, the difference between the freight rate New York–London and the through bill of lading rate New York–Far East, namely between ¾% and 1%, or, ¼% difference will be returned to the silver shipper in New York upon instructions to have the silver delivered in London instead of having it go forward to the Far East.

Shipment New York–Bombay. — Silver shipped directly from New York to Bombay can be laid down in Bombay at about the same price that silver would cost CIF London. These sailings from New York to Bombay, however, are irregular, a steamer about every two or three weeks; the freight rate is only satisfactory if shipment is made of ½ million ounces or more. Silver from New York to Bombay is mostly shipped on through bill of lading via London, in which case the shipping charges New York–

Bombay amount to 1¾% against 1.16% London–Bombay. Taking in consideration that silver can practically always be bought in New York 1% below the London quotation, these shipments from New York to Bombay either directly or via London leave a sufficient margin that should be an inducement to every Bombay silver buyer to buy in New York directly instead of in London, provided the silver can be obtained in New York ¾% to 1% below the London price.

Shipments New York–Hongkong.—When shipping silver from New York to Hongkong, the following routes may be considered:

(*a*) From New York directly to Hongkong at a shipping cost of 1.84%
(*b*) From New York via London to Hongkong at a shipping cost of 1.95%
(*c*) From New York via Vancouver, Victoria or Seattle to Hongkong at a shipping cost of 2.04%

These charges compare with shipping charges from San Francisco to Hongkong of 1.02%. When money is cheap and the silver not needed, it may be profitable to have the silver shipped from New York directly to Hongkong or via London.

Routing via Vancouver, Victoria or Seattle has the advantage, at a slightly higher shipping charge than directly or via London, that silver will reach its destination within a month or less. Express charges from NEW YORK to SAN FRANCISCO, SEATTLE, VICTORIA or VANCOUVER are the same, and including interest at 5% amount to 1.18%. When silver is shipped from New York, the Northern route is usually preferred because that route affords quicker transportation facilities than shipment from New York via San Francisco to either Shanghai or Hongkong.

In New York–Shanghai silver shipments we have to consider the following: The shipping charge from New York by direct steamer to Shanghai amounts to 1.84% which compares with the shipping charge from New York, via Vancouver, Victoria or Seattle of 1.97%, or via London of 2.09%. Unless money is cheap and silver little needed in Shanghai, the routing of the silver from New York via Vancouver, Victoria or Seattle will always be preferred because it affords the quickest connection and consignees have expressed themselves always very satisfactorily in regard to the prompt manner in which the silver is being delivered at destination; in Shanghai or Hongkong. Unless contracted for delivery in San Francisco, silver is hardly shipped from New York via San Francisco to the Far East because this procedure works out uneconomically.

There will seldom be occasion to ship silver from San Francisco via Seattle, Victoria or Vancouver to the Far East because charges for expressage from San Francisco to these northern points would become prohibitive, compared to any interest calculations. Where silver is bought partly for delivery in New York, and partly for delivery in San Francisco, and where it has to be shipped to either Hongkong or Shanghai, it will in many cases be preferable to ship the New York silver via the northern route directly to destination and to ship the San Francisco silver on separate steamer, instead of trying to join both shipments in San Francisco. The slight saving that might be obtained in regard to the freight by increasing the shipment in San Francisco, will be offset through loss of interest and handling expenses on shipments from New York to the Far East via San Francisco.

Bullion from American Pacific Coast ports to China are subject to the following graduated freight rates:

Value $10,000 and under	1.00%
10,000 to $50,000	.75%
50,000 „ 100,000	.625%
100,000 „ 150,000	.50%
150,000 „ 200,000	.475%
200,000 „ 250,000	.45%
250,000 „ 300,000	.425%
300,000 „ 350,000	.40%
350,000 and over	.375%

China will always buy in San Francisco at the China silver price less actual shipping expenses. Under above schedule, a China buyer can pay for 50,000 ounces only less ¾% freight. A larger buyer may obtain freight at ⅜%. The smaller buyer is therefore discriminated against to the extent of the difference in the freight rates. Since regular profits in these transactions do not exceed between 1/10% to ¼% at the very most, the difference in the freight rate is actually more than the profit involved and the average China bank drops out of the American market, because they can do their business in London without being penalized through graduated freight rates. They may buy and sell in London and in their calculations they need pay no attention just how much silver they are going to ship; the freight rate remains the same, no matter whether they ship 50,000 ounces or 500,000 ounces. Since there are in San Francisco always only a very few shippers who can ship at the minimum freight rate, the competition for silver shipments from San Francisco is very much restricted and as a result there are only few buyers. This would be entirely different, if ALL China banks could compete on EVEN TERMS. There are at least 20 banks in San Francisco and 50 institutions in New York which act for account of China banking institutions, and if a UNIFORM FREIGHT RATE of ½% should be quoted for any quantity of silver in excess of $20,000, the cause of "orderly marketing of silver" would automatically be more advanced than any centralized selling organization can accomplish. Instead of a stifled competition as at present, we would have a wide individual competition and each silver producer whether selling 30,000 ounces or 200,000 ounces at a time would be able to make his top price individually, directly and at no extra expense to him. The steamship companies would carry the same amount of silver as under present conditions, but the silver producer would obtain a better price. It is therefore up to the producer to use his influence to get the freight rates changed.

The freight rate on silver between NEW YORK and INDIA on direct steamers is at present ½%: minimum $50,000. This minimum should be reduced to $25,000. India has entered the New York market during the last few weeks as an important factor for direct shipments in competition with London and as a result, since India can often pay better prices than London, the London quotations are no longer of as much influence in the New York market as they were formerly. When buying, India can pay in New York the same price that they may pay in London; in other words, shipping charges New York–London need no longer be deducted from the London official price; the producer may receive approximately the FULL London equivalent for delivery in New York.

China and India being the principal buyers, and both buying and competing directly in San Francisco and New York, London can buy here only when willing to pay more f.o.b. steamer New York than China or India are willing to bid.

Silver from territory adjacent to MEXICO CITY is at present being shipped to both New York and San Francisco BY RAIL at an express charge of about 1½%, roughly. Producers should bear in mind that if they can arrange shipments VIA VERA CRUZ to NEW YORK and provided a freight rate of ¼% can be obtained as same was quoted before war time, the producer in Mexico can obtain a better net price by shipping by water to New York instead of shipping by rail. The express charge Mexico–Vera Cruz is approximately .35%, handling charges in Vera Cruz should under no circumstances exceed .15% and a freight rate of .25% should make the business as attractive to steamship companies as before the war. It should be taken into consideration that a freight rate New York–India is quoted at .50% and from Pacific Coast port to China at ⅜%. A freight rate of ¾% for Vera Cruz New York shipments is entirely out of proportion.

"TABLE OF SHIPPING CHARGES ON SILVER" *Overleaf*

SHIPPING CHARGES ON SILVER

From New York—	Cartage %	Freight %	Insurance %	Days in Transit	Interest @ 5%	Dealers or, % Banks, Commission	Total % Charges
to Bombay by direct steamer.....	.05	.50	.17	35	.48	.06	1.26
to Calcutta via Bombay steamer .	.05	.05	.20	55	.76	.06	1.57
to Bombay via London on through Bill of Lading................	.04	1.	.17	34	.48	.06	1.75
to Calcutta via London on through Bill of Lading................	.04	1.	.17	40	.56	.06	1.83
to Shanghai, direct steamer or on through Bill of Lading by steamer via San Francisco.........	.05	Min. .75	.20	40—50	.65	.06	1.71
to Hongkong by direct steamer or on through Bill of Lading by steamer via San Francisco.....	.05	Min. .75	.22	50	.70	.06	1.78
to Shanghai or Hongkong by rail on through Bill of Lading via Seattle, Victoria or Vancouver	...	Min. 1.50	.13	22—28	.36	.06	2.05
to San Francisco by steamer via Panama........................	.05	.38	.10	16—24	.30	.06	.89
to San Francisco by rail.........	...	1.10	...	5	.07	.06	1.23
to London from N. Y. every Tuesday and Saturday............	.04	.75	.05	8	.11	.06	1.01
From San Francisco—							
to New York by rail............	...	1.10	...	5	.07	.06	1.23
to New York by water via Panama Canal........................	.04	.38	.10	16—24	.28	.06	.86
to Shanghai or Hongkong........	.04	.38	.13	22—28	.36	.06	.97
to India via Shanghai or Hongkong........................	.04	1.25	.25	—50	.70	.06	2.30
From London—							
to New York....................	.04	.75	.05	8	.11	.06	1.01
to Bombay......................	.04	.75	.05	22	.31	.06	1.21
to Calcutta.....................	.04	.75	.13	30	.42	.06	1.40
to Hongkong....................	.04	.75	.18	36	.50	.06	1.54
to Shanghai.....................	.04	.75	.20	42	.59	.06	1.64

With regard to the graduated freight rates from American Pacific coast ports it was ascertained in November, 1925, upon inquiring at the steamship company at Shanghai, that the same scale was then still in force without alteration.

As concerns the above table (Shipping charges on silver) it should be noted that (1) In September, 1924, the freight rate on bar silver from London to China and Japan has been reduced from ¾% to ⅝%, in order better to be able to compete with U.S.A. Consequently the last item should now read "1.52%." (2) Reduction in the freight rate from New York to India have been made simultaneously, viz., from ¾% to ½%, so that the total charges should be changed accordingly. (3) The freight rates indicated in the schedule of shipping charges (for instance, San Francisco–Shanghai 0.375%) refer to quantities valued at $350,000 and over. If $100,000 worth of silver is shipped from San Francisco to China, the freight rate would be $\frac{5}{8}$%,—same as from London.

It will be noticed that conditions prevailing on the American silver market are somewhat peculiar; they differ from those in vogue at London in many respects, but notably in the following points:—

(1) The New York official silver quotation (per ounce fine) is hardly ever the price at which business is done in America, while the London official quotation (per standard ounce) represents the actual market price.

(2) The express and the steamer freight rates in and from America are not uniform, but subject to reduction in the same proportion as the quantity increases in value. London quotes uniform freight rates for any quantity, instead of graduated rates.

(3) Transactions in bar silver in London are subject to the uniform rate of a brokerage of $\frac{1}{8}$% on the cost of the silver, always payable by the buyer.

Conditions are vitally different in New York, where the brokerage is not always uniform, but where it is always payable by the seller.

In the spring, 1923, the brokerage on bar silver sold in New York was $\frac{1}{16}$ cent per ounce fine. In the autumn of the same year it was stipulated that "quotations should be understood silver delivered at banks' vaults per troy ounce 999 fine net to buyer and 1000 fine net to seller—including brokerage."

In the spring of 1925 the same firm of New York bullion brokers announced that New York brokerage rates were $30.00 per 100,000 ounces of fine silver, any delivery.

In answer to an inquiry on the subject made in 1923, the following letter has been received from the Vernon Metal and Produce Co., Inc., New York:—

Regarding your question as to the silver prices which are cabled to you, the price which you apparently had in mind is the so called "New York Official Price" quoted daily by Messrs. Handy & Harman, which as you correctly say, governs the price which the melters and refiners pay for silver. The actual market price of bars is usually higher, though rarely as much as you say in your letter. We would estimate that the premium above the New York Official price is approximately 3 cents per fine ounce on an average, but it fluctuates very considerably. We have seen bar silver sell below the New York Official Price and have seen premiums of over 1 cent, while we would say that ¼ cent to ¾ cent is a normal premium.

The premium depends mainly on the supply and demand and from the above will note that there is no way for you to know what the premium was on each day, unless you make arrangements for somebody to cable you the actual rates at which business was done.

The difference between the San Francisco and the New York price of silver depends chiefly on the demand from China. The express rates on Bar silver from New York to San Francisco are now $12.47 per $1,000 for shipment up to $50,000 value and $11.09 per $1,000 for shipments of above $50,000 value. With silver at about 68 cents per ounce the latter figure would amount to a freight rate of about ¾ cent per ounce, plus approximately five days interest charge. The San Francisco price will naturally not exceed the New York price plus freight and interest charges, unless there should be a keen demand for San Francisco silver for immediate delivery not leaving time to make shipment from New York, in which case a higher price might be paid at San Francisco than the New York price plus shipping charge and interest; such cases however are very rare.

On the other hand, when the demand from China is weak silver at San Francisco might sell very near to the New York price, and we have occasionally seen San Francisco silver sell even slightly below the New York price. Such a condition, however, will hardly last for any length of time, because most of the "foreign" silver originates from Mexico, and inasmuch as the freight rate from Mexico to San Francisco is slightly higher than from Mexico to New York, silver producers will speedily divert their silver shipments to New York instead of to San Francisco if they cannot get a higher price at San Francisco than at New York.

American Silver Invoices.

The following are three examples of invoices for silver shipped from the United States to China. These invoices do not contain any provision for interest, which has to be added to the total, and which varies according to conditions prevailing on the money market. No account has been taken of landing charges and coolie hire at destination. These charges, though small, have to be considered.

The price of bar silver at San Francisco is higher than at New York, the difference being accounted for by the cost of freighting from New York to San Francisco, inclusive of interest. Proforma Notes No. 2 and 3 will illustrate what has just been said.

Invoice for 56 bars silver shipped from San Francisco to Hongkong:—

Proforma Note No. 1.

56 bars or 70,828 ounces @ $72\frac{1}{16}$ per ounce	$51,040.43
Cost of telegram to San Francisco . . .	.75
Premium on insurance	68.75
Cost of cable to Shanghai	14.10
Telegram to San Francisco	2.66
Drayage	13.12
Clearing and marking	7.63
Ocean freight	328.13
Our San Francisco correspondents' charge for handling, supervising and storing silver	32.52
Total	U.S.$51,508.09

Proforma Note No. 2.

250,000 ounces silver shipped from San Francisco at 70 cents per ounce 999 fine San Francisco delivery . . .	$175,000.00
Ocean Freight to Shanghai option Hongkong $4.75 per $1,000 (on amounts of $150,001 to $200,000)	831.25
⅛% Insurance covering all risks on $179,500	223.13
Trucking, Cleaning and incidental charges	70.00
Total	U.S.$176,124.38

Proforma Note No. 3.

250,000 ounces silver shipped from New York via San Francisco, Seattle, Vancouver or Victoria at cents 69.20 per ounce 999 fine New York delivery .	$173,000.00
Expressage (New York to Pacific Port $11.09 per $1,000)	1,918.57
Ocean Freight (Pacific port to Shanghai option Hongkong) $4.75 per $1,000 (on amounts of $150,001 to $200,000) .	830.86
⅛% Insurance covering all risks at $178,500	223.13
Trucking, Cleaning and incidental charges	70.00
Total	U.S.$176,042.56

N.B.—When comparing cost of shipping from New York with that from San Francisco, it should be remembered that the former figures do not allow for additional loss of interest for the time the silver is in transit from New York to the Pacific Coast.

Conversion of American Bar Silver into Shanghai Taels.

If the bar silver imported from America is to be melted down in Shanghai, in order to be converted into sycee taels, the local smelting shops, called Loofangs (爐房), will return to the bank 111 Shanghai taels (currency) for every 100 Canton taels weight of American bar silver (0.999 fine). This proportion was fixed in 1920. Before that year the outturn would have been 111.30 Shanghai taels. As a reason for the reduced result the smelters indicate the higher cost of labor and coal.

It has happened in the years 1922 to 1925 that American bar silver was sold locally at premiums varying from ¼% to 1%. In such cases the bar silver was not wanted for conversion into sycee, but for coinage purposes. Some of the provincial Mints thought that they could afford to pay a premium, as even under these circumstances they made sufficiently large profits. American bar silver was frequently sold at Shanghai during the period indicated at 111.50 and even as high as 112 Shanghai taels for every

100 Canton taels weight. 1 Canton tael weight is 579.84 grains, or 1.208 ounces troy.

100 Shanghai taels are 108.6212 ounces troy in weight. The parity between American bar silver and the Shanghai rate for telegraphic transfer on America can be established by means of the following:—

Formula I.

? U.S.$	: 100 Shanghai taels currency
111 Shanghai taels currency	: 100 Canton taels weight
1 Canton tael weight	: 579.84 grains
480 grains	: 1 ounce
1 ounce	: New York silver price

$$\frac{100 \times 100 \times 579.84}{111 \times 480} = \mathit{108.828}$$

The figure of 108.828 is a constant.—It does not include charges and interest, which have to be added according to conditions prevailing at the time of making calculations. These charges vary not only in course of time, but their total is influenced by the rate of interest prevailing on the money market. The total is furthermore subject to a graduated scale of freight rates, according to the quantity shipped.

In the autumn of 1925 the expenses for shipping U.S. $100,000 worth of bar silver from San Francisco to Shanghai would have been as follows:

Freight ⅝%	$625.00
Insurance ⅛%	125.00
Bank's commission 1/16%	62.50
Interest for 25 days at 5% (about) . . .	340.00
Landing expenses, coolie hire at Shanghai, cable and incidentals	60.00
Cartage at Frisco 25 cents per bar . . .	37.50
Total charges . .	$1,250.00
or 1¼%.	

The constant is	108.828
Add 1¼% charges	1.360
	110.188

In order to obtain the parity of telegraphic transfer in Shanghai, multiply the constant, plus charges, by the price at which silver is actually obtainable at San Francisco.

If, for example, the actual price per ounce 0.999 fine is 70 cents, the parity for T.T. on America will be $110.188 \times 70 = 77.1316$ U.S.$.

Provided telegraphic transfer at Shanghai can be bought at say 77½ U.S.$ for 100 taels, it will be remunerative to buy bar silver at San Francisco at a price of 70 cents an ounce and have it shipped to Shanghai.

Formula II.

? U.S.$	: 1 Shanghai tael currency
111 Shanghai taels	: 100 Canton taels weight
82.7815 Canton taels	: 100 ounces fine
1 fine ounce	: U.S.$ price

$$\frac{100 \times 100}{111 \times 82.7815} = 1.0882877$$

To the constant of 1.08829 add the amount of charges and interest.

100,000 ounces of American silver (0.999 fine), if turned into Shanghai sycee, will produce Shanghai taels 91,887.27.

New York and London Quotations Compared.

The following comparative table of daily silver prices is one of the regular monthly publications, issued by Messrs. Kracht & Murphy, Far Eastern Exchange and Bullion Brokers, New York City. It shows the daily quotations for bar silver for near and forward delivery at New York, San Francisco and London and means to prove that silver prices in the United States are almost invariably below London prices. The table referred to is also meant to indicate valuable arbitrage possibilities.

The table of comparative silver quotations is followed here by some general remarks, contained in a previous

THE CURRENCIES OF CHINA—BAR SILVER AND CHINA

COMPARATIVE SILVER QUOTATIONS, NEW YORK—SAN FRANCISCO—LONDON—SHANGHAI

New York March 31, 1925.

THE FOLLOWING QUOTATIONS REPRESENT RELIABLY NEW YORK'S OPEN MARKET FROM 9:30 A.M. TO 4:30 P.M.

All following silver quotations are per troy ounce 999 fine silver delivered at banks' vaults. London quotations represent the equivalent of the London official prices converted at cable exchange rates prevailing at the moment of announcement.

	2	3	4	5	6	7	9	10	11	12	13	14	16	17	18	19	20	21	23	24	25	26	27	28	30	31	+ or —	Price
New York—one week Low	6830	6845	6850	6825	6810	6820	6845	6820	6820	6800	6800	6800	6800	6800	6800	6800	6780	6765	6745	6722	6725	6744	6738	6750	6730	6720		
High	6845	6855	6856	6840	6830	6840	6850	6830	6830	6790	6810	6818	6820	6840	6820	6820	6810	6785	6775	6738	6740	6758	6756	6760	6750	6740		
Average	6838	6850	6853	6833	6820	6830	6847	6825	6825	6795	6805	6806	6810	6820	6810	6810	6795	6775	6760	6730	6733	6715	6747	6755	6740	6730		6795

We indicate below the corresponding points premium (+) and discount (—) as compared to the New York prompt average price. Fluctuations of these points from day to day and their relation to each other indicate clearly valuable arbitrage possibilities.

	2	3	4	5	6	7	9	10	11	12	13	14	16	17	18	19	20	21	23	24	25	26	27	28	30	31	+ or —	Price
New York—2 mos. fwd.	—25	—40	—45	—50	—30	—25	—40	—35	—40	—35	—40	—50	—60	—40	—50	—50	—50	—50	—40	—30	—35	—50	—30	—20	—25	—30	—39	6756
San Francisco—one week	—40	—50	—50	—60	—45	—30	—40	—60	—40	—30	—30	—30	—40	—50	—40	—60	—45	—35	—30	—30	—35	—10	—10	—10	—15	—30	—36	6759
San Francisco—2 mos. fwd.	—40	—60	—75	—70	—70	—30	—65	—80	—60	—55	—50	—60	—65	—70	—60	—80	—70	—65	—50	—50	—55	—60	—30	—30	—25	—30	—56	6739
London official—prompt	+55	+46	+50	+54	+76	+75	+62	+72	+75	+69	+79	+72	+74	+81	+81	+87	+88	+54	+69	+62	+64	+59	+65	+82	+88	+79	+70	6865
London Official—2 mos. fwd.	+59	+22	+26	+17	+35	+37	+24	+00	+25	+28	+42	+22	+20	+28	+28	+33	+34	+14	+29	+36	+24	+19	+37	+69	+62	+51	+32	6827
Shanghai Tael T. T. parity @ 111/8278/999 fine	+30	—12	—19	—51	—11	—12	—29	—66	—76	—59	—65	—64	—60	—70	—45	—68	—53	—56	—39	—00	+03	—09	+13	+27	+42	+32	—28	6767

BULLION SHIPPING CHARGES, COMPRISING: FREIGHT, INSURANCE and TRANSIT INTEREST @ 4% p.a. (but not including storage, cartage and handling commission in N. Y. and S. F. for which .05% to .15% should be added when silver is purchased delivered at banks' vaults and when actual shipment has to be made)

	BOMBAY	CALCUTTA	SHANGHAI	LONDON
From New York direct to..	1.00%	1.20%	1.10%	.90%
From New York via London to..	1.30%	1.40%	1.70%	—
From San Francisco to	—	1.25%	.75%	1.13%
From London to	.85%	.95%	1.20%	

NEW YORK'S BROKERAGE RATES:

$10.00 per 100,000 Yen or Rupees.

$25.00 per 100,000 Shanghai Taels or Hongkong Dollars,

$30.00 per 100,000 ounces of fine silver, any delivery.

$62.50 per 100,000 pounds sterling.

circular issued by the same firm and containing some useful hints of intending operators in silver bullion.

Our comparative silver price quotation sheets show that New York and San Francisco prices are almost invariably—often considerably—below London prices. Our quotations are absolutely reliable. They represent actual figures at which business was done or could have been done in the open market in New York on the date given. There is hardly any transaction taking place of which we do not hear.

New York is not only an excellent buying market for silver; it is as well a reliable selling market for forward deliveries on a large scale. There are not enough selling orders for forward deliveries in this market; producers prefer to sell for spot delivery. The forward market is broad, deliveries up to 6 months are traded in regularly. They are not for a fixed date: always seller's option for the period contracted, either first or second half of the month, or, mostly, for the whole month.

New York and San Francisco deliveries are continually exchanged against each other for all deliveries. This makes the market very broad and elastic. It permits regularly small arbitrage profits, as soon as the buying trend changes from India to China, or from Europe to either India or China. London deliveries can be readily exchanged against New York or San Francisco, on dollar or sterling basis.

China buying orders can be most advantageously executed on a C.I.F. (cost, insurance, freight to destination) basis. In many cases we should be able to realize extra profits for our clients where their limit is C.I.F. Shanghai and/or Hongkong and where we have time and occasion to exchange New York for San Francisco delivery or vice-versa. We might be able to first buy New York 1¼% below San Francisco and later sell New York buying simultaneously San Francisco or Vancouver delivery at a smaller difference than the original 1¼%.

Estimating America's total production at about 150,000,000 ounces annually, conditions being about equal, 7,000,000 are likely to come monthly into New York and about 5,000,000 ounces monthly into San Francisco.

In most cases the banks effect shipment at $\frac{1}{16}$% commission. Where a bank should not be familiar with this shipping service, we gladly arrange for them, free of charge. Where they do not desire to attend to shipments, we arrange with one of the above banks to do so at $\frac{1}{16}$% commission to the buyer.

Cartage is 25 cents per bar in New York and custom brokers charge $5.00 for attending to customs entry and making up of shipping documents.

American Silver Parities and Shanghai–New York T.T. Quotations.

The following excellent table has been compiled by Messrs. Kracht & Murphy, Far Eastern Exchange and Bullion Brokers, New York City. It shows the shipping points of American silver, at five different percentages of charges and interest, as well as the theoretical par for rates ranging from U.S.$65 to 85 per 100 Shanghai taels.

SHANGHAI TAEL—DOLLAR—SILVER PARITIES

Cents per Tael	Par @ 111.30	111 Shanghai Taels = 100 Canton Weight 82.78 Canton Weight = 100 ozs. Troy 999 Fine Deducting Shipping Charges: @ 111	.85%	1%	1.10%	1¼%	1½%
6500	5989	5973	5920	5913	5907	5898	5883
65⅛	6000	5984	5931	5924	5918	5909	5893
65¼	6012	5996	5943	5936	5930	5921	5906
65⅜	6023	6007	5954	5947	5941	5932	5917
65½	6035	6019	5966	5958	5952	5943	5928
65⅝	6046	6030	5977	5970	5964	5955	5940
65¾	6058	6041	5988	5981	5975	5966	5951
65⅞	6069	6053	6000	5992	5986	5977	5962
6600	6081	6064	6011	6004	5998	5989	5973
66⅛	6092	6076	6022	6015	6009	6000	5985
66¼	6104	6087	6034	6027	6020	6011	5996
66⅜	6115	6099	6045	6038	6032	6023	6007
66½	6127	6110	6057	6049	6043	6034	6019
66⅝	6138	6122	6068	6061	6055	6045	6030
66¾	6150	6133	6079	6072	6066	6057	6041
66⅞	6161	6145	6091	6083	6077	6068	6053
6700	6173	6156	6102	6095	6089	6079	6064
67⅛	6185	6168	6114	6106	6100	6091	6075
67¼	6196	6179	6125	6118	6111	6102	6087
67⅜	6208	6191	6136	6129	6123	6113	6098
67½	6219	6202	6148	6140	6134	6125	6109
67⅝	6231	6214	6159	6152	6145	6136	6121
67¾	6242	6225	6170	6163	6157	6147	6132
67⅞	6254	6237	6182	6174	6168	6159	6143
6800	6265	6248	6193	6186	6180	6170	6155
68⅛	6277	6260	6205	6197	6191	6181	6166
68¼	6288	6271	6216	6208	6202	6193	6177
68⅜	6300	6283	6227	6220	6214	6204	6188
68½	6311	6294	6239	6231	6225	6215	6200
68⅝	6323	6306	6250	6243	6236	6226	6211
68¾	6334	6317	6262	6253	6248	6238	6222
68⅞	6346	6329	6273	6265	6259	6250	6234
6900	6357	6340	6284	6277	6270	6261	6245
69⅛	6369	6352	6296	6288	6282	6272	6256
69¼	6380	6363	6307	6300	6293	6284	6268
69⅜	6392	6375	6318	6311	6304	6295	6279
69½	6403	6386	6330	6322	6316	6306	6290
69⅝	6415	6398	6341	6334	6327	6318	6302
69¾	6426	6409	6353	6344	6339	6329	6313
69⅞	6438	6421	6364	6356	6350	6340	6324
7000	6449	6432	6375	6368	6361	6352	6336
70⅛	6461	6443	6387	6379	6373	6363	6347
70¼	6472	6455	6398	6390	6384	6374	6358
70⅜	6484	6466	6410	6402	6395	6386	6369
70½	6495	6478	6421	6413	6407	6397	6381
70⅝	6507	6489	6432	6425	6418	6408	6392
70¾	6518	6501	6444	6436	6429	6420	6403
70⅞	6530	6512	6455	6447	6441	6431	6415
7100	6542	6524	6466	6459	6452	6442	6426
71⅛	6553	6535	6478	6470	6463	6454	6437
71¼	6565	6547	6489	6481	6475	6465	6449
71⅜	6576	6558	6510	6493	6486	6476	6460
71½	6588	6570	6512	6504	6498	6488	6471
71⅝	6599	6581	6523	6516	6509	6500	6483

SHANGHAI TAEL—DOLLAR—SILVER PARITIES

Cents per Tael	Par @ 111.30	111 Shanghai Taels = 100 Canton Weight 82.78 Canton Weight = 100 ozs. Troy 999 Fine Deducting Shipping Charges: @ 111	.85%	1%	1.10%	1¼%	1½%
71¾	6611	6593	6535	6527	6521	6510	6494
71⅞	6622	6604	6546	6538	6532	6522	6505
7200	6634	6616	6558	6550	6543	6533	6517
72⅛	6645	6627	6569	6561	6554	6544	6528
72¼	6657	6639	6580	6572	6566	6556	6539
72⅜	6668	6650	6592	6584	6577	6567	6550
72½	6680	6662	6603	6595	6588	6578	6562
72⅝	6691	6673	6614	6606	6600	6590	6573
72¾	6703	6685	6626	6618	6611	6601	6584
72⅞	6714	6696	6637	6629	6623	6612	6596
7300	6726	6708	6649	6641	6634	6624	6607
73⅛	6737	6719	6660	6652	6645	6635	6618
73¼	6749	6731	6671	6663	6657	6646	6630
73⅜	6760	6742	6683	6675	6668	6658	6641
73½	6772	6754	6694	6686	6679	6669	6652
73⅝	6783	6765	6706	6697	6691	6681	6664
73¾	6795	6777	6717	6709	6702	6692	6675
73⅞	6806	6788	6728	6720	6713	6703	6686
7400	6818	6800	6740	6732	6725	6715	6698
74⅛	6829	6811	6751	6743	6736	6726	6709
74¼	6841	6823	6762	6754	6748	6737	6720
74⅜	6852	6834	6774	6766	6759	6749	6731
74½	6864	6845	6785	6777	6770	6760	6743
74⅝	6876	6857	6797	6788	6782	6771	6754
74¾	6887	6868	6808	6800	6793	6783	6765
74⅞	6899	6880	6819	6811	6804	6794	6777
7500	6910	6891	6831	6823	6816	6805	6788
75⅛	6922	6903	6842	6834	6827	6817	6800
75¼	6933	6914	6854	6845	6838	6828	6811
75⅜	6945	6926	6865	6857	6850	6839	6822
75½	6956	6937	6876	6868	6861	6851	6833
75⅝	6968	6949	6888	6879	6872	6862	6845
75¾	6979	6960	6900	6891	6884	6873	6856
75⅞	6991	6972	6910	6902	6895	6885	6867
7600	7002	6983	6922	6914	6907	6896	6879
76⅛	7014	6995	6933	6925	6918	6907	6890
76¼	7025	7007	6945	6936	6929	6919	6901
76⅜	7037	7018	6956	6948	6941	6930	6913
76½	7048	7029	6967	6959	6952	6941	6924
76⅝	7060	7041	6979	6970	6963	6953	6935
76¾	7071	7052	6990	6982	6975	6964	6946
76⅞	7083	7064	7002	6993	6986	6975	6958
7700	7094	7075	7013	7004	6997	6987	6969
77⅛	7106	7087	7024	7016	7009	6998	6980
77¼	7117	7098	7036	7027	7020	7009	6992
77⅜	7129	7110	7047	7039	7031	7021	7003
77½	7140	7121	7058	7050	7043	7032	7014
77⅝	7152	7133	7070	7061	7054	7043	7026
77¾	7163	7144	7081	7073	7066	7055	7037
77⅞	7175	7156	7093	7084	7077	7066	7048
7800	7186	7167	7104	7095	7088	7078	7060
78⅛	7198	7179	7115	7107	7100	7089	7071
78¼	7209	7191	7127	7118	7111	7100	7082
78⅜	7221	7202	7138	7130	7122	7112	7094

SHANGHAI TAEL—DOLLAR—SILVER PARITIES

Cents per Tael	Par @ 111.30	111 Shanghai Taels = 100 Canton Weight 82.78 Canton Weight = 100 ozs. Troy 999 Fine Deducting Shipping Charges: @ 111	.85%	1%	1.10%	1¼%	1½%
78½	7233	7213	7150	7141	7134	7123	7105
78⅝	7244	7225	7161	7152	7145	7134	7116
78¾	7256	7236	7172	7164	7156	7146	7127
78⅞	7267	7247	7184	7175	7168	7157	7139
7900	7279	7259	7195	7186	7179	7168	7150
79⅛	7290	7270	7206	7198	7190	7180	7161
79¼	7302	7282	7218	7209	7202	7191	7173
79⅜	7313	7293	7229	7220	7213	7202	7184
79½	7325	7305	7241	7232	7225	7214	7196
79⅝	7336	7316	7252	7243	7236	7225	7207
79¾	7348	7328	7263	7255	7247	7236	7218
79⅞	7359	7339	7275	7266	7259	7248	7229
8000	7371	7351	7286	7277	7270	7259	7241
80⅛	7382	7362	7298	7289	7281	7270	7252
80¼	7394	7374	7309	7300	7293	7282	7263
80⅜	7405	7385	7320	7311	7304	7293	7275
80½	7417	7397	7332	7323	7315	7304	7286
80⅝	7428	7408	7343	7334	7327	7316	7297
80¾	7440	7420	7354	7346	7338	7327	7308
80⅞	7451	7441	7366	7357	7350	7338	7320
8100	7463	7443	7377	7368	7361	7350	7331
81⅛	7474	7454	7389	7380	7372	7361	7342
81¼	7486	7466	7400	7391	7384	7373	7354
81⅜	7497	7477	7411	7402	7395	7384	7365
81½	7509	7489	7423	7414	7406	7395	7376
81⅝	7520	7500	7434	7425	7418	7406	7388
81¾	7532	7512	7446	7437	7429	7418	7399
81⅞	7543	7523	7457	7448	7440	7429	7410
8200	7555	7535	7468	7459	7452	7440	7422
82⅛	7567	7546	7480	7471	7463	7452	7433
82¼	7578	7558	7491	7482	7474	7463	7444
82⅜	7590	7569	7502	7493	7486	7474	7456
82½	7601	7581	7514	7505	7497	7486	7467
82⅝	7613	7592	7525	7516	7509	7497	7478
82¾	7624	7604	7537	7528	7520	7509	7489
82⅞	7636	7615	7548	7539	7531	7520	7501
8300	7647	7627	7559	7550	7543	7531	7512
83⅛	7659	7638	7571	7562	7554	7543	7523
83¼	7670	7649	7582	7573	7565	7554	7535
83⅜	7682	7661	7594	7584	7577	7565	7546
83½	7693	7672	7605	7596	7588	7577	7557
83⅝	7705	7684	7616	7607	7600	7588	7569
83¾	7716	7695	7628	7618	7611	7600	7580
83⅞	7728	7707	7639	7630	7622	7611	7591
8400	7739	7718	7650	7641	7634	7622	7603
84⅛	7751	7730	7662	7653	7645	7633	7614
84¼	7762	7741	7673	7664	7656	7645	7625
84⅜	7774	7753	7685	7675	7668	7656	7637
84½	7785	7764	7696	7687	7679	7667	7648
84⅝	7797	7776	7707	7698	7690	7679	7659
84¾	7808	7787	7719	7709	7702	7690	7671
84⅞	7820	7799	7730	7721	7713	7701	7682
8500	7831	7810	7742	7732	7724	7713	7693

Bar Silver from London.

FACTS AND FIGURES.

Until the outbreak of the World War London was the only market of importance for bar silver. During a certain period of the war exports of silver from England had to be discontinued. As New York was well able to take care of the silver market matters developed rapidly, and since that time New York has not only held its own, but conjointly with San Francisco, has taken the lead.

The world's production of silver was:

In 1924	237,043,000	ounces
„ 1923	242,418,000	„
„ 1922	213,542,000	„
„ 1921	171,286,000	„
„ 1920	174,213,000	„

Since the beginning of the current century, *i.e.*, during the years 1901 to 1924 the total of the world's silver production amounted to 4,622,000,000 ounces, which means an annual average of 192,583,000 ounces, for the first 24 years of the twentieth century.

Distributed as to the sources of production the averages for the same period are as follows (in million of ounces fine):

United States.	61.10
Mexico	62.50
Canada	18.70
South America	15.70
Total for the Americas .	157.80
Australasia	12.30
Other countries	22.30
Total average world's production .	192.40 million ounces.

The world's production of silver, divided as to percentages of producing countries, shows the following averages for the years 1901 to 1924 inclusive:

United States	31.75%
Mexico	32.50%
Canada	9.60%
South America	8.15%
Total for the Americas	82.00%
Australasia	6.40%
Other countries	11.60%
Total	100.00%

Practically all of America's silver production is now being sold in the United States. India and China, since 1923, are taking the bulk of their requirements from America direct, instead of from England, as was done formerly.

The figures contained in the following tables are meant to illustrate our statement.

(a) *Export of bar silver from London to the Orient.*

	To China.	*To India.*	
1916	£ 69,000	£4,799,000	World War.
1917	£ —	£ —	
1918	£ —	£ —	
1919	£ 725,000	£ —	
1920	£4,928,000	£4,057,000	
1921	£3,558,000	£6,368,000	
1922	£3,320,000	£7,085,000	
1923	£2,058,000	£8,562,000	
1924	£ 365,000	£3,496,000	

(b) *Imports to and Exports from London of bar silver in troy ounces.*

Imports.	*1923*	*1924*
United States	21,051,000 ounces	53,250,000 ounces
Netherlands	10,420,000 „	1,523,000 „
Canada	3,119,000 „	4,418,000 „
West Africa	4,000,000 „	—
Russia	—	7,881,000 „
Belgium	—	1,387,000 „
France	—	2,420,000 „
Other Countries	25,840,000 „	4,914,000 „
Total	64,430,000 „	75,793,000 „

Exports.	*1923*	*1924*
British India	62,899,000 ounces	29,475,000 ounces
China	14,743,000 "	2,459,000 "
Russia	—	19,787,000 "
France	1,415,000 "	3,424,000 "
Other Countries	4,127,000 "	12,260,000 "
Total	83,184,000 "	67,405,000 "

(c) *Direct silver exports from the United States.*
(To London and to the Orient.)

	To London	*To India*	*To China & Hongkong*
1913	$41,596,000	$ 1,418,000	$ 1,114,000
1922	$10,685,000	$11,972,000	$33,077,000
1923	$ 6,319,000	$23,721,000	$38,310,000
1924	$23,421,000	$54,119,000	$24,233,000

(d) *Import of bar silver into Shanghai.*

	From U.S.A.	*From London*	*Re-shipments from Eastern ports*
1922	23,107 bars	17,541 bars	167 bars
1923	50,204 "	14,750 "	6,394 "
1924	31,796 "	10,642 "	2,316 "
	105,107 "	42,933 "	8,877 "

In spite of these facts the London silver market undoubtedly retains a good deal of its old glory and importance. It has served as a basis for quotations in silver-using countries for many decennaries, and it continues to exercise this function, notwithstanding the limitation of supplies and the fluctuations in the value of the pound sterling.

The London Bar Silver Market.

Silver bars have the shape of bricks and weigh usually from 30½ to 37 kilograms, *i.e.*, 980 to 1,190 ounces troy. This description is applicable to English as well as American bar silver.

English bars, destined for export abroad, are 0.998 and 0.999 fine, but bars of a fineness of 0.996 and 0.997 are admissible and do occur, though in small proportions only.

The British standard for silver is 0.925, which means that in 240 parts of alloy 222 parts of pure silver are contained $\frac{222}{240} = \frac{37}{40}$ or *0.925.*

As bar silver exported from London to China and India is usually 0.998 fine, it is 17½ better than the English standard $\frac{222 + 17\frac{1}{2}}{240} = \frac{239\frac{1}{2}}{240} = 0.998.$

Bar silver is a commodity in London, and its price subject to the proportion of demand to supply. All official transactions have to pass through one of the four old-established firms of bullion brokers who meet daily, in order to fix silver quotations in harmony with orders on hand.

There are two official silver quotations issued in London; one for spot delivery (which means within seven days) and one for two months from date of making the contract. But unofficially it can be arranged that delivery is made at any particular day within two months, at a price to be specially arranged.

As there is a difference of eight hours in time between Shanghai and London (Shanghai being earlier), China can only operate on London's quotations of the previous day.

Every bar of silver is clearly marked so as to be easily identified. It shows the weight (within ¼ oz.), the fineness, initials and numbers. It is accompanied by a chip (about ¼ oz. in weight) and a testimony of assay.

There are only four firms of silver brokers guiding the London silver market. All of them are old-established, of excellent standing and enjoying the confidence of all parties interested in silver transactions. These firms are: Messrs. Mocatta & Goldsmid; Pixley and Abel; Samuel,

Montague & Co. and Sharps & Wilkins. They meet daily for the purpose of "fixing" the official price of bar silver. As a rule the four representatives of the firms of silver brokers will merely disclose the balance of their orders to be bought or sold, and not the totals. On the basis of those balances the official quotations are "fixed" daily at 1.45 p.m.

In order to safeguard the confidence placed in the assay of London silver all bars are assayed by one of the four official assayers of the Bank of England, respectively the Royal Mint, whose findings are indisputable. The following are the names of the four firms of official assayers: Messrs. Johnson & Sons, D. C. Griffith & Co., F. C. Claudet and Johnson, Matthey & Co.

English Bar Silver Shipped to China.

English bar silver is bought by China either for export to this latter country or for forward delivery as cover for a purchase of sterling drafts or T.T., with the idea to reverse the transaction as soon as the parity will permit.

The import of bar silver into China serves entirely currency purposes, which means that the silver is melted after arrival in this country and then converted into sycee taels, or dollars, or subsidiary coins. Here is a copy of an invoice relating to a shipment of bar silver from London to Shanghai.

Invoice of 279 silver bars Marked X.Y.Z. shipped per s.s. to Shanghai, optional Hongkong.

SHANGHAI.

(Various numbers as per weight list herewith.)

Ounces 300,455.50

ounces	284,830.50	.999	ounces	standard	307,616.94
„	8,315.75	.998	„	„	8,972.02
„	7,309.25	.997	„	„	7,878.19
„	300,455.50		„	„	324,467.15

Ounces Standard 324,467.15

12/11/1924.]	at 33⅝ pence .	£45,459. 4. 0
	Commission ⅛%	56.16. 6
		£45,516. 0. 6
	Freight, £45,500 at ⅝%	284. 7. 6
	Dock Dues	3.15.10
	Bill/Lading	2. 6
	Insurance £48,300 at 2*s*./0% . . .	48. 6. 0
	Policy Duty	. 2
	Marking, etc.	13.19. 0
	Value 12/1/1925	£45,866.11. 6

E. & O. E.

London, January 16, 1925.

Contrary to established usage in America the brokerage on bar silver, amounting to ⅛%, is payable by the buyer.

Other charges fluctuate. So, for example, has the freight from London to China been reduced in September 1924, from ¾% to ⅝%, in order to be better able to compete with New York.

Insurance is now 1 per mille. Dock charges, marking, etc., at London and landing charges at Shanghai may be put at ¼%.

Interest varies greatly and depends not only on the state of the money market, but also on the ability of the importer to finance the shipment (until arrival at Shanghai) by means of sterling or by means of taels. In the former case the rate of interest will be much lower, as money at Shanghai commands usually much higher rates of interest.

Bar silver is bought and sold in London in gross ounces, but quotations are in standard ounces (0.925 fine). One can have orders executed in standard ounces just as well, but this would have to be distinctly stated when placing the order. "Buy 100,000 ounces spot delivery, at best," means 100,000 ounces troy. Orders may also be placed for a specified amount in sterling: "Buy at a limit of . . .*d.*, £25,000 bar silver, forward delivery."

Conversion of English Bar Silver into Shanghai Taels.

As already stated English bar silver imported into Shanghai is usually 0.998 and 0.999 fine, but some bars show a fineness of 0.997 and 0.996 only.

The smelting shops at Shanghai have agreed to return for each 100 Canton taels weight of bar silver 110.90 Shanghai taels currency, provided the fineness is 0.998.

For bars 0.997 fine the return will be Shanghai taels 110.80 (currency). For bars of a fineness of 0.996 the return will be 110.70 Shanghai taels currency.

There are two questions immediately connected with the conversion of bar silver into sycee taels: Firstly, how many Shanghai taels currency are 100,000 troy ounces of bar silver 0.998 fine?

Formula:

? Shanghai taels	:	100,000 ounces silver 0.998 fine
1.208 ounces	:	1 Canton tael weight
100 Canton taels weight of bar silver 0.998 fine	:	equal 110.90 Shanghai taels (currency)

$$\frac{100{,}000 \times 0.998 \times 110.90}{1.208 \times 100 \times 0.998} = \textit{91,804.64 Shanghai taels}$$

The second problem, which is of more importance, resolves itself in establishing a basis for the parity of the pound sterling and the Shanghai tael.

The constant derived from the following formulæ, multiplied by the London price per ounce standard of bar silver, will give the theoretical par between London and Shanghai. The addition of charges and interest will produce the actual parity between the Shanghai tael and the pound. Charges fluctuate and may be considered (until further notice) to consist of the following items:

Freight—London–Shanghai	0.625%
Insurance	0.100%
Dock charges, marking, landing	0.250%
London brokerage	0.125%
	1.10 %

Interest for 45 days to be added according to the rate at which one is willing to invest funds, or at which one can borrow money.

The origin of most of the links in the chain constituting the following formulæ are plain, except perhaps the presence of the Canton taels weight. The reason why the Canton tael is introduced into our calculations is that, when foreign banks first entered the field at Shanghai, they brought along with them Cantonese Compradores, who were accustomed to the Canton taels weight. To this day the original standard has been maintained.

Another link in the chain probably needs elucidation, namely why 100 Canton taels weight of bar silver, 0.998 fine, equals 110.90 Shanghai taels currency. For some decades the constant has been 111.20 Shanghai taels, and only on the plea of higher workmen's wages and dearer coal prices the Shanghai smelters have created, in 1920, the reduced constant of 110.90. The original figure of 111.20 has the following origin:

In Shanghai bar silver is weighed by the Canton tael weight, which is converted into Chauping taels weight. When selling sycee the Chinese reckon 100 Canton taels = 102.5 Chauping taels weight; when buying sycee they reckon only 102.4 Chauping taels = 100 Canton taels.

Formula:

? Shanghai taels currency	: 100 Canton taels weight
100 Canton taels weight	: 102.4 Chauping taels weight
930 Chauping taels weight	: 1000 Shanghai taels currency
	X = 110.10
Add: 1% premium for fineness	= 1.10
Shanghai taels	= 111.20

The relation of 930 Chauping taels weight to 1,000 Shanghai taels currency represents sycee of a fineness of 0.98565.

As stated already the Shanghai smelters will pay 110.90 Shanghai taels for every 100 Canton taels weight of silver

0.998 fine. Sometimes provincial Mints will offer higher rates, as much as 111.50 taels. In such an event the premium has to be considered in the calculation.

The following are four formulæ, built up somewhat differently, but identical in their results:

Formula I.

? pence	: 1 Shanghai tael currency
110.90 Shanghai taels	: 100 Canton taels weight
1 Canton tael weight	: 1.208 ounces, 0.998 fine
1 ounce, 0.925 fine	: London price in pence

$$\frac{100 \times 1.208 \times 0.998}{110.90 \times 0.925} = 1.175234$$

Formula II.

? pence	: 1 Shanghai tael currency
110.90 Shanghai taels	: 100 Canton taels weight
82.7815 Canton taels	: 100 ounces troy
100 ounces troy (of 17½ betterness)	: 107.8829 ounces standard
1 ounce standard	: London price in pence

$$\frac{100 \times 100 \times 107.8829}{110.90 \times 82.7815 \times 100} = 1.175135$$

Formula III.

? pence	: 1 Shanghai tael currency
110.90 Shanghai taels	: 100 Canton taels weight
1 Canton tael weight	: 579.84 grains
222 grains (of 17½ betterness)	: 239½ grains standard silver
480 grains	: 1 ounce
1 ounce	: London price in pence

$$\frac{100 \times 579.84 \times 239.5}{110.90 \times 222 \times 480} = 1.175135$$

Formula IV.

? pence	: 1 Shanghai tael currency
110.90 Shanghai taels	: 100 Canton taels weight
1 Canton tael weight	: 579.84 grains
480 grains	: 1 ounce 0.998 fine
222 ounces fine	: 240 ounces standard
1 ounce standard	: London price in pence

$$\frac{100 \times 579.84 \times 0.998 \times 240}{110.90 \times 480 \times 222} = 1.175234$$

The constant is 1.175.—Say the price of bar silver in London per ounce standard is 35⅝*d.* for spot delivery—

Multiply by the constant of 1.175.	35,625 × 1.175 =	41.859375*d.*
Add charges 1.1% (variable)		0.460453*d.*
„ interest for 45 days, 4% (variable)		0.231472*d.*
	Parity . .	42.5513 *d.*

for 1 Shanghai tael, or 3*s.*/6 9/16 *d.*

If, for example, T.T. on London is obtainable in Shanghai at 3*s.*/7*d.* for ready delivery, it will be remunerative to buy T.T. in Shanghai, remit to London and purchase bar silver there for ready shipment. If, on the other hand, T.T. on London can be sold at Shanghai below the parity just demonstrated (3*s.*/6 9/16 *d.*), say at 3*s.*/6*d.* for forward delivery, it will prove remunerative to sell sterling at Shanghai and cover by selling simultaneously silver in London, for forward delivery.

This means that if the rate for telegraphic transfer is above parity of bar silver, it induces purchase of silver in London (import into China). If below parity, it favors sale of silver in London (export of silver from Shanghai).

It has been asserted that the Shanghai Loofangs have fixed the proceeds of bar silver according to the following scale:

Silver 0.999 fine will yield Shanghai taels 111.00 for 100 Canton taels.

Silver 0.998 fine will yield Shanghai taels 110.90 for 100 Canton taels.

These figures mean a reduction from the previous standard, which used to be 111.30 and 111.20 taels respectively. In view of the fact that the provincial Mints have continued to acquire bar silver at the original prices (and even higher), the Shanghai Loofangs have been forced to go back to the old limits, at least on occasions. This means that one has to bargain with the smelting shops (which are not controlled by the Government). If there are small stocks of bar silver at Shanghai and comparatively many buyers, the Loofangs will have to revert to the old figures. If, however, stocks of bar silver are in excess of Mint requirements, the smelters will return no more than 111 and 110.90 Shanghai taels currency for 100 Canton taels weight.

It is essential to bear these eventualities in mind when making calculations and working on a " constant," which may easily prove to be rather fickle.

To summarize, it may be stated that, if the smelters will return for every 100 Canton taels weight of silver—

110.90 Shanghai taels, the constant will be 1.1857, or if
111.20 " " " 1.1820.

Both these figures include a hypothetical total of 0.90% for shipping charges, but they do not contain a provision for interest.

Import of Bar Silver from France.

France is neither a silver-producing country, nor a market for bar silver. These facts did not prevent the said country from exporting, in 1920, considerable quantities of bar silver to China and to London. The source of the supply was French five franc pieces, melted down and sold in bars, 0.900 fine. The principal reason which induced the Government to turn a seller of bar silver was the exceptionally high price which was then prevailing in the world's silver markets. Probably economic causes were also forming a lever towards the policy of selling silver.

The French five franc piece is 0.900 fine and weighs 25 grams gross, or 22.5 grams fine silver. It is legal tender up to any amount.

The silver could not very well be shipped from France in its original shape of coins, owing to the fact that these had lost in weight through wear and tear, and also because of the legally permitted shortage under the style of *remedium.* Therefore it was turned into bars before being shipped.

In England French bar silver would be refined and remelted into bars 0.998 fine (for export to the Far East) or it would be turned into British standard silver (0.925 fine). The parity price of French and English standard silver can be established by means of the following:

Formula:

? francs	: 1,000 grams pure silver
31.1035 grams	: 1 ounce
925 ounces	: 1,000 ounces standard price
1 ounce	: London quotation in pence
240 pence	: francs cross rate in £

$$\frac{\text{London silver price} \times \text{cheque cross rate}}{6{,}905}$$

In Shanghai, French bar silver will have to be refined and a good deal of alloy will have to be extracted, before it can be converted into Shanghai sycee. This extra labor explains why the smelting shops at Shanghai will return for French bar silver 0.900 fine, for every 100,000 ounces troy, only Shanghai taels 81,950 as compared with U.S.A. silver, 0.999 fine, Shanghai taels 91,887.27, and compared with English silver, 0.998 fine, Shanghai taels 91,804.04. *N.B.*—Bear in mind what has been said regarding the temporary increase of these prices, when the demand for bar silver is large in Shanghai.

Formula:

? francs	: 1 Shanghai tael currency
81.95 Shanghai taels	: 100 oz. troy silver 0.900 fine
32.1507 ounces troy	: 1 kilogram
1 kilogram (1000 fine)	: Paris price for silver

$$\frac{100 \times 0.900}{81.95 \times 32.1507} = 0.034158$$

Multiply the constant of 0.034158 by the price of bar silver per kilogram at Paris, in order to obtain the Shanghai parity for T.T. on France. Add charges and interest.

Charges fluctuate and may be considered on the following lines:

Railway freight Paris–Marseilles	about	0.550%
Freight Marseilles–Shanghai	„	1.200%
Insurance	„	0.250%
Total		2.00 %
Interest 60 days at 6%		1.00 %
Total expense		3. %

Outturn of a shipment of French bar silver, derived from melted five franc coins, 0.900 fine.

169 bars of silver, weighing 5,000 kilograms at say francs 360 per kilogram	= francs	1,800,000.00
Add charges 2%	„	36,000.00
„ interest 60 days at 6%	„	18,000.00
Total cost	„	1,854,000.00

Converted in Shanghai into sycee:

5,000 kilograms silver are 160,753.50 ounces troy, at taels 81.95 per 100 ounces		Shanghai taels 131,737.49
Less: Wharfage dues	taels 75.00	
„ Compradore's commission	„ 65.54	
„ Coolie hire	„ 10.00	
		150.54
Net proceeds		Shanghai taels 131,586.95

1,854,000 ÷ 131,587 = *francs 14.09 parity per Shanghai tael.*

Import of Bar Silver from India.

The quotation for bar silver in India is in rupees for 100 tolas. 1 tola=180 grains=3/8ths of one ounce or 11.66 grams; this means that eight tolas equal three ounces troy.

Whenever Bombay exports bar silver to Shanghai, which is rarely enough the case, it becomes merely a question of arbitrage. India is not a silver producing country, and the bar silver possibly finding its way into Shanghai from there is of American (0.999) or English origin (0.998).

In importing bar silver from Bombay, payment by Shanghai is to be rendered in rupees by cable transfer. The whole question therefore resolves itself as to whether or not the remitting rate to India in Shanghai is above silver parity. In order to test this, we refer to the following:

Formula:

? rupees	: 100 Shanghai taels currency
110.90 Shanghai taels	: 100 Canton taels weight
82.7815 Canton taels	: 100 ounces
3 ounces	: 8 tolas
100 tolas	: Price of silver in rupees

$$\frac{100 \times 100 \times 100 \times 8}{110.90 \times 82.7815 \times 3 \times 100} = \textit{2.9047 as constant.}$$

Multiply same by the price of bar silver in Bombay in order to find the parity for cable transfer on India at Shanghai. Add charges and interest (variable). The price of bar silver (0.998) at Bombay is say 92 rupees per tola:

$$2.9047 \times 92 = \textit{267.23 rupees}$$

Mint par works out at	rupees	267.23
Add ¾% charges and insurance, say .	„	2.00
„ interest for 30 d/s at 6%, say. .	„	1.35
Total cost .	„	270.58

It will pay to import bar silver from Bombay to Shanghai, at rupees 92 per tola, if one can obtain T.T. in cover at a rate above rupees 270.58.

Here is a practical example: Shanghai buys in India 800 bars of silver for delivery on settlement day in about a month. Each bar, for purposes of making the contract, is supposed to weigh 1,050 ounces troy and to be of a fineness of 0.998. The silver is acquired at varying prices, as follows:

200 bars	=	560,000	tolas	@	rupees	90.11.00	=	rupees	507,850
100 „	=	280,000	„	@	„	91.00.00	=	„	254,800
500 „	=	1,400,000	„	@	„	91. 3.00	=	„	1,276,625
800 „	=	2,240,000	„				=	„	2,039,275

2,240,000 tolas = 840,000 ounces troy; at 91,804.64 per 100 ounces = Shanghai taels 771,158.98.

This means rupees 268.679 for 100 Shanghai taels. Brokerage and Bombay agents' commission to be added. If the parity permits, the transaction will be reversed before settlement day. If the silver is to be shipped on to Shanghai, charges and interest will have to be added to the cost in rupees. Compare with the T.T. rupees remitting rate in order to determine the rentability.

Merely for the purpose of three-cornered arbitrage the following formulæ are hereby quoted as supplied by Messrs. Kracht & Murphy (Far Eastern Exchange and Bullion Brokers):

EXAMPLES OF SILVER PARITIES:

Between NEW YORK and INDIA		Between INDIA and NEW YORK	
? rupees	: 100 tolas fine	? cents	: 1 ounce 999 fine
8 tolas fine	: 3 ounces fine	3 ounces fine	: 8 tolas fine
1 ounce 999 fine	: 64 cents	100 tolas	: 77-12-0 rupees
30.90 cents	: 1 rupee	1 rupee	: 30.90 cents
rupees 77-1230		*64 cents (per ounce 999 fine)*	

? rupees	: 100 tolas fine	? cents	: 1 ounce 999 fine
8 tolas fine	: 3 ounces fine	3 ounces fine	: 8 tolas fine
1 ounce 999 fine	: 64 cents	100 tolas fine	: 78-5-5 rupees
460 cents	: 240 pence	1 rupee	: 16 pence
16 pence	: 1 rupee	240 pence	: 460 cents
rupees 78-5-5		*64.009 cents*	

? rupees	: 100 tolas fine	? cents	: 1 ounce 999 fine
8 tolas fine	: 3 ounces fine	1000 ounces 999 fine	: 999 ounces fine
999 ounces fine	: 1000 ounces 999 fine	3 ounces fine	: 8 tolas fine
1 ounce 999 fine	: 64 cents	100 tolas fine	: 78-0-6 rupees
48.80 cents	: 100 yen	158.50 rupees	: 100 yen
100 yen	: 158.50 rupees	100 yen	: 48.80 cents
rupees 78-0-6		*64.00 cents*	

Approximate cost for import from New York to India:

Freight on direct steamer New York—Bombay	0.50%
Insurance	.15%
Buying brokerage, paid by seller and therefore included in buying price 1/16th cent	
Cartage, storage (can be saved at times) Bill/Lading	.05%
Bank's shipping commission in New York	.06%
	0.76%
Transit time New York—Bombay direct: 32-40 days. Interest @ 5% for 36 days.	.51%
	1.27%

Plus landing charges in Bombay.

Naturally some of the above figures have to be altered according to conditions actually prevailing. This refers notably to the cross rates, which form part of the above examples.

With the same idea the following examples *re* London–Bombay parity are hereby quoted:

Formula I.

? rupees	: 100 tolas silver, 0.998 fine
8 tolas	: 3 ounces
1 ounce, 0.925 fine	: Price in pence per rupee

$$\frac{100 \times 0.998 \times 3}{8 \times 0.925} = 40.459 \text{ as constant}$$

In order to obtain the London–Bombay cross rate, multiply the constant by the silver price in London and divide the product by the Indian price for bar silver. Add charges and interest (variable).

Example: Constant	40.459
Charges and interest say	.541
	41.00

London price of bar silver per ounce standard *35 pence.*
Bombay price *82 rupees* per 100 tolas.

$$\frac{41 \times 35}{82} = 17\tfrac{1}{2} \text{ pence per rupee}$$

Indian parity is:

$$41 \times \frac{\text{London silver price}}{\text{Bombay silver price}}$$

Formula II.

? pence	: 1 ounce silver, 0.925 fine
3 ounces	: 8 tolas
1 tola, 0.998 fine	: Bombay silver price in rupees
1 rupee	: X pence

$$\frac{0.925 \times 8}{3 \times 0.998} = \textit{0.24716 as constant.}$$

Multiply the constant (after deducting charges and interest—variable) by the Bombay–London T.T. rate and multiply the product by the Bombay silver price, in order to obtain the London–Bombay bar silver parity.

Say London–Bombay is 1*s.*/5*d.* The price per 100 tolas of silver is rupees 75.5:

Constant	0.24716
Less: Charges and interest, say	0.00216
	0.245

$$17 \times 75.5 \times 0.245 = \textit{31.446 pence per ounce standard silver.}$$

The Indian Bar Silver Market.

British India is by far the largest user of bar silver, which is exported there from America, London and, by way of re-shipment, from China. It will, therefore, be justified to insert here a short description of conditions prevailing on the Indian silver markets. Bombay is the most important place for dealings in silver; next in importance comes Calcutta. Silver is imported into India by the foreign banks established there; in the majority of cases for account of the Indian buyer, at a price fixed before shipment from New York or London. In course of 1924 direct shipments from U.S.A. to India totalled about 80,000,000 ounces as compared with less than 30,000,000 ounces shipped there from London.

The large Indian bullion merchants are styled "Chokseys." In Bombay they practically control the silver market; there are only about twenty-five of them in existence. Closely allied with the Chokseys are the "Shroffs"; these are native bankers, acting as intermediaries between the Chokseys and the dealers situated in the interior of the country. The Shroffs work on a commission basis. Next in importance comes the crowd of professional speculators in silver, and finally the hundreds of silver brokers.

The monthly settlement day is five days after the full moon day. Bar silver 0.996 and higher is acceptable as good delivery. Purchases are made at so many rupees per tola 0.998 fine; bars are supposed to weigh 2,800 tolas each, and any eventual difference in weight is adjusted on the basis of the quotation ruling at noon on settlement day. The Calcutta settlement follows three days after that in Bombay.

Hamburg Silver.

Bar silver destined for Chinese Turkestan is imported in small bars, owing to the immense difficulties of transport, and also on account of the necessity of its being handled and moved about by a population that is largely composed of nomads. Such silver is usually cast in small flat cakes, which weigh about 4½ kilograms and which are 0.999 fine. They used to be cast in Hamburg (hence the name) and exported to Turkestan, either overland *via* Russia, or through China. Dealings in those bars require an exact knowledge of the cost of transport (inclusive of interest during a long journey), which means many factors of a changeable nature. As Hamburg silver would be handled in the majority of cases by banks situated in Russia, we give herewith particulars in connection with Russian requirements.

Formula:

? roubles	: 1 Russian pound of fine silver
1 Russian pound	: 409.512 grams
1000 grams	: price of silver in Hamburg in mark
100 mark	: X roubles (sight rate Moscow-Hamburg)

$$X = \frac{409.512 \times \text{Hamburg silver price} \times \text{Moscow-Hamburg cross rate}}{1000 \times 100}$$

Charges and interest to be added.

In the book entitled *North Manchuria and the Chinese Eastern Railway* (Harbin, 1924) we find the following vivid description of causes leading up to the use of "Hamburg silver."

As a rule larger sycee shoes are cut or hewn into smaller pieces when necessary for minor payments. A most complete and vivid picture of this process of minor payments made through the medium of silver ingots may be observed at the famous Hunchur Fair (in Barga), at which the largest trading transactions in cattle take place. The local government authorities arrange for the period of this fair a special smithy in a native hut, where full-weight silver ingots are being cut into smaller pieces. This hut is usually leased to an exchange shop for the entire period of the market, and this shop supervises the work performed there. The breaking up of the ingots is done by smiths on ordinary forges. The silver ingots are clenched by tongs, heated over the furnace, and thereafter small pieces of the necessary size are cleft off with a hammer. A part of the smith's remuneration is paid by the remaining waste of silver crumbs.

The form of the sycee, especially of the larger pieces, is extremely unsuited for such work; in the majority of cases a piece of the necessary value is only obtained after a whole series of consecutive divisions of the piece originally cleft off. Therefore this process entails a considerable loss, owing to the fact that a large percentage of silver is lost in the shape of small crumbs. This is why the so-called *Hamburg Silver* in the shape of thin plates, resembling chocolate tablets, with incisions indicating fractions, became so very popular at the Hunchur Fair.

The silver was purchased by Russian merchants in Frankfurt on the Main, or in Hamburg. These two kinds of silver bullion differed by the size of the plates and their marks. The former bore the mark:—"Deutsche Gold-und Silber Scheide Anstalt vorm. Roessler, Frankfurt a/M," and the latter:—"Norddeutsche Affinerie, Hamburg;" this is why the silver bullion received the name of "Hamburg Silver."

Standarding.

Bar silver sold in London is usually 0.998 and 0.999 fine, but some bars are 0.997 fine and others 0.996. No bar silver is shipped to China and India, excepting these four grades.

The price of silver bought and sold in London is quoted per ounce standard, which means 925/1000ths fine. The following figures are meant to serve as a rapid way of converting bar silver of a fineness of 0.996 to 0.999 into silver 0.925 fine, *i.e.*, from ounces fine (4 grades) into ounces standard.

Silver Standarding Tables.

	Fineness 0.996		*Fineness 0.997*
1	1.076756757	1	1.077837837
2	2.153513513	2	2.155675676
3	3.230270270	3	3.233513513
4	4.307027027	4	4.311351351
5	5.383783784	5	5.389189189
6	6.460540541	6	6.467027027
7	7.537297298	7	7.544864865
8	8.614054054	8	8.622702703
9	9.690810811	9	9.700540540
	Fineness 0.998		*Fineness 0.999*
1	1.078918919	1	1.080000000
2	2.157837838	2	2.160000000
3	3.236756767	3	3.240000000
4	4.315675676	4	4.320000000
5	5.394594595	5	5.400000000
6	6.473613514	6	6.480000000
7	7.552432432	7	7.560000000
8	8.631351351	8	8.640000000
9	9.710270270	9	9.720000000

Example:

London has sold 120,000 ounces of bar silver at 35½ pence per standard ounce and ships 109 bars to Shanghai, invoiced as follows:

92 bars, ozs, troy	102,310.50	= 0.998 fine	=	oz. std.	110,384.773
13 ,, ,,	13,802.25	= 0.997 ,,		,, ,,	14,876. 58
4 ,, ,,	4,018.70	= 0.996 ,,		,, ,,	4,327. 16
109 bars, ozs. troy	120,131.45	=		oz. std.	129,588. 47
Standard ounces 129,588.47 @ 35½d		=			*£19,168/5/10*

The foregoing example shows how bars of varying fineness are converted into standard ounces weight. All London silver is quoted in standard ounces (0.925 fine) only.

For standarding American silver 0.999 fine, the table referred to can be used to advantage. Example: 50,000 troy ounces of American silver, 0.999 fine, are 54,000 standard ounces.

For converting the American silver price into the London equivalent, refer to the following:

Formula:

? pence	: 1 ounce silver, 0.925 fine
1 ounce silver, 0.999 fine	: X U.S.$
1 U.S.$	: 49.316 pence

$$X = \frac{49.316 \times 0.925}{0.999} = .45663$$

This figure is *a constant,* as long as the pound sterling remains at mint par with the U.S. dollar. Multiply the constant by the American silver price, in order to obtain the English parity quotation.

If, for example, New York quotes 70 cents per ounce 0.999 fine, the parity price for English silver per standard ounce (0.925 fine) will be 31.964 pence (£1 = U.S.$4.8666).

If the £ has lost in value and is quoted at say $4.45, there will have to be a reconstruction of the

Formula:

? pence	: 1 ounce of silver 0.925 fine
1 ounce of silver, 0.999 fine	: U.S.$ .70
U.S.$4.45	: 240 pence

$$X = \frac{0.925 \times 0.70 \times 240}{0.999 \times 4.45} = 34.956$$

The English parity quotation in this instance will be 34.956 pence per standard ounce.

If we have the London bar silver price per standard ounce, and if we desire to find the parity price for American silver, we shall have recourse to a constant, derived from the following:

Formula:

? U.S.$	: 1 ounce silver, 0.999 fine
1 ounce silver, 0.925 fine	: X pence
49.316 pence	: 1 U.S.$

$$\frac{0.999}{0.925 \times 49.316} = 2.189958$$

This constant, multiplied by the London silver price, will give the American parity quotation—always provided that the pound sterling is at mint par ($4.8666).

For example: Bar silver price in London per standard ounce is 31½ pence. The New York parity would then be 68 cents per ounce, 0.999 fine.

Export of Bar Silver from Shanghai.

As will be seen from the foregoing treatise, as well as from the Customs statistics quoted on page 166, the import into China of large quantities of bar silver has become a regular feature. Nevertheless Shanghai not infrequently also exports bar silver, by way of re-shipment to other China ports or to certain places abroad. Such re-exports are taking place whenever the stocks of silver held by Shanghai banks exceed local requirements, or when a premium over the regular *Loofang* outturn is offered. It has already been stated that, when bar silver is melted at Shanghai, in order to be turned into sycee, the yield will be 110.90 Shanghai taels currency for each 100 Canton taels weight of silver, 0.998 fine; or 111 Shanghai taels currency for 100 Canton taels weight of bar silver, 0.999 fine. Whenever a price is offered by one or the other of China's numerous provincial Mints, exceeding these fixed limits, Shanghai will readily sell its stocks of bar silver and obtain the normal equivalent, plus the market premium.

The following instances are quoted from actual experience.

Export of Bar Silver from Shanghai to Tientsin.

The import into Tientsin of bar silver depends principally on the Tientsin–Shanghai market rate. Bar silver is used at Tientsin for conversion into high-grade sycee, or for minting silver dollars or small coin currency. The following problems may arise in connection with the import of bar silver into Tientsin.

Tientsin currency taels are known under the designation of *Hongping Hua Pao. Hongping* means Tientsin tael *weight,* while *Hua Pao* refers to the *touch.*

1. How many Tientsin (Hongping) taels weight are 100 Shanghai (currency) taels worth of bar silver, 0.998 fine?

2. How many Tientsin taels will it cost to import 100 ounces of bar silver into Tientsin?

3. How many Tientsin taels will 1000 ounces of bar silver realise, which have been contracted for sale at Tientsin at say 21 per mille premium?

4. If a certain market premium for bar silver is offered at Tientsin, for example 21 per mille, how will the Tientsin-Shanghai drawing rate work out?

Formula I.

? Tientsin Hongping taels	:	100 Shanghai taels currency
110.90 Shanghai taels currency	:	100 Canton taels weight
82.7815 Canton taels weight	:	100 ounces (0.998 fine)
116.28 ounces (0.998 fine)	:	100 Tientsin Hongping taels

$$X = \frac{100 \times 100 \times 100 \times 100}{110.90 \times 82.7815 \times 116.28} = \mathit{93.6768}$$

This means that 93.6768 Tientsin taels are equal to 100 Shanghai taels; or, 106.7505 Shanghai taels are the equivalent of 100 Tientsin taels, if measured by bar silver, 0.998 fine, imported from Shanghai into Tientsin.

The figure of *106.7505 is a constant.* If this constant is divided by the Tientsin–Shanghai drawing rate, the result will indicate the premium which has to be charged at Tientsin. In connection with the Shanghai tael currency one has to divide by the convention ratio of 98. At Tientsin a market premium is being added instead.

If, for example, the Tientsin–Shanghai drawing rate is 1055, the market premium will be 16.15 taels on every

1000 Tientsin taels, if weight of bars is given for weight of Tientsin (Hongping) taels.

$$106.7505 \div 1055 = \mathit{1011.85}$$

Add charges which are variable and which, in the spring of 1925, were as follows:

Freight	2.50	per mille
Insurance	0.50	,,
Coolie hire	0.05	,,
Wharfage dues	0.30	,,
Interest 5 days at 7%	0.95	,,
Total	4.30	,,

To the result of	1011.85
Add charges and interest	4.30
Total	1016.15

which means that, in the case under discussion, the Tientsin market premium will amount to 16.15 per mille.

Regarding freight charges, these were quoted by one of the Shanghai shipping companies at 2½ per mille, but at only 2 per mille, if the value of the shipment exceeded 500,000 taels. Another Shanghai shipping company quoted 2½ per mille, subject to a 5% discount.

Insurance was five tael cents per 100 taels for shipment by steamer direct to Tientsin, but six cents if shipped *via* Chinwangtao; and 20 cents if despatched by rail from Shanghai to Tientsin. These rates comprise "all risks," including that of piracy. Another Insurance Company quoted 0.34 per mille only for shipments of treasure from Shanghai to Tientsin direct or *via* Chinwangtao.

A second problem is the following: What is the cost in Tientsin taels of 100 ounces of bar silver, 0.998 fine, imported into Tientsin from Shanghai, if the Tientsin–Shanghai parity rate is 1054.85?

Formula II.

? Tientsin Hongping Hua Pao taels	: 100 ounces bar silver 0.998 fine
100 ounces bar silver 0.998 fine	: 82.7815 Canton taels weight
100 Canton taels weight	: 110.90 Shanghai taels currency
1054.85 Shanghai taels currency	: 1000 Tientsin taels currency

$$X = \frac{100 \times 82.7815 \times 110.90 \times 1000}{100 \times 100 \times 1054.85} = 87.031$$

Add charges, say 4.30 per mille (variable) .	0.374
Cost of 100 ounces bar silver, 0.998 fine, delivered c.i.f. Tientsin . . Tientsin Tls.	87.405

The next question is: How many Tientsin taels will 1000 ounces of bar silver realise, which Tientsin has contracted to sell at say 21 per mille market premium?

Formula III.

? Tientsin taels currency	: 1000 ounces silver
116.28 ounces bar silver	: 1000 Tientsin taels weight
1000 Tientsin taels weight	: 1021 Tientsin taels currency

$$X = \frac{1000 \times 1000 \times 1021}{116.28 \times 1000} = 878.05295 \textit{ Tientsin taels}$$

The last of the four problems is: If a certain market premium for bar silver is offered at Tientsin, for instance 21 per mille, how does the Tientsin–Shanghai remitting rate work out?

Divide the constant resulting from *Formula I* (106.7505), consider charges, and divide by 1021.

$$107.1805 \div 1021 = \textit{1049.75 Shanghai taels.}$$

Export of Bar Silver from Shanghai to Hongkong and Canton.

Hongkong is not importing bar silver for own account, as no Mint is situated there. Bar silver consigned to Hongkong is meant either for the Canton Mint or for transshipment; there is also a moderate demand for the art industries, which have been flourishing at Canton for generations. But, speaking generally, Hongkong is importing bar silver at certain occasions only and then mostly for account of Canton.

Shanghai will be induced to ship bar silver to Hongkong and/or to Canton in the event of these places offering higher outturns than what is obtainable on the Shanghai market. The smelting establishments return invariably 110.90 Shanghai taels currency for each 100 Canton taels weight of bar silver 0.998 fine, and 111 Shanghai taels currency for silver 0.999 fine. Some of the provincial Mints offer prices considerably above these limits, the highest of which, according to our experience, so far has been 112.50 Shanghai taels for American silver.

Bullion melted in China is weighed by means of the local tael. In Shanghai gold bars as well as sycee are weighed in Chauping taels. Bullion imported from abroad is weighed in terms of the Canton tael; 100 ounces troy are equal to 82.7815 Canton taels weight. Therefore, supposing the weight of a silver bar to be 1000 ounces, and the market price Shanghai taels 111.50, the total cost per bar would be

$$82.7815 \times 111.50 = \textit{923.01 Shanghai taels}$$

Add charges and interest. These are variable and are approximately as follows (Shanghai to Hongkong):

Freight ¼%	0.25%
Wharfage dues	0.03%
Insurance ½‰	0.05%
Coolie hire, commission, etc.	0.09%
5 days interest at 6% per annum	0.08%
Total	0.50%

If shipment is made from Shanghai to Canton, with trans-shipment at Hongkong, the charges from Hongkong to Canton would be approximately as follows:

20 cents per ounce of silver, which is . .	0.150%
Insurance ¼°/oo.	0.025%
Coolie hire, etc. ½°/oo	0.050%
2 days interest at 6% per annum	0.030%
Total . .	0.255%

In case of shipment being made by direct steamer from Shanghai to Canton, charges would be approximately as follows:

Freight ½%	0.500%
Insurance ¾°/oo	0.075%
Coolie hire, wharfage dues, etc.	0.075%
8 days interest at 6% per annum	0.125%
Total . .	0.775%

With brokerage or compradore's commission, landing charges and insurance against piracy the total charges will amount to at least 1%.

Bar silver is weighed on the Canton tael scales and sold in Hongkong at the fixed rate of 71.70 Canton taels weight equal to 100 Hongkong dollars currency, plus a varying market premium. As 100 troy ounces of bar silver weigh 82.7815 Canton taels, 100,000 troy ounces of bar silver will realise 115,455.30 Hongkong dollars, plus the market premium of the day, according to the following:

Formula:

? Hongkong dollars	: 100,000 troy ounces of bar silver
100 troy ounces of bar silver	: 82.7815 Canton taels weight
71.7 Canton taels weight	: 100 Hongkong dollars

$$X = \frac{100{,}000 \times 82.7815 \times 100}{100 \times 71.7} = \textit{115,455.30 Hongkong dollars, as a constant}$$

Multiply the constant by the market premium in order to obtain the cost in Hongkong dollars of 1000 troy ounces of bar silver. For example, if the market premium on bar silver in Hongkong should be 8%, multiply the constant of 115,455.30 × 108 = 1246.92 Hongkong dollars for 1000 troy ounces of bar silver.

Shanghai exports surplus bar silver to Hongkong and Canton against payment in Shanghai taels, whenever the premium (over 110.90 Shanghai taels for silver 0.998 fine) warrants this. A sale of bar silver by Shanghai to Hongkong or Canton is, as far as the outturn is concerned, entirely for account of the Southern ports.

Shanghai may be induced to sell bar silver to Hongkong or Canton in Hongkong dollar currency, in which event the transaction turns into an arbitrage operation on the part of the Shanghai seller.

Formula:

? Shanghai taels	: 100 Hongkong dollars
115,455.30 Hongkong dollars	: 100,000 troy ounces bar silver
100,000 troy ounces bar silver	: 91,804.04 Shanghai taels

$$X = \frac{100 \times 100{,}000 \times 91{,}804.04}{115{,}455.30 \times 100{,}000} = 79.515 \textit{ Shanghai taels as a constant}$$

The last mentioned link in the chain represents the amount in Shanghai taels, which the Loofang will pay at Shanghai at the basis of 100 Canton taels weight of bar silver, 0.998 fine, equals 110.90 Shanghai taels currency.

To the constant of	79.515
Add charges and interest, say	0.500
Total . .	80.015

Divide by 100, plus the Hongkong premium of the day, say 7%, in order to obtain the parity quotation between Shanghai and Hongkong.

$$80.015 \div 107 = 74.78 \textit{ Shanghai taels.}$$

If it is feasible to sell at Shanghai telegraphic transfer on Hongkong at a rate higher than 74.78, plus $\frac{1}{16}$% brokerage, (0.0467) there will remain a margin of profit.

In case shipment is made to Canton, it will be essential to consider the enhanced charges, as outlined on page 230.

The bulk of the bar silver shipped to Hongkong and Canton in course of the years 1919 to 1923 was destined for the Canton Mint, where enormous quantities of 20 cents coins were turned out.

Export of Bar Silver from Shanghai to Yunnanfu.

Bar silver is exported to Yunnanfu for the manufacture there of silver coins. For Shanghai the operation is a clean sale against Shanghai taels, at the rate of 111 taels currency (plus a certain premium) for each 100 Canton taels weight. The charges are for account of the importer. Shipment is made *via* Haiphong by French steamer, or by coasting steamer, with trans-shipment at Hongkong.

Charges vary and may be considered to approximate the following figures:

Charges and interest to Hongkong	0.50%
Freight Hongkong–Haiphong	0.50%
Trans-shipment	0.04%
Interest 5 days @ 6% Hongkong–Haiphong .	0.08%
Insurance ½°/∞ Hongkong–Haiphong . .	0.05%
Total . .	1.17%

To this figure has to be added the railway freight from Haiphong to Yunnanfu, loading and unloading charges, interest and insurance for the period of the railway journey, and incidentals.

Export of Bar Silver from Shanghai to Mukden.

Mukden at times imports bar silver from Shanghai for the requirements of the provincial Mint situated there. The importer has to consider how many Shanghai taels currency will 100 Mukden taels weight of bar silver cost, c.i.f. Mukden.

Formula:

? Shanghai taels currency	: 100 Mukden taels weight of bar
100 Mukden taels weight	: 35.95 grams bar
31.1035 grams bar	: 1 troy ounce bar
100 troy ounces bar	: 998 ounces fine
925 ounces fine	: 100 ounce standard
100 ounces standard	: 82.7815 Canton taels weight
100 Canton taels weight	: 110.90 Shanghai taels currency

$$X = \frac{100 \times 35.95 \times 998 \times 100 \times 82.7815 \times 110.90}{100 \times 31.1035 \times 100 \times 925 \times 100 \times 100} = 114.486$$

Shanghai taels as constant.

100 Mukden taels weight = Shanghai taels currency 114.486

Add charges:	
Freight 4½ °/₀₀	0.4500
Insurance ⅝ °/₀₀	0.0625
Coolie hire, wharfage dues, etc.	0.0750
8 days interest at 6%	0.1250
Total Shanghai taels .	115.1985

a figure which needs revising owing to the frequent changes in freight and insurance rates applicable in Manchuria.

Export of Bar Silver from Shanghai to India.

In considering export of bar silver from Shanghai to Bombay we should like to refer to our remarks under the heading "Import of Bar Silver from British India," page 216. The analogous principle applies here, but the reasoning has just the reverse effect. Charges and interest have to be deducted from, instead of added to, the proceeds.

Take the constant		2.9047
Deduct charges ¾%	0.0218	
„ interest 6% for 30 d/s	0.0145	
		0.0363
		2.8684

In multiplying this constant by the forward (30 days) price of bar silver in rupees per 100 tolas, the product will represent the Shanghai parity. For example, the forward quotation for bar silver in Bombay is 82 rupees per 100 tolas.

$$2.8684 \times 82 = 235.208 \textit{ rupees.}$$

If Shanghai can sell telegraphic transfer on Bombay below 2.35 rupees per tael, it will be remunerative to ship bar silver from Shanghai to India. It should be borne in mind that the charges, and especially the rate of interest, are variable and that brokerage on the sale of telegraphic transfer on Bombay should be considered in the calculation.

Take a practical example: Shanghai has 100 bars of surplus silver, 0.998 fine, and desires to export these to Bombay. The total weight of the 100 bars is 105,000 ounces troy, or 280.000 tolas.

If melted in Shanghai the bar silver will net Shanghai taels 96,394.87. If exported to Bombay and contracted for sale there at the price of say 82 rupees per 100 tolas, the proceeds will be—

			rupees 229.600
Less freight and insurance, etc., ¾%	rupees	1722	
„ 8% interest for 30 days . .	„	1530	
„ Correspondents' commission, etc., 1°/oo	„	230	
			„ 3.482
			rupees 226.118

This corresponds to a Shanghai—

Bombay T. T. rate of	rupees 234.58
Less: ⅛% brokerage	„ .29
	Net rupees 234.29

If Shanghai can sell telegraphic transfer on Bombay at or below 234¼, against the proceeds of this particular shipment, it will be feasible to export bar silver to Bombay.

Supposing the T.T. rate Bombay–Shanghai is known (say 236 rupees equal to 100 taels) and the parity price quotation of bar silver in Bombay is wanted:

Formula:

? rupees	: 100 tolas bar silver
8 tolas	: 3 ounces troy
100 ounces troy	: 82.7815 Canton taels weight
100 Canton taels weight of silver	: 110.90 Shanghai taels currency
100 taels currency	: 236 rupees

$$X = \frac{100 \times 3 \times 82.7815 \times 110.90 \times 236}{8 \times 100 \times 100 \times 100} = \mathit{81.247\ rupees}$$

for 100 tolas of silver, 0.998 fine.

The arbitrated parity quotation per 100 tolas is therefore	81.247 rupees
Deduct charges and interest, say ½% . . .	1.217 ,,
Net proceeds per 100 tolas .	80.03 ,,

In short, in order to find the parity quotation between bar silver in India and the Shanghai Bombay cross rate, divide the latter by the constant of 2.9047 and deduct charges and interest.

$$236 \div 2.9047 = \mathit{81.247145}$$

less charges and interest.

It does happen at times that Shanghai is requested to ship some of its surplus bar silver to Bombay against payment by telegraphic transfer on London in £. As such transactions are not directly connected with Chinese currency, the instance is merely recorded here without further comment.

CHAPTER X

TAELS

What is a tael ?

THE tael is of considerable importance to commercial and financial life in China. The name is neither Chinese, nor is it derived from the English language. In searching for the etymology of the expression one is inclined to think of the Indian weight, the "tola," notwithstanding the fact that the two are not synonymous as measures of weight.

The term "tael" signifies either a weight or a currency. The tael is really a weight, namely the Chinese ounce. It is true that there is no uniformity regarding ounces in China; the ounce weight of one town differing from that of another, and if possible, the ounce of the seller will weigh more heavily than the ounce of the buyer. But the tael is also a unit of silver money in China.

In Chinese it is not difficult to differentiate between the two meanings, which in almost all foreign tongues, happen to be expressed in a single word. If the tael of weight is meant, the Chinese ounce, the Chinese will use the word "liang," (兩); for the money tael they will employ the expression "liang yindze" (兩銀子), tael of silver.

And this is exactly what the money tael represents—an ounce of silver. It is beside the point to draw attention to the fact that there are hundreds of different kinds of ounces in use within China, and probably just as many degrees of fineness in the silver making up a part of the country's currency.

If silver of a fineness of at least 0.935 is cast into ingots of varying weights, such money taels will be called collectively "sycee." The origin of this name also cannot be authenticated, but it is most probably derived from the Cantonese expression "Si-soi" (細絲), meaning "fine silk." Some students interpret the word to mean that pure silver can be drawn out by the use of heat into thin thread; others say that pure silver is glossy like silk.

The Chinese Government does not deem it its duty to define and control the weights used within the country, and neither does it interfere as regards the fineness of bullion. All this is left to the local governing bodies, to Chambers of Commerce and like corporations.

As will be shown later on, the taels current in various parts of China differ considerably from each other, not only with regard to weight, but also in respect to the standard of fineness. Local taels of certain denomination represent a *quasi* standard of weight. But the fineness of the silver contained in the sycee is not uniform on account of the primitive methods of smelting, and also owing to different institutions manufacturing sycee without regard to standardized methods. This shortcoming is made good by an assay instituted by the "Kung-ku-chu" (公估局), the public assaying office.

Tael Coins.

The tael does not exist in China, Proper, in the shape of a coin. It is chronicled that silver coins were for the first time made in A.D. 1183 in five denominations, weighing one, two, three, five and 10 taels respectively.[1] Those silver coins were called *Ch'eng-an,* current money. Owing to fraudulent cutting out of particles of silver by some people, and on account of the manufacture of inferior imitation coins by some others, the Government ceased to mint those coins after three years' trial. In A.D. 1200 an edict declared that the coins referred to would cease to be legal tender.

In A.D. 1793 two tael subsidiary coins were cast in Tibet by order of the Chinese Government, namely one *ch'ien*

[1] *Banking and Prices in China,* By J. Edkins. (1905).

and five *fen, i.e.*, 10 and five taels cents.[1] It is curious to learn that one tael of silver exchanged for only nine of the one *ch'ien* coins, which means that the Mint's profit was 10%.

There was an attempt to produce a silver coin for circulation in Fukien province as early as 1835;[2] this coin was supposed to have weighed 517 grains. One side showed the image of the God of Longevity and an inscription denoting that it was a cake of pure silver weighing seven mace and two candareens and that it had been cast during the reign of Tao-kwang.

At the same time another silver coin was issued for the purpose of paying the troops stationed in Fukien and Formosa. The coin bore the inscription "Pure silver for current use from the Changchow Commissariat; seven mace, two candareens."

It may be disputable whether the two coins just described are to be considered tael or dollar coins. At that time China had no dollar piece of her own, all such coins circulating in the ports being of foreign origin. The inscription "Seven mace, two candareens" refers to the subdivision of the weight tael and approximates the weight of the foreign dollar. Probably the authorities merely intended to produce a silver coin, without attempting to investigate whether it was a tael or a dollar coin that had been created by them.

In A.D. 1867, when the Crown Colony of Hongkong still owned a Mint, a Shanghai money tael was coined there by way of trial. The coin was 0.982 fine, weighed 36.67 grams and was intended to replace the theoretical Shanghai currency tael; but it never succeeded in achieving its aim. In 1905, when China endeavored to introduce a uniform currency for the entire country, the K'uping tael was chosen as the new unit. In Wuchang tael coins, to

---

[1] *Journal of the Royal Asiatic Society*, Vol. XXXII. Article by Dr. S. W. Bushell.

[2] *The Middle Kingdom*. By S. Wells Williams.

the extent of 648,000, with a fineness of 0.877 and a gross weight of 37.3 grams, were then coined by way of experiment, but as the scheme in its entirety failed, those coins were soon withdrawn again.

There exists another remnant of a rather peculiar type of tael coin. In Changsha, the capital of Hunan province, bankers were in the habit of sending into the provincial Mint small flat lumps of silver, where the latter were die-impressed with the name of the bank and the weight. These taels existed in denominations of one tael, seven mace and five mace, and were in circulation throughout Hunan province for about 10 years, up to 1915, when they completely disappeared from public hands.

In Chinese Turkestan (Hsin-kiang) tael coins have been in circulation since the reign of Kuang Hsu. They were minted in Urumchi in denominations of one tael, five, four, three, two and one mace coins. The tael piece is known there as the "Sar," and the mace pieces as "Miskal."

The Mint at Tientsin, during the closing days of the Manchu regime, struck one tael coins, but merely by way of experiment.

Since the establishment of the Chinese Republic tael coins have been minted in Hsinkiang (Chinese Turkestan) only. Two kinds of one tael coins have been issued, both being 39 m.m. in diameter, but one varying slightly from the other in the design of the flag and in the shape of the two characters denoting the year of issue (1912-1913). The legend, contained within a beaded circle, written in Chinese characters only, reads, when translated "One tael, revenue silver." Around it, in an outer circle, is written in Chinese "First year of the Republic of China."

Besides the one tael coins there exist some half tael silver coins of Hsinkiang issue.

One of these, inscribed "five mace," was issued simultaneously with the one tael piece. It measures 33½ m.m. in diameter and is similar in design to the tael coin.

In addition to these there was another five mace coin issued in Kashgar, made of silver and measuring 32.5 m.m. in diameter. The obverse shows two crossed republican flags and the legend in Turki, denoting the date 1331 as the year of issue (the Mohammedan year 1331 began on 11th December, 1912, and expired on 13th November, 1913). The reverse bears four Chinese characters, denoting "The Republic of China," within a beaded circle. Around the latter is written in Chinese "Five mace, revenue silver," and below "Made in Kashgar, Hsinkiang."

A year later a similar five mace coin was issued in Kashgar. It measures 33 m.m. in diameter and is similar in design to the coin just described, except that it bears "1332" as year of issue.

The subsidiary coins, viz. one, two, three and four mace, republican issues, also exist in silver.

The Money Tael.

The currency tael is the principal medium for financing wholesale transactions and for the payment of Customs duties in China. It exists in denominations of from ½ tael up to 100 taels, but in the majority of cases circulates in "shoes" of about 50 taels. In chapter IX "Bar Silver and China" it has been explained how imported silver is converted into currency taels,—into sycee. The smelting is done by a few privileged firms of old standing.

We have endeavored to ascertain the period in which taels in the shape of "shoes" made their first appearance, but have not been able to obtain absolutely reliable data on this question. According to one authority sycee in the shape of "shoes" was for the first time manufactured under Kublai Khan, the Mongol emperor, who ruled from A.D. 1260–1295. According to a memorial on currency reform submitted by the Minister of Finance to the President in 1918, sycee was known to exist in China during the Sung dynasty (A.D. 960–1280). Undoubtedly

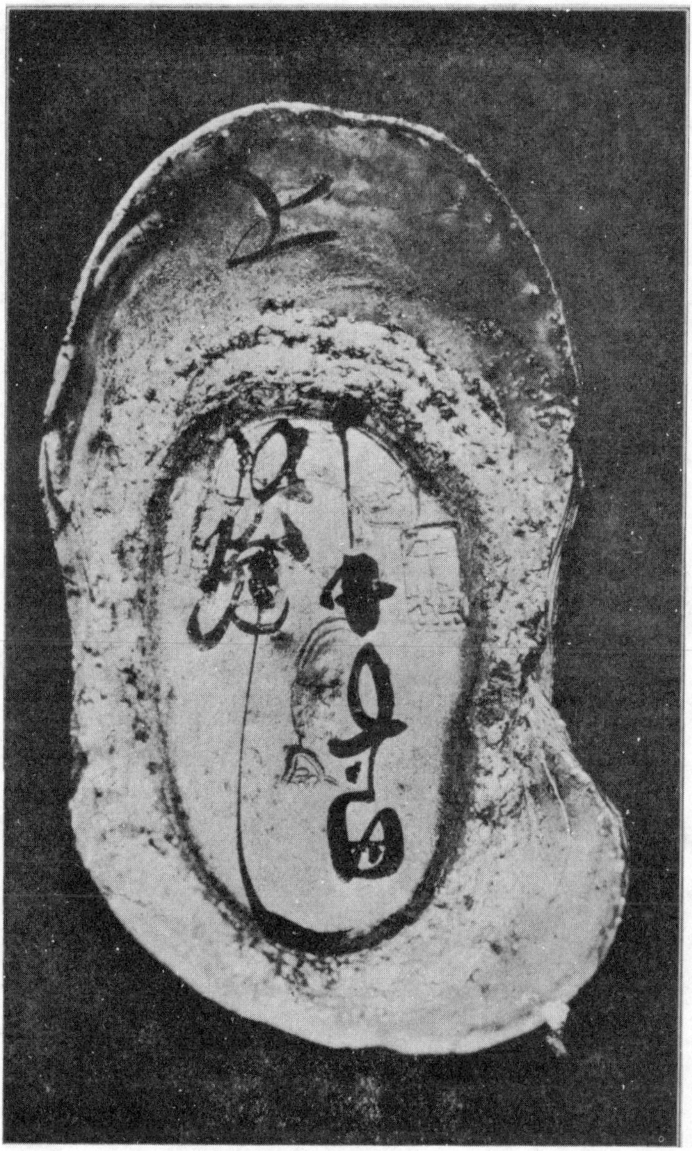

TOP VIEW OF A SHOE OF SHANGHAI SYCEE.
Value about 50 taels. Showing the Kungku's ink inscriptions.
Nearly actual Size.

Side View of a Shoe of Shanghai Sycee. Value About 50 Taels.
Nearly actual Size.

silver currency in the shape of sycee is of very old standing in China and has undergone but little change in its composition and handling during the centuries of its existence.

The bulk of the sycee in circulation has its origin from imported bar silver. At times the parity permits it to melt dollars, or small coin dollars, and convert these into sycee, but this is not often feasible. The melting is entrusted to a few private concerns, styled "Loofangs" (爐房). Every shoe of silver bears the firm name of the Loofang, the town where its business is situated and the number of the furnace from which the shoe of sycee originates; these particulars are stamped upon the shoe with dies. In Szechuen province as well as in Peking (Sungkiang tael) are found ingots of a value of 10 taels. Shanghai shoes weigh very closely on 50 taels; the same refers to Hankow and Tientsin sycee. In Nanchang (Kiangsi) the "shoe" weighs also about 50 taels, but is rectangular in shape. Newchwang taels weigh on an average 53½ taels.

Some kinds of money taels exist as book currency only; they are never to be found in the shape of silver ingots or, in fact, in any shape. These remarks refer notably to the *Haikwan* tael (the Customs tael) and to the *K'uping* tael, (the Treasury tael). The numerous kinds of money taels current in China do not by any means tally regarding the number of fine contents of silver. This is not surprising since each town has its own ideas on this question. Even the currency taels produced in one place and current there are by no means uniform in fineness and, of course, neither are they uniform in weight. Therefore these all-important points have to be adjusted by an official body, called the Kung-ku-chu, the public assay office, which is appointed by the Native Banks and/or the Chamber of Commerce and whose assay is taken as final. The delegate from the Kung-ku-chu takes the silver "shoes" as they come from the smelter's hands. First he weighs each ingot and writes the weight in Chinese ink on the upper surface of the "shoe."

After this procedure is completed he assays the sycee, in order to determine its fineness by means of an estimate (the estimate of a connoisseur), *i.e.*, by judging according to the colour, the lustre and the general appearance of the silver; or the Kung-ku man employs the touchstone, in order to determine the fineness. As soon as he has made his decision he adds, also in Chinese ink, the fineness, and/or the premium, which corresponds to a certain degree of fineness.

In spite of the very primitive manner of assaying it must be emphasized that the results, upon examination within the country and also abroad, have invariably shown the honesty of the assayer as well as the correctness of his judgment.

The tael is subdivided as follows:

1 tael (liang) = 10 mace (chien)
1 mace (chien) = 10 candareens (fen)
1 candareen (fen) = 10 cash (li)

It is essential to clearly keep apart the tael of weight and the tael of currency. The former is a measure of weight,—the Chinese ounce. The tael of value is a piece of silver, with a clearly defined weight and fineness. This definition holds good in face of the fact that taels of account do not exist in substance, though they do exist in theory and in practice as currency of account.

Simple Truths?

The tael as a measure of values, having celebrated its millenium in China, has always been an object of genuine interest. And yet there are very few people who know the genesis of the tael. Amongst those who have to admit their ignorance on this particular subject are multitudes of Chinese, many of whom are in constant touch with practical finance. Of foreigners residing in China but a very small portion has endeavored to investigate the mysteries surrounding the romance of the tael, yet only a small fraction of those attempting to seek the truth has succeeded. The subject, as well as the object itself, is somewhat intricate; otherwise they could not have afforded for centuries a living to millions of people.

Recognised foreign authorities have given their definitions. These were as correct as they possibly could be. If, in spite thereof, they have failed to enlighten and convince the man in the street, it may possibly be ascribed to their assumption that their fellow-citizens are as equally well posted as themselves in the rudiments of the subject.

By way of illustration we shall let the authorities speak:

The value of the Shanghai tael is made up of three elements—the weight, the quality of silver, and a convention. The weight on the scale is the Tsaoping tael of 565.65 grains, the silver is reduced to a standard of 944 fine on the Kuping basis of 1000 fine, and the convention is that 98 taels of this weight and this silver settle a liability of 100 taels Shanghai convention currency.—(H. B. Morse).

A quantity of silver weighing 935.40 Shanghai taels of the denomination 98/100—*i.e.*, 916.66 Shanghai taels (weight) of the denomination 1000/1000—has the conventional value of 1000 taels currency. In other words, 1 tael of silver Shanghai weight of the standard denomination 9354/9800 or 916.666/1000, is equivalent to 1 tael of Shanghai currency within a fraction of two or three thousandths, more or less.—(G. Pietsch).

The average fineness is from 985 to 986, but the sycee circulates at its value in Shanghai currency based upon a standard of 913 for sycee silver.—(W. F. Spalding).

The silver which circulates in China as the medium of exchange has the shape of broad shoes and is therefore called "shoe." The weight of these shoes varies from ½ tael up to 100 taels, their lowest degree of fineness is 0.935. Currency silver of a higher degree is named "sycee." The most current sycee is nearly 0.986 fine.—(Henry Deutsch).

These notes on the fineness of the Shanghai tael were written by some of the foremost authorities on the subject. To the reader with experience in Chinese financial matters they are very instructive, but the uninitiated are likely to become confused. Every kind of tael in China tells its own tale.

Once upon a time, to wit in A.D. 1905, it was decreed that China's new and universal currency should have a silver tael coin as its legally recognised unit. Yet it came otherwise; this means it did not come at all. To-day, twenty years thereafter, the currency is what it was a thousand years ago,—sycee taels.

The attempt to introduce a tael coin into China induced a correspondent in Shanghai to write to the London *Times*, giving his expert views on the subject of "taels" in general. Here is his personal opinion:

CHINA'S NEW SILVER COINAGE.

(From a correspondent)

Shanghai, December 29th, 1905.

Parturiunt montes and for result—a mouse. For three years the Chinese Government has had before it the dual task of creating a uniform currency as required by treaty and of establishing that currency on a fixed basis as demanded by economic laws. Stability of exchange with other commercial nations has not been required by treaty, and has no very considerable pressure behind it to overcome the inertia of the mercantile world of China: its establishment on a solid basis must call for large sums to be set aside as a banking or reserve fund. The recent rise in the value of silver has removed the pressure on the Government and much water will flow under the bridges before the official world will take the requisite steps to confer this boon upon the nation. For the creation of a uniform currency, however, the initial steps have been taken, authorized by an Imperial decree which appeared on November 20.

China has had silver coins since 1889, issued by the various provincial mints. The very idea of legal tender is repugnant to the Chinese mind, and for the major operations of trade these coins have served only as bullion with a more or less guaranteed quality, passing by count only in retail transactions. The coins were the dollar of silver and its fractional part, but no steps were taken to assimilate them to the tael; and, while the dollar was inscribed 72/100ths of a tael, the coins have never been issued or received by the Government at their face value to make up sums expressed in taels. They had, however, in one respect, the true characteristic of a coin, in that the inscribed weight (or face value) was the weight of the coin itself, and did not express the value of the silver contained in it. These coins were issued in denominations of one dollar and ½ dollar of silver 900 fine, and 20 cents and 10 cents pieces owing to the greater amount of seignorage for minting them.

The Imperial "tael."

All this coinage is now to be jettisoned and the new Imperial "uniform currency" is to be the tael. The official mind has not yet grasped the functions of a coin, and the new coin which is to represent the tael is emphatically not a tael either in weight or in value. When the Englishman wishes to explain to his friend from Mars the currency which he uses, he takes a sovereign from his pocket and says, "That is a pound." The Martian naturally asks "What is a pound?" and the reply comes promptly "A pound is that;" there is nothing more that need be said. But when the inquisitive Martian comes to China in the course of his travels, his Chinese friend must enter into an explanation;—"That is a tael. At least it is not exactly a tael, but it is supposed to represent the value of one K'uping tael. Now K'uping tael silver is supposed to be pure, but it is not, it is only 989 fine; and, besides, the Government must allow something for its own trouble and the cost of minting; and of pure silver the coin contains 96 per cent. of the face value. Then all standard coins must contain 10 per cent. of alloy to harden the silver, so the Government adds of copper 10 per cent. not of the actual weight of the coin nor of the silver in it, but of the nominal face value. So though I call it a tael, it is not really a tael. A thousand of them represent a thousand taels, weight 1060 taels, are supposed to contain 989 taels, and actually contain 960 taels of silver."

This is not burlesque, it is a fair paraphrase of the words of the regulations put in force by the decree; the words are as follows:

The best quality of sycee which is now in circulation is found by chemical analysis to consist of 98.9 per cent. of pure silver. Allowing two or three per cent. for loss in minting, the new tael coin is to be minted of a mixture of 0.96 tael pure silver and 0.10 tael copper as equal to one K'uping tael of full touch.

The Regulations for the New Tael Currency.

The observations of the London *Times* correspondent were very much to the point, notwithstanding the fact that destiny willed that the new currency unit should never be adopted in practice. As a historical record the following official regulations will be of interest:

THE REGULATIONS OF NOVEMBER 19, 1905.[1]

1. The new silver currency should be purer in quality than the dollars heretofor coined in various provinces and the standard unit of value must be heavier to be suitable as a national coin. The purest silver in circulation in China to-day is shown by chemical analysis to contain not more than 98 or 99 per cent. of pure silver, but a deduction of two or three per cent. should be allowed in minting the new coin to cover the cost of coinage, and it is proposed to make the new tael of nine mace six candareens of pure silver, mixed with one mace's weight of pure copper, to be fixed as the equivalent of one K'uping tael of full touch.

The fractional currency shall consist (*a*) of a piece containing four mace eight candareens' weight of K'uping silver mixed with five candareens' weight of pure copper which shall be declared the equivalent of five mace K'uping silver full touch; (*b*) a piece of one mace seven candareens' weight of K'uping silver mixed with three candareens of pure copper, to be the equivalent of two mace K'uping silver of full touch; and (*c*) a piece of the weight of eight candareens five *li* of pure K'uping silver mixed with one candareen five *li* of pure copper, as the smallest piece, to be the equivalent of one mace of K'uping silver, full touch. It is also decided that in every ten pieces minted four shall be of one tael's value and two of the denomination of five mace, two of two mace and two of one mace. This shall be the rule, but, if there shall be a demand for a larger proportion of any particular denomination, orders shall be issued to make a careful investigation as to the real amount (in circulation) and report upon the matter to the Financial Commission and the Board of Revenue, who shall consult together and make reply, and only if they consent may the additional amount be minted. As to these coins the central and branch mints must make them exactly of the same weight and fineness, and assay and inspection must be made according to the rules for the regulation of the coinage already submitted by us and approved by the Throne.

2. The one tael coin shall be equal to two five mace coins or five two mace coins, or ten one mace coins. The small fractional coins of less than five mace shall exchange among themselves at this rate, and in all monetary transactions, public or private, they must be paid out and received at this rate; under no circumstances may a discount be charged. Any disobedience will be punished according to law.

3. The one tael coin being the standard monetary unit, there shall be no limit to its circulation. The five mace and other fractional silver pieces shall be legal tender in every transaction to the amount of ten taels, *i.e.*, to the value of ten of the one tael

[1] In the *Report of the Director of the Mint of the U. S.*, 1906, pp. 198-200. Translation made by Mr. E. T. Williams, of the American Legation, Peking.

coins. They must not be used to pay in full amounts over ten taels, and if offered they may be refused in amounts over the sum specified. The rate of exchange between the copper coins and the silver and the limit of circulation of the former will be determined after the provincial authorities have complied with the regulations already submitted, by which they are required to investigate and report to the Board of Revenue the facts as to the circulation of copper coins.

4. As to the minting of the silver coins, it is proposed that, the Board of Revenue having been ordered to coin, the central mint will coin several million pieces and send them to the bank, and the Board of Revenue shall send dies to the provincial mints of Chili, Kiangsu, Hupeh and Kuangtung, which shall at the same time mint several million pieces, whereupon the bank of the Board of Revenue shall print paper money to the full amount of the silver coins minted and fix a date upon which it shall be put into circulation. After its issue the Treasury of the Board of Revenue and the treasuries of the provinces mentioned shall first receive it in a fixed proportion, and thereafter all the provinces, the railways, the (China Merchants) steamship Company, and the Telegraph Administration shall receive it in the same proportion. There must be no discrimination against it by the said official companies on the ground that it is not issued in their provinces. The method of arranging the proportions shall be to fix the proportion payable in silver coins and that payable in paper money of the bank of the Board of Revenue, and for the present the remainder may be paid in other silver—that is, in lump silver or the old dollars—but afterwards as the coinage of the new pieces increases in amount the proportion payable in this may be increased until finally payments will be made entirely in the new silver coins. We request that orders be issued to all the Tartar generals, viceroys, and governors, as well as to the superintendent of railways, of the China Merchants Steam Navigation Company, and the Telegraph Administration to comply with this regulation.

5. All provincial taxes levied in K'uping taels shall be payable in the same amount of the new tael coins. The collectors should have salaries definitely fixed, *i.e.*, not be allowed to make their living by charges for exchange, etc., as heretofore. Aside from the legal charge of meltage, no other charge shall be added to the sum levied under the name of "assaying charges," etc. All other moneys heretofore collected or paid in taels of another scale shall be converted, according to the value of the tael used, into their equivalent in K'uping taels of full touch, and the conversion having once been made, these sums shall forever hereafter be receivable and payable in that amount of the new one tael coins, and no variation from the rule will be allowed. We have also to request that orders be issued to all the provincial authorities to comply with this rule.

6. As China is now entering into new commercial treaties with the various foreign powers which provide for the adoption of a uniform national coinage which the merchants of foreign nationalities residing in China shall use, it becomes necessary to request that the Board of Foreign Affairs be instructed that at the time of the issue of the new coinage dispatches must be sent to the various foreign ministers and to the consuls at the various treaty ports and notifications made to the commissioners of customs that they may all hereafter uniformly use the new coins. The customs duties have heretofore been levied and collected in Haikwan taels, and orders must be issued to the commissioners of customs thereafter in accordance with the provisions of the commercial treaties to convert the duties levied in Haikwan taels into their equivalent in K'uping taels and collect accordingly.

7. On the day when the new coins are put into circulation the viceroys and governors of the various provinces must issue instructions to the local authorities to put out proclamations informing the merchants and all people that whatever accounts they may have, old or new, and whatever commercial transactions may take place in the markets, the original amounts, according to the value of the taels in which they may be reckoned, must be converted to their equivalents in K'uping taels of full touch, and paid in that amount of the new silver coins, and such payment may not be refused.

8. As all viceroys, governors, other officials, merchants, soldiers and common people in all the provinces must use the new coins, all may send their silver to be minted, and the central mint and the branch mints at Tientsin, Nanking, Wuchang and Canton will coin it for them. Every tael of K'uping silver of full touch will be refined to pure silver 0.985 fine, or finer, in return for which (0.985 tael) they will receive one of the new tael dollars. Fractional coins of the denomination of five mace, two mace, and one mace will also be minted for them in the proportions set forth above.

The excess in the fineness of the silver will pay the cost of minting, and thus there will be nothing to make good on either side.

Silver of inferior quality, foreign silver coins, and the silver dollars heretofore minted in the various provinces may also be sent in to be reminted, the amount of the new coins given in exchange being determined by the amount of pure silver contained —that is, their value will be determined in K'uping taels of full touch, and new coins issued accordingly.

9. When the new coins are first issued and the people are unfamiliar with them, there will almost surely be attempts made among the merchants in exchanging them to discriminate against them (boycott them), or to discount them. The Bank of the Board of Revenue, the customs banks in the various provinces, and other

official banks and cash shops must be charged with the responsibility of seeing that any one bringing the new silver coins to exchange for paper money, bullion, or copper coins, or desiring to exchange paper money, silver bullion, or copper coins for the new silver coins, shall receive just treatment on the basis of one K'uping tael being the equivalent of one tael in the new coinage. There must be no extortion. Orders must be given also to investigate the markets, and if any mercantile firms are found raising or lowering the rate of exchange at their own pleasure, report shall be made for cases in Peking to the Financial Commission and to the Board of Revenue, and for the provinces to the Tartar generals, viceroys and the governors concerned, who shall investigate and severely punish the offence, so as to enforce the coinage regulations.

10. These regulations must be published in the official gazettes for the information of the people, and we have to request that orders be issued to the Tartar generals, viceroys and governors of the various provinces that at the time when the new coins are issued they must instruct the department and district magistrates to print these regulations in large characters in proclamations which must be posted in all the cities, villages and market towns in their jurisdictions, that the people on seeing the same may become thoroughly acquainted with the matter, and thus the yamen clerks may be kept from cheating them.

An Attempt to Explain.

It cannot be denied that the question of taels and of sycee bristles with complications. These arise principally out of the fact that every commercial center has its own tael weight, or rather weights, of which there are several " standards " side by side. But this is not all, as the silver which is weighed out in any particular locality is by no means of uniform degree of fineness. A correct definition is at times rendered difficult by the confusion caused by the term of " tael," which happens to represent a unit of weight and simultaneously a measure of value.

Nevertheless we should like to make an attempt at presenting an explanation regarding the *raison d'être* of the sycee tael. Owing to its prime importance the Shanghai currency tael has been chosen here for " vivisection." Be it remembered that every currency tael is made up at least by a clearly determined weight of silver and by a stipulated degree of fineness of that particular lump of silver.

The tael weight current at Shanghai is the Chauping tael (漕平), which is often pronounced "Tsaoping" tael. It forms the weight element of a currency tael which is recognised in the provinces of Chekiang, Kiangsu, Anhwei and Kiangsi, and it is also in regular use in Chefoo. It is known under the name of "Tribute" tael, because it is current principally in those provinces which used to send rice as tribute to Peking. The weight of the Chauping tael is 565.65 grains (36.64 grams). In order to avoid confusion we shall henceforth call the Chauping tael "Chauping ounce."

After these preliminaries comes the question: what are the elements comprising the Shanghai tael?

1. The Shanghai currency tael weighs one Chauping ounce, which means 565.65 grains, or 36.64 grams.

No comment is needed here.

2. 98 Chauping ounces of silver are counted and universally accepted as 100 Shanghai currency taels.

Why? By convention from times immemorial. Since this convention is invariably a condition *sine qua non,* it is, and must be, accepted as a fact which is not subject to discussion.

3. What is the fineness of the Shanghai currency tael?

(*a*) In practice as near as possible 0.980.

(*b*) By convention 0.935374.

(*c*) In theory $0.916\frac{2}{3}$.

Now, which of these three disparate figures has a claim to authenticity? Every one of the trio is correct in its own way.

So far we have had smooth sailing, and just when nearing the end of the trail, difficulties threaten to arise. Yet, in reality, matters are easily capable of explanation. Let us begin at the end, with (*c*) "in theory $0.916\frac{2}{3}$."

Everybody familiar with the rudiments of finance is aware of the fact that the standard fineness for the British sovereign, and for gold in England generally, is $0.916\frac{2}{3}$. The Indian silver rupee is likewise 11/12ths fine, which means $0.916\frac{2}{3}$. By chance the standard fineness of the Shanghai money tael is also $0.916\frac{2}{3}$. In other words, 1000 Shanghai currency taels are equal to 1000 Chauping ounces, containing 11 parts pure silver and 1 part alloy. (11/12ths fine, or 0.916.666).

Neither doubt nor objection can be raised against this statement of facts.

Our next step is to elucidate (*b*) "by convention 0.935374."

Why this deviation from the theoretical standard? Because here enters the old convention, discussed under (2), according to which 980 Chauping ounces on the scale will irrevocably be accepted in settlement of a liability of 1000 Shanghai currency taels.

$$916.6666 \div 980 = \mathit{0.935374}$$

The figure of 0.935374 is accepted as the conventional standard for sycee.

As this point has now also been satisfactorily explained, it remains only to solve the last "mystery," mentioned under (*a*) "In practice Shanghai sycee is as nearly as possible 0.980 fine."

As a matter of fact, this point requires the least explanation. It is immaterial whether Shanghai sycee is 0.975 or 0.990 fine, as every degree above the standard of 0.935374 is marked down on the sycee shoe in form of a premium and charged for accordingly.

Here we have an analogous practice to the treatment of bar silver in England. There the standard for silver is 0.925. Anything above this fineness is marked down as B (betterness). Bar silver shipped to China from England is usually 0.998 fine, which means $17\frac{1}{2}$ better than the British standard.

Here is a practical example.

The standard fineness for Shanghai sycee is .	0.935374
Plus a premium of 5%	0.046768
	0.982142

Shanghai sycee, 0.982 fine, corresponds to a premium of 5%.

This is the whole essence of the Shanghai tael in a nutshell.

Theoretical and Practical Parities.

In attempting to determine the theoretical and practical parities between the Shanghai tael and imported bar silver we have first of all to recall the hypothesis that the Shanghai currency tael weighs one Chauping ounce of silver 0.916 $\frac{2}{3}$ fine. Based on this figure the *theoretical parity* between the Shanghai currency tael and bar silver can be determined by multiplying the *constant of 1.168* by the price of bar silver in London per standard ounce; charges and interest are not included in the calculation. In practice currency taels do not exist as such, and therefore the theoretical parity is of importance only for the purpose of fixing the relation of currency taels to sycee.

One Shanghai currency tael equal[1]

1.	Chauping	ounce	or	1.178	ounces	silver	0.916.2/3	fine,	or
0.991	,,	ounces	,,	1.168	,,	,,	0.925	,,	or
0.980	,,	,,	,,	1.155	,,	,,	0.935	,,	or
0 930	,,	,,	,,	1.097	,,	,,	0.985	,,	or
0.918	,,	,,	,,	1.082	,,	,,	0.998	,,	or
0.916.2/3	,,	,,	,,	1.080	,,	,,	1000	,,	

1000 Chauping ounces of silver, 0.985 fine, equals 1075.25 Shanghai currency taels.

In fixing the *actual parity* between the Shanghai currency tael and bar silver one has to know how many currency taels the Loofangs (smelting shops) will return for 100 Canton taels weight of bar silver. It has already been stated in Chapter IX, page 211, that since 1920 the tariff provides for a nominal return of 110.90 Shanghai taels for every 100 Canton taels of bar silver, 0.998 fine, tendered. On this basis silver 0.996 fine will realize

[1] C. Champkin, *Bullion Operations in China.*

110.70 Shanghai taels, and silver 0.999 fine will give a return of 111 Shanghai taels. But whenever the demand for bar silver is strong, these figures will be improved upon. The following table shows what the proceeds of 100,000 troy ounces of bar silver will be, if converted into Shanghai sycee at varying constants.

If the Loofangs return for every 100 Canton taels weight of silver Shanghai taels currency:	*The proceeds for 100,000 troy ounces of bar silver will be:*
110.70 taels	91,639.07 Shanghai taels
110.80 „	91,721.85 „ „
110.90 „	91,804.04 „ „
111.00 „	91,887.27 „ „
111.10 „	91,970.20 „ „
111.20 „	92,053.00 „ „
111.30 „	92,135.77 „ „
111.40 „	92,218.55 „ „
111.50 „	92,301.33 „ „

Classification of Taels.

The different species of the currency tael may conveniently be grouped as follows:

(*a*) Taels in shape of coins.
(*b*) Taels as money of account.
(*c*) Transfer taels.
(*d*) Sycee taels.

We have already spoken of tael coins and need not therefore revert to the matter.

Regarding taels as money of account the most prominent amongst these is the *Haikwan* (or Customs) tael. It is a purely fictitious money, an arbitrary unit, a book currency. The Haikwan tael is the standard in which the Chinese Maritime Customs levies all duties and in which the imports and exports are valued and recorded. Though all Customs dues are prescribed in this non-existent currency, they are collected in local money at rates of exchange fixed by the Customs authorities.

The Haikwan tael is supposed to be 1000 fine. Its theoretic weight is about 583.30 grains, but estimates vary considerably. The equivalent of 100 Haikwan taels has always been 111.40 Shanghai taels.

Another prominent theoretical tael is the *K'uping* (or Treasury) tael. Under the rule of the Manchu dynasty this imaginary currency was adopted for the collection of most of the taxes. It has also repeatedly served as the unit for the currency in which the capital of some of the banks (with government participation) was subscribed. The K'uping tael is supposed to be 1000 fine and to weigh 575.8 grains, but also here the authorities are not of one mind. Besides, the receiving and paying out of silver are governed by different weights. The fixed rate of conversion is 109.60 Shanghai taels equals 100 K'uping taels.

The K'uping tael in its original composition was undoubtedly a theoretical currency. But there was an endeavour on the part of the treasurers of the Imperial Court at Peking to keep the silver reserves of the Imperial family in K'uping tael sycee. This could be obtained either from the conversion of imported bar silver into sycee, or from refining up to the highest degree of locally circulating silver supplies. The Mints in the North also required K'uping silver for coinage purposes. This means that K'uping tael sycee had been in existence until the closing days of the Manchu regime, but with a fineness of " as nearly as possible 1000 " and not actually 1000 fine.

The *transfer tael*, referred to under (*c*) is likewise a mere book currency. But its characteristic difference from the taels grouped under (*b*) is that it does not pretend to have a certain fineness or a certain weight;—in fact any weight at all. It is a theoretical book unit with a varying market value attached to it. The transfer currency system is liable to force itself by circumstances on any business center in China. As a matter of fact it has been in vogue temporarily in sundry commercial places, but its real and more permanent home is Newchwang.

The origin of the transfer tael system is closely connected with the prolonged dearth of hard metal. The former is employed for the settlement of business transactions. Its principal characteristics are that the bank credits the account of the client at the time of deposit, and likewise on each quarterly settlement day, with a fluctuating market premium.

The working of the system will be described later on.[1] Suffice it to say that it is far from being an ideal medium of finance. The frequent serious monetary disturbances in Newchwang have had their foundation in the disadvantages of the unscientific system of the transfer tael, the value of the latter having been reduced considerably as a consequence thereof.

The *sycee tael,* the last of the group, is considered the most important and the most substantial standard of currency in China. It is conspicuous not only by reason of its varieties, but also because of the equally large number of variations within those varieties. Yet in spite of its unwieldly form and the clumsiness of its composition, it has faithfully and truly served the needs of the country and has proved to be what it pretended to represent. Since the advent of modern minting methods in China the number of counterfeiters has been legion; while even those who are in authority have often misused their powers by giving to the country intentionally depreciated coins, and to themselves revenue. But sycee taels are not tampered with.

How many different kinds of sycee taels are there in existence? Many hundred. Lack of uniformity limits the circulation of sycee taels to the locality for which they were originally created, and when obliged to migrate they are first cleaned in their new home, re-assayed and re-valued.

---

[1] See Appendix III.

We have heard it said that 98 Chauping taels weight of silver will settle an account of 100 Shanghai money taels. Why?—convention, popularly known as "old custom."

In searching for the origin of this remarkable convention one finds recorded in a dusty chronicle the following interesting points: "Once upon a time, before Shanghai was open to foreign trade, the bean merchants used small, round pieces of sycee, of a value of about one tael, as medium of currency. The quality of the silver making up the grain merchants' sycee (called *Tou-kuei-yin* 豆規銀), is said to have been 2% below the standard of the sycee as assayed by the Kung-ku office. This is the only available attempt at a solution regarding the origin of the old convention." *Crede quod habes, et habes.* (Believe that you have it, and you have it).

The good old sycee tael has held out for a thousand years and has not been conquered yet.

Regarding the period of origin of the Shanghai money tael it can be stated with accuracy that this currency was adopted in A.D. 1856. Until that year the banks used to keep books in Carolus dollars. Only when the supply of these latter gave out, and their market value rose considerably above the intrinsic value, was it decided at Shanghai to do away with the Carolus dollar as money of account and to substitute for it the Shanghai sycee tael.

Some of the Principal Taels Current in China.

The following is a list of the principal taels current in China: [1]

---

[1]The list (opposite) has appeared in S. R. Wagel's *Finance in China* (1914), in the Shanghai weekly *Finance and Commerce*, (1921), and in the *China Year Book* (1925), etc.

It will be more to the point, if the heading of the last column would contain the designation of "Shanghai taels" (which are undoubtedly meant), in place of "Tsaoping taels".

Place.	Name of Tael.	Silver in Tael Grains.	Value Compared with 100 Ku'ping Taels.	Value Compared with 100 Tsaoping Taels.
Government	K'uping	—	—	—
Customs	Haikwan	583.3	98.384	—
Shantung	Tsinanfu	—	101.600	—
„	Chefoo	548.2	104.681	—
„	Tungchang money	—	—	99.80
„	Haw'ping	—	—	92.70
Shensi	King-pu-p'ing	—	101.456	—
„	Sin-ngan-p'ing	—	—	99.40
Kansu	Lan-pu-p'ing	—	102.470	—
„	Lan-p'ing	—	104.500	—
Honan	Shih-p'ing	—	101.317	—
„	Kaifeng money	—	—	99.85
„	Chowkiakow (South)	—	—	99.55
„	Chowkiakow (North)	—	—	99.35
„	Taokow money	—	—	98.63
Hupeh	Hankow	536.4	—	101.70
„	Laohokow	—	—	102.33
„	Shasi	—	—	101.55
„	Fancheng	—	—	102.30
Kiangsi	Han-p'ing	548.8	104.573	—
„	Nanchang	—	—	100.25
„	Hukow	560.0	—	103.50
Anhwei	Wuhu	—	102.484	—
Kiangsu	Soochow	—	—	98.00
„	Chinkiang	560.0	102.484	—
„	Shanghai Teo-Kwai	—	—	107.55
Chekiang	Ningpo	523.6	109.600	—
„	Wenchow	561.7	102.200	—
„	Hangchow treasury	—	—	98.14
„	Hangchow market	—	—	99.72
Fukien	Foochow Ssu-ma-p'ing	523.5	108.498	—
„	Amoy	516.0	109.945	—
Kwangtung	Swatow guild	517.5	—	—
„	„ market	522.0	—	—
„	Kwei-ling Kung-fah	—	—	99.90
Kwangsi	Lungchow	519.4	102.612	—
Hunan	Changsha money	—	—	101.75
„	Siangtan market	—	—	102.10
„	Changteh	—	—	99.85
„	Siangkiang market	—	—	100.74
Kweichow	Kweiyang money	—	—	100.80
„	„ market	—	—	100.56
„	„ treasury	—	—	98.69
Szechuen	Chengtu treasury	—	—	103.00
„	Chungking Yu	—	—	102.25
„	Chungking Sha-tsien-tao	—	—	101.50
Shansi	Taiyuanfu	—	—	99.36
„	Kweihwating money	—	—	98.15
„	Hu-hao	—	—	100.75
„	Lucheng money	—	—	100.80
„	Ping-yao market	—	—	101.30
Yunnan	Provincial Capital	—	—	100.75
Manchuria	Kingchow	—	—	99.90
„	Newchwang	—	—	101.22
„	Shanhaikwan	—	—	98.82
„	Fung-hwang-ch'en	—	—	99.82
„	Kwangchengtze	—	—	101.38
„	Liaoyang	—	—	99.52
„	Kirin	—	—	101.82
„	Kirin, western Kung-fah	—	—	101.66
Chihli	Tientsin Kung-fah	—	—	101.10
„	„ Hong.	—	—	101.60
„	„ Taotai's	—	—	98.20
„	„ I-fah	—	—	101.80
„	Han-P'ing	554.4	103.515	—
„	Hsiang-p'ing	554.5	103.500	—
„	Ho-si-wu	—	—	99.44
„	Tungchow market	—	—	98.10
„	Tsangchow	—	—	98.20
„	Pao-ting	—	—	99.22
„	Taku	—	—	98.30
„	Kung-fah	—	—	101.32

Haikwan Taels.

100 Haikwan taels (at 583.3 grains, 1000 fine) are equal to:

Amoy	Taels	(廈 門)	101.75
Chefoo	,,	(煙 台)	106.40
Chingkiangpu	,,	(清江浦)	104.16
Foochow	,,	(福 州)	110.00
Hankow	,,	(漢 口)	108.75
Hoikow	,,	(海 河)	113.76
Ichang	,,	(宜 昌)	109.65
Kiukiang	,,	(九 江)	104.37
Newchwang	,,	(牛 莊)	108.50
Ningpo	,,	(甯 波)	105.83
Pakhoi	,,	(北 海)	110.57
Shanghai	,,	(上 海)	111.40
Swatow	,,	(汕 頭)	110.15
Takow	,,	(大 沽)	101.11
Tamsui	,,	(淡 水)	111.32
Tientsin	,,	(天 津)	105.00
Wenchow	,,	(溫 州)	103.00
Wuhu	,,	(蕪 湖)	104.16

The following table has been published by the Chinese Bureau of Economic Information in its *Weekly Bulletin* (1924).

Comparative Value of Shanghai Tael.

The exchange value of the Shanghai tael as compared with the tael in other places is shown in the following table:—

Shanghai Taels				*Taels of Other Ports*
1,045.00	Equals	Peking		1,000.00
1,053.00	,,	Tientsin		1,000.00
1,000.00	,,	Soochow		965.00
1,000.00	,,	Hankow		99.00
1,000.00	,,	Tsinan	(濟 南)	1,060.00
1,045.00	,,	Chungking	(重 慶)	1,000.00
1,065.00	,,	Chengtu	(成 都)	1,000.00
1,060.00	,,	Whahsien	(萬 縣)	1,000.00
1,000.00	,,	Nanking		960.00
1,000.00	,,	Chinkiang	(鎭 江)	937.00
1,000.00	,,	Yangchow	(揚 州)	934.00

Shanghai Taels				*Taels of Other Ports*
882.50	Equals	Canton		1,000.00
1,045.00	„	Chefoo		1,000.00
1,037.00	„	Ichang		1,000.00
1,067.00	„	Tsingtao		1,000.00
1,052.00	„	Sian	(西 安)	1,000.00
1,000.00	„	Kiukiang	(九 江)	931.00
1,000.00	„	Wuhu	(蕪 湖)	964.50
1,106.00	„	Kweiyang	(貴 陽)	1,000.00
1,000.00	„	Swatow		1,050.00
1,000.00	„	Shasi	(沙 市)	940.00
964.00	„	Changsucheng	(樟樹鎮)	1,000.00
1,055.00	„	Hwaian	(淮 安)	1,000.00
1,059.00	„	Chingkiangpu	(清江浦)	1,000.00
1,066.00	„	Pangpu	(板 浦)	1,000.00
1,111.60	„	Anking	(安 慶)	1,000.00
1,000.00	„	Tatung	(大 通)	940.00
1,096.00	„	Hangchow	(杭 州)	1,000.00
1,000.00	„	Antung	(安 東)	1,180.00
1,035.00	„	Changchun	(長 春)	902.00
1,099.80	„	Kalgan		1,000.00
1,082.00	„	Paoting	(保 定)	1,000.00
1,098.80	„	Loyang	(洛 陽)	1,000.00
1,078.65	„	Chowchikow	(周家口)	1,000.00
1,085.00	„	Hsuchow	(許 州)	1,000.00
1,000.00	„	Sinyangchow	(信陽州)	910.00
1,066.67	„	Kaifeng	(開 封)	1,000.00
1,088.00	„	Tatung	(大 同)	1,000.00
1,096.00	„	Shansi		1,000.00
800.00	„	Yunnan		1,000.00
1,014.00	„	Hongkong		1,000.00

Taels Parity Table.

The following parity table of thirteen different kinds of taels was compiled by the late Mr. Pokotiloff, when he was the Peking representative of the Russo-Chinese Bank. It will be observed that the weight and fineness of most of the taels referred to vary somewhat from the figures indicated by other writers. But this is not to be wondered at in view of the fact that there is no fixed standard, in the full sense of the term, existing in China.

TABLE OF PRINCIPAL TAELS CURRENT IN CHINA, WITH WEIGHT, FINENESS AND PARITY

Kind of Tael	Weight in Grammes	Fineness	Peking Kung Fah Tael	Peking Ku Ping Tael	Peking Shi Ping Tael	Peking Er Liang Tael	Tientsin Tael (Hongping)	Kalgan Tael	Shanghai Tsao Ping Tael	Hankow Tael	Chefoo Tael	Newchwang Tael	Mukden Tael	Tsitsikar Tael	Kirin Tael
I Peking Kung Fah Tael........(公　砝)	33.99	0.987	I	0.9664	1.0061	1.0280	1.0066	0 9607	0.9850	1.0264	0.9906	1.0011	1.0021	1.0076	1.0035
I Peking Ku Ping Tael.........(庫　秤)	37.24	„	1.0347	I	1.0411	1.0637	1.0416	0.9941	1.0193	1.0620	1.0251	1.0358	1.0369	1.0426	1.0384
I Peking Shi Ping Tael.........(市　秤)	35.77	„	0.9939	0.9605	I	1 0217	1.0005	0.9548	0.9790	1.0201	0.9846	0.9948	0.9960	1.0015	0.9974
I Peking Er Liang Tsin Ping Tael(二兩秤)	35.01	„	0.9728	0.9401	0.9790	I	0.9792	0.9345	0.9582	0.9984	0.9637	0.9737	0.9748	0.9802	0.9762
I Tientsin Tael (Hong Ping)....(行　化)	36.12	0.977	0 9934	0.9601	0.9995	1.0212	I	0.9544	0.9786	1.0196	0.9841	0.9945	0.9955	1.0010	0 9969
I Kalgan Tael..................(張家口)	37.5	0.986	1.0409	1.0060	1.0473	1.0701	1.0478	I	1.0253	1.0684	1.0312	1.0419	1.0431	1.0489	1.0446
I Shanghai Tsao Ping Tael.....(糟　秤)	36.61	0.985	1.0152	0.9811	1.0214	1.0436	1.0219	0.9753	I	1.0419	1.0057	1.0162	1.0173	1.0229	1.0188
I Hankow Tael...............(洋　例)	35.1	0.986	0.9743	0.9416	0.9803	1.0016	0.9807	0.9360	0.9597	I	0.9652	0.9753	0.9764	0.9817	0.9777
I Chefoo Tael..................(烟　秤)	36.44	0.984	1.0094	0.9756	1.0156	1.0377	1.0161	0.9698	0.9943	1.0361	I	1.0105	1.0116	1.0171	1.0130
I Newchwang Tael............(牛莊秤)	35.99	0.986	0.9990	0.9654	1.0051	1.0269	1.0056	0.9597	0.9840	1.0253	0.9896	I	1.0011	1.0066	1.0025
I Mukden Tael................(奉天秤)	35.95	0.986	0.9979	0.9644	1.0040	1.0258	1.0045	0.9587	0.9830	1.0242	0.9885	0.9989	I	1.0055	1.0014
I Tsitsikar Tael...............(齊齊哈)	35.9	0.982	0.9924	0.9591	0.9985	1.0202	0.9990	0.9534	0.9776	1.0186	0.9831	0.9934	0.9945	I	0.9959
I Kirin Tael...................(吉林秤)	35.9	0.986	0.9965	0.9630	1.0026	1.0244	1.0031	0.9573	0.9816	1.0228	0.9872	0.9975	0.9986	1.0041	I

CHAPTER XI

TRANSACTIONS WITH SYCEE

IF the balance of trade between two given commercial ports in China favors one of those business centers for a prolonged period or to a very large extent, it will most likely have to be settled by means of shipments of sycee. By par of exchange between silver using places is understood the intrinsic value of sycee taels, of a given place, expressed in terms of another, also employing taels as medium of circulation.

Usually the balance of interport trade is adjusted by means of telegraphic transfers or by bills of exchange. If the rate of exchange is excessively high, the debtor port will ship specie instead of making remittances through banks. If, on the other hand, the rate of exchange is extremely low, the creditor port will demand payment in shape of hard sycee. This example illustrates the two silver points, which really mean the par of exchange plus, respectively minus, the shipping charges.

Shipments of sycee are made either in settlement of trade balances or, at times, sycee is shipped for the requirements of provincial Mints. Sycee does not yield the same satisfactory outturn as bar silver, but the margin of profit which is left to the Mint authorities is not tending to obviate its movement. Finally sycee is shipped from China to India or Great Britain, simply as an arbitrage transaction, when parities permit it; but this is extremely rare.

Export of Shanghai Sycee to Tientsin.

The rentability of importing sycee from Shanghai depends on the Tientsin–Shanghai drawing rate, respectively on the market premium for silver prevailing in Tientsin. The following reasoning will explain matters from the practical point of view.

1,000 Shanghai taels weight is of an average premium of 2.7 per shoe of Tls. 50.00, which means a premium over the Shanghai standard of 5.4 per 100 taels.

Taels 1000 + 54 = Tls. 1054 weight

This, divided by the Shanghai convention of 98, gives 1075.50 Shanghai currency taels.

1075.50 Shanghai currency taels equals 1013.5 Tientsin Hongping taels weight.

1075.50 ÷ 1013.5 = 1061.17 Shanghai taels weight (equal to 1000 Tientsin taels weight).

Kungku premium at Tientsin is from 5.6 on every 1000 taels Shanghai (Yentaihwa) of 2.7 premium, because the Tientsin standard fineness

is	992.
the Shanghai standard fineness is	935.4
Difference .	56.6

	1061.17 Shanghai taels weight
Less:	5.64 Kungku premium
	1055.53 Shanghai currency = 1000 Tientsin taels currency.

1000 Tientsin taels currency equals . . . 1055.53 Shanghai taels

Add:	Freight	2.50 °/oo				
„	Insurance . . .	0.50 °/oo				
„	Interest . . .	1.00 °/oo				
„	Boxes, coolie hire .	0.47 °/oo	(variable)	4.47	„	„
		4.47 °/oo		1060.00	„	„

The market premium for Kungku sycee is varying from ½ to 7 per mille.

	1060.00
Less:	2.50 market premium on 20 shoes
	1057.50 Shanghai taels per 1000 Tientsin taels.

Under the conditions as described above (market premiums) it will pay to import Shanghai sycee to Tientsin if the market (T.T. drawing) rate is above 1057.50 Shanghai taels.

In order to establish the mint parity between the Shanghai currency tael and the Tientsin currency tael refer to the following:

Formula:

? Shanghai taels currency	:	1000 Tientsin taels (Hongping Hua Pao)
(weight) 1013.5 Tientsin taels (Hongping)	:	1000 Chauping taels (weight)
(touch) 1006 Tientsin taels (Hua Pao)	:	Chauping taels 1054 (weight)
98 Chauping taels weight (convention)	:	100 Shanghai taels (currency)

$$\frac{1000 \times 1000 \times 1054 \times 100}{1013.3 \times 1006 \times 98} = \textit{1054.85 Shanghai taels currency.}$$

This figure does not include charges and interest, which approximate 4.5 per mile (variable).

Export of Shanghai Sycee to Chefoo.

Shanghai sycee shipped to Chefoo is not melted there, but instead converted into Chefoo currency taels after re-assay through the Kung-ku office at Chefoo. First of all the ink inscriptions, put on at Shanghai, are washed off; then the shoes are re-weighed, one by one, and marked with the Chefoo weight. Finally the fineness is determined by estimate and also recorded on the shoe in Chinese ink. Shipping charges and interest to be considered.

Export of Shanghai Sycee to Hankow.

The procedure relating to Chefoo is also applicable to Hankow.

Export of Shanghai Sycee to Manchuria.

Sycee shipped to Mukden or Changchun is always paid for in Shanghai currency, plus actual charges and a small commission. The outturn is always for account of the Manchurian buyer, who is often synonymous with the Mint.

Export of Shanghai Sycee to Hongkong and Canton.

Sycee is shipped to either of the two Southern ports for the manufacture by the Canton Mint of subsidiary coins, though bar silver is generally preferred.

Shanghai sycee is sold in Hongkong at the basis of 71.70 Canton taels weight equal to 100 Hongkong dollars, plus the market premium. Speaking generally, the equivalent in Chauping taels of 100 taels Shanghai convention currency will produce 90.55 Canton taels weight which, at 71.70, is equal to Hongkong dollars 126.30, plus X% market premium.

Merely as a trial, one case of Shanghai sycee shipped to Canton produced the undermentioned result:

60 shoes weighing	Chauping taels 2994.93
Premium	„ „ 163.60
	Total Chauping taels 3158.53

@ 98 = *3,222.99 Shanghai currency taels.*

Shipping charges:

Freight	Taels 8.00
Boxes and coolie hire	„ 1.10
Wharfage dues	„ 0.96
Insurance ¾ ‰	„ 2.40
Interest 8 days at 6%	„ 4.04
	Total taels 16.50

In Canton quotations are as follows:

X Canton taels weight @ 72 = X Hongkong dollars plus the market premium.

The box of sycee shipped from Shanghai, costing Shanghai taels 3,222.99, gave an outturn of Canton taels weight 2,929.68. At 72 this amounted to Hongkong dollars 4,069, plus a market premium of 15% equals Hongkong dollars 4,679.35. Deduct compradore's commission and landing charges at Canton, say ¼% ($11.70), so that the net yield was Hongkong dollars 4,667.65.

$$3206.49 \div 4667.65 = \textit{68.69 Shanghai taels.}$$

This outturn proves that this particular sycee shipment to South China was not remunerative. In the case under discussion it should be noted that the freight charges on larger shipments are considerably cheaper.

Export of Shanghai Sycee to Bombay.

Sycee exported to India is bought there by dealers as "country silver" at ¾ to 1 rupee below the market rate for silver. This fact, combined with the heavy shipping expenses, permits shipments only when the Bombay–Shanghai quotations are at a considerable disparity. It should be borne in mind that 1000 Chauping taels weight, with the average premium of 2.7 taels per shoe of 50 taels, equals 1054 Chauping taels. This figure, divided by the convention of 98, represents 1075.50 Shanghai currency taels. But it must not be lost sight of that the figure of 1075.50 is not a constant, as the premium is not uniform on each shoe.

Sycee in its original shape has no regular quotation on the Bombay silver market, because its fineness varies considerably and cannot therefore be guaranteed. In Bombay sycee from China will either be sold as fine silver, or it will be remelted into bars and sold in that shape as country silver, at a price which is somewhat below the quotation for London or New York silver bars.

Before converting the sycee into bars (of country silver) the Mint certifies the weight before melting; as a rule it turns out to be below the weight marked by the *Kung-ku-chu,* the deficiency being 0.2% on an average. It also certifies the weight of the silver after melting, which usually results in a loss of 0.4%. On the other hand the degree of the fineness after the melting of the sycee is somewhat higher than the fineness inscribed on the shoes; this in view of the loss in weight of the sycee.

Formula I.

? rupees	: 100 Shanghai taels currency
107.55 Shanghai taels	: 100 Chauping taels weight
1 Chauping tael	: 565.7 grains
180 grains	: 1 tola
1000 tolas	: 983 fine
100 fine	: price in rupees in India

$$X = \frac{100 \times 100 \times 565.7 \times 983}{107.55 \times 180 \times 1000 \times 100} = \textit{2.8724 as constant.}$$

The constant of 2.8724 holds good as long as the premium on sycee is 5.4 taels per 100 taels and as long as the fineness of Shanghai sycee is 0.983 (a fair average). Deduct charges and interest, which are variable.

Freight ½%	0.50%
Insurance	0.15%
Wharfage dues, boxes, coolie hire	0.15%
6% interest for 30 days	0.50%
Total	1.30%

Constant	2.8724
Less charges and interest 1.30%	0.0373
Net	2.8351

Multiply this figure by the price of silver for 100 tolas in India, in order to find the parity for the Shanghai–Bombay T.T. rate. If, for example, the Bombay silver price is 90 rupees: 2.8351 × 90 = 255.159 rupees for 100 Shanghai taels. Do not overlook that Shanghai sycee is at a discount, because it is considered as "country silver." Eventual agents' commission and Bombay landing charges have not been taken into account.

The following instance represents the results of an actual shipment to Bombay of Shanghai sycee:

Shipped Chauping taels weight . . .	249,007.90
Costing Shanghai currency taels . . .	267,789.89
The sycee, before melting, was 0.983021 fine and weighed.	782,390 tolas
After melting in Bombay it proved to be 0.98641 fine and to weigh . . .	779,696 „
This means 1000 fine	769,106 „

Assuming the price of silver in Bombay for 18 B to be 60 rupees per 100 tolas, the value of the Shanghai sycee shipped would be (per 100 tolas) as follows:

Formula II.

? rupees	: 100 tolas Shanghai sycee
782,390 tolas	: 769,106 tolas fine silver
100 tolas	: 60 rupees

$$X = \frac{100 \times 769{,}106 \times 60}{782{,}390 \times 100} = 58{,}981 \textit{ rupees.}$$

Or, on the basis of the outturn of that particular shipment, the parity between the Shanghai tael and the rupee can be established according to the following:

Formula III.

? rupees	: 100 Shanghai taels currency
107.55 taels (variable)	: 100 Chauping taels weight
1 Chauping tael	: 565.7 grains
180 grains	: 1 tola
782,390 tolas (before melting)	: 769,106 tolas (after melting)

$$X = \frac{100 \times 100 \times 565.7 \times 769{,}106}{107.55 \times 180 \times 782{,}390} = 2.8725$$

Here we find the constant which resulted from Formula I. When multiplied by the price of silver (country silver) in Bombay per 100 tolas, it will give the Shanghai–Bombay T.T. quotation on the basis of sycee shipped. Deduct charges and interest.

If, for example, the Bombay price for 100 tolas country silver is 60 rupees:

2.8725 × 60	172.35	rupees
Less charges and 6% interest . . .	2.24	„
Shanghai–Bombay parity .	170.11	„

Export of Shanghai Sycee to London.

The export of sycee from Shanghai to London would only be feasible if the Shanghai quotation for T.T. on London was considerably below parity. It must also be taken into account that the assays in London might produce different results from those decreed at Shanghai.

Taking it for granted that the Kungku assay at Shanghai was correct, the following formulæ should be representative of the outturn and of the theoretical parity:

Formula I.

? standard ounces	: 1 Chauping ounce
102.5 Chauping ounces	: 100 Canton taels weight
1 Canton tael weight	: 579.84 grains troy
222 grains troy	: 239½ grains (17½ B.)
480 grains	: 1 standard ounce

$$X = \frac{100 \times 579.84 \times 239.5}{102.5 \times 222 \times 480} = \textit{127.144 as constant.}$$

Formula II.

? standard ounces	: 1 Chauping ounce
102.5 Chauping ounces	: 100 Canton taels weight
1 Canton tael weight	: 1.208 ounces troy
100 ounces troy (17½ B.)	: 107.8829 standard ounces

$$\frac{100 \times 1.208 \times 107.8829}{102.5 \times 100} = \textit{127.144 as constant.}$$

Formula III.

? pence	: 1 Shanghai tael currency
107.55 Shanghai taels	: 100 Chauping taels weight
1 Chauping tael	: 565.7 grains
480 grains	: 1 ounce standard
925 ounces	: 983 ounces
1 ounce	: price in pence in London

$$\frac{100 \times 565.7 \times 983}{107.55 \times 480 \times 925} = \textit{1.1663}$$

Charges:

Freight ⅝%	0.625%
Insurance 1°/oo	0.100%
Wharfage dues	0.030%
Boxes, coolie hire, etc.	0.020%
London landing charges	0.100%
London refining charges	1.000%
45 days interest at 6%	0.750%
Total . .	2.625%

The constant is subject to the fineness of Shanghai sycee being 0.983, and furthermore to the premium being 5.4 per 100, so that the figure of 107.55 is applicable.

If the bar silver price in London is say 32*d.* per standard ounce, the Shanghai tael parity, on the basis of sycee shipped, would be

$$1.1663 \times 32 = 37.3216 \textit{ pence } (3s./1\tfrac{3}{8}d.).$$

	pence
Theoretical parity	37.3216
Deduct charges and interest 2⅝% . . .	0.9797
Net . .	36.3419

Unless the Shanghai–London £ T.T. market rate is below 3*s.*/0⅜*d.* (when bar silver in London is 32*d.* per standard ounce) it will not pay to ship sycee to London.

Export of Sycee from Tientsin to Changchun.

Sycee imported into Manchuria from Tientsin is of the highest fineness and is accounted for per K'uping tael, at the fixed ratio of 1033.40, plus the market premium.

	Tientsin taels
K'uping taels 1000	1033.40
Add premium 9 per mille (variable) .	9.30
	1042.70
Charges:	
Freight 2½°/oo (variable)	2.60
Insurance ½°/oo (variable)	0.52
Coolie hire (variable)	0.08
Total . .	1045.90

If the Tientsin–Shanghai drawing rate is 1057, the cost will be 1105.52 Shanghai taels for 1000 K'uping taels.

Consider interest, wooden boxes, agent's commission, etc.

Import of Sycee into Shanghai.

It is only on rare occasions that Shanghai imports sycee from outports. The principal reason for such eventual imports is a very low outport-Shanghai cross-rate. If the Tientsin drawing rate is, for example, 104 (Shanghai taels), it will prove remunerative to ship sycee to Shanghai, instead of remitting by T.T. or demand draft through banks. The principles applying here are identical with those explained already, when discussing the export of bar silver from Shanghai. But instead of adding charges and interest, these will have to be deducted from the mint-par figure.

Sycee brought into Shanghai is either re-kungku-ed there and treated in the same manner as described in "Export of Shanghai sycee to Chefoo"; or else, if the shoes vary to any extent in shape, weight or fineness from those current in Shanghai, the sycee will have to be re-melted in order to better conform to the Shanghai standard.

Besides sycee from other Chinese ports Shanghai imports silver in the shape of coins of native and foreign origin. Usually such coins are melted and converted into local sycee.

During the upheaval in Siberia, 1918 to 1920, large quantities of Russian silver coins were brought into Shanghai and converted there into sycee. Chinese subsidiary coins were shipped to Shanghai from various parts of the country for account of Canton (1919 to 1924), in order to be converted into sycee. With the proceeds Canton purchased bar silver on the Shanghai market, for the purpose of coining therefrom new subsidiary coins of a considerably lower fineness.

The problem of importing into Shanghai silver derived from foreign coins has already been elucidated, when discussing the import of bar silver from France.

If it is a question of bringing silver *coins* into China, the following points have to be taken account of:

(*a*) The weight and the fineness of the coin.

(*b*) The *remedium* fixed by law for either one of the two factors.

(*c*) The loss of weight through wear and tear of the coins.

(*d*) The price obtainable at Shanghai for the various categories of silver. By this is meant the price paid by the Shanghai smelting shops for silver, according to the degree of fineness. It must be pointed out once more that silver 0.900 fine is more than 10% below the price of silver 0.999 fine, because the former needs refining (extraction of alloy), while the latter has alloy added to it. Furthermore, although the proceeds of foreign silver are fixed at certain prices, these latter are in fact not absolutely "fixed"; at times it is possible to bargain with the Loofangs and obtain a better price than originally decreed. The Shanghai "constant" for silver of a touch of 0.900 is Shanghai taels 81,950 for 100,000 troy ounces, which means 98,995.60 Shanghai taels currency for 100 Canton taels weight of silver 0.900 fine. But possibly one may succeed in bargaining for Shanghai taels 82.05 to 82.10 for 100 troy ounces of such silver.

By way of illustration we shall consider the import into Shanghai of Russian one-rouble silver coins.

The old Russian silver rouble is 0.900 fine and weighs 19.99568 grams. Out of 1000 grams fine silver 55.5672 roubles were minted. The law provides for no remedy for fineness, but permits two per mille for weight.

The question for the importing bank will be: how many Shanghai taels are obtainable for 100 silver roubles, respectively how many silver roubles are needed to produce 100 Shanghai taels sycee?

For the exporting party in Russia the problem will resolve itself into the question: Is it better to sell the silver roubles at Shanghai, buying there simultaneously gold currency, or will it prove more remunerative to dispose of the silver on the London or New York market?

On the particular day when these investigations were made price conditions were as follows:

SHANGHAI:	T.T. on London	3*s*./1⅝*d*.
	T.T. on New York	76
	100 ounces silver, 0.900 fine	81.95 taels
LONDON:	Bar silver	31 11/16*d*.
NEW YORK:	Bar silver	68¾ cents

Charges, interest, commissions and remedy are not being considered in either case. The refining fee in London and New York is taken at 1%; for Shanghai it is included in the price of 81.95.

Formula A. *(Shanghai)*

? Shanghai taels currency	: 100 silver roubles (0.900 fine)
1 silver rouble	: 20 grams
31.1035 grams	: 1 ounce troy
100 ounces troy (0.900 fine)	: 81.95 Shanghai taels currency

X = 52.695 taels.

Formula B. *(Shanghai)*

? silver roubles	: 100 Shanghai taels currency
81.95 Shanghai taels	: 100 ounces troy, (0.900 fine)
32.1507 ounces troy	: 1000 grams
20 grams, (0.900 fine)	: 1 rouble silver

X = 189.771 silver roubles.

Formula C. *(London)*

? pence	: 1 silver rouble
1 silver rouble	: 20 grams, 0.900 fine
31.1035 grams	: 1 ounce troy
1 ounce, 0.925 fine	: 31 11/16 pence

	X = 19.824 pence
Less 1% refining fee	0.198 „
	19.626 „

equal to £8/1*s*./6*d*. per 100 silver roubles, as compared with taels 52.695 @ 3*s*./1⅝*d*. = £8/5*s*./2*d*. per 100 silver roubles.

Formula D. *(New York)*

? U.S. dollars	: 1 silver rouble
1 silver rouble	: 20 grams, 0.900 fine
31.1035 grams	: 1 ounce troy
1 ounce troy, 0.999 fine	: 68¾ U.S. dollars
	X = 39.826 U.S. dollars
Less: 1% refining fee	0.398 „
1 silver rouble is worth	39.428 „

as compared with $40.05 via Shanghai. (Tls. 52.695 @ 76).

The same principles apply to other countries' silver coins and, at the same time, to silver coins current in China. If the touch of the silver contained in the coins is 0.800, instead of 0.900, the proceeds will be inferior by more than 11%, owing to the additional cost of extracting the alloy. It is essential that the extent of proceeds of coins to be melted in Shanghai should be bargained for with the Loofangs in advance.

CHAPTER XII.

FOREIGN EXCHANGE IN CHINA

CHINA is a silver using country, and is therefore obliged to derive its parity quotations from the price of silver in some important bar silver market. Such markets have up to the present existed in London and in New York only. It is therefore immaterial whether the parity of the Shanghai tael is based on the price of one standard ounce of silver (0.925 fine) in London, or on the price in New York of one troy ounce of silver 0.999 fine.

As shown in Chapter VIII (Import of Bar Silver from London and from New York) the theoretical conversion of bar silver into Shanghai sycee will result in constants for England of 1.1752, and 108.228 for America. Multiply these constants by the price quoted for bar silver at either London or New York, add charges and interest, in order to obtain the parity quotations for one Shanghai tael in shillings and pence, respectively in U.S. dollars.

Having either one of these two rates, all other currencies are brought to the taels parity by introducing into the problem the cross rate. That is to say that, in order to issue parity rates at Shanghai, it is necessary to receive telegraphically the price of bar silver, the cross rates between the principal trade centers and the discount rates; the latter only, whenever a change in discount rates occurs.

It needs no emphasizing that the official rates of exchange, as issued every morning at 9.30 by the Hongkong and Shanghai Banking Corporation, Shanghai, do not necessarily correspond to the parity. In fact they are usually above or below parity, according to conditions ruling on the home and/or the local money markets. It must also be clearly understood that exchange business in Shanghai is done at widely and frequently fluctuating rates. The official quotations are likely to guide or influence the trend of the market, but usually they fail to check activities created by either a genuine demand or by speculators.

The Official *Exchange Bulletin* as issued at Shanghai every morning at 10.30 a.m., reads as follows:

RATES OF EXCHANGE

Shanghai, Saturday, 5th September, 1925.

(A)	BAR SILVER Spot	33 3/16	—	3/3¼
(B)	„ „ Forward	33⅛		
(C)	CHINESE DOLLARS MARKET RATE			72.45
(D)	„ „ BUYING „			
(E)	„ „ SELLING „			
(F)	NATIVE INTEREST			.05

H. & S. B. C. OPENING QUOTATIONS 9.30 A.M.

BANKS' SELLING RATES.

(G)	LONDON	T.T.	3/3
(H)	„	Demand	3/3 1/16
(I)	„	4 m.s.	3/3¼
(J)	INDIA	T.T.	214
(K)	FRANCE	T.T.	1680
(L)	AMERICA	T.T.	79
(M)	HONGKONG	T.T.	77
(N)	JAPAN	T.T.	51½
(O)	BATAVIA	T.T.	194¼
(P)	STRAITS	T.T.	72½

BANKS' BUYING RATES.

(Q)	LONDON	4 m.s. Credits	3/4¼
(R)	„	4 m.s. Docts.	3/4⅜
(S)	„	6 m.s. Credits	3/4⅝
(T)	„	6 m.s. Docts.	
(U)	FRANCE	4 m.s.	1755
(V)	AMERICA	4 m.s. L/c.	81
(W)	„	Docts.	81¼

Exchange Brokers Association.

For the sake of reference only each quotation is preceded by progressive letters.

(A) *BAR SILVER SPOT* . . 33 3/16*d.*, parity 3*s.*/3¼*d.*
This is the bar silver quotation of the previous day, as cabled from London, for one standard ounce of bar silver. The parity of 3/3¼ is the theoretical parity, based on the constant of 1.182; it includes charges, but not interest, and is based on 111.20 Shanghai taels currency being equal to 100 Canton taels weight.

(B) *BAR SILVER FORWARD* . . . . 33⅛*d.*
This is the London official quotation for two months delivery of bar silver. In some cases it coincides with the rate for spot delivery, but at times it may be higher, at other times lower than spot.

(C) *CHINESE DOLLARS* (*Market Rate*) . . 72.45
The quotation is fixed and issued twice daily, in the morning and in the afternoon, by the Chinese Native Bankers' Guild. It is the proportion of Shanghai taels to 100 silver dollars (local currency). Foreign banks have very little influence over this quotation.

(D) *CHINESE DOLLARS BUYING* . . —

(E) *CHINESE DOLLARS SELLING* . . —

Ordinarily the foreign banks are quoting for transactions over the counter 20 decimal points below the market rate for buying dollars, and 20 decimal points above the market rate for selling dollars. In this particular case the bank is prepared to buy 100 dollars for 72.25 taels and to sell 100 dollars for 72.65 taels.

(F) *NATIVE INTEREST* 05
This is the official interest rate, issued every day anew, by the Native Bankers' Guild, uninfluenced by the foreign and modern Chinese Commercial Banks. It is a good barometer for the state and tendency of the local money market.

The quotation refers to so many candareens per 1,000 taels per day. The maximum rate permitted by the Guild is 70 candareens. In order to compare with percentage, multiply the rate by 365. Thus a quotation of 20 candareens equals 7.30% per annum.

(G) *LONDON T.T.* . . . . 3*s.*/3*d.*

This quotation means that the bank is prepared to sell telegraphic transfer on London, payable there on the same day, and give 3/3 in exchange for every Shanghai tael. The rate in this instance is below silver parity, which fact does not favor imports of bar silver. However, it must not be overlooked that the official rate is not necessarily the market rate. In fact, on September 5 business was done at quotations considerably above the official rate.

(H) *LONDON DEMAND* . . . . . 3*s.*/3$\frac{1}{16}$*d.*

The banks sell checks at a slightly higher rate than T.T., the difference representing about 15 days interest at the London discount rate.

(I) *LONDON 4 MONTHS* . . . . . 3*s.*/3¼*d.*

The same remarks apply here. Interest for five months to be added to the T.T. rate. In this case the rate of interest works out at 1½% per annum, which does not induce the remittance of money to London by bank draft, payable there four months after sight. As a matter of fact, this mode of remitting is very rarely used, unless the difference between T.T. and four months sight is much wider.

(J) *INDIA T.T.* 214

The quotation for India (214 rupees = 100 Shanghai taels), as well as all other rates following here (except M.) are based on the rate for T.T. London, taken in conjunction with the cross rates, as per

Formula:

? rupees	: 1 Shanghai tael
1 Shanghai tael	: 39 pence
18.1875 pence	: 1 rupee

$$X = 214.43$$

The London–Bombay cross rate was cabled as 1*s.*/6$\frac{3}{16}$*d.* for 1 rupee.

(K) *FRANCE T.T.* 1680

The quotation for 100 taels equals 1680 francs. In order to ascertain the cross rate, on which the Hongkong and Shanghai Bank has based its calculation, use chain rule.

Formula:

? francs	: £1
£1	: 240 pence
39 pence	: 1 tael
1 tael	: 16.80 francs

$$\frac{240 \times 16.80}{39} = 103.38 \textit{ francs.}$$

The London–Paris cross rate in this instance was 103.38 francs equals £1.

(L) *AMERICA T.T.* 79

Formula:

? U.S. dollars	: 100 taels
1 tael	: 39 pence
240 pence	: 4.85 U.S. dollars

$$X = 78.81 \textit{ dollars.}$$

(M) *HONGKONG T.T.* 77

This quotation is, contrary to most others on the bulletin, in taels, and not in foreign money. It means that the bank will sell 100 Hongkong dollars, telegraphic transfer, for 77 Shanghai taels. The quotation is subject to demand and inquiry and may fluctuate up to the shipping point, always provided that there is no embargo on the export of silver dollars from Hongkong. As the

Hongkong and Shanghai Bank is the principal note-issuing bank in Hongkong, it is in a position to control Hongkong-Shanghai quotations.

(N) *JAPAN T.T.* . . . . $51\frac{1}{2}$

As in the previous instance the Japan rate is quoted in China in taels per 100 yen. It is obtained by applying the cross-rate between London and Japan. In normal times the mint parity is 24.576 pence per 1 yen. In 1919 the cross rate had surpassed 2*s.*/10*d.*, and in 1925 it had dropped to 1*s.*/8*d.* per yen.

Formula:

? taels	: 100 yen
1 yen	: 20.0625 pence
39 pence	: 1 tael

X = 51.442 taels.

(O) *BATAVIA T.T.* . . . . $194\frac{1}{2}$

There is but little direct trade between Holland and China, but a good deal of direct business is done between the Dutch East Indies and China, notably in sugar. Usually the rate for florins payable in Holland is somewhat higher than the quotation for florins (guilders) on the Dutch East Indies. Through chain rule, in the usual manner, we can ascertain on what cross rate the above quotation of $194\frac{1}{2}$ florins for 100 taels is based.

Formula:

? florins	: £1
£1	: 240 pence
39 pence	: 1 tael
100 taels	: $194\frac{1}{2}$ florins

£1 = *12 florins.*

(P) *STRAITS T.T.* . . . . $72\frac{1}{2}$

This quotation is in taels for 100 Singapore dollars. It is obtained by applying the cross rate, which was then 2*s.*/$4\frac{1}{4}$*d.* for one Straits dollar.

Formula:

? taels	: 100 Straits dollars
1 Straits dollar	: 28.25 pence
39 pence	: 1 tael

100 Straits dollars = *72.436 taels.*

Banks' Buying Rates.

The foregoing sixteen quotations are banks' selling rates, while the following seven are buying quotations. These are obtained by adding to the selling rates interest for the period during which the drafts are *en route;* plus interest for the time the draft has still to run. The official buying rates are often too high to allow for business being transacted. Therefore they may be considered as nominal.

In making calculations for buying rates, the bank has to add to the quotation at which it can actually sell, firstly, brokerage; secondly, interest for the time the draft is *en route;* thirdly, interest for the period the draft has to run; this means the rate at which it can be discounted after acceptance; and last, a margin of profit. In some countries there are also revenue stamps and collection charges to be considered. Let us examine the remaining quotations in this light.

(Q) *LONDON* (*4 Months Credits*) . . 3*s.*/4¼*d.*

The quotation refers to drafts negotiated under confirmed banker's credit and therefore easily discountable. Say on September 5, 1925, a Shanghai bank had to sell T.T. on London at 3*s.*/3¼*d.* per tael:

Selling rate	39.250	pence
⅛% brokerage	.049	„
30 days interest at 6% (en route) . .	.196	„
120 days discount at 4%	.516	„
Profit	.250	„
Bill stamps, postage and petties . . .	.029	„
	40.20	„

(R) *LONDON (4 Months Documents)* . . 3*s.*/4⅜*d.*
The rate is ⅛*d.* above the 4 months credits quotation, partly because the draft is either not discountable, or only at a higher rate of discount; therefore the interest charge is above the cost discussed in the previous example. Besides this there is an added risk in negotiating documentary drafts drawn on firms or individuals.

(S) *LONDON (6 months Credits)* . . 3*s.*/4⅝*d.*
The extended usance, as well as the higher rate of discount for 6 months drafts, are the principal factors for an increased quotation.

(T) *LONDON (6 Months Documents)* . . —
No quotation is given here, as it is not customary to draw 6 months, D/P. However, such paper is sometimes in the market, and as banks are not keen to compete for this class of bills, the drawer will have to accept a rather unfavorable rate.

(U) *FRANCE (4 Months)* 1755
It is not customary to negotiate drafts on France under L/C. Practically all export drafts from China are drawn on firms (chiefly against shipment of raw silk), either D/P or D/A. Discounts are usually 1% below the official Banque de France rate, but no standing rule can be established in this connection.

Say on September 5, 1925, a bank could sell T.T. on Paris at	Frs.	1,680.00
Add ⅛% brokerage	„	2.10
¼% profit	„	4.20
Bill stamps, commissions	„	5.00
150 days interest at 6%	„	42.00
	„	1,733.30

The Bank would probably buy 4 months documentary drafts at the rate of 1740 francs for 100 taels.

(v) *AMERICA (4 Months L/C)* 81

If the Bank could have sold T.T. on America at say 79, it would have bought 4 months credit bills at 81.

T.T. selling	$79.00
⅛% brokerage	0.10
¼% profit	0.20
1 month's interest at 6%	0.40
4 months' discount at 4%	1.05
Postage and petties	0.05
	$80.80

(w) *AMERICA (4 Months Documents)* . . 81¼

The calculation is similar to the preceding example, except for a higher rate of interest, as the draft is hardly discountable.

The Shanghai Exchange Market.

The importance of Shanghai as a center for international exchange transactions is too well known to need emphasis. The elucidative discussion of the official exchange bulletin renders it unnecessary to re-examine the fundamentals of the principles involved. It therefore remains to record here the customs and rules prevailing on the Shanghai market. In the autumn of 1925 there were 23 foreign banks established at Shanghai, of whom 21 were members of the Shanghai Foreign Bankers' Association. All of these banks were conducting foreign exchange business. According to nationalities the foreign banks are to be grouped as follows:

Japanese	6
British	4
American	4
French	2
Dutch	2
Russian	2
German	1
Belgian	1
Italian	1

The Sino-Foreign banks have not been included in this list.

Of the modern Chinese commercial banks 23 are united in the Chinese Bankers' Association. Out of these, eight are conducting a regular foreign exchange business.

Exchange transactions, as they are occurring on the Shanghai market, may be divided as follows:

(*a*) Mercantile requirements.

These comprise exchange operations between importers and/or exporters on the one hand and banks on the other hand. Terms of exchange requirements range from telegraphic transfers to 6 months after sight drafts. In the ordinary course of events the option for taking up exchange contracts for forward delivery (or portions thereof) rests with the merchants.

(*b*) Interbank requirements.

Usually for obtaining cover for its own transactions one bank will buy from, or sell to, another bank,—as a rule through the intermediary of a broker. Often interbank transactions have their origin in orders received from other commercial centers. At times such operations are concluded with the idea of creating a speculative exchange position.

(*c*) Speculative requirements.

It must be admitted that these are paramount in Shanghai and that they are really shaping the market. The group of Chinese gold dealers, operating on or from their own Gold Exchange, has become very powerful. Their commitments are so enormous at times, that they influence some of the world's markets. The organisation of the gold dealers, appropriately called "the speculators," has been described in detail in the first section of this volume. Apart from the gold dealers there is a fair number of individuals or firms trying their luck in exchange gambles.

Closely allied with the Shanghai exchange market is the Shanghai Exchange Brokers' Association with a membership, at present limited to 53 foreign brokers. There is also a Chinese Brokers' Association in existence, but members do not call on the foreign exchange banks.

Rates of brokerage, as at present in force, are as follows:

$\frac{1}{8}$% on merchants business.
$\frac{1}{16}$% on interbank business.
$\frac{1}{16}$% on speculative exchange contracts.
$\frac{1}{32}$% on cross-transactions.

Brokerage is payable at the end of every calendar month, and invariably by the seller of gold currency. Brokers are required to guarantee the performance of exchange contracts concluded with banks on behalf of "the speculators."

Exchange business is carried on at Shanghai daily, except on Sundays and bank-holidays, from 9.30 a.m. to 12 noon, and in the afternoon (Wednesday and Saturday afternoons excepted) from 2.30 to 4.30.

Bar Silver as Cover for Forward Transactions.

If the speculators decide to take an oversold gold position, they will sell gold currencies and gold bars for forward delivery. Banks buying at inflated quotations will find it convenient to cover themselves by purchasing bar silver for forward delivery in London and/or New York. The result of such purchases will be a rise in the price of the white metal and a consequent strengthening of exchange, inducing the Chinese operators to continue their speculative sales of gold. The consequence will be a further rise in the price of silver. And so the game will continue until either natural factors intervene, making a further rise questionable, or until the speculators have reached the limit of their credit or the limit of their courage.

The bar silver which banks were thus forced to acquire in London will not as a rule be shipped to China. As the origin of those purchases is entirely unconnected with legitimate requirements, the silver will not be needed in the country. It will probably serve as cover for the inevitable sales which are bound to follow as soon as the turn comes. Then the drop in the exchange rates of gold currencies is likely to be accelerated by the resales of bar silver recently acquired by banks as cover for their purchases from speculators.

It is more convenient for China banks to buy silver in London and/or New York for forward delivery than to sell silver short on the markets there, because stocks can on due date be brought out to China. But to sell largely for forward delivery is tantamount to creating a bear position of silver abroad, an action which may prove a source of great danger.

Speculative sales of gold currencies on the Shanghai market will cause a rise in the price of silver; but such rise does not represent an element of strength,—unless stocks of silver in China are below the average. On the contrary, a rise brought by speculation means an accumulation of silver stocks in London and/or New York for account of banks in China. Thus the probability of a sharp drop in the price of silver becomes apparent, as soon as a reactionary movement sets in.

Yet the element of danger is less pronounced in the case just cited than in the event of a speculative bear position being covered by sales of silver. Purchases of gold currencies can be covered by purchases of bar silver abroad. But a bear position cannot be covered by silver, except by hedging on its forward quotation. If the silver market turns distinctly weak, the difference between the quotation for ready and that for delivery 2 months hence, would become so wide as to make the position very uncomfortable.

Options.

For genuine mercantile exchange transactions with a stipulated term of delivery the option of taking the exchange contract up rests entirely with the merchant. In all other cases it is clearly understood that the option of taking delivery within the stipulated term remains with the buyer of gold currency.

The question of the option of delivery plays a very important rôle in the Shanghai exchange market. Factors enter here of which the more important ones are: the state of the local money market in general, a bank's own cash requirements, respectively its superabundance of funds, credit or debit balances with correspondents abroad, and discount rates prevailing abroad. It is the custom in Shanghai to demand and to obtain extended options on exchange contracts, usually from 3 to 6 months, but not infrequently for a whole year. Usually such long options are subject to a graduated scale of rates of exchange which, as a rule, are lower for forward than for near delivery. But it is impossible to generalise regarding this question. At times the contract calls for one "flat" rate during its entire term; sometimes the quotations are higher for forward delivery than for near. It all depends on the factors previously cited.

For the banker the question of options is a very thorny and risky problem. He has to carefully dovetail his exchange operations and to be able to forecast the movement of silver stocks, in order to defend his position. He must always attempt to have sufficient silver funds at his command (if not in stock), to take care of his future engagements in the event of his purchases being taken up before his sales are applied for. Take a practical case.

A Bank of Shanghai buys on a certain day the following export paper:

£65,000, 4 months Credit, delivery June–October.
U.S.$ 80,000 sight drafts, delivery June–August.
Francs 1,000,000 4 m.s. D/P bills, delivery June–December.

In cover the bank sells on the same day:

£40,000 T.T. (to other banks) delivery July.
£20,000 T.T. (to other banks) delivery June.
£5,000 T.T. (to merchants) delivery July–November.
G.$150,000 T.T. (to merchants) delivery August–December.

In June a political crisis breaks out all of a sudden and throws the Shanghai money market into confusion. Most of the export paper is sent into the bank for negotiation during the opening days of June, but the funds to be derived from the bank's sales are not forthcoming when needed. In such an event the bank will probably have to sell for cash and buy simultaneously for forward delivery at a difference which may cause it severe losses.

Such cases are not of uncommon occurrence in Shanghai. During the closing months of 1923, when stocks of silver were much depleted there, a premium of one penny per month was frequently paid to buyers of sterling T.T. for spot delivery, as compared with delivery one month hence; this corresponds to an interest rate of 33% per annum on the then prevailing T.T. quotation of 3*s*./3½*d*.

The difficulties a Shanghai banker dealing in foreign exchanges has to contend with are really very great, for apart from the often very complicated local conditions and internal difficulties he has to watch foreign cross-rates and international discount quotations. Shanghai is the clearing house for the entire country and as such of paramount importance to the whole of China as well as to the outside world.

Cross-Transactions.

Besides the usual exchange transactions, which culminate in either purchase or sale of foreign currencies against local money, the Shanghai banker is not infrequently called upon to " cross " one foreign currency with another one. This can be accomplished either direct (gold against gold), or *via* the tael.

The motives inducing cross-transactions are either genuine requirements for own purposes, or speculation, or orders from abroad.

If a bank at Shanghai sells, for example, £50,000, but cannot find immediate cover, except in the shape of

U.S.$245,000, it might take these for the moment. But on the following morning the bank will endeavour to sell U.S.$, buying at the same time £50,000 for deliveries to correspond with the original terms.

When the world was afflicted with disjointed cross-rates, say from 1918 onwards, Shanghai became a favorite hunting ground for cross-rate transactions. In some instances Shanghai even strongly influenced the trend of such quotations.

When it becomes difficult to find adequate cover for foreign exchange transactions in Japan, in New York or in Bombay, these places cable orders for execution to Shanghai. The volume of business transacted there usually permits the absorption of such orders, provided the price levels suit the requirements or ideas of the Shanghai operators.

Let us consider some practical examples.

Kobe cables to Shanghai to sell yen 250,000—against £ T.T., delivery next month, at 1*s.*/8¼*d.* per yen. The operation might not be capable of execution, because a certain Shanghai bank, though in need of yen, might not desire to sell £. Therefore the transaction will have to pass through two banks, usually through the intermediary of a broker. The latter will have to part it into two distinct operations, with two distinct parties, but in both cases *via* the tael. A buyer of yen against taels will have to be found, and at the same time, a seller of sterling against taels. Banks are selling at 3*s.*/1½*d.*

Formula I.

? Shanghai taels	: 100 yen
1 yen	: 20¼ pence
37½ pence	: 1 tael

X = *54 taels* (for 100 yen)

If the yen-taels rate is known (say 53⅛) and the "cross" required is to be based on a Japan–London quotation of

1*s.*/8$\frac{7}{32}$*d.*, the corresponding £ price in Shanghai can be ascertained through the following:

Formula II.

? pence	: 1 Shanghai tael
53.375 taels	: 100 yen
1 yen	: 20.21875 pence

X = *3s./1⅞d.* (per 1 tael)

The problems are identical if the £ rate is substituted by U.S.$, rupees, francs, etc.

If £ are to be crossed in the Shanghai market with U.S.$, the proposition would appear as follows: Say the £ T.T. selling rate on the Shanghai market is 3*s.*/2¾*d.* per tael. The cross is to be effected on a basis of 485½ U.S.$ per £1. At what rate will the Shanghai bank have to buy T.T. on New York?

Formula III.

? U.S.$	: 1 tael
1 tael	: 38.75 pence
240 pence	: 485.5 U.S.$

X = *78.346 U.S.$*

Say T.T. on New York is obtainable in Shanghai at 75½. It is desired to buy U.S.$ and sell simultaneously sterling T.T. at the basis of a London–New York cross-rate of 486½.

Formula IV.

? pence	: 1 tael
1 tael	: 75.5 U.S.$
486.5 U.S.$	: 240 pence

X = *3s./1¼d. per tael.*

Apart from the usual cross-transactions, there may arise the necessity for the Shanghai operator to enter into so-called " three-cornered " arbitrage transactions.

Let us assume that Japan makes a firm offer to sell to Shanghai U.S.$ at the rate of 43¾ net equals 100 yen. The banker at Shanghai desires to sell locally £ against U.S.$

at a limit of 486⅜. At that moment there are buyers in Shanghai for £ T.T. at 3*s.*/1½*d.* per tael. But there are no sellers for U.S.$ at reasonable quotations. Therefore the arbitragist will consider the offer from Japan, which will enable him to obtain his U.S. currency. But, in order to complete the transaction, he will have to sell yen T.T. on Japan. At what price he can afford to do so will be seen from the following

Formula:

? Shanghai taels	: 100 yen
100 yen	: 43.75 U.S.$
486.375 U.S.$	: 240 pence
37.5 pence	: 1 Shanghai tael

$$X = \frac{100 \times 43.75 \times 240}{100 \times 486.375 \times 37.5} = 57.72 \textit{ taels.}$$

The arbitragist at Shanghai, in order to effect his "cross" at 486⅜, will sell £ in Shanghai at 3*s.*/1½*d.* and yen also in Shanghai at 57¾; at the same time he will accept Japan's firm offer and purchase U.S.$ there at $43¾.

The principles applying to cross-transactions on the Shanghai market can be briefly recorded in the shape of permanent formulæ.

(1) £—U.S.$ CROSS.

(*a*) When £ rate known at Shanghai.

$$\frac{\text{£ rate} \times \text{New York–London rate}}{240}$$

(*b*) When U.S.$ rate known at Shanghai.

$$\frac{\text{U.S.\$ rate} \times 240}{\text{New York–London rate}}$$

(2) £—FRANCS CROSS.

(*a*) When £ rate known at Shanghai.

$$\frac{\text{£ rate} \times \text{Paris–London rate}}{240}$$

(*b*) When Francs rate known at Shanghai.

$$\frac{\text{Francs rate} \times 240}{\text{Paris–London rate}}$$

(3) £—RUPEES CROSS.

(*a*) When £ rate known at Shanghai.

$$\frac{\text{£ rate}}{\text{Bombay–London rate}}$$

(*b*) When rupees rate known at Shanghai.

$$\text{Rupees rate} \times \text{Bombay–London rate}$$

(4) £—GUILDERS CROSS.

(*a*) When £ rate known at Shanghai.

$$\frac{\text{£ rate} \times \text{Amsterdam–London rate}}{240}$$

(*b*) When guilder rate known at Shanghai.

$$\frac{\text{Guilders rate} \times 240}{\text{Amsterdam–London rate}}$$

(5) £—YEN CROSS.

(*a*) When £ rate known at Shanghai.

$$\frac{\text{£ T.T. in Japan}}{\text{£ T.T. in Shanghai}}$$

(*b*) When yen rate known in Shanghai.

$$\frac{\text{£ T.T. in Japan}}{\text{Yen T.T. in Shanghai}}$$

(6) U.S.\$—YEN CROSS.

(*a*) When U.S.$ rate known at Shanghai.

$$\frac{\text{U.S.\$ T.T. in Japan}}{\text{U.S.\$ T.T. in Shanghai}}$$

(*b*) When yen rate known at Shanghai.

$$\frac{\text{U.S.\$ T.T. in Japan}}{\text{Yen T.T. in Shanghai}}$$

Exchange Quotations at other ports in China.

The following exchange bulletins issued in Hongkong, Hankow and Tientsin are added to this chapter for purposes of reference.

OPENING EXCHANGE QUOTATIONS

Thursday, 6th August, 1925.

SELLING

Previous day.		*To-day.*
2/3 7/8	T.T.	2/3 7/8
2/3 15/16	Demand	2/3 15/16
2/4 1/8	4 m.s.	2/4 1/8
nom.	T.T. Shanghai	nom.
99 1/4	T.T. Singapore	99 1/4
136 1/4	T.T. Japan	136 1/4
153 3/4	T.T. India	153 3/4
56 3/8	T.T. San Francisco & New York	56 3/8
138	T.T. Java	138
11.90	T.T. Francs	12.00
10$59	T.T. Escudos Es.	10$59

BUYING

2/4 15/16	4 m.s. L/C.	2/4 15/16
2/5 1/16	4 m.s. D/P.	2/5 1/16
2/5 1/4	6 m.s. L/C	2/5 1/4
2/5 3/8	30 d.s. Sydney & Melbourne	2/5 3/8
57 5/8	30 d.s. San Francisco & New York	57 5/8
12.60	4 m.s. Francs	12.70
12.80	6 m.s. Francs	12.90
32	Bar Silver Ready	32
32 1/8	Bar Silver Forward	32 1/16
4.85 11/16	New York–London	4.85 11/16

With the Compliments of

HONGKONG EXCHANGE BROKERS' ASSOCIATION

RATES OF EXCHANGE

Hankow, Monday, 7th September, 1925.

READY SILVER	33 7/16	—	33⅜	Forward.
HUPEH DOLLARS	69.90	—	70.50	„

H. & S. B. C. Opening Quotations.

Banks' Selling Rates.

LONDON	T.T.	3/4 9/16
„	D/D	3/4½
INDIA	T.T.	2.22
FRANCE	T.T.	17.45
AMERICA	T.T.	82.
HONGKONG	T.T.	72⅜
JAPAN	T.T.	50.
SHANGHAI	T.T.	97.

Banks' Buying Rates.

LONDON	4 m.s. Credits	3/5¾
„	4 m.s. Docts	3/6.
„	6 m.s. Credits	3/6⅛
FRANCE	4 m.s.	18.75
AMERICA	4 m.s.	85.
JAPAN	30 d.s.	
London–New York		485.
Paris–London		103.42

HANKOW EXCHANGE BROKERS' ASSOCIATION

RATES OF EXCHANGE

Tientsin, 5th September, 1925.

Bar Silver

Spot	33 3/16
Forward	33⅛

Dollars

Buying	68.30
Selling	68.70

H. & S. B. C. Official Opening Quotations.

Banks' Selling Rates.

LONDON	T.T.	3.5
„	Demand	3.5 1/16
FRANCE	T.T.	17.50
AMERICA	T.T.	83.
HONGKONG	T.T.	72½
JAPAN	T.T.	49¼
SHANGHAI	T.T.	105.30

Banks' Buying Rates.

LONDON	4 m.s. Credits	3.6¾
„	4 m.s. Docts	3.7
FRANCE	4 m.s.	—
AMERICA	4 m.s. Credits	86
„	4 m.s. Docts	86½
JAPAN	30 d.s.	46¼
SHANGHAI	3 d.s.	106.
„	10 d.s.	106.20
„	30 d.s.	106.50

TIENTSIN EXCHANGE BROKERS' ASSOCIATION

CHAPTER XIII

SILVER DOLLARS

Varieties of Dollars in China.

DOLLARS were first introduced into China early in the 16th century. Spanish traders, from their base on the Philippine Islands, first brought the Spanish dollar to China. In the course of centuries other dollars made their appearance there, until China decided to mint dollar coins within the country. In trying to classify the varieties of dollars which, at one time or another, were current in China, we arrive at the following result:

A. *Foreign Dollars.*

(1) Carolus dollar
(2) Bolivian dollar
(3) Chilean dollar
(4) Peruvian dollar
(5) Mexican dollar
(6) American trade dollar
(7) Saigon piastre
(8) Japanese silver yen
(9) British dollar

B. *Chinese Dollars.*

(1) Dragon dollars
(2) Republican dollars

FOREIGN DOLLARS

The Carolus Dollar.

From A.D. 1757 Canton was the only port open to foreign trade, and it retained that monopoly for about a century. The largest commercial corporation in those times was the East India Company, which exported tea, silk, porcelains and other China produce, from Canton, paying for its purchases with Carolus dollars. In the course of time the said dollar, which was the only silver coin in circulation, penetrated into the interior of the provinces of Kwangtung, Fukien, Kiangsu, Chekiang, Anhui and Chihli. Until A.D. 1856 the Spanish (or Carolus) dollar was the local currency along the Yangtze valley, inclusive of Shanghai. All commercial transactions were conducted in that currency, and banks' exchange quotations were based thereon. The minting of the Carolus dollar having been discontinued in the early forties of the nineteenth century, supplies became scarce. Very soon the local value advanced to premiums varying between 20% and 30% above the intrinsic value of the coin. This naturally meant a serious dislocation of trade. In 1855 the Shanghai Taotai issued a proclamation, decreeing that all dollars should be accepted in payment without distinction, as long as they were identical in fineness and weight. A few years before the situation had become acute, the Mexican and some South American dollar coins entered China, likewise through Canton, whence they spread up to the Yangtze basin. It is a well-known fact that the Mexican dollar has won the fight, effectively replacing the Carolus dollar. The latter was the currency unit in Formosa (as "chopped" dollar at its intrinsic value) until the Japanese took possession of that island 1895.

The Carolus dollar, usually styled "Spanish dollar," was actually minted in Mexico. It had adopted a second name for the reason that Mexico was at the time a colony of Spain, and also because it showed the portraits of some of the Spanish kings. Already during the Middle Ages Mexico was the richest silver producing country. Its Mint, erected in Mexico City in A.D. 1535, converted the huge quantities of silver mined within the country into coins, which were exported to Spain, India and the Philippine Islands. From there the channels of trade brought the Carolus dollar into China. It was the first foreign coin which entered the country in quantities and which was destined to form, for more than a century, a most popular medium of circulation.

Encouraged by the permanent hold which the Carolus dollar had gained on the mercantile community in the principal trade centers, the Chinese officials, towards the close of the eighteenth century, desired to halt the further inflow of foreign coins. They therefore induced some of the Chinese silversmiths to manufacture dollars, in every respect similar to the Carolus dollar. Apart from the impossibility of obtaining uniformity in design and weight,—the coins being produced by numerous artisans working quite independently from each other,—the tendency became discernible on the part of the silversmiths to adulterate the home-made coins by reducing their fine contents. In order to reap benefits for themselves the silversmiths added alloy up to 50% (instead of the legally permitted 10%). These malpractices had the inevitable effect of causing confusion and losses to the commercial community, which resulted in the prohibition of the further manufacture by the silversmiths of silver dollars.

The harm done was aggravated by forgeries committed by private parties, who had been secretly carrying on their nefarious work. In order to give some guarantee to the public, exchange shops impressed every genuine dollar handed out with a tiny ideogram. This is the origin of the "chopped dollar."

Towards the middle of the nineteenth century the supply of Carolus dollars became limited to such an extent, that in China they commanded heavy premiums, at times up to 50%. The commercial community, therefore, was forced to abandon the Carolus dollar. At Shanghai it was replaced, in 1856, as currency of account by the Shanghai tael; other districts gradually agreed to replace the Spanish dollar by the then new Mexican dollar. It is of interest to note that when, in 1856, the Shanghai banks and commercial houses had consented to change the book currency from Carolus dollars to Shanghai taels, the former stood already at a market premium, which made it equal in value to the Shanghai tael. It was, therefore, simply a matter of substituting the name of one currency for another, without altering the figures.

The Carolus dollars with the bust of Charles III. (A.D. 1772–1788) and of Charles IV. (A.D. 1788–1808) are also known under the style of "Pillar" dollars, owing to the pillars of Hercules being included in their design. Now, in 1925, the Carolus dollar having been "demonetised" by circumstances, it no longer forms a part of Chinese currencies.

Bolivian, Chilean and Peruvian Dollars.

The motives underlying the issue and distribution of dollar coins by the above countries are closely connected with the rich silver deposits which were worked there during the Middle Ages. Spanish traders acted as distributors for the silver dollars minted in Chile, Bolivia and Peru. Through that channel they entered China along with the Carolus dollars. While the latter lived up to its reputation as to weight and fineness, the South American dollars were manufactured, even in the middle of the seventeenth century, with the admixture of larger quantities of alloy than what they pretended to contain. In consequence they lost favor with the public. Coins of these issues, which may be found in China nowadays, are to be regarded as a curiosity, and not as media of circulation.

The American Trade Dollar.

The silver resources of the United States began to be developed only during the sixties of the nineteenth century. In order to find a market for their huge output of silver the mine owners solicited and obtained the support of Congress. In A.D. 1873 they were granted permission to have their silver coined at the government Mint for special requirements of the Far East. At that time the Mexican dollar ruled supreme and the demand on the part of Eastern commerce was so great, that the coin commanded a premium in foreign markets. This in spite of the fact that the Mexican Government was then levying a tax of 8% on their export. It was anticipated that, as a logical consequence of these abnormal conditions, the newly issued American Trade dollar ought to have a splendid reception in the Far East, superseding the Mexican dollar in course of time. These arguments were based on the more precise weight of the coins and of their superior silver contents. The American Trade dollar was minted at a weight of 420 grains, (or 27.215 grams) being 0.900 fine; this means that its contents of fine silver were 378 grains, as compared with 377¼ grains of pure silver contained in the Mexican dollar.

The new American Trade dollar was indeed well received in the Far East; it promised to become so popular that in Germany it was seriously contemplated, in 1877, to similarly mint there a Trade dollar for use in the East, in order to dispose of Germany's stocks of surplus silver.

The American Trade dollar gained wide circulation in the Straits Settlements, in Indo-China, at Hongkong and at the principal Chinese trade ports. It soon became a serious rival to the Mexican dollar, beside which it was declared legal tender. There is evidence available to show that the American dollar was threatening to make very swift inroads upon the territory in the Orient where the Mexican dollar was then ruling supreme. Suddenly circumstances presented themselves which caused the hasty discontinuance of its coinage and its final withdrawal from circulation.

When the American Trade dollar was first produced in 1873 it was worth, at the ratio of exchange then prevailing, a little over $1.04 in gold, thus making the coin not only popular in the East, but simultaneously preventing its invasion of the homeland. With the serious decline in the price of the white metal, four years after the issue of the new dollar, the fine silver contained therein was worth less than a gold dollar and also less than the depreciated dollar bank notes, which were then the principal medium of circulation in the United States. Notwithstanding the fact that these coins were not legal tender in America, they were in those days frequently tendered and accepted in payment, since they bore the inscription "United States of America." Herein lies the chief cause of the withdrawal and disappearance from circulation of the American Trade dollar, of which about 36,000,000 had been coined between A.D. 1873 and 1887. The stocks, which had not found their way back to America, went into the melting pots of the Orient. Some writers maintain that the superior weight of the American Trade dollar, as compared with the Mexican, induced the shrewd people of the Orient to melt the former as fast as it appeared on the market. In fact, both causes cited are responsible for the total disappearance of what was once the American Trade dollar.

While the American Trade dollar had been circulating in the home country and tendered and accepted there at its face value, it must not be overlooked that the Government had never decreed it legal tender. But the inscription on the Trade dollar read "United States of America," and there was, therefore, a sort of moral guarantee on the part of the Government. The latter's dilemma turned into confusion when—by Act of February 25, 1878—Congress agreed to the resumption of the coinage of the old U.S. standard dollar. This was tantamount to a circulation under the authority of Government, at par with the gold dollar, of a silver coin of inferior intrinsic worth than that of the Trade dollar.

In this way the latter, originating from the identical government Mint, was to be of a lesser value than the U.S. standard dollar. In order to end the anomaly the Treasury decreed on October 15, 1877, that the minting of Trade dollars should be stopped. Yet there remained another difficulty to be overcome, namely, the solution of the problem how to dispose of the considerable quantity of Trade dollars still in circulation in the home land. Finally an Act was passed by Congress on March 3, 1887, authorising the redemption at par, within the next six months, of Trade dollars presented for re-minting into standard dollars. Although a fair quantity of Trade dollars had been re-imported from abroad after passage of the new law, the total amount presented for redemption aggregated 7,689,036 dollars. The balance of the entire amount produced in the United States, viz.: $28,276,888, has never been returned to the homeland.

Thus ended the promising career of the American Trade dollar.

The Saigon Dollar.

In Indo-China the Carolus dollar, and later on the Mexican dollar, have for a considerable time circulated side by side with the native currency. Indo-China became a French colony in 1862. A year thereafter the currency of France was made legal tender in the new colonial possessions without, however, obtaining much popularity. When the heavy fall in the price of silver occurred some years later, the French silver coins circulating in Indo-China flowed back to the home country, where they retained their fixed value of exchange. By virtue of proximity the trade of Indo-China was principally with Hongkong, Singapore and China proper, where the French coins were neither available nor acceptable. Originally the British Government had made endeavors to introduce its own gold currency system into Hongkong, but, after unsuccessfully experimenting, it reverted to the silver dollar standard. The French Government tried to proceed on the same lines and arrived at the same results.

Thereupon the French authorities decided to strike their own silver dollars, with a view of displacing the Mexican and the American Trade dollars. The experiment was inaugurated with the minting, in 1879, of subsidiary silver coins. In 1885 the new Saigon dollar *(Piastre de Commerce)* began to be minted. It was a prototype of the American Trade dollar in regard to its weight (420 grains gross, or 27.215 grams, equalling 378 grains, or 24.493 grams of pure silver), fineness (0.900 fine) and uniformity; and it shared the fate of those American Trade dollars which had not been reshipped to the homeland, namely, the melting pot. More than 13,000,000 Saigon piastres were struck in the course of the first ten years, but hardly any ever served the purposes of trade as, owing to their superiority over the Mexican dollars, they were either hoarded or melted down.

In order to remedy this state of affairs another Saigon piastre was struck in 1895. Its weight was reduced to 416.2/3 grains, (27 grams) the fineness remaining at 0.900; its contents of pure silver are therefore 375 grains or 24.3 grams. All these items are below the standard of the Mexican dollar.

These fresh measures had the desired effect, inasmuch as the new Saigon piastre has driven the Mexican dollar out of circulation in Indo-China. Between A.D. 1895 and the end of 1903 over 55 million dollars of the new series have been struck and are freely circulating. The Chinese province of Yünnan, which is bordering on Indo-China, has adopted the Saigon piastre as part of its medium of circulation.

Being one of the numerous kinds of moneys current in certain parts of China, it will be of interest to establish the intrinsic value in pence of the Saigon piastre.

Fineness of the piastre	0.900	
Weight of the piastre	27	grams

Contents of pure silver	24.3 grams
Contents in English standard silver. .	26.27 ,,
1 troy ounce	31.1035 ,,

Formula:

? pence	: 1 Saigon piastre
1 Saigon piastre	: 26.27 grains silver, English standard
31.1035 grams	: 1 ounce
1 ounce	: Price of silver in pence

$$X = \frac{26.27}{31.1035} = \mathit{0.844599\ as\ constant.}$$

Multiply the constant by the price of bar silver in London in order to obtain the intrinsic value of the Saigon piastre.

The Japanese Silver Yen.

As was the case in most Eastern countries, the Mexican dollar had gained a strong foothold in Japan. It is only natural that the Government there should have endeavored to replace the foreign coin with a locally minted dollar. This opportunity had arisen when, in 1868, Japan had purchased from the Hongkong Government the entire mint machinery, which had proved a failure there.

By a law of May 10, 1871, the Japanese authorities provided for the minting of silver coins at the newly established government Mint at Osaka. These coins were to be called "yen"; they were 0.900 fine, weighing 416 grains gross (26.956 grams) and containing $374\frac{2}{5}$ grains of pure silver. The new coin, which was distinctly intended to replace the Mexican dollar, was made legal tender in Japan's treaty ports. After a few years' experience it was ascertained that the prime object had not been attained and that the Mexican dollar continued to circulate freely throughout Japan. This fact was attributed to the inferior weight of the Japanese yen.

In consequence thereof the Japanese Government decided to raise the weight of the silver yen from 416 to 420 grains, to make it harmonise with the American Trade dollar. Simultaneously the name of the coin was changed from "yen" to "Boyeki Gin," which signifies "Trade dollar".

The new measures which the Japanese authorities had adopted yielded effects which were just contrary to their original purpose. In fact, the undesired coins were attracted to Japan, replacing the heavier Japanese dollar pieces. Therefore, in 1878, the Government came to the conclusion that the further coinage of the heavier trade yen should be discontinued and that the Mint should revert to the production of the lighter coin; this latter was to be legal tender throughout Japan.

With the decline in the price of bar silver the Japanese Mint was required to produce silver yen on an ever-increasing scale. If one may judge by the fact that, between the years 1871 and 1897, more than 165 million silver yen were produced (of which over 110 millions had been shipped abroad), it would appear that the Japanese silver yen had become a very valiant rival of the Mexican dollar. Prior to the appearance of the British dollar (in 1895) the silver yen constituted the principal currency in the Malay Peninsula and in the Straits Settlements. Gradually it had succeeded in ousting the Mexican dollar from Japan and in becoming its serious competitor in the principal ports of China, Korea, French Indo-China and Siam.

In 1897, when the silver yen stood at the height of its glory, Japan adopted the gold-standard and began its demonetisation within her own borders. This new measure became the signal for the discontinuance of the coinage of the silver yen. About 46 million of these coins were redeemed in gold before April 30, 1898, when the further circulation of that currency in Japan was forbidden.

According to an analysis made by the Nanking Mint, the average weight of the silver yen is 0.7213 K'uping taels, and its contents of pure silver are given as 0.6473 K'uping taels weight.

The silver yen was destined to vanish from China, as were also other foreign coins. But circumstances gave the silver yen *currency* a new lease of life in China. As a result of the Russo-Japanese war (1904–1905), the silver yen gained a foothold in the Kwangtung Leased Territory and the adjacent parts of Manchuria. It is true that the silver yen plays its principal rôle in those districts either as banknotes (not redeemable against silver yen coins) or as book-currency. Yet its importance there as a medium of currency has remained paramount for a considerable number of years, notwithstanding the fact that the actual stocks of coined silver yen in Manchuria are rather small.

In 1900 the Newchwang branch of the Yokohama Specie Bank made its first issue of banknotes in silver yen, but subsequently these were withdrawn from circulation. The permanent issue of banknotes calling for silver yen was effected in 1904, and since that time has become of great importance to the economic life of South Manchuria. The place of issue for these banknotes is Newchwang, but they are used principally along the entire South Manchuria railway line, from Dairen to Changchun. There have been repeated attempts on the part of the Japanese Government to replace the silver yen by the gold yen, the currency of the homeland. In view of the serious opposition raised by the Chinese population inhabiting South Manchuria, it was thought imperative to let matters remain in abeyance. All quotations for soya beans and other cereals are officially issued throughout South Manchuria in silver yen currency. Though the banknotes in circulation there are not redeemable in silver coin, they are readily convertible into transfers on Shanghai and other commercial centers in China in taels, at rates of exchange fixed from time to time by the issuing bank. Needless to say, there is a certain stock of actual silver yen coins still in existence within South Manchuria, but the quantity is not large. On the other hand it can be safely asserted that the silver yen *currency* is now, at the close of 1925, the backbone of trade in South Manchuria.

The British Dollar.

The Spanish dollar—and later on the Mexican dollar—had firmly established themselves in Great Britain's Far Eastern possessions. From the beginning the home Government did its utmost to dislodge the alien coins, and to replace them with British money. At first there promised to be a certain amount of success, but in the end the Government's endeavors proved futile.

In 1893 a further attempt was made to repeat the first experiment and to strike another British dollar for circulation in the Straits Settlements and in Hongkong. As the Indian government Mints were just then without work, it was agreed, in February of 1895, to mint British dollars on behalf of the public, in consideration of a royalty of 1%; since 1903 the coinage fee has been raised to 2%.

After the adoption of the gold exchange standard system by the Straits Settlements a new dollar was struck there in 1906 weighing 312 grains, for circulation throughout the Crown colony and the Malayan States, dislodging the British dollar. The latter, nevertheless, was coined by the Royal Mints in Bombay and Calcutta in ever-increasing quantities. A new field had been found for the British dollar in many parts of China; it had become a serious rival to the Mexican dollar.

In composition the new British dollar is identical with the original coin minted in Hongkong in 1866, namely, fineness 0.900, weight 416 grains (26.95636 grams), that is to say the contents of pure silver are 374⅖ grains, exactly as is the case with the silver yen.

In the course of time the British dollar became the favorite currency in North China, where huge quantities were imported, especially during the period of 1909 to 1912. These coins went into the interior and became so popular there that they commanded a small premium over the Chinese dragon dollars, as well as over the Mexicans. Apart from Hongkong the British dollar is also legal tender in Labuan. The obverse of the coin shows the figure of Britannia standing on a rock rising from the sea. Her right hand holds a trident, while her left arm rests upon a shield. Both the obverse and the reverse are encircled by an ornamental border in Chinese style. On a scroll on the reverse are inscribed the value of the coin in both Chinese and Malayan characters. The total amount of British dollars coined by the Bombay Mint, from 1895 till the end of 1914, was $217,860,285.

Since the beginning of the nineteenth century the British Government was doing its utmost to banish the Mexican dollar from her colonies and to substitute it by the English currency system. The latter measure has failed completely, but in the course of years the continued efforts on the part of the British Government to dislodge the Mexican dollar began to bear fruit, by finally driving it out from Great Britain's American colonies and by directing its channels to the Far East.

As is known Hongkong became a British colony in A.D. 1841. In 1844 a proclamation was issued there, declaring English coins the standard currency for the new Colony. In endeavoring to replace the dollar by the English coinage system no regard seems to have been taken of the low intrinsic value of British silver coins. Besides, the Chinese mercantile community was in the habit of taking silver by weight only, so that the newly-adopted coins were doomed to be accepted at their silver value only, which means that they would have been subjected to a heavy discount. After it had become evident to the authorities that the Mexican dollar was not to be banished from Hongkong by proclamations, it was decided, in A.D. 1864, to erect a Mint in the Colony for the purpose of producing a dollar which would be capable of ousting the Mexican dollar from the territorial limits of Hongkong by means of its weight, size, fineness and general appearance.

In A.D. 1866 the first British dollar was coined in Hongkong. Its contents of pure silver were three grains less than the standard of the Mexican dollar. For this reason the new coin was not welcomed by the Chinese community and would to all appearances circulate at a discount only. This fact discouraged the colonial authorities who, after having watched results for two years, sold the entire mint machinery, in 1868, to Japan. Altogether only 2,000,000 British dollars were struck at Hongkong.

The results of the first experiment were certainly not encouraging enough to accede to the recurring requests for a repetition of the tentative experiment. Such requests came on several occasions from the trading communities domiciled in the Straits Settlements, the Malay Peninsula and at Hongkong. Many years passed by until numerous factors induced the British Government to attempt a repetition of its first experiment. In 1893 the Indian Mints had to cease work, owing to a suspension of rupee coinage.

By a law of February 2, 1895, the British Government authorised the Mints of Bombay and Calcutta to mint British dollars according to the requirements of the public, on payment of a coinage fee of 1%. The second experiment has proved an unbounded success, if one may judge by the large amount of British dollars coined in the intervening period. The new coin gained wide circulation in the Straits Settlements, in the Malay States, in Labuan and in Hongkong. Only the success attained by the Yuan Shih Kai dollar, combined with the export embargo of silver during the World War from India, as well as Hongkong, caused an interruption of the triumphant march of the British dollar into the Northern commercial fields of China. The Straits Settlements have since adopted the gold-standard, discarding the original British dollar and replacing it by a token coin. Since Hongkong has placed an embargo on the export of silver dollars from the Crown colony (in 1922), the circulation within its precincts is negligible in size.

Between 1895 and 1903 over 151 million British dollars have been issued, and in the course of the succeeding 10 years, until the outbreak of the Great War, this figure has been considerably augmented. Particulars about coinage statistics for the first eight years are as follows:[1]

Year	*Number*
1895-1896	3,316,063
1896-1897	6,135,617
1897-1898	21,286,427
1898-1899	21,545,564
1899-1900	30,743,159
1900-1901	9,464,991
1901-1902	27,198,656
1902-1903	31,671,117
Total for eight years	151,361,594

Changing conditions (due to the World War) have been responsible for a considerable reduction in the size of the circulation of the British dollar, but yet it remains the unit of currency in Hongkong and it is still to be found circulating in certain parts of South China and North China.

It is a peculiar fact that while the British dollar was popular in many parts of China, it was never current in Shanghai,—the great emporium of trade. Like many another foreign coin, the British dollar is vanishing from circulation in China, making room for the native-made Yuan Shih Kai dollar.

From an analysis made by the Nanking Mint it appears that the gross weight of the British dollar is 0.7243 K'uping taels, and its net weight 0.6478 K'uping taels.

Before turning to the discussion of the principal dollar, the Mexican, it may be advisable to refer briefly to other

[1] A. Platt Andrews. *Quarterly Journal of Economics*, May 1904.

silver dollars of foreign origin, which may at times have been found in circulation in China.

The Spanish Philippine dollar of 1897, gross weight 385⅘ grains, 0.900 fine, pure silver 347⅕ grains.

The American Philippine Peso of 1903, 416 grains gross, 0.900 fine, pure silver 374⅖ grains.

The Straits Settlements dollar of 1903, 416 grains gross, 0.900 fine, pure silver 374⅖ grains. The foregoing was changed in 1906 to 312 grains gross weight, 0.900 fine, pure silver 280.80 grains.

The Austrian Maria Theresia Thaler of 1751, gross weight 433 grains, 0.833½ fine, pure silver 361 grains.

According to the Maritime Customs Decennial Reports (1902–1911) there existed then a Chinese rupee coin, minted in Chengtu, Szechuen, for use along the Tibetan border. It is made to look as much like a rupee as possible, but bears, on the obverse side, what purports to be the effigy of the emperor *Kuang Hsu.*

The Mexican Dollar.

The rightful successor of the Spanish and the Carolus dollar is the Mexican dollar, which, for some decades, had the distinction of being the most widely-used coin known in history. As stated on page 296, the Spanish dollar was not minted in Spain, but in Mexico which, until the beginning of the nineteenth century, was one of Spain's colonial possessions. The Spanish dollar was first produced in A.D. 1497. It contained originally 937/1000ths parts of pure silver. For some centuries this standard was maintained. The first government Mint was opened in the city of Mexico in A.D. 1535. The percentage of fine silver in the Spanish dollar was reduced to 916/1000ths, in 1728, and the weight of the coin was likewise reduced 1½%. In A.D. 1772 there was a further diminution of the coin's fine contents, which were then fixed at 0.902.7/9, a level at which it has remained ever since. The Spanish dollar, and later on its successor, the Mexican, were never called "dollar" in the home country. There it is known as "peso," or "piece of eight," *i.e.*, a coin, representing eight Reales.

In 1821 Mexico ceased to be a Spanish colony, becoming a republic. Shortly before that period, under the rule of Ferdinand VII (1808–1821), five other Mints were opened in Mexico. In course of time six further Mints were established there.

The first Mexican (Republican) dollar was issued in A.D. 1824, and even when the Hapspurg emperor Maximilian was placed on the Mexican throne, the coins continued to be issued, in 1865 and 1866, with the inscription "Republica Mexicana." Until 1868 the legend on the reverse was "8 R.M.", meaning 8 Reales. In 1898 the legend was changed to read "Un Peso."

The reverse of the Republican Mexican dollar bears the Cap of Liberty and the word "Libertad" across it, surrounded by 32 rays of the sun. Beneath inscribed is the value, the mark of the Mint and the year of issue. On the obverse is seen an eagle, with outstretched wings, holding a snake in its beak and standing on a cactus. This picture is the national emblem. Above it is inscribed the legend "Republica Mexicana," below a wreath of oak leaves.

Apart from the coin just described there is a recent issue, showing a female figure on horseback. Yet this coin circulates only in the homeland, and is entirely unknown in the Far East.

By A.D. 1870 the Mexican peso was current not only in the two American continents, in the West Indies, in the islands of the Pacific and in Japan, but throughout the greater portion of Asia, from the arctic Siberian shores down to the tropics.

The principal causes for this phenomenal success were the superior fine contents of silver, as found in the Mexican dollar, and its uniformity and reliability during the many decades of its existence. The widest circulation has been attained by the Mexican dollar in China.

According to reliable estimates the total amount of these coins circulating and being hoarded in China in 1911 (when the Republic was founded) was between 400 and 500 million dollars. It was in A.D. 1854 that the Mexican dollar first invaded China, where it ruled supreme for about 60 years. But then its glory began to wane.

In the various subsections of this chapter have been described the endeavors to oust the Mexican dollar from its strongholds all over the East. The attempts on the part of China to coin and circulate her own silver dollars began to bear fruit shortly after the establishment of the republic. In 1925 one rarely met the Mexican dollar in circulation in China. Old stocks have been re-melted or exported. There is a fair quantity of Mexicans still being hoarded in China. Yet undoubtedly the deathknell of the coin, which has performed highly useful service in China and which gladdened many a heart there for years, has been sounded. The Mexican dollar is departing from China for ever.

The following instructive table shows Mexico's export of dollars from 1881 to 1903. It also shows her exports of silver in Mexican dollars, the percentage of silver exports to total exports and the percentage of coined silver in silver exports.

EXPORTS OF MEXICO.

(Exports expressed in millions.)

YEAR	*Total exports in Mexican dollars.*	*Exports of silver in Mexican dollars.*	*Percentage of silver exports to total exports.*	*Percentage of coined silver in silver exports.*
	—	—	—	—
1881–1882	29,207	15,822	54.17	73.69
1882–1883	41,919	28,601	68.22	80.72
1883–1884	46,861	32,524	69.40	80.45
1884–1885	46,812	32,878	70.23	77.47
1885–1886	43,797	29,243	66.77	75.28
1886–1887	49,330	33,041	66.98	67.26
1887–1888	49,079	30,399	61.93	55.39
1888–1889	60,380	38,157	63.19	59.87

EXPORTS OF MEXICO—*cont.*

(Exports expressed in millions.)

YEAR	*Total exports in Mexican dollars.*	*Exports of silver in Mexican dollars.*	*Percentage of silver exports to total exports.*	*Percentage of coined silver in silver exports.*
1889–1890	62,680	38,054	60.71	60.89
1890–1891	43,426	35,489	81.72	49.98
1891–1892	75,661	48,145	63.63	55.48
1892–1893	88,045	55,479	63.01	48.97
1893–1894	80,084	45,620	56.96	38.11
1894–1895	95,020	48,138	50.60	35.47
1895–1896	110,022	59,056	53.67	34.50
1896–1897	117,784	59,578	50.58	24.47
1897–1898	138,068	67,637	48.98	26.90
1898–1899	148,454	67,281	45.32	20.98
1899–1900	158,248	63,584	40.17	17.10
1900–1901	158,009	72,421	45.83	22.27
1901–1902	168,041	59,582	35.45	19.05
1902–1903	197,729	77,555	39.22	27.21

According to law the Mexican dollar should weigh 417.8 grains and ought to be 902.65/72 fine; consequently its contents of pure silver ought to amount to 377.14 grains. In fact the average weight of the coin is only 416½ grains, the average fineness not more than 0.898 and its average contents of pure silver 374 grains, which latter corresponds to 404.32 grains of English standard silver. When tabulated, this means:

Average gross weight: 416½ grains=27 grams=0.8677 ounces.
Average fine weight: 374 grains=24.24 grams=0.7791 ounces.
Average content of English standard silver weight 404.32 grains=26.20 grams=0.8423 ounces.

According to an analysis undertaken by the Nanking Mint the gross and net weight of the Mexican dollar is as follows:

(1) 0.7284 K'uping taels weight, or net 0.6569 K'uping taels.
(2) 0.7222 K'uping taels weight, or net 0.6534 K'uping taels.

It is not without interest to establish the intrinsic value of the Mexican dollar, and also the market value of one ounce Mexican dollar:

Formula I.

? pence	: 1 Mexican dollar
1 Mexican dollar	: 0.8423 ounces English standard
1 standard ounce	: London price in pence

$$X = 0.8423 \text{ as constant.}$$

Multiply the constant by the London silver price, in order to obtain the value of one Mexican dollar.

Formula II.

? pence	: 1 ounce Mexican dollar
867.7 ounces	: 1,000 Mexican dollars
1,000 Mexican dollars	: 842.3 ounces standard
1 ounce standard	: London price in pence

$$X = \frac{1000 \times 842.3}{867.7 \times 1000} = 0.97073 \text{ as constant.}$$

Multiply the constant by the London silver price in order to obtain the value of one ounce of silver as contained in the Mexican dollar.

As the gross weight of the Mexican dollar is 0.8677 ounces, it follows that one ounce weight corresponds to 1.15247 dollar pieces.

As from May 1, 1905, a gold currency standard has been established in Mexico, the unit being the gold peso, which is to contain 75 centigrams of pure gold. Thereby the good, old Mexican dollar has been banished from its own homeland.

Chopped Dollars.

The free circulation of the Carolus dollar in China induced the silversmiths in the South to manufacture, with the connivance of the officials, similar coins within the country. The home-made product proved, however, to be only a poor imitation of the original—not only in workmanship, but also as regards the excessive contents of alloy in the coin. In order to protect themselves against such irregularities, Chinese money changers and bankers started to stamp (chop) the silver dollars with an ideogram, thus giving a pledge of genuineness. This happened first towards the close of the eighteenth century in the city of Canton.

In certain portions of South China, notably at Foochow, Amoy and Swatow, the chopped dollar is to this day in circulation, though only to an ever-decreasing degree. With every infliction of an additional chop, with a tiny steel chisel, a minute portion of silver is removed from the coin. Slowly its surface becomes defaced, and finally the flat disc is turned into a cup-shaped coin. It is therefore obvious that, wherever the chopped dollar is current, it is tendered and accepted by weight only at the fixed price of 71.7 Canton taels weight of chopped dollars as equalling 100 dollars.

In Shanghai and North China money changers affix to the dollar coin their sign in ink, by way of guarantee. Sometimes a chop is hammered into the coin, but never in such a way as to deface, as the same would then cease to be acceptable.

CHINESE DOLLARS.

Dragon Dollars.

During the eighties of the bygone century the first government Mint was established in China for the purpose of turning out copper cash. These had hitherto been cast from moulds. The precisely-stamped new copper cash failed to obtain the favor of the public, and the minting therefore had to be discontinued.

It was in the Spring of 1887 that the then Viceroy of Kwangtung, Chang Chi-tung, petitioned the emperor to sanction the coinage of Chinese dollars, bearing the emblem of the dragon. Chang pointed out that throughout almost all provinces of China the Mexican dollar ruled supreme, and that the appearance of the newly-proposed Chinese dragon dollar would tend to dislodge the foreign currency. The petition of Chang Chi-tung obtained imperial sanction; whereupon the Canton Mint began (in 1889) to strike the first dragon dollar.

The gross weight of the new coinage, styled Kwangsu currency, was 0.73 Chauping taels or 0.7245 K'uping taels; its contents of fine silver weighed 0.6540 K'uping taels, which corresponds to the fineness of the Mexican dollar, viz., $902\frac{7}{1000}$ths. The dollar coin bore inscriptions in English and Chinese. It was decreed that the new dragon dollar should be legal tender, and acceptable as such in payment of taxes, likin, customs dues and official salaries.

The coining of these dollars left practically no profits to the Mint, a factor which favored adulteration. As a matter of fact, the new dollars were not favorably received by the public and were accepted by the latter by weight, instead of by count. After all, they were issued by a province which was sufficient to make them acceptable outside that province only at a discount.

The Lack of Uniformity of the Dragon Dollar.

Although the Empress Dowager had sanctioned the memorial regarding silver coinage, as submitted by Chang Chi-tung in 1887, it was not until 1890 that the first silver dollar, produced by the newly-erected provincial Mint at Canton, made its appearance on the market. Other provinces followed suit in the course of years. In 1895 Wuchang established a Mint, in 1896 Tientsin did likewise, and within ten years there were as many provincial Mints operating in China. Their doings were not subjected to government control. This explains the lack of uniformity of, and the subsequent confusion caused by, the coins turned out by the numerous Mints.

The Peking Government supported the endeavors of the provinces to erect individual Mints. The consequences were not foreseen: first, there was lack of uniformity; secondly, every province manufacturing dragon dollars embossed the name of the respective province thereon, thus hindering and curtailing circulation throughout the country; and finally there soon was overproduction. These circumstances induced the Board of Revenue to pass new coinage laws in 1898. These regulations provided *inter alia* that every type of dragon dollar minted should be authorised by the Peking Government; but the new decree did not attempt to order the production of one uniform dollar. Therefore it remained a dead letter.

The situation had grown so bad that, in 1905, the Board of Revenue petitioned the throne to put a stop to the calamity caused to the financial market by the irregularities committed by the provinces in the coinage of the national dollar. The following is a translation of the petition referred to:[1]

> The primary purpose of allowing Kwangtung to issue dragon dollars was to stop the import of Mexican dollars from abroad and drive out those already in. Accordingly, the mints there together with those of other provinces, have been issuing a flood of coins, and the production has constantly increased. However, they have been using different stamps, and their coins are naturally different in size and composition. Constant debasement has also reduced them far below the original weight, so that they differ considerably in purchasing power from one another, and even the same coin has different purchasing power at different times and places. The people of one province hesitate to accept the coins issued in the other, every province considering the coins of every other province as debased. This attracts the Mexican dollars back into circulation and makes the condition worse than ever. It would be wise at present to legalise the use of uniform coins, coins of a standard weight and composition, and to have them coined at the national mint. The mints of Kwangtung and Hupeh, and the Peiyang and Nanyang mints might well be changed to branch factories, and the moulds of the standard coin be distributed by the National mint.

The result of this petition was an order to discontinue coinage at the provincial Mints. However, already in 1906, Yunnan province succeeded in obtaining permission

[1] Chang Kia Ngau, "The Vanishing Mexican Dollars" *(Millard's Review, 1917)*.

to coin her own dollars. This was the signal for most of the other provinces to resume the minting of dragon dollars. The latter at no time bore the inscription "dollar," but instead "7 mace and 2 candareens."

The following provinces were inscribed on dragon dollars minted there:

Anhwei	Hupeh	Manchuria
Chekiang	Kiangnan	Peiyang
Fengtien	Kiangsu	Shantung
Fokien	Kiangsi	Szechuen
Honan	Kirin	Wuchang
Hunan	Kwangtung	Yunnan

Apart from the provincial issues there exists a dragon dollar intended for general circulation and belonging to the *Ta Ching Ti Kuo* series. This dollar bears on the obverse two dragons, in the center the denomination in Chinese, and in the lower circle the inscription in English "ONE DOLLAR."

In 1913 the Board of Finance attempted to obtain statistics relating to the total output of dragon dollars. The result of the endeavor was the figure of 206 millions. This is probably an under-estimate, and 225 million dollars is considered much more accurate.

The following table, compiled by Mr. Chang Kia Ngau, gives particulars as to weight, fineness and year of issue of dragon dollars produced by some of the principal Mints of China.

Name of Mint	*Year of Establishment or Date of First issue*	*Gross Weight in K'uping or Treasury tael*	*Pure Content of Silver*	*Weight of Copper*
Kwangtung	Kwangsu	.7245	.6540	.0705
Hupeh	Kwangsu	.7226	.6530	.0696
Hupeh	Hsientung	.7261	.6547	.0714
Kiangnan	1898	.7243	.6538	.0705
Kiangnan	1902	.7074	.6386	.0688
Peiyang Machine Factory	1898	.7289	.6492	.0797
Peh Yang	1897	.7396	.6582	.0814
Fengtien Machine Factory	1899	.7247	.6207	.1040

Name of Mint	*Year of Establishment or Date of First issue*	*Gross Weight in K'uping or Treasury tael*	*Pure Content of Silver*	*Weight of Copper*
Fengtien	1903	.7074	.5959	.1097
Manchuria	1907	.7191	.6400	.0799
Kirin	1900	.6988	.6178	.0810
Kirin	1905	.6977	.6249	.0728
Szechuen	Kwangsu	.7179	.6437	.0742
Anhwei	1898	.7229	.6477	.0762
Central	Kwangsu	.7209	.6521	.0688

A Chinese Standard Dollar.

The coining of dragon dollars had in the course of years become a matter of business for the provinces. There was lack of uniformity in the weight of the coins and also in the fineness. The latter (according to Mr. Chang Kia Ngau) was as follows:

Produced by Mint	*Fine Content of Silver.*
Tientsin Central	900.30
Peyang branch	888.90
Peyang Machine Factory	890.00
Tai Ching	894.50
Manchuria	889.50
Fengtien	843.50
Fengtien Machine Factory	843.50
Kirin	889.40
Anhwei	887.20
Hupeh	900.10
Kiangnan	899.50
Szechuan	886.80
Szechuan Military Government	878.60
Kwangtung	899.60
Yunnan	888.80

These coins began to circulate during the first decade of the twentieth century, at a time when the Chinese authorities were bent on instituting effective reforms in the currency system of the country. The entire lack of uniformity of the Chinese dragon dollars in circulation induced the Board of Finance to promulgate regulations with regard to a new and uniform Chinese standard dollar.

The new law was issued in the 3rd moon of the 2nd year of Hsuan Tung (May, 1910). It provided that the new standard coin should be styled "Yuan"; it was also known under the name of Ta Ching Yen-pi (Silver coin of the Ta Ching dynasty). The steel dies were engraved by the head Mint at Tientsin and submitted for approval of the design to the Imperial Court. The new standard dollar was to weigh 0.72 K'uping taels and to be 0.900 fine. The Mints at Wuchang and Nanking started to strike the standard *yuan* in July, 1911, with the intention of putting it into circulation during December of the same year. However, when the revolution broke out in October, 1911, the soldiers were paid with the new dollar (in Nanking and Wuchang). Thus the new Ta Ching dollar was put into circulation without ceremony.

A few years later the province of Szechuen coined another new-design dollar, styled the Ta Han Yen-pi (Silver coin of the great Han dynasty). This was the last of the "imperial dollar."

A rough estimate places the total amount of dragon dollars produced in China within approximately 25 years at 250 million dollars.

The law relating to the coinage of the new standard dollar was promulgated on May 24, 1910, and reads as follows:

REGULATIONS FOR THE NATIONAL COINAGE OF MAY 24, 1910[1]
(WITH ORIGINAL EXPLANATORY NOTES).

ART. 1. The monetary unit of the Ta Ch'ing Empire shall be called the dollar (yuan).[2]

ART. 2. The different coins shall be as follows:

Silver coins: (1) One-dollar coins; (2) fifty-cent coins; (3) twenty-five-cent coins; (4) ten-cent coins.

Nickel coins: (1) Five-cent coins.

The coinage of this nickel coin will be delayed pending an investigation into mines and methods of mintage.

[1] In *U. S. Mint Report*, 1911, pp. 236-8. Translation by Dr. C. D. Tenney, of the American Legation, Peking.

[2] The monetary unit means that used in computations above unity. Below unity the reckoning is decimal.

Copper coins: (1) Two-cent coins; (2) one-cent coins; (3) five-mill coins; (4) one-mill coins.

The coinage of the one-cent copper coins will be postponed, owing to the danger of their being confounded with the ten-cash coins formerly minted.

ART. 3. The dollar (yuan) will be the standard coin, and the coins from the fifty-cents and under will be considered subsidiary coinage, and will be in the decimal system. One dollar will be ten dimes. One dime will be ten cents. One-cent will be ten mills. All exchanges must be at this rate.

ART. 4. The weight and fineness of the silver coins will be as follows: The weight of one dollar will be seventy-two hundredths of a K'uping tael, and the fineness ninety per cent, amounting to six hundred and forty-eight thousandths of a tael of silver.

The weight of the fifty-cent pieces will be thirty-six hundredths of a K'uping tael and eighty per cent fineness, amounting to two hundred and eighty-eight thousands of a tael of silver.

The weight of the twenty-five cent piece will be eighteen hundredths of a K'uping tael, and the fineness eighty per cent, amounting to one hundred and forty-four thousandths of a tael of silver.

The weight of the ten-cent piece will be 864/10000ths of a K'uping tael, and the fineness sixty-five per cent, so containing 5616/100000ths of a tael of silver.

The weight and fineness of the nickel and copper coins will be determined later.[1]

ART. 5. There will be no limitation in the use of the standard dollar.

The subsidiary silver coins may not be offered in excess of five dollars' worth in any one payment. The nickel and copper subsidiary coins may not be offered in excess of half a dollar's worth in any one payment.

Payment of the subsidiary coins in excess of the above amounts may be refused, but this does not apply to the Ta Ch'ing Bank or any of its branches in the exchange of coins.[2]

---

[1] In these regulations the "K'u-p'ing tael" refers to the K'u-p'ing tael as determined in response to the joint memorial of the Board of Agriculture, Industry, and Commerce, and the Board of Finance in regard to uniform weights and measures. Therein it was specified that the K'u-p'ing tael would be reckoned as equivalent to thirty-seven and three hundred and one one-thousandths (37.301) grams by the French metric system. The silver referred to is to be absolutely pure silver.

[2] Therefore in all financial operations the dollar will be current, whether the transactions are in tens, hundreds, thousands, or tens of thousands. The purpose in minting the subsidiary coins is to provide for small transactions in trade and for reckoning change; so the limit for the use of them must be clearly defined. But exchanging coins and using them are different, and therefore there is no limit in matters of exchange. So the subsidiary coinage is protected and the people's confidence in it will not be impaired. If it be found that the absence of a limitation in the matter of exchanging coins will lead to the banks receiving large amounts of the subsidiary coins so that they cannot avoid offering temptation to counterfeiters, it should be remembered that there is a fixed limit to the number of subsidiary coins that may be minted and those who care to exchange them will naturally be few. Also there is a regular medium of exchange so that the counterfeiting may be easily discovered. So no fear need be entertained on this score.

ART. 6. On one face of the silver dollar will be a dragon and on the other face the characters "Ta Ch'ing Silver Coin, One Dollar." The subsidiary coins of silver, nickel, and copper will be minted on the same general model.[1]

ART. 7. No dollar may differ from the legal weight by more than two one-thousandths of a K'uping tael. One thousand coins weighed together must not differ more than three one-thousandths of the legal weight.[2]

ART. 8. The fineness of silver coins must not differ from the legal standard more than 3/1000.[3]

ART. 9. When a dollar coin has been so abraded by use that its weight has fallen below seventy-one one-hundredths tael, and when the fractional coins, whether of silver, nickel, or copper of fifty-cents and under, show signs of abrasion, they may be taken to the mint or to the Ta Ch'ing Bank to be exchanged for new coins.[4]

ART. 10. No one can be compelled to accept mutilated coins, when the mutilation can be shown to be intentional.[5]

ART. 11. The Board of Finance will fix the limit for the amount of coinage of the subsidiary coins.[6]

Supplementary Articles

ART. 12. The Ta Ch'ing Bank will appoint a special official to control carefully all matters connected with the exchanging of coins, both old and new.[7]

ART. 13. During the introductory period of issuing the new coins, one dollar and fifty-cents will be reckoned as one tael of the Board of Finance Treasury weight, standard silver.[8]

ART. 14. In places where the new coins have been issued, the large and small coins previously minted may continue to circulate

[1] The exact forms of the silver, nickel, and copper coins will be sent to all the Provinces.

[2] In enforcing the first and second parts of this article some liberality may be shown in reckoning and passing single silver dollars, but the reckoning by thousands will be strictly observed.

[3] Differences in weight in numbers of coins will be determined according to the provisions of the last Article, but differences in fineness according to this Article.

[4] Silver coins used in trade cannot fail to be abraded, therefore the limit of seventy-one one-hundredths tael will be set for abrasion. When this limit of abrasion is exceeded the coins must be exchanged to secure confidence.

[5] The last Article provides for the exchange of coins abraded by use, and this Article forbids the exchange of coins deliberately mutilated, in order to prevent the people from boring holes, affixing stamps, or grinding off the coins.

[6] The coinage of the subsidiary coins must be limited, and they must not be issued in excessive quantities to avoid injuring their currency as subsidiary coins.

[7] The exchanging of the old and new coins is the special business of the bank, but since the business of the bank is complicated, a special bank officer will be deputed to control this department so that it may be properly managed.

[8] This Article fixes the exchange value of the new and old money and the standard for discounting. By standard silver is meant silver of nine hundred and eighty-five one-thousandths fineness.

temporarily at their market value. On the one hand, the Government mints and the Ta Ch'ing Bank will gradually withdraw them at the market rate to be reminted into the new coinage; and on the other hand, the Board of Finance will take all the circumstances into consideration, and fix a limit of time for this to continue. After the time fixed, all such circulation will cease, and the mints and the Ta Ch'ing Bank will exchange the old coins as silver bullion.

ART. 15. The copper coins previously minted in the Provinces will continue to circulate at their market value and the Board of Finance will regulate this matter in accordance with circumstances.[1]

ART. 16. After the regulations have been approved by imperial rescript, a limit of one year will be granted within which period all regular official receipts and disbursements will be converted into Treasury taels of standard silver and then reckoned in the new monetary unit.[2]

ART. 17. A limit of one year will be fixed after the date of the imperial sanction of these regulations, and within this time all official receipts and disbursements regularly made in copper cash or silver shall be reckoned in Treasury taels and thence converted into national dollars. In cases where silver dollars or other coins have hitherto been used, the same method shall be followed.[3]

ART. 18. All customs, postal, telegraph, steamer, and railway accounts shall be tendered in the national coinage after being first changed into Treasury taels by the heads of the offices concerned according to the weights and purity of the money received or disbursed, within one year of the time when these regulations receive the imperial sanction.[4]

---

[1] In regard to the method of treating the old coinage as laid down in Articles 14 and 15, the Board of Finance will determine a special method of treatment after considering the conditions and will memorialize the throne on the subject.

[2] In order to unify the currency system all accounts and public documents will first use the new monetary denominations. This is to hasten the adoption of the new monetary unit, and the resulting advantages in making and auditing the budgets will be many. Therefore before the new coins have been issued there is no difficulty about fixing a limit of time within which the new terminology shall replace the old. So if the former reckoning in taels is changed to dollars it will not be troublesome to use the ratio of exchange laid down in Article 13. Therefore fixing a year as the limit for the change is not too rapid. If it is found that the new coins will not be immediately sufficient for use till after the change of name, the silver bullion and old coins may continue to be used and the actual receipts and disbursements may be reckoned in Treasury taels of standard silver and then reckoned in the national coin. This will cause no inconvenience.

[3] In changing the unit of reckoning according to this Article, public accounts and documents shall be first changed and the market rate for the day fixed by the throne, on memorial, shall be used in order to prevent brokers from lowering or raising the exchange and to avoid dispute about exchange. The method of carrying out this provision shall be for the Board of Finance to telegraph to every Province, obtaining the market rates for all sorts of silver money in every *fu*, *ting*, *chou*, and *hsien*, which the Board will publish in every locality.

[4] Since the large customs accounts and the communication accounts have an important influence upon currency, they should be first changed so as to promote the use of the new currency.

ART. 19. All debts of the common people which are reckoned in silver shall be reckoned in Treasury taels according to the weight and fineness of silver in the locality concerned and then reckoned in the national coinage. When they are reckoned in the old silver dollars, copper-minted coins, copper cash, or any other kind of money they shall be reckoned in Treasury taels according to the market rate for the place, fixed by decree on memorial as provided in these regulations, and then reckoned in the national coinage. In all cases, in which the documents have not been reckoned in the national coinage, as laid down in this Article, if there shall be any litigation, judgment shall be given according to the rate for the day fixed by edict, on memorial, as prescribed in these regulations.[1]

ART. 20. From the date when these regulations receive the imperial sanction, all mintage of large and small silver and copper coins in the Provinces shall cease.

ART. 21. The Board of Finance will establish an assay office and engage an expert to take charge of it. Specimen coins will be taken from the coins minted by the mints, which shall be assayed and the analysis will be published.[2]

ART. 22. Throughout the Ta Ch'ing Empire when the Ta Ch'ing national coins are offered in payment, no matter who the person may be or what the account may be, the national money may not be refused.[3]

ART. 23. Any one who violates the provisions of Article 3 or Article 22 may be accused in court by the person concerned. After conviction a fine of from $10 to $1,000 will be inflicted.[4]

ART. 24. If these regulations require alteration, the Board of Finance will memorialize the Throne publicly thereon.

The Yuan Shih Kai Dollar.

Christmas eve, in A.D. 1914, was the date on which the Yuan Shih Kai dollar was officially issued for the first time. Since then it has made enormous strides and is fulfilling its mission to replace not only the Mexican and other foreign dollars, but also the heterogeneous collection of Chinese dragon dollars. After an existence of ten years

[1] The different kinds of money alluded to in this Article and Article 17 are the Tientsin "ching ch'ien," Hsinchiang "hung ch'ien," and other such coins.

[2] The coins selected will be either from those already in circulation or from those just minted, and the analysis will be for the purpose of maintaining confidence.

[3] This article defines the legal-tender quality of the national coins, and is in accordance with the regulations of all countries.

[4] Violating Article 3 means forcing one to discount coins, so interfering with the decimal value of the subsidiary coins. Violating Article 22 means that when the national currency is offered one refuses to accept it.

the Yuan Shih Kai dollar has penetrated to even the most out-of-the-way places of China's outlying provinces, and bids fair to remain in popular favor throughout the vast country.

The origin of the Yuan Shih Kai dollar dates back to February 1914, when new National Currency Regulations were promulgated. Yuan Shih Kai was then President of the Republic which, at the time, was in the third year of its existence. According to the provisions of the new law (*see* pages 328–332) the Yuan Shih Kai dollar was to be 0.900 fine and to weigh 72 candareens in K'uping taels; that is to say, the contents of pure silver were to be 0.648 K'uping taels in weight.

However, the coining of the new Yuan Shih Kai dollar was closely connected with the withdrawal and re-minting of the existing 250 million dragon dollars, the fineness of which was considerably below the new standard. As the Government had not the means at its disposal to make good the considerable difference, it was resolved to alter the degree of fineness of the Yuan Shih Kai dollar from 0.900 to 0.890, but to retain the former *remedium* of 0.003. This means that the contents of pure silver in the new coin were not to exceed 892.67 per mille, or be less than 887.33 per mille.

The first output of Yuan Shih Kai dollars came from the Mints at Tientsin and Nanking. Since then some of the provincial Mints have contributed their quota, large quantities coming from the Mint at Hangchow. In order to facilitate the introduction of the new coin the Government arranged that the Bank of China, the Bank of Communications and the official provincial banks should exchange, free of charge, the old dragon dollars against the new Yuan Shih Kai dollars. This measure was welcomed by the commercial community, as it facilitated the introduction of the new coin. During the period from 1914 to July 1917, about 30 million Mexican dollars were exported from China, and in addition 19 millions were melted by the Mints for re-coinage. Both these measures continued in an extended form during the following five years, thus making room for the new Yuan Shih Kai dollar which, by 1919, had succeeded in firmly establishing itself.

The original design differed somewhat from the finally adopted type. It showed Yuan Shih Kai's bust in half profile to the left, and was designed by L. Giorgi, at that time engraver at the Tientsin Mint.[1] That coin exists only in proof state and was not adopted. A second design was made, showing Yuan Shih Kai in profile to the left, and the dies were distributed by the Tientsin (Central) Mint to the various provinces. In course of time the dies were worn and had to be either retouched or re-engraved. In this way it happened that many varieties of the Yuan Shih Kai dollar came into being. In 1920 two new types made their appearance which, though very similar in design to the original type, showed differences in the legend, which read "eighth year" and "ninth year," in place of the original inscription of "third year."

Above the head of Yuan Shih Kai, in a half circle, are found the Chinese characters (造年三國民華中), denoting "Third year of the Republic of China." The reverse is occupied by an open wreath of grain, enclosing the two characters (圓壹), meaning "One Dollar."

Mr. A. Tracey Woodward supplies the following particulars regarding the Yuan Shih Kai dollar:

	Weight	*Fineness*	*Diameter*	*Thickness*
Third year:	414.73 grains	0.880	38.75 m.m.	2.66 m.m.
Eighth year:	413.37 „	0.880	38.75 „ „	2.66 „ „
Ninth year:	413.99 „	0.880	38.75 „ „	2.66 „ „
Tenth year:	414.66 „	0.880	38.75 „ „	2.50 „ „

Dr. Giuseppe Bos, another authority on Chinese coins, gives the diameter of the Yuan Shih Kai dollar as 39 m.m., the weight (3rd year) as 27 grams and the fineness 88%.

[1] Mr. A. Tracey Woodward *The Influence of Yuan Shih Kai on Chinese Coins* (1922)

With regard to the last named point there would appear to be a misconception, since the standard has not only been fixed by law at 0.890, but subsequent independent analysis by foreign Mints has shown that the coins are really of a fineness exceeding 0.890.

In 1924 an assay was made by the government Mint at Osaka of Yuan Shih Kai dollars minted in Nanking and in Hangchow; the result was as follows:

> Dollar minted in Nanking, inscribed as having been struck in the 3rd year of the Republic, but actually coined in the 12th year:
>
> Weight 414.7747 grains troy. Fineness 0.891.
>
> Dollar minted in Hangchow, marked as having been coined in the 10th year of the Chinese Republic, but actually produced in the 12th year:
>
> Weight 412.2994 grains troy. Fineness 0.8898.

Debasing the Yuan Shih Kai Dollar.

There were two attempts, made under official auspices, to debase the fine contents of the Yuan Shih Kai dollar. The first incident is the more condemnable, as the schemers were the authorities in charge of the government Mint at Anking, the capital of Anhwei province. The underlying motives were connected entirely with profit making, irrespective of the interests of the community and of state finance. Luckily the fraudulent practice was detected in good time, and the alarm raised immediately. When, in the summer of 1924, Yuan Shih Kai dollars, inscribed as of the 8th year of the Chinese Republic, emanated from the Anking Mint, it was soon ascertained that the coins had been adulterated. This fact was widely advertised, with the result that the Customs authorities placed an embargo on the export of the debased dollar coins. Apart from the adulteration there was a remarkable disregard of accuracy in the weight and composition of the output of the Anking Mint.

An analysis carried out by the Japanese government Mint at Osaka produced the following results:

	Weight grains troy.	*Fineness.*	*Contents of pure silver in grains troy.*
(*a*)	418.4095	0.8231	344.3929
(*b*)	417.8308	0.8281	346.0857
(*c*)	421.3031	0.7449	313.8287

Towards the end of August, 1925, it was brought to light that debased Yuan Shih Kai dollars were circulating in Shanghai. The first analysis resulted in proving a fine contents of only 0.763, while subsequent analysis showed that the coins were still further adulterated, namely to the extent of 660 parts of fine silver in one case, and about 560 in the second instance.

It is generally surmised that the debased dollars have been turned out at Shanghai unofficially by a powerful government functionary, with machinery secretly imported. It is estimated that the capacity of the said plant was $40,000 *per diem* and that altogether about $250,000 had been produced and placed in circulation. The object of this shady manœuvre was personal gain and greed, with an entire disregard of public welfare and the reputation of national finance.

The Genesis of the Yuan Shih Kai Dollar.

The inauguration of the Yuan Shih Kai dollar was the result of the currency regulations of January 1914, already referred to. These, and the regulations for the enforcement of the new law, read in translation as follows (according to the *China Year Book*, 1924):

National Currency Regulations.

Art. 1. The right of minting and issuance of national currency shall belong solely to the Government.

Art. 2. The unit of the national coin shall be called *yuan*, and the yuan shall contain six mace, four candareens and eight *li* *(k'uping weight)* or 23.97795048 grammes of pure silver.

ART. 3. The different kinds of national coins are as follows:—

A. Four kinds of silver coins are—

(1) 1 *yuan.*

(2) ½ *yuan.*

(3) 20 cents piece.

(4) 10 cents piece.

B. One kind of nickel coin—

(1) 5 cents piece.

C. Five kinds of copper coins—

(1) 2 cent copper piece.

(2) 1 cent copper piece.

(3) 5 *li* piece.

(4) 2 *li* piece.

(5) 1 *li* piece.

ART. 4. The value of the national coin shall be in decimal progression. One-tenth of a *yuan* shall make a *chu* or a 10 cent piece. One-hundredth of a *yuan* shall make 1 *feng* or cent, and one-thousandth of a *yuan* shall make 1 *li.*

ART. 5. The weight and fineness of the coins shall be as follows:—

1. 1 *yuan,* gross weight 72 candareens with 90[1] per cent. silver and 10 per cent. copper.

2. 50 cent piece, gross weight 32.4 candareens with 70 per cent. silver and 30 per cent. copper.

3. 20 cent piece, gross weight 12 candareens with 70 per cent. silver and 30 per cent. copper.

4. 10 cent piece, gross weight 6 candareens with 70 per cent. silver and 30 per cent. copper.

5. 5 cent nickel piece, gross weight 7 candareens with 25 per cent. nickel and 75 per cent. copper.

6. 2 cent copper piece, gross weight 28 candareens with 95 per cent. copper and 4 per cent. pewter and 1 per cent. lead.

7. 1 cent copper piece, gross weight 18 candareens with its fineness same as 2 cent copper piece.

8. 5 *li* copper piece, gross weight 9 candareens with its fineness same as above.

9. 2 *li* copper piece, gross weight 4-5 candareens with its fineness same as above.

10. 1 *li* copper piece, gross weight 2.5 candareens with its fineness same as above.

ART. 6. No restrictions shall be placed upon the use of 1 *yuan* piece. The amount of 50 cents pieces involved in one transaction shall not exceed twenty dollars. The amount of 20 cents and 10 cents pieces involved in one transaction shall not exceed five dollars. The amount of nickel or copper pieces involved in one transaction shall not exceed one dollar. This restriction shall not

[1] Since changed to 89 per cent. silver and 11 per cent. copper.

be applied to the collection of taxes and the exchanges in the national banks.

ART. 7. The designs of the national coins shall be promulgated by a Provisional Order.

ART. 8. The ratio of the difference between the weight of silver coins and that of the legal tender shall not exceed 3/1000.

The ratio of the difference between the total weight of per 1000 pieces of the silver coins and the legal weight of that amount of coins shall not exceed 3/10,000.

ART. 9. The ratio of the difference between the fineness of any piece of silver coins and the legal fineness shall not exceed 3/1000.

ART. 10. When, on account of wear and tear, 1 *yuan* silver piece loses one per cent. of its weight, it may be exchanged at the Government banks for a new dollar. When, on account of wear and tear, the 50 cents silver piece and other kinds of coins lose five per cent. of the legal weight, they may be exchanged at the Government bank for new coins.

ART. 11. When a coin is found to be mutilated purposely, no one shall be compelled to accept it.

ART. 12. When the Government consents to coin 1 *yuan* silver pieces for those who give to it silver bullion, 6 *li* per yuan shall be charged as minting fee.

ART. 13. This law shall be in force on the day of its promulgation.

REGULATIONS FOR THE ENFORCEMENT OF THE CURRENCY LAW.

ART. 1. The national coins must be used as medium in the transaction of any financial dealings in the country. Special regulations in the Currency Regulations must also be observed.

ART. 2. The Government shall exchange the silver dollars coined by the old mints with the national coins and remint the dollars.

Within a certain period, the old dollar shall possess the same value as the national *yuan,* but as to the length of that period, a Provisional Order shall be issued to fix it.

ART. 3. The Government shall replace all the old silver pieces of the different denominations, old copper pieces and cash with the national coins. After recalling them, the Government shall remint them, but within a certain fixed period the old coins shall be allowed to be circulated at the market prices.

If the old coins are used to pay taxes, every month all the public offices shall issue notices fixing the current rate at which the offices shall receive old coins. The offices shall take as the current rate an average of the rates of exchange during the previous month. The period for the circulation of the old coins shall be fixed by a Provisional Order.

ART. 4. If taxes are remitted with silver bullion or if anyone wants the Government to mint silver coins for him, in the calculation one dollar shall contain 65.4 candareens. Bullion of other fineness and weight shall be converted according to a Table to be attached.

ART. 5. In the public offices where the receipts and expenditures are calculated in taels, the amount should be converted into the term of *yuan* in accordance with Article 4. At places where the receipts and disbursement consist of copper coins and cash, the public office shall report to the Ministry of Finance the actual sum of receipts and disbursements with the request for permission to convert the coin into the term of *yuan*.

ART. 6. In the collection of various revenues and taxes, Articles 4, 5 and 6 shall be observed. In the calculation, the *li* shall be the smallest of denominations. All the decimal fractions of the *li* shall be treated thus:—when the figure is 4, it shall be discarded, and when it is 5, it shall be considered as one to be added to the other integers.

ART. 7. When the debts among the people themselves are calculated in the term to taels, they should be converted into the term of the national coin. Where the old subsidiary coins are involved, Article 6 shall be observed in the conversion into the national coins. If the sums in the deeds, contracts and promissory notes are not converted into the term of *yuan*, and if any law suit arises, the exchange rate on the day of the promulgations shall be considered as a standard.

ART. 8. Within the domain of China no one shall object to the use of the national coins.

ART. 9. If anybody disregards Article 4 of the law for the national currency and Article 8 of the regulations for the enforcement of the law of the national currency, the concerned may bring a law suit against him, and when convicted, a fine of from 10 dollars to 1,000 dollars shall be imposed on the offender. Any official or any member connected with the Government enterprises who commits the same offence, is liable to pay a fine of from 50 to 3,000 dollars after the same procedure has been observed.

ART. 10. The area and the date for the enforcement of these regulations shall be fixed by a Provisional Order.

Criticism was directed against this Currency Law on the following grounds *(inter alia)*:—

1. The omission of a definite statement to the effect that Goverment institutions will always accept the token coins at their face value.
2. The excessive margin of minting profit in the case of 2 cent coins (Article 5), which should weigh 36 per cent. more (222 grains instead of 163 grains), if they are to have the same intrinsic value in relation to face value as the present 10 cash copper coins.
3. The 5 cent nickel coin (Article 5), would represent even a greater margin of minting profit, as its intrinsic value would be only about one-tenth of its face value.

It was noted that, in spite of the declared intention of the Government to regulate the output of its mints to the needs of the country, enormous quantities of 10 cash copper coins were issued by the Government mints within six to twelve months after the publication of the Currency Law, with the result that the whole copper coinage was still further depreciated. According to a statement in the Chinese press in October, 1915, the Ministry of Finance had already instructed the Yunnan Mint to proceed with the issue of 5 cent nickel coins.

In a statement issued by the Ministry of Finance to a foreign newspaper *(The China Press,* Shanghai), in October, 1915, the steps taken towards currency reform are thus described: "The plan was to coin first new coins of one dollar, in order to secure uniformity, the mould to be manufactured and issued to the branch mints by the Central Mint. Coining is now in progress in the Tientsin and Nanking mints, and the coins are gradually issued. The old dollars are now permitted to be circulated with the new coins, and are gradually being called in by the Bank of China and the Bank of Communications to be re-minted. Subsidiary coins of 10 cents and 20 cents will also shortly be struck and issued. Two half dollars, twenty 5 cents, or ten 10 cent pieces will be changed for a new dollar permanently without change. The subsidiary coins for legal tender will be restricted in conformity with the general rules of currency. The old subsidiary coins will, after the issue of the new coins, be current according to their market value for a time, and then be gradually called in and re-coined.

Chinese Dollars Versus Sycee.

The desirability of substituting the dollar for the sycee tael as a medium of currency has been recognised by the foreign as well as the Chinese commercial community. The change involved one prime condition, namely that the dollar should be a coin with uniform weight, size, design and fineness. Uniformity was obtainable only if the coin would emanate from one and the same Mint, which would have to be equipped with the latest appliances and directed by a highly-skilled staff of engineers and chemists. It was proposed and agreed that the most suitable location for such an establishment would be at Shanghai.

In 1921 a loan for $2,500,000 was obtained from a Chinese Banking Group for the purpose of providing land, buildings, machinery and equipment for the new Central Mint. When, in 1923, the buildings had been completed and the bulk of the machinery had arrived, the total expenditure was estimated at about six million dollars. But unfortunately a large portion of the capital required was not forthcoming, so that the principal machinery could not be paid for and installed after its arrival at Shanghai. The situation was still unchanged in the autumn of 1925, when it was feared that a portion of the delicate machinery might meanwhile have gone to ruin.

Cost of Producing Dollars.

Dollars are minted from bar silver or, if this is not available, from sycee. Let us consider the theoretical cost of producing Yuan Shih Kai dollars.

(a) *Minted from bar silver, 0.998 fine.*

Formula I.

? Shanghai taels	: 100 Yuan Shih Kai dollars
1 Yuan Shih Kai dollar	: 416 grains, 0.890 fine
480 grains	: 1 ounce
100 ounces (0.998 fine)	: 91.804 Shanghai taels

$$X = \frac{100 \times 416 \times 0.890 \times 91.804}{480 \times 100} = 70.811 \text{ taels.}$$

The theoretical cost of producing 100 dollars appears to be 70.811 Shanghai taels, provided English bar silver can be obtained at 110.90 Shanghai taels (currency) for 100 Canton taels weight. The cost of minting, freight, interest, commission, etc., is not included.

Another example of producing dollars from bar silver gives the identical result.

Formula II.

? Shanghai taels	: 100 Yuan Shih Kai dollars
1 Yuan Shih Kai dollar	: 26.9514 grams, 0.890 fine
31.1035 grams	: 1 ounce
100 ounces (0.998 fine)	: 82.7815 Canton taels weight
100 Canton taels weight	: 110.90 Shanghai taels

$$X = \frac{26.9514 \times 0.890 \times 82.7815 \times 110.90}{31.0977 \times 100 \times 100} = 70.811 \text{ taels.}$$

Formula III.

? Shanghai taels	: 100 Yuan Shih Kai dollars
1 dollar	: 416 grains, 0.890 fine
480 grains	: 1 ounce
1.208 ounces	: 1.109 Shanghai taels

$$X = \frac{100 \times 416 \times 0.890 \times 1.109}{480 \times 1.208} = \textit{70.811 taels.}$$

(b) *Minted from Shanghai sycee.*

Formula IV.

? Shanghai taels	: 100 Yuan Shih Kai dollars
1 Yuan Shih Kai dollar	: 416 grains, 0.890 fine
516.82 grains, 1000 fine	: 1 Shanghai tael

$$X = \frac{100 \times 416 \times 0.890}{516.82 \times 1000} = \textit{71.638 taels.}$$

It will be noted that the cost of minting dollars from Shanghai sycee is considerably higher than the cost of coining them from bar silver.

(c) *Minted at Tientsin from Bai-bao sycee.*

Formula V.

? Tientsin taels (Hongping Hua Pao)	: 1,000 Yuan Shih Kai dollars
1 Yuan Shih Kai dollar	: 0.72 K'uping taels weight 0.890 fine
100 K'uping taels weight	: 103.34 Hongping taels weight, Bai-bao sycee
1,000 taels Bai-bao sycee	: 1008 taels (Hongping Hua Pao) with premium

$$X = \frac{1000 \times 0.72 \times 0.890 \times 103.34 \times 1008}{100 \times 1000} = \textit{66.744 Tientsin taels.}$$

This means that 100 Yuan Shih Kai dollars have an intrinsic value of 66.744 Tientsin taels.

(d) *The Mint's figures.*

According to the estimate of the government Mint in Nanking, the cost of coining a dollar coin is equivalent to Shanghai taels 0.727984. The Mint has a capacity for turning out 120,000 coins a day and the cost, including running and overhead expenses as shown below, amounts in total to K'uping Tls. 79,705.88; that is, K'uping Tls. 6,642.157, or Shanghai Tls. 7,279.84 for every 10,000 dollars coined. The tael used in the following list is the K'uping tael:—

	Taels.
Price of bullion	78,067.005
Cost of copper ball for alloy	142.558
Loss of weight in bullion caused by smelting	234.201
Loss of weight caused by re-smelting of discarded coins	99.066
Loss caused by coin-assaying	57.38
Loss caused by Assaying and Chemical Analysis	9.83
Loss caused by smelting of copper balls	0.774
Daily depreciation on tools and equipment, etc.	187.273
Daily cost of coal	282.192
Daily wages for mint operatives	97.485
Railway freight for Bullion transportation from Shanghai to Nanking	180.08
Daily expenses for upkeep of machinery	12.827
Interest on capital	134.426
Daily miscellaneous expenses	46.69
Daily salaries for executive staff	154.1
Total	79,705.88

N.B.—100 K'uping taels = 109.60 Shanghai taels.

Although these figures have been supplied from official sources, we venture to doubt their accuracy. According to the official statement the cost of producing 1,000 dollars is Shanghai taels 727.984. But this figure does not include the freight to Shanghai (or elsewhere) of the minted dollars, nor the cost of boxes and finally interest, of which no account has been taken. Furthermore, the statement is based on the supposition that the Nanking Mint is worked to full capacity during every one of the 365 days of the year. This assumption is, of course, not in accordance with facts. Taking these points into consideration, we arrive at a mint cost of about 73 Shanghai taels for 100 dollars.

In practice one can observe the Mints at Nanking and at Hangchow minting silver dollars at a time when the market price at Shanghai is 72.3, and even less, for 100 silver dollars. Therefore the official estimate appears to be either hypothetical or ultra-conservative.

Transactions with Dollars.

The use of the dollar for currency purposes is constantly on the increase in China. Taxes, railway fares, postage and salt revenue are officially prescribed in dollars. As in years gone by, in most of the commercial places in China, various currencies are still circulating side by side. This fact is conducive to the creation of exchange transactions between the "big dollar" and the swarm of other media of circulation, as taels, small coin dollars, copper cents and depreciated banknotes.

In Shanghai at the meetings of representatives of the Native Banks, held daily in the morning and early afternoon, the official rate of exchange between the silver dollar and the Shanghai tael is fixed in accordance with actual demand and supply. Quotations are issued (per 100 dollars) in Shanghai taels, with 4 decimals, the last 3 of which are always expressed in "eighths"; for instance, 100 dollars are Shanghai taels 72.4875.

As a rule, transactions in dollars are for ready delivery. In Shanghai forward sales in dollars are permissible and customary only a few weeks before the opening of the cocoon season, when large quantities of silver dollars are needed for despatch into the interior.

Of considerable interest is the structure of interport transactions in silver dollars. In theory China has one uniform silver dollar, therefore the transfer from one place to another through the intermediary of a bank ought to be a simple matter. But it should not be overlooked that there is no institution operating in China which could carry out the functions pertaining to a government bank.

In consequence thereof the transfer by draft of dollars is subject to demand and supply. During the cocoon season in May the district of Wusih will be in need of large quantities of silver dollars; in the late summer the vicinity of Tsinanfu will require that commodity to pay the farmers for the tobacco harvested there; in the autumn considerable quantities of hard dollars are needed in the Tungchow and other cotton-growing districts. During those seasons banks situated in the places mentioned will be prepared to issue drafts on Shanghai, payable in dollars, at par, and sometimes even at a discount.

Speaking generally, the cost of transfering dollars in China from one place to another ought not to exceed the cost of actually shipping the coins, though it must not be lost sight of that, at times, an embargo is issued against the export of treasure from a certain province. In such an event there will be a discount on the dollar current in the district which has placed the embargo on the shipment of hard dollars.

The following is a *pro formâ* note relating to the shipment made in 1925 of 100,000 Yuan Shih Kai dollars from Shanghai to Tientsin:

Tls.	72,500.00	$100,000
	181.25	2½‰ freight
	36.25	5 cents per $100 insurance
	108.75	1½‰ interest
	14.50	boxes
	4.30	coolie hire
	21.75	wharfage due
	50.00	charge for picking out Yuan Shih Kai dollar.
Total Tls. .	72,916.80	

Ordinarily, when Shanghai is requested to draw in dollars on an outport, say on Tientsin, both these places are required to forget that a uniform dollar is supposed to be current in China. The transaction will invariably be coupled with the tael current in both places. Shanghai, when drawing dollars on Tientsin, will have to ascertain firstly the Tientsin selling rate for dollars against Tientsin taels, and secondly Tientsin's buying rate for Shanghai taels against Tientsin taels. In purchasing drafts drawn in dollars on Tientsin, Shanghai will have to reverse its reasoning, with the result that there will be a considerable difference between buying and selling Tientsin dollars at one and the same time.

Example: *Tientsin, November 25, 1925.*

Dollars buying . . .	69.10	Dollars selling . . .	69.40
Shanghai taels buying .	105.60	Shanghai taels selling .	105.30

(*a*) If Shanghai wants to draw (sell) dollars on Tientsin:
69.40 × 105.60 = Shanghai taels 73.28 for 100 Tientsin dollars.

(*b*) If Shanghai wants to remit (buy) dollars to Tientsin:
69.10 × 105.30 = Shanghai taels 72.76 for 100 Tientsin dollars.

N.B.—On the same day the market rate for dollars at Shanghai was 72.5875 Shanghai taels.

Even in places where the currency tael plays a secondary rôle, the premium or discount on transfers in dollars is closely allied with the tael. Take the example of Tsinanfu, the capital of Shantung province:

The Tsinan–Shanghai premium on dollar transfer is based on the cross-rate between Shanghai taels and Tsinan taels, and the cross-rate between Shanghai taels and Shanghai dollars. The Tsinan tael dollar rate is fixed at 70 (that is, 7 mace = 1 dollar), but the Shanghai tael and Tsinan tael cross-rate, as well as that between Shanghai tael and dollar, is subject to constant fluctuations, according to the supply and demand of tael bills on Shanghai. (Curiously enough all such bills traded in the Commercial Guild, where the daily rate is made, are in the form of five days' sight drafts).

Say, for example, the official cross-rate between Tsinan taels and Shanghai taels is 104.50 for drafts drawn five days after sight. Multiply by 0.7 and deduct from the product five days interest at the basis of the Native interest rate ruling at Shanghai; say 8% per annum.

104.50 × 0.7	73.150
Less: 5 days interest at 8% per annum .	.081
Taels . .	73.069

which represents the cross-rate between Tsinan dollars and Shanghai taels (sight). On the same day the official dollar rate ruling at Shanghai is, say 72.625. Hence the premium collectable at Tsinanfu will be at least 0.434 taels, or $0.60 per cent. Consequently, when selling demand draft in dollars on Shanghai, Tsinanfu will have to charge on that particular day a premium of at least $0.60 per cent. as otherwise it would be more remunerative to purchase five days after sight drafts on Shanghai.

Other Republican Dollars.

Apart from the Yuan Shih Ḳai dollar, described already, there are a number of Republican dollars in existence, though not necessarily in circulation. Most of these coins were struck in commemoration of important events connected with the republican regime.

(*a*) 1 dollar, 39.3 m.m. in diameter. Showing on the obverse the bust of Sun Yat Sen in profile, looking to the left. Within a beaded circle is to be found the inscription (in Chinese only) "The Republic of China," and below "Coin commemorative of the change of régime."

The reverse shows in the centre an open wreath of grain and the Chinese inscription of 1 dollar. Around the circle is inscribed in English "* Memento * Birth of the Republic of China."

(*b*) 1 dollar. Same as the preceding, except that the legend in English has been altered to read "The Republic of China * One dollar *." Both these coins were struck in Nanking in 1912, the engraver being Ho Tze-liang.

(*c*) 1 dollar, 39.5 m.m. in diameter. Showing President Li Yuan Hung's portrait in military uniform *(en face)*. Design and legend are similar to the patterns of the two previously described coins.

(*d*) 1 dollar. Also bearing the portrait of President Li Yuan Hung, but in a different pose and without cap. Otherwise similar in design to the previous item. Both

Li Yuan Hung dollars have been coined at Wuchang, the die having been made by Chu Tse-fang in 1912.

(*e*) 1 dollar. 39 m.m. in diameter, with the portrait of Yuan Shih Kai in general's uniform with feathers on the military cap. Weight 26.04 grams, fineness 0.900. Engraved by L. Giorgi and coined in 1914 by the Tientsin Mint; total issue 20,000 pieces only.

The reverse of the coin contains, enclosed in an open wreath of barley, the Chinese characters for "One dollar." Above the legend in Chinese "The Republic of China—Coin Commemorative of the Republic." Below in English "One dollar."

(*f*) 1 dollar. Showing the bust of President Tsao Kung in military uniform. This coin was struck by the Tientsin Mint in 1923, in commemoration of the promulgation of the country's constitution. 50,000 of these coins were sent to Nanking at the time for distribution in Kiangsu province.

(*g*) 1 dollar. 39 m.m. in diameter. Issued by the provincial government of Szechuen during the first year of the Republic. Meant to serve as currency within the province. The design is entirely different from the dollar pieces described so far. Inscriptions in Chinese characters only. There is a second specimen of this coin existing, varying slightly from the original design.[1] According to reports emanating from the Maritime Customs the republican Szechuen dollar has been found, after analysis, to be 0.872 fine. The meaning of the inscription on the reverse is "Made by the Military Government."

(*h*) 1 dollar. On the occasion of the 14th anniversary of the foundation of the Chinese Republic the Peking Government ordered the Mint at Tientsin to strike 100,000 dollars of a special design. The first instalment of $20,000 was issued on October 10, 1925.

[1] For full details of Republican coins see "Coins of the Republic of China" in Aolume XLVIII, 1917, in the *Journal of the North China Branch of the Royal Vsiatic Society*.

CHAPTER XIV

SUBSIDIARY SILVER COINS

THE coining of the silver dollar in China was a step in the right direction and constituted a great convenience to financial circles within the country. But the value of the dollar was too great to serve the purpose of China's enormous population, the bulk of which is notoriously poor and accustomed to handle the mediæval copper cash.

The Mint at Canton produced subsidiary silver coins for the first time in A.D. 1890. These were of a fineness of 0.820, as compared with 0.900, the fine contents of the dragon dollar. The new coins were well received by the public and as they left a wide margin of profit to the Mint authorities, their existence would have proved a great convenience to all those concerned, had it not been for the unpreventable tendency of competition. As soon as the other provinces realised the enormous possibilities in connection with the production of subsidiary silver coins, they all strove to open Mints within their domains. Unfortunately they were successful in carrying out their plans. The immediate result was an enormous overproduction of subsidiary silver coins and a consequent fall in their market value. Although a ten-cents piece was meant to represent one-tenth part of a dragon dollar, it soon became apparent that, owing to a production of small silver coins far in excess of actual requirements, the value of those coins had depreciated and was subject to constant fluctuations. Competition between provincial Mints became so keen, and the market price of silver subsidiary coins declined to such an extent, that the authorities in charge had recourse to the doubtful expedient of reducing the fine contents of the coins. This policy was carried out secretly, but the public learned soon enough of those dubious practices and tried to defend its position by accepting the adulterated coins at a further discount only. If it is taken into consideration that certain provinces offered their Mint for rent to the highest bidder, who worked practically uncontrolled; that other provinces placed their Mints at the disposal of military chiefs, who were bent on paying their armies with the profits from minting operations, with complete disregard of public welfare; that the Central Government in Peking was powerless to interfere, it will be understood that there could not remain even a semblance of uniformity in weight, fineness or market value. The chaotic conditions with regard to the subsidiary silver coinage were aggravated by the nefarious work of forgers, who were quite prominent in 1924 and 1925. Probably it could be rightly argued that the output of professional counterfeiters was not worse than the authentic production of certain provincial Mints which were under the "protection" of military chiefs.

Subsidiary silver coins in China exist in denominations of 50, 20, 10 and 5 cents. The 50 cents piece is to be found in certain provinces only, while the 5 cents silver coin is now obsolete. The 10 cents piece is also slowly disappearing from circulation. Most of these coins have been melted, in order to be re-minted into 20 cents pieces, the latter with a lesser degree of fineness. The 20 cents piece, in 1925, ruled supreme. The bulk of the 20 cents coins in actual circulation within the country, in the autumn of that year, had been turned out by the Canton Mint. Most of the old subsidiary silver coins with the dragon design have mysteriously disappeared from circulation, in order to be replaced and augmented by the prolific production of the Canton Mint. The old dragon design 20 cents piece minted at Canton was of an average fineness of 0.800, weighing about 5.30 grams. The new 20 cents piece (which is designed similarly to the subsidiary coins current in the Straits Settlements) was, until 1921, of an average fineness of 0.700, and weighed about 5.30 grams. This means that the contents of fine silver in the old coin was on an average 4.24 grams, as compared with 3.71 grams in the new 20 cents piece. Since 1921 the degree of fineness of the subsidiary silver coins minted at Canton has been further reduced to figures which cannot be indicated owing to their instability.

Although subsidiary silver coins are current all over the country, they are accepted only at their market value. But in certain provinces the small coin dollar forms the official currency, notably in Kwangtung, Kwangsi and Fengtien provinces.

Classification of Subsidiary Coins.

It would mean entering the realm of numismatics were we to attempt to give particulars regarding all subsidiary silver coins minted in China. Accurate statistics concerning the output and the composition of these coins are conspicuous by their absence. Suffice it to say that half dollar pieces with the dragon design were produced by the Mints of Canton, Wuchang, Tientsin and Mukden. Nearly all the provincial Mints in operation, until 1912, turned out 10 and 20 cents pieces.

During the republican regime appallingly large quantities of subsidiary silver coins have been forced on the public. In trying to classify these we have to consider:

(*a*) *Issues in commemoration of the Revolution.*—Only the 20 cents coin with the bust of Dr. Sun Yat Sen belongs to this category. Although it is a legalised coin, it was produced in 1912 in small quantities as a souvenir and was never put in circulation.

(*b*) *Provincial Issues.*—Space does not permit our entering into a detailed description of the numerous provincial issues, therefore only some of the peculiarities are to be recorded here.

The first production of a republican 20 cents piece dates back to February 1913, when the Foochow Mint turned out a newly-designed coin with the old inscription of "1 mace and 4.4 candareens."

The province of Szechuen produced the 50, 20 and 10 cents pieces, all of which are of a distinctive and peculiar design; the inscription is in Chinese characters only. The denominations are termed 5 *chio,* 2 *chio* and 1 *chio* respectively. These coins are dated the first year of the Republic.

Canton has flooded the country with its newly-designed 20 cents pieces, which are distinguished by the large figure of 20 on the obverse of the coin, the reverse of which contains Chinese characters only, indicating the province, the year of issue and the value (2 *hao* silver coin).

There are many minor variations which are distinguished from each other by the different year of issue. Besides the 20 cents piece there exists a 10 cents silver coin turned out by the Canton Mint in an identical design. The lavishness of the output of 20 cents pieces by the Canton Mint may be seen from the following figures of production:

1912	. . . .	87,000,000 pieces
1913	. . . .	109,974,000 „
1914	. . . .	41,691,000 „
1915	. . . .	22,332,000 „
1919	. . . .	195,000,000 „
1920	. . . .	197,000,000 „
1921	. . . .	402,250,000 „

The European war interrupted silver supplies to a large extent but, beginning from 1919, the Mint at Canton resumed its activities with renewed vigor, flooding the entire country with its enhanced output of 20 cents coins.

In the summer of 1924 the Mint at Hangchow struck new 20 cents and 10 cents coins to the extent of about $500,000 worth. But the experiment was discontinued for the time being, as it was said to be unremunerative.

The governor of Yunnan province, T'ang Chi-Yao, ordered the Mint at Yunnanfu, in 1918, to strike a 50 cent piece. The coin shows his bust in military uniform and the inscription above (T'ang, Governor-General of the Military Government). On the obverse are shown the national and military flags crossed; between the inner and outer circles above 擁護共和紀念 (Commemorating the defense of the Republic); below 庫平三錢六分 (3 mace and 6 candareens K'uping). Size 33¼ m.m., weight 13½ grams. This coin was soon withdrawn from circulation in order to be replaced by a similar piece. The obverse remained practically of the identical design, but the reverse was changed into an *en face* portrait of His Excellency. The new coin succeeded in gaining wide popularity, obtaining a large circulation not only within Yunnan, but equally throughout Szechuen province.[1]

(c) *Full value subsidiary coins.*—From the text of the National Currency Regulations published in the previous chapter it can be seen that already in 1914 the Government had decided to issue subsidiary silver coins, 0.700 fine, which were to pass at their full value, based on the decimal system. However, it was not until the beginning of 1917 that the portion of the scheme, relating to subsidiary silver coins, could be put into effect; even then it had been somewhat modified. The following is a translation of the proclamation issued early in 1917 by the Minister of Finance:

The public is hereby notified that the Ministry of Finance has been advised by the Head Mint at Tientsin that the three kinds of subsidiary silver coins, the half *yuan* piece, the 20 cents piece, and the 10 cents piece, newly minted as per order of the Ministry have all been issued and put in circulation. They are considered

[1] Mr. A. Tracey Woodward in the *New China Review*, No. 3, June 1921.

the most convenient in every respect by the business circle as well as the people in general. Now, again; the two kinds of subsidiary copper coins, the 1 cent piece and the ½ cent piece, newly minted as per order of the Ministry have all been duly minted and ready for issue. Their weight and fineness and the legal allowance for variations of the same all conform to the provisions of the National Currency Law.

Other Ministries and the Provincial Authorities have been informed by this Ministry to the effect and local officials pertaining thereto are to be instructed as well by the Governors concerned that in collecting taxes, duties, likin, and other revenue, the receipts from the Post Office, the Telegraphic Administration, Railways and other governmental enterprises, the above mentioned coins shall hereafter be accepted in the manner as stated in the National Currency Law.

These coins are to be exchanged for one another on a decimal basis, *i.e.,* 10 pieces of a lower denomination shall exchange for 1 piece of the immediate higher denomination, and vice versa, and no premium nor discount is allowed in exchange. Whoever shall violate this prescription will be punished in accordance with Article 9 of the regulations for the execution of the National Currency Law.

These new subsidiary coins being of the decimal system, have the advantage of simplicity and uniformity over the corresponding old coins. They may be presented to the Government Banks for exchange at any time, one *yuan* can exchange for ten 10-cents pieces, or for one hundred 1-cent pieces and vice versa. No limit is set as to amount that may be exchanged for one time, the exchange rate being of course the same for paying out as well as for receiving in to the Bank.

The following are particulars of the three subsidiary coins which were then actually issued:

(1.) Half dollar, 0.800 fine, weight 207.49 grains (13.5 grams), diameter 31.5 m.m., thickness 2 m.m.

The half dollar piece is similar in design to the Yuan Shih Kai dollar of the third year of the Republic. The obverse is identical, in proportionately reduced dimensions. On the reverse is stated, in Chinese characters: "Each two pieces are equal to one dollar."

(2.) The 20-cents piece (called 2 *chio,* or two-tenths dollar). This coin is 0.700 fine, weighs 82.57 grains (5.35 grams), is 1.66 m.m. thick, and 22.5 m.m. in diameter. The design is similar to the preceding, except the wording of the Chinese inscription which reads: "Two *chio*" and "Each five pieces are equal to one dollar."

(3.) The 10-cents piece (called 1 *chio*). Fineness 0.700, weight 41.09 grains (2.65 grams), diameter 18.5 m.m., thickness 1.33 m.m. The design is similar to the preceding ones. The Chinese inscription on the reverse reads: "Each ten pieces are equal to one dollar."

These three coins have been produced by the Mints at Tientsin and Nanking. They soon become current in Peking and Tientsin, but the Chinese public at Shanghai and in the interior of the country showed signs of distrust, so that the innovation proved unsuccessful. This, in spite of the fact that the post office, as well as the railways, accepted the new coins freely as "big money." But a fixed value attached to coins was against the interest of the multitude of money changers, who make their living on the fluctuations of the country's currencies. Apathy gradually turned into open opposition and, as the Central Government lacked the power to enforce its decrees, the "big money" was automatically degraded into "small money." Here is another sad example regarding the impotency of the Government to impose its will on the people, even in a matter of national importance, and with far-reaching benefits to the trade of the entire country.

The output of large quantities of debased subsidiary silver coins by the various Mints in Fukien province, combined with the issue there, on the part of numerous private banks, of fractional currency notes, caused the authorities to seek a way out of the chaos. In August of 1925 it was contemplated to recall all fractional banknotes and prohibit their issue in future; and furthermore, to replace the debased subsidiary silver coins by the "big money," represented by 10 cents and 20 cents subsidiary silver coins in fractions of the dollar, as provided by the currency law of 1914.

Small coin has become merchandise in China. Apart from the size of the output, and the actual demand, there is the question of fineness to be considered. On the Shanghai market there are daily quotations for dragon subsidiary coins, and also for silver coins of Canton origin. As may be seen from the following bulletin of October 12, 1925, there was then a difference of about 10% between the value of Canton and Kiangnan subsidiary silver coins.

NATIVE INTEREST AND COPPER EXCHANGE

Native Interest per day: a.m. Taels 0.23 per Taels 1,000; p.m. Taels 0.24 per Taels 1,000.

Mexican and Chinese Dollars: a.m. Taels 72.3375 per 100 dollars; p.m. Taels 72.625 per 100 dollars.

Kiangnan Cents: a.m. Taels 60.70 per 100 cents (silver); p.m. Taels 60.70 per 100 cents (silver).

Canton Cents: a.m. Taels 54.925 per 100 cents (silver); p.m. Taels 55.000 per 100 cents (silver).

Coppers: a.m. 342,000, per Taels 100; p.m. 342,000 per Taels 100.

Exchange: dollar 1 = 12 silver 20 cents pieces, 19 coppers.
dollar 1 = 242 coppers.
10 cents = 18 coppers.
10 cents big money = 6 coppers.

In order to avoid disputes regarding the rates of exchange between the silver dollar and subsidiary coins the foreign banks of Shanghai have (on May 11, 1925) issued the following notice relative to the exchange of "small money" into "big money," as these commodities are popularly termed in China.

SHANGHAI FOREIGN EXCHANGE BANKERS' ASSOCIATION.

Members of the above Association have agreed that, on 11th instant and until further notice, subsidiary coins will be received and paid out at the following ratio:—

Big Money		*Subsidiary Coins*			
(Dollars) 10 cents	=	10 cents	silver and	5	coppers
20 „	=	20 „	„ „	11	„
30 „	=	40 „	„ „	1	„
40 „	=	50 „	„ „	6	„
50 „	=	60 „	„ „	11	„
60 „	=	80 „	„ „	2	„
70 „	=	90 „	„ „	7	„
80 „	=	100 „	„ „	12	„
90 „	=	120 „	„ „	2	„

To show how intricate the question of dealings with subsidiary coin was at the close of the first quarter of the twentieth century, we append hereto an official notification issued by the Chinese Post Office at Shanghai. It will be observed that the official notice knows only the "Mexican or Dragon Dollar,"—both of which are actually vanishing from circulation, having been replaced by the Yuan Shih Kai dollar.

POST OFFICE.

NOTIFICATION.

Subsidiary coins tendered for the payment of taxed mail matter will be accepted at the following rates:—

One Mexican or Dragon Dollar equals Copper Cash 2500.

One Mexican or Dragon Dollar equals Copper Cents 250.

One Mexican or Dragon Dollar equals 13 10-cents pieces, 9 Copper cents and 5 cash.

For one 10 cents piece may be obtained stamps to the face value of 7 cents plus 10 cash.

A 10 cents stamp costs one 10 cents piece 6 copper cents, and 5 cash.

A 3 cents stamp costs 7 copper cents plus 5 cash.

A 1 cent stamp costs 2 copper cents plus 5 cash.

CHINESE POST OFFICE,
Shanghai, October 2, 1925.

E. TOLLEFSON,
Postal Commissioner.

Cost of Minting Canton Subsidiary Coins.

The Mint at Canton strikes subsidiary coins from bar silver, which is imported either direct from San Francisco, or bought at Shanghai against taels. Or, at other times, small coin dollars are produced from imported sycee or from melted coins of a degree of fineness which is above the standard of the new coins.

In considering the theoretical cost of minting Canton 20-cents pieces, we shall base our calculations on bar silver bought at Shanghai at a premium, costing with brokerage 111.50 Shanghai taels for each 100 Canton taels weight. The average weight of a Canton 20-cents coin is 5.40 grams and its average fineness is taken at 0.650. Therefore the contents of pure silver would be 3.51 grams. Charges and interest on shipments from Shanghai to Canton are here taken at 1%.

For further details concerning the export of bar silver to South China refer to Chapter IX, "Bar Silver and China."

Formula I.

? Canton dollars (in 20 cents pieces)	: are minted out of 100 ounces silver (0.999 fine)
100 ounces silver	: 82.7815 Canton taels weight
100 Canton taels weight (0.999 fine)	: cost 111.50 Shanghai taels
1 Shanghai tael	: 565.70 grains
480 grains	: 31.1035 grams
3.51 grams (pure silver)	: are contained in 0.20 Canton dollars

$$X = \frac{100 \times 82.7815 \times 111.50 \times 565.70 \times 31.1035 \times 0.20}{100 \times 100 \times 480 \times 3.51} = 192.7985$$

Less charges and interest, 1%	1.9279
Small coin . .	$190.8706

Minting charges to be taken into consideration.

If the transaction is made through Hongkong the result will be similar:

Formula II.

? Canton small coin dollars	: 100 ounces bar silver (0.999 fine)
100 ounces bar silver	: 115.4553 Hongkong dollars (with X% premium)
100 Hongkong dollars	: 71.70 Canton taels weight of silver
100 Canton taels weight	: 111.50 Shanghai taels
1 Shanghai tael	: 565.70 grains
480 grains	: 31.1035 grams
540 grams, 0.650 fine	: 0.20 Canton small coin dollars

$$X = \frac{100 \times 115.4553 \times 71.70 \times 111.50 \times 565.70 \times 31.1035 \times 0.20}{100 \times 100 \times 100 \times 480 \times 540 \times 0.650} = 192.7985$$

Less charges and interest, 1%	1.9279
Small coin .	$190.8706

Minting charges to be considered.

Most of the figures quoted are permanent, but the following items are variable:

The price at Shanghai of 100 Canton taels weight of bar silver.

The fineness and weight of the Canton 20-cents piece.

In order to obtain Shanghai taels, Canton is obliged to sell subsidiary coins against Hongkong dollars, and employ the latter for the purchase of Shanghai taels.

Say that 125 Canton small coin dollars will realise 100 Hongkong dollars; on the same day the latter will exchange for 74 Shanghai taels.

Formula:

? Canton small coin dollars	: 100 Shanghai taels
74 Shanghai taels	: 100 Hongkong dollars
100 Hongkong dollars	: 125 Canton small coin dollars

$$X = \frac{100 \times 100 \times 125}{74 \times 100} = \textit{168.919 small coin dollars.}$$

Nickel Coins.

Apart from silver subsidiary coins there are, or were, nickel token coins in use in certain districts of China. The first coins made of nickel were issued, in denominations of 5 and 10 cents, in the then German colony of Kiaochow. Later on Kwangtung province circulated a 5 cents nickel coin (with a hole in the center); this coin was also current in Kwangsi province. Yunnan province minted 5 and 10 cents nickel coins for circulation there. Speaking generally, it cannot be asserted that coins made from nickel have become popular in China, or that their use has become an extended one.

CHAPTER XV

THE PRODUCTION OF SILVER IN CHINA

Historical Notes.

CHINA is the second largest silver-consuming country in the world. Only infinitely small quantities of the white metal have been found within the boundaries of the huge country and its outlying dependencies. Yet in spite thereof there have been determined endeavors on the part of China's officials to prospect for silver, and to work existing silver mines. The results have at no time fulfilled anticipated hopes, but the risks were not great, considering that mining operations were carried out by commandeered labor.

The earliest period in which Egyptian silver was known dates back to 2400 B.C. In the *Book of History* it is stated that during the Yin dynasty—which ruled over the five Northern provinces from 1765–1122 B.C.—". . . silver overflowed from the hills." From this statement it is not necessarily to be deduced that, measured by modern methods, the mines of Northern China were rich in silver deposits. Undoubtedly silver was obtained in ancient China principally through cupellation of lead. It was originally employed chiefly for incrustations on bronze articles.

The Chinese character for "silver" (銀) is interpreted as meaning the (艮) *ken* or "obstinate metal," because it is so hard to find in China,[1] or more likely as the "difficult metal," owing to its not being obtainable by a direct process from galena.[2] Since about 200 B.C. silver has been

[1] *Glossary of Chinese Terms.* By H. A. Giles.

[2] *Mineral Enterprise in China.* By W. F. Collins

known in Chinese writings as *Bai Chin* (白金), "white metal."

Owing to the small quantities of silver produced within the borders of old China, its uses were rather limited during the first few centuries of the Christian era. There are reasons to suppose that mining in general received a certain amount of encouragement during the reign of the T'ang dynasty (A.D. 618 to 907).

The working of silver mines in China was always subject to permission from the emperor. Such permission was often granted, but not infrequently withdrawn again. On various occasions, a general interdiction of silver mining throughout the country was decreed. So, for instance, it was commanded in A.D. 807, by order of emperor *Hsien Tung,* to refrain from the search for silver on pain of banishment.

As a result of war with the Sung emperors the Kins entered the latter's capital, Kaifengfu in Honan, and demanded an indemnity of 5 million ounces of gold, 50 million ounces of silver, silk and horses. Although the payment of so heavy an indemnity was agreed to, it soon became apparent that no more than 200,000 taels weight of gold and 5 million taels weight of silver could be procured.

During the fifteenth century prohibitions relating to the mining of silver were renewed. In 1440 it was proclaimed that any person found secretly smelting silver be executed, and all his relatives banished to the outlying barren provinces. In A.D. 1444 the Government agreed to re-open the silver mines in Fukien and Chekiang provinces. Six years later these silver mines were again closed down.

In A.D. 1460 the Chinese Government despatched criminals to Hsin Hsing, in Yunnan province, to work the silver mines there. Three years later work was discontinued, apparently owing to heavy earthquakes having occurred in those districts. This was the signal to once more proclaim the closing down of all silver mines throughout the country.

A few years thereafter silver mining was resumed by the government authorities, the miners being recruited principally from the ranks of soldiers. It seems that the notoriously poor silver deposits had given out, for in A.D. 1473 most of the soldiers could no longer pay the mining taxes, except by selling their children. Others abandoned their unremunerative work and became bandits. In A.D. 1511 fresh earthquakes did considerable damage in Yunnan province. This fact induced the governor there to petition the throne to once more close down the silver mines situated in Yunnan province. But they were again re-opened in A.D. 1514.

Six years later another general prohibition against silver mining in China was issued. The embargo was extended in A.D. 1530, to provide for capital punishment of any person crossing the Yellow River with silver ore, melted silver, or even mining utensils. But after a few years' interval mining operations were again permitted, and in A.D. 1556 the officials were even requested to encourage mining, in order to assist in the raising of funds needed for the construction of the emperor's palace.

In 1568 mining within the provinces of Chihli, Kwangsi and Chekiang was again interdicted, and in 1584 the prohibition was applied to the whole country. The embargo was proved to be of little consequence to the economic life of China, as the existing mines had yielded only insignificant quantities of silver. Besides, considerable quantities of the white metal from America had already found their way into the interior of China through the port of Canton.

Chinese Silver Mining in Modern Times.

Some of the conditions that militated against the success of silver mining operations during the Middle Ages have applied to successive centuries and up to this day. Paramount amongst these are poor natural deposits, lack of communications and general insecurity.

The quantity of silver used for currency purposes in modern China is enormous, but the silver deposits in the home country are not capable of contributing a percentage of the country's silver requirements worth mentioning. The hopelessly small quantities of silver produced in China are obtained mostly as a bye-product from the refinery of lead or zinc. The following list of places, where silver mining in China has been tried, is to be considered merely as an endeavor to present an authoritative record.

On the subject of silver deposits in China the *Encyclopædia Sinica* has the following to remark:

> Silver is widely distributed in West China, chiefly in the form of argentiferous galena, which is present in every prefecture of Yunnan and West Kueichou. The chief workings are in Yunnan, at Tungchwan, Tali (in conjunction with arsenic and zinc), near Likiang (with copper) and at Talang and Weiyuan in the Shan States region. In Kuangsi, Kueichou, and Kuangtung galena exists over a Y-shaped area, the prong pointing about N.W., and the foot touching the coast near Swatow. Silver also occurs on the tributaries of the West River; there is a rich mine at Yunning, Kuangsi; in Lopingchou and North of Weining, Kucichou, and in the Hweilichou district of Ssuch'uan.

The sources of information contained in the succeeding paragraphs are indicated by figures, viz.:

(1.) *Chinese Maritime Customs Decennial Reports.*
(2.) *Chinese Economic Bulletin* (1924 and 1925).
(3.) *The Chinese Economic Monthly* (1923 and 1925).
(4.) J. Edkins, *Chinese Currency* (1901).
(5.) Rea's *Far Eastern Manual* (1923).
(6.) Sir Alexander Hosie, *Szechwan.*

Silver Mining in Kwangsi Province.

Kanning—(Kwangsi). (1911).

The silver mines in the San Ch'a Mountains (三叉山) have been exploited for nearly 16 years, without financial success, by various Chinese companies. It is said that more silver has been put into these mines for machinery, experts, etc., than has ever been taken out. Silver deposits are also found near Kweiping (桂平縣) and in the T'ien P'ing Mountains (天平山), near Kweihsien (貴縣);

the lodes are worked, on the surface only, by a Chinese syndicate with a considerable capital.—(1).

Wuchow—(Kwangsi). (1911).

Mines.—The silver mines at T'ien P'ing Shan (天平山) and San Ch'a Shan (三叉山) were worked by various native syndicates during the past decade, but all to no purpose; for, though the mines undoubtedly contain rich ore, in no one instance, due probably to the lack of proper supervision and to the crude methods of smelting, did the mines prove a financial success, and they are now shut down.—(1).

San Ch'a Mountain Silver Mines.—Location: Near Kweihsien, Kwangsi Province. Remarks: Several different Chinese companies have exploited these mines in the last twenty years, but without financial success. Considerable modern machinery has been used and experts have been employed at different times. It is said that "more silver has been put into these mines for equipment and experts than has been taken out."—(5).

T'ien P'ing Mountain Silver Mines.—Location: Near Kweihsien, Kwangsi Province. Remarks: The lodes are worked on the surface only by a Chinese syndicate, said to have a capital of $2,000,000. A Chinese mining engineer, educated in America, surveyed the field and reported the existence of no less than twenty veins of silver, some of the ore averaging 10 ounces of silver to each 100 pounds of ore. In addition to the silver there are small deposits of gold, copper and lead. The concessionaires planned to turn out 100 tons of ore per day but working reports are not available. —(5).

According to reports emanating from the Chinese Maritime Customs, Wuchow, an attempt was made in 1912 to revive the mine at San Ch'a Shan (三叉山), which, together with that at T'ien P'ing Shan (天平山), formed the enterprise known under the general title of the Kwaiyuen Silver Mine, in which money had been lost by various Chinese companies during the past twenty years,—and a new syndicate with a working capital of $100,000 was formed. During the political troubles in the province, the promoters decamped with all the available funds; subsequently the mine had to be finally abandoned. At the outset the results were promising, but later on the cost of production exceeded the value of silver produced, and by the year 1912 the loss incurred exceeded half a million dollars. The machinery and the methods adopted were rather modern.—(1).

Silver Mining in Chihli Province.

Jehol Silver Mines.—Location: 45 Miles NE of Chengteh (Jehol), Chihli Province. (North of the Great Wall). The mines have been worked by the natives for about 75 years.

Annual Output: 75,000 ounces (average for a period of years). The Jehol Mines embrace two workings, 5 miles apart—the Ku Shan Tze Mine and the Yen Tung Shan Mine.

Geology: The upper part of the vein is galena mixed with iron-stone, and is 2 feet to 4 feet thick. At lower levels the veins are composed of silver-lead ore running between quartz-porphyry walls. Limestone, talc and black shale, colored by graphite are found in other parts of the mine.

Mining: A small inclined shaft, 4 feet by 4 feet, is sunk in the vein stuff where the appearances are most favorable. Another shaft is sunk 20 or 30 yards away for ventilation. The shaft follows the vein in whatever direction it appears to be richest. Timber is used only in soft ground. In some places, instead of using ladders, steps are cut in the rock. The deepest native workings are 400 feet below the surface. As the workings are above water-level, very little water is met with.

Smelting: The ore is first dressed by breaking it into small pieces about 1½-in. square and picking out the waste rock. The waste ore is concentrated by washing. The dressed and concentrated ore is then roasted in a primitive roasting-furnace—a round wall of blue bricks, perforated at intervals to allow the escape of gases. When cold, the roasted ore is transferred to a small smelting-furnace, built of sun-dried bricks, 3 feet high and 1 foot in internal diameter, cone-shaped and open at the top so that the ore and flux can be fed in. Ore and flux are added until there are about 100 lbs. of silver-lead in the bottom. The lead is extracted in the form of a round cake. It is cleaned and transferred to a crude cupel-furnace, about 4 feet long, 3 feet wide and 2½ feet high, and built of rough mud bricks. These furnaces are located in groups of a dozen or more, as occasion may require. The complete cupellation of 100 lbs. of lead takes about 10 hours. When the silver brightens, water is poured on and it is extracted with tongs, washed and cleaned with brushes. It is then cut up, and is ready to be made into sycee-shoes, which weigh from 5 to 50 ounces each. The fineness of the silver is 995.—(5).

Silver Mining in Shantung Province.

Silver Mine discovered at Taian, Shantung.—A silver mine is reported to have been discovered at Kun Li Shan (滚栗山). Taian (泰安), Shantung province. Certain local capitalists have petitioned the Shantung provincial authorities for permission to work the mine, says the "Yih Shih Pao."—(2).

The Paishiling (白石嶺) silver mine is located in the district of Ankiu (安邱), Shantung Province. For more than fifty years, during the reign of the Ming Dynasty, it was under the control of the Imperial household. But at the commencement of the Manchu regime it was abandoned.—(1).

Silver Mining in Szechuen Province.

In the province of Szechuen, at Ningyuan (甯遠) a silver mine is situated, but same is not worked.—(1).

Szechwan, so far as I have been able to ascertain, is not particularly rich in silver ores, but metal is found in the districts situated in the north-west, west, and south-west of the province. They are T'ien-ch'uan Chou, Lu-shan Hsien, and Ta-chien-lu T'ing (in the Ya-chou Prefecture), Sung-p'an T'ing, Li-fan T'ing, Moukung T'ing, Mao Chou, Chiung Chou, and Kuan Hsien, and in Hui-li Chou, Yueh-hsi (sui) T'ing, Yen-yuan Hsien, and Mien-ning Hsien, in the south-western Prefecture of Ning-yuan. The ore is smelted with charcoal in furnaces erected at the mines, and the alloys, such as lead, are removed by means of saltpetre and borax. —(6).

Silver Mining in Kiangsi Province.

Silver Mine in Kiangsi.—Chiang Sze-chih (姜思治) is raising capital to operate a silver mine at Likangshan (裏坑山), Shangyao (上饒), Kiangsi province. The mine has been prospected by an American engineer and reported to be workable, the analysis of the ore showing a good percentage of silver. Several other silver mines have also been reported in the same district.—(2).

Silver Mining in Shansi Province.

In the spring of 1924 a company was organized by Shansi merchants for the purpose of exploiting silver mines at Yinkowtun (銀溝屯) on the border of Chinyuan (沁源) and Hwohsien (霍縣) in the province of Shansi. From the announcement that "over 10,000 dollars capital has been subscribed" it may be inferred that the enterprise is a very small concern.—(1).

Silver Mining in Kwangtung Province.

Lien Chow in Canton Province produces silver. Shun-Te near Canton also produces silver. The white metal was also obtained in Shao-Chou-Fu, a prefecture in the northern part of Kwangtung province. In the southeast part of the same province silver is also found in the prefectures of Hwei-Chou and Ch'ao-Chou. In the western prefectures of Kao-chou and Chao-ch'ing the same mineral occurs.—(4).

Silver Mining in Kirin Province.

Kirin—(Manchuria). (1911).

A silver mine at Shaoerhhata(少爾哈達), situated in the Hwatien district (樺甸縣), will shortly be opened; and a prospecting license for a lead mine at Kwanmatsui (官馬嘴), situated in the Panshih district, was issued a few months ago to a merchant with $100,000 capital.

The T'ien Pao Shan (天寶山) copper and silver mine is the largest and most important in this part of Manchuria, and, in fact, the only one which has been worked on a large scale. It is located in the western part of the district, about 40 miles from Lungchingtsun, and has an altitude of 5,000 feet above sea level.

The mine first began to be worked on a small scale in 1889, only about 40 coolies being employed. Four years after an official in Chutzekai was deputed by the Tartar General in Kirin to raise subscriptions and work it on a large scale. A foreign smelting furnace was purchased, and the number of miners was increased from year to year until at one time some 2,000 were employed. At first the amount of silver produced was small, averaging about 12 taels to 10 piculs of ore; but as the mine was developed the deposits became richer, and although the methods of extraction were very crude, yet at one time 10 piculs of ore produced some 32 taels of silver. Although the ore is richer in copper than in silver, no attempt was made to extract it. After a few years of working, greater difficulties were experienced on account of the accumulation of water in the mine, until after 1897, the work was so retarded that the mine was worked at a loss, and in 1900 it was closed. In 1902 the Tartar General in Kirin sold a concession to an American, and a joint company was formed to work the mine. Before the machinery arrived, however, the Russo-Japanese war broke out, and soon after the Tartar General dying, the company's plans were never realised. In 1907 the local official, who had previously worked the mine, sold a concession to a Japanese company, it being agreed that the work was to be carried on jointly by Chinese and Japanese. Some engineers and miners were brought from Japan; but again work had no more than commenced when the Governor, hearing of it, disclaimed any responsibility for the action of the official, declared the concession to be illegal, and ordered that the mine should be closed. Since then, as the parties concerned have been unable to come to any agreement in regard to working the mine, and as the attempts on the part of the Chinese to buy back the concession have been without avail, the price offered not being acceptable to the Japanese company, the mine has remained closed.—(1).

In Kirin Province, at T'ien Pao Shan, (天寶山) a silver mine is situated, about the prospects of which little is known.—(1).

T'ien Pao Shan Copper and Silver Mine.—Location: T'ien Pao Shan, Yenki, Kirin Province; 40 miles N.W. of Lungchingtsun, and 10 miles S.W. of Laotowkow, Chientao. Operated by the South Manchuria Development (Tashing) Co., a Sino-Japanese concern.

Annual Output.—The ore production increased from 218 tons in 1917, to 10,157 tons in 1920. The ore is copper pyrites and argentine of passable quality and found in fair quantity. The company has a large modern refinery, and operates a trolley line from the mines to the Laotowkow coal-field; completed in 1920.

Light Railway.—The construction of a 68 mile light rail line from the Tumen River bank to T'ien Pao Shan, was ratified by the Peking Government on March 16, 1918, after four years of obstruction on the part of the Kirin provincial authorities, it is now to be carried out.—(5).

The *Chinese Economic Monthly,* in its issue No. 2 of November 1923, gives the following particulars about silver mines in Kirin Province:

District	*Location*	*Area*	*Remarks*
Mengkiang (濛江)	Aherhhung (阿爾蟲)	2,700 mow	1918, Chen Yung-chang (陳用章)
Yenki (延吉)	Tienpaoshan (天寶山)	32,400 „	1916, Liu Shao-wen (劉紹文)
Hwatien (樺甸)	Shaoerhata (少爾哈達)	2,139 „	1918, Sun Wen-pu (孫文圃)
Kirin (吉林)	Kiutai (九台)		Applications for licenses were made prior to the establishment of the Kirin Industrial Commissioner's Office and are still awaiting Government sanction.
Itung (依通)	Heitingtze (黑頂子)		
Do.	Yukiafen (于家墳)		
Do.	Changkiawan (張家灣)		Do.
Do.	Lungwangmiao (龍王廟)		Do.
Mengkiang (濛江)	Shwangkowtze (雙溝子)		Do.
Hwatien (樺甸)	Taipingkow (太平溝)		Do.
Wuchang (五常)	Changshowshan (長壽山)		Do.
Yenki (延吉)	Erhtaokow (二道溝)		Do.
Ningan (甯河)	Yaolungtun (腰龍屯)		Do.
Tungning (東甯)	Laoheishan (老黑山)		Do.
Omu (額穆)	Malukow (馬鹿溝)		Do.
Shwangcheng (雙城)	Kwangtungtzekow (鑛洞子溝)		Do.
Acheng (河城)	Tungtzekow (洞子溝)		Do.

Silver Mining in Yunnan Province.

Ming Hsing Mining Company.—Head Office: Yunnanfu, Yunnan Province. Established: September, 1918, jointly by the Yunnan Provincial Government and the Orient Mines Co., of New York

City. It is a Sino-American enterprise, but the corporation is Chinese, operating under a Chinese charter.

Capital: G.$2,000,000.

Particulars: More than 30 American mining engineers were engaged in the preliminary field work. The forming of the company cost about $1,000,000. It is reported that silver and lead in large deposits have been discovered on the concession.—(5).

Yunnan Ming Hsing Mining Co., Ltd.—Established: at the beginning of 1920 at Tatongchwang, 40 miles north of Tengyueh, Yunnan Province, for the purpose of locating the mother-lode of a silver working; ceased operations in June, 1921.—(5).

Szemao—(Yunnan). (1911).

About 80 *li* north-west of the town of Talang, silver, too, is to be found. A silver mine was secretly opened there by the natives in the reign of Chia Ch'ing (嘉慶), A.D. 1796. It is on record that some travellers passing by that part of the country found by chance two bars of silver. News of this reached the ears of the natives, and, search having proved fruitful, a mine was opened by them. Their luck, however, did not last long, as it was closed soon after by the authorities, on the ground that it had been opened without their knowledge and consent. It seems that from 5 to 8 candareens of silver could be realised from each catty of the ore. To the west of Chenpienting (鎮邊廳), at Monachang (募乃廠), a place bordering on that wild country inhabited by the savage tribe of the Was (猢), there is another important silver mine. It is, however, very little worked, and only enough silver is extracted to meet the needs of the people there. Silver is also found in the neighbourhood of Puerh, but it is not worked to any extent. There are gold, silver, copper, and lead mines in the sub-prefecture of Weiyuan (威遠); but as the officials fear that, if opened, the "foreigners" from the near countries of Burma and Tonkin might come and turn them to their own profit, no work has yet been done.—(1).

Silver Mining in Chahar.

Location: Taoshutisiatseng, Kuyuanhsien (沽源縣,桃樹底下村), owner Yeh Hsiang-lin (葉詳麟). Area 1753 Mow, registered in March, 1924.—(2).

Location: Miaotzekow, Kuyuanhsien (沽源縣,黑河廟子溝), owner Nien Tseng-mou (佟增茂). Area 5400 Mow, registered January, 1923.—(2).

Silver Mining in Hsinkiang.

Silver is produced in small quantities at Yen-chi-hsien (焉耆縣), Hami, Tsi-wei-hsien (且末縣), Wusu (烏蘇), Tihua, Tarbagatai, Eli and Hsi-hu (西湖). The silver mine jointly operated by Sino-Russian interests has been abandoned recently, owing to insufficient output.—(3).

CHAPTER XVI

HONGKONG'S CURRENCY

Historical Retrospect.

HONGKONG, an island in South China, became a British Colony in 1842 in accordance with the treaty of Nanking. In 1861 the peninsula of Kowloon was ceded to Great Britain and is now administered as a portion of the Crown Colony of Hongkong.

Although in fact the colonial possession of a foreign country, Hongkong is, in the full sense of the word, Chinese, though not China. It is Chinese by virtue of its geographical position and owing to its overwhelmingly large Chinese population. Its importance must be ascribed to its enormous trade with China. Consequently its currency has been shaped to harmonise with Chinese ideas and requirements. Therefore it is essential to include in our discussion a short treatise on Hongkong's currency.

Towards the close of the sixteenth century the Spaniards inaugurated trade relations with South China from their base at the Philippine Islands.

From the principal trade centers, Amoy and Canton, the Spanish trade dollar, in course of years, drifted into Hongkong. Soon after the occupation of the Island by the British the Carolus dollar, the Mexican as well as other silver dollars, the rupee issued by the East India Company, and finally the copper cash of China, were all permitted to circulate as legal tender. But by a government proclamation published in April, 1842, the Mexican and other Republican dollars were made the standard currency of Hongkong.

In 1844 the British Government decided that British silver should be the nominal standard for Hongkong, though the currencies already referred to were to be permitted to circulate. Apart from the government offices, where accounts were henceforth kept in sterling, the proclamation remained a dead letter, as the Chinese insisted on ignoring the new proclamation and continued to trade by the intermediary of the silver dollar (see R. Chalmers' *History of Colonial Currency*).

In April, 1853, a law was enacted according to which Hongkong was to have a gold currency. Seeing that the endeavors of the Colonial Office in London bore no fruit and that the Chinese bought and sold in silver dollars only (principally Mexican), the authorities, in 1863, cancelled all previous proclamations regarding currency standards and decreed that the Mexican and other silver dollars of an equivalent value should become the sole legal tender.

In 1866 the Government decided to erect a Mint in Hongkong and to coin there a British dollar. The new coin was designed to be similar in size and weight to the Mexican dollar (0.900 fine, 416 grains weight), and to bear a British emblem. For two years the Mint was worked, but its output did not find favor with the Chinese and was accepted with a discount of 1% and more. Subsequently the Mint was dismantled and sold to the Japanese Government.

In the course of years the British dollar began to find favor with the native population, but the subsidiary coins of 50, 20, 10 and 5 cents depreciated up to 35% at first. Gradually they not only rose to par, but at times even commanded a premium. Altogether 2,108,054 dollars were struck at Hongkong.

In 1895 a new law was passed, in terms of which another British dollar was struck at the Royal Mints in Bombay and Calcutta, and later on also in London. This dollar, equal in weight and fineness to the former British dollar, had meanwhile found great favor, not only in the Colony itself, but equally in North China, where, up to the revolution in 1911, it was imported in huge quantities. It must not be forgotten that up to this day Mexican as well as chopped dollars are still legal tender in Hongkong. Chopped dollars are not taken by count, but by weight only, *viz.*, 717 Canton taels weight are equal to 1,000 dollars. Mexicans have practically vanished from China and are no more met with in Hongkong.

The coins circulating at present officially in Hongkong are:

			Weight		
1 silver dollar,	0.900 fine,	416.	grains or	26.957	grams
50 cents piece	0.800 „	209.52	„ „	13.576	„
20 „ „	0.800 „	83.81	„ „	5.430	„
10 „ „	0.800 „	41.80	„ „	2.715	„
5 „ „	0.800 „	20.95	„ „	1.357	„
1 cent copper piece.					

Hongkong Parities.

Hongkong is a place of great importance to the world's commerce and shipping, and consequently also with regard to finance. There is constant demand not only for Chinese moneys and Saigon piastres, but also for gold currencies of practically all countries. The mint parity between the Saigon piastre and the British dollar is easily established, by taking into consideration that both are 0.900 fine and that the weight of the former is 27 grams, as against the British dollar's weight of 26.9564 grams. The seigniorage on the latter is 2%, and the charges for bringing it to Hongkong about 1%.

As the British dollar is minted outside the Colony, Hongkong does not figure as an importer of bar silver, except for the purpose of transhipment or re-export. Only small lots of bars are retained for industrial purposes.

All silver (bars, chopped dollars, etc.) is weighed at Hongkong with the Canton tael weight and is paid for at the fixed rate of 71.7 Canton taels weight equal to 100 Hongkong dollars, plus a variable market premium. The parity between the Shanghai tael and the Hongkong dollar, on the basis of silver bars and/or sycee shipped from Shanghai to Hongkong, has already been discussed in chapters IX and XI.

Before turning to the discussion of parities between Hongkong dollars and gold currencies it will be advisable to show the cost in Hongkong dollars of coins minted either in India or in London for account of Hongkong.

Minted in London.

Formula I.

? pence	: 1 British dollar
1 British dollar	: 415.985 grains
480 grains	: 1 ounce
925 oz. fine (London)	: 900 oz. fine (Hongkong)
1 ounce	: London price in pence

0.843212 as constant.

Charges are:

Seigniorage	2%
Freight, insurance, brokerage, etc.	1%
Total	3%

The charges, apart from minting charges, are variable. Interest fluctuates according to market rates and must be taken into account. If, for example, 5% for 40 days, the percentage would be 0.555%.

Therefore: Constant	0.843212
Seigniorage 2%	0.001686
Charges (about) 1%	0.008432
Interest 5% 40 days	0.004670
Total	0.858000

This means that one minted British dollar = *0.858 ounces standard silver.*

Minted in Bombay.

For the mint-parity of British dollars coined in India turn to:

Formula II.

? rupees	: 1 British dollar
1 British dollar	: 415.985 grains
998 grains (English silver)	: 900 grains (Hongkong dollars)
180 grains	: 1 tola
100 tolas	: Price in rupees of silver

0.02084 as constant.

Multiply the constant by the Bombay price for 100 tolas of bar silver, 0.998 fine, in order to obtain the mint parity between the British dollar and the rupee.

The Bombay Mint charges for seigniorage 2%. Expenses fluctuate and may be taken at about 1%. Interest varies considerably. Say, for 30 days, at the rate of 6% per annum, *i.e.* ½% per mensem.

Constant	0.02084
Seigniorage 2%	0.00417
Charges, etc., 1% (variable)	0.00208
Interest, say 6% for 30 days	0.00104
Total	0.02813

T.T. Parity London–Hongkong.

These calculations refer to the import of British dollars from London or Bombay. If it is required to establish the parity between London T.T. and Hongkong currency, take the constant from Formula I and add charges and interest (both fluctuating).

Constant	0.843212
Charges, interest, brokerage, landing, etc., say 2%	0.016864
Total	0.860076

Multiply by the London price for bar silver, in order to obtain the equivalent of Hongkong telegraphic transfer on London.

There is another method of finding the parity between Hongkong currency and T.T. on London.

Formula III.

? pence	:	1 Hongkong dollar
Hongkong price for bar silver	:	71.7 Canton taels weight
1 Canton tael weight	:	1.208 ounces
1,000 ounces silver	:	998 ounces fine
925 ounces fine	:	1,000 ounces standard
1 ounce standard	:	London price in pence

$$X = 93.45 \times \frac{\text{London price per ounce standard}}{\text{Hongkong price for bar silver.}}$$

When the quotation for cable transfer Hongkong–London is known, it will be possible to find the parity rate for bar silver in London by means of

Formula IV.

? pence	:	1 ounce standard
1000 ounces standard	:	925 ounces fine
998 ounces fine	:	1000 ounces bar silver
1208 ounces troy	:	1000 Canton taels weight
71.7 Canton taels weight	:	100 Hongkong dollars, plus the premium
1 Hongkong dollar	:	*X* pence (T.T. Hongkong–London)

$$X = \frac{925 \times 1000 \times 1000 \times 100 \text{ Hongkong \$ (plus premium)} \times \text{T.T. London}}{1000 \times 998 \times 1208 \times 71.7}$$

In order to complete the chain of parities it is thought advisable to add

Formula V.

? Hongkong dollars	:	1 ounce of bar silver (0.998 fine)
1.208 ounces troy	:	1 Canton tael weight
717 Canton taels weight (0.998 fine)	:	1000 Hongkong dollars

$$X = \frac{1000}{1.208 \times 717} = 1.15455309 \text{ as constant.}$$

Regarding Hongkong's relations to bar silver we refer the reader to the exhaustive description of conditions prevailing there, as set forth in chapter IX, "Bar Silver and China," under the sub-heading "Export of Bar Silver from Shanghai to Hongkong and Canton."

Parity New York–Hongkong.

As to the parity between Hongkong currency and T.T. on U.S.A. refer to

Formula VI.

? U.S. dollars	: 1 Hongkong dollar
Hongkong price of silver in dollars	: 71.7 Canton taels weight
1 Canton tael weight	: 1.208 ounces
1 ounce 0.999 fine	: New York price of silver

$$X = 86.70 \times \frac{\text{New York price of silver}}{\text{Hongkong price of silver}}$$

Parity India–Hongkong.

The parity between the Indian rupee and the Hongkong dollar on the basis of bar silver is derived from

Formula VII.

? rupees	: 100 Hongkong dollars
Hongkong price for bar silver	: 71.7 Canton taels weight
1 Canton tael	: 1.208 ounces
0.375 ounces	: 1 tola
100 tolas	: Price of bar silver in rupees

$$X = 230.9 \times \frac{\text{Price of bar silver in rupees}}{\text{Hongkong price for bar silver}}$$

Export of British Dollars from Hongkong.

In 1922 the export of silver coins from Hongkong was forbidden by proclamation. Before the World War huge quantities were shipped out of Hongkong, notably to North China, where they were very popular, often commanding a premium. The transaction resolved itself in a simple question of arbitrage. As long as cover in the shape of telegraphic transfer on Hongkong (either direct from Tientsin or *via* Shanghai) was obtainable against taels, at a rate below the one obtainable for the imported dollars, it was possible to do the business.

Since the embargo was imposed, the public was forced to recognise that the payment in banknotes is the basis for all exchange and business operations; hence it follows that in finding the exchange parity between Hongkong and London, besides the charges as set up in Formula II to be added to the constant, the premium or discount of Hongkong banknotes must also be added to, or substracted from, the above sum, as the case may be.

The proclamation concerning the embargo on the export from Hongkong of silver coins is hereby quoted *verbatim:*

Hongkong Government Gazette, June 30, 1922.

Order made by the Governor in Council under Sections three and four of the Importation and Exportation Ordinance, 1915, Ordinance No. 32 of 1915, on April 13, 1922.

I. (1) No person shall, except with the express permission of the Superintendent, *export* any of the following articles to any destination:—

Hongkong silver subsidiary coins, provided that a bona fide traveller leaving the Colony may take with him Hongkong silver subsidiary coins of the total face value of not more than fifty dollars.

Silver dollars. Provided that this paragraph shall not apply to Chinese dollars, or to silver dollars which pass through the waters of the Colony in transit, that is to say, without landing or transshipment.

II. No person shall, except with the express permission of the Superintendent, export any Chinese cash except to China.

Banknotes Issue in Hongkong.

Banknotes in Hongkong are being issued by British banks only, in denominations of dollars 1,000, 500, 100, 50, 25, 10, 5 and 1. The Colonial Government controls the issue and demands adequate reserves in the shape of bullion, coin or government securities, usually up to two-thirds of the amount of notes in circulation. This rule refers to the issues of the Hongkong and Shanghai Banking Corporation and also to the banknotes issued by the Chartered Bank of India, Australia and China, but not to the circulation of the Mercantile Bank of India. The latter is required to deposit at all times with the Crown Agents securities to be approved by the Secretary of State, to an amount equal in value to the face value of the notes in circulation, with the addition of 5 per cent. of such value or, at its option, the company shall deposit, and at all times keep deposited, with the Treasurer, coin which is unlimited legal tender in the Colony to an amount equal to the face value of the notes in circulation; or at its like option the company shall deposit and at all times keep deposited securities, so approved as aforesaid with the Crown Agents, and coin, which is unlimited legal tender in the Colony, with the Treasurer, in which case the amount of such securities shall be equal in value to the difference between the amount of the coin deposited and the face value of the notes in circulation with the addition of 5 per cent.

Returns of the Average Amount of Bank Notes in circulation and of specie in Reserve in Hongkong during the month ended 30th April 1925, as certified by the Managers of the respective Banks.

(Hongkong Government Gazette, May 8, 1925).

Banks.	*Average Amount.*	*Specie in Reserve.*
Chartered Bank of India, Australia & China	$11,133,438	$5,000,000 [1]
Hongkong & Shanghai Banking Corporation	39,090,933	29,900,000 [2]
Mercantile Bank of India, Ltd.	1,240,510	550,000 [3]
Total . .	51,464,881	35,450,000

In 1922 the Hongkong and Shanghai Banking Corporation applied for an amendment of its statutes of 1866. The amendment contains details regarding issue of banknotes and reserves to be held against the issue. It is here quoted in full:

[1] Sterling Securities deposited with the Crown Agents valued at £1,044,300.
[2] Securities with the Crown Agents and Straits Government £3,091,000.
[3] Securities with the Crown Agents £130,000 in 5½% Treasury Bonds repayable @ 100 in 1930, present price 101½—102.

To all whom it may concern.

NOTICE is hereby given that the Hongkong and Shanghai Banking Corporation intends at an early date to apply to the Legislative Council of Hongkong for a Bill authorizing the Corporation from time to time to increase the capital of the Corporation from the existing limit of $20,000,000 to a total of $50,000,000 and to increase its ordinary note issue to $20,000,000 and making certain modifications in the existing requirements as regards the deposit of security in respect of its note issue.

Dated 17th day of February, 1922.

JOHNSON, STOKES & MASTER,
Solicitors for and on behalf of
The Hongkong & Shanghai Banking Corporation.

A BILL INTITULED

An Ordinance to amend the Hongkong & Shanghai Bank Ordinance, 1866.

Be it enacted by the Governor of Hongkong, with the advice and consent of the Legislative Council thereof, as follows:

I. (1.) This Ordinance may be cited as the Hongkong & Shanghai Bank Amendment Ordinance, 1922.

(2.) The Hongkong & Shanghai Banking Bank Ordinance 1866, hereinafter referred to as the principal Ordinance and the Hongkong & Shanghai Bank amendment Ordinance, 1914, and this Ordinance, may be cited together as the Hongkong & Shanghai Bank Ordinances 1866 to 1922.

II. Section 13 of the principal Ordinance is repealed and the following section is substituted therefore:—

Re Limit of amount of issue of bills and notes.

13 (1.) The total amount of the bills and notes of the company payable to bearer on demand actually in circulation shall not at any time exceed the sum of 20,000,000 dollars.

Re Security required in respect of ordinary note issue.

(2). The Company shall at all times keep deposited, either with the Crown Agents or with trustees to be appointed by the Secretary of State, or partly with the Crown Agents and partly with such trustees, coin of denominations to be approved by the Secretary of State, or, at the option of the company securities to be so approved, or, at the like option, partly such coin and partly such securities, equal to two-thirds of the said amount of $20,000,000, such coin or securities or such coin and securities to be held by the Crown Agents or by the said trustees, separately or jointly as special funds exclusively available for the redemption of the bills and notes payable to bearer on demand issued by the Company, and, in the event of the company becoming insolvent, to be applied accordingly so far as may be necessary, but without prejudice to the rights of the holders of such bills and notes to rank with other creditors of the company against the assets of the company.

Re Security required in respect of excess note issue.

(3.) Notwithstanding the restriction imposed by sub-section (1) of this section upon the total number of the bills and notes of the company payable to bearer on demand actually in circulation, bills and notes of the company payable to bearer on demand may be issued and be in actual circulation to an amount in excess of the said sum of 20,000,000 dollars if there has been specially deposited and is kept in the custody of the Colonial Secretary and the Colonial Treasurer an amount of coin, or bullion, or coin and bullion, equal to the whole value of such excess issue for the time being actually in circulation, to be held by the said Colonial Secretary and Colonial Treasurer exclusively for the redemption of such bills and notes, wherever the same may have been issued; Provided nevertheless that nothing herein contained shall exempt the company from the operation of any laws restricting or regulating the issue of bills or notes in the Colony or in any place outside the Colony where the company has banks or branch banks.

Part of security for excess note issue may be kept in such places and under such conditions as the Governor may approve.

(4.) Notwithstanding anything contained in sub-section (3) of this section, portions of the security in coin or bullion provided for by the said sub-section may be kept deposited in such places outside the Colony, with such persons, to such amounts, and subject to such conditions, as may at any time and from time to time be approved by the Governor.

Amendment of Ordinance No. 2 of 1866, s. 22.

III. Section 22 of the principal Ordinance is amended as follows:

(*a*) 50,000,000 is substituted for 20,000,000 in the eleventh line thereof.

(*b*) 20,000,000 is substituted for 10,000,000 in the fifteenth line thereof.

(*c*) The second proviso thereto, that is to say, all the words after the words "herein provided" in the eighteenth line thereof, is repealed.

Saving of the rights of the Crown and of certain other rights.

IV. Nothing in this Ordinance shall affect or be deemed to affect the rights of His Majesty the King, His heirs and successors, or the rights of any body politic or corporate or of any other person, except such as are mentioned in this Ordinance and those claiming by from or under them.

Objects and Reasons.

(1.) The objects of this bill are:—

(*a*) To give the Corporation power to increase its capital, with the consent of the Governor, up to $50,000,000. The present limit is $20,000,000.

(*b*) So increase the limit of the ordinary note issue from $15,000,000 to $20,000,000.

(*c*) To revise the requirements of the law as to the security to be held against the ordinary note issue.

(*d*) To enable the Corporation to keep at certain places outside the Colony part of the security held against the excess note issue.

(2.) Under the existing law the excess note issue must be fully covered by coin or bullion, under the control of custodians independent of the Corporation, and this will be so under the new Ordinance also. In future, however, the excess note issue will mean any issue in excess of $20,000,000 instead of $15,000,000 as at present.

(3.) The present requirements of the law as to the security to be held against the ordinary note issue are that coins or securities approved by the Secretary of State must be kept with the Crown Agents, or with trustees appointed by the Secretary of State, equal in value to one-third of the first $10,000,000 of the issue, and that the remaining $5,000,000 of the issue must be fully covered by such coin or securities, so deposited. The new Ordinance will provide simply that two-thirds of the ordinary issue, which issue will in future amount to $20,000,000, must be so covered.

(4.) The comparison between the existing law and the new Ordinance can also be made in the following way, as regards the first $20,000,000 of the total issue.

Security under present law:—

1/3rd of $10,000,000 *in coin or securities.*
— $ 5,000,000 *in coin or securities.*
— $ 5,000,000 *in coin or bullion.*

Security under *new* Ordinance:—

2/3rds of $20,000,000 *in coin or securities.*

It will thus be seen that the value of the security will not be altered, but that the Corporation will be relieved from the necessity of keeping coin or bullion against any part of the first $20,000,000 of the total note issue.

(5.) It will be noted that one provision disappears in the proposed new section 13, *i.e.*, the requirement of the latter part of the present section 13 (I) that the Corporation must keep at each of its establishments an amount of coin or bullion equal in value to one-third at least of the notes issued from such establishment and actually in circulation. It is considered that this may be left to the discretion of the Corporation.

(6.) Sub-section (4) of section 13 will enable the Corporation, subject in all respects to the approval of the Governer, to keep, in places outside the Colony where notes may be issued by the Corporation, part of the excess note issue security, which must of course be in coin or bullion. The bringing of this section into practical operation is of course dependent upon the arrangement of a satisfactory scheme for the custody of the coin or bullion.

(7.) Clause 4 is the usual saving clause.

SECTION 3

COPPER AND COPPER COINAGE

CHAPTER XVII

OLD CHINESE COPPER COINAGE

Introductory.

FOR thousands of years copper currency has formed the principal medium of circulation in China. The subject deserves therefore close investigation and discussion. While there exists but scanty literature on the use of the precious metals for currency purposes in China, it should be emphasised that the topic of copper currency within the country has been very exhaustively and ably dealt which by authoritative writers. It stands to reason that while bronze and copper coins have been the mute witnesses of the vicissitudes of a country's development during thousands of years, the shape, the design and the composition have been subjected to considerable changes. It will readily be understood that the extent of varieties within the realm of China's copper coinage is colossal, thus forming an inexhaustible source for research by the archæologist, the historian and, above all, the numismatist. China's copper coinage has hardly any direct bearing on world commerce, and neither does it offer a field of activity to the international arbitragist. These facts absolve us from the advisability of attempting to enter into a discussion of the details pertaining to the development of China's copper currency, notwithstanding the fact that copper coins have formed the principal medium of exchange in China for many centuries; even to this day the currency of the Chinese people consists indisputably of copper coins.

Another factor, which absolves us from the task of attempting a detailed discussion of China's copper coinage, is to be found in the existence of excellent works on this particular subject. These have served as the principal source of information for the succeeding brief outline of China's ancient copper coinage. The following are some of the authentic works, to which the reader is referred for more detailed and authoritative information:

Catalogue of Chinese Coins, from the seventh century B.C. to A.D. 621, by Terrien de Lacouperie, London, 1892.

The Stewart Lockhart Collection of Chinese Coins, by Sir James H. Stewart Lockhart. Kelly & Walsh, Ltd., Shanghai, 1915.

Chinese Early Barter and Uninscribed Money, by H. A. Ramsden, Jun Kobayagawa Co., Yokohama, 1912.

China's ancient copper (bronze) coins were cast from copper mined within the country. Practically all of China's "cash" coins,—not to speak of the ancient *knife*—and *Pu-money*—was cast in moulds, and not struck by machinery. The moulds were in stone, in earthenware, beaten clay, bronze, and sometimes, but rarely, in iron. The casting of the coins was carried out singly or in pairs, or in a circle, or arranged in clusters like a tree with its branches.

Originally, merchants' guilds and town communities were at liberty to issue their own copper coins, bearing a distinctive symbol. This prerogative was, however, subject to the regulation by the State of pattern and weight of the coinage. In 336 B.C. the State itself issued round bronze coins. There are undoubted proofs existing regarding the prevalence during the entire history of Chinese copper coinage of counterfeiting.

Origin of Metallic Money in China.

The investigation regarding the earliest attempts on the part of ancient China to introduce metallic currency, is rendered exceedingly difficult by the absence of authoritative evidence. The only available sources of information on this particular subject are the old Chinese chronicles which unfortunately are not always convincingly accurate and which, moreover, differ frequently in their estimates. According to the *Shih Chi* (史記) or Historical Records of *Ssu-ma Ch'ien,* it is stated that the media of exchange of the emperor *Shun,* (2255 B.C.), and of the *Hsia* dynasty, (1105–1818 B.C.), were three kinds of metal: yellow (gold); white (silver); and red (copper).[1] Copper money is said to have then existed in three categories, namely *Ch'ien* (錢); *Pu* (布); and *Dao* (刀).

The author of the *Pen Ts'ao Kang Mu* (本草綱目), maintains that the origin of money in China was the casting of *Pi* (幣) by the emperor *Yu* (禹), who ruled 2205–2197 B.C. The purpose of casting metallic money was supposed to have been connected with the intention to relieve the distress caused by five successive years of drought. The production of metallic currency ceased with the disappearance of the drought.

Another Chinese writer[2] asserts that money first came into existence during the reign of *T'ai Hao* (太昊), *i.e.,* from 2953 B.C., onwards. The second coin is supposed to have been cast 2838 B.C. These statements can hardly be supported by historical data. Therefore more weight is attached to the theory, according to which the first *Pu* coins were created 2255 B.C.

According to Terrien de Lacouperie *(Catalogue of Chinese Coins,* London, 1892), the first attempt to introduce metallic currency in ancient China dates back to about 1100 B.C. In the *Tsien Han Shu* (The Annals of the former Han Dynasty) the historical statement is contained that ". . . gold was in square inch, weighing one *kin,* bronze money was round (or in rings), tongue-

---

[1] *The Stewart Lockhart Collection of Chinese Coins.* (Kelly & Walsh, Ltd. Shanghai, 1915.)

[2] Ma Tuan Lin, in *Wen Hsien T'ung Kao,* published in A.D. 1321.

like (or in boards) and in squares (or ingots) and their weight was ascertained by *tchus*."

The beginnings of coinage in the Occident dates back to 750 B.C., when *Pheidon*, King of Argos, established a Mint for metallic currency. Those early coins were bean-shaped, stamped with a distinctive emblem and minted from silver and also from electrum.

From these statements it may be deduced that China was the first of all the countries in the world to create a metallic currency.

Uninscribed Barter Money.

The original and primitive metallic currency of ancient China appeared at first as articles of utility and primitive ornaments, and was by natural growth slowly transformed into inscribed money. The historian chronicles that the very first specimens of bronze money were round. There is abundant evidence available that these token coins were really armlets or rings of bronze, used as ornaments, without any emblem or legend. This primitive money was the precursor of the first inscribed round bronze coins, with a hole in the center, which gradually developed into the familiar *cash*.

The population of ancient China lived principally on the production of the soil. Hence an implement which was universally employed was the spade. Owing to its convenient size it lent itself as medium of exchange. So it came about that the bronze spade, in its original size and uninscribed, became a recognised medium of currency in that primitive age. Probably it will be more correct to substitute the word "currency" by "barter."

At first the spade was employed for daily use and simultaneously as recognised medium for barter. Gradually spades were produced which, though retaining their original sizes, ceased to be implements, becoming measures of value, yet still without distinctive marks. This particular "currency" became the forerunner of the inscribed spade money.

Another implement which was universally used, already during early civilization in China, is the knife. It was made of one piece and employed for domestic as well as for hunting purposes; special types of knives served for the incision of ideographic inscriptions on bamboo or bone. Knives originating from that prehistoric period were characterised by the handle ending in a circular ring. Those implements served practical purposes and became a recognised medium for barter. They were precursory to the inscribed knife money of ancient China.

Amongst the oldest implements employed in ancient China were bells of various shapes. Apparently these were found suitable for the purpose of barter. Many kinds of bells of a prehistoric age, too miniature for practical use, have been found in China, thus strengthening the assumption that bells have served as a medium of exchange.

Other media of barter were uninscribed bronze articles, as for instance, tablets with dragon designs, metallic seals, arrow heads, miniature shields, flat discs, etc. The best known of the small objects which, on account of their metallic value, have served as currency media, are familiar under the style of bridge money. In ancient China the cicada was closely connected with immortality, and thus it is not strange that this particular insect was used as model for barter money. Made of bronze it served also practical purposes by being fastened to wearing apparel as buttons or ornaments.

Inscribed Early Coins.

Somewhat more authentic particulars are available regarding China's early inscribed copper (bronze) coinage. The first round coin with inscription was turned out under the rule of *Ch'eng Wang* (成王), 1115–1079 B.C., of the *Chou* dynasty. The coin just referred to exists in various collections and undoubtedly was originated during the *Chou* dynasty, but if it is considered that the reign of that dynasty lasted from 1122–255 B.C., it is quite feasible that—as some writers assert—the first round coins in China were produced only in *c.* 660 B.C. The coin referred to is about one inch in diameter and has a square hole in the center. The obverse bears two Chinese characters, of which one is 寶 (valuable) and the other 化 (coin); the reverse is uninscribed.

The round coin issued next is supposed to date back to *c.* 540 B.C. It shows on the obverse the character for "valuable," and besides 四化 meaning "coin exchangeable for four."

Inscribed spade money dates back to *c.* 600 B.C. On the obverse of the earliest specimen is to be found as legend the name of the city in which the money was produced, and besides the character 化, denoting its function as a coin. The reverse was adorned usually by three perpendicular lines. From the inscription of the earliest spade money it may be gathered that it originated in Shantung province. One of the early specimens bears the characters for "officially examined," which probably means that the coin was issued with the Government's approval. Similar spade money was produced in Honan and Shansi provinces.

Spade money developed gradually into *Pu* coins with either square or pointed feet. As far as can be ascertained *Pu* money made its first appearance *c.* 475 B.C.

The introduction of inscribed *knife money* dates back to *c.* 680 B.C. It undoubtedly had its origin in the archaic knife money which, in prehistoric times, served as a measure of value for barter. Inscribed knife money distinguishes itself from its contemporaries by its precise inscriptions, indicating that it represents token money, besides showing the place of issue.

The legend on the obverse on the original issues reads, when translated: "Valuable coin of the State of *Ch'i,*" (by which is meant the present province of Shantung). The reverse bears merely the character 化 (coin), and a few ornamental lines.

In 221 B.C. the king of *Ts'in*[1] assumed the title of *She Hwan-ti* (the first universal emperor). At that occasion the use of cowries, tortoise-shells, pearls, gems and tin for currency purposes was prohibited. A new and more convenient bronze coinage, inscribed "B'an liang," (meaning half a tael in weight) in round pieces with a square hole, was introduced instead.

The successor of the *Ts'in* dynasty was the Western *Han* dynasty which provided China with fifteen rulers, between 206 B.C. to A.D. 24. They began their rule by giving permission to the people to cast their own metallic currency. Due to the absence of an official standard there was soon an odd variety of small coins, irregular in weight, size and design; some of these coins were quite plain, while others bore the legend "B'an liang" on the obverse.

In 186 B.C. empress *Liu Shih Kao Hou* ordered the issue of bronze coins weighing eight *tchu,* which were equal in value to the half-ounce currency of the preceding dynasty.[2] The new money was supposed to take the place of the irregular issues; but the circulation of the latter was so profuse that it had to remain in use. The employment of a thoroughly debased coinage caused so much harm that it induced emperor *Heng Hiao Wen-ti,* in 175 B.C., to have new coins cast. These weighed only four *tchu,* but nevertheless they had the same former legend inscribed which read "B'an liang" (half an ounce). The minting was then allowed as a private enterprise. But the irregularities thereupon grew so glaring that steps had to be taken officially to have counterfeiting stopped, by forbidding the private casting of coins.

[1] The Ts'in dynasty ruled from 255 B.C. to 206 B.C.

[2] Terrien de Lacouperie.

The "B'an liang" currency in circulation had, through excessive debasement, deteriorated to such an extent, that it was decided by the authorities to withdraw all the metallic currency from circulation, in order to replace it by a uniform coin. In 118 B.C. the famous *Wu-tschu cash,* the standard coin of the *Han* dynasty, was created. It succeeded to remain in uninterrupted circulation for seven hundred years, notwithstanding other coinages which were occasionally attempted.

In spite of the initial success which accompanied the *Wu-tschu cash* the legion of counterfeiters grew stronger from day to day, their number was reputed, about 40 B.C., to have exceeded 100,000 persons. The disorders brought about by their malicious practices were so great that counsellors of the throne pleaded for the abolishment of metallic currency and its replacement by silk, grain, cloth and tortoise-shell, as in vogue in byegone centuries. After careful consideration it was determined to continue the circulation of metallic currency.

Copper Coinage since the beginning of the Christian Era.

The emperor *Ping-ti* was a boy of only nine years of age when he ascended the throne. This was in A.D. 2. Four years thereafter he was poisoned by his Prime Minister, *Siu Wang Mang,* who thereupon usurped the throne. *Wang Mang,* in A.D. 7, declared the decrees of the *Han* dynasty, relative to the coinage, null and void; at the same time he expressed the desire to revert to the coinage system of the *Tchou* dynasty.

The new ruler introduced the old *knife* money in a somewhat different and more convenient shape. The handle of the *knife* money was a regular round coin of the familiar *cash* pattern, bearing the inscription *"K'i-dao,"* while a second kind was inscribed with *"I-dao."* The blade of the knife was immediately connected with the round coin and showed on the obverse the legend "Five hundred" in the first, and "Equal to five thousand" in the other instance. The reverse remained plain. Besides these pieces *Wang Mang* placed into circulation six series of new coins. In A.D. 10 he suppressed the *knife* money which, only two years previously, had been inaugurated by himself.

The coins issued during the later *Han* dynasty (A.D. 25–220), as well as those circulated by the minor *Han* dynasty (A.D. 223–262), were of the familiar *cash* pattern, based on the *Wu tchu* (5 tchu) piece. These coins were rich in variations, but all of them, as well as the succeeding issues, until A.D. 454, were characterised by having a legend on the obverse only, while the reverse remained blank.

At the beginning of his reign *Sung Hiao Wu-ti* issued, in A.D. 454, a new currency, which showed on the obverse the year of issue and on the reverse—for the first time—the denomination, "four tchu."

The story of the development of China's bronze currency is a long one, but it concerns chiefly the realm of numismatics. It will therefore be permissible to be brief here. The army of counterfeiters, which has always been more or less active within the country, grew alarmingly bold in the period of about A.D. 500. The practice of issuing coins with inscriptions on both the obverse and reverse was soon abandoned in favor of the original order of things.

The five tchu money, after having circulated in China for seven hundred years, came to an end with the *Sui* dynasty in A.D. 618.

With the inauguration of the *T'ang* dynasty, in A.D. 618, begins the Golden Age of China. The copper coinage issued by that dynasty is distinguished from its predecessors by the inscription in modern square characters. as compared with the ancient seal script to be found on all previous issues of Chinese coins. Furthermore, the coins issued by the *T'ang* dynasty were 24.13 mm. in diameter, a size which remained the standard for many succeeding centuries. The first Chinese copper coins which were inscribed with the title of the ruling emperor, were cast during the reign of *Kien Feng*, A.D. 666–668.

During these remote ages the quantity of coinage actually in circulation was comparatively small. This fact may be explained by circumstances which made an extensive use of coins unnecessary. Government dues were then payable in kind, in silk or in grain. Trade and means of communications were undeveloped, and the usual manner of exchange was barter. Under the *T'ang* dynasty commerce developed rapidly, which event brought about a much enlarged circulation of copper coins. It must be admitted that, until the end of the nineteenth century, none of the Chinese government authorities have attempted to derive profits from coinage.

The variations to be found in the composition and inscription of Chinese copper coins of the *cash* pattern, issued in course of the following thousand years, are immense. Their description is not within the realm of this essay and is therefore left to the numismatist for investigation.

With the advent of the entry into China of the Manchus as rulers, from A.D. 1616 onwards, the copper coins almost invariably show on the obverse inscriptions in Manchu.

In 1851 the *T'aiping* rebellion broke out, lasting until 1864. The originator, *Hung Hsiu Ch'uan*, declared himself emperor, adopting the dynastic title of "The Celestial Kingdom of Great Peace." Eight copper coins of the usual *cash* pattern were cast during the *T'aiping's* regime. They are distinguished by their inscriptions, some of which read: "Sacred coinage of the Celestial Kingdom;" or, "Celestial Kingdom of great peace;" or, "Sacred coinage;" or, "Currency of the Emperor."

The rightful ruler, *Hsien Feng*, had to undergo serious difficulties while the *T'aiping* rebellion lasted. Owing to much reduced government revenues, and also on account of the impossibility to obtain sufficient supplies of copper, the Treasury had, for the first time in China's history, to have recourse to the issue of token coins. These latter were cast in multiples of the original *cash,* namely in the following denominations 5, 8, 10, 20, 30, 50, 100, 200, 500 and 1,000 *cash.*[1]

The idea of using token coins was strange to the Chinese people and has remained so to this day. Therefore it is not to be wondered at that they soon disappeared from circulation. Only the 10 *cash* coin survived and became the principal medium of circulation in Peking for about sixty years. Yet the 10 *cash* piece was never accepted there at its inscribed value, but instead at its intrinsic worth, which is subjected to constant fluctuations.

All the copper *cash* coins issued in China were cast in moulds, except one single specimen which, in about 1890, was struck by modern minting machinery in Canton. It failed, however, to find popular favor and its existence was therefore only shortlived. This particular coin was the last specimen of the *cash* pattern with a square hole in the center.

In the beginning of the twentieth century one could still find in actual circulation copper *cash,* the origin of which dates back a thousand years.

With the appearance in China of modern copper coins (without hole in the center) all further supply of *cash* coins ceased. Existing stocks gradually went out of circulation, in the same measure as the price of copper made the melting down of coins profitable. During the World War the market value of copper rose by leaps and bounds. This was the signal (in 1915) for an organised campaign to collect all the old copper coins that became available and melt them down for export abroad, notwithstanding the existing embargo regarding the melting down of coins and the shipping of copper from China.

[1] H.B. Morse *The Trade and Administration of the Chinese Empire.* Kelly & Walsh, Limited, Shanghai, 1908.

By the end of 1925 the old copper *cash* was still current in China, though the total amount in actual circulation was then not large.

Other base metals used for coinage.

In order to complete the discussion of China's metallic currencies this chapter is supplemented by a brief reference to other base metals which, at one time or another, have served coinage purposes.

In the year 120 B.C. coins were cast by *Hsia Wu-ti* in *white metal.* They were in circulation for five years only and consisted of a series in three denominations. The first coin was inscribed "3000 *ch'ien*"; it was round in shape and showed a dragon as emblem. The second piece was of a value of 500 *ch'ien;* its shape was a square, ornamented by a horse. The third kind was oblong, worth 300 *ch'ien* and embellished with the shell of a tortoise.

Lead was only rarely employed for coinage purposes. According to Chinese writers a coin made of lead by emperor *Hsuan-ti* (Northern *Chou* dynasty) was issued in A.D. 579.

Brass has been largely used for the manufacture of *cash* coins, especially in modern times.

Iron was used during exceptional times for coinage purposes in China. It was probably first employed in this capacity in 206 B.C. After *Kung Sun Shuh* had taken possession, in 23 B.C., of Szechuan province, he issued iron coins there, prohibiting the use of bronze coins. The people objected to the innovation which therefore lasted for a short period only.

In A.D. 523, during the *Liang* dynasty, iron money was issued which bore the inscription "Greatly lucky" and "5 *Chu.*" In A.D. 527 another issue of iron money was made with the legend "5 *Chu* of (the) *Tatung* (period)." Two iron coins were to be of the value of one copper coin. But as iron could be procured cheaply, counterfeiters became very active and flooded the market with spurious coins. In A.D. 546 the iron currency was only worth one-third of its original value. Iron coins became therefore most unpopular and had to be gradually replaced by copper pieces. In the course of the tenth century iron money was in general circulation in Western China.

For the last time there was an issue of iron coins during the *T'aiping* rebellion (1851–1864) when, owing to a shortage of copper, emperor *Hsien Feng* was forced to issue iron money. In 1857 the people rose in protest, whereupon the new measure had to be withdrawn.

CHAPTER XVIII

MODERN CHINESE COPPER COINAGE

The Authorities determine to discontinue the ancient coinage.

FROM the brief description contained in the preceding chapter it will have been inferred that currency conditions in China, as far as they related to copper coinage, have remained practically unchanged during two thousand years. The unsettled state of the huge country, its seclusion from Western civilisation and its conservative attitude in general, were some of the factors responsible for the existence and maintenance of a prehistoric currency system which succeeded in lasting practically changeless until the commencement of the twentieth century.

After having been in touch for centuries with Western nations, and after having had the opportunity of observing the advantages which a regulated currency system provides, it began to dawn on the Chinese authorities that the country's coinage was cumbersome and disadvantageous. All the copper *cash* were cast in moulds and not struck by machinery, a factor which facilitated counterfeiting. This malpractice was flourishing in China at all times, to the great detriment of the nation as a whole. *Chang Chi T'ung*, one of the most enlightened statesmen China ever possessed, introduced the first modern minting plant in Canton (A.D. 1889), at a time when he was viceroy there. But the real impetus for the discontinuance of the archaic copper coinage was the outbreak of the Boxer movement, as a result of which many far-reaching reforms were initiated. One of the most important amongst these was the determination to discontinue the casting of copper *cash* and the substitution of the latter by modern copper coins.

Disadvantages of the antiquated copper-cash.

In prehistoric times, when trade within China was still undeveloped, primitive bronze coinage may have answered the modest requirements of the country. It is, therefore, unnecessary to enlarge here on a subject which, being self-satisfied with its achievements, needs no elucidation. On the other hand it is very interesting to review the status of the *cash* currency in the second half of the nineteenth century, a period which followed more than 200 years after the opening of direct foreign trade relations.

The succeeding examples are some of the characteristic circumstances connected with the circulation of China's antiquated bronze coinage as they presented themselves to the observer in A.D. 1900. The instances cited here are merely instances for the shortcomings of an unscientific system. They are not systematically arranged, but taken at random, solely for the purpose of recording some of the peculiarities of a method which dominated China for thousands of years; and which had been restlessly striving for a complete change of basic conditions. Radical alterations in China's copper coinage have since been accomplished,—hypothetically for the better, yet in practice far from ideal. But this is another story which it is not intended to relate at this stage.

All the *cash* coins circulating in China were provided with a square hole in the center; the opening was meant to facilitate the stringing of the coins. Each string was supposed to contain 100 *cash* coins, and 10 such strings formed one *tiao*. In Tientsin, for instance, in A.D. 1900, each *tiao* consisted of ten strings containing 974 good *cash* reckoned as full thousand. In every *tiao* there were eight strings, each containing 98 coins, and besides two strings, each consisting of 95 coins only. The latter was styled

"Tidze" and was known by a knot on the end of every string. Every string was permitted to contain two or three counterfeit coins; in fact the percentage was usually larger than that.

The quantity of spurious *cash* coins actually found in circulation was so large that they were often sorted out and strung separately. They had a market value according to their intrinsic worth.

So, for instance, was there a counterfeit coin, made of red copper and called "Hung Ch'ien." The best quality of these used to pass as 900 for 1000 adulterated *cash;* the medium grade of the same coin was accepted at 800 good *cash* for 1000 spurious coins, while 1000 of the poorest quality were counted as 700 good *cash.* There were various other kinds of spurious *cash* coins in large quantities in circulation which had a market value according to the quality of the ingredients.

The peculiarities of the *cash* coinage system showed their effects in a hundred ways, and it would lead too far if we were to attempt to enlarge on a subject, on which so much excellent literature exists already. It would be difficult to describe conditions relating to the vagaries of the *cash* coinage system, as they existed during the closing years of the nineteenth century, with as much skill and precision as J. Edkins has done. His article on this particular subject[1] is a rare specimen of intimate knowledge of a question worthy of close attention and thorough study. We quote *verbatim:*

The subject of Chinese currency demands not a brief paragraph, but a comprehensive essay, or rather a volume. Its chaotic eccentricities would drive any occidental nation to madness in a single generation, or more probably such gigantic evils would speedily work their own cure. In speaking of the disregard of accuracy we have mentioned a few of the more prominent annoyances. One hundred cash are not 100, and 1,000 cash are not 1,000, but some other and totally uncertain number, to be ascertained only by experience. In wide regions of the Empire

[1] See North China Herald, 1889, fol. 411.

1 cash counts for 2, that is, it does so in numbers above 20, so that when one hears that he is to be paid 500 cash he understands that he will receive 250 pieces, less the local abatement, which perpetually shifts in different places. There is a constant intermixture of small or spurious cash, leading to inevitable disputes between dealers in any commodity. At irregular intervals the local magistrates become impressed with the evil of this debasement of the currency and issue stern proclamations against it. This gives the swarm of underlings in the magistrate's yamen an opportunity to levy squeezes on all the cash shops in the district and to make the transaction of all business more or less difficult. Prices at once rise to meet the temporary necessity for pure cash. As soon as the paying ore in this vein is exhausted, and it is not worked to any extent, the bad cash return, but prices do not fall. Thus the irrepressible law by which the worse currency drives out the better is never for an instant suspended. The condition of the cash becomes worse and worse until, as in some parts of the Province of Honan, everyone goes to market with two entirely distinct sets of cash, one of which is the ordinary mixture of good with bad, and the other is composed exclusively of counterfeit pieces. Certain articles are paid for with the spurious cash only. But in regard to other commodities this is matter of special bargain, and accordingly there is for these articles a double market price. That enormous losses must result from such a state of things is, to any westerner, obvious at a glance, although the Chinese are so accustomed to inconveniences of this sort that they seem almost unconscious of their existence, and the evils are felt only as the pressure of the atmosphere is felt. Chinese cash is emphatically "filthy lucre." It cannot be handled without contamination. The strings of 500 or 1,000 (nominal) pieces are exceedingly liable to break, which involves great trouble in recounting and retying. There is no uniformity of weight in the current copper cash, but all is both bulky and heavy. Cash to the value of a Mexican dollar weigh not less than 8 pounds avoirdupois. A few hundred cash are all that anyone can carry about in the little bags which are suspended for this purpose from the girdle. If it is desired to use a larger sum than a few strings the transportation becomes a serious matter. The losses on transactions in ingots of sycee are always great, and the person who uses them is inevitably cheated, both in buying and in selling. If he employs the bills of cash shops the difficulty is not greatly relieved, since those of one region are either wholly uncurrent in another region not far away, or will be taken only at a heavy discount, while the person who at last takes them to be redeemed has in prospect a certain battle with the harpies of the shop by which the bills were issued as to the quality of the cash which is to be paid for them. Under these grave disabilities the wonder is that the Chinese are able to do any business at all, and yet, as we daily perceive, they are so accustomed to these annoyances

that their burden appears scarcely felt, and the only serious complaint on this score comes from foreigners.

In summarising it may be asserted that the following causes have lead to the abolition of China's ancient copper-cash currency:

(*a*) Sentimental reasons, according to which China desired to have a coinage on lines which were similar to the system employed by all modern countries.

(*b*) With the increase in the intrinsic value of the *cash* coins the latter were promptly melted down. In course of time the deficiency made itself keenly felt, but the Government was unable to supply the wastage. This fact lead to serious troubles and was the cause of riots in some instances.

(*c*) The multitude of different specimens of *cash* coins, genuine and spurious, circulating side by side at unstable market rates,—one a thousand years old and the next one cast only yesterday,—brought hardships in its wake which only a people, with the proverbial patience of the Chinese, would consent to bear for so long.

The Beginning of Modern Copper Coinage in China.

As stated on page 388 viceroy *Chang Chi T'ung* established the first modern Mint in Canton in 1889, the machinery having been ordered from England at a cost of 1 million dollars. Minting operations were started in the summer of 1890, the first output being silver dollars. These were soon followed by large quantities of subsidiary silver coins. The coinage of copper began only ten years after the opening of the Mint, *i.e.*, in A.D. 1900.

The production by the Canton Mint of modern copper coins marks an important stage in the development of China's coinage system. The workmanship of the first specimens is excellent and represents probably the best work which may be found amongst the modern copper coins struck in China in course of the first quarter of the twentieth century.

The design of the modern Chinese copper coinage is characterised by an allegorical emblem; furthermore the inscriptions (with only rare exceptions) on the obverse are in the English language; finally in many cases the date of issue is inscribed. The square hole in the center, so characteristic of ancient *cash* coins, is no more there. These are the most important of the innovations, which distinguish the new coinage from the antiquated issue of copper *cash*.

It is not intended to enter here the realm of numismatics; only for record's sake are the following particulars, relative to China's first modern copper coin, noted down at this stage:

The first modern copper coin produced in Canton is 28 m.m. in diameter; it is composed of red copper. The obverse shows within an inner circle the dragon emblem, while the outer circle bears the inscription *"Kwangtung. One cent."* The reverse has inscriptions in Chinese and Manchu characters. The denomination "One cent" was soon altered to "Ten cash," an inscription which all Chinese copper coins of that value showed during the imperial regime. The vicinity of Hongkong surely left its influence on the (Chinese) inscription of the first modern 1 cent copper coin produced by the Canton Mint, because it reads (圓一換枚百每), meaning "One hundred to the dollar." This innovation is remarkable, if it is taken into account that hitherto all inscriptions on Chinese coins were in terms of the tael and its subdivisions.

The Government's Part in the New Coinage.

The experiments carried on by the Canton Mint during the first ten years of its existence were more or less undertaken by the provincial authorities with the cognisance of Peking, but not under the imperial Government's control. In other words, the activity of the Canton Mint was a provincial affair, unconnected with the principles of a national currency system.

The conclusion of peace in 1901, after the Boxer rebellion, was the signal for far-reaching reforms in every branch of China's national life. Amongst other reform edicts the following rather primitive proclamation, relating to the new copper coinage, was issued [1] under date of February 2, 1902:

For some time past the legal currency in the various Provinces has been insufficient for use. Formerly the two Provinces of Fuchien and Kwangtung minted some large, round copper coins of excellent workmanship that were said, by the people after they were put into circulation, to be convenient.

The Province of Kiangsu has now taken up with the same plan and finds it very convenient and beneficial, and moreover, a check upon the evil practices of illicit coining and illicit melting.

Let the viceroys and governers of the Provinces along the River Yangtsze and the seacoast provide the necessary funds and adopt the aforesaid plan and at once mint these coins in addition to the others being made by them, that they may be put into general circulation. The legal cash of the capital ought also to be of the same sort; therefore, let the Provinces of Fuchien, Kwangtung, and Kiangsu at once forward to the Board of Revenue several hundred thousand each of the copper coins minted by them, that the said Board may pay them out and get them into use, which we hope will be beneficial and convenient to the people and prove a help to the currency. Respect this.

The order of the Peking Government was promptly obeyed by the provinces, most of which foresaw the prospects of obtaining large profits from minting. Provincial Mints sprung up like mushrooms. Their output of new copper cents was readily taken by the people, not only at the face-value of 100 to the dollar, but not infrequently at a premium. According to reports emanating from the Chinese Customs 80 coppers exchanged, before 1905, in Kiaochow for 1 dollar; during the same year 95 coins of 10 *cash* each equalled one dollar in Anking; in 1902 the equivalent of 1 dollar at Soochow was 88 coppers; at about the same time copper cents were issued at Hangchow at 90 for the dollar; in Ningpo the quotation in 1905 averaged 95 coppers for the dollar; at Shanghai 92 to 95 coppers were obtained for a dollar in 1905.

[1] Wen Pin Wei, *The Currency Problem of China*, New York, 1914.

These few examples will clearly show that the new copper coins were eagerly taken by the people. Although the issue price was 100 to the dollar there was a premium of from 5 to 15% on the new 10-cash copper coin. The success and the minting profits obtained by the provinces, which were in possession of coinage plants, caused jealously amongst some of the governors of other less fortunate provinces. This lead to the importation of further minting machinery and to feverish activity, resulting in the output of enormous quantities of copper coins. Mints increased rapidly and coinage of money became a favorite means, on the part of the provincial authorities, of raising revenues.

The embargo which was placed by some of the provinces on the import of coppers from neighboring districts, and the lack of uniformity which characterised the production of the heterogeneous Mints, were responsible, *inter alia,* for depreciations from the original value and for considerable disturbances in the money markets of China. Finally the Government was roused to take action. The decision was reached to reform the country's currency. A set of regulations consisting of ten parts was granted imperial approval, on August 22, 1905. The rules relating to copper coinage provided that there should be no more new copper Mints and that those already existing should be permitted to continue operations in accordance with a set of uniform rules. These provided that China's copper coins were to contain 95% pure copper and 5% zinc. The proportion of the coins issued should be as follows:

20 cash . .	10%	of entire	issue,	weight	4	mace	K'uping.
10 ,, . .	50%	,,	,,	,,	2	,,	,,
5 ,, . .	20%	,,	,,	,,	1	,,	,,
2 ,, . .	20%	,,	,,	,,	4	cand.	,,

By imperial edict of December 7, 1905, operations in all of China's copper Mints were suspended for three months, in order to be resumed thereafter with renewed vigor, nominally under the direction of the Board of Revenue. In fact, the currency regulations of 1905 were never carried into effect. In the course of the following three years the provincial Mints continued to strike fabulously large quantities of copper coins, thereby adding chaos to the already existing confusion. In 1909 most of the copper Mints were obliged to close down, the market being overflooded with coppers.

In 1910 the Government issued a Currency Reform Act, in terms of which the existing copper coins were to be permitted to circulate for a few years, while the reformed coins were gradually being introduced. The new national currency (the unit of which was the new silver *yuan*) was to be on a decimal basis. The weight and fineness of the reformed copper coinage was scheduled to be as follows:

	Gross weight			*Composition*
2 *fen* . . .	28/100	K'uping tael		95% copper, 4% zinc, 1% lead.
1 *fen* . . .	18/100	,,	,,	
5 *li* . . .	9/100	,,	,,	
2 *li* . . .	45/1000	,,	,,	
1 *li* . . .	25/1000	,,	,,	

As is known this Act, like many another reform measure, was never carried into effect.

The Depreciation of Copper Coins.

The total issues of copper coins for 1904 were estimated at 1,693,700,000 pieces; in 1905 the total had risen to 7,500,000,000 coins. By the end of that year there were 16 copper Mints operating in 12 provinces with 846 coinage presses which, if worked to their full capacity, were liable to produce 16 billion copper coins per annum.[1]

[1] Wen Pin Wei *The Currency Problem in China*, New York, 1914.

It is estimated that during the years 1906–1908 the following additional quantities of copper coins were turned out by China's provincial Mints:

1906	1,709,384,000	pieces
1907	2,851,200,000	„
1908	1,428,000,000	„

During 1909 coinage of copper coins was suspended in most of the Mints. The Government in 1910 estimated the new copper coinage at a silver value of 100 million taels.[1]

And yet there would have been no cause for anxiety, had it not been for the intervention of the following factors:

(*a*) The absence of adequate transportation facilities, which prevented the rapid and organised distribution. Some of the outlying districts which had been clamouring for the new copper coins, could not always obtain them, while the producing centers became congested with an enormous output which could not readily be consumed on the spot.

(*b*) Speculation which grew very extensive. The copper cent is distinctly a token coin of an intrinsic value inferior to its face amount. The Chinese as a nation have not yet learned to think in terms of coins; hence the copper cent has become an article of fluctuating value and an excellent object to speculate in.

(*c*) Ignorance and avarice displayed by some of China's officials. In Foochow, for instance, where the provincial Mint was busy turning out copper coins, there was stationed, as representative of the Manchus, a Tartar-General who desired to share the spoils from modern minting. He therefore opened his own competing Mint in the same town. Another typical example was supplied in 1906 by the director of the arsenal at Shanghai who received large quantities of copper coins from the pro-

---

[1] Wen Pin Wei *The Currency Problem in China*, New York, 1914.

vincial authorities for payment of workmen's wages. One day he felt that he was also entitled to participate in the profits from seigniorage. He therefore announced that in future coppers would be received by him only after a deduction of a discount of 10%. This measure brought about a marked depreciation at Shanghai in the value of copper cents.

(*d*) The prohibition on the part of one province to permit the importation into its own domains of coppers produced in another province.

(*e*) The deliberate adulteration of the metallic contents of the coins, reduction of their size and weight and very inferior workmanship.

(*f*) The refusal of all government offices to accept the new coins at their face value (100 to the dollar), but instead only at their market value.

The amount of copper coins produced in China will probably never be known. In view of the fact that the direction of the Mints was, and still is, in the hands of the provincial authorities, and not under the control of the Peking Government, statistics, as far as they have been made available, are very incomplete and inaccurate.

According to information derived from the Weekly Bulletin (No. 228), the total output from 1900 till the end of 1917 was:

1 cent pieces	31,682,102,308
2 cents pieces	386,292,308

The same authority (No. 27), indicates the total quantity of copper coins produced, between 1900 and the end of 1921, by the undermentioned Mints as follows:

Old design:	*10 cash*	*20 cash*
Tientsin, Nanking, Wuchang, Anhwei and Shensi . . .	14,235,476,568	1,426,994,702
New design:	*10 cash*	*5 cash*
Tientsin, Nanking, Wuchang, Anhwei	16,964,238	1,728,380

The figures are fragmentary evidence only and are merely intended to hint at the possibilities regarding the plethora of modern copper coins which have been turned out with the object of obtaining huge profits. The Mint in Hupeh, for example, imported in 1902, 6,860 piculs of copper; in 1903, 36,870 piculs; in 1904, 103,670 piculs. Each picul yielded 8,000 coins of 1-cent each. Although a good portion of the metal was re-exported, it is estimated that in 1904 alone 560 million 1-cent pieces were thrown on the market by the Wuchang Mint alone.

It would lead too far if the attempt was made here to trace the depreciation of the copper cent in the various provinces of China during its career of 25 years. Suffice it to say that the 10 *cash* coins have, during that period, depreciated from 80 copper cents (lowest) to 300 copper cents to the dollar (highest). It need scarcely be pointed out that this alarming loss in value has brought untold hardships in its wake, especially to the multitude of toilers who form the bulk of China's population and whose currency the copper cent remains.

One of the large enterprises whose income is composed of copper coins, is the Shanghai Tramway Co. This concern started operations in 1908, when the ratio of depreciation to gross receipts was 14¾% and the total loss $50,812.00. The percentage of loss in converting the depreciated copper coinage into local dollars had grown, in 1925, to 56.74% which, when applied to the actual total receipts for 1925, is represented by the enormous deficiency of $2,536,239. The Shanghai Tramway Co. are operating in the foreign Settlement only and represent an infinitesimal part of the numerous sufferers from a steadily depreciating currency system. For record's sake the following official and reliable figures, as published by the Shanghai Electric Construction Co., Ltd., are quoted here.

Table overleaf.

Period.		Amount of loss in converting depreciated subsidiary coinage into Mex. $	Ratio to gross receipts collected on the cars.
Year to 31st December	1909	116,089	24.01%
" "	1910	155,184	24.91%
" "	1911	168,848	22.93%
" "	1912	239,375	24.55%
" "	1913	258,810	23.19%
" "	1914	316,670	26.04%
" "	1915	362,368	28.58%
" "	1916	387,510	26.72%
" "	1917	354,776	23.26%
" "	1918	390,377	23.95%
" "	1919	521,385	26.21%
" "	1920	658,572	27.93%
" "	1921	937,313	33.04%
" "	1922	1,397,579	40.68%
" "	1923	1,684,500	43.91%
" "	1924	2,126,882	48.36%
" "	1925	2,536,239	56.74%

Classification and denominations.

The numerous issues of modern Chinese copper coins may conveniently be classified into the following divisions:

(1) Tai Ching Ti Kuo Series,
(2) Regular Provincial Series, } Empire.

(3) Commemorative Series,
(4) Regular Provincial Series,
(5) Coins for General Use,
(6) "Big money" copper Series, } Republic.

(1) Under this heading are included all the copper coins issued under the Manchu regime bearing the inscription "Tai-Ching-Ti-Kuo Copper Coin." The reverse shows Chinese and Manchu inscriptions and, incised in the center, the countermark indicating the place in which the coin is meant to circulate; besides the year of issue

is shown. From the last mentioned information it can be seen that the coins of this group were minted between A.D. 1905 and 1909; in the majority of cases the year 1906 is incised on the coin. The following table, composed by the late Mr. H. A. Ramsden,[1] gives particulars of the denominations and the origin of China's copper coins of the Tai-Ching-Ti-Kuo Series:

Name	*20 cash.*	*10 cash.*	*5 cash.*	*2 cash.*
(a) General use	x	x	x	x
(b) An Hwei	..	x	..	x
(c) Che Chiang	x	x	x	..
(d) Chi Li	..	x	..	..
(e) Foo Kien	..	x	..	..
(f) Fung Tien	x	..	..	..
(g) Ho Nan	..	x	..	..
(h) Hu Nan	..	x	..	..
(i) Hu Peh	..	x	x	..
(j) Kiang Soo	x	x	..	..
(k) Kwang Tung or Kwang Si .	..	x	..	..
(l) Nan King	..	x	..	..
(m) Shang Tung	..	x	..	..
(n) Yu Nan	..	x	..	..
Totals . .	4	13	3	2

(2) Regular Provincial Series.

From the same source we have obtained the information contained in the following account:

Name	*20 cash.*	*10 cash.*	*5 cash.*	*1 cash.*
(a) An Hwei	x	x	..	..
(b) Che Chiang	x	x	..	..
(c) Chin Kiang, *see* Tsing Kiang	..	x	..	..
(d) Foo Kien	x	x	x	..
(e) F.K. Custom House . . .	..	x	..	..
(f) Fen Tieng, *see* Fung Tien .	..	x	..	..
(g) Fung Tien, *see* Fen Tieng .	..	x	..	..
(h) Ho Nan	..	x	..	..
(i) Hu Nan	..	x	..	..
(j) Hu Peh	..	x	..	x
(k) Hu Poo	x	x	x	..
(l) Kiang See, *see* Kiang Si .	..	x	..	..

[1] "Modern Chinese Copper Coins," The Numismatist Press, Worcester, Mass., 1911

	Name	*20 cash.*	*10 cash.*	*5 cash.*	*1 cash.*
(*m*)	Kiang Si, *see* Kiang See	..	x	..	..
(*n*)	Kiang Nan	..	x	..	..
(*o*)	Kiang Soo	x	x	x	..
(*p*)	Kirin	x	x	..	..
(*q*)	Kwang Tung	..	x	..	..
(*r*)	Pei Yang	x	x	..	..
(*s*)	Shang Tung	..	x	..	..
(*t*)	Tsing Kiang, *see* Chin Kiang	..	x	..	..
(*u*)	Miscellaneous	..	x	..	..
	Totals	8	20	3	3

Most of the coins of this group, in common with the foregoing series, contains in the center on the obverse the dragon emblem. The inscription on the reverse is in Chinese and Manchu, signifying the Mint at which the coin was manufactured, the value and the remark "Original coin of the *Kwang Su* period." The metal employed in all these series was either red copper with a slight admixture of zinc or, more rarely, yellow brass. The size of the coins is fairly uniform and may be indicated as averaging:

33 m.m. for the 20 cash piece,
28 ,, ,, ,, 10 ,, ,, ,
23 ,, ,, ,, 5 ,, ,, ,
17 ,, ,, ,, 2 ,, ,, ,
16 ,, ,, ,, 1 ,, ,, .

Although differing in the minor detals of the design, almost all the series are characterised by a more or less uniform design, the outstanding feature of which is the dragon, surrounded by clouds or waves. All the series issued under the Manchu regime bear English inscriptions (on the obverse), apart from the Chinese and Manchu legends (on the reverse); except the coins issued in Chekiang province. These contain no foreign letters.

The "imperial" series exist in denominations of 20, 10, 5, 2 and 1 *cash*. The average weight of the 10-cash piece is from 112 to 115 grains; the pure copper contained in the 10-cash coin has been found to weight 7.25 grams.

(3) Commemorative Series.

These were issued in the first year of the Republic, either in its commemoration or in commemoration of the revolution.

Of the latter series only the 10 cash and 5 cash pieces exist in copper. The obverse shows the military and national flags in the center. Above the inscription 中華民國, meaning "The Republic of China" 開國紀念幣 signifying "Coin commemorative of the change of the regime." The center on the reverse is occupied by an open wreath and the inscription of the value (十文), meaning "10 *cash*." Around the circle is found the legend "The Republic of China * Ten cash *. Of this denomination there are known about ten varieties; diameter from 28. to 28.9 m.m. The 5 cash piece is 23 m.m. in diameter and was produced by the Wuchang Mint which is also responsible for the output of some of the varieties of the 10 cash coin. The larger portion of the latter were, however, minted in Nanking.

Of the copper coins issued in commemoration of the Republic there was only one denomination issued, *viz.*, the 10 cash piece. It is similar in design, except that the only inscription it bears in English reads "Ten cash," while the Chinese legend on the obverse reads 共和紀念幣 meaning "Coin commemorative of the Republic." The second specimen of a 10 cash coin belonging to this group is of an entirely different design. On the obverse it shows the portrait of Yuan Shih Kai in full military uniform, while the reverse contains the denomination 十文 (10 *cash*) within a wreath, and also the legend 共和紀念 denoting "Souvenir of the Republic."

(4) Provincial issues.

The provincial issues produced until the end of 1925 are conspicuous by their inconstancy with regard to weight, size, design, composition and workmanship. These series exist in denominations of 200, 100, 50, 10, 5, 2 and 1 *cash*.

The most common denomination is the 10 cash coin, the design of which differs according to the province from which it emanated. The following denominations have been minted as provincial issues:

	200 cash.	*100 cash.*	*50 cash.*	*20 cash.*	*10 cash.*	*5 cash.*	*2 cash.*	*1 cash.*
Fukien					x		x	x
Honan					x			
Hunan				x	x			
Kiangsi					x			
Kwangtung					x			
Sinkiang				x	x	x		
Szechuen	x	x	x	x	x			

Besides these series there was an issue of two types of copper coins in 1916 in Yunnan province, showing the portrait of governor T'ang Chi Yao in profile and also *en face.*

It would lead too far if an attempt was made here to describe the heterogeneous provincial issues of copper coins which distinguish themselves by the independence displayed in the variation of the design. Special mention ought to be made of the existence of a 1 cash and a 2 cash brass coin, minted by Fukien province, with a round hole in the center. It should also be pointed out that the provincial series of the 10 cash pieces, coined by the Kwangtung Mint, is inscribed "1 cent," instead of "10 Cash."

(4) Coins for the General Use in the Republic. The design on the obverse was an open wreath of vine enclosing an emblem resembling the chrysanthemum flower. Outside the circle is to be found the legend "The Republic of China * Ten Cash*. The center of the reverse is occupied by the national and military flags. Around the outer circle, above, is written 中華民國 (The Republic of China); below 當十銅元 (Copper coin of the value of ten cash). Since this original coin was struck there were hundreds of variations, many of which deviate in all essential points from the first design. Some of the 10 cash coins belonging to this group minted after 1919 bear no foreign characters in their inscription.

In 1913 the Tientsin Mint produced sample coins of the denomination of 1 *cash*. These were made from iron and had a square hole in the center. But they never exceeded the experimental stage.

(5) "Big money" copper series.
In connection with the attempt of reforming the national currency of China a series of new subsidiary coins was issued. The proclamation relating thereto was quoted in Chapter XIV, "Subsidiary Silver Coins." Two copper coins were issued by the Tientsin Mint, in denominations of 1 *fen* and 5 *li*, representing the one-hundredth, respectively two-hundredth, part of a silver dollar.

The 1 *fen* piece is 26 m.m. in diameter and uninscribed on the obverse, apart from a tasteful design, representing ears of grain. The coin has a small central hole. On the obverse is to be found the denomination 壹分 (1 cent), above 中華民國五年 (Fifth year of the Republic of China), below 每一百枚當壹圓 (Each hundred pieces equal to 1 dollar).

The other "big money" copper coin exists in the denomination of half-a-cent. It has a small central hole and is similar in design to the 1 cent coin; the denomination reads, when translated, "Each two-hundred pieces equal to one dollar." In the beginning these coins were accepted as "big money," at least in North China. But gradually they vanished from circulation, having failed to accomplish the purpose for which they had been created.

In conclusion mention ought to be made of a certain number of copper coins which were issued in commemoration of the existence of more or less important personages. As is known preparations were made in 1916 to elevate Yuan Shih Kai from the presidency to the throne of China. These preparations included also the minting of special coins, showing the new emperor in his imperial garb. The Mint at *Changsha* prematurely issued some of the new copper coins; these were quickly withdrawn and destroyed when it was seen that Yuan Shih Kai's unfortunate attempt was bound to fail.

Composition and debasement.

It has already been pointed out that the 10 cash coins were supposed to consist of 95% copper and 5% zinc. There is a moderate quantity of yellow brass coins in circulation, which contain about 80% of copper and 20% of spelter. Copper coins are not token money in China. They are merchandise, subject to violent fluctuations. The main causes for the steady decline in the value of China's modern copper coinage have been discussed already on page 397. An additional factor, contributing indirectly towards the decline in value of China's copper currency system, is to be found in the uncontrolled issue of vast quantities of copper cash notes. These are emitted not only by provincial banks, but also by private bankers, by cash-shops, by pawn-shops and by dealers in merchandise who have sufficient standing to induce the people to accept such notes. Often these are covered merely by promises to pay and backed solely by the reputation of the issuer. The prolific circulation of such cash-notes, which have frequently proved to be unredeemable, has been causing untold harm to China's population and has coincidentally been helpful in the further depreciation of copper-cent coins. But the principal cause of the debacle is to be found in the desire to derive undue profits from minting. This selfish policy, enhanced by the deliberate debasement of the coins' ingredients, was the chief cause for the failure experienced in connection with China's copper coinage system. In ancient times the authorities, when casting copper coins, never looked for minting profits. There are examples showing the unselfish attitude on the part of the Chinese Government which deliberately took upon itself a considerable loss when attempting to alleviate the inconveniences caused by the melting down of large quantities of copper cash. This happened in the course of the last few years of the existence of old copper cash, and shortly before the termination of the Manchu regime. When the great change took place China's modern copper coins were fairly uniform in composition and size. The depreciation, which had taken place between the years 1906 and 1911, was due to overproduction, and not to adulteration of the metal contents. But shortly after the inauguration of the republican regime, and especially after the ending of the World War in 1919, the production of copper coins became so prolific and the metal contents so variable that, within five years, the situation had become desperate. In certain districts of the country not less than 300 copper cents had to be tendered for a dollar, in 1924. Occasional analysis of the fine contents of 10 cash pieces showed that there were debased coins in circulation which deviated up to 25% from the standard weight of 18 candareens.

In attempting to consider the cost of producing copper coins in China one has to bear in mind, firstly, the cost of copper in terms of gold and, simultaneously, the relation between gold and silver. In other words, the rentability or otherwise of producing copper coins depends on the price in silver of copper ingots laid down in China. If copper is cheap and the price of silver high, it will be possible to strike copper coins in China at a low cost. Some authorities are inclined to believe that, even considering the enormous output of copper coins, there is really no superfluity on the market, especially if the total quantity is brought into relation with the enormous population of the country. What is harmful is the unstable value of the copper coin in relation to the commodities it is meant to purchase. In other words, China's copper coinage of to-day is not a medium of exchange with a clearly defined standard, but merely a commodity with a continually fluctuating price. For the definite stabilisation of copper coins it would be essential that the Government should proclaim all copper coins as token coins and, moreover, be able to enforce its decree. Needless to say, such an attempt could only be made if all the Mints would produce uniform copper coins under strict government control.

The manager of the Shanghai Electric Construction Co., Ltd., being particularly interested in copper currency questions, has made a close study of the subject.[1] He estimates that until the end of 1915 the total number of 1 cent pieces in circulation in China amounted to 22 billion pieces. During the European war raw copper was too high in price to allow of extensive minting operations. But during the years 1919–1920 coinage of copper coins was resumed in China, resulting in an estimated additional output of 3.080 billions of 1 cent coins. Mr. McColl opines that the net profit derived by the provincial Mints by this additional production may be put at 3,500,000 dollars.

Owing to the unstable price of raw copper, and also in view of the ever fluctuating price of silver, it is impossible to indicate for general purposes the cost of producing copper cent coins. In the essay already referred to Mr. McColl views the position, in 1920, in connection with the production of 1-cent and 2-cents coins, in the following light:

	1 cent coin.	*2 cents coins.*
Weight (candareens)	17.72	29.20
Intrinsic (or metal) value computed on—		
Copper (93%) per ton	$700.56	$700.56
Zinc (7%) per ton	279.89	279.89
Minting labour, etc., per 10,000 coins	9.50	17.00
7% interest on Capital Investment=per day	160.00	160.00
Face value	1.000	2.000
Depreciation	0.301	0.767
Circulating rate	0.699	1.233
Intrinsic (or metal) value	0.583	0.976
Minting profit	0.116	0.257
Ratio of intrinsic (or metal) value to face value	58.3%	48.8%
Circulating rate (cents per $)	143[2]	162.26[2]

[1] "Chinese Subsidiary Currency", by Donald McColl, Shanghai 1921.
[3] At Hankow.
Average of different Cities.[2]

CHAPTER XIX

THE PRODUCTION OF COPPER IN CHINA

In Ancient Times.

COPPER was mined and utilised in China already about 3000 B.C. The following paragraphs, relating to copper production in prehistoric times, have been extracted from William F. Collins' interesting work, entitled *Mineral Enterprise in China:*

The Chinese Emperors have always consistently discouraged mining of the metals and minerals except to provide currency as the wherewithal to pay indemnities, and as a convenient commodity for the payment of the troops. Coal, salt and sometimes iron may be considered as exceptions to this rule. A history of mining and metals in China must consequently be largely a history of the currency.

Metallic currency has been known from the earliest historical time in China. "In T'ai Hao's time (2852–2737 B.C.), money ch'ien (錢) was used. At that time money was also called "chin" (金), remarks one of the Chinese canonical books. T'ai Hao (Fu Hsi) was the first of the five rulers. He taught the people to fish with nets, regulated the marriage laws and invented Chinese writing. Another of the most reliable Chinese authorities remarks that chin (gold, copper, or simply metal) was then melted down for making tools.

Even before the Hsia and Shang Dynasties (1990–1050 B.C.), there were three kinds of money, gold (yellow metal), silver (white metal), and copper (red metal).

Copper is mentioned as having been mined in Shansi in the reign of Yu (2205–2198 B.C.).

Copper, or a cupreous mixture, was highly valued during the three ancient dynasties. It is also often referred to in the older books under the name of "chin" (金), having been the metal "par excellence" of the period. The distinctive name of ch'e chin, or (red metal), referring clearly to copper, was in ancient days occasionally used.

The best modern Chinese name for copper is hung or ch'e t'ung (銅), literally red copper. The common name T'ung has as character (䥫), made up of the character chin (金) and t'ung (銅), indicating, according to Chinese commentators, sound, harmony and assembling, possible because metallic mixtures, such as brass or bronze, may have been known to the Chinese as composite before pure copper was known to them. The radical chin of the modern compound t'ung (銅) was, according to Bushell, added later.

The Emperor Chow (1000–946 B.C.), fixed commutations of penalties mentioned in the Shu Ching for crime in huang t'ieh (yellow iron), which appears to indicate brass. In a commentary of the Han period (206 B.C. to A.D. 23), it is remarked that the "yellow iron" (黃 鐵) of the Shu Ching is the t'ung (銅) modern times. This Han period t'ung (銅) was obviously yellow and, therefore, could scarcely have been pure copper. This being so the Chinese were probably the first to make brass. Gowland in the absence of information as to Chinese metallurgy has remarked that the Romans were the earliest nation to make brass.

The "yellow iron" of the Emperor Chow must have been too plentiful to be gold, for a penalty such as the cutting off of the nose of a culprit was commutable to a fine of 100 lbs., of the metal. Incidentally it may be added that the same commentator remarks, "in ancient times gold (金), silver, (銀) copper (銅), and iron (鐵) were all named Chin (金). Bushell states that bronze has been known in China from prehistoric times under the name T'ung (銅). T'ung is loosely used by modern Chinese to indicate copper, bronze and brass, or any other metallic mixture of cupreous colour. Brass is usually known as Huang T'ung (黃銅), yellow copper, and Pai T'ung (白銅) white copper. Copper was precipitated from vitriol (硫銅) solution by iron in two works, as early as in 1090 and A.D. 1097. They had outputs of 50,000 and 380,000 catties of copper respectively. The iron consumed was in the proportion of 2.4: 1 of copper.

China's coinage has been based on copper for at least twenty-five centuries, but it must be remembered that her currency has frequently been largely non-metallic. Japanese copper cash were first cast in A.D. 708.

Records of the Chow Dynasty (1142–249 B.C.), indicate the composition of the Chinese metal-mixture for making bells, hatchets, spears, swords, arrow-heads and boring instruments of that period as being true bronze, for it was an alloy varying in copper-tin content of from 5 to 1. From this evidence iron was probably rare and expensive at that time.

Bushell remarks that the tin of ancient Chinese bronze is rarely, if ever, composed of pure tin, but contains in addition notable proportions of zinc and lead. Many of the more recent so-called Chinese "bronze" are undoubtedly brasses, for like the cash currency they are commonly of gold-yellow colour. Manufacture of Chinese cash currency is described in A.D. 968, and early in the seventh century, as being made by a melting down of the following percentages of metal-copper 65.8, lead 21.1, and tin 13. Cash may be considered to be impure brass.

During A.D. 808, copper mining was encouraged, while silver mining was again prohibited, "because copper was used for minting coins, while silver was valueless to the people."

Between A.D. 937 and A.D. 946 the Liao Dynasty, which ruled from A.D. 916–1122, found much copper ore. This was smelted and used for coinage and was one of the reasons for the country's becoming an Empire.

In 1078 the recorded output of the mines was:—

Gold . . .	10,710 liang (14,280 ounce).
Silver . . .	215,385 liang (287,180 ounce).
Copper . .	14,605,959 catties (8693 tons 292 lbs.).
Iron . . .	5,501,097 catties (3274 tons 1033 lbs.).
Lead . . .	9,197,335 catties (5474 tons 1353 lbs.).
Tin. . . .	2,321,898 catties (1382 tons 184 lbs.).
Mercury . .	4,456 catties (2 tons 1461 lbs.).
Cinnabar . .	3,640 catties (2 tons 373 lbs.).

The increase in copper-production to so large a figure as 14½ million catties (about 8631 tons) at a period when the Yunnan mines were not available as a source of copper seems altogether remarkable, and is clear evidence of the existence of considerable copper resources in China outside Yunnan.

Betwen 1078 and 1084 an Imperial Order prohibiting mining appears to have been issued, and the industry never again reached such high development.

In 1102 an important advance in copper mining and metallurgy was registered. The coppery solution from certain mines had begun in 1090 to be treated with iron for the deposition of copper, and the rice official of Kwangtung reported a considerable improvement in copper production, so that one district increased its copper output by 661,000 catties (about 394 tons). One work had an annual output of 380,000 catties (about 226 tons) of copper.

The Mongol rulers felt, perhaps in a primitive sort of way, that existence of a metal currency was necessary to strengthen their enormous issues of notes. In 1286 export of gold, silver and copper coins was forbidden. This was repeated seven years later, when export of gold, silver, copper and iron was placed under a prohibition. This was again repeated sixteen years later; and in 1439 foreigners were forbidden to buy copper or iron goods.

Historical Notes on Copper in China.

Copper occurs widely in all parts of China, and copper mining is one of the most ancient metal industries. Its history is exceedingly instructive and may prove important in the reopening of the old mines by indicating the favourable localities for prospecting with modern methods. Briefly, in the days of the Han dynasty the centre of the copper industry was in Honan and later on in Chekiang; for example, the famous Copper Hill of Tengt'ung is in the Chiyuan district in Honan, and that of Wupi is in Anchi in Chekiang. In the T'ang dynasty it was at first in southern Fukien and on the Kiangsi border. The Yunnan and Szechwan deposits from which most of the copper of to-day is produced were not worked to any extent until the time of the Mings. On the average none of these localities lasted more than three centuries because copper, being the metal for coinage, has always been minutely prospected for and every bit of outcrop discovered and worked, but native methods of mining have their limit in depth owing to ventilation and drainage difficulties. For example, the well-known districts of Tungch'uan in Yunnan and Hweili in Szechwan are among the most recent discoveries, hence they are still producing some copper. But the annual output of the metal has decreased from over 6,000 tons in the time of Ch'ien Lung to about 800 tons at the present day. Owing to the lack of outcrop and the drowning of old shafts it is exceedingly difficult to express any opinion about the value of most deposits, but in general it may be said that most of the districts mentioned above should be well worth while reopening with a view to prospecting thoroughly by modern methods, for the continuation of many of the rich ore bodies may still be found in the depth; and there is also a great hope that the old miners left untouched the low grade ore, the working of which has proved such a success in the United States.

Before 1911 copper was a government monopoly and no private mines were allowed to exist. After the first Revolution, however, the T'ungch'uan copper mine fell into the hands of a private company. It is still the largest copper producing district in China. The annual production varies between 700–800 tons, and because it is a monopoly it pays a handsome profit.

The Penghsien copper mining administration belongs to the Provincial Government of Szechwan and was organized in 1911 with a capital of Tls. 41,020. It possesses a unique modern smelting plant provided with reverbatory furnace of Japanese type; the copper produced is of high purity 99.5% *cu.* Owing to the unsettled political conditions of the province, the production is rapidly declining.

Year	*1918*	*1919*	*1920*	*1921*	*1922*	*1923*
Copper (tons)	68	43	43	34	27	5

In Kirin province, the government mine of Panshih has been stopped since 1918. The T'ienpao shan mine in Yenchi district worked by a Sino-Japanese Co., has the following production of ore with a content averaging about 2%.

Year	*1918*	*1919*	*1920*
Copper Ore (tons)	11,275	9,089	10,158

In Hupeh, the provincial governmental mining bureau has made several attempts to mine and smelt the copper ores of contact metamorphic type in Ta-yeh and Yang-sing districts; so far they have totally failed with quite serious losses of capital. Some private companies have been active in working the Chushan mine in Northern Hupeh.

Several mines are producing copper in Sinkiang but the methods of mining and smelting are very primitive and output quite small.—(*China Year Book, 1925*).

The copper deposits of Yunnan have yielded in the past practically all the copper required for minting and other purposes in China and Burma. The Tungchwan hills have been the chief source of supply; the mines were organized in 1697, and mining made a government monopoly in 1738, for the increased demand for brass coinage (the little copper produced in Hupei, Shansi, and Chihli being insufficient). Four thousand tons were sent to Peking annually thenceforward, until the outbreak of the great Mahommedan rebellion in Yunnan in 1858 put a stop to work for nearly 20 years, since when the output has never reached figures approaching the 8,000 tons which were averaged at the close of the eighteenth century. At present only ten thousand to thirteen thousand piculs are mined yearly. Other mines in Yunnan are those N. of Tali Lake, where the ores worked are chiefly oxides and carbonates; here also great development is possible. In the Shan State of Hswenli there are workings at Malipa.

The ores mined at Tungchwan are malachite, azuirite, cuprite, pyrites, etc.

In Yungchangfu on the extreme west there are mines which before the rebellion produced 10,000 piculs annually.

In Ssuch'uan a little copper is mined in the rich region of Hweilichow.

The export in 1916 was piculs 564,818, value Tls. 9,066,681.

(From "*Encyclopedia Sinica*").

In Modern Times.

The following paragraphs contain information on some of the present-day copper mines in China. Sources of information are indicated by figures as follows:

(1) Maritime Customs Decennial Reports, 1902–1921,
(2) China Press, December, 1924,
(3) Chinese Economic Monthly, 1924–1925,
(4) Chinese Economic Bulletin, 1924–1925,
(5) Finance and Commerce, 1925,
(6) Rea's Far Eastern Mannual, 1923,
(7) Sir Alexander Hosie's "Szechwan."

Copper Mines in Hunan.

The following is a list of copper mints in Hunan province:—

LOCATION	OPERATED BY	LOCATION	OPERATED BY
Tung Changkai, Suanninghsien (綏甯銅場界)	Hunan Government Mining Bureau (湖南官礦局)	Taitsingshan, Lihsien (澧縣太淸山)	Kai Tai Company (開泰公司)
Tungchungmen. Shenkuhsien (辰谿銅冲門)	,,	Tangkingkun, Sinninghsien (新甯唐金崙)	,,
Lokungtang, Shenkuhsien (辰谿羅公塘)	,,	Lutzefang, Kweiyanghsien (桂陽綠紫坳)	,,
Szetuping, Shenkuhsien (辰谿四都平)	,,	Takai, Kweiyanghsien (桂陽大開)	,,
Shihmapo, Yuanlinghsien (沅陵石馬坡)	,,	Wanfalung, Kweiyanghsien (桂陽萬發窿)	,,
Chenkaishan, Yuanlinghsien (沅陵陳家山)	,,	Fenghwangshan, Kweiyanghsien (桂陽鳳凰山)	,,
Chuankiyih, Yuanlinghsien (沅陵船溪驛)	,,	Nanchungwei, Huitunghsien (會同南冲尾)	Pao Ho Company (寶和公司)
Tingshaoling, Mayanghsien (麻陽汀邵嶺)	Feng Hao Company (豐厚公司)	Tientaikun, Huitunghsien (會同天台崙)	,,
Lungchangya, Mayanghsien (麻陽龍長埡)	,,	Kungkiawan, Huitunghsien (會同龔家灣)	,,
Nuikuling, Mayanghsien (麻陽牛谷嶺)	,,	Ssutzelao, Huitunghsien (會同獅子腦)	,,
Hungyehki, Huitunghsien (會同紅岩溪)	Chung Hsin Co. (中興公司)	Yangkiachow, Changninghsien (常甯楊家洲)	,,
Lungkitow, Huitunghsien (會同龍溪頭)	,,	Changshantang, Changninghsien (常甯樟山塘)	,,
Tafengyue, Huitunghsien (會同大風坳)	,,	Mashihling, Changninghsien (常甯麻石嶺)	,,
Hweikiho, Taoyuanhsien (桃源灰溪河)	Pao Hsiang Chen (保湘城)	Tungkang, Changninghsien, (常甯銅坑)	Yu Hua Company (裕華公司)
Kiutoushan, Sangchihhsien (桑直九斗山)	,,	Fenghwangpo, Hsiangtanhsien (湘潭鳳凰坡)	,,
Shanyangki, Shihmenhsien (石門山羊溪)	,,	Wuchushan, Paochinghsien (寶慶烏竹山)	,,
Paotzekia, Yungtinghsien (永定保子界)	,,	Yaowan, Taoyuanhsien (桃源窰灣)	Yu Chang Company (裕場公司)
Tangchung, Yunghsinhsien (永興塘冲)	,,	Lenshiuki, Loukihsien (屢溪冷水溪)	Ta Li Company (達利公司)
Meihwaching, Yunghsinhsien (永興梅花井)	,,	Hsiangfengshan, Chihyanghsien (祁陽象飛山)	,,
Siamatang, Yunghsinhsien (永興下馬塘)	,,	Maolientang, Chihyanghsien (祁陽毛鐮塘)	,,

LOCATION	OPERATED BY	LOCATION	OPERATED BY
Tungpienlung, Yunghsinhsien (永興東邊蔭)	Pao Hsiang Chen (保湘城)	Tungkangli, Chihyanghsien (祁陽銅坑里)	Pao Shan Company (寶善公司)
Sinkangling, Yunghsinhsien (永興新坑嶺)	Yu Sin Company (玉鑫公司)	Yingtsengkwan, Liuyanghsien (瀏陽隱眞觀)	”
Meihwaching, Yunghsinhsien (永興梅花井)	Hung Ta Co. (宏大公司)	Ssutzeyao, Liuyanghsien (瀏陽獅子腰)	”
Tungtangchung, Yunghsinhsien (永興銅塘冲)	”	Tungpangling, Liuyanghsien (瀏陽銅盆嶺)	”
Maanpo, Liuyanghsien (瀏陽馬鞍坡)	”	Luweichung, Liuyanghsien (瀏陽六尾冲)	Pao Hsin Company (寶興公司)
Shanyangki, Shihmenhsien (石門山羊溪)	Hao Sun Company (厚生公司)	Tungchangyu, Shihmenhsien (石門銅廠坳)	”

(4.)

Copper Mining in Honan Province.

Tsiyuan (濟源), Honan province, is 40 *li* north of the Yellow River, 110 *li* from Tsinhwachen (清化鎮), and 120 *li* from Loyang (洛陽). A copper deposit occurs about 70 *li* northwest of hsien city, extending for a distance of 50 *li*. Outcrops of copper-bearing quartz, varying from fractions of a Chinese foot to several feet in width, appear at Sunchenjenfen (孫眞人墳), Hwangtuyao (黃土窰), Chimayao (芝蔴窰), Jinyukow (銀魚溝), Kungho (宮河), Shuikochien (水格澗), Matowshan (馬頭山), and other localities. Old pits are numerous, but mostly shallow. Exploitation probably dates back to the reign of Wen Ti of the Han dynasty (漢文帝) 220–226, as pointed out by the existence of the Teng Tung Temple (鄧通廟) at Chinghsukung (清虛宮) in the mine area. Teng Tung was the richest man in the history of Han days; the Emperor bestowed on him a hill named Tungshan (銅山), or "copper hill," in Szechwan province. The copper ore found in Tsiyuan is chalcopyrite, cuprite, malachite, and bornite. The deposit is probably an impregnation or a dissemination. It is particularly rich in the point of contact between quartz and schist. The mother rock is granite or schist, sometimes both. Metamorphism is shown by the appearance of quartzite and crystalline schists. Schists are seen from Yinyukow until Hungchitashan (紅圪塔山) is reached, where red shale, common limestone, make their appearance. The geology is probably of the Cambrian Age, while the origin of schists may be Pre-Cambrian. The result of analysis of the cuperiferous ore in the following locations is shown below:

Location	Ore	Percentage of Copper	Gold Contents
Yinyukow, West	Pyrite and chalcopyrite	11.50 %	1.25 oz. per ton
" "	Pyrite in schist	1.66 %	Minute quantity
" "	Pyrite in limestone	Minute quantity	——
" East	Pyrite in quartz	1.24 %	Minute quantity
Sunchenjenfen	Chalcopyrite and bornite	15.11 %	" "
Hwangtuyao	Chalcopyrite and bornite	18.06 %	——
Matowshan	Cuprite	28.85 %	——
Kungho	Chalcopyrite and copyrite	18.06 %	——

(4.)

Copper Mining in Kiangsi Province.

Chang Pai-ling Copper Mines.—Location: Chang Pai-ling in the Kanchow Prefecture, in the southern part of Kiangsi Province.

Remarks: Operated by the Chinese Government. They were worked for a number of years by native methods; recently modern machinery was installed. Engineers who inspected the mines in 1908, made a favorable report, both on the quantity of ore available, and on the quality. Some samples obtained contained 40 per cent. copper.

(6.)

Government-owned mines are operated at Chang Pai-ling in Kiangsi. The quality of the ore is excellent, running as high as 42% of copper.

(5.)

Copper Mining Chihli Province.

Jui Sheng Copper Mining Co., Ltd.—Location: Tashihtso, Chengwumen West, Peking. Established: November, 1914; Registered: May, 1915. Capital: $100,000 (潤盛銅鑛有限公司).

(6.)

Copper Mining in Szechwan Province.

The copper reefs of the Provinces of Kweichow and Yunnan run north-west into Szechwan, where the Yangtsze makes its sweep southwards after its junction with the Ya-lung, and the southern half of the Prefecture of Ning-yuan, including the Department of Hui-li Chou and the two districts of Hsi-ch'ang Hsien and Yen-yuan Hsien, is rich in this metal. Hui-li Chou especially is noted for its copper mines, which mainly supply the wants of the whole province. In that department both red and white copper are found, the latter, which is not artificially produced, being smelted from a combination of ores found in situ. The smelting is done by packing layers of ore with alternate layers of charcoal in cone-shaped furnaces. The contents are brought to a red heat by means of a bellows made of part of the hollowed-out trunk of Sterculia platanifolia, in blowing which five or six men are engaged at one time. The smelting occupies a day, and when this has been effected dry rice and rice with the water in which it has been milled are poured into each furnace to bring out the colour in the copper which is afterwards drawn out in round rough layers of the diameter of the furnace, and, therefore, differing in size and weight according to their position in the cone. It is again fused and run into slabs.

The copper reefs are not, however, confined to the south-west of the province. They are found further north in the district of T'ien-ch'uan Chou, Ming-shan Hsien, Lu-shan Hsien, and Jung-ching Hsien in the Prefecture of Ya-chou Fu, in Ma-pien T'ing and Lei-po T'ing and the district of P'ing-shan Hsien, in the Prefecture of Hsu-chou Fu, to the north-east of Hui-li Chou, and the Chien-ch'ang Valley, and in the mountains in the west of the districts of Kuan Hsien and P'eng Hsien, in the Ch'engtu Prefecture. Copper mines are worked at a place called Pai-shui Ho, in the Mi-chia Shan hills, 90 *li* from the city of P'eng Hsien, and the copper is brought to Ch'engtu for use in the Arsenal and Mint and for copper and brass ware generally. From the Ning-yuan Valley the copper comes to Ch'engtu in slabs, weighing from 35 to 40 catties, and is valued here at T. 0.3.8 per catty, while the circular blocks from P'eng Hsien weigh from 40 to 60 catties worth T. 0.2.8 a catty. White copper costs T. 0.7.0 a catty.

Ch'engtu is a great centre for the manufacture of copper and brass ware. Kitchen utensils of all kinds, such as pots, pans, basins and spoons, tobacco pipes, lamps, candle-sticks, locks, hinges, buttons, images, bells, gongs, musical instruments, weighing scales, and other articles too numerous to mention are here made of copper or a mixture of copper and zinc. Copper mixed with tin is also minted into cash, and it is likewise used as an alloy in the manufacture of silver dollars, Chinese rupees for use in Tibet, and subsidiary silver coins.

In the manufacture of red copper or brass ware, 5 to 6 ounces of zinc are added to every pound of copper, while for yellow brass ware 10 to 11 ounces are required. (7.)

Copper Mining at Peng Hsien, Szechwan.—Sixteen samples of refined copper have been turned out by the Copper Mining Bureau at Peng Hsien (彭縣), Szechwan province, and are now exhibited in the Ch'engtu public library. A copper smelting plant has been established at Chuanho(泉河), Peng Hsien, near the copper mines. (1925). (4.)

Szechwan.—Found in several areas, and although the Kololo mine, near Maha, has not been worked for a number of years, there are indications that the mining operations in this locality were formerly very extensive. In this region there are great possibilities for copper mining on modern lines.

(5.)

Chungking—(Szechuen). (1921).

Copper ore is found in the Peng Hsien (彭縣) mines.

Location	*Owner*	*Sino-British*
Tapaoshan, Peng-hsien, Szechwan (四川彭縣大寶山)	Tapaoshan Mining Bureau (大寶山鑛務局)	Operated by the Provincial Government.

(1925). (3.)

Copper Mining in Hupeh Province.

Ichang—(Hupeh). (1911).

Several years ago the Chinese commenced to work a copper mine near Twanpaosze (團寶寺), in the Lichwan (利川) district; but the mine unfortunately got flooded by heavy rains and was abandoned, owing to the Chinese being unable to pump out the water with the primitive appliances at their disposal. It is said that the ore is abundant and of very good quality, and that with proper gear the pumping out of the water would present no difficulties. (1.)

Mines, equipped with modern machiinery, are working in seveal districts. Abundant ore of good quality is found in a mine near Twanpaosze in the Lichwan district, but its working has been checked by the inrush of water, which cannot be dealt with in the absence of modern machinery.

(5.)

Location of Mines	*Owners*
Hunglitienshan, Yangsinhsien, Hupeh (湖北陽新縣洪李田山)	Pao Yuan Company (寶源公司)
Fengshihtung, Chushanhsien, Hupeh (湖北竹山縣豐石洞)	Hwa Hsin Company (華興公司)
Chenkiashan, Chushanhsien, Hupeh	Wu Yin Company (五盈公司)

(1925). (3.)

Copper Mining in Kirin Province.

District	*Location*	*Area*	*Remarks*
Panshih (磐石)	Tsingshihtsui (青石咀)	400 mow	Formerly jointly operated by Provincial Government and merchants; later converted into a Provincial Government concern.

District	*Location*	*Area*	*Remarks*
Hwatien (樺甸)	Pichowshao (皮州哨)	2,700 mow	1915, Pao Tsang Hsing Copper Mining Co. (寶藏興銅鑛公司)
Yenki (延吉)	Tienpaoshan (天寶山)	32,400 „	1916, Liu Shao-wen (劉紹文)
Do.	Ilankow (依蘭溝)	1,755 „	1919, Cheng Ya-Chieh (提亞階)
Kirin (吉林)	Hwanhsiling (歡喜嶺)	3,985 „	1918, Fan Yu (范孺) To prospect
Panshih (磐石)	Liangpactai (亮寶台)		1918, Su Yen-mo (蘇炎槙) To operate
Do.	Itzeshantun (椅子山屯)		Applications for license made, but still awaiting Government sanction.
Yenki (延吉)	Kunniushihtze (滚牛碣子)		Do.
Do.	Erhtaokow (二道溝)		Do.

(1923). (3.)

At Tienpaoshan (吉林延吉縣天寶山) in Kirin province there exists a copper mine which has been organised as a Sino-Japanese joint concern, with a capital of 600,000 Yen. The company has erected a smelting plant, but owing to the excessive cost of coal the enterprise has proved to be unremunerative.

In Kirin there is a fine lode of copper at Shihtsuitze, which has been worked with success for a number of years.

Another Kirin mine of importance is the Tienpaoshan copper and silver field. This is situated about 40 miles north-west of Lungchingtsun, and at one time over 2,000 workmen were employed at the mine. (5.)

A fine lode of copper exists at Shihtsuitze (石咀子), situated in the Panshih district (磐石縣). In April 1907 the mine was taken over by the provincial government, which provided a capital of Tls. 30,000 and appointed an official manager to carry on mining and smelting according to native methods. 1,000,000 catties of ore were raised and smelted into 50,000 catties of copper in the first half-year. The prospect of the mine being thus shown to be strikingly good, samples were sent to Japan, a mining expert was employed, and machinery was bought. In November 1910, with a view to developing the mine on an extensive scale, permission was granted to a Shanghai merchantn, named T'ANG CHIEN-CHANG (唐鑑章), to form the Panshih Mining Company, Limited (磐石鑛務有限公司), with a capital of $500,000, the provincial government being given shares in the new company to the extent of the capital originally subscribed by it. Much of the output of the mine finds its way to Japan, 198,000 catties of copper having been sold to Japanese merchants in 1910.

(1.)

Panshin Mining Co., Ltd. — Copper Mines: Shihtsuitze, near Panshih, Kirin Province.

Established: 1910.

Capital: $500,000, of which the Kirin Provincial Government holds $40,000.

Ore: Copper pyrites and malachite of fine quality but found in meager quantity. The copper content is about 10 per cent. Work at the mines has been under suspension part of the time since the formation of the company. (6.)

Location	*Owner*
Shihtsuitze, Panshihhsien, Kirin (吉林石咀子磐石縣)	Panshih Mining Co., Ltd. (磐石礦務有限公司)

(4.)

Copper Mining in Shantung Province.

The Taoko(桃科) copper mine, in the district of Lishan(歷山) which has a long past history, is now managed by a Tsinan merchant. The amount of output is unknown. According to the essay of a specialist, the mineral rock contains 16 per cent. copper and 24 per cent. nickel. Copper is also found in the districts of Fushan (福山), Kiaochow, Chu, Ishui (沂山), and Sincheng.

(1.)

Copper Mining in Kweichow Province.

With the exception of the mines at Weiningchow, where copper oxides are worked, the industry is neglected in this province, though the existence of rich copper deposits is well known, and Kungshan (near Tungchwanfu in Yunnan) is so near the border that a proportion of that output finds its way into Kweichow.

(5.)

Copper Mining in Kansu Province.

Found in several areas, from the Tsinyuan district, large quantities of copper are obtained, and the Chinese Government formerly established smelting works at Yaokai to deal with the output. Owing to the difficulty in bringing the ore to the smelters, the works have long been in a condition of suspended animation.

The plant is capable of turning out four tons of copper in 24 hours from 7½% ore. (5.)

Copper Mining in Yunnan.

Location	*Owners*
Tamankiao, Lotsehsien (羅次縣大滿橋)	Chang Lu-chen (張魯臣)
Likwanchang, Lotsehsien (羅次縣李官場)	Chang Lu-chen (張魯臣)
Malutsun, Imenhsien (易門縣馬鹿村)	Chu Teh-chang (褚德章)
Tungchwanhsien, Yunnan (雲南東川縣)	Tung Chwan Mining Company (東川鑛業公司)

(1925). (4.)

The copper mines of Yunnan are the most important in China. In the past Yunnan yielded nearly all the copper used for coinage and other purposes in China and Burma. Up to the time of the Mohammedan rebellion, the yield was said to have been 100,000 piculs annually, mostly from the Malipa and Tungchwan workings. The oldest known workings in Yunnan are these at Malipa and Taotsutai. At the latter workings the metal obtained by native smelting analyses are as follows:—

Copper	. 93.4%.
Silver	. 26 ounce per ton.
Gold.	. 0.4532 ounce per ton.
Tin	. 0.134%.
Iron	. 0.567%.

Among other places in Yunnan where copper is mined are Kutsingfu, Yungchangfu and Talifu. The product of the mines at the latter place, which is technically known on the London market at "Chinese rough copper," gives the following yield on analysis:—

Copper	. 95.78%.
Silver	. 32.78 ounce per ton.
Gold.	. 0.514 ounce per ton.
Zinc	. 1.11%.
Iron	. 0.87%.

Specimens from the Tungchwan mines assayed as high as 43.65 ounces of silver to the ton. (5.)

Szemao— (Yunnan).

Copper is to be found in many places. Two notable mines were opened at Puerh and at Szemao, but later on closed. The Pailung

(白龍) copper mine, in the Puerh prefecture, was first opened in the 44th year of K'ANG-HSI (康熙), by the Viceroy PEI HUO-NO (貝和諾). It was subsequently closed in the reign of CH'IEN LUNG (乾隆). In the 20th year of KUANG HSU (光緒) a Prefect, by name HSU CHI-CHAO (舒之翹), called on the merchants to subscribe funds to open it again, and a petition was sent to the Viceroy for permission, which was granted. Owing, however, to the output being too small, the mine had to be closed. The copper mine in the Szemao sub-prefecture, which bears two names—Kan Kou Shan (乾溝山) and Meng Sa Shan (猛薩山),— was opened in the 44th year of K'ang Hsi, and eventually closed in the 14th year of CH'IEN LUNG (乾隆).

(1.)

Tengyueh—(Yunnan).

Of mining under native methods one of the latest local ventures is a copper mine at Paitachen (擺達鎮), some two days' journey east of Lungling. This mine, operated by a Tengyueh company, started work a year or so ago and is said to be producing between 200 and 300 piculs of copper a year, nearly all of which is consumed on the Tengyueh market. (1.)

Copper Mining in Anwhei Province.

Location	*Owner*	*Sino-British*
Tungkwanshan, Tunglinghsien, Anhwei (安徽銅陵縣銅官山)	Tungkwanshan Iron & Copper Mines (銅官山鐵銅礦)	Originally conceded to the London and China Syndicate, a British concern.

(1925). (3.)

Copper Mining in Kwangsi Province.

Location	*Owner*
Changpailing, Kanchow, Kwangsi (廣西贛州長白嶺)	Chang Pailing Copper Mines (長白嶺銅礦)

(1925). (3.)

Copper Mining in Fukien Province.

American mining experts have recently made a report on the Nam Ping copper mine area in Fukien province, owned by the Wha Pao Mining Co. This property lies in the mountains on the south side of the Min River and is said to be easy of access. Some of the principal points in the report on the mine follow.

This mine was once worked no later than the Ming dynasty by the ancients and their slag-dump, an old open pit and numerous pieces of discarded ore remain as evidences of their work. The slag is remarkably free from shot copper, showing a very easy smelting ore.

The prospecting work has furnished some specimens of ore such as the ancients mined and such as it is expected to find when the untouched vein is reached. The specimens assays are as follows:

No. 1.	Copper	18.27%.
	Silver	19 ounce per ton.
	Gold.	1/40 ounce per ton.
No. 2.	Copper	14.00%.
	Silver	20 ounce per ton.
	Gold.	1/40 ounce per ton.

When the zone of secondary enrichment is reached ore of much higher grade should be found. This prospect has many points of similarity to the prospects at the Suan Copper Mines in Korea. It is said that The Wha Pao Mining Company will soon be re-organised in order to take in new stocks for developing this mine. (2.)

Copper Mining in Hsinkiang.

Copper Mines at Ili were worked as early as 1776, but the output has since declined. The best producing mine at present is at Pai-chen (拜城), while small workings are found at Aksu, Yenchihsien Wushihsien (烏什) and Tihua.

(1925). (3.)

CHAPTER XX

MINTS IN CHINA

IN ANCIENT TIMES

Introductory.

THE value of money circulating in ancient China was invariably determined by weight, in close relation to the intrinsic worth of the metal. The principle defining the valuation of China's metallic currency still applies to the country's present day conditions, for the value of the sycee currency tael, the minted silver dollar and the humble copper cent depends upon the weight and fine contents of metal composing the modern currency of China.

The exchange of commodities in prehistoric China was carried on by barter. For this purpose metallic implements were used, besides lumps of metal which passed according to their weight. Gradually sham tools were cast of bronze, for the purpose of barter only. These were notably small, uninscribed spades, knives, bells, arrow-heads, etc.

According to tradition the casting of metallic currency was carried on for the first time in ancient China, in 1985 B.C., and repeated by the founder of the *Shang* dynasty, in 1556 B.C. However, this statement cannot be authenticated.

In 1032 B.C., *Ch'eng,* the second king of the Chou dynasty, promulgated certain currency regulations, in terms of which metallic lumps should henceforth be exchangeable according to their weight.[1] Apparently those rules remained in abeyance for centuries, until

[1] Terrien de Lacouperie "Catalogue of Chinese Coins" London, 1892.

Duke *Huan* of *T'si* (685–645 B.C.), put them into force. From that period onwards money began to appear in regular shapes and sizes.

In ancient China the casting of money was not a government monopoly. Private persons, guilds, town communities and other corporations were authorised to issue metallic money. During those remote times means of communications were very poor, so that trading—and consequently the circulation of money—was limited to rather small districts. Originally the problem of a national or uniform currency was neither known in China, nor was its realisation intended. Therefore the circulation of privately issued metallic currency did not, as a rule, exceed the boundaries of the region for the use of which it had been designed. All that the State required was that it should retain the prerogative to fix and control the weight and general design of privately issued coins.

The materials used in ancient times in China for coinage purposes,—or unminted, as media of exchange,—consisted mainly of bronze; but besides gold, silver, copper, lead, tin and iron were used for currency purposes. Owing to the great scarcity of silver deposits within China its employment, in olden times, for currency purposes was very limited; iron was utilised in Szechuen province, from where its use spread to China proper; the knowledge of bronze was introduced into China from the West, in the middle of the eighteenth century B.C.

Until A.D. 1890, Chinese coins were produced by the casting process; the crudeness connected with that method gave incessant opportunities to counterfeiters, forcing the authorities to institute frequent alterations in the design of the coinage.

Casting and Moulding.

Existing records regarding the beginning of the utilisation of metals for currency purposes are not very reliable, seeing that all written statements are based on tradition only. It may, however, be accepted as tolerably accurate that gold in cubic inch was officially issued as currency in 1032 B.C. But there is reason to surmise that the gold cube currency has been very shortlived. In the course of centuries its place was taken by bars which slowly developed into the so-called shoe-shaped ingots which are in general use to this day. Silver ingots, styled "shoes," but which others appropriately compare to the shape of a boat, are still, at the close of the year 1925, the principal currency for the financing of wholesale trade. Gold in the shape of shoes is only rarely met with nowadays; it occurs still in the Peking district in ingots of 10 taels weight and as nearly as possible 1000 fine. It is, however, on record that, in the course of the sixteenth and seventeenth centuries, China exported gold in "shoe" shape to India.

The principal medium of circulation in China during prehistoric times, and also during the Middle Ages, consisted of bronze coins. Bronze money in the shape of either small implements or flat rings, which gradually developed into coins with a hole in the center, were invariably cast from moulds. The latter were made from beaten clay, from stone, earthenware, bronze, and rarely from iron. Their legends were plain or reverted, sunk or in relief. The moulds bore sometimes the inscription on the reverse of the year of issue, principally as a record for the mint officials. The habit of dating coins originated only about fifty years before the Christian era. It is noteworthy that the old Chinese circular bronze money was inscribed on the obverse only, at least until 118 B.C., when the *Wu-chu* coins made their appearance with the reverse also inscribed. The casting was done singly, or in clusters, or arranged on the tree shape.

According to *de Lacouperie*[1] the inside of the moulds "was sprinkled with fine sand to avoid adhesion, and the

[1] Terrien de Lacouperie "Catalogue of Chinese Coins" London, 1892.

metal was poured in through an opening of the cover for those made flat, or through a running channel from the top when held vertically." Another method of moulding is described by the same author as follows: "Two tiles or bricks, fine grained, are chosen; one face of each ground smooth, that they may lie close; and stops and holes made in the bricks to hold them together. The mould is cut out with great care from the face of the brick, one half in each brick; a channel for the metal to run in is next cut; then the bricks are tied together with a piece of string, and the mould is ready for use." According to *W. S. Bushell,* under the *T'ang* dynasty a model of the coin in the required shape was made of wax, in order to be enclosed in an earthen matrix and exposed to the action of heat. The melted wax ran out from an opening left for the purpose, leaving a cavity into which the bronze was poured.

Government Assumes the Coinage Monopoly.

The coining of bronze currency, though in principle a governmental prerogative, was frequently left in the hands of private parties and corporations. Yet the authorities reserved to themselves the right to control weight and design. In 135 B.C., all private casting was strictly forbidden. Nineteen years thereafter *Han Wu-Ti* placed the affairs of the government Mint under the authority of three high officials. All the metallic currency previously in circulation was called back and brought to the *Shang-lin* Mint, established in the capital for the purpose of being re-melted and re-cast. All coins not emanating from the government Mint were regarded illegal.

In A.D. 598, under the *Sui* dynasty, five Imperial money foundries were established in *Chengtingfu (Chihli).* Shortly thereafter the emperor decreed that ten foundries of money should be opened in *Hupeh* province, where copper was available; besides five more foundries were erected in *Szechuen* province.

The casting of copper "cash" continued until about A.D. 1890, when it was essayed by the Kwangtung Mint to produce copper "cash" by modern minting methods. This only attempt proved futile, as the precisely struck new "cash" failed to win the favor of the populace.

Minting Statistics of Copper "cash."

According to J. Edkins' *Chinese Currencies* the following was the

Annual Amount of Cash Coined.

Shun Chih	1	A.D.	1644	71,663,900	cash
,, ,,	2	,,	1645	443,751,760	,,
,, ,,	3	,,	1646	624,823,960	,,
,, ,,	4	,,	1647	1,333,384,194	,,
,, ,,	5	,,	1648	1,449,494,200	,,
,, ,,	7	,,	1650	1,682,424,510	,,
,, ,,	9	,,	1652	2,097,632,850	,,
,, ,,	10	,,	1653	2,521,663,740	,,
,, ,,	11	,,	1654	2,488,544,460	,,
,, ,,	12	,,	1655	2,413,878,080	,,
,, ,,	17	,,	1660	280,394,280	,,
,, ,,	18	,,	1661	291,584,600	,,
,, ,,	5	,,	1666	295,879,800	,,
,, ,,	10	,,	1671	290,475,830	,,
,, ,,	15	,,	1676	231,365,360	,,
,, ,,	20	,,	1681	231,398,600	,,
,, ,,	25	,,	1686	289,936,700	,,
,, ,,	30	,,	1691	289,925,400	,,
,, ,,	35	,,	1696	237,063,050	,,
,, ,,	40	,,	1701	238,065,800	,,
,, ,,	45	,,	1706	238,075,800	,,
,, ,,	50	,,	1711	374,933,400	,,
,, ,,	56	,,	1717	399,167,300	,,
,, ,,	60	,,	1721	437,325,800	,,
,, ,,	1	,,	1723	499,200	,,
,, ,,	4	,,	1726	675,160	,,
,, ,,	5	,,	1727	723,528,000	,,
,, ,,	6	,,	1728	746,304,000	,,
,, ,,	8	,,	1730	757,865,000	,,
,, ,,	9	,,	1731	1,048,759,660	,,

In the reign of Shun Chih two million strings of cash were cast during several successive years, that is, from 1652 to 1655. But in

A.D. 1660 the quantity was thought too great for the need of traders. After this time 300,000 strings were believed to be sufficient. This continued to be the number of new copper cash made down to 1711, when the quantity was increased to about 380,000.

In the Hu-pu Regulations of the year A.D. 1831 the number of cash made yearly in each province is recorded. They amount in all to two million and fifty thousand strings of cash. These regulations were in use in the reign of Chia Ching and Tao Kuang, that is, from about A.D. 1800–1830. This number of new cash sufficed in those times when the population was increasing from 300 millions in A.D. 1800 to 394 millions in 1830.

According to S. W. Bushell the following list shows the Mints existing in China in 1865 and their output of copper "cash" during that year.

Table of Mints and Annual Coinage (1865):

Province.	*City.*	*Mint Name.*	*Annual Coinage.*
Chihli	Peking	Pao ch'uan	899,856,000
Chihli	Peking	Pao yuan	449,928,000
Chihli	Paotingfu	Pao chih	60,756,840
Shansi	T'aiyuanfu	Pao tsin	17,472,000
Kiangsu	Suchoufu	Pao su	111,992,052
Kiangsi	Nanch'angfu	Pao ch'ang	42,037,992
Fukien	Fuchoufu	Pao fu	43,200,000
Chekiang	Hangchoufu	Pao che	129,600,000
Hupei	Wuch'angfu	Pao wu	84,420,000
Hunan	Ch'angshafu	Pao nan	48,054,000
Shensi	Sianfu	Pao shan	94,589,040
Ssuch'uan	Ch'engtufu	Pao ch'uan	157,733,333
Kuangtung	Kuangchoufu	Pao kuang	34,560,000
Kuangsi	Kueilinfu	Pao kuei	24,000,000
Yunnan	Yunnanfu	Pao yun	125,682,480
Yunnan	Tungch'uanfu	Pao tung	44,886,600
Kueichou	Kueiyangfu	Pao ch'ien	67,329,900
Kueichou	Tatingfu	Pao ch'ien	22,443,300
Ili	Kuldja	Pao i	1,122,000

Under the *Manchus* the following government Mints were opened for casting copper "cash":

Location.	*Province.*	*Period opened.*
Hsuanhuafu	Chihli	A.D. 1645
Chichou	Chihli	1645
Miyun	Chihli	1645
Paoting	Chihli	1796–1820
Taiyuanfu	Shansi	1645
Yangho	Shansi	1649
Tatung	Shansi	1645
Kaifeng	Honan	1647
Foochow	Fukien	1649
Changchou	Fukien	1649
Ningpo	Chekiang	1680
Hangchow	Chekiang	1649
Tsinan	Shantung	1649
Linching	Shantung	1644
Chingchow	Hupeh	1646
Wuchang	Hupeh	1650
Hsianyang	Hupeh	1650
Yenshui	Shensi	1644
Changsha	Hunan	1667
Changteh	Hunan	1851–1862
Kueilin	Kwangsi	1667
Yunnanfu	Yunnan	1662–1722
Tungch'uan	Yunnan	1851–1862
Canton	Kwangtung	1622–1722
Taiwan	Formosa	1689
	Annam	1736–1795
K'ungch'ang	Kansu	1723–1735
Tihua	Kansu	1851–1862
Anking	Anhui	1723–1735
Nanking	Kiangsu	1723–1735
Soochow	Kiangsu	1736–1795
Nanchang	Kiangsi	1723–1735
Kuldja	Ili	1851–1862
Yarkand	Turkestan	1736–1795
Aksu	Turkestan	1796–1820
Wu-Shih	Turkestan	1736–1795
Board of Works	Chihli (Peking)	1644
Board of Revenue	Chihli (Peking)	1644

IN MODERN TIMES.

The following is a list of the principal Mints in China. It would be incorrect to classify these as "government" Mints, for the reason that the authorities in Peking have really no say in the policy and management of the numerous Mints, which are under the control of the provincial authorities.

Situated at.	Province.	Established.	Remarks.
Shanghai	Kiangsu	1921	Still uncompleted in 1925.
Nanking	,,	1901	British & German machinery.
Tsinkiangpu	,,	1905	Coppers only. Closed.
Hangchow	Chekiang	1901	Capacity about $200,000 daily.
Anking	Anhwei	1902	Under military "protection".
Foochow	Fukien	1901	Under provincial governor.
Hungshanchao	,,	1905	Under military control.
Makiang	,,	1905	Under naval authorities' control.
Shahshien	,,	1905	Under military control.
Amoy	,,	1924	Organised by merchants.
Nanning	Kiangsi	1905	Stopped work in 1921.
Wuchow	,,	1920	Intended to coin copper.
Kweilin	Kweichow	1905	Principally copper coins.
Canton	Kwangtung	1887	Since 1920 producing subsidiary silver coins.
Yunnanfu	Yunnan	1905	German machinery.
Wuchang	Hupeh	1893	American machinery.
Nanchang	Kiangsi	1901	Coppers & silver coins.
Changsha	Hunan	1901	Copper coinage. British machinery.
Chengtu	Szechuen	1898	American & Japanese machinery.
Chungking	,,	1913	American & British machinery.
Sianfu	Shensi		Coppers only.
Lanchowfu	Kansuh		Coppers only.
Kaifengfu	Honan	1901	Closed in 1914.
Taiyuanfu	Shansi	1919	Coppers & subsidiary silver coins.
Tsinanfu	Shantung	1905	At the beginning of 1925 still idle.
Tientsin	Chihli	1901	Central Mint. Rebuilt 1914.
Peyang	,,	1905	Branch Mint of Central Mint.
Kalgan	Chahar	1923	Copper coins only.
Mukden	Fengtien	1901	German & American machinery.
Kirin	Kirin	1901	Silver & copper coinage.
Urumchi	Turkestan		Silver & copper coinage.

The establishment of Mints in China is of recent date, yet owing to decentralisation these have had very varied careers.

The first government Mint in China was established at *Canton,* KWANGTUNG, in 1887, on the initiative of Viceroy *Chang Chi Tung,* who ordered a modern minting plant from England at a cost of 1 million dollars; it began operations in the summer of 1890; in the beginning the Canton Mint confined its activities to the production of silver dollars. Shortly thereafter subsidiary coins were struck there. In 1900 the Canton Mint was authorised to turn out 10-cash copper coins (1 cent), the first of their kind in China.

During the republican regime the Canton Mint became a business concern, uninfluenced by governmental instructions or restrictions. The whole outfit was at certain periods let out by tender to the highest bidder, thus securing a fixed income to the provincial authorities. Needless to say the tenantry was bent on recovering not only the rentals paid in advance, but also on reaping profits commensurate to the extent of the investments and risks connected therewith. This could only be accomplished by deliberately debasing the fine contents of the silver coins produced. Canton thus became the originator of debased silver coinage in China, a title which it retains to this day.

During certain periods in the beginning of the republican regime there was a good deal of civil strife in Kwangtung province. On such occasions work at the Canton Mint had to be stopped altogether for fear of looting by the soldiery. Not infrequently the Canton provincial authorities would run the Mint on their own account, but even then the tendency to continue the process of vitiation was clearly discernible; in fact it became bolder in the same measure as the fine contents of silver in the coins were systematically reduced. Other reasons for the temporary closing down of the Canton Mint were lack of credit in connection with the purchase of bar silver supplies or, at other times, an over-supply of adulterated coins which the people finally refused to receive, except at a discount.

The main object of the Mint authorities at Canton has been to make money from coining money. The requirements and views of the country were of secondary consideration. In June of 1924 the then Mint director went so far as to take a loan from a foreign group of capitalists and to register the *Chinese Government Mint* of Canton with the Hongkong Government as a British joint stock company.

It should be added that the Mint at Canton was one of the few establishments which have produced Yuan Shih-Kai dollars. A limited quantity of such coins, marked "3rd year of the Republic" was struck there.

In 1902 the Canton Mint turned out a large number of 10 cents coins, and two years later a considerable supply of 20 cents subsidiary coins was placed in circulation. But the intrinsic value of the silver contents were not satisfactory to the people in the South. This fact gave the impetus to the establishment of a Government Bank at Canton with the privilege of issuing small coin banknotes. As soon became apparent, this measure made matters still worse, as the notes were rendered practically unredeemable.

In 1917, during the World War, supplies of bar silver from England ceased. Hongkong placed an embargo on the export of silver and gold coins or bullion; and Canton saw itself forced to do likewise. When the embargo was lifted by the Canton Government in 1918, a prohibition relating to the import of Canton small coin was pronounced by the Central Government, owing to the inferior fine contents of the Canton subsidiary coinage. In 1914 the Hongkong Government declared the output of the Canton Mint as illegal tender within the colony of Hongkong. In 1917 and 1918, owing to the acute shortage of supplies of bar silver, the Canton Mint produced copper cents of a new design, the raw material for which was taken from old cannon. It was the Canton Mint which collected the old dragon-design subsidiary silver coinage of China, in order to melt it down and re-mint it with an ever-decreasing degree of fineness.

In 1900 the privilege of opening a Mint was granted to the province of FUKIEN. In 1902 the Mint at *Foochow* began operations by supplying, first, copper cents, and subsequently, dragon dollars, and 20, 10 and 5 cents silver subsidiary coins. In 1905 two more Mints were established at Foochow, one at the Arms Factory, the other, at the Mamoi Arsenal. The three Mints had a combined daily output of 2 million copper cents; this soon caused a depreciation of copper cents, whereupon the Peking Government prohibited the export to other provinces, limiting the daily production to 300,000 pieces. The two branch Mints were thus forced to close.

The Foochow Mint, during the years 1907–1910, experimented with a new 2 cash coin, but closed down towards the end of 1910. It re-opened for active operations in 1920. The two branch Mints reopened in 1924, devoting their energy to the manufacture of debased subsidiary silver coins. These coins are circulating only within the radius of influence of the respective military or naval commander, under whose orders the Mint works. The fine contents of the coins were lamentably short of the prescribed standard, and, besides, there was a remarkable lack of uniformity in weight and fineness. The latter ranged from 50% to 30% pure silver. The governor of Fukien province was obliged to announce repeatedly that only the coins produced by the Foochow Mint would be considered legal tender. Taking advantage of the confused state of currency, certain unscrupulous people forged the already debased silver coinage of Fukien province, thereby adding further chaos to the already existing confusion.

A fifth Mint was established in Fukien province in 1924, at *Amoy*, by merchants who invested in the new enterprise 400,000 dollars, with the object of making money, in every sense of the word.

The first Mint established in CHEKIANG province was inaugurated at *Hangchow* by imperial edict in 1901. But five years later operations ceased, the Mint being amalgamated with the one operating at Foochow. In 1919 the Hangchow Mint was re-opened, operating ever since in a businesslike manner. The Hangchow Mint is one of the principal sources of supply of Yuan Shih-Kai dollars. From time to time it is necessary to discontinue operations, either on account of civil commotion or because the tael price of the Yuan Shih-Kai dollar reaches a point which is below cost of production. In the summer of 1924 a new type of 10 and 20 cents pieces, 0.650 fine, was struck by the Hangchow Mint, in order to replace the debased Canton subsidiary coins which were then flooding the country. On account of warfare carried on in and around Chekiang province, in the autumn of 1924, minting operations had to be suspended and were not resumed until February of the following year, when the output consisted again of Yuan Shih-Kai dollars. It is reliably reported that the minting of new 10 and 20 cents pieces has proved unremunerative.

Originally there were three Mints in Hangchow: One silver Mint, where dollars and subsidiary silver coins were struck between 1897 and 1903, when it was closed, remaining idle for 16 years. Besides these two Mints were opened in Hangchow in 1903 and 1905, but both were definitely closed in 1906.

The opening of a government Mint at *Nanking,* KIANGSU province, also dates back to September, 1901. There dragon dollars were turned out and also subsidiary silver coins. In 1912, after the establishment of the Republic, the Nanking Mint still continued to strike Kiangnan dragon dollars. But since that time Nanking has been one of the chief sources of supply of Yuan Shih-Kai dollars. Its operations are not infrequently suspended for reasons coinciding with those applicable to the Chekiang Mint.

In 1919 the Nanking Mint produced enormous quantities of light weight 1 cent pieces of a new design and without foreign inscriptions. The debased coinage caused serious dislocation of trade, so that its import into Shanghai had to be prohibited by the Customs. Yet large quantities were nevertheless smuggled into Shanghai and other commercial centers. Another attempt on the part of the Nanking Mint authorities, put forth at the close of 1924, to devote their activities to the production of copper cents, resulted in the most strenuous opposition on the part of Shanghai's commercial community, whereupon the project had to be abandoned for the time being.

During the first seven years of its existence the Nanking Mint worked chiefly on copper cents and silver subsidiary coins, which it supplied so lavishly that it became largely responsible for their depreciation. In 1908, for instance, 300 million copper cents and 60 million 10 and 20 cents pieces, were turned out by the Nanking Mint, which thereafter was forced to temporarily close down.

There were two more Mints situated in Kiangsu province, namely at *Soochow.* These were opened in 1898 and 1904 respectively for the minting of copper coins only. Both were dismantled in 1906.

As a matter of fact, another Mint had been established in 1905 in *Tsinkiangpu,* Kiangsu province, with the sole object of supplying the district with copper coins. During the first year of its existence 339 million copper blanks and 5,000 piculs of copper were imported. But it was closed down some years thereafter. The Tsinkiangpu Mint had a capacity of 1 million 1 cent copper pieces per diem.

The universal recognition of the necessity of providing the country with a uniform currency, based on a coin with a clearly fixed standard weight and fineness, led to the determination on the part of all factors concerned to erect a modern coinage plant for the purpose of striking silver coins. After careful consideration *Shanghai* was chosen as the most suitable place where the new Mint should be erected. It was to be provided with the most modern machinery, capable of producing 500,000 silver dollars a day.

On March 3, 1921, a contract was signed by a Chinese banking group on the one part, the Minister of Finance and the Director of the Currency Bureau on the other, providing for a loan of $2,500,000.00. The major portion of this sum served for the purchase of land, for the erection of the numerous buildings and for administrative expenses. It proved, however, insufficient to meet the cost of the extensive plant, which though it had arrived in Shanghai, could not be installed owing to lack of funds.

In such circumstances the Ministry of Finance was forced to temporarily suspend work on the Shanghai Mint; on August 18, 1924, a Presidental mandate was issued accordingly. The affairs of the Shanghai administrative Mint office were wound up and the entire Mint property placed under the custody of the Shanghai Bankers Association.

The project lay still dormant at the close of 1925, waiting for the time when the Peking Government would wield sufficient power to enforce its regulations.

The Mint for CHIHLI province was established by imperial edict at *Tientsin,* in 1901, and began operations in 1904. It produced dragon dollars and subsidiary silver coins. When new national currency regulations were promulgated in 1910, it was decreed that the Tientsin establishment should be the Central Mint for China. Its administration was placed under a Director-General, styled *Chiento.* The moulds and dies were to be made at the Central Mint at Tientsin and supplied to the numerous establishments in the provinces, thus ensuring uniformity in the design of the coins. The outbreak of the revolution in October of 1911 and the subsequent looting and burning by the mob of the Tientsin Central Mint in March, 1912, frustrated the realisation of prearranged plans.

The Tientsin Central Mint was resuscitated in 1914. Supplied with new and modern machinery, it was responsible for the designing and manufacture of the Yuan Shih-Kai dollar, the dies for which were supplied to the Mints situated in the other provinces. In the course of the general tendency to decentralise, the latter became quite independent from the Central Mint at Tientsin, obeying exclusively the dictates of the provincial authorities.

Seeing that there was practically no profit connected with the minting of dollar coins, the Tientsin Central Mint turned its attention, towards the close of 1923, to the manufacture of 10, 20 and 50 cents silver coins. Its activities soon resulted in overproduction and subsequent depreciation of auxiliary silver coinage, so that work on this particular line had to be stopped after a few months trial. Then followed another attempt to turn out copper coins, notably 2 cents pieces. In the beginning the venture proved very profitable indeed, but an oversupply resulted in a depreciation of copper cents which, in the summer of 1924, fell to 260 cents to the dollar. The market soon became saturated with the deluge of those double-cents pieces and declined to take any more. But the Mint went on with the production of coppers, pledging these as security with local banks, in consideration of loans obtained. In the autumn of 1924 work had to be stopped by the Central Mint at Tientsin. Apart from the considerations already cited, rumours were then current in connection with defalcations committed by some members of the administrative staff of the Mint.

There is a second Mint in existence in Tientsin, established during the opening years of the twentieth century. It is styled the *Peyang* Mint, was intended primarily for the manufacture of copper coins and is being treated as a branch of the Tientsin Central Mint.

The Provincial Mint of HUPEH is situated in the capital *Wuchang*. It was founded in 1893 by Viceroy *Chang Chih-tung,* who had been transferred from Canton to Hupeh province. Operations had already been started in the following year, when dragon dollars were turned out. The Wuchang Mint began to produce copper cents for the first time in 1900. Modern equipment was purchased in 1902 for the manufacture of copper coins; the latter were in constant demand in those times, so that it was deemed expedient to open another copper Mint in 1905 (as a branch of the Wuchang establishment) at Hanyang. It was, however, closed again in 1906.

Owing to its excessive production of copper coins the Wuchang Mint was closed in 1909, only to be reopened a year later under the direction of the Peking authorities. After the outbreak of the revolution the management of the Mint reverted to the governor of Hupeh, and though the Mint is supposed to be once more under the control of the Central Government (since 1914), it is merely so in name.

The provincial Mint at Wuchang is responsible for the output of excessive quantities of 1 cent and, since 1917, also of 2 cents copper coins. But it has also produced large quantities of dragon dollars and Yuan Shih-Kai dollars; the latter were turned out during a part of the years 1924 and 1925 at the rate of $120,000 a day.

The Wuchang Mint is well equipped and boasts of 240 furnaces for smelting and beating. There are 11 engines and boilers, 105 stamping machines, 23 rolling machines, 2 electric light and power plants, 29 chimneys, etc.

The Mint of HUNAN province, situated at *Changsha,* dates back to 1901. At times it attempted silver coinage, but its principal activities were devoted to coinage of copper. The quantities of 10 and 20 cash coins turned out were so great that the ratio between the silver dollar and the copper cent reached 1 to 300 in 1924. This fact, together with official accusations regarding "squeeze," made advisable a temporary closing down of the Mint in 1925.

The provincial Mint of ANHWEI, established in 1902, is situated in *Anking.*

It succeeded another coinage plant which had been dismantled there in 1899. The Anking Mint began its career by striking 5 and 10-cash coins. The production of the 5-cash pieces was soon abandoned, but the coining of the 10-cash copper coins continued for several years. The output of 1 cent coppers, in 1905, by the Anking Mint was estimated at 240 million pieces. During that year one Mexican dollar exchanged at Anking for 95 coppers on an average. The production of copper coins by the Anhwei provincial Mint, during the following two years, had grown so prolific, that the Anking Mint had to close down in 1907, seeing that the market was overflooded with 10-cash coins. In the course of the following years the Anhwei provincial Mint had a checkered career. It re-started operations in December, 1919, having a capacity of 1 million coppers a day.

The Mint became notorious in the summer of 1924, when it supplied the country with debased Yuan Shih-Kai dollars, marked eighth years of the Republic. The outcry against the authorities' malpractices became so great that the Maritime Customs was obliged to interfere by preventing silver shipments, destined for Anhwei province, from passing Nanking. An official investigation into the shady doings of the Mint authorities was demanded and promised towards the close of 1924. But as the Mint was then under the "protection" of the military, nothing tangible could be done in the matter. Apart from adulterated Yuan Shih-Kai dollars, Anking also supplied the country with debased 10 and 20 cents pieces.

In common with most of the other provincial Mints KIANGSI had its Mint decreed in 1901. But the Mint at *Nanchang* was closed in 1905 and so remained for a time. More than twenty years after its inception the Kiangsi

Mint was converted into a semi-official concern, one of the shareholders being the Kiangsi Provincial Bank. A novel scheme provided that the coins turned out by the Nanchang Mint should be lodged with the said bank, in order to form a specie reserve against the latter's bank-notes issue. But complications arose when the time came to determine the rights and duties of the parties concerned, and furthermore, the actual identity of these parties. This dispute caused the Mint to close down temporarily towards the end of 1924,—a blessing in disguise. For it is not further supplies of copper cents that the country is in need of.

During the spring of 1925 the Mint at Nanchang, as also the Nanchang Provincial Bank, ceased to be a semi-official concern and returned to its old status of a purely government institution. In the summer of 1925 the new director of the Kiangsi Mint was endeavoring to raise a loan of $500,000.00 for the purpose of reorganising the undertaking. It is intended that hereafter the Mint should turn out silver coins.

The provincial Mint at Wuchang had contracted to deliver large supplies of silver dollars during the autumn of 1925. As its own plant was not able promptly to cope with the task, the authorities passed an order to the Mint at Nanchang, for the supply of 2,500,000 silver dollars. The Nanchang Mint has a capacity of 100,000 dollars a day and was supposed to complete the order by the end of September, 1925.

Of more recent origin is the Mint of YUNNAN which was founded in 1905. It is situated at *Kunming*. Originally established for the purpose of producing copper coins, it began operations in 1908, turning out dragon dollars, subsidiary silver coins and copper cents. Since August, 1907, copper coins, struck by the Szechuen Mint, for Yunnan province, (with the name of the latter province on the reverse) have been in circulation there.

Though nominally placed under the control of the Board of Revenue, Peking, the Mint at Yunnan soon became independent. Immediately after the revolution (October, 1911) it began to follow its own policy.

One of the results of the World War was the embargo in 1917 on the export of bullion from Hongkong and Tonkin. Thus sources of supply of precious metals were cut off from Yunnan. The melting of good dollars and re-minting of bad dollars and subsidiary coins was the consequent result of a desperate situation. There were coins manufactured by the Yunnan Mint which, beginning from 1915, bore the effigy of the energetic provincial governor, T'ang Chi-yao. Due to the peculiar conditions just described the good T'ang Chi-yao dollar, 0.862 fine, was driven out by a new dragon dollar, made by the Yunnan Mint, which was only 0.602 fine, and by a half dollar, containing a lesser quantity of silver.

The Yunnan Mint was the first to mint, in 1919, gold coins in quantity. Needless to say, the Yunnan Mint has also produced copper and subsidiary silver coins in large quantities. In the autumn of 1924 the Yunnan Mint imported new German machinery. A remarkable feature of the silver subsidiary coins is that these were actually decimal subdivisions of the Yunnan dollar; 10 coins of a face value of 10 cents each, or 5 coins of 20 cents each, to exchange for one dollar.

This has possibly been accomplished through the rigid observation relating to the prohibition of the importation of other provinces' subsidiary coins.

The Mint for the province of SHANTUNG was opened at *Tsinanfu* in 1905. It began its career by producing copper cent pieces and, during the first eighteen months of its existence, managed to realise a profit of about 30%. The deliberate overproduction, combined with the influx of similar copper coins from neighbouring provinces, caused the exchange value of the 10-cash piece to drop from 100–130 to the silver dollar. This was the position in October, 1907. The people began to object to the gradual absorption of the old cash coins, as the new 10 cash pieces could not replace the former. The old Mint was closed in 1906 and remained closed for years, its administrative staff having been transferred to Tientsin. In 1922 preparations were made for the re-opening of the Tsinan Mint, but early in 1925 matters had not yet progressed sufficiently to permit of the resumption of work.

The province of SZECHUEN is supplied with two Mints, of which the older one dates back to 1901; it is situated at the capital, *Chengtu*. The other Mint is operating at *Chungking*.

Until 1902 only copper cash and sycee were current in Szechuen. In course of that year the Chengtu Mint supplied the market with dragon dollars, with silver coins of 20, 10 and 5 cents face value, and with 1 cent copper pieces. The innovation met with but scanty success, in spite of the Viceroy's proclamation ordering the use of the new coins and permitting their acceptance in payment of taxes and dues. But it required years before the coins began to circulate freely.

Since the advent of the Republic the two Mints at Szechuen have been supplying the province with numerous specimens of a coin, which distinguish themselves by design, entirely different from the regular series, and also by inferior fine contents. The issues include $1, 50, 20 and 10 cents, in silver; and 200, 100, 50, 20 and 10 cash, in copper.

In August, 1925, on the occasion of one of the numerous civil wars, soldiers entering Chengtu looted the Mint there, carrying away all the silver and copper on which they could lay their hands.

The province of KUANGSI boasts of two Mints. The original institution was created by imperial decree at the capital *Nanning*, in 1905. It deemed its mission to supply the province with coppers and subsidiary silver coins. After having stood idle for some years the Mint, in 1919, recommenced operations. But owing to lack of raw material and subsequent hostilities with the neighboring province of Kwangtung, operations were suspended after a few months' working. In 1925 the Nanning Mint was still idle.

A second provincial Mint is located at *Wuchow.* This establishment was created in 1920 for the purpose of turning out subsidiary silver coins. The larger portion of the machinery arrived in January, 1921, but owing to the invasion of the province by the Kwangtung troops the question of starting operations was left in abeyance.

The province of SHANSI has its Mint since 1919, at the capital *Taiyuanfu.* During the World War the price of copper rose considerably, so that there was a universal attempt throughout China to collect the circulating copper cash coins and replace them with 1 cent copper pieces. The provincial authorities were not slow in realizing opportunities which were then offering; so they ordered their own coinage equipment. In the beginning the Mint's output was well received and proved useful in replacing the rapidly disappearing copper cash. But as elsewhere in China there soon was an overproduction of coppers, which found expression in the following quotations: During the first 2 years of the Shansi Mint's career (in 1919 and 1920) one dollar exchanged on an average for 150–160 coppers; in 1924 the ratio had exceeded 200. During the early autumn of 1925 the supply of locally minted 1 cent copper coins had become so prolific that 300 would exchange for one dollar.

The Mint for HONAN province is situated in the capital, *Kaifengfu.* It produced copper coins only, all of the 10 *cash* pattern. In the early days of the Republic it turned out 10 cash pieces with the Chia-ho pattern on the reverse and the nine-pointed republican star on the obverse.

The Kaifengfu Mint was definitely closed in November, 1914.

The province of SHENSI is in possession of a copper Mint. Nevertheless the governor, in 1923, ordered from Germany complete minting machinery with a capacity of 500,000 copper coins a day. The new Mint was to be erected in the capital *Sianfu.* The plant arrived in Shanghai in the early summer of 1924 and was forwarded to Hankow for transport to its destination. However, shortly thereafter governor *Liu* of Shensi province decided to go on the war-path. In order to obtain a supply of ammunition from the neighboring province he was obliged to pledge the mint machinery and other factory equipment (then still lying at Hankow) to the governor of Shansi province. *Liu* lost his little war and simultaneously the new coinage equipment.

Output of Mints.

On account of the scant importance attached in China to the value of statistics, and owing to the decentralisation of government functions, reliable statistical material is very difficult to obtain in this country.

The following figures are merely fragmentary evidence of some of the Chinese Mint's doings during certain periods. Most of the provincial Mint authorities do not see any advantage in publishing particulars relative to the outputs of the coinage plants under their control.

Output of dollar coins by the Mints at:

Year	*Nanking*	*Hangchow*	*Tientsin*	*Wuchang*
1923 . . .	$58,017,000	$50,000,000	$7,950,000	—
1922 . . .	$25,673,000	—	—	—
1921 . . .	$15,594,000	—	$7,158,000	$4,500,000

Date and Mint Inscriptions.

The first round coin bearing an inscription was issued during the rule of the *Chou* dynasty (1122–255 B.C.). The following characters are to be found on coins cast during those remote times: 寶化, *Pao hua,* meaning "valuable coin," 寶四化, *Pao Ssu Hua,* denoting "valuable four coins," and 寶六化, *Pao Liu Hua,* signifying "valuable six coins," by which is meant, coin equal in weight to four, respectively six, units of the first mentioned coin. These coins are interesting as being the first on which appears the character 寶 *Pao,* which became ultimately one of the terms in the combinations 通寶, current valuable coin, which is still employed on the modern Chinese copper coins. 通寶 *T'ung Pao* is translated as meaning "currency."[1]

The custom to inscribe the copper coins with the title of the period of the reign of the imperial family has been a very old one. It dates back to the *Han* dynasty (140–86 B.C.), but at that time the inscribing of the 年號 *Nien Hao,* on coins was not a regular practice in China. But it became such from the commencement of the rule of the *T'ang* dynasty, in A.D. 618, and lasted without interruption until the end of the Manchu dynasty, in A.D. 1911.

The copper coins issued during the Manchu regime (A.D. 1616–1911), bear inscriptions which are fashioned after one pattern. On the obverse one reads: *Shun Chih T'ung Pao,* meaning "Currency of the *Shun Chih* period." On the reverse one Chinese character indicates the Mint, at which the coin was cast; for instance, 原 *Yüan* standing for 太原 *T'ai Yüan,* the capital of Shansi province.

Turning to the issue of modern coins, and especially these of the *Tai Ching Ti Kuo* series, one observes that the date of issue is inscribed on the reverse, mostly by means of the symbols of the Ten Celestial Stems, combined with those of the Twelve Branches. The following list indicates those characters in numerical order:[2]

---

[1] Sir James H. Stewart Lockhart, "The Stewart Lockhart Collection of Chinese Copper Coins," Kelly & Walsh, Ltd., Shanghai 1915.

[2] H. A. Ramsden "Modern Chinese Copper Coins," 1911.

Ten Celestial Stems (天 干)		*Twelve Branches* (十 二 支)	
(1) 甲 Chia	(6) 己 Chi	(1) 子 Tzu	(7) 午 Wu
(2) 乙 Yi	(7) 庚 Keng	(2) 丑 Ch'ou	(8) 未 Wei
(3) 丙 Ping	(8) 辛 Hsin	(3) 寅 Yin	(9) 申 Shen
(4) 丁 Ting	(9) 壬 Jen	(4) 卯 Mao	(10) 酉 Yu
(5) 戊 Hou	(10) 癸 Kuei	(5) 辰 Shen	(11) 戌 Hsu
		(6) 巳 Ssu	(12) 亥 Hai

The issues of the *T'ai Ching Ti Kuo* series have one single character in the center of the reverse of the coin, representing the province where it is meant to circulate. Coins intended for general circulation within the empire bore no character whatsoever. On all others one of the following characters is to be found:

(1) 皖 for An Hwei
(2) 浙 ,, Che Chiang
(3) 直 ,, Chih Li
(4) 閩 ,, Fu Kien
(5) 奉 ,, Fung Tien
(6) 汴 ,, Ho Nan
(7) 湘 ,, Hu Nan
(8) 鄂 for Hu Peh
(9) 粵 ,, Kwang Tung or Kwang Si
(10) 甯 ,, Nan King
(11) 東 ,, Shan Tung
(12) 滇 ,, Yu Nan

APPENDIX I.

REVISED REGULATIONS OF
THE SHANGHAI GOLD STOCK EXCHANGE, LD.

(A rough translation from the Chinese text.)

Chapter I.

GENERAL INTRODUCTION.

Art. 1. This Exchange is engaged in buying and selling gold for cash and forward delivery.

Chapter II.

BUSINESS HOURS AND HOLIDAYS.

Art. 2. Transactions for forward delivery take place from 9-12 in the morning and 2-4 in the afternoon every day. But on Saturday the afternoon market is closed, while on Sunday the market is open from 11-12 A.M. On the 16th of every month, old contracts will be carried forward. The morning market commences at 8.30 and lasts until 12 noon.

Should transactions not be completed at the closing time of the market an extension of not more than 30 minutes may be allowed.

This Exchange is closed in the afternoon on Saturdays and Sundays and on all bank holidays.

Art. 3. Cash transactions can be fixed at any time when required.

Chapter III.

BROKERS AND THEIR AGENTS.

Art. 4. Brokers must be managers of the members' firms of the Shanghai Gold Dealers' Association. When the manager is elected as director or superintendent of this Exchange, he may appoint any qualified member of his firm to be his agent. The above mentioned brokers are required each to file an application and a statement giving the particulars of their business to the Exchange, and the latter will forward same to the Ministry of Agriculture and Commerce for registration and license. If a broker's firm has a partner, the name of the firm, the copy of the partnership agreement, the application of their representative and particulars of his business career must be sent to the Exchange.

Whoever has any one of the attributes mentioned in article XII of the Produce Exchange Law is debarred from becoming a broker.

Art. 5. The number of brokers of this Exchange is fixed at 138.

Art. 6. Brokers and their agents are not allowed to get into the market without wearing their badges, issued by this Exchange.

The badge should not be lent or given to another party. In case of loss or damage, a new badge may be issued against payment of two Shanghai taels.

Art. 7. Should a broker fail to carry out his contracts, either for cash or forward delivery, he will be disqualified as a broker; his shares in the Exchange, together with his margin money, will be detained for the settlement of his obligations.

Art. 8. All unfinished transactions handled by a broker so disqualified must be settled by that broker himself, or by any other broker appointed by the Exchange. After settlement, any balance of the value of his shares or of his margin money is to be returned to the said broker; should his shares and margin money be insufficient for making the settlement, the shareholders of the Gold Shop, which is represented by the said broker, are liable to make up the deficiency in proportion to to the shares they hold.

Art. 9. Brokers should return their licences and badges to the Exchange on their retirement.

Art. 10. Brokers are supposed to be cognizant of and to observe all bye-laws, regulations and other necessary announcements of this Exchange, immediately after publication.

Art. 11. Should the account books of the broker's firm be kept in any way contrary to the regulations of this Exchange, the Exchange has the right to examine them, and any question put by the Exchange should be answered fully by the broker's firm.

Art. 12. Brokers shall not refuse to allow the Exchange to take any or all of their documents, whenever necessary.

Art. 13. This Exchange will ask the Ministry of Agriculture and Commerce to withdraw the registration and licence of any broker who is discovered and reported by the Brokers' Association to have become a broker in another Exchange of the same nature.

Art. 14. Every broker may appoint five agents to transact business for him at this Exchange.

This Exchange may dismiss any agent or deny him entrance whenever he is considered to be unfit.

Chapter IV.

BROKERS' ASSOCIATION.

Art. 15. All the brokers should organize themselves into an Association for the purpose of promoting business interests and rectifying abusive practices.

Art. 16. The revision of any part or the whole of the rules, regulations and resolutions of the Brokers' Association may be ordered by this Exchange, if they are considered unsuitable.

Officers of the Brokers' Association can be dismissed or re-elected by order of this Exchange, when they are found to be inefficient in the performance of their duties.

The Chairman and other Directors of this Exchange may be present at any meeting convened by the Brokers' Association, whenever their presence is considered to be absolutely necessary.

Chapter V.

BUYING AND SELLING ORDERS.

Art. 17. All privileges and duties between brokers and customers shall, apart from conforming to the Regulations issued by the Ministry of Agriculture and Commerce, be in accordance with the bye-laws, regulations, and other specifications of this Exchange as well as the Rules of the Brokers' Association.

Brokers may settle any contract for their customer even without his consent in case of his non-observance of the above mentioned rules, and dispose of his margin money and other securities. When any case, such as the one mentioned above, happens, the broker shall at once report it to this Exchange, and notification will be posted in the market.

Art. 18. When a transaction is completed, the broker must notify his customer immediately, taking care to tell him precisely the number of bars sold or bought, the price, date of delivery, and other particulars.

Art. 19. In accepting an order, the broker shall at the same time collect the margin money or other securities in lieu thereof from the customer, all of which must not be returned until the transaction is completely settled.

Art. 20. Should the customer fail to deliver to his broker the margin money, or the commodity, or its equivalent value, or the amount of loss or any other thing or money for the settlement of his expired contract, the broker may dispose of the funds and other commodities he has collected, as mentioned in the foregoing article, at his own discretion.

The customer will be held liable to pay the balance in case his funds and securities should prove insufficient to settle his debt.

Chapter VI.

BUYING AND SELLING TRANSACTIONS.

Art. 21. Commodities transacted at this Exchange are articles of yellow gold:—(1) Gold produced in China, (2) Gold bullions & coins of all countries, (3) Gold bars (Standard fineness usually accepted in Shanghai is 978. Each ping is 70 Chaoping taels in weight,—a ping consists of seven bars—and is the unit adopted in transactions. The price quoted is for 10 taels), (4) Red Gold Bars (this gold is the pure gold used by goldsmiths and gold shops in the provinces and at Shanghai. Each ping is 50 Chaoping taels in weight and it is the unit in buying and selling. The price quoted is for 10 taels.) The bidding unit is five Shanghai taels cents.

Art. 22. This Exchange transacts business both for cash and for forward delivery. Our method is to find a buyer for a seller, or vice versa.

Art. 23. Transactions for cash delivery should be settled on the same day: while contracts for forward delivery are limited to two months. Gold bars for any month's delivery may be bought or sold or settled at any time, provided it is done within the time limit (before the delivery falls due).

Art. 24. The contract of each transaction, after being sealed and checked by brokers of both buying and selling parties, should be handed to Market Service Department for evidence. If any mistake is found, the buying and selling brokers must make another contract and hand it to the above department.

Before handing the contract to the Book Department for accounting, this Exchange may grant any request for correction with the consent of both buyer and seller; but this Exchange may refuse the request, if it is made after the contract has been handed in for accounting and when no mistake is discoverable.

Art. 25. The number of bars, price, the numbers of buyer and seller, and the date of a cash transaction shall be reported to the Market Service Department for record.

Art. 26. Unfixed date transactions by mutual agreement will be arranged by the Board of Directors, when necessary, after this Exchange has commenced business.

CHAPTER VII.

PERSONAL GUARANTEE AND TRANSACTION SECURITY FUNDS.

ART. 27. Brokers doing business at this Exchange must each deposit with this Exchange, as personal guarantee, 200 shares of this Exchange, for which a receipt will be issued, but this receipt must not be bartered away or mortgaged for any loan from outsiders.

ART. 28. For forward transactions, margin money is divided into three classes:—(1) margin money for the present transaction, (2) margin money paid in advance, and (3) special margin money.

ART. 29. The brokers shall pay Tls. 10 as margin money for every bar bought or sold, after balancing their account of previous transactions, according to the price announced by the Booking Department. The same procedure shall be followed the next day; the price of the Booking Department shall be the standard price; if the balance falls short of Tls. 10 per bar, the deficit must be made up; if it is more, the surplus will be paid back upon application.

Margin money for the morning market should be paid before 2 P.M. and for the afternoon market before 6 P.M.. Any broker failing to do so, will forfeit his qualifications immediately.

ART. 30. When a broker has transacted business up to several thousand bars already, and wants to buy or sell some more, he is required to deposit some margin money in advance, should the Exchange consider his operations too risky. Such margin money should be handed to the Exchange immediately when called for. He shall not be allowed to make any more new contracts, unless such preliminary margin has been paid; this margin will be applied to cover any further business he may do.

ART. 31. When the market fluctuates extraordinarily, or in case of an emergency, this Exchange may ask for special margin, on part or whole of the unsettled contracts, when it deems its payment necessary. Amount and term of such special margin will be fixed by this Exchange.

ART. 32. In place of cash, various bonds, if recognized by this Exchange, and capital stocks of this Exchange may be accepted as first margin, at a price to be fixed by this Exchange from time to time.

CHAPTER VIII.

COMMISSION AND BONUS.

ART. 33. This Exchange charges commission from both sides, buyer and seller, amounting to Shanghai Taels 0.06 per bar; 75% of which is given to the broker and 25% to this Exchange. Commission shall be collected at the same time when the first margin is received.

This Exchange will give one quarter of the 25% to the respective brokers as bonus.

CHAPTER IX.

OFFICIAL MARKET PRICE AND CALCULATION.

ART. 34. The price fixed by the Booking Department at noon for the morning market shall be the standard price binding on all forward transactions; the amount of difference will be calculated thereby, the minimum unit will be one tael, that is, 4 mace will be cast off and 5 mace will be counted for one tael. At 4 P.M. the afternoon market is closed, when the margin shall be readjusted, if there is a difference of Tls. 5 per bar; if not, readjustment may take place next day.

ART. 35. The difference between the book-value and the average value of all selling and buying done by a broker shall be fully paid by native banks clearing check every day; otherwise, the said broker is to be suspended from doing further business.

Balance of cash margin, if any, can be transferred and applied in paying the amount of difference; but bonds and capital stocks are not transferable.

Art. 36. Should a broker be entitled to receive cash for one item and pay out money on account of another, at the same time, he may square his account of difference, commission and first margin, by the process of arithmetic cancellation.

Chapter X.

SETTLEMENT.

Art. 37. On the monthly expiration of forward delivery the seller can take delivery at any time from the beginning to the end of that month, except Sundays and Holidays.

Art. 38. Should the actual gold be delivered against contract for forward delivery, the seller has to hand his invoice to this Exchange before 5 P.M. on the previous day; and the Exchange will notify the buyer before 7 P.M. On the day of settlement, the seller must deliver his goods to this Exchange before 11.30 A.M., and the buyer must procure from the Exchange the goods against payment of the price, (only native bank's clearing check will be acceptable) ruling on the previous day.

Before the delivery of gold bars to the buyer, the seller is responsible for any shortage in their weight. Shortage in weight of every seven bars must not exceed five mace. Only Gold bars whose marks have been approved by the Gold Dealers' Association will be accepted in settlement when the seller shall bring the Certificate of Marks issued by the Association. Any shortage can be made up according to this Certificate as well as a report of analysis signed by a foreign assayer, at a price fixed by this Exchange.

Art. 39. If the buying party is composed of more than two persons, the gold bars are to be distributed proportionally in the presence of a representative of this Exchange. Should the broker, who makes the transaction, be absent at the time of delivery, this Exchange has the right to act for him.

Art. 40. At the time of delivering the actual gold bars, the parties concerned must accept the rate given by the Public Assaying Office (Kung-Ku) as standard (of fineness & weight).

Art. 41. In case of cash delivery only the American gold dollar and the Japanese yen are accepted for settlement. One bar equals G$ 240 or Yen 480. In such case the seller has to pay to the buyer 5 mace a bar to cover mint expenses.

Art. 42. If the goods covered by a forward contract cannot be delivered when due, (for example, the seller purchases gold coins from abroad, but owing to delay on the way, he has nothing to deliver on due date), such contract is to be settled according to the first official rate for telegraphic transfer of yen quoted by the Hongkong and Shanghai Bank on the day (yen 480 makes one bar), three taels is to be paid on each bar for freight which is stipulated in the bye-laws of the Gold Dealers' Association, against which the buyer must not protest, nor must he refuse acceptance.

Chapter XI.

ARBITRATION.

Art. 43. If any dispute should arise between brokers, or between a broker and a customer, in connection with their business, upon application by the parties concerned stating that they will not bring the matter to the court, this Exchange will nominate three arbitrators from the officers of the Brokers' Association to hear and decide the case. After this, no further protest should be raised by either party.

CHAPTER XII.

PUNISHMENT.

ART. 44. When deceit in transaction is found out on the part of a broker, the Exchange will have to cancel the transaction and dismiss the broker.

ART. 45. Brokers who make any private transactions will be fined $500 and deprived of the bonus which they may be entitled to receive from this Exchange.

ART. 46. Brokers may be suspended from doing business by the Exchange for any one of the following offences:—

(1) Anyone who has intentionally upset the market or acted violently.
(2) Violating the bye-laws, regulations, announcements, and directions of this Exchange or the Brokers' Association.
(3) Contravention of any business etiquette which this Exchange may consider harmful to the credit of brokers.
(4) Disturbing the market with false rumours and improper dealings.
(5) Attempting to obtain compensation from this Exchange by unfair means.

ART. 47. After the suspension of his business, a broker is, however, allowed to buy or sell within a definite time sufficient goods to settle his old contracts.

ART. 48. In enforcing these regulations, opinions of the Brokers' Association may be taken into consideration whenever necessary.

CHAPTER XIII.

VAULT.

ART. 49. A vault is provided for the safe-keeping of books, securities and other articles concerning the business of this Exchange.

CHAPTER XIV.

APPENDIX.

ART. 50. Each of the following items will be announced in the market:—

(1) Orders and proclamations of the Government.
(2) Bye-laws, rules and regulations of this Exchange.
(3) Foreign and local financial news.
(4) Forfeiture of qualifications or death of a broker.
(5) The closing of any broker's firm.
(6) Suspension and recovery of a broker's business.
(7) The holding of an Extraordinary Meeting and alteration of the meeting time.
(8) Announcement of the market rate.
(9) Fixing or altering the rate of commission.
(10) Amount of margin fixed by the Brokers' Association.
(11) Matters in connection with a settlement.
(12) Matters in connection with arbitration.
(13) The imposition of a penalty.
(14) Anything considered necessary by the Brokers' Association.
(15) Alteration of the value of any security.
(16) Other essential questions.

Art. 51. Should any question arise in the course of this Exchange's business which is not mentioned in the present bye-laws of this Exchange, the bye-laws and other obligations of the Produce Exchange may be applied in dealing with the said question, provided the opinion of the Brokers' Association is respected. The decision shall be announced in the market.

Art. 52. Any alteration of the bye-laws of this Exchange must be decided by the Board of Directors and approved by the Ministry of Agriculture and Commerce. The above bye-laws have been approved by the Ministry of Agriculture and Commerce, and registered in the Mixed Court of the International Settlement of Shanghai, for observance by this Exchange.

APPENDIX II.

WORLD'S PRODUCTION OF GOLD SINCE THE DISCOVERY OF AMERICA.

Period.	Average annual for period.		Total for period.	
	Fine ounces.	Value.	Fine ounces.	Value.
1493-1520	186,470	$3,855,000	5,221,160	$107,931,000
1521-1544	230,194	4,759,000	5,524,656	114,205,000
1545-1560	273,596	5,656,000	4,377,544	90,492,000
1561-1580	219,906	4,546,000	4,398,120	90,917,000
1581-1600	237,267	4,905,000	4,745,340	98,095,000
1601-1620	273,918	5,662,000	5,478,360	113,248,000
1621-1640	266,845	5,516,000	5,336,900	110,324,000
1641-1660	281,955	5,828,000	5,639,110	116,571,000
1661-1680	297,709	6,154,000	5,954,180	123,084,000
1681-1700	346,095	7,154,000	6,921,895	143,088,000
1701-1720	412,163	8,520,000	8,243,260	170,403,000
1721-1740	613,422	12,681,000	12,268,440	253,611,000
1741-1760	791,211	16,356,000	15,824,230	327,116,000
1761-1780	665,666	13,761,000	13,313,315	275,211,000
1781-1800	571,948	11,823,000	11,438,970	236,464,000
1801-1810	571,563	11,815,000	5,715,627	118,152,000
1811-1820	367,957	7,606,000	3,679,568	76,063,000
1821-1830	457,044	9,448,000	4,570,444	94,479,000
1831-1840	652,291	13,484,000	6,522,913	134,841,000
1841-1850	1,760,502	36,393,000	17,605,018	363,928,000
1851-1855	6,410,324	132,513,000	32,051,621	662,566,000
1856-1860	6,486,262	134,083,000	32,431,312	670,415,000
1861-1865	5,949,582	122,989,000	29,747,913	614,944,000
1866-1870	6,270,086	129,614,000	31,350,430	648,071,000
1871-1875	5,591,014	115,577,000	27,955,068	577,883,000
1876-1880	5,543,110	114,586,000	27,715,550	572,931,000
1881-1885	4,794,755	99,116,000	23,973,773	495,582,000
1886-1890	5,461,282	112,895,000	27,306,411	564,474,000
1891-1895	7,882,565	162,947,000	39,412,823	814,736,000
1896			9,783,914	202,251,600
1897			11,420,068	236,073,700
1898			13,877,806	286,879,700
1890			14,837,775	306,724,100
1900			12,315,135	254,576,300
1901			12,625,527	260,992,900
1902			14,321,360	296,048,800
1903			15,747,378	325,527,200
1904			16,739,448	346,034,500
1905			18,599,937	384,495,700
1906			19,471,080	402,503,000
1907			19,977,260	412,966,600
1908			21,422,244	442,836,900
1909			21,965,111	454,059,100
1910			22,022,180	455,239,100
1911			22,348,313	461,939,700
1912			22,549,335	466,136,100
1913			22,249,596	459,941,100
1914			22,039,548	455,676,600
1915			22,674,568	468,724,918
1916			22,107,669	457,006,045
1917			21,240,416	439,078,260
1918			18,557,000	383,606,000
1919			17,695,000	365,789,000
1920			16,303,000	337,019,000
1921			15,939,000	330,232,000
1922			15,440,200	319,178,000
1923			17,772,200	366,940,884
1924			18,596,000	384,278,000

The data from 1493 to 1885 is from a table of averages, compiled by Dr. Adolph Soetbeer. From 1886 onwards the figures represent the estimate of the U.S.A. Bureau of the Mint. The figures since 1918 are compiled on the basis of estimates contained in various financial Journals and are to be considered as approximate only.

SOURCES OF GOLD PRODUCTION FOR THE YEARS 1921 TO 1924.

In order to show the principal sources of gold production the following table, taken from Samuel Montagu & Co's., London, Annual Bullion Letter, 1924, is quoted here:

	1924 (est.)	1923.	1922.	1921.
TRANSVAAL	£40,800,000	£38,800,000	£29,800,000	£34,500,000
CANADA	6,500,000	5,200,000	5,400,000	3,900,000
AUSTRALASIA	3,500,000	3,700,000	3,900,000	3,800,000
RHODESIA	2,600,000	2,700,000	2,800,000	2,500,000
INDIA	1,800,000	1,600,000	1,800,000	1,800,000
WEST AFRICA	800,000	800,000	900,000	900,000
TOTAL	£56,000,000	£52,800,000	£44,600,000	£47,400,000
Approximate World's Total ..	£79,000,000	£75,500,000	£65,500,000	£68,000,000
British percentage of Total ..	70·9	69·9	68·1	69·7

APPENDIX III.

SOME AUTHORITIES ON THE TAEL

The tael as measure of values has, during many centuries, been of prime importance to the destinies of China and deserves closer investigation and description. Not many economists have chosen the intricacies of the tael currency as object for research work. Of the existing treatise on the tael some of the more important and authoritative versions are quoted here in detail.

Gratitude is due to the Chinese Maritime Customs for having investigated and reported on currency questions within China with just as much exactitude as authority. The complexities and the variations of Chinese currency questions are watched and carefully recorded by the numerous Customs stations which are spread all over the vast country, and particulars are made known to the world through the excellent periodical Customs reports.

As an individual authority no one has so far excelled H. B. Morse, formerly Commissioner of Customs, who has written some masterly essays on things Chinese in general, and on currency questions in particular. His writings are often cited and justly taken as *dictum.*

Though exceedingly brief in space only, Henry Deutsch, in his well-known work, entitled *Arbitrage,* (London, 1910), has given the world an excellent definition of the tael.

During recent years the bulletins issued by the *Chinese Government Bureau of Economic Information* are endeavoring to contribute towards the knowledge of China's currency systems.

The following interesting particulars are quoted *verbatim* as contained in *Gold Standard in International Trade* (Washington, 1904) p.p. 227 to 249. The contents of the report relate to the period from 1864 to 1895, but it should be taken into consideration that the statements contained therein are just as true to-day as they were when originally written.

SYCEE: WEIGHT, VALUE, TOUCH—V. OFFICE SERIES:

CUSTOMS PAPERS NO. 47.

[Translation of a memorandum on the weights and monetary system of Shanghai, drawn up by Mons. G. Pietsch, of the Comptoir d'Escompte de Paris, and dated July, 1864.]

Weights.

The tael is a weight which is in use all over China; its weight varies considerably in the different cities of the Empire.

In transactions between Chinese and foreigners the Canton tael is the one in general use, as the port from which it takes its name is the one which was first opened to foreign trade in China.

In Shanghai use is made in business of two weights: (1) The Canton tael, for goods imported, viz., for silver in bars, whether from England, France, or America. (2) The Shanghai tael, for goods of Chinese origin, viz., for gold, bar and leaf; also for "sycee" silver. This question, however, will be gone into further on. According to local usage 100 Canton taels equal 102½ Shanghai taels.

I. CANTON TAEL.

According to the supplementary Franco-Chinese and Anglo-Chinese treaties signed at Shanghai in November, 1858, the Canton tael ought to weigh in French weight, 37.783 grams; in English weight, 1.333 ounces avoirdupois equals 1.215 ounces troy, or equals 24.30 pennyweights, equals 583.20 grains. These proportions are based on the convention made at Canton in 1770 between the supercargoes of the old East India Company and the privileged Chinese merchants who formerly there possessed the monopoly of the trade with foreigners. But in reality the Canton tael as in ordinary use in China is one-half per cent. lighter than the above-mentioned standard, and does not weigh more than 37.58 French grams (according to the scales of the agency of the Comptoir d'Escompte de Paris); according to the basis adopted by the English banks, 1.208 ounces troy weight, 24.16 pennyweights, 579.84 grains; 3,000 taels equal 302 pounds troy, or, better, equal 3,624 ounces troy; according to the standard of India equals 3.221⅓ tolahs (the weight known in India as a tolah being 180 grains troy or 11.662 grams).

According to Article XXVI of the French treaty of June 27, 1858, and Article XXIV of the English treaty of the same month, the head of the customs in each of the ports opened to trade ought to receive for himself and also deposit at the French and English consulates official (légales) scales both for goods and money, as well as weights and measures in exact conformity with the weights and measures in use at the Canton customs, marked with a stamp and a certificate (cachet) stating that they so conform to their standard. These standards were intended to serve as a basis for all payments of customs duties or to the Chinese Government; also that recourse might be had to them in all cases where there might be disagreement as to the weight or measure of goods.

II. SHANGHAI TAEL.

Having found that, contrary to the above-mentioned stipulation, the Chinese Government has not deposited at the consulates any standards of weights and that the weights in ordinary local use do not bear any official stamp of the Chinese Government, which does not usually interfere in such matters, I went to the Chinese custom-house of this city to compare the weights which are in use there with those employed by the agency of the Comptoir d'Escompte. After making myself acquainted with the conformity of the two weights, I made with some legal French weights a series of comparative weighings, which give the result that the

Shanghai tael weighs 36.64 French grams; 565.70 grains troy (perhaps only 565.43 grains—the English, as it appears, reckon it as 566 grains in round numbers); 3.143 Indian tolahs.

The Shanghai tael is therefore a real weight, and not one merely in name, as was told me on my arrival here.

At the Shanghai custom-house I found another weight, which is called the "Haikwan" or "Customs" tael. One hundred Haikwan taels weigh 102.90 Shanghai taels. This tael, it appears, is not in use commercially.

III. WEIGHTS IN USE FOR MERCHANDISE.

Besides the tael, there are other weights in use in China for goods. Subjoined is a list. The tael is the unit.

1 grain millet is a shu.
10 shu =1 lei.
10 lei =1 chu (pearl).
24 chu =1 liang (tael) =1.333 ounces avoirdupois or 37.873 grams.
16 liang=1 chin (catty)=1.333 pounds avoirdupois or 604.53 grams.
2 chin =1 yin.
30 chin =1 chün.
100 chin =1 tan (picul) =$133\frac{1}{3}$ pounds avoirdupois or 60.453 kilograms.
120 chin =1 shih (stone)=159.99 pounds avoirdupois or 72.544 kilograms.

In dealings where valuable goods are concerned the tael is subdivided into decimal fractional parts, as indicated in the table below, where the tael is dealt with as a monetary designation.

Monetary System.

I. MONEYS.

The tael is not only a weight, it is also an ideal value or monetary account term (monnaie de compte) in use in all the ports of north China.

In the English colony of Hongkong the current value is the Mexican dollar, but I am ignorant as to what is the usage in the Chinese southern ports, such as Canton, Foochow, Amoy and Formosa.

The value of the tael varies in the different cities in the same way as its weight. Considered in either sense there are considerable differences between the taels of Peking, Tientsin, Hankow, Kiukiang, Shanghai, Chefoo, Ningpo, etc. To estimate these differences properly it would be necessary to give oneself up specially to the study of the usage of each town. This is how the case stands in Shanghai.

(*a*) *Nominal money.*— Accounts are reckoned and kept in Shanghai currency taels. This standard of value serves equally well for exchange or ordinary business (matières et marchandises).

The subdivisions of the tael and their relations are:

Tael (Liang).	Mace (Ch'ien).	Candarin (Fên).	Cash (Li.)
1	10	100	1,000
	1	10	100
		1	10

(*b*) *Actual money.*—The only actual coined money is the li (small coins of copper), called by the English "cash" and by the French sapèque (from the Portuguese word sapeca).

It has been in use in China for more than 3,000 years. Its value as money is reckoned, as stated above, as the one-thousandth part of a tael; in reality, it has deteriorated, and its price is variable, according to the demand for the interior. At the moment the rate is 1,370 cash for 1 tael, which gives the value of a single cash as a little over half a French centime.

II. MONEY IN CIRCULATION.

Sycee.—For commercial transactions on a large scale a monetary unit so small as a cash would be of no use. All payments are made in silver bullion (sycee), a term employed in banking to express fine silver, in consequence of its resemblance to sai ssŭ, "fine silk."

The expression in ordinary use among the natives is not, however, sycee, but wên yin, "pure silver." The ingots are of different sizes. The ordinary weight is about 50 taels; there are some of 5 taels weight or less. Their form bears some resemblance to that of the Chinese shoe, from which "shoes" is the designation ordinarily given them by foreigners.

I shall keep to this expression, in order to distinguish these Chinese ingots from bars coming from Europe and America.

Although these shoes of sycee are the principal element in the monetary circulation in China, the Chinese Government does not take any cognizance of the making or issue of them, which matter is in the hands of those who cast them and of the bankers and money changers.

The money cast into shoes is as much made from ingots and moneys imported from foreign parts as from native sources, but it is impossible to estimate how much China can draw annually from its own mines.

At Hoshan (Yunnan), and at Tungsing, on the borders of Cochin China, there are silver mines farmed out by the Government, the renters of which employ from 40,000 to 50,000 workmen. The annual product is estimated at 2,000,000 taels. There are, besides, other mines in the interior of the Empire less rich than these if considered individually, but whose united product would be, in all probability, something considerable.

Refined silver is cast into sycee. The name of the caster and the date and place of the casting are stamped on the shoes.

For any fraud discovered afterwards, no matter at what period, the founder remains responsible and liable to severe punishment.

On leaving the hands of the founder the shoes are submitted to the inspection of a Government officer or public appraiser, called Kung-ku. After having examined them, he places on them two marks in Chinese ink, one to indicate the weight, the other to indicate the fineness. Marked with this official stamp (cachet) the shoes go into circulation as a current value.

The assays of the Chinese are exceedingly primitive and imperfect; shoes are received always and everywhere in payment without question at a conventional value based on the marks of the Kung-ku, which will be explained further on.

The fineness of the shoes of silver taken separately is not uniform, but operating on some quantities experience has shown that their average standard is ninety-eight one-hundredths or 98 touch —touch, as they say here, being equivalent to assay.

The designation of the standard of fineness is, then, as in France, 98 touch, signifying ninety-eight one-hundredths or nine hundred and eighty one-thousandths.

Three remittances of silver received from Shanghai by the agency in Calcutta on the 29th May and 15th and 20th December, 1862, and melted at the Calcutta mint were recognized as of an average fineness of 15½ to 16 B, *i.e.*, nine hundred and eighty-two one thousandths.

To wit: standard of silver in India	220 —240	220—240
Better	15½	16
	235½—240	236—240
or	981.25	983.33
	982/1000 as an average.[1]	

To form a basis on which to establish the value of sycee silver the Chinese take the weight and the touch marked on the shoes by the Kung-ku, making therefore some odd enough calculations, as may be seen from some figures which follow.

Chinese memorandum, giving, weight, fineness, and value of 38 shoes of sycee counted and verified at the agency of the Comptoir d'Escompte de Paris at Shanghai on the 16th March, 1864:

Shoes.	Weight in Shanghai taels.	Premium for betterness in Shanghai taels.	Shoes.	Weight in Shanghai taels.	Premium for betterness in Shanghai taels.	Shoes.	Weight in Shanghai taels.	Premium for betterness in Shanghai taels.
1	49.90	2.60	1	49.83	2.10	1	48.94	1.40
1	51.15	2.80	1	50.06	2.65	1	49.93	2.40
1	49.95	2.60	1	50.55	0.80	1	50.88	2.30
1	49.87	1.90	1	50.01	2.00	1	50.02	2.50
1	46.30	1.90	1	50.80	2.75	1	50.24	2.75
1	49.67	2.20	1	50.00	2.50	1	50.43	2.70
1	50.94	2.75	1	51.09	2.75	1	50.00	2.00
1	50.56	2.10	1	51 42	2.80	1	49.58	2.10
1	49.98	2.60	1	50.26	2.50	1	50.58	2.30
1	50.20	2.75	1	41.52	1.65	1	51.08	2.80
1	49.57	2.10	1	50.54	2.50	1	50.97	2.75
1	40.62	1.50	1	50.42	2.65			
1	50.90	2.80	1	51.42	2.80	38	1,890.12	89.70
1	49.94	2.65						

In all, 1,979.82 taels of Shanghai weight, equalling, at the rate of 100 taels currency equals 98 taels of Shanghai weight (fixed rate), 2,020.22 taels current.

---

[1] This seems to mean as follows:

The standard of silver in currency in India is 220 parts of pure silver in 240 of coinage; to put this in decimal form it means that 1,000 parts contain 916.66 of pure silver.

Betterness seems to mean that 240 parts of a mixture contain (220 + B) parts of pure silver.

In this instance 15½ betterness put in decimal form=15½ parts in 240 or 64.583 per 1,000.

In the same way: 16 betterness=16 parts in 240 or 66.66 per 1,000.

Therefore, $\frac{916.66}{1,000}$ fine better by $\frac{15\frac{1}{2}}{240}$ or $\frac{64.583}{1,000}=\frac{916.666+64.583}{1,000}$ =approximately $\frac{981.25}{1,000}$ as above.

Similarly, a betterness of 16 produces $\frac{983.33}{1,000}$, or an average of about $\frac{982}{1,000}$ as given above.

Memorandum of a similar verification made in May, 1864, at the Agra Bank, Shanghai, which has had the goodness to place the information at my disposal:

(1) 69 shoes weighing.............	3,000.48	taels Shanghai weight.
(2) Premium for betterness.......	140.50	,, ,, ,,
	3,140.98	,, ,, ,,
(3) At $^{100}/_{98}$ =	3,205.01	Shanghai currency taels.

Memorandum of another verification made in June, 1864, at the agency of the Comptoir d'Escompte:

(1) 20 shoes weighing.............	980.54	taels Shanghai weight.
(2) Premium for betterness.......	48.60	,, ,, ,,
	1,029.14	,, ,, ,,
(3) At $^{100}/_{98}$ =	1,050.14	Shanghai currency taels.

Few persons are familiar with these calculations, many are entirely ignorant of them, others have adopted them mechanically without taking any notice of the basis on which they stand. Strange to say, I have never found in Shanghai anyone who has been able to give me conclusive explanations in this particular matter.

Left to my own reflections and calculations, I have arrived by induction at the following theory, which appears to me to be in perfect accord with the actual state of the case.

In each of these calculations, which are always the same, there are three striking figures which present themselves:

(1) The first indicates the weight of the shoes in Shanghai taels.

(2) The second expresses a difference between two degrees of fineness of about 4½ to 5 per cent., the real standard of the shoes being 98. It appears to me that after deducting this difference of 4.5, the remaining cipher, 93.5, would be the standard touch in the sense indicated farther on.

In practice this calculation bears a close resemblance to that in use in England, where the standard touch is the invariable basis of price for precious metals—when an ingot is of a touch above or below, it is brought by a calculation to the standard touch by adding or substracting a quantity of proportional weight.

(3) The third cipher indicates the conventional value of the shoes in currency taels of Shanghai at the fixed rate of 100 current taels for 98 taels weight of Shanghai taels.

By analysing and recasting into a European mould these calculations, at first sight so confused, I have arrived at the following results:

?Taels weight Shanghai.	1,000 currency taels.	?Taels.		1,000 currency taels.
2,020.22	1,890.60	or better	2,020.22	1,890.60
	935.60 taels (of a touch of 98)		100	98
				916.88 taels of $^{1000}/_{1000}$
?Taels weight Shanghai.	1,000 currency taels.	?Taels.		1,000 currency taels.
3,205.01	3,000.48	or better	3,205.01	3,000.48
	936.18 taels (of a touch of 98)		100	98
				917.14 taels of $^{1000}/_{1000}$
?Taels weight Shanghai.	1,000 currency taels.	?Taels.		1,000 currency taels.
1,050.14	980.54	or better	1,050.14	980.54
	933.72 taels (of a touch of 98)		100	98
				915.05 taels of $^{1000}/_{1000}$
Mean	935.40 of $^{98}/_{100}$	or		916.66 of $^{100}/_{100}$

It will be seen that this figure varies infinitely without the variations exceeding some thousandths.

After a number of weighings and calculations, which have always come to the same result, I believe I can assert that the following proportions represent correctly the actual basis of the monetary system of Shanghai.

A quantity of silver weighing 935.40 Shanghai taels of the denomination $\frac{98}{100}$—*i.e.*, 916.66 Shanghai taels (weight) of the denomination $\frac{1000}{1000}$—has the conventional value of 1,000 taels currency. In other words, 1 tael of silver Shanghai weight of the standard denomination $\frac{9354}{9800}$ or $\frac{916^2/_3}{1000}$ is equivalent to 1 tael of Shanghai currency within a margin of 2 or 3 thousands, more or less.

If a Shanghai currency tael, instead of being a simple "money of account," were good and proper silver money struck into real coin it would weigh 1 Shanghai tael or 36.64 grams, its standard of touch would be $\frac{916^2/_3}{1000}$, and its intrinsic value francs 7.35 $\frac{18}{100}$ (calculating silver at the par value of francs 218.89 for 1 kilogram of $\frac{1000}{1000}$)

Calculation: (x) ? francs=1,000 currency taels.
1,000 currency taels=916²/₃ taels weight of Shanghai fineness.
1=36.64 grams.
1,000=1 kilogram,
1=218.89.

$$10{,}000 = x \text{ (francs)} = 916^2/_3 \times 36.64 \times 218.89$$

$$x = \frac{916^2/_3 \times 36.64 \times 218.89}{10{,}000} = 735.18$$

intrinsic par value, premium on silver at Paris and freight from Paris to Shanghai not included.

But as the currency tael of Shanghai is no more than an ideal value, it cannot be better defined than by designating it as a sign representing the proportion of weight and fineness above mentioned.

Let us now examine if the result obtained at the Calcutta Mint confirms the theory set forth above. According to this theory, the result ought to be as follows:

(x) ? rupees=100 currency taels.
1,000=916²/₃ taels weight of Shanghai fineness.
1=3.143 tolahs fine.
916²/₃=1,000 tolahs standard.
1=1 rupee.

		(x)=314.30 rupees.
Less mintage, 2.1 per cent	6.60 }	7.23
Loss in casting, 2 per mill	0.63 }	
		307.07 rupees,
Commission	¼ per cent.	
Freight	1½ ,,	
Insurance	⅝ ,,	
Landing and shipping	⅛ ,,	
Contingencies	⅛ ,,	
Interest (note below).		
	2⅝ ,,	= 8.07
Net		299.00 rupees.

See now the actual result:

1862 Cost at Shanghai.

Sent first time	Tls. 48,852.13	=	Rs. 149,796. 6.11	or Rs. 306.63	per Tls. 100.
Sent second time	10,000.	=	30,574.11. 9	305.75	100.
Sent third time	16,500.	=	50,469. 6. 7	305.88	100.
Total	Tls. 75,352.13	=	Rs. 230,840. 9. 3	or Rs. 306.35	average
From this deduct, as above, 2⅝ per cent.		=		8.04	
				Rs. 298.31	

(Loss of interest for one month is compensated for by the interest gained on the drafts made against the sycee).

To two-thousandths or thereabouts the reality and the theory agree.

These small differences will always exist; they are unimportant and result from the fact that the purity, and even the standard, of sycee silver is not always the same.

The conclusions to be drawn from the above calculations have some interest:

(1) The standard of the currency tael of Shanghai of $\frac{916^{2}/_{3}}{1000}$ is in conformity with the rupee standard of 220–240.

(2) The cost of Shanghai sycee and its out-turn at the mint receiving houses in India stand on fixed bases.

(3) The intrinsic par value (per Shanghai 100 taels to 2 per mill or thereabouts) of Rs. 314.30 and the net par value of Rs. 299 (298 at the lowest) is the rate which represents a minimum out-turn on which an exporter of sycee can count in any case.

The result of this is that whenever the exchange for three days' sight bank bills on Calcutta or Bombay falls below 298, drafts may be sold and covered by sycee with the absolute certainty of making money. In 1861 and 1862 the course of exchange was often enough in this position.

Whether or not my theory relative to the monetary system of this place be confirmed or modified by experience, this is certain: The verification of a box of sycee does not present any difficulty, and the operation can be performed without its being necessary to have anything to say to or to be done by the comprador. Rules to be followed:

(1) Verify your weights and assure yourself that your Shanghai tael has the required weight of 36.64 grams.

(2) Then weigh your shoes; ascertain the total weight and calculate the value, reckoning 100 taels current for 93.54 Shanghai taels (weight).

In this way you will be sure of finding out to a few thousandths the current value of your sycee.

When a great number of shoes pass through one's hands such an operation can not take place every day, but in any well-ordered financial establishment it ought to be made at least once or twice a month, it being of course understood that a daily approximate verification should be made.

The entire mechanism of China for keeping money in motion is extremely crude and inconvenient. Silver is ordinarily packed in boxes, each containing about 60 shoes, weighing altogether a little over 3,000 taels or 110 kilograms. To carry one such case two coolies must be paid, by the trip, at the rate of 50 cash (25 centimes French money) a head.

To pay 100,000 taels (800,000 francs) 66 coolies are consequently required.

From a bank to a private person this expenditure is charged to the latter; from one bank to another, to the one buying.

One can readily imagine the inconveniences of such a system. The simplest means of obviating it would be the establishment of a clearing house, which would, so to speak, represent generally the coffers of all the bankers and merchants, through the medium of which they would effect all their receipts and payments; but the place is not yet ripe for institutions of this sort.

Some of the English banks issue bank notes payable to bearer, but I do not know to what extent or if the notes issued remain long in circulation.

SHANGHAI, *July, 1864.*

Weighing trial, August, 1880.

SHANGHAI TAEL.

Weight in grains.	Weight in grams (0.0648=1 grain).
(1) According to Mr. Veitch, of the Hongkong & Shanghai Banking Corporation...... 565.973	(1) No information obtainable.
(2) By weighing trials at this office obtained 564.229	(2) By calculation of Mr. Veitch's statement, 565.973 grains × 0.0648 gram 36.6750504
(3) Average.................... 565.101	(3) By calculation of what I found the S'hai tael, 564.229 grains × 0.0648 gram........ 36.562
	(4) By weighing trials at this office obtained 36.555
	(5) Average 36.59735

HAIKWAN TAEL.

(1) According to the Hongkong and Shanghai Banking Corporation, 102.90 Shanghai taels=100 Haikwan taels, and 1 Shanghai tael=565.973 grains; thus, 1 Haikwan tael 582.3862	(1) No information obtainable.
(2) According to Mr. Veitch, of the Hongkong and Shanghai Banking Corporation 581.630	(2) By calculation of Mr. Veitch's statement, 581.630 grains × 0.0648 gram 37.689624
(3) By weighing trials at this office obtained 581.938	(3) By calculation of what I found the Haikwan tael, 581.938 grains×0.0648 gram 37.7096
(4) Average.................. 581.984	(4) By weighing trials at this office obtained 37.686
	(5) Average 37.69504

K'UPING TAEL.

(1) According to the Hongkong and Shanghai Banking Corporation, 101.80 Shanghai taels=100 K'u-p'ing taels, and 1 Shanghai tael=565.973 grains; thus, 1 K'u-p'ing tael.......... 576.160514	(1) No information obtainable.
(2) The Hongkong and Shanghai Banking Corporation can not give any information respecting the K'u-p'ing tael.	(2) By calculation of weight given by Hongkong and Shanghai Banking Corporation, 576.1605 grains×0.0648 gram 37.3352
(3) By weighing trials at this office obtained 576.339	(3) By calculation of what I found the K'uping tael, 576.339 grains × 0.0648 gram 37.336
(4) Average.................. 576.2497	(4) By weighing trials at this office obtained with two different weights—1 tael weight ..... 37.320 6 mace and 4 mace (=1 tael). 37.258
	(5) Average 37.3173

TOUCH OR FINENESS.

There is no positive standard of touch or fineness for the different taels.

STATISTICAL DEPARTMENT, G. H. NOETZLI.
Shanghai, August 28, 1880.

New weighing trial, September, 1880.

SHANGHAI TAEL.

Weight in grains.		Weight in grams (0.0648=1 grain).	
(1) 1 tael weighed	564.954	(1) 1 tael weighed	36.590
2 taels weighed	1,130.201	2 taels weighed	73.117
1 tael=	565.100	1 tael=	36.558
3 taels weighed	1,695.448	3 taels weighed	109.777
1 tael=	565.149	1 tael=	36.592
5 mace weighed...........	282.614	5 mace weighed	18.275
1 tael=	565.228	1 tael=	36.550
Average	565.117	Average	36.587
		No information obtainable as to the weight in grams.	
(2) According to the information of Mr. Veitch, of the Hongkong and Shanghai Banking Corporation......	565.973	(2) By calculation of Mr. Veitch's statement, 565.973 grains × 0.0648 gram...............	36.675
(3) By my first weighing trial, 28th August, 1880 (weights procured from Hongkong and Shanghai Banking Corporation)	564.229	(3) By my first weighing trial, 28th August, 1880	36.555
		(4) By calculation, 565.117 grains × 0.0648 gram	36.6195

The fundamental difficulty is that the weights do not agree among themselves, so that it is impossible to know which is the correct weight On the whole, I would not hesitate to take 565.10 grains and 36.56 grams as the weight of a Shanghai tael.

HAIKWAN TAEL.

Weight in grains.		Weight in grams (0.0648=1 grain).	
(1) 1 tael weighed	582.031	(1) 1 tael weighed	37.677
2 taels weighed	1,163.861	2 taels weighed	75.350
1 tael=	581.930	1 tael=	37.675
3 taels weighed	1,743.741	3 taels weighed	112.894
1 tael=	581.247	1 tael=	37.631
9 mace and 1 mace (=1 tael) weighed	584.309	9 mace and 1 mace (=1 tael) weighed	37.845
7 mace and 3 mace (=1 tael) weighed	582.864	7 mace and 3 mace (=1 tael) weighed	37.740
6 mace and 4 mace (=1 tael) weighed	580.938	6 mace and 4 mace (=1 tael) weighed	37.602
5 mace, 4 mace, and 1 mace (=1 tael) weighed	584.463	5 mace, 4 mace, and 1 mace (=1 tael) weighed	37.847
Average	582.2207	Average	37.6955
		No information obtainable as to the weight in grams.	
(2) According to the Hongkong and Shanghai Banking Corporation, 102.90 Shanghai taels=100 Haikwan taels, and 1 Shanghai tael =565.973 grains, thus, 1 Haikwan tael	582.3862	(2) By calculation, 582.3862 grains×0.0648 gram	37.7386
(3) Mr. Veitch, of the Hongkong and Shanghai Banking Corporation, gives	581.630	(3) By calculation, 581.630 grains ×0.0648 gram	37.6896
(4) By my first weighing trial, 28th August, 1880	581.938	(4) By my first weighing trial, 28th August, 1880	37.686
(5) If 102.90 Shanghai taels= 100 Haikwan taels, and 1 Shanghai tael, as found by the new weighing trial,= 565.117 grains, then 1 Haikwan tael is	581.5053	(5) By calculation, 581.5053 grains×0.0648 gram	37.6815

The weights (a new set) for the new weighing trial were obtained from the Haikwan Bank, after some delay for the purpose of having them assayed. The above figures, however, show how imperfectly the task was performed. I am under the impression that the bank forgot to have the weights assayed, and when I called for them was ashamed to say so. I would be inclined to take 581.938 grains and 37.686 grams as the most approximate. This weight is thirty one-hundredths grain above Mr. Veitch's statement, thirty one-hundredths grain below the found average, and equal to the 2 taels weight.

K'U-P'ING TAEL.

Weight in grains.		Weight in grams (0.0648=1 grain).	
(1) 1 tael weighed	575.463	(1) 1 tael weighed	37.254
2 taels weighed	1,151.846	2 taels weighed	74.550
1 tael=	575.923	1 tael=	37.275
3 taels weighed	1,726.962	3 taels weighed	111.970
1 tael=	575.654	1 tael=	37.323
8 mace and 2 mace (=1 tael) weighed................	575.494	8 mace and 2 mace (=1 tael) weighed	37.257
7 mace and 3 mace (=1 tael) weighed................	576.571	7 mace and 3 mace (=1 tael) weighed	37.330
5 mace, 3 mace, and 2 mace (=1 tael) weighed......	576.309	5 mace, 3 mace, and 2 mace (=1 tael) weighed........	37.314
Average	575.849	Average	37.297
		No information obtainable as to weight in grams.	
(2) According to the Hongkong and Shanghai Banking Corporation, 101.80 Shanghai taels=100 K'u-p'ing taels, and 1 Shanghai tael=565.973 grains; thus, 1 K'u-p'ing tael	576.1605	(2) By calculation, 576.1605 grains × 0.0648 gram	37.3352
(2a) At 565.117 grains for the Shanghai tael, 1 K'u-p'ing tael would be	575.289	(2a) By calculation, 575.289 grains ×0.0648 gram	37.2787
(3) By my first weighing trial, 28th August, 1880	576.339	(3) By calculation of my first weighing trial, 576.339 grains ×0.0648 gram	37.346
(4) Dr. S. Wells Williams, in his Chinese Commercial Guide, page 275, gives......	579.	(4) By my first weighing trial, 28th August, 1880	37.320 37.258

The weights used in the above trial were procured from the Haikwan Bank, after waiting for some time to have them assayed; but here also thev were found to differ among themselves. I would be inclined to take the result of the weighings of the 2 taels and 3 taels—575.923 and 575.654 grains, giving an average of 575.788 grains, 37.275 and 37.323 grams, giving an average of 37.299 grams—as the weight most likely to be correct.

TOUCH OR FINENESS.

There is no standard as to touch or fineness for the different taels.

G. H. Noetzli.

Statistical Department,
Shanghai, 30th September, 1880.

Memorandum.

1. *The Shanghai market (or Kuei-p'ing) tael* (not a weight).—Fineness –2 or 2 per cent. discount.

The Shanghai or Kuei-p'ing tael used in the record of values has no corresponding weight. There are copper or brass weights for Haikwan or Ssŭ-p'ing taels, for K'uping taels, and for Ts'aoping taels; but I am told that there are no copper or brass weights called Kuei-p'ing weights. Shanghai sycee is known as tou-kuei yin, also as chiu pa yin.

2. The Kuei-p'ing tael is not a weight, but is the result of a calculation, the elements in which are the actual weight of the silver in Ts'aop'ing taels. The addition to this of whatever percentage is indorsed by the Kung-ku on each shoe for its quality or betterness. The conversion of the total of the two sums into the so-called Kuei-p'ing taels at the rate Ts'ao-p'ing taels 98 = Kuei-p'ing taels 100.

For example, a shoe of sycee that has to be valued is taken to the Kung-ku office; there the weight, say, 50 Ts'ao-p'ing taels, is written on the shoe; also the premium for quality, say, Ts'ao-p'ing taels 2.70. The owner can then say that he has 50 Ts'ao-p'ing taels of sycee of 2.70 premium. Should he wish, however, to express the value of his sycee in the so-called Kuei-p'ing tael, the total of the two figures must be divided by 0.98 ($\frac{98}{100}$) or multiplied by $\frac{100}{98}$, *e.g.*, 1 shoe 50 Ts'ao-p'ing taels weight + premium Ts'ao-p'ing taels 2.70 = Ts'ao-p'ing taels 52.70 ÷ 0.98 = Kuei-p'ing taels 53.77.

	Ts'ao-p'ing taels.
Weight..........................	50.00
Premium	2.70
	.98) 52.70 (53.77
	490
	370
	294
	760
	686
	740
	686

The following is a copy of the tally of box No. 1 of the remittance of sycee from Chefoo ex "Fungshun" on 26th July last, the valuation being made at the Haikwan Bank on the 27th July by deputies from the Kung-ku office:

Shoes.	Actual weight.	Premium for quality of sycee per shoe.
	Ts'ao-p'ing Tls.	*Ts'ao-p'ing taels.*
1......	51.37	2.80 }
2......	50.97	“ } 3 at 2.80=Tls. 8.40
3......	50.82	“ }
4......	50.03	2.75 }
5......	50.02	“
6......	50.92	“
7......	50.72	“
8......	50.72	“
9......	50.84	“
10......	50.50	“
11......	49.95	“
12......	50.21	“
13......	50.36	“ } 18 at 2.75=Tls. 49.50
14......	49.90	“
15......	50.94	“
16......	49.87	“
17......	50.81	“
18......	51.30	“
19......	50.02	“
20......	50.36	“
21......	50.02	“ }

Shoes.	Actual weight.	Premium for quality of sycee per shoe.
	Ts'ao-p'ing Tls.	*Ts'ao-p'ing taels.*
22......	50.10	2.70 }
23......	50.97	“
24......	50.60	“
25......	50.60	“
26......	50.13	“
27......	51.15	“
28......	50.80	“
29......	50.19	“
30......	50.24	“ } 17 at 2.70=Tls. 45.90
31......	50.20	“
32......	50.84	“
33......	49.94	“
34......	50.28	“
35......	49.87	“
36......	51.25	“
37......	50.18	“
38......	50.95	“ }
39......	50.14	2.65 } 2 at 2.65=Tls.5.30
40......	50.30	“ }
		Total premium 109.10 taels.

2,019.38 total weight.
109.10 premium in Ts'ao-p'ing taels.

.98) 2, 128.48 (2,171.918
196
168
98
704
686
188
98
900
882
180
98
820
784
36

The object of the two foregoing operations is, first, to reduce sycee of a given premium to its equivalent in terms of a sycee without premium, and, second, to reduce that figure to its equivalent in terms of a sycee that is either 2 per cent. inferior to sycee that bears no premium or that is subject to a discount in weighing.

I have been told that 98 Ts'ao-p'ing taels are taken to equal 100 taels kuei yin as a mere discount on weight. I have also been told that the relation of 98 to 100 is set down to the inferiority of the original kuei yin sycee as compared with the present standard of the Kung-ku office. In Edkins's Progressive Lessons in Chinese, page 29, the following definition is given: “Kiu-pah yin, Shanghai sycee, literally, sycee at 2 per cent. discount.”

On inquiry at the Kung-ku office[1] I obtained a memorandum in answer to certain questions to the effect that the weight adopted

[1] I have not been able to find any confirmation of the statement that Shanghai sycee is sycee of the dollar purity; my authority from the Kung-ku office says that it differs somewhat in fineness from the dollar.

by the Kung-ku is the Ts'ao-p'ing weight used, before the opening of Shanghai to foreign trade, by the merchants in the pulse and grain trade; that the sycee used by the trade was called yüan-ssŭ yin, and was cast in small round cakes of about a tael's weight each, which were current much as dollars now are; that it was also called tou-kuei yin, because it was the regulation sycee of the pulse and grain trade; and that compared with the present standard of the Kung-ku, kuei yin sycee would have its quality expressed by the term chü hsui erh shi—that is, each 100 taels weight of such sycee would have a discount of 2 taels and be taken only as 98 taels.

On the Kung-ku scale of touches, then, this yüan-ssŭ yin would have its standard expressed by minus two (–2), *e.g.:*

	Haikwan.		K'uping.	Ts'ao-p'ing.							Kuei yin		
Percentages..	(+6.168),	+6	(+5.6)	+5,	+4,	+3,	+2,	+1,	0,	—1,	—2,	—3,	4,

Degrees of betterness (+6.168 to +1). Degrees of worseness (—1 to 4).

The scale proceeds by 5 candarins per 50 taels or 1 mace per 100 taels, but for sake of brevity the whole numbers only are given in the illustration.

The Yüan-ssŭ or kuei yin is no longer met with, the current sycee varying from 4 to 6 degrees of betterness, but the denomination of value is kept up, and all values are expressed in their equivalents in the imaginary kuei yin.

The term Kuei-p'ing seems somewhat misleading (there being no weight of that name), so, instead of writing 100 taels Kuei-p'ing, we might preferably write 100 taels of kuei yin.

The following calculation is submitted for finding the rate of exchange between, say, Ts'ao-p'ing sycee and kuei yin:

Scale.

		Percentages.
Degrees of betterness.	*a.*	(106.168) Haikwan.
	b.	106.
	c.	(105.6) K'u-p'ing.
	d.	105 Ts'ao-p'ing
	e.	104
	f.	103
	g.	102
	h.	101
	x.	100
Degrees of worseness	*i.*	99
	j.	98 Kuei yin.
	k.	97

To find the relation which sycee of the *d.* qualty bears to the sycee of the *j.* quality:

$$\left(j=\frac{98}{100}x\right) \text{ or}$$

$$100j=98x$$

$$105x=100d$$

$$d=\text{Ans. } 1.071428j$$

$$\frac{100j\times105x\times d}{98x\times100d}=\frac{105j}{98}$$

Or by analysis:

$$100d=105x$$

$$98x=100j$$

$$x=\frac{100j}{98}$$

$$100d=\frac{105\times100j}{98}$$

$$d=\frac{105j}{98}$$

One of the premises of the calculation is that $j=\frac{98}{100}x$; this is merely a comparison of percentages. It follows that 100 taels of the *j* quality equal 98 taels of the *x* quality, and that $x=\frac{100}{99}j$; and 1 tael of the *x* quality equals $\frac{100}{98}$ taels of the *j* quality:

$$j=\frac{98}{100}x$$
$$100j=98x$$
$$\frac{100j}{98}=x$$

In the foregoing calculations sycee of different grades has had its value expressed in terms of sycee of the *x* quality by adding the percentage of premium to the weight; by the above formula *x* equals $\frac{100}{98}j$, so whatever coefficient there may be of *x*, whether it be 52.70, as in the first example, or 2,128.48, as in the second example, may be multiplied by $\frac{100}{98}j$ in lieu of *x*, the answer being the equivalent in kuei yin sycee. In the calculations, in place of multiplying by 100 and dividing by 98 a step is saved by dividing by the decimal 0.98.

The Chinese method of making the calculation on the suan-pan to find the equivalent in kuei yin of 100 Ts'ao-p'ing taels weight of sycee at 5 per cent. premium is—

	Ts'ao-p'ing taels.
To	100.00
Add for premium	5.00
For 100 taels add 2 per cent.	2.00 called shên shang shên chia êrh.
For 7 taels add 2 per cent.	0.14
For 0.14 taels add 2 per cent.	0.0028
For 0.0028 taels add 2 per cent.	0.000056
	Ts'ao-p'ing taels 107.142856 +

The process may be carried on until the repeating decimal 0.142857 is obtained in the answer. The direct division of 105 by 98 gives the same answer: 107.142857, 142857, etc.

3. *Fineness.*—I was told at the Oriental Bank that through remittances to India the average fineness of Shanghai sycee, as assayed by the mints in India, was found to be 982, and at the Comptoir d'Escompte that it was 980 or 982. The comprador of the Oriental Bank Corporation stated that the Chinese term 2.70 premium (per 50 taels) corresponded to 986,[1] but it is hardly worth while to make a calculation on the basis of a single statement. Were, however, a certified statement obtainable of the out-turn as to fineness of a shipment of sycee in which each shoe had been marked by the Kung-ku as of a given premium—say, 2.70—then a basis would be obtained from which the foreign expressions corresponding to the terms for betterness of sycee, such as 2.6, 2.65, 2.7, 2.75, etc., could be calculated and given in thousandths ($\frac{1000}{1000}$).

The out-turn of several remittances to India can be referred to, but the records do not state that the sycee experimented on was of a uniform touch. In the foregoing tally of 40 shoes it is seen that the shoes of sycee in one box were of four different grades

[1] My authority from the Kung-ku office considers that—

2.70 corresponds to	988	2.95 corresponds to	993	3.15 corresponds to	997
2.75	989	3.00	994	3.20	998
2.80	990	3.05	995	3.25	999
2.85	991	3.10	996	3.30	1000
2.90	992				

taking as his basis that foreign bar silver is stamped as 998; but never having had occasion to make the calculation, gives these figures as approximate only.

of fineness. A "lot" of sycee may contain shoes from different provinces and varying in betterness from 2 taels or less up to 3 taels premium (per 50 taels weight, or double these figures per 100 taels weight).

I am further told that the smelting establishments which convert bar silver or dollars into sycee, and which recast certain sycee for the percentage of gold contained in it, have no fixed standard of fineness; the shoes turned out will enter into the currency of the place whether they be of 2.6, 2.65, 2.7, or 2.75 touch.

It appears, then, that in the absence of further information as to the Chinese standard of the sycee sent to India no conclusion can be come to as to the proper foreign equivalents for the terms in the Chinese scale of touches.

The required touch or premium for K'uping taels is taken as 2.8 per 50 taels, or 5.6 taels per 100 taels weight; it would appear, then, that the fineness of K'uping sycee could be ascertained approximately by having a number of shoes, certified to by the Kung-ku as being of this exact quality, submitted to a foreign mint for assay. From the result the entire Chinese scale of touches could be calculated, or the same experiment might be made with sycee picked at the Ts'ao-p'ing or at the Haikwan standard; in any case a basis would be obtained for calculating the requirements for a coin equivalent to the Haikwan, K'uping, Ts'ao-p'ing, or Shanghai tael. It would, however, still be a question whether the Kung-ku offices at different places have a common standard of valuation,[1] and whether a valuation made by an unofficial Kung-ku office would be accepted at a provincial treasury.

4. *Haikwan taels:*

Weight each	581.47 grains.
Fineness...........................	6 Haikwan taels premium per 100.

Distinction has to be made between a tael's weight and a tael's value.

As to weight: I procured from the Haikwan Bank manager a set of weights called kuan or Ssŭ-p'ing fa-ma, made of brass, with the exception of the weights for candarins, which are of ivory in small strips. The 50-tael weight has cast on it the characters (Chinese).

These weights I have compared with a set of troy weights belonging to the Comptoir d'Escompte, obtaining results varying from 581.71 grains to 581.60 grains per tael; but as in weighing the subdivisions or lesser Haikwan weights had to be used, which were found not to agree closely with the 50-tael weight, it may be better to arrive at the weight of the Haikwan tael by multiplying the weight obtained for the Ts'ao-p'ing tael, viz., 565.637 grains, by the accepted proportion, 100 Haikwan taels weigh 102.80 Ts'ao-p'ing taels.

565.637×102.80=581.47 grains, weight of 1 Haikwan tael.
1 Haikwan tael weighs (or should weigh) 581.47 grains.

At the Kung-ku office the Haikwan 50-tael weight was considered to be the most reliable of the set. Furthermore, its ascertained weight in Ts'ao-p'ing taels agrees with the figure used by the Haikwan Bank in its calculation on page 23.

---

[1] I have been informed since writing the above that sycee, considered at Shanghai to bear a premium of 3.2 taels per 100, at Chefoo would only be considered as of the unity standard—that is, as having no premium and no discount.

Shanghai premium, 3.2 taels said to equal unity standard at Chefoo.
Shanghai premium, 4.8 taels said to equal unity standard at Hankow.
Shanghai premium, 2.7 taels said to equal unity standard at Soochow.

By using a set of gram weights belonging to the Comptoir I found 1 Haikwan tael to weigh 37.68 grams, and on another trial to weigh 37.66 grams. The first result is verified as follows: Multiply the weight taken for the Ts'ao-p'ing tael, 36.6527 grams, by the proportion 100 Haikwan taels weigh 101.80 Ts'ao-p'ing taels.

36.6527×102.80=37.6789 grams, weight of 1 Haikwan tael.
1 Haikwan tael weighs (or should weigh) 37.68 grams.

If the figures 37.6789 be multiplied by 15.432349 (the number of grains equivalent to a gram) the result is 581.47 grains—the weight submitted above for the Haikwan tael.

In the Reports on the Haikwan Banking System, page 100, it is stated that tael weights from the [Wuhu] Haikwan Bank were weighed by Mr. Taintor, the Haikwan tael being found to weigh 582.94 grains troy, and the Wuhu tael, 565.7035 grains. On page 97, Mr. Kopsch gives the weight of 1 Haikwan tael as 38.08 grams nearly; multiplying this figure by 15.432349, the equivalent 587.66 grains is obtained. According to Mr. Taintor, 1 Haikwan tael weighed 582.94 grains; according to Mr. Kopsch, 1 Haikwan tael weighed 587.66 grains. As given above, 1 Haikwan tael weighs 581.47 grains. The 50-tael weight mentioned above was found at the Kung-ku office to weigh 51.40 Ts'ao-p'ing taels and indorsed to that effect; hence, 100 Haikwan taels weigh 102.80 Ts'ao-p'ing taels.

The Haikwan tael as a denomination of value: In practice in Shanghai the Haikwan tael is not a denomination of weight, but of value; it may theoretically be a tael's weight of sycee of 6 taels touch or premium per 100; but as such sycee is not generally current at Shanghai, the equivalent in Shanghai taels is accepted in the collection of duties, the calculation being:—

As the Haikwan tael weight of brass bears to the Ts'ao-p'ing tael weight the proportion 100:102.80:

	Shanghai Ts'ao-p'ing taels.
To	100.000
Add for difference in weight	2.800
Add for touch or premium, 6×102.8 Haikwan taels	6.168
Meltage fee, etc.	.204
Ts'ao-p'ing taels	109.172

(That is, 109.172 Ts'ao-p'ing taels (without premium), less meltage fee, equals 100 Haikwan taels of the standard 6 taels premium).

Ninety-eight Ts'ao-p'ing taels being taken to equal 100 Shanghai taels, we have the proportion:—

Ts'ao-p'ing Tls. 98: Shanghai Tls. 100:: Ts'ao-p'ing Tls. 109.172:111.4

```
98) 109.172 (111.4
    98
    ---
    111
     98
    ---
     137
      98
     ---
      392
      392
      ---
```

Haikwan taels, 100=Shanghai taels, 111.4.

To pay 100 Haikwan taels one must hand the bank sycee or dollars or cash at the market rate, or the tael notes issued by the foreign banks, to the value of 111.4 Shanghai taels. The calculation, however, includes a meltage fee, and the item of premium, 6 taels, is in excess of what is generally required, 2.8 taels per weight of 50 taels, or 5.6 taels per weight of 100 taels, being said to be the standard for K'uping, or provincial treasurer's, sycee.[1] Why the meltage fee should be charged when the bank is not forced to take a given weight of dollars is not apparent. Were the meltage, etc., fee dropped out and the standard for K'u-p'ing sycee taken, the calculation would be:—

100+2.80+5.60=108.40÷98=110.61 Shanghai taels.

The calculation given above is that communicated by the Haikwan Bank manager and printed in the Shanghai Report on the Haikwan Banking System, page 111.

5. *K'uping taels:—*

Weight, each	575.82 grains.
Fineness	5.60 taels per 100.

Distinction has to be made between a tael's weight and a tael's value.

As to weight: I procured from the Haikwan Bank a set of brass weights with the characters K'uping cut on them, which were compared for me at the Kung-ku office with the sets of troy and gram weights from the Comptoir as well as with the Kung-ku Ts'ao-p'ing weights. It was found that the 50-tael K'uping weight weighed 50.90 Ts'ao-p'ing taels, and it was indorsed accordingly; hence:—

100 K'u-p'ing taels weigh 101.80 Ts'ao-p'ing taels;

also that 1 K'uping tael weighed 575.812 grains.

For the sake of uniformity we may multiply the weight obtained for the Ts'ao-p'ing tael, viz., 565.637 grains, by 101.80, the proportion given above, and take the result, 575.818 grains, as the weight of the K'uping tael.

1 K'u-p'ing tael weighs (or should weigh) 575.82 grains.

In grams the K'u-p'ing tael was found to weigh 37.30. If, however, the weight of the Ts'ao-p'ing tael in grams, 36.6527, be multiplied by 101.80, the fixed proportion, the result obtained is 37.312 grams; the same figure is obtained by dividing 575.818 by 15.432349, to reduce grains to grams.

1 K'u-p'ing tael weighs (or should weigh) 37.312 grams.

As regards value and fineness: The standard for K'uping sycee is said to be 2.80 taels premium per shoe of 50 taels weight, or 5.60 taels per 100 taels weight.

The rate for converting K'uping into Shanghai taels is 100 K'uping taels = 109.6 Shanghai (kuei yin) taels, and is arrived at as shown in the following calculation:

As the K'uping tael weight of brass bears to the Ts'ao-p'ing tael weight the proportion 100 : 101.80, so:—

	Shanghai Ts'ao-p'ing Tls.
To	100.00
Add for difference in weight	1.80
Add for touch or premiun	5.60
Ts'ao-p'ing taels	107.40

(That is, 107.40 Ts'ao-p'ing taels (without premium) equal 100 K'uping taels of the standard 5.60 taels premium).

[1] 2.8 or 5.6 is the touch used in calculating the official rate of exchange between K'u-p'ing and Shanghai taels; 2.8 is, however, considerably below the pure silver which the Chinese may lay claim to collect.

Ninety-eight Ts'ao-p'ing taels being taken to equal 100 Shanghai taels, we have the proportion:—

Ts'ao-p'ing Tls. 98 : Shanghai Tls. 100 : : Ts'ao-p'ing Tls. 107.40 : 109.6.

```
98) 107.40 (109.592
    98
    ---
     940
     882
     ---
      580
      490
      ---
       900
       882
       ---
        180
```

100 K'uping taels=kuei yin or 109.60 Shanghai taels.

The above calculation differs from that for the conversion of Haikwan into Shanghai taels in that the premium is considered as expressed in Ts'ao-p'ing taels, and that no meltage fee enters into the calculation.

I have been told in the Haikwan Bank that a remittance would not necessarily be of sycee picked for the 2.80 touch. To remit 2,000 K'uping taels, the sycee would be put up in packets of 100 K'uping taels weight each, the cover of the packet would be marked with the touch of the sycee, say 2.75 taels per 50 taels, or 5.50 taels per packet; the difference between 5.50 taels and the standard 5.60 taels, viz., 1 mace for each packet, would have to be made good, and to make up the 2,000 K'uping taels an additional 2 K'uping taels weight of broken sycee would have to be put in the box.

On the 21st or 22nd ultimo I took advantage of the Kung-ku appraisers being at the Haikwan Bank to have compared a bank weight, marked with Chinese characters expressing the fact that it is the standard treasury weight of that locality, with the weights brought from the Kung-ku office, with the result that it weighed 101.80 Ts'ao-p'ing taels.

6. *Ts'ao-p'ing taels:*—

Weight each....................	565.637 grains.
Fineness......................	5.50 taels per 100 Kung-ku standard. 5.00 taels per 100 official.

As to weight: The Ts'ao-p'ing tael weight[1] of brass is the basis of all monetary calculations when the value of sycee is in question, it being used for weighing the sycee.

I have compared the troy weights of the Comptoir with the Ts'ao-p'ing weights at the Comptoir, the Haikwan Bank, and the Kung-ku office, with results varying from 565.72 grains to 565.56 grains as the weight of 1 Ts'ao-p'ing tael; but as the weights of the Kung-ku office are accepted as the local standard, and their balances considered to be accurate, I prefer taking the weight ascertained there to an average of several weighings at different places. By the Kung-ku weights a brass weight of 100 ounces troy weighed 84.86 Ts'ao-p'ing taels.

100 ounces=48,000 grains÷84.86=565.6375.
1 Ts'ao-p'ing tael weighs 565.6375 grains.

In this experiment the balance between the 100-ounce weight and the 84.86 taels was considered exact. The Chinese in weighing do not use any fractional part of a candarin, but were a half

[1] Not uniform at different places.

candarin (5 *li*) added to or subtracted from 84.86 taels the difference in the result would only be 0.033 of a grain.

At the Kung-ku office I found 950 grams to balance 25.93 Ts'ao-p'ing taels; the result worked out is 1 Ts'ao-p'ing tael weighs 36.64 grams. But as in this case the weight in taels is small and the possible discrepancy of a half candarin in weighing would have a greater effect on the answer than in the foregoing calculation, I prefer to take the Ts'ao-p'ing tael as equal to 565.6375 grains, and to ascertain the equivalent in grams by dividing that figure by 15.432349, the number of grains equal to 1 gram.

565.6375÷15.432349=36.6527.
1 Ts'ao-p'ing tael weighs (or should weigh) 36.6527 grams.

Also by the Kung-ku weights:—

102.80 Ts'ao-p'ing taels weight=100 Haikwan taels weight.
101.80 Ts'ao-p'ing taels weight=100 K'u-p'ing taels weight.

In 1864 the manager of the Comptoir d'Escompte at Shanghai gave the weight of the Shanghai tael as "troy grains 565.70, perhaps only 565.43;" the present manager of that bank gives the weight as 565.63 grains.

As regards value and fineness: The standard for Ts'ao-p'ing sycee is said to be 2.75 per 50 taels weight, or 5.50 taels premium per 100 taels weight; that is, for tsu-sê Ts'ao-p'ing sycee. In written bank orders, to prevent dispute, the standard of the sycee must be specified.

The writer Sun tells me that when salaries were paid in Ts'ao-p'ing taels the equivalent realized for 100 taels was 107.143 Shanghai taels, the calculation being:—

	Ts'ao-p'ing taels.
To	100.00
Add for premiun	5.00
Ts'ao-p'ing taels	105.00

(That is, 105 taels Ts'ao-p'ing (without premium) equal 100 Ts'ao-p'ing taels with 5 taels premium as the standard).

98 Ts'ao-p'ing taels being taken to equal 100 Shanghai taels:—

Ts'ao-p'ing Tls. 98 : Shanghai Tls. 100 : : Ts'ao-p'ing Tls. 105 : 107.1428.

```
98 ) 105 ( 107.1428
     98
     ---
     700
     686
     ---
      140
       98
      ---
       420
       392
       ---
        280
        196
        ---
         840
         784
         ---
          56
```

100 Ts'ao-p'ing taels weight of sycee at 2.5 premium=107.143 taels Shanghai.

I am far from submitting these notes as authoritative; but offer them mainly with a view to indicating the field for inquiry in this connexion.

PASCAL MARTIN.

SHANGHAI, *October 20, 1880.*

COPY OF A LIST PREPARED BY THE WRITER SUN.

Haikwan Tls. 100	=Shanghai Tls.	111.4.0.0	
	=K'u-p'ing Tls.	101.6.4.2	(from multiplying 91.24 by 111.4)
	=Ts'ao-p'ing Tls.	103.9.7.3	(from multiplying 93.333 by 111.4)
Shanghai Tls. 100	=K'u-p'ing Tls.	91.2.4.0	
	=Haikwan Tls.	89.7.6.6	
	=Ts'ao-p,ing Tls.	93.3.3.3	
Ts'ao-p'ing Tls. 100	=Shanghai Tls.	107.1.4.3	
K'u-p'ing Tls. 100	=Shanghai Tls.	109.6.0.0	

Memo. re silver of various sorts at Shanghai, with values and weights; 1895.

1. Shanghai is the great trading center; all kinds of merchandise arrive and depart and many banks are open there, doing large business.

2. Accounts are kept in Shanghai taels, called kuei yin, also called tau qui yin, also called chiao pai yin.

3. There are also Ts'ao-p'ing taels and K'uping taels and Kuan-p'ing taels.

4. For Ts'ao-p'ing and K'u-p'ing taels there are scales and weights, but the Kuei-p'ing and Kuan-p'ing taels are names or designations of value simply, and there are no corresponding scales and weights.

5. There is a Kung-ku office for testing and valuing silver at Shanghai.

6. When silver is brought to this Kung-ku office it is weighed with the Ts'ao-p'ing scales and weights which were used by the merchants in the grain and pulse trade before the treaties opened the port. The office then writes on the silver its weight in Ts'ao-p'ing taels and also its touch or quality. A subsequent calculation has to be made to fix its value in Kuei-p'ing, K'uping, or Kuan-p'ing taels.

7. Ninety-eight Ts'ao-p'ing taels are equal to 100 kuei yin taels; but as there are no Kuei-p'ing scales and weights, it is not known whether this difference is a discount on weight or on touch. Formerly the tau kuei yin was styled ——— or yüan-ssŭ yin, and then was made up of small round cakes weighing about 1 tael each; and as for kuei yin, when compared with the Kung-ku's present standard, its quality is expressed thus: Chü hsui erh shi, which means 100 taels weight of kuei yin silver has a discount of 2 taels and is taken as being only 98 taels.

8. The yüan-ssŭ silver is now not met with. Current silver or sycee varies in touch from 4 to 6 degrees of betterness; and these degrees are expressed in kuei yin taels.

9. When asked to calculate on the suan-pan the value of 100 taels Ts'ao-p'ing in kuei yin silver, a Shanghai banker:—

	Taels.
Will first put down	100
Will add for betterness 5 per cent	5 [105]
For Tls. 100 will add 2 per cent	2 [107]
For Tls. 7 will add 2 per cent	0.14
For Tls. 0.14 will add 2 per cent	0.0028
For Tls. 0.0028 will add 2 per cent	0.000056
And the result will be Shanghai silver	107.142856

10. Similarly, if the value of 100 K'uping taels is to be expressed in Shanghai silver—seeing that the standard for K'uping silver

is said to be 5.60 taels and that 100 K'uping taels equal 101.80 Ts'ao-p'ing taels in weight, a banker would:—

	Taels.
First of all set down	100
Add for weight	1.80
Add for touch	5.60
Thus making Ts'ao-p'ing taels	107.40

equal to 100 K'uping taels, and further calculation shows that as 98 Ts'ao-p'ing taels are equal to 100 Shanghai taels, so 107.40 Ts'ao-p'ing taels are equal to 109.60 Shanghai taels; therefore, 100 K'uping taels equal 109.60 Shanghai taels.

11. So, too, in the case of the Haikwan tael—inasmuch as 100 Haikwan taels equal in weight 102.80 Ts'ao-p'ing taels and the touch is said to be 6 taels on 100 taels weight, a banker would:—

	Taels.
First of all set down	100
Add for weight	2.80
Add for touch, at Haikwan taels 6 per cent on 102.80	6.168
Add for meltage	0.204
Thus making Ts'ao-p'ing taels	109.172

equal 100 Haikwan taels. But as 98 Ts'ao-p'ing taels are equal to 100 Shanghai taels, so 109.172 Ts'ao-p'ing taels are equal to 111.4 Shanghai taels; that is, 100 Haikwan taels equal 111.4 Shanghai taels.

12. As regards comparative values, therefore, the following may be taken as the standard:—

Ts'ao-p'ing Tls.	100	=	Shanghai Tls.	107.1.4.3
Kuping Tls.	100	=	Shanghai Tls.	109.6.0.0
Haikwan Tls.	100	=	Shanghai Tls.	111.4.0.0
Shanghai Tls.	100	=	Kuping Tls.	91.2.4.0
			i.e., Haikwan Tls.	89.7.6.6
			i.e., Ts'ao-p'ing Tls.	93.3.3.3

13. What precedes refers chiefly to comparative values; accordingly, if one desires to know how many English pounds sterling can be bought in London with so much Haikwan or K'uping or Ts'ao-p'ing silver at Shanghai, he has only to ask the market remitting rate for Shanghai kuei yin and calculate accordingly. Just now 3 English shillings is the exchange value of the Shanghai kuei yin tael; that is, 1,000 Shanghai taels will buy a draft for 3,000 shillings, *i.e.*, £150.

14. If one asks about weights without reference to touch of silver or any such items, the following figures give the results of comparisons of weights made at the Kung-ku, Taot'ai's yamên, and foreign French and English banks at Shanghai (the Ts'ao-p'ing scales and weights are the bases of all calculations):—

101.80 Ts'ao-p'ing taels=100 Kuping taels.
102.80 Ts'ao-p'ing taels=100 Haikwan taels.
1 Ts'ao-p'ing tael in English weight weighs 564.6375 grains.
1 Ts'ao-p'ing tael in French weight weighs 36.6527 grams.

1 Kuping tael weighs	575.82 grains. / 37.312 grams.
1 Haikwan tael should weigh	581.47 grains. / 37.68 grams.

15. Accordingly, if we discuss money and remittances from Shanghai to London, and if 1,096 Shanghai taels equal 1,000 K'uping taels, and if the exchange value of the Shanghai tael is 3 shillings, then 200,000,000 K'uping taels are equal to 219,200,000 Shanghai taels, and therefore would buy £32,880,000. If we discuss weights and purchase of the commodity silver by weight, then, inasmuch as 480 grains equal one ounce, and one K'uping tael

weighs 575.82 grains, 200,000,000 K'uping taels weight will equal 115,164,000,000 grains, *i.e.*, 239,925,000 ounces; and, further, seeing that at present bar silver is quoted at $30\frac{9}{16}$*d.* per ounce, 239,925,000 ounces of silver would cost in London £30,552,949/4*s.*/4½*d.* But of course the simultaneous purchase of so large a quantity of silver would probably send up its price, and freight, etc., would have to be paid on it from London to Shanghai; so that to lay down in Shanghai 200,000,000 K'uping taels weight of bar silver bought in London would in the end cost more than 3,055 wan pounds sterling of mere figuring calculation. There would, besides, be the time required to bring out so much—possibly two or three months.

16. If it is said that a Chinese tael weight is equal to 579.84 grains, the tael spoken of is the Canton tael and originated in 1770 (Chien Lung 34th year) with the 13 factories at Canton before the treaties. According to the treaty tariff rules 100 Chinese catties are equal to $133\frac{1}{3}$ pounds $\frac{\text{coarse weight}}{\text{avoirdupois}}$; therefore, one Chinese tael will weigh $\frac{1.333}{1\frac{1}{3}}$ ounces $\frac{\text{coarse weight}}{\text{avoirdupois}}$, *i.e.*, 1,215 ounces, *i.e.*, 583.20 grains $\frac{\text{fine weight}}{\text{troy}}$, or French weight 37.783 grams. But really the Canton tael ordinarily used is one-half per cent. lighter, weighing only 37.58 French grams, or 579.84 English grains.—20th October, 1895.

The following remarks relating to sycee taels in China are taken from the Chinese Maritime Customs Decennial Reports, covering the period from 1902 to 1921; except two items, which are from the weekly bulletin, issued (1925) by the Chinese Bureau of Economic Information, and the *China Year Book* (1925).

Kongmoon—(Kuangtung).

For this district we find the Kongmoon tael, the Sailam tael, the Haikwan tael and the Native Customs tael.

Chungking—(Szechuen).

The great variety of taels formerly in use in this province—almost every district and trade center had its own weight—caused many inconveniences. In 1908 the Industrial Taotai introduced one uniform tael for the whole province, the Chiu-ch'i-p'ing tael (九 七 平); its relation is Hk. Tls. 100 = Szechwan Tls. 107.075.

Wanhsien—(Szechuen).

The Szechuen tael, commonly called Chiu-chi-p'ing, which name indicates that 100 Szechwan taels equal 97 K'uping taels, is universally used in trade transactions. The sycee occurs usually in shoes of about 10 taels weight. To become current it must be passed by the Kung-ku Chu, or Assay Office, and each parcel of sycee must contain a slip stamped by this office and indicating the weight. Wanhsien sycee is of inferior quality and, when exported to other places, is subject to heavy discount.

Lungkow—(Shantung).

The sycee current in Lungkow is styled Kao Pao Yin (國寶銀), and is cast in shoes of from Tls. 53 to 54 in the Hwanghsien and Lungkow *lu-fang* (smelting houses). It is in use in this and neighbouring *hsien;* and it is found also in Chefoo, where it is popularly known as the "two-four-shoe" because its colour is 2.4 per cent. higher than the Chefoo silver.

The tael used for commercial purposes is the Huangp'ing (黃 平) tael. Its exchange value, according to the Bank of Communications, is as follows:—

Huangp'ing	Tls.	1000	=	Peking	Tls.	958
"	"		=	Tsinan	"	938
"	"		=	Tientsin	"	961
"	"		=	Chefoo	"	943
"	"		=	Shanghai	"	1012.37
"	"	1105	=	Haikwan	"	1000
"	"	1082	=	K'up'ing	"	1000

All these values are not in proper ratio with one another. It may be assumed that they were fixed by arrangement with the exchange bureaux and without strict regard to mathematical accuracy.

Wuhu—(Anhwei).

Sycee has disappeared from the market, and for all practical purposes the dollar has become the local unit of silver. The Wuhu tael, though it exists only in name, is still the standard by which dollar rates are fixed, though the natives no longer speak of the price of cash in relation to the tael. (1921).

Foochow—(Fukien).

The accepted standard tael is the *Hsin-i-p'ing* (新 議 平) and the currency the t'ai-fu or paper dollar. The practice in Foochow of chopping dollars, compels the banks to accept it by weight instead of at its face value. The tael weight used for this purpose is the Yang-p'ing, of which 71.7 equal 100 chopped dollars. The Native banks, on the other hand, accept these dollars at the rate of *Hsin-i-p'ing* taels 74.16 per hundred.

Tengyueh—(Yunnan).

In addition to the two local silver standards, *wen yin,* or pure silver, and Kung-ku yin, or assay silver, is sometimes used. The local scale differs from the provincial one by 2.5 per cent. *(Sheng-p'ing* taels 102.5 = *Tengyueh* taels 100); the touch of all assay silver, whether local or provincial, is the same and is 0.028 below that of pure silver. Since 1920 taels have become exceedingly scarce, said to be due partly to the long-continued drain to Burma to meet the adverse balance of trade and partly to the increased demands of the Provincial Mint for coinage purposes.

The *Kung-ku-yin* is cast generally in oblong cakes and is normally employed in government payments. The *wen-yin* is cast in semispheroidal cakes, is at a premium of taels 0.028 as compared with *Kung-ku-yin,* and is the standard chiefly employed in commercial transactions.

Szemao—(Yunnan).

Szemao tael. Of the old silver currencies the following were still in use in 1912: Kung-ku-yin (公 估 銀) the weight ranging from 4 to 5 taels a piece. Wen-yin (紋 銀) small cakes of pure silver, 1 tael each. *Shi-yin* (市 銀) that weighs 5 to 10 taels.

Nanking—(Kiangsu).

By the close of the past decade Nanking had become almost entirely a dollar-using port. With the elimination of the white metal from the market, the Nanking tael (漕 平) exists no longer in reality but only as a fictitious unit of account kept by bankers and merchants. The Nanking tael having now assumed the character of a bank unit, it is circulated in the shape of native orders (莊票), and if payments have to be liquidated in cash, they must be made in silver dollars or dollar notes, or copper cents in the case of minor payments. But this bank unit is more particularly made use of in transfers from bank account to bank account for the settlement of mercantile transactions. The transformation of the Nanking tael from an ounce of silver (the standard weight of the Nanking tael was 565.30 troy grains, and the standard fineness of the local silver shoes hovered round 946) into a book unit was not the outcome of any concerted action by interested parties. The change took place simultaneously with the gradual disappearance of sycee from the market, and the system of credit was thus unconsciously created, affording to merchants greater banking facilities than formerly. The rate of this fictitious tael unit fluctuates daily and is determined by applying both the dollar Shanghai tael rate and the Nanking–Shanghai cross rate. The tael-dollar rate thus obtained varies for buying and selling within a margin of 2 mace and 4 candareens below or above this rate. The calculations may be shown by the following formula:—

Nanking-Shanghai cross rate: 100 Shanghai taels = x Nanking Tls.
Dollar-Shanghai tael rate: $100 = y Shanghai taels.
Hence, in Nanking the tael-dollar rate is:—

$$\$100 = \frac{xy}{100} = Z \text{ Nanking taels;}$$

and —

Banker's buying rate = $Z \times 0.2/0.04$.
Banker's selling rate $Z - 0.2/0.04$.

Wuchow—(Kwangsi).

Banking and mercantile operations are conducted in *P'aip'ing taels.*

Lungchow—(Kwangsi).

The local tael is the *Shihp'ing* (市平) tael, the official ratio of which to the Haikwan tael is Hk. Tls. 100 = *Shihp'ing* taels 113, when paying in to the Bank, but Shihp'ing taels 116 when drawing on the bank in the former currency. The military are paid through the bank in Hunan taels, of which there exist two kinds, the *Hsiangp'ing* (湘平) and the *Hsin Hsiangp'ing* (新湘平). There are besides accounts to be rendered in K'uping taels, the value of which in *Shengp'ing, Shihp'ing, Hsiangp'ing,* and the *Hsin Hsiangp'ing* taels are respectively as follows: viz. 0.980, 0.960, 0.940.

Antung—(Manchuria).

The purity of the Chenp'ing tael, which is the medium of local commercial transactions, has recently been more strictly observed than in former years. The assaying concerns which used to be private institutions were amalgamated in 1918, and an office named Kung-ku Chu was established by the local Chamber of Commerce, which in 1919 changed the local standard sycee from Chenp'ing Tls. 108.50 = Hk. Tls. 100 to Chenp'ing Tls. 109.92 = Hk. Tls. 100. This Chu remains omnipotent in regulating local finance. (1921.)

The standard touch of Antung sycee was originally fixed at .992 purity; but the assaying offices have not continued to produce sycee of this fineness. It is even said that it has fallen as low as .970. There are three assaying offices . . . . all under the supervision of the local Chamber of Commerce and Merchants' Guild. The local officials have nothing to do with their control, and permission to open an assaying office must be obtained from the Merchants' Guild. The Antung or Chenp'ing tael is the medium in which all the staple products such as timber, wild raw silk, and beans, are bought and sold. When trade is brisk, silver ingots are nearly twice as numerous as in the slack season. (1911.)

Manchuria.

Sycee or silver ingot is also a common medium of exchange in Manchuria. Generally speaking, there are two kinds, one known as "ting ning" (丁銀) and the other known as "lu ning" (爐銀) The unit for both is the tael, whose weight varies at different places. The Newchwang tael is most commonly adopted. The difference between the "ting ning" and "lu ning" is that the former is the common sycee, which has a variety of weight and fineness at different places. The "luning" is said to have been assayed and standardised by the Lu Fang (爐房), an institution partaking of the nature of a native bank and a silver smelting plant, and is more or less uniform in weight and fineness.

Chinese Turkestan. (From *China Year Book,* 1925).

The monetary system differs from that of China. The dollar is not current, and the Sinkiang tael is the principal medium of currency; but the Chinese and Turki methods of subdividing the tael differ considerably. The Chinese and Turki denominations and values of current coins are as follows:

Chinese.		*Turki.*	
4 red cash	1 fen	2 pul	1 red cash
10 fen	1 chien (miscal)	25 red cash	1 tenga
10 chien	1 tael (sar)	16 tengas	1 tael
50 taels	1 yuan pao (yambu)	50 taels	1 yambu

Of the above, however, the pul and tenga do not exist as coins, though the Turkis always reckon in this way. The tael or sar was originally worth 1.33 ounce of pure silver, but the local tael coins are now much debased in value and a real Chinese yuan pao (*i.e.,* shoe weighing 50 *liang* or 66.65 ounces of pure silver) now fetches about 65 sars. Silver is, however, rarely seen, except in the circuit of the Kashgar Taoyin. Even in Kashgar more notes are now seen than silver, but the notes retain their face value. In Urumchi paper money is worth about 40 per cent. of its face value, and the Ili notes are worth still less.

Newchwang Transfer money. (1901).

Nearly all local mercantile business is done in transfer money, passing through the hands of the Lu Fang.

An account in transfer money may be started as follows:

(*a*) By a credit allowed on the strength of good recommendation

(*b*) By sale of goods

(*c*) By paying in hard *sycee* and converting it into *transfer money.*

Hard sycee, when paid into a Lu Fang is allowed a premium, ranging on an average, from Tls. 0.10 to Tls. 3 (fluctuating according to demand and supply) per shoe of about Tls. 53.50; with this premium added on it is placed to the credit of the depositor as *transfer money,* which on settling days—1st day of the 3rd, 6th, 9th, and 12th moons—again becomes hard *sycee;* but as the Lu Fang like to keep the money in their hands, transfer money is on settling days of late only called *hard transfer money,* which may again be converted into transfer money by adding the premium (chia sai) of the day; but if demanded in hard sycee, a premium is charged by the Lu Fang.

Transfer money cannot be withdrawn in hard sycee, except on settling days, unless the premium of the day is paid, but as the foreign expression implies, may be transferred to another person's account in payment for goods, etc.; if that person keeps his account with another Lu Fang, the amount can be transferred to his credit there without any charge being made.

Nearly all business among the Natives being done by word of mouth only, thousands of taels are transferred from one person to another without cheque or other receipt being issued, the Lu Fang's books being the only written evidence of the transaction.

Drafts on all principal coast ports and inland places may be obtained at time sight, according to the distance of the place, through the Hui Tui Chuang, or the large firms who have branches at the various places.

All exchange quotations for drafts are in transfer money, so that when wishing to remit hard sycee the chia-sai has first to be added. For instance, I wish to remit equivalent of 100 shoes of sycee (say, Tls. 5,350) to Shanghai, sycee premium (chia-sai) being Tls. 1.50, exchange (hui-shui), 3½ per cent.

Newchwang Tls.	5,350.00	
	150.00	chia-sai for 100 shoes
	5,500.00	
	192.50	hui-shui at 3½ per cent.
I receive Shanghai Tls.	5,692.50	draft on Shanghai.

Exchange is usually so arranged that money is not likely to be withdrawn in large sums, except when really necessary, rates on other places being usually low when local rate (chia-sai) is high, and *vice-versa,* so that it pays better to leave the money in the Lu Fang's hands at local rates.

Nanning—(Kwangsi). (Transfer money). (1911).

The financial basis of all commercial transactions is the "transfer money"; this term signifies the transcribing at fixed periods from account to account of the moneys deposited with banks. The periods of transfer, or settlement of accounts, vary from a fortnight to six months and bear close connexion to the commodity concerned. Hard cash is hardly ever paid into banks, the latter receiving the first as well as all following deposits from the depositors in bills on other banks, local or elsewhere. The system of transfer money is, however, not exclusively applied to mercantile transactions; it is also used by all classes of the population who have a reliable income; they, similarly, settle their accounts for their daily necessities by cheque with the local shopkeepers. Nearly all transfer money accounts are kept in local, or Yungp'ing, taels (邕平). The Yungp'ing, or Nanning, tael weighs 572.35 grains of silver 1,000 fine; but there is, of course, the difference between the receiving and paying rates. When received or paid out on the scale in metal (not in bills of transfer money), which happens rarely enough, the Yungp'ing tael is weighed in subsidiary coin, and not in sycee or any other kind of silver. Transactions are rarely done by count of coin, and even if so, the payment is effected at a rate varying from $138.50 to $142, or, in other words, for every Yungp'ing Tls. 100, subsidiary silver coins amounting to from $138.50 to $142 are paid out. Hard cash is always at a premium, varying, with the demand for metal, from 1 to 4 per cent., and even more.

H. B. Morse's views.

In his standard work *The Trade and Administration of the Chinese Empire* (Kelly & Walsh, Ltd., Shanghai, 1908), pp. 149–162, Hosea Ballou Morse, gives the following version about "taels":

THE TAEL

It is not always possible to keep them apart in writing, but in reading it is necessary always to bear in mind the distinction between the tael of value and the tael of weight. At Tientsin, by "Tientsin tael" is meant one *Hang-ping* tael in weight of silver of the *Hwa-pao* standard 992 fine; by "Hangping tael" is meant one Hangping tael in weight of silver or any other commodity, and, if of silver, it may be of Hwapao or any other stipulated standard; to express fully what the foreigner calls the "Tientsin tael," the Chinese would say "Hang-ping tael of hwa-pao silver." It is not possible to use different words for the two meanings thus connoted, since they are interwoven; and always to distinguish them otherwise would involve the use of much circumlocution. It must be left to the reader to make the distinction, since, even without this, there will be found to be enough of "proving axioms" to break constantly the thread of thought.

THE TAEL OF WEIGHT

The tael is the "ounce" of China, of which, as in England and America, 16 make one catty,[1] or Chinese "pound." In weighing the precious metals, however, the tael is the heaviest unit, and it has decimal subdivisions, each with its own name, down to the one thousand-million-millionth $\left(\frac{1}{1,000,000,000,000,000}\right)$ part of a tael, those in daily use being the following:—

10 Li (cash)	=	1 Fên (Candarin)
10 Fên	=	1 Tsien (Mace)
10 Tsien	=	1 Liang (Tael).

Seven places of decimals (the ten-millionth part) of a tael are frequently, even regularly, seen in statements of account of revenue and expenditure submitted to the Throne. This is the tael of the arithmetics, but its actual weight will best be considered under the head of the tael of currency; it is sufficient here to say that the weight ranges, at different places and in the same place, from 540 to 583 grains.

THE TAEL OF CURRENCY

Of the various taels of currency two may be considered to have a universal range, the Haikwan, or "Customs" tael, and the K'uping, or "Treasury" tael; and a third, the Tsaoping, or "Tribute" tael, is current over a wide area.

Haikwan Tael.

The Haikwan tael is the currency in which duties are levied by the Imperial Maritime Customs, but it is a purely fictitious and non-existent currency. Inquiry leads to no indication that it ever has been an existent currency at any time since the opening of the Inspectorate General of Customs, and it is certain that it is

[1] Catty or Kati—Malayan for pound.

not in current use at the present day. At no Custom House does any merchant tender Haikwan taels in payment of duties, and the invariable practice is to pay all Customs obligations in local currency at a rate of conversion settled on the opening of each of the several Customs Offices, now forty in number. The actual theoretic weight, apart from any question of the quality of silver, is not ascertainable with any degree of certainty. Using an official weight of 100 taels dated 1867, which had been verified at Canton by a weight of 1846, it has been found to be 581.55 grains. The result of independent tests at Canton in the same year (1905) gave a weight of 581.83 grains, while other estimates range from 581 to 589 grains. The only outside authority to which appeal can be made is in the Treaties. By the Trade Regulations annexed to the British Treaty of 1858 the "picul of one hundred catties is held to be equal to one hundred and thirty-three and one-third pounds, avoirdupois," giving a catty of $1^1/_3$ lb. av. and a tael of $1^1/_3$ ounce av., equal to 583.3 grains; while the Regulations annexed to the French Treaty of 1858 fix the picul at 60 kilograms and 453 grammes, which gives a resultant tael of 37.783 grammes or 583.1 grains.

Taking the Haikwan tael, then, as being purely a money of account, and not an existing currency of the Empire, the place at which its value may be most conveniently found is Shanghai, at which port were paid in 1905 duties to the extent of 34 per cent., of the total Customs collection of the year. Here since the opening of the port, half a century ago, the rate of conversion has been Haikwan Tls. 100 = Shanghai Tls. 111.40 worked out as follows:—

Weight on local scale	100.0.0.0
Add for difference in weight	2.8.0.0
Add for touch	6.1.6.8
Add for expenses of melting, etc.	0.2.0.4
Divide by the "Shanghai Convention," 0.98 ..	109.1.7.2
	111.4.0.0

(*N.B.*—The proper name for the Shanghai tael is "Convention Currency," referring to the convention, or understanding, by which 98 taels on the scale settle a liability of 100 taels in money of account.)

It remains to ascertain the true value of the Shanghai tael. The weight used as the basis of this is the Tsaop'ing tael, and the equivalence is worked out as follows:

Weight on scale	100.0.0.0
Add for touch	5.6.0.0
Divide by the "Shanghai Convention," 0.98 ..	105.6.0.0
Tsaoping taels 100 Shanghai taels ..	107.7.5.5

The Tsaop'ing tael has been found to weigh 565.65 grains; and if in 100 Tsaop'ing taels of pure silver there are 107.7.5.5 taels of Shanghai convention currency, then the latter will contain 525 grains of pure silver of K'uping standard. On this basis the Haikwan tael is the equivalent of 584.85 grains of pure silver; but note has now to be taken of the quality of the silver.

Introduced under the treaty of Nanking (1842), the lapse of sixty years has not sufficed to create modifications in this standard, which, moreover, is current for revenue purposes in all the ports open to foreign trade. Even with this currency, however, this immutability has to be taken with some reservation. It seldom happens that the merchant has at hand to pay his duties the fine silver (1,000) which is, theoretically, the standard for all payments to government; and tendering other silver, commonly the ordinary trade silver of the place, the rate at which it shall be accepted becomes a matter of arrangement with the banker; the latter, having to account to the government for a certain weight of silver 1,000 fine, will be careful to receive an amount in other silver fully sufficient in value to cover his liability. Another element of variation, even in this currency, is the difference between the receiving and paying rates in force in all government treasuries, all banks, and with those merchants of sufficiently strong standing to make their own counting-house rules; this difference, usually between a quarter and a half of one per cent., is made not by charging a commission, but by boldly using two sets of weights, one for receiving and one for paying, and is intended to compensate for the labor of weighing ingots and lumps of silver of no fixed weight, and for the risk incurred and expert knowledge requisite for taking in silver of unknown degrees of fineness. The practice is defended on the same ground as that of the foreign exchange banks in quoting different buying and selling rates for bills of exchange.

K'uping Tael.

The K'uping tael is the currency in which are collected all other dues to the government than Customs duties, excepting only those which are levied in kind (such as the grain tribute) or in copper cash. Theoretically uniform throughout the Empire, there are still differences to be observed apart from the differentiated receiving and paying rates referred to above. In one aspect this tael may be considered as "bank money"—a fictitious medium of exchange from one currency to another—as when we find that (with normal exchange at 1,200 cash to the tael) 2,000 or 3,000 or 4,000 cash or more are levied where a tax, assessed in taels, is collected in cash, while the exchange is fixed at 800 cash or less where a tax, assessed in cash, is collected in silver. This, however, from another point of view, may be taken as an eccentricity of the Chinese taxing offices. The normal standard K'uping tael is 575.8 grains of silver 1,000 fine; this is the receiving rate (the paying rate being 0.2 per cent. lighter) at the Imperial Treasury, and the several provincial treasuries vary from this standard in some instances as much as one per cent. Where the foreign obligations of the Imperial Government are concerned the equivalence of the several currencies is taken as follows:—

100 Haikwan taels = 101·642335 K'uping taels.
100 K'uping taels = 109·60 Shanghai taels.

Tsaoping Taels.

As the weight element of a currency tael, the Tsaoping tael is current throughout the provinces contributing tribute in kind (mainly rice) which is forwarded to the capital, either by sea or by the Grand Canal, viz. in the provinces of Kiangsi, Anhwei, Kiangsu and Chekiang; it is also the regular tael in use at Chefoo, on the sea route to the north, but is not known at Tientsin, the northern terminus of the Grand Canal and the port of disembarkation by the sea route. It may be stated with some degree of confidence to weigh 565.65 grains, subject always to the possibility of oscillation in the standard. While the weight is more or less constant, varying between one place and another by no more than a tenth to a half per cent. (100 Soochow Tsaoping taels = 99.90 Shanghai Tsaoping taels by weight), the tael of currency is based in different places on different standards of silver. At Chefoo the standard is 976, at Kiukiang and Wuhu 994, at Hangchow 997. In places where the standard of silver is quoted by degrees of betterness, as at Shanghai and on the lower Yangtze, the standard for Tsaoping is 2.75 silver which, referred to a K'uping standard, is 999.

Local Taels

It may be said that every commercial place has, apart from the various government taels, its half-dozen, or dozen, or score of local taels, all generally recognised and all current; *i.e.,* each of them is a recognised currency when it is so stipulated, as we have seen in the case of the currencies of Chungking. Usually, however, if not generally, among these various taels there is one which is recognised as the currency of the place, in which payments would be made when there is no stipulation to the contrary, which will be commonly stipulated, and into which remittances are made from other places; for even in China the necessity is felt for some limitation on the kaleidoscopic varieties which would otherwise perplex the minds of even Chinese bankers. Sometimes, but by no means generally, this recognised local tael will extend its influence over the surrounding country within a limited radius; but ordinarily the right of even the country banker to live is fully recognised, and every place is privileged to adopt its own standards. I have notes of 170 well-recognised and different currencies, gathered mainly from the Treaty ports and their immediate vicinity.

Peking Taels.

The capital, Peking, is one place, it may be said the one place of importance, in which no one currency has emerged as the one local tael. Being the capital, the K'uping tael is of course much in evidence as the currency of all official government transactions. Besides this there are three standards of tael weight—the Kung-fa of 555.7 grains, the Market of 552.4 grains, and the Metropolitan or Two-tael[1] scale of 541.7 grains—and two recognised standards of silver, 1,000 and 980 fine respectively. Each standard of weight (except the K'uping) is expressed in each of the two standards of silver, with the result that there are at Peking seven taels all equally current. The foreign banks established there have within a few years adopted the Kung-fa tael of 1,000 silver as their currency of account. Each of these currencies, except the K'uping and Kung-fa, is further subject to a difference of 0.6 to 0.9 per cent. according as it is "equalised" or "empty" or "mercantile" or "complete"; thus 100 Kung-fa taels are equivalent to Metropolitan taels 102.80 if mercantile, 102.70 if empty, 102.60 if equalised, but only 102.00 if complete.

Tientsin Taels.

At Tientsin I have note of nine taels generally known, and two standards to which silver is reduced. Of these, the tael which for forty years past has been recognised as "the Tientsin tael" is the Merchants tael weighing 557.4 grains of silver 992 fine. For some

[1] The addition of 2 taels in the hundred, 2 per cent., will bring this to the value of the Market tael; hence probably the name.

occult reason there has lately (since 1900) been introduced a "New Merchants" tael of 557.6 grains, differing from the old established local tael by only 0.00038 part of itself or less than $\frac{4}{100}$ of one per cent., the standard of silver remaining the same; this new tael has not yet worked its way into general acceptance. As an illustration of the ordinary Chinese rough-and-ready methods of banking it may be noted that the true equivalence of Haikwan Tls. 100 is Tientein Tls. 105.215; and that for many years, in paying Customs duties, for every 100 Haikwan taels Chinese merchants paid Tientsin Tls. 106, foreign merchants in general paid Tientsin Tls. 105, and Russian merchants for tea paid Tientsin Tls. 104.

Hankow Taels.

At Hankow one tael stands out above the rest as "the Hankow tael"; and, though the triple city at Hankow is a great commercial emporium not created by foreign trade, this is the "Foreign rule" tael, weighing 554.7 grains, of "Foreign rule" silver 967 fine.

Canton Tael.

At Canton, and for a considerable area commercially tributary to it, extending beyond the limits of the province of Kwangtung, the standard tael is the Sze-ma tael, weighing 579.85 grains, being the heaviest mercantile tael in the Empire; silver was originally, and is in theory, reduced to the standard of 1,000 fine. This sounds as if we had here a departure from the prevailing diversity of currency, and could point to a tael, uniform in weight and value, not confined to one city, but current through a large commercial area. The bankers must, however, be reckoned with; and, both in Canton and thoroughout the whole area, while we find the Sze-ma to be the standard of weight, it is usually varied by being subject to discounts, fixed for each sub-standard, but supplying that variability which is demanded for all transfers in China from place to place, from bank to bank, or from account to account. These sub-standards are known by the per-mill proportion to the Sze-ma standard; and I have note of taels of the 998, 996, 995, 993, 992, 990, 988, and 986 scale, being respectively 0.2, 0.4, 0.5, 0.7, 0.8, 1.0, 1.2, and 1.4 per cent. lighter than standard Sze-ma in weight. Formerly the silver was always taken as 1,000 fine, but in the last half-century dollars, mainly Mexican, more or less battered and chopped, have entirely supplanted ingots; for large transactions payment is always made by weight, and never by count. The result is a curious medley, it being always necessary to express clearly if the tael is of "foreign silver" (900 fine) or of "pure silver"; in the latter case payment is effected by weighing out 10 per cent. additional of the dollar silver. The question is even further complicated by a practice, which has crept in of recent years, of making 20 per cent. of payments in subsidiary silver coins (800 fine), with perhaps some bargaining as to whether the proportion shall be 15 or 25 per cent. Here we have a case of degeneration within the memory of men now living. Disregarding any question of what constitutes "pure silver," a tael containing 579.85 grains of fine silver becomes one of 574.1 grains, and ultimately one of 561.4 grains; and, as there is a tendency now (1906) to substitute 20 cent pieces entirely for dollars, the tael is on the way to become one containing 510.3 grains of fine silver. These figures are all subject to proportionate reduction for each of the various sub-standards of weight.

Shanghai Taels.

I come now to the consideration of the currency at Shanghai, the commercial metropolis of China. Omitting the government and other exceptional taels, I must first note the exclusive use of the Canton standard (tael = 579.85 grains) for dealings in foreign bar silver; a practice originating when foreign trade was centred at Canton and continued when the foreign banks and merchants brought Cantonese as their first compradors and shroffs to Shanghai, has been sanctified by use and by the ingrained habit of introducing, whenever possible, further elements of conversion into all dealings with the precious metals. Then the Tsaoping tael, described above, is fully current and fully recognised at Shanghai and in a large area around, and is the ordinary currency for Chinese remittances through Chinese banks to places in China, *e.g.*, a remittance to Hankow is converted from "Shanghai taels" to Tsaoping taels and thence to "Hankow taels." Finally the legitimate banking and trading currency of the place is the "Shanghai tael" or "Shanghai convention currency," which is also the standard of international exchange for the trade of North China and the Yangtze basin, all other quotations in local currencies being re-conversions from the rate for Shanghai currency. The rate of the day is accepted by merchants as the rate of conversion between two fixed currencies; and yet, if we take exchange on London as an example, one of the currencies stands for the immutable in finance, while in the other it is doubtful if many of the foreign merchants who so blindly base their operations on this exchange quotation could go into the treasury of a Chinese bank and weigh out for themselves a Shanghai tael, assuming even that they could read the inscriptions on the weights they used. The value of the Shanghai tael is made up of three elements—the weight, the quality of silver, and a convention. The weight on the scale is the Tsaoping tael of 565.65 grains, the silver is reduced to a standard of 944 fine on the K'uping basis of 1,000 fine, and the convention is that 98 taels of this weight and this silver settle a liability of 100 taels "Shanghai convention currency." In order fully to understand what is a Shanghai tael, how it may be ascertained, and what may be done with it when once ascertained, let us consider the processes to be gone through in an exchange operation under present conditions. Of course, in Shanghai as in London, the merchant will ordinarily draw his cheque, against which the bank will give him its bill of exchange; but somewhere, and some time, there will be a cash transaction; and thoroughly to understand the situation we must see what, in Shanghai, corresponds to the act of a London merchant who takes a thousand sovereigns to the bank and gets a draft on Paris for 25,150 *f.* or 25,175 *f.* according to the exchange. Let us assume the simple case where our Shanghai merchant wishes to remit the contents of a box full of silver (if he wishes to make up an exact sum in Shanghai currency, certain complications are added). The silver in the box will be in the shape of "shoes" of "sycee" of about 50 taels each, and of varying "touch" (degrees of fineness). If these shoes are marked, in ink, with the results of a previous assay at the Assay Office for the Foreign Settlement, the preliminary stage becomes unnecessary; but if they have come in the course of trade from another port, or if their last previous assay was made by the Assay Office for the Chinese City, then all existing marks are washed off and the silver must be sent to the proper office. Here each shoe is weighed and the result written on one side; it is then "touched" and the difference (usually an addition) from a certain standard, as indicated by the colour on the touchstone, is written on the other side. This difference for touch is so much for the shoe irrespective of its exact weight, which is anything between 49 and 54 taels, but an allowance of 0.05 tael is added for each tael by which the weight of the shoe exceeds 50 taels; thus if the quality of the silver is 2.70, the addition for a shoe weighing 49.75 or one of 50.05 taels is 2.70, for one of 51.25 taels is 2.75, for one of 52.15 taels is 2.80, and so on. Let us take two such shoes weighing 50 and 51 taels and having 2.60 and 2.40 respectively added for touch, making for the two 50 + 2.60 + 51 + 2.40 = 106.00; this result, divided by 0.98 (the Shanghai "convention") gives 108.163 as the number of Shanghai taels in our two shoes. If the transaction is one in Shanghai currency only, this ends it, the whole operation corresponding to the single action of the London merchant who takes £108/3*s.*/4*d.* from his cash to pay a bill; but we have now to connect this with foreign exchange. First, it is to be noted that at the present day no other currency is used at Shanghai, all others being reduced to Shanghai taels. The government, for example, in making payments for indebtedness or indemnity, does not use the K'uping ("Treasury") tael weights or the pure silver (1,000 fine), which make up the K'uping tael currency, but pays in Shanghai currency at the rate of 109.60, calculated as follows:

K'uping taels 100 weight = Tsaoping taels	101.800
Add for touch of pure silver on two shoes	5.600
	107.400
Divide by the "convention" 0.98	109.592
Add for meltage fee	.008
	109.600

So with Customs duties, merchants pay in Shanghai taels at the fixed rate 111.40 and never tender the "Haikwan tael-weight of pure silver" specified by treaty.

Coming now to the exchange operation, we have first to find our parity of exchange, and to do this we must get the equivalence in foreign notation. The weight used for Shanghai currency is the Tsaoping tael, and this is 565.65 grains; for pure silver the addition for touch is 2.8 per shoe, which the Chinese treat as if it were 5.6 per cent.; and the "convention" is 0.98. One Tsaoping tael of pure silver is, therefore, 1.07755 Shanghai tael; and one Shanghai tael contains 524.93 grains of fine silver. In one ounce of silver British Standard (0.925) are 444 grains of fine silver, or 84.6 per cent. of the amount in the Shanghai tael; and to get the parity of exchange for the latter the London price of bar silver must be divided by 0.846.[1] The actual rate of exchange is, of course, affected by the demand and supply of bills wanted and offered, but in the great and frequent fluctuations in the value of silver bullion we have an everpresent element of instability which must be taken into account. Our Shanghai merchant, who has once gone through such a series of manipulations and calculations, is likely to consider his time of too much value to repeat the transaction, and, as is actually the case, will leave such operations in future to his comprador, until such time as he is put on the same footing as his London brother.

[1] Subject to modification by consideration of the true standard of quality of silver.

Newchwang Transfer Money

One currency practice, recalling the "bank money" of the old Amsterdamsche Wisselbank, must be referred to. At Newchwang the local tael is 555.1 grains of silver 992 fine. Except of copper there is (or, as the war may have caused a change, has been) little of the metals in circulation, silver being commonly deposited at the banks, which permit removal only on the first days of the third, sixth, ninth, and twelfth months, but allow transfers from account to account. This "transfer money" is exclusively used in the settlement of all mercantile transactions. On deposit, and for renewal on each quarter day, the depositor is credited with a premium which varies with the demand for money, but which, in ordinary peaceful times, ranges from 0.20 to 6 per cent. Exchange quotations also are always quoted in transfer money, not in hard silver. An ordinary exchange operation would be as follows:—

Silver deposited, Newchwang taels..	100.00
Premium on deposit 1·60 per shoe	3.00
Transfer money credited	103.00
Exchange premium 3¼ per cent.	3.35
Shanghai taels	106.35

It may be noted that the parity of exchange is 100 Newchwang taels of silver = 104.89 Shanghai taels. The rates of premium given above are, as has been stated, those of ordinary conditions; the effect of the stress of war on the money market and the financial position of the bankers may be seen from the quotations of the last day of 1904: Silver Tls. 1,000 = Transfer-money Tls. 1,358.50 (quoted Tls. 72 per shoe); Transfer Tls. 1,000 = Shanghai Tls. 785.

These figures show the banker protecting his reserves, apparently giving 36 per cent. premium for deposits and charging 22 per cent. discount for withdrawals instead of giving a premium. This works out to a rate of exchange for cash transactions, however, of Newchwang Tls. 100 = Shanghai Tls. 105.65.

Henry Deutsch's explanation.

The following concise description about sycee and about the Shanghai tael is found on fol. 66–71 of Deutsch's work, entitled *Arbitrage:*

Sycee.

The silver which circulates in China as the medium of exchange has the shape of broad shoes, and is therefore called "shoe." The weight of these shoes varies from ½ tael up to 100 taels, their lowest degree of fineness is 0.935. Currency silver of a higher degree is named "sycee." *The most current sycee is nearly 0.986 fine.*

Before a "shoe" is put into circulation, its weight and fineness are fixed, and the result of the examination is marked on the shoe by the "Kung-ku."

A silver piece marked by the "Kung-ku" is ripe for circulation. Obviously, that process for creating medium of exchange is a very primitive one, but it must be admitted that the examination is carried through in a very careful and irreproachable manner.

The conversion of sycee into Shanghai money taels is somewhat complicated. But it will appear more simple if we remember that the Shanghai money tael is 11/12 fine silver of the weight of 1 Shanghai (Chauping) tael.

We therefore have the following equations:—

1000 Shanghai money taels equal 1000 Chauping taels $\frac{11}{12}$ fine silver
,, 91666 ,, ,, pure silver
(1000 × $\frac{11}{12}$ equal 916.66)
1000 ,, ,, ,, ,, 980 Chauping taels silver
0.935374 fine
(980 × 0.935374 equals 916.$\frac{2}{3}$).

The last named equation forms the basis for the conversion of sycee into Shanghai money taels.

The Chinese take silver of a fineness of 0.935374 as the standard for the circulating silver, and mark it with a premium of "0%."

As the *lowest grade* sycee is marked with "0" a premium of "4%," must be of a fineness of 0.9728, because

standard equals	0,935374	
4% excess of standard ,,	0.037414	(0.935374 × 0.04)
	0.972788	

and we find that the equivalent to 1000 Shanghai money taels, in *such* a quality of sycee, is silver of the weight of 942.31 Chauping taels, because $\frac{916.2/3}{0.9728}$ equals 942.31. In a similar way we may establish the metal quantity which corresponds to sycee mark d 4¼—4½—4¾ and upwards to 6%.

Sycee of a higher mark than 6% does not circulate. Pure silver would have to be marked "6.91" because

standard equals	935.37
Plus 6.91% of ,, ,,	64.63
	1000.

Putting together the results of these calculations, we obtain the following table:—

Chinese Marks	Degree of silver Fineness.	Equivalent to 1000 Shanghai Money Taels in Chauping Taels Silver.
0	935.374	980
4	972.788	942.31
4¼	975.127	940.04
4½	977.466	937.80
4¾	979.804	935.56
5	982.142	933.34
5¼	984.481	931.13
5⅜	985.650	930.01
5½	986.819	929.05
5¾	989.158	926.71
6	991.496	924.53
6.91	1000.000	916.67

The above-mentioned equation:—

1000 money taels equals 980 Chauping taels weight (0.935) can also be written:—

100 money taels equal 1 Chauping tael (0.935).

If we call the quantity of silver to be valued *q*, its money value would be $q \times \frac{100}{98}$, or as the Chinese mark silver, 0.935 fine, "0."

$$q \times \frac{(100 \times 0)}{98} \text{ equals } q \times 1.0204.$$

If the quantity of silver were 0.972 fine (or according to the Chinese way of writing "4") the money value would be

$$q \times \frac{(100 \times 4)}{98} \text{ equals } q \times 1.06122.$$

The money value of silver 0.9868 fine would be

$$q \times \frac{(100\ 5.\ 5)}{98} \text{ equals } q \times 1.07653.$$

The multiplicators to be used would therefore be:—

1.0204—1.06122—1.07653

From this we are able to establish the money value of a sycee remittance by the following methods:—

Sycee is generally packed in boxes containing 60 shoes of a weight of about 50 Chauping taels each.

I.

Presuming a total weight of 3,000 taels (60 × 50 equals 3000), and the surplus in value of 2¾ taels for each shoe or 5½% of 3000 (60 × 2¾ equals 165), we arrive at the figure *3165,* which, divided by 98, gives Tls. 3229.59 Shanghai money taels as value of the remittance.

II.

The multiplicator which is to be used for 5½ sycee (or 2¾% for 50 taels) is 1.07653, therefore 3000 × 1.07653 equals Tls. 3229.59 as the result of the calculation.

III.

The table for converting sycee into money taels gives 929.05 Chauping taels silver with the mark 5½ as equivalent to 1000 Shanghai money taels, the money value of 3000 Chauping taels of *such* silver must therefore be $1000 \times \frac{3000}{929.05}$ equals *$3229.59.*

Shanghai Currency Taels.

As the silver which circulates in China does not possess a uniform degree of fineness, payments there are not so quickly effected as in this country. They always require the fixing of weights and calculations in which the Chinese excel. If we consider that the Chinese scales leave much to be desired, and that the existing currency is the result of many alterations of preceding currencies, it is not surprising that the definitions of the Shanghai money tael differ. Some years ago—in 1867—the mint in Hongkong coined, by way of trial, a Shanghai money tael, and made it 36.67 grammes 0.982 fine (*i.e.,* 36 grammes pure silver) and intended it to replace the theoretical Shanghai currency tael which contains about 2½ grammes less pure silver.

Of all existing definitions of the Shanghai money tael, the following seem to be the most simple:—

The Shanghai currency (money) tael can be taken *theoretically* as equivalent to one Shanghai (Chauping) tael weight of silver 11/12 fine, *i.e.*, silver of the fineness of the Indian rupee.

It therefore represents, theoretically 518.555 grains. Troy pure silver equals 33.59 grammes ($565.697 \times 11/12$ equals 518.555). But in reality its content of silver is 1/3% less, *i.e., 516.82 grains equal 1.0767 ounce equals 33.48 grammes pure silver.*

As the Shanghai money tael corresponds to 1.0767 ounce pure silver, and the Shanghai (Chauping) tael weighs 1.17853 ounce, we find the Shanghai currency based upon silver of the fineness of 0.91323, because $\frac{1.0767}{1.17853}$ equals 0.91323.

As 1.0767 ounce pure silver corresponds to 1.164 ounce standard silver $\left(\frac{1.0767}{0.925}\right)$ we find the *London parity of the Shanghai currency equals 1.164 × London price of silver.*

At a silver price of 25*d.*, the parity would be 29.1*d.*, equals 2*s.*/5⅛*d.*

Shanghai Weight Tael.

That tael is the most important of all taels, as it forms the basis of international payments, it weighs *565.697* grains troy equals 1.17853 ounces troy equals 36.65 grammes equals 3.1426 tolas, and is therefore 2½% lighter than the Canton tael, so that

100 Canton taels equal 102.5 Shanghai weight taels

(100×579.84 equals 102.50×565.697).

The weight of gold is always expressed in Shanghai weight taels.

D. K. Lieu's views on the Chauping Tael.

The following essay on the Chauping (Tsaoping) tael has been kindly supplied, at the special request of the author, by the Chief of the Investigation Department of the Government Bureau of Economic Information, Peking. We maintain that the Chauping tael exists at present merely as a unit of weight, and not as a money tael. The Shanghai currency tael is frequently,—and we venture to say—erroneously,—called "Chauping" tael. Mr. D. K. Lieu, while not opposing our views, proves that there was, in the fifties of the past century, a Chauping currency tael, though no such currency tael, with a standard weight and standard fineness, is in circulation nowadays.

Origin and Meaning of the Shanghai and Tsaoping Taels.

Before the establishment of Foreign Settlements in Shanghai, the principal business section was at Nantao. The Tsaoping sycee in current use at that time had a fineness of 935.374. This was what the authorities claimed for it, although personally I think the fineness was only approximately so, that is, somewhere between 935.3 and 935.4, as we can hardly expect silversmiths of that time to have produced shoes of uniform fineness with so great accuracy. When the Newchwang bean merchants traded with Shanghai, they brought their own sycee with them in payment of accounts, and it was subject to a two per cent. discount, because its fineness was 916.666, or 11 parts silver and 1 part alloy. It was consequently called the "chiu pa tou kwei yuan" (九八荳規元)

meaning "98 bean kweiyuan" or "98 bean tael." On account of the simplicity of its composition, perhaps, it later became the standard currency of account in Shanghai.

After the Settlements were established, a new sycee appeared, called the "yi chang hsin" (夷場新) or "new sycee for the Foreign Settlements." Because its fineness was 986.837, also approximately, which was 5½ per cent. higher than that of the old Tsaoping sycee, it commanded a premium of 5.5 taels for each 100 taels, or 2.75 taels for each actual sycee shoe of 50 taels. It was therefore known as "Tsaoping er chi pao," or "Tsaoping 2.7 sycee" (漕平二七寶).

From the above it will be seen that there was actual sycee representing the old Tsaoping tael of 935.374 fineness. There is also actual sycee representing the er-chi-pao of 986.837 fineness. Moreover, if we trace still further back to its origin, the term "Tsaoping tael" stood for a standard grade of sycee used by the Collectorate of the Rice Tribute, known as "Tsao liang" (漕糧), in Kiangsu and other rice-producing provinces. All receipts and payments of that Collectorate were in Tsaoping taels, or were converted into such. There were actual sycee shoes of a definite fineness in the vaults of that office, just as there was K'uping sycee in the Imperial Treasury of Peking, or Fan K'uping (藩庫平) sycee in some of the provincial treasuries. The word Tsaoping itself represented a weight system, used by the same Collectorate and is still now used in many Kiangsu cities, but the original Tsaoping tael was represented by actual sycee and had a definite fineness. This is important because it explains why the Shanghai tael is called the "98 kwei yuan." If there were no actual sycee with a fineness taken as 100 (only in comparison, and not meaning 1000 fine), how is the two per cent. discount calculated? Why should "kwei yuan" be at a discount and the er-chi-pao at a premium, both on account of their fineness, if the standard to which both of them are referred in comparison (*i.e.*, the Tsaoping tael) had no definite fineness of its own?

In Chinese financial practice, all silver taels have "ping" (平), or weight standard, and "se" (色), or fineness. The word *Tsaoping* itself stands for a weight, but the Tsaoping *tael* has a definite "se" or fineness. The Tsaoping taels of different localities are of different fineness, because they are variations of the original Tsaoping tael. Similarly, K'uping is a weight standard, but the K'uping tael of the Manchu Imperial Government had a fineness nearest to 1000 of all Chinese silver sycee, while the K'uping of Taian (泰安), Shantung, Yuncheng (運城), Shansi, etc., are its variations.

A Shanghai Banker's Views.

Mr. C. Champkin, Manager of the Peninsular & Oriental Banking Corporation, Shanghai, has kindly given his permission to reproduce a chapter from his privately circulated publication, entitled *Bullion Operations in China* (1923). The said chapter treats of the interesting subject of

Mint Shops and Sycee.

The difference between the theoretical parity of monetary taels with standard silver 1.168 × London price per ounce and the actual parity without charges 1.175 × London price per ounce is due to the fact that *the conversion rate of 110.90 monetary taels per 100 Canton taels weight of bar silver 998 fine is arbitrarily fixed by the Mint shops on a principle that cannot be reconciled with exactness to any formula,* as "olo custom" and "squeeze" interpose at every step of the process. Thus when the Mint shops buy bar silver they reckon 102.5 Chauping taels are equal to 100 Canton taels; when they sell sycee they reckon only 102.4 as the equivalent. Also in the formula they nominally use to arrive at the conversion rate of 110.90 they allow only 1 per cent. for the superior fineness of bar silver over sycee. As the latter is reduced by copper alloy to about 985 fine this assumes that bar silver is about 995 fine instead of 998 fine, the difference being an additional profit to the Mint shops. Even allowing for about .3 per cent. on fineness and about .1 per cent. on weight there is still a further "squeeze" of nearly .3 per cent. as shown in the following formula, but, as no charge is actually quoted or made for the cost of melting and making, due allowance must be made for this and the matter is perhaps better expressed by stating that *through devious ways the Mint shops arrive at a fixed rate for the conversion of bar silver into sycee that includes a total charge of .7 per cent. for their services.* The charge seems unduly high, especially when it is considered that the sycee delivered in payment is neither of the fineness nor the weight it purports to be, though as it circulates locally at its purported fineness and weight this fact means no loss to the banks unless they export it for remelting into bars, when an average loss of .2 per cent. on fineness and .2 per cent. on weight has to be allowed for on this account. Actually therefore the Mint shops charge about 1.1 per cent. for converting bar silver into sycee, of which about .4 per cent. is concealed by the issue of debased currency. There is also some profitable and inexplicable huggermugger in the further theoretical conversion of this sycee into monetary taels that will be dealt with later.

The outturn of bar silver 998 fine in Shanghai, making no allowance for Mint shop charges is:—

Theoretical conversion of bar silver in Shanghai into monetary taels payable in sycee 985 fine

? monetary taels	=	100 Canton taels
100		102.5 Chauping taels
100 } 985 fine }		{ 1000 { 998 fine

Outturn 111.66 monetary taels per 100 Canton taels weight

The difference between this and the fixed rate 110.90 represents allowance for melting and making, to which must be added the fact that the sycee delivered in payment is deficient in weight and fineness. The effect of this is that:—

Sycee paid in exchange for monetary taels is theoretically 985 fine.

Sycee paid in exchange for bar silver is theoretically 991.75 fine. The difference between this and 985 is Mint shop charges and squeeze.

Sycee on assay averages 983 fine. The difference between this and 985 is Mint shop squeeze.

Sycee on test by weight averages a shortage of .2 per cent. This difference also is Mint shop squeeze.

A hundred ounces troy is equal to 82.78 Canton taels, so that the value of a bar of silver weighing 1158.25 ounce 998 fine would be $1158.25 \times 82.78 \div 100 = 958.80$ Canton taels at 110.90 per cent. = 1063.31 monetary taels.

It is obvious that in any well ordered currency system Mint shops would be impossible, but the system in China being what it is they have necessarily to be accepted as part of that system. Mint shops are under no supervision by government but are members of a guild and command general, if somewhat misplaced, confidence locally. Each is responsible for any deficiency in sycee bearing his "chop" though as shoes circulate locally at their marked value he is never called upon for a refund and as shoes lose their identity in the process of melting when exported it is difficult to see how in that case a claim for shortage could be brought home to the maker.

In addition to the Mint shops there is an official called a *"Kongku,"* who may be described as a public valuer, to whom all shoes of sycee are sent by the Mint shops to be attested before being put into circulation. This official, who is appointed by the Mint shops, tests each shoe in a perfunctory way with a touchstone, but judges it principally by its general appearance. He marks in ink on each shoe his opinion of its weight and fineness and for obvious reasons he is more apt to overvalue a shoe than otherwise.

The fineness is assessed by the "Kongku" at a premium on 935, which may conveniently be called the *standard fineness of sycee.* Shoes of a lower fineness than 935 do not exist.

Practically all sycee in general circulation is marked from 2.65 to 2.75 premium. *This is premium per shoe, not the premium per cent.* A shoe being about 50 Chauping taels weight the premium per cent. is about double the premium per shoe, varying of course with the weight. Therefore a shoe weighing exactly 50 Chauping taels and marked in Chinese characters "2.65 premium" would be about 984½ fine because:—

Standard	935
Add 5.3 per cent premium	49.55
	984.55

Mint shops do not ordinarily calculate the fineness of sycee, but adopt an arbitrary scale of nominal finenesses as under:—

Premium per shoe	*Nominal Fineness*
2.80	987
2.75	986
2.70	985
2.65	984
2.60	983
2.55	982
2.50	981

There is simply no explanation of this scale and as the weight of shoes varies appreciably it is obvious that no scale of fineness can be correct that is based on the premium per shoe with no regard to its weight. The matter however is of no importance to banks as the scale has a merely local application and no actual calculations are locally based on the millesimal fineness of sycee. Its only use apparently is as a means of ready reference by which the Mint shops discard for re-melting up-country shoes that fall below a certain standard and are therefore not good delivery. The minimum standard is 2.60.

An actual test covering 20,000 shoes of *new sycee* shipped during the War gave an average weight of 49.88 Chauping taels and an average premium of 2.72 per shoe according to the Kongku's marking, this giving a fineness by calculation of 985.98 as under:—

Standard	935
Add 5.453 per cent. premium	50.98
(equivalent of 2.72 on 49.88)	985.98

These shoes were specially made for export and, on account of their superior fineness over ordinary shoes 985 fine a special premium of 1/32 per cent. was charged *over and above their calculated value.* It has to be recorded that their actual fineness as assayed by the Bombay Mint was 983.95 and their shortage by weight was .2 per cent. The exporting bank therefore lost .20 per cent. on fineness, .20 per cent. on weight and .03 per cent. premium paid, a total of .43 per cent., or say over Tls. 4,000 on the consignment. *It is probable that the ordinary sycee in circulation averages a fineness of 985 by calculation and 983 by assay.*

For the *conversion of sycee into monetary taels* the rule is that 98 Chauping taels of sycee 935 fine are equal to 100 monetary taels, as stated in the table headed *theoretical parity between monetary taels and silver.* This, as already explained, is an anomaly if regarded in connection with the conversion of bar silver into monetary taels, depending as it does on the theory that a monetary tael is equal in value to a Chauping tael of silver 916.2/3 fine, which would make a parity without charges between the monetary tael and standard silver of 1.168 × London price of silver whereas the actual constant without charges is 1.175. Still, the conversion of bar silver into monetary taels and the conversion of sycee into monetary taels are separate and distinct operations each subject to its own peculiarities, and since the rule is that 98 Chauping taels of sycee 935 fine are equal to 100 monetary taels, a shoe of sycee weighing exactly 50 Chauping taels and marked "2.65 premium" would be worth:—

50+2.65×100÷98 = 53.72 monetary taels or, 930 Chauping taels = 1000 monetary taels and 1000 Chauping taels = 1075.25 monetary taels.

In most calculations affecting sycee there are discrepancies due to certain conventional principles in force in commercial dealings that are not in accordance with actual fact, that difference being "squeeze." In so far as local usages are concerned, it is immaterial whether a shoe of sycee purporting to be worth 53.72 monetary taels by calculation, is in fact worth only 53.62 monetary taels by assay, provided it passes locally for its face value as certified by the "Kongku."

In the example given it is shown that 2.65 premium sycee is 984.55 fine, and also that 50 Chauping taels weight of 2.65 premium sycee is worth 53.72 monetary taels. The latter agrees with the convention that 1000 Chauping taels is equal to 1075.25 monetary taels but this convention presupposes that sycee of this value is 985 fine because it is based essentially on the fundamental theory that 1 monetary tael = 1 Chauping tael of silver 916.2/3 fine.

It must therefore be obvious that either the standard, the premium, the value and the fundamental theory, or one or more of them, is wrong, or that the Mint shops have succeeded in confounding Euclid by producing two things that are equal to the same thing yet differing one from the other. It may be assumed that the example proceeds *a priori* from a fixed standard of 935 to a certified fineness of 984.55 and that sycee of this fineness is then conventionally regarded as being 985 fine for the purpose of effecting payment in monetary taels; or it may be perhaps more properly assumed that as the only fixed and certain factor, locally regarded, is the amount in monetary taels received for sycee purporting to be, and accepted as being, 985 fine, then the example should proceed *a posteriori* from this fixed fineness of 985 to the fixed standard of 935, in which case the premium should be 2.67 since:—

Standard	935
Add 2.67 per cent premium	50
	985

A third assumption is possible, *i.e.,* that the fineness is 985 as accepted, the premium 2.65 as marked and the standard 935.42 since:—

Standard	935.42
Add 5.3 per cent premium	49.58
	985.00

The fact is of course that *there can be no real standard of sycee when the price is fixed and every other factor is not only juggled with in theory but subjected to fluctuating "squeeze" in practice.* Every actual outturn provides its own standard according to the vagaries of the Mint shops and the "Kongku." The only local safeguard is the conventional acceptance of the probity of these time-honoured institutions and the only danger is in placing any reliance on that probity when sycee is exported and assayed.

Sycee exported to India may be remelted into bars or sold outright as sycee. In the former case it is classed as *country silver,* the quotation for which is always lower than that for bar silver. The quotation for sycee on a basis of fine silver is about 8 annas per 100 tolas lower than the quotation for country silver 998 fine, the difference being approximately the Mint charges for melting. Sycee, however, is not ordinarily quoted on the Bombay market, for the very good reason that it is impossible to guarantee its fineness.

During the war large shipments of sycee were made to Bombay for sale to the Government of India. Payment was made in London at the contracted price per ounce standard. 95 per cent. of the estimated value of each consignment was paid on receipt of cabled advice in London that the shipment had arrived in Bombay. The balance was paid on the final report of the result of the Mint's assay.

The Shanghai value weight and fineness of a shipment of sycee is calculated from the average per box of sixty shoes. Thus the contents of a box of new sycee may weigh 2990.82 Chauping taels and the total premium on the sixty shoes may be 164.05. In that case its value would be:—

$2990.82 + 164.05 \times 100 \div 98 = 3219.26$ monetary taels and the fineness of the sycee by calculation would be:—

$164.05 \div 60 = 2.73$ premium per shoe

$2990.82 \div 60 = 49.84$ Chauping taels weight per shoe

$935.374 + 51.23$ (5.477% premium) $= 986.6$ fineness of sycee.

The fineness by calculation based on the "Kongku's" marking is not reliable since it is invariably higher than the fineness by assay. In the remelting of sycee into bars of country silver the Mint publishes the "weight before melting" which shows a loss of about .2 per cent. from the Kongku's marked weight, the "weight after melting" which shows a loss of about .4 per cent., and the "fineness after melting" which in view of the loss in weight is higher than the marked fineness of the shoes. From these figures the "fineness before melting" can be calculated and compared with the reputed fineness of the sycee, allowance being made for the disparity in weight between the Kongku's marking and the Mint's weighing.

Exports of bar silver from Shanghai to India are sometimes made, but these are re-exports of English, Australian or American bars. *There is no real market for bar silver in Shanghai and no bars are made locally.* Bar silver on arrival in Shanghai is usually converted at once into sycee. It may, however, be held in reserve by the importing banks if money is plentiful, and it is from these reserves that re-exports are made when prices in India are favourable. *It is rarely that banks are able to buy bar silver in Shanghai* as the Mint shops are prejudiced against a bank selling bar silver, at a better price than can be realised by having it converted into sycee. A banker who did not respect this prejudice would probably find that when next he sent bar silver to the Mint shops for conversion into sycee he would be kept waiting under one pretext or another four or five days longer for his money than would otherwise have been the case.

From these notes and calculations may be deduced the following definite rules of practice that cover all that is necessary in the working of silver operations in Shanghai:—

1. The *conventional fineness of sycee* in Shanghai is 985 and on this basis 1000 Chauping taels = 1075.25 monetary taels and 930 Chauping taels = 1000 monetary taels.

2. The *actual fineness of sycee* by assay is about 983 but the fineness varies and this can be accepted only as an average.

3. The *actual weight of sycee* averages .2 per cent. less than the marked weight.

4. To find the *value in monetary taels of a bar silver* in Shanghai, convert at the following rates:—

Bar 999 fine = ·9188	monetary	taels	per	ounce	troy
,, 998 ,, = ·9180	,,	,,	,,	,,	,,
,, 997 ,, = ·9172	,,	,,	,,	,,	,,
,, 996 ,, = ·9154	,,	,,	,,	,,	,,

5. To find the *value in monetary taels of a shoe of* sycee in Shanghai:—

Add the weight in Chauping taels to the marked premium per shoe, multiply by 100 and divide by 98.

APPENDIX IV.

REPORTS ON SILVER DOLLARS AND SUBSIDIARY COINS

Customs Reports on Silver Dollars.

The following remarks relating to dollars circulating in China, foreign as well as locally coined, are taken from the Maritime Customs Decennial Reports, covering the period 1902 to 1921.

***Foochow*—(Fukien). (1911).**

A feature of Foochow currency is the chopped, or rather the scooped, the scraped, the cut, the punched, dollars. This maltreatment often obliterates all trace of the original markings, some assuming the shape and appearance of a mushroom suffering from small-pox. It is obvious that such coins must pass by weight, and so in local business circles they do; for example, $1,000 mean a certain weight, and not 1,000 individual dollars. At the foreign banks the ratio adopted is 717 Yangp'ing taels for 1,000 dollars, while the large native banks weigh in at Hsini Tls. 741.6 and weigh out at Hsini Tls. 740.66: the Haikwan Bank takes the equivalence to be Hsini Tls. 742.742, the Yangp'ing being to the Hsini scale as 717 to 741.6. Dollars are put up in bags of $1,000 each, and in one of these bags there may be found as many as 14 varieties Mexican, Hongkong, Straits Settlements, and Indo-China dollars, Philippine pesos, Japanese yen, etc. In 1902 there was but one Mint for the province, the Foochow city Mint, which supplied sufficient subsidiary currency for provincial use and even furnished a surplus for export. The chopping of the dollar, a system in vogue in Foochow of imprinting a firm's or money-shop's name or mark on the coin by means of a sharp die, cannot be too strongly condemned. Not only does it deface the coin, but, by removing a portion of the silver, compels the banks to accept it by weight instead of at its face value. The tael weight used for this purpose is the Yangp'ing (洋平), of which 71.7 equal 100 chopped dollars. The native banks, on the other hand, accept these dollars at the rate of Hsin-i-p'ing Tls. 74.16 per hundred. It is certainly very annoying to be unable to withdraw the same number of dollars from the bank which you have paid in and almost as irritating to tender a chopped dollar to the Chinese Post Office and to be refused a dollar's worth of stamps. But, after all, it is only our individual feelings which are injured, not trade, which on its t'ai-fu basis pursues "the even tenor of its way" quite regardless of the chopping of the dollar.

***Amoy*—(Fukien). (1921).**

The Spanish dollar, a fictitious currency which held the paramount position in local business for a number of years, finally disappeared in 1921, being superseded by the Chinese silver dollar. Bank-notes issued by the Bank of Taiwan were entirely

driven out of the Amoy market as a consequence of the boycott against Japanese goods in June 1919, and only the bank-notes issued by the Bank of China and the Fukien Bank are circulating in Amoy at present. Chopped dollars (which were usually discounted $3 or $4 per $1,000 against clean dollars) have gradually disappeared from the Amoy market, as people are unwilling to accept them for ordinary transactions, and they now pass only as bullion for melting purposes. Silver dollars of foreign countries have gradually been forced out of circulation by the more popular Yuan Shih-kai dollar. The following table shows the approximate proportion of the various silver dollars in circulation in Amoy:—

DOLLAR.	Weight.	Fineness.	Proportion.	
			1916. Per cent.	1921. Per cent.
Yuan Shih-kai	26.8835	891.47	10	70
Hongkong	26.9560	900.00	30	15
Japanese	26.9563	900.00	50	15
New Mexican	27.0300	unknown	10	—

Pakhoi—(Kwangtung). (1921).

Most local prices are quoted in subsidiary silver coin, the value of which at present may range from $1.10 to $1.18 vis-a-vis the large silver dollar. This latter, as remarked in the last Decennial Report, is requisite for dealings with the Maritime Customs or the Chinese Post Office, and almost any silver dollar which makes its appearance in the port seems to pass current. One finds Yuan Shih-kai dollars, British trade dollars, Japanese yen, and Tonkin piastres—many of which, however, are chopped or defaced in some way and exchange (*e.g.*, in Hongkong) only at a discount in normal times. Chopped dollars sent to Hongkong towards the end of 1921, however, were exchanging at quite an appreciable premium. The Mexican dollar is seen at times, but is not now in use locally to any great extent.

Canton—(Kwangtung). (1921).

In 1919 there was an unprecedented rise, and the Canton Mint became active with this influx. Nearly 6 million silver dollars were placed on the market in 1915 and 1916, but they are now seldom seen. The export of Canton Mint silver coin was prohibited in 1917 and 1918, and shortly after this embargo was lifted their import into northern ports was forbidden by the Peking Government, owing, it is alleged, to their inferior quality.

Mengtze—(Yunnan). (1911).

The year 1902 found both sycee and silver dollars used concurrently locally, while dollars were still accepted with difficulty inland. However, French dollars (piastres de commerce) were put in circulation by the French in erecting buildings for the railway staff, the French hospital, the French post office, and particularly in paying the railway staff and the army of labourers employed for construction work on the railway track. From 1902 to 1908 inclusive not less than Hk. Tls. 7,955,485 of these French dollars were imported, and against this only Hk. Tls. 69,422 were exported, the explanation given for this discrepancy between imports and exports being that the dollars were melted into sycee, with a profit of 1½ per cent. From 1909, when trains reached Mengtze, up to the end of 1911 the importation of dollars has been increasing, but mostly from Hongkong, viz., from Tonkin Hk. Tls. 814,952, and from Hongkong Hk. Tls. 5,406,197; exports to Tonkin amounted to Hk. Tls. 123,333. This large increase in the importation of dollars from Hongkong is accounted for by a corresponding increase in the output and export of tin, while the decrease in Tonkin dollars was due to the railway nearing completion. Dollars of all kinds, including Hongkong and Mexican dollars, but principally dollars from the Kwangtung and Hupeh provincial Mints, and also Hupeh subsidiary silver coins and Fukien copper cents, found their way from Hongkong, and sycee was gradually absorbed by the provincial Mint erected at Yunnanfu in 1907, and which began in 1908 to turn out dollars, subsidiary silver coins, and copper cents. The only good silver coins were driven out of circulation; these were dollars and half-dollars bearing, as the gold issue, the effigy of T'ang Chi-yao and were of 862 fineness, whereas the Yunnan dragon dollar contained only 60.2 per cent. silver and the dragon half-dollar probably less. At the end of the decade the silver in circulation was composed of the dragon dollar, dragon half-dollar, 20-cents and 10-cents pieces, and also a few Hupeh and Szechwan dollars and subsidiary coins, which were mostly brought back by the troops when they returned from Szechwan. Of such poor quality is the Yunnan dollar that it requires $232.66 of them to produce Hk. Tls. 100 of pure silver.

The only good point regarding Yunnan currency, which is worthy of note, is the normal exchange in the province of ten 10-cents or five 20-cents pieces for 1 dollar. This has never changed and is in all probability due to the fact that the circulation of subsidiary coins of other provinces is restricted.

Szemao—(Yunnan). (1921).

The complete disappearance of all silver dollars, including Yunnan and other Chinese dollars, Tonkin piastres, and Mexican and Hongkong dollars, and the great depreciation of copper cash are the two most noteworthy features under this heading. During the past three years or so the financial standing of this province was greatly affected by adverse trade circumstances, and Yunnan, which in former years was always a creditor in Hongkong and coast ports, became a debtor. The Yunnan dollar, which in 1918 was at a small premium in Hongkong, suddenly dropped in 1919, during which year it stood as low as $1.40 to Hongkong dollar. This great depreciation of the Yunnan dollar, which has since only recovered about 10 per cent., is responsible for the disappearance of silver dollars, whose intrinsic value was realised by exporting these coins to other provinces and to Tonkin. Silver, however, has never been scarce in Szemao, for this market has always been well supplied with half-dollar silver coins from the Yunnanfu Mint. In fact, the present currency consists entirely of these coins and of the Futien Bank notes of $100, $50, $10, $5, and $1 denominations.

Lungchow—(Yunnan). (1911).

Of dollars, the French Indo-China piastre de commerce is the favourite and the one almost exclusively used. Chinese dollars are not accepted. Mexican dollars are occasionally met with, but are not in favour. The dollar exchanges, according to the local market rate, from $1.03 to $1.15 in subsidiary coin. Indo-China paper money is largely employed for settlement of trade transactions with Tonkin, there being no other means of remitting.

Nanning—(Kwangsi). (1911).

The unchopped clean Indo-China trade dollar, or French piastre, has been within the last three years the only silver dollar in circulation in this part of the province. The French piastre is now largely used in the cattle, ground-nut, and sugar trades: inland selling agents refuse any other kind of payment. Formerly the French piastre ruled also in the paper trade; but of late the local buying firms have enforced trade terms in local taels. The relationship between the French piastre and the current subsidiary coin (and, consequently, also the copper cash) showed in former years extraordinary fluctuations; it has, however, become more stable since the establishment of regular quick motor-boat communication with Wuchow, which has rendered it more difficult for individual merchants to make corners in any kind of cash.

Hankow—(Hupeh). (1911).

Here sycee practically passed only in 50 taels shoes, as in smaller bits the exchange value of the silver depreciated with its size. Dollars and subsidiary coins were used for sums under Tls. 50. Any variety of dollar was current at a price, the Mexican dollar being the standard. There was no local dollar until, in 1903, the Hupeh government dollar made its first appearance, at a discount compared with others.

Wuhu—(Anhwei). (1911).

Coins of 1789 bear the names of both CAROLUS III and CAROLUS IV; whilst those of 1790 bear inscriptions either CAROLUS IIII or CAROLUS IV.

Sycee has disappeared from the market, and for all practical purposes the dollar has become the local unit of silver. The Wuhu tael, though it exists only in name, is still the standard by which dollar rates are fixed, though the natives no longer speak of the price of cash in relation to the tael, quoting the exchange of copper cents to the dollar. The most acceptable dollars are the Hsin-pi or Yuan Shih-kai dollars, the Ta Ch'ing, Hupeh, and Anhwei dollars. Mexican and Carolus dollars are out of circulation, but the latter are offered as a relic of the past at a discount of 2 per cent. The Carolus dollar was once the only tender insisted upon in certain produce markets, and it was then worth as much as 50 per cent. over its intrinsic value. Subsidiary silver coins of 50, 20, and 10 cents are also current, and, as exchange for 1 cent pieces, some shops issue small slips of bamboo with nominal values inscribed. The dollar rates of exchange fluctuate largely, following Wuhu tael and Shanghai dollar rates, on which they depend.

Lungchingtsun—(Manchuria). (1921).

An attempt was made to introduce silver dollars into circulation, but without success: a certain number find their way into the markets, but they have been little in demand, and the complete absence of small money makes their use inconvenient.

Chungking—(Szechuen). (1921).

There exist in circulation in the province two different types of silver dollars minted at Chengtu, a pre-Revolution and Republican coin, both taken at the fixed rate of Szechwan Tls. 0.71 in monetary transactions. The pre-Revolution or dragon dollar has a face value of K'uping tael 0.72, while the Republican dollar, which was put into circulation shortly after the Revolution, bears no inscription of denomination. Although the new coin has a weight and diameter both smaller than the old coin, it is accepted at par with the dragon dollar. The respective fineness of the two Szechwan coins was ascertained in 1916 through a test made by the Shanghai Assay Office as follows:—

DENOMINATION.	Weight in Ts'ao-p'ing taels.			Number Equivalent to Hk. Tls. 100 in sycee.	
	Before Melting.	After Melting.	Touch or Fineness.	Dollars.	Half-Dollars.
Kuang Hsu dollars	0.730	0.630	875	161.84	—
Hsuan T'ung dollars	0.730	0.636	871	162.55	—
Chun-cheng-fu or Republican dollars	0.702	0.612	872	168.93	—
Kuang Hsu half-dollars	0.362	0.303	837	(170.60)	341.20
Hsuan T'ung half-dollars ..	0.360	0.287	797	(180.11)	360.22
Chun-cheng-fu or Republican half-dollars	0.349	0.291	833	(177.88)	355.76

Silver coins of other provinces, such as Hupeh, Kiangsu, Yunnan, and the Yuan Shih-kai dollars, are also in circulation but in limited quantities. They are accepted at the same fixed rate and without any discrimination. Merchants prefer to accept these dollars for exportation to down-river ports when the remittance rate is unfavourable, as the Szechwan dollars are not negotiable lower than Ichang. Subsidiary coins of 10 cents and 20 cents denominations have also been minted, but are not used to any extent.

Tientsin—(Chihli). (1921).

The Tientsin Mint was destroyed and its contents looted in 1912 during the revolutionary riots, but was soon rebuilt. The present standard Yuan Shih-kai dollar was first minted in 1914 by this Mint, under the National Currency Regulations promulgated in that year, which rule that the national coin shall be called the yuan, and the yuan shall contain 6 mace 4 candareens, and 8 *li* (K'uping) or 23.97795048 grammes of pure silver, and that its weight and fineness shall be gross weight 72 candareens, with 89 per cent. silver and 11 per cent. copper. This dollar still keeps up to specification, though it is not yet the national coin with respect to duty payments and mercantile dealings—the tael still holding its place. Subsidiary coins of 10, 20 and 50 cents denominations are in two grades, those bearing the image of Yuan Shih-kai and known as the Republican are current at par, while the dragon coins (mostly from the Manchurian provinces) are usually at about 15 per cent. discount.

The other dollars circulating at par are the dragon dollar (four varieties), Hongkong dollar, and Mexican dollar, though the last mentioned is not popular in Chihli.

Nanking—(Kiangsu). (1921).

Many varieties of silver dollars are in circulation. The standard imperial, or dragon dollar, introduced by the Edict of the 24th May 1910, has, since the promulgation of the National Coinage Law in March 1914, been succeeded by the national or Yuan Shin-k'ai dollar, authorised to be coined by the Nanking Mint. The weight and fineness of the new standard dollar turned out by the local Mint from the 2nd February 1915 have been fixed with the following notations: weight, 0.72 tael K'up'ing scale; fineness, 890; and the maximum variation in weight and fineness allowed is $\frac{3}{1000}$

The net amount of pure silver in each dollar being $0.72 \times 890 = 64.08$ candareens, and the ratio between K'uping taels and Shanghai taels being K'up'ing Tls. 100 = Shanghai taels 109.60, the Mint par of exchange between the national dollar and the Shanghai tael is therefore as follows:—

$$\$100 = \frac{109.60 \times 64.08}{100} = 70.23 \text{ Shanghai taels.}$$

and as the Mint charges are Shanghai Tls. 1.454 per $100, the cost of minting is, exclusive of Mint expenses, Shanghai Tls. 70.231×1.454 (Shanghai Tls. 71.685). From 1912 to 1921 the output of the Nanking Mint was 281,646,132 silver dollars, 263,000 silver half-dollars, 2,344,100 silver 20-cent pieces, 851,200 silver 10-cent pieces, and 2,152,333,634 copper cents.

Chinkiang—(Kiangsu). (1921).

The currency of this port consists of Mexican and Chinese dollars, 20-cent and 10-cent silver coins, and 20-cash and 10-cash copper coins. At one time Japanese and Spanish dollars were in circulation, but they have totally disappeared since 1912. The Chinese dollars, having three varieties of equal value—the dragon, the Peiyang, and those issued by the Nanking Mint,—are generally preferred to the Mexican, because in the case of the latter it requires much skill to recognise forgery.

Customs Reports on Subsidiary Coins.

The following remarks, relating to small coin dollars in circulation in China, are taken from the Chinese Maritime Customs Decennial Reports, covering the period 1902 to 1921.

Mukden—(Manchuria). (1921).

Of silver coins the dollar (大洋) has circulated but little in Manchuria owing to the smallness of the amount minted, a good part of which was further driven out of circulation by the smaller silver coins. The circulation of silver subsidiary coins was so universal at one time in Fengtien province that it did not seem unlikely that the provincial currency might be unified on that basis. Unfortunately, financial embarrassment of the provincial government, coupled with the world-wide appreciation in the price of silver consequent on the European War, restricted the minting of silver coins, with the result that there was a large increase in the issue of notes, nominally against silver subsidiary coin, known generally as feng-p'iao (奉票). Towards the end of 1913 the conversion of these feng-p'iao into specie became impossible owing to over-issue of notes without adequate specie reserve, resulting in a great depreciation in the value of the notes as compared with that of actual cash, and in February 1914 the export of silver and copper coins was prohibited with a view to checking further depreciation of this paper currency.

In its issue of September 25, 1925, (No. 240) the *Chinese Economic Bulletin* writes as follows about Small coin dollars circulating in Fengtien Province:

Currency in Fengtien Province.

To understand the currency in Fengtien province, the expressions "small money," or *hsiao yang* (小 洋), and "big money," or *ta yang* (大 洋), the popular money units in Fengtien as well as in other provinces, must first be made clear. By small money, or *hsiao yang,* in general is meant fractional silver coins, such as 10 cents or 20 cents pieces, the exchange rate of which varies according to the supply of copper coins, among other factors. By big money, or *ta yang,* in general is meant silver dollars. Small money, or fractional silver coins, must not be confused with subsidiary silver coins, issued in the denominations of 10 cents, 20 cents, and 50 cents, of which 100 cents are originally exchangeable for one dollar.

A 10 cents fractional silver coin of the Fengtien currency was formerly exchangeable for 10 coppers. Later, silver notes were issued in Mukden in two units; the *hsiao yang,* or fractional silver notes, Fengtien currency (奉 大 洋 票), and the *ta yang* notes, Fengtien currency (奉 小 洋 票). The ratio of the *hsiao yang* notes is 2 : 1. *Ta yang* of the Fengtien currency is, therefore, quite different from *ta yang,* or "big money" of the national currency. The official exchange rate in Mukden is fixed at a dollar of Fengtien *hsiao yang* currency for 100 coppers. In 1923, the exchange rate of a 10 cent Fengtien *hsiao yang* note rose to 14 coppers, or of one dollar in Fengtien *hsiao yang* notes to 140 coppers. In 1924, the former rate of 10 coppers to 10 silver cents, Fengtien currency, was restored. Copper, however, was then legal tender only for 10 cents, above which amount silver or silver notes must be used. But the accumulation of copper in retailers' shops has caused the actual rate of exchange to drop to 12 coppers for 10 silver cents. A dollar of the national currency is at present exchangeable for $2.20, Fengtien small money, or for over 220 coppers.

Samshui—(Kwangtung). (1911).

20 cents pieces, or silver coins marked "1 mace and 44 candareens," are the coins mostly used by merchants in larger business transactions, the practice being not to accept them at face value but according to weight.

Previous to 1912 the currency used by merchants in large business tran·actions was the 10 cents or 20 cents piece. These were accepted according to weight and not at face value. Customs duties theoretically were received in pure silver. These subsidiary coins, if tendered in quantities above $1, were discounted at the market rate, varying from 5 to 8 per cent. discount. In April 1912 the Kwangtung Military Governor endeavoured to relieve the stringency of the local money market and put into circulation new bank-notes on an extensive scale without having in stock a safe reserve of sycee. The result was that the public did not freely support the scheme.

Kongmoon—(Kwangtung). (1921).

During the decade the silver dollar and, to a large extent, cash have completely disappeared from the district, and, to all intents and purposes, the only currency in use consists of copper cents, provincial and Hongkong 20 cents pieces, and notes issued by foreign banks in Hongkong. Business transactions are, however, in many cases still made in taels. The Hongkong 10 cents piece, which was a popular coin before the enactment by the British Government in 1914 of the ordinance prohibiting the use of

Chinese subsidiary coins in the Colony, has since been conspicuous by its absence. The fineness of silver in the provincial 20 cents piece, as at present minted in Canton, is less than 50 per cent., compared with 78 per cent. in the old coin and 80 per cent. in the coinage issued by the Hongkong Government.

Canton—(Kwangtung). (1921).

Table showing minting of coin is appended:—

	Dollars.	20-Cent Pieces.	10-Cent Pieces.	5-Cent Pieces (Nickel).	Copper Cents
	Million.	Million.	Million.	Million.	Million.
1912	..	87	..	..	19
1913	..	110	1½	..	..
1914	..	42	½	..	14¾
1915	2¾	22	¾	..	6
1916	3	..	1/7	..	18
1917	..	..	..	..	43
1918	..	..	..	..	..
1919	..	195	..	1/6	..
1920	..	197	..	¾	..
1921	..	402¼	..	2/3	..

Wuchow—(Kwangsi). (1921).

During the decade 10 cents pieces as well as copper cash have almost disappeared and are now found in the market only to a very small extent. The currency during the last 10 years has been Cantonese 20 cents pieces, copper cents, and Kwangsi notes.

Szemao—(Yunnan). (1921).

Subsidiary silver coins of 20 and 10 cents are rather rare in Szemao, but five of the former and 10 of the latter have always exchanged for a large dollar or its present-day equivalent of two 50 cents coins. This is due to the limited issue of these coins by the Yunnanfu Mint and to the prohibition, strictly enforced, against the importation of similar coins from other provinces. The old silver currencies, or the various standards of bullion sycee, are no longer in use, and all business transactions are now made on the dollar basis.

Foochow—(Fukien).

The following remarks are contained in the Chinese Economic Bulletin (April, 1925).

Foochow Fractional Currency.—Five mints at Foochow, Yenping (延 平), Shahsien (沙 縣), Yuki (尤 溪) and Mamoi (馬 尾) are minting 20 cents subsidiary coins for Fukien province. In addition to these, spurious coins are put out by counterfeiters. The result has been a drop in the market rate to 66 cash per 10 cents piece. Coppers have also depreciated to 50 per cent. below par owing to smuggling of debased coppers from other provinces. A copper reputed to be equivalent to 10 cash now exchanges for only five in Foochow.

Nanking—(Kiangsu).

The same source has supplied the following notes:

There are also new and old subsidiary silver coins. Of the former the 10 cents, the 20 cents, and the half dollar pieces are engraved with the portrait of Yuan Shih-kai and were formerly accepted at their face value. But at present, with the exception of the half dollar, they have depreciated considerably. The old subsidiary silver coins are of two kinds, the 10 cents and 20 cents. Those commonly accepted are those issued by the Nanyang, Kwangtung and Hupeh Mints before the Republic. Those coined in Hunan, Anhwei, Chekiang, Fukien, Kirin, and Hongkong, are accepted at a discount of six or seven cents for each 10 dimes. There is no discrimination between the copper coins of the various provinces.

Chinkiang—(Kiangsu). (1921).

Throughout the last decade the subsidiary silver coins have been circulated at 12 per cent. discount. Previous to the Revolution only those issued by Kiangsu and Hupeh were freely accepted, but since 1912 the Kwangtung 20 cents pieces have been made popular in the market, while those from other sources, chiefly from the Three Eastern Provinces, Chekiang, and Fukien, are still reckoned as inferior coins and can only pass in circulation at a discount of 5 to 10 cash for every 10 cents; to this class also belongs the new issue 1921 by the Nanking Mint.

Counterfeiting of Subsidiary Silver Coins.

The already much abused small coin dollars became an object of much interest to professional forgers, whose activities were rather prominent in 1925. The following cutting is taken from the *North China Daily News* (Spring of 1925) and refers to subsidiary coins produced by provincial Mints, which are under military "protection."

The present outcry against the debasement of small coins in circulation in Shanghai may be taken as an indication that the nuisance has about reached its limit. The present stage is the logical outcome of a process which has been going on slowly for some few years, resulting in the domination of the local currency by small coins of the Kwangtung Mint, practically to the exclusion of all others. At first, the depreciation was slight, but it was profitable and increasingly lucrative production led to further debasement, the gross weight being maintained but with a gradually diminishing amount of silver. Such depreciation being common to China, where there is no legal tender, the new issues were tolerated as they appeared.

The phenomenon was not a new one, for the Chinese have always been prone to compromise in this respect, even their old time "cash" having a normal depreciation of 10 per cent. In these circumstances, there came into play the Gresham Law, which is briefly that where two coins, one of which is inferior, are accepted without distinction, the inferior coin will gradually drive out the good one; and this law has effectually operated in Shanghai, practically the whole of the good coins having been exported.

We have now apparently reached the point of reaction. Debasement has been carried to its limit, public patience and toleration are exhausted, and tradesmen and others are refusing to accept the inferior coins. This is the true and the only remedy, and when the refusal to accept becomes general, importation of the coins must cease, for they will have lost their value.

Thus, to a very large extent, the public has the remedy in its own hands, but there is need for a strong initiative by people in authority, the Chambers of Commerce, the banks etc. In one sense, the small coinage problem has been nobody's problem. It has been allowed to take care of itself for the simple reason that the interests involved were diffuse and scattered, outside the scope of big organizations and affecting only workpeople and others whose daily financial transactions are minute. Those are the people who are the greatest sufferers, the loss of a few cents in purchasing power being a matter of considerable importance where wages are counted in cents, a factor which has been the cause of more than one recent strike.

Under date of March 6, 1925, the *Manchuria Daily News*, published in Dairen, contained the following paragraph on debased 20-cents silver coins, which it says, were produced in Canton.

20 Sen Silver Coins Minted at Canton.

The local residents are warned against new 20 sen silver coins minted at Canton, in the 11th and 12th years of the Chinese Republic (1922 and 1923). The new coins contain much less silver, its percentage proving barely 27–31 per cent. against 60 per cent. of copper according to an assaying test made at the Chinese Guild, Shokoshi. The local exchange-brokers will refuse to accept them. Something like S.Yen 30,000 in such coins is supposed to have been dumped on Dairen, with a tendency for further influx.

Shortly after the publication of the news from Dairen came the report (as published in the Shanghai *Evening News* of March 18, 1925) that the headquarters of the counterfeiters was situated at Dairen.

EXISTENCE OF NEW AND POWERFUL RING OF COUNTERFEITERS IN DALNY REVEALED

While information recently gathered by foreign and Chinese authorities is being closely kept within official archives, it became known today that a powerful ring of foreign and Chinese counterfeiters and smugglers is directly responsible for the flooding of Shanghai with inferior subsidiary coins through the manufacture and circulation of which they are reaping a huge profit.

The headquarters of this organization are known to be in Dalny, and it is from the Manchurian city that this stream of inferior and light-weight money has been poured into Shanghai. Evidence of these new counterfeiting activities came to light a few weeks ago when a limited number of base 20 cents coins were put into circulation locally.

Find Quick Market.

These cheap disks were offered exchange shop keepers in the city at a discount of 40 per cent, the dealers being given, in some cases, as many as 10 such coins for one dollar. Confronted with such get-rich-quick possibilities, many exchange men seized the opportunity and commenced sliding the counterfeits across the counter to customers. Foreigners mainly are the victims, the natives being too suspicious to accept the bright coins tendered.

Suspicion was born when many such shopkeepers refused to exchange the new coins at the regular rates. This led to inquiries by the local authorities and the source of the counterfeits was traced to the Northern port.

Traffic is Heavy.

While no exact figure can be given, it has been estimated that several hundred thousand of the new 20 cents pieces have been smuggled into the various districts of Shanghai. This confirmed the belief that the counterfeiting ring is involved in a far-reaching plan which will eventually involve the whole of the country.

A number of new Yuan Shih-kai dollars, accredited to the same source, suddenly popped up here but the quantity of these circulated has been so small that considerable difficulty is being experienced in reaching dealers who originally handled the coins.

It is strongly suspected by the local authorities that the same counterfeiting-smuggling gang in Dalny have commenced with the 20 cents pieces with a view to issuing later the inferior dollar coins which they now are manufacturing.

The same journal, under date of August 15, 1925, revaled further activities of forgers of silver subsidiary coins. Such and similar reports are by no means rare, and the few instances cited are merely intended to show in a general way how common the practice has become in this country.

Revelations concerning the inner workings of many of Shanghai's thousands of little exchange shops, are expected to follow the arrest late yesterday afternoon of a band of counterfeiters who virtually have flooded Shanghai with spurious twenty cents coins. The roundup of the crooks was made in Chapei by detectives of the French Police.

A complete counterfeiter's plant which included four machines, moulds, stamping equipment, metal in various stages, as well as hundreds of the base 20 cents pieces manufactured on the premises, were seized in the raid.

The coins made in the Chapei counterfeiters' headquarters were of the eighth and tenth years of the Republic, and had been so manufactured that they did not look like new coins. The counterfeits were pronounced perfect by one of the detectives, who admitted that had they been tendered him in the ordinary way he would have accepted them without question.

While no statement has been issued by the French Police, it has been divulged that the fake 20 cents pieces have been widely-circulated in Shanghai and have made their way into the market through countless unscrupulous exchange shops which have reaped a rich profit in the nefarious trade.

Many more arrests are expected to follow in the wake of last evening's raid which, it is believed, will lead to startling disclosures in the very near future.

Mr. Holdo Stromwall, a merchant residing in Shanghai, has published the following interesting study on small coins in the *North China Daily News* of December 18, 1925:—

Our 20-cents Coins.

Ever since subsidiary silver-coins were introduced into China, they have proved to be a very attractive object of profit-making, the 20-cents coins in particular. We, the public, being financially concerned in the matter, have a decided interest in establishing our position with regard to same. I will try to make this our position clear.

We accepted at one time the Nanking Mint's imperial 20-cents coins as legal tender, *i.e.*, legal in practice, because their intrinsic value did practically correspond to the exchange value. It is in this particular instance of no importance whether the intrinsic value of the 20-cents coins is one fifth or one tenth of a dollar. In other words, as long as we actually receive what we know we are entitled to, there is no room for dissatisfaction, but if we receive a 20-cents coin which we attach a value of 15-cents, but which is worth only 10-cents we naturally object.

On the first appearance of the 7th year 20-cents coins of the Canton Mint we accepted them though under protest, not because of their value being less than those of the Nanking Mint above referred to, but because they did not give in exchange what they were supposed to give. Immediately the exchange value of the new coins was adjusted to their intrinsic value, all justified cause for dissatisfaction had passed, and the Mint was ready for another attack on the public wealth. The following table showing the fineness of some 20-cents coins, will tell the story of the policy pursued by the Canton Mint since it captured the Shanghai market. The various issues have been mentioned in chronological order as they appeared on the market. The imperial coin is from the Nanking Mint, the rest from the Canton Mint.

	Fineness
Imperial	813.9
7th year of Rep.	748.7
8th year of Rep.	702.5
9th year (1920)	673.0
10th year	698.8
11th year	517.7
14th year (1925) minted but dated 9th year	526.8

The purchasing power of the 20-cents coins as expressed through the exchange value is presently adjusted to the intrinsic value of the regular 9th year's coin, *i.e.*, to 20-cents coins of a fineness of round 670 or more. This adjustment of values has, however, not been attained without difficulties and "financial sacrifices," as will be seen from the fineness of the 10th year coin. Had the Mint continued to pursue the policy of reducing the silver-content gradually within reasonable limits, they would, with only a tame objection, in course of time have been able to enforce 20-cents coins of a fineness of about 520 as legal tender in practice, for the same reason as the "legal tender" has presently a fineness of round 670 or more. The Mint is, however, apparently determined to get a firm footing for their new 20-cents coins within the shortest possible time, having made at least two attempts during this year. Since the Mint is now openly counterfeiting its own coins the prospects of success are very bright. Should they actually succeed, the exchange, which now is the theoretically and practically 130 silver-cents 673 fine, will gradually drop until it again has stablized and at about 170 silver-cents about 520 fine. The rates mentioned are based on the regular silver-dollar with a fineness of 889. The transition period will be characterized by suffering and loud protests and complaints about increased cost of living among wage-earners and possible strikes. We have already experienced this for years, but a reduction of the silver-content of 25 per cent. in one year or two, as it may prove to be, is more serious than a reduction of 17 per cent. spread over 7 years. Should the Mint choose to counterfeit the

7th, 8th and 10th year's issues as they have done with the 9th year coin, values will soon have to adjust themselves to coins of a fineness of about 520. The public's resistance will weaken with every successful or partly successful attempt made by the Mint. As soon as these latter coins represent fully 50 per cent. of all 20-cents coins in circulation there is nothing but a full value coin that will prevent all values to adjust themselves to the intrinsic value of the coins 520 fine.

For reasons which everybody with a knowledge of political economy will understand, the interests of the Canton Mint are diametrically opposite to those of their clients, *i.e.,* the public. The wider the difference between the exchange value and the intrinsic value in favour of the former, the bigger the profit for those who control the output of the Mint, and the more the sufferings of the public, since these profits are illegally drawn from the public. As soon as all values have adjusted themselves to the intrinsic value of the coin which, through quantity, the majority must recognise as "legal tender," the profits of the mint will practically have been reduced to nil, and the sufferings of the public will also practically have come to an end. An equilibrium has been established and so the scale of justice is once more tampered with until justice is again administered by the economical laws and equilibrium reached.

APPENDIX V.

PRACTICAL SUGGESTIONS FROM FOREIGN AND CHINESE BANKERS REGARDING THE INTRODUCTION OF A UNIFORM DOLLAR

The following interesting remarks on the above subject and, in conjunction therewith, on the establishment of the Shanghai Mint have been taken from the *China Year Book* (1923).

The following extracts from an address by Mr. G. H. Stitt, Manager of the Hongkong & Shanghai Banking Corporation at Shanghai, at the Annual Conference of British Chambers of Commerce in Shanghai in November 1920 will convey a clear idea of the present situation:

> The following memorandum, drawn up by the Shanghai Foreign Exchange Bankers' Association, was also forwarded to the Ministry of Finance, Peking, in the early part of this year, a copy being sent to H. M. Minister:—
>
> "The Foreign Exchange Banks have heard that a resolution was passed at the Conference of the British Chambers of Commerce held in Shanghai last November to the following effect:—
>
> "'That the Chinese Government be strongly urged to bring an end to the use of sycee: to establish a uniform currency of dollars, subsidiary silver and copper coinage throughout the country: to open a mint in Shanghai for the free coinage of dollars and to place the mints under efficient control, so that uniformity of standard may be preserved.'"
>
> "The Foreign Exchange Banks have also been informed that H. M. Minister has recommended this resolution to the Chinese Government and it is reported in the public press that the Government is according favourable consideration to it."
>
> "In October, 1917, the Foreign Exchange Banks' representatives had the privilege of exchanging views on this subject with Messrs. Wang and Yee, of the Ministry of Finance, and on that occasion they put their views on record in the following words:—
>
> "The Banks recognize the great advantage that would ensue to trade generally by the entire abolition of the tael and the substitution therefor of a uniform Chinese silver dollar which would be currency throughout China, and although this would deprive the Banks of a certain profit which they at present secure from interport exchange, they are so convinced that the change would be of such ultimate benefit to trade and to themselves that the Government may count on their wholehearted support to the measures necessary to bring this about. In the adoption of a uniform Chinese dollar it is absolutely essential that care be taken

that whatever weight and fineness is decided upon, that weight and fineness must be as invariable and as reliable as the weight and fineness of a British sovereign, or of the current gold coins of other countries. The dollars coined by the Chinese Mints have not been of uniform fineness and composition, and to establish general confidence in the new Chinese dollar expert foreign supervision in the Mints would be necessary, for a time at least."

"The exchange of sycee and of Mexican dollars for the new dollar should present no difficulties, but it would be necessary that a Mint should be established in Shanghai, which is the principal port of entry of silver from abroad and the source from which most other treaty ports derive their supplies of currency."

"The Foreign Exchange Banks have seen no reason to change the views as expressed above and they wish therefore to record their support to the resolution of the British Chambers of Commerce.

Practical Suggestions.

"The following suggestions may be of use to the Chinese Government if they decide to give effect to the resolution:—

(1) The Mint should be established within easy distance of the business centre of the International Settlement of Shanghai, and should be under the direct control of the Central Government.

(2) The control should be vested in the hands of a Chinese Director-General, with a Foreign Associate Director-General.

To ensure uniformity of coinage and proper workmanship, also the efficient handling of silver tendered to the Mint, it would be necessary to employ two foreign Assayers, three Inspectors and one Accountant.

Note:—When the Japanese Government first began minting coins which went into circulation in the East in competition with the coins of foreign countries, they employed ten foreign experts. There is, however, so much efficient Chinese labour available which is skilled in the handling of metals, that we consider a minimum of foreign supervision would be sufficient.

(3) The Mint should be capable of manufacturing one million coins daily. One million dollars or half dollars daily.

(4) When it is in full working order, the coinage of dollars must be discontinued by the other Mints in China, unless these Mints are controlled by the Central Government and placed under expert foreign supervision, similar to that of the Shanghai Mint.

(5) A new die should be made so that the new dollars will be readily distinguishable from those already in circulation.

(6) Silver should be tendered direct by the Banks and the public to the Mint, which, in order to simplify the procedure, can stipulate that no silver under 0.890 fine will be received for coinage.

Dollars should be delivered by the Mint to the Banks and the public in the same rotation as the silver has been received.

(7) With regard to the weight and fineness of the new dollar, in view of the considerable quantities of Provincial Mint dollars already in circulation, it would be desirable that the new coin should approximate as closely to them as possible, in order that no discrimination would be made by the public against one or other of the coins.

From a series of tests made at the Indian Government Mint at Bombay, it has been ascertained that the Nanking Mint dollars, although very uneven, average 891.15 fine and weigh 414.589 grains.

These dollars are considered to be equal to those coined by the Tientsin and Wuchang Mints. The new coin might, therefore, be fixed at 416 grains weight, 890 fine, and it should be received at par with the existing recognized dollars by the Government and the public. The Mint should, however, be prepared to recoin the existing dollars into the new dollar free coins.

(8) As it is proposed to consider the question of subsidiary coinage at this time, the Foreign Exchange Banks are of opinion that it would be a public convenience if a half dollar were coined, the weight and fineness of which should correspond with the dollar, viz.: 208 grains weight and 890 fine.

(9) The rate of conversion of the existing stocks of sycee to dollars can be fixed by arrangement with the Chinese Government and the Foreign Banks, on the basis of the actual amount of pure silver contained in the sycee. It should be coined free of charge as it is not desirable to compel the public to bear the expenses of the change.

(10) The rate of seigniorage might be agreed on at 2 per cent., which is what the Indian Government charged when the Mints in India were open to the public for the coinage of rupees—Presumably that was considered a fair charge to the public and to the Government.

(11) It is recognized that the expense of establishing a Mint may be inconvenient to the Chinese Government at present. The Foreign Banks, therefore, would be willing to give what temporary financial assistance might be necessary for the purchase of land and machinery and the erection of suitable buildings."

The Chinese Government has accepted the advice so far as the establishing of a Mint in Shanghai is concerned, but appears unwilling to place such Mint under expert foreign control.

As pointed out in the above memorandum, it is a cardinal essential to the success of the proposal that the weight and fineness of the new coins be absolutely reliable and invariable. Without this essential it would be quite impossible for Foreign Banks to accept the new dollar currency in substitution for sycee, the reliability of which has stood the test of time, or for the foreign trade of the country to be conducted in it. There can be no doubt, however, that the introduction of a thoroughly reliable coin, circulating freely throughout the whole country, would prove an immense stimulus to trade, a large increase in the volume of which could confidently be looked for as a result of such reform. The country is ripe for its introduction, for public confidence in paper issues, unsupported by adequate metallic reserves as they have been, has of late years received a rude shock, and dollars minted at existing mints, variable, as I will show them to be, have been going freely into the interior, while considerable quantities of silver must also have been hoarded there.

Results of Recent Assays.

In 1908 two parcels of silver dollars, minted at a Chinese Mint which I will refer to as A, were forwarded to the Indian Government Mint in Calcutta for assay. The result was:—

(1)	A dollar weighing	415.26	grains	899.5	fine
(2)	,,	414.90	,,	897.8	,,
	Average	415.08	,,	898.65	,,
	Variation	*.276%*			

You will note that the fineness is much higher than that of the dollars being minted to-day. The reason no doubt is that in those days the desire was to produce a dollar which could circulate at par with a British or Mexican dollar, rather than form a new National Currency. I mention this assay, however, as I will draw your attention presently to a curious coincidence in connexion with the large variation of more than ¼ per cent. between these two assays.

The following assays of Chinese silver dollars have all been made at the Indian Government Mint, Bombay. In each case two parcels were sent and each parcel was assayed separately:—

MINT B.

1916	(1)	Weight	414.80	grains	891.	fine
	(2)	,,	414.80	,,	891.2	,,
		Average	414.60	,,	891.1	,,
		Variation	*.074%*			
1920	(1)	Weight	414.20	grains	890.3	fine
	(2)	,,	414.	,,	889.8	,,
		Average	414.10	,,	890.05	,,
		Variation	*.104%*			

It will be noted that there was less variation between the dollars minted at this Mint in 1916 than between those minted in 1920, while the value of the 1916 dollars is .239% higher than that of the 1920 one.

MINT C.

1920	(1)	Weight	414.48	grains	891.	fine
	(2)	,,	414.20	,,	891.1	,,
		Average	414.34	,,	891.05	,,
		Variation	*.056%*			

MINT D.

1915	(1)	Weight	414.639	grains	889.6	fine
	(2)	,,	414.639	,,	889.5	,,
		Average	414.639	,,	889.55	,,
		Variation	*.0112%*			

In these assays the weight is constant, while the variation is only .0112 per cent. From that point of view this is the best assay obtained.

1918	(1)	Weight	414.76	grains	891.4	fine
	(2)	,,	414.32	,,	890.9	,,
		Average	414.54	,,	891.15	,,
		Variation	*.162%*			
1919	(1)	Weight	415.80	grains	891.4	fine
	(2)	,,	415.20	,,	890.5	,,
		Average	415.50	,,	890.45	,,
		Variation	*.133%*			
1920	(1)	Weight	415.40	grains	890.8	fine
	(2)	,,	414.40	,,	890.5	,,
		Average	414.90	,,	890.65	,,
		Variation	*.275%*			

While there was a gradual improvement in dollars minted at this Mint up to 1919, there has been a depreciation of .122 per cent. in the dollars minted in the early part of this year—as compared with those minted last year. It is also noticeable that the variation between the 1920 dollars is practically the same as the variation between dollars minted as A in 1908, viz.: .276 per cent.

Dollars as variable as these are not coins in the technical sense, for they have no definite intrinsic value. At the best they are but a commodity whose expressed value in the accepted tael unit must necessarily fluctuate considerably.

The cost of minting $100 weighing 416 grains of silver 890 fine, exclusive of mint expenses, is Shanghai currency taels 71.685. At current prices it would not be a profitable transaction to mint such coins under the present system on which Chinese Mints are conducted—a further depreciation of their dollars would probably result if that system is continued. The first step on the road to currency reform is the minting of an absolutely invariable dollar for circulation throughout the country. If this step be now taken by placing the proposed Shanghai Mint effectively under efficient technical control, it should not prove a very costly one for the Government, while the increased volume of trade which should result will more than repay the country. The longer the minting of the present unreliable dollar is continued, the more expensive must reform become. If the trade of the country were to be financed through the medium of a dollar as variable as those at present available, an unnecessary tax would be placed on it, which could not but retard its full development.

The Shanghai Mint.

The recommendations of the Foreign Exchange Banks have not yet been accepted *in toto* by the Chinese Government. But on March 3, 1921, a Loan Agreement was signed between the Ministry of Finance, and a Chinese Banking Group, almost identical with that which arranged the Railway Car Loan for the erection and equipment of a modern Mint at Shanghai. The amount of the Loan is $2,500,000 Chinese Currency, and the main provisions of the contract are printed below. Special importance attaches to the Memorandum from the Chinese Banking Group to the Minister of Finance and Director of the Currency Bureau, recommending the procedure to be adopted to standardize the new dollar currency, which is reproduced in full. It will be seen that several of the recommendations of the Foreign Exchange Banks have been adopted, others modified, and some not referred to at all.

Summary or Loan Contract.

The contract for the Shanghai Mint Loan, of $2,500,000 in Chinese currency, was signed on March 3, by the Minister of Finance, the Director of the Currency Bureau and representatives of the Shanghai Mint Loan Chinese banking group. The contract makes the following stipulations:—

(1) Treasury notes will be issued in accordance with regulations to be announced by the Ministry of Finance.

(2) The money derived from these notes is to be exclusively used for the purchase of land, the building of the mint and its equipment with machinery. Within one month of the signing of the contract the parties of the first part will instruct the officers

of the Shanghai mint, and their engineers and contractors, to draw up a detailed plan for the approval of the parties of the second part. Upon the latter's approval the building of the mint will proceed without delay, and an immediate order for the required machinery will be placed.

(3) In accordance with the Shanghai Mint Treasury notes regulations, the parties of the first part will receive $93 for every $100 note, and the parties of the second part will sell for the actual amount received by the parties of the second part.

(4) The notes will bear nine per cent. interest.

(5) On the day of the signing of the contract, the parties of the second part will place to the credit of the Shanghai mint account the net sum of $2,325,000 upon the notes that have been underwritten, as a deposit bearing four per cent. interest, all the interest on the notes being debited to the account of the Shanghai mint from the deposit above-mentioned.

(6) The parties of the second part will bear all the expenses involved in the sale of the notes, telegrams, posting, advertising, etc., the second parties receiving not more than one per cent. of the total value of the notes as commission.

(7) A monthly redemption of $70,000 will be effected from April, 1921, to May, 1924, for which the first parties will instruct the Salt Administration to make such payment to the Bank of China and the Bank of Communications in Shanghai, which will in turn hand over the money to the second parties for the redemption of the notes.

(8) Upon the completion of the Shanghai mint, the first parties will hand over the documents in relation to the ownership of the land, machinery, equipment, etc., to the second parties.

(9) This deals with the profits, which cannot be taken out by the first parties until all the notes have been redeemed.

The remainder is unimportant. The banking group concerned is practically the same as the one which contracted for the railway-car loan.

Chinese Bankers' Recommendations.

The following correspondence has been exchanged between the Chinese Banking Group associated in the Mint Loan and the Ministry of Finance and the Currency Bureau:

To The Minister of Finance and the Director of the Currency Bureau:

We have been taking great interest in the proposition put before us by your Ministry and the Currency Bureau, concerning the issue of $2,500,000 Shanghai Mint Loan Treasury Notes: and a contract has been entered into between your Ministry and ourselves, signed on March 3, 1921, by which we will be the underwriters of the issue of the full amount of the notes.

Owing to the fact that Shanghai is the trading as well as the financial centre of the whole of China, both Chinese and foreign commercial circles here, desiring to see the realization of financial stability and commercial development of China, have been most urgently looking forward to the establishment of a modern and efficient mint at Shanghai in the immediate future. Political conditions in the country during the past few years have been very unfavourable to trade activities, and lack of adequate communication has shaken the financial equilibrium of the nation. The uncertainty of transportation, which prevents the free movement of dollars and often enhances their value, unnecessarily and abruptly made the situation still worse. It is true that we have several mints in different provinces; but it is equally true that the provincial authorities have been taking these mints as provincial property and conducting them on a purely business basis. When any profit is seen, then dollars are minted; and when there is no prospective profit to be realized, the operations of the mints are stopped, whether the Central Government approves or not. As a result, the existing mints in China have ceased to perform their functions as stabilizing agents of national finance. Therefore the establishment of a centralized and efficiently managed mint in China is not merely a matter of importance but also a matter of necessity.

We are glad to see that the loan contract for the establishment of such a mint has been signed, and we are sure that we shall see the mint in operation before long. However, our interest regarding the establishment of the Shanghai Mint does not end with the mere creation of an additional manufacturing house where dollars and cents will be produced. Our interest goes far beyond that. We hope to see in this mint a stepping stone towards the abolition of bullion sycee, towards the nationalization of the currency system, and towards the reconstruction of the whole financial structure of the nation. In connexion with such a great expectation as ours, we cannot but offer our suggestions regarding the coinage system as well as the ways and means by which the mint can maintain its independence and efficiency. We therefore make the following suggestions:—

Suggestions Concerning Mint.

1. *Weight and fineness of the coins.*

According to the regulations governing national coinage, issued in the year 1914, the dollar should contain .648 of a K'uping tael, or 23.97795048 grammes of silver, and the fineness should be 900.00, the other 100.00 being copper. But these stipulations have not been carried out. The Yuan Shih-kai dollar has a fineness of 890.00, and there are more than 400,000,000 of such dollars in circulation. It seems to us that it would be wise to adopt the fineness of the Yuan dollar, *i.e.,* 890.00 as the fineness for the new dollars to be coined by the Shanghai Mint, containing a weight of .6408 of K'uping tael, *i.e.,* 23.9024808 grammes. This adoption will avoid unnecessary changes. The 1914 Coinage Regulations should be revised according to the above conditions, so that the laws will not be merely empty words.

2. *The die of the coins.*

The coins now circulating have been coined after the model of 1914, bearing a picture of Yuan Shih-kai. A new die should be adopted for the Shanghai Mint, and a special mark should be put on the coins so as to distinguish them from the existing issues. The new die should be adopted by a Presidential mandate, and mention should be made in the Mandate to the effect that the old and new coins are to be circulated at the same par value.

3. *Remedy.*

The weight, fineness and remedy should be definitely fixed by a certain set of regulations, as was done in 1914. The remedy between the actual weight of a dollar and the authorized weight should not exceed .03 per cent., the remedy between the total weight of 1,000 dollars and the authorized weight, should not exceed .003 per cent. The remedy between the fineness of one dollar and the authorized fineness should not exceed .03 per cent.

4. *Coinage system.*

For the purpose of the abolition of sycee and the standardization of coinage, the system of free coinage should be adopted. According to the 1914 regulations, a seigniorage of .006 tael is to be charged. A dollar would contain .648 of a tael if the same regulations were observed. The reason why the seigniorage of .006 tael was added was so that the dollar would approach the then market value of .66 taels, Tientsin currency, and .71 taels, Shanghai currency. The British Chamber of Commerce at Shanghai proposed to charge a seigniorage of 2 per cent. If we reckon that a dollar contains a silver equivalent of .6408 taels, a seigniorage of .0128 would be charged. This seigniorage as proposed by the British Chamber of Commerce nearly doubles that provided in the regulations. It seems to be altogether too high. The .006 tael seigniorage is a just one; but as the price of commodities at present is very high, and if the Shanghai Mint is not going to coin subsidiary coins for the time being, it is feared that .006 seigniorage would not be enough to maintain operating expenses. The loss on the part of the mint would be still greater, when the old dollars are to be recoined. So it seems that a seigniorage charge of more than .006 tael would be necessary. According to the report made by the Currency Bureau in May, 1915, it stated that the minimum cost of .65 taels should be maintained, that is, .01 tael should be the minimum seigniorage charge. If the .01 tael seigniorage should be adopted as the standard seigniorage, it would mean a seigniorage of 1.5 per cent. This seems to be a just charge. Then a dollar would contain .6508 K'uping tael. However, should the 1.5 per cent. seigniorage become too high at a future date, it could be reduced by a Presidential Mandate.

If the free coinage system should be adopted, the mint should not accept for minting any bullion, the fineness of which is below 890.00; and for the sake of ensuring efficiency, the English system of receiving and paying out the money to be coined should be adopted, that is, the Chinese banks at Shanghai would elect representatives to whom the mint could entrust the task of receiving bullion for coinage, and paying out the coins minted. The Chinese Bankers' Association at Shanghai and the Shanghai Mint will work together and fix the amount of money that the mint should coin every day or every month.

However, prior to the adoption of the free coinage system, the question of abolition of bullion sycee and the tael standard should first be definitely settled. If the bullion sycee and the tael standard are to be allowed to remain, dollars will still have a market exchange quotation daily. When the exchange rate is high, people bring their bullion to the mint for coinage, and when the rate drops, the mint would cease coining altogether. Therefore, if China should adopt a system of free coinage, bullion sycee and the tael standard should be first totally abolished. The Government should entrust the Chinese Bankers' Association, the Chinese Chamber of Commerce and the Domestic Bankers' Association to work together with the Foreign Bankers' Association and the officials of the Customs to organize a special committee to look into this matter. If the methods could be outlined before the opening of the mint, so much the better.

If the abolition of bullion sycee and the tael standard cannot be realized at an early date, and the free coinage system could not be adopted before the mint starts operations, then the precedents of the present working in the Tientsin and Nanking Mints should be followed. All the member banks of the Shanghai Mint Loan Banking Group, when they want to have coins minted, can apply for procedure from the Bank of China and the Bank of Communications.

5. *The organization of the Mint.*

The control of the Shanghai Mint should be in the hands of the Ministry of Finance and the Currency Bureau. The Chief and other members of the staff should be appointed by the Ministry of Finance directly. These officials should be appointed according to their real qualifications both regarding knowledge and experience, and once appointed, they should not be changed or shifted too often so as to ensure efficiency of the mint management and production. The Shanghai Mint should also employ a foreign assaying expert to take charge of the work of the assaying office and for testing the variations and fineness of the coins minted. His investigations should be published from time to time, so that the public will have full confidence in the mint's work.

6. *Production of the Mint.*

According to the present estimate the amount of money daily needed in Shanghai now is somewhere between $500,000 and $600,000. If we calculate on the basis of daily production $600,000, a sum of Tls. 12,000,000 is needed every month. It seems that it would be enough to start the initial production at that rate. If the mint is in need of further funds for its expansion and enlargement, we, the Shanghai Mint Loan Banking Group, will be willing to supply such funds. The present plan of the mint should leave plenty of room for further expansion so that enlargement plans to the extent of $1,000,000 daily production can be formulated whenever necessary.

7. *Special Committee.*

In order to make certain of the abolition of the tael standard and bullion sycee, the Shanghai Mint should appoint a Special Committee. Any persons, whether Chinese or foreign, who have close connexions with the question of the tael and dollar, should be represented by members of the Committee, for instance, the members of the Chinese Bankers' Association, members of the Native Bankers' Association, members of the Chinese General Chamber of Commerce, members of the staff of the Customs (who have great interest in this proposition in so far as they are concerned in the question of abolishing the Haikwan tael and the payment of foreign loan obligations on the basis of dollars instead of taels) the members of the Foreign Bankers' Association (who also have considerable interest in this question because they have a great deal to do in connexion with settlement of foreign loans, both in principal redemption and interest payment) The Committee should from time to time discuss ways and means of how to abolish bullion sycee and the tael standard, as well as to test the fineness of coins and supervise the coinage of the mint, and to make suggestions for general efficiency of the mint. This committee will cease to function only when the reform of currency throughout the country has been completely carried out.

We, the Shanghai Mint Loan Banking Group, sincerely submit the above suggestions for the consideration of you, the Minister

of Finance and Director of the Currency Bureau. As the matter is one of importance and urgency, we beg to request that you will give serious consideration to these suggestions.

Reply from the Ministry of Finance and the Currency Bureau.

We are in receipt of your letter submitting suggestions concerning the weight and fineness of National coins, the die of coins, remedy, coinage system, the organization of the Mint, production of the mint, and special committee, which have received our hearty approval. We have duly instructed the Shanghai Mint to act upon them. In case we desire to make any changes we will discuss first with you on the subject.

APPENDIX VI.

REPORTS ON MODERN COPPER COINS OF CHINA.

The following paragraphs relating to modern Chinese copper coinage are from the Maritime Customs Decennial Reports, 1902–1921:

Chefoo—(Shantung). (1911).

The decade will hereafter be famous for the imposition of the copper 10-cash coin, introduced into Shantung in 1905. Though obviously far below its fiat value, it was at first pretty generally accepted by trader and peasant at that value, here as elsewhere. Soon, in obedience to a well-known law, the large copper cash (制 錢) itself—a clumsy but honest coin began to disappear rapidly; the new coin depreciated; and the Chinese people found themselves suffering from all the evils of a debased currency. It may be possible some day to estimate the extent of these evils and the part they have played in the financial exhaustion of the Empire. Various attempts were made by the Central Government to check the mischief by restrictions on the inter-provincial movement of the coins, the effect of which was merely to hamper trade and encourage the coiner of counterfeit. Finally, in 1907, the majority of the provincial Mints were closed. The Tientsin and Canton Mints, however, continued to issue the light coin, which by this time had become the only available currency, eked out by "small," *i.e.*, spurious, cash (私 錢). The Shantung Mint was closed in 1906, but the province has always been well supplied with the copper coinage of its neighbours.

(1921).

In 1915 Japanese bought up copper cash, melted it down and exported it to Japan by tons: this is said to have been most profitable to them, but it stripped and completely upset the money market. Cash now are only used for sums under 1 cent, or only for ½ cent postage stamp, the only things said to cost less than a 10-cash coin. The depreciation of copper 10-cash coins was pointed out in the last report: it has grown ever worse, as debased coins have poured in from other provinces in spite of occasional prohibition of import; 475 millions are on record as imported. Practically the value of everything here is quoted in or determined by these coins in tiao, even land, and they are the medium for purchase of all daily necessaries; consequently, depreciation has meant a general rise in prices and hardship on all save the coin importers.

Lungkow—(Shantung). (1921).

Copper 10-cash pieces have largely taken the place of the old square-holed cash. Their introduction dates from the outbreak of the European War, when so much of the old cash in circulation in the promontory was collected and melted down for export. These old cash are now used only to make up fractional parts of a copper cent, though all business dealings are based on cash quotations. The tiao quoted for this purpose is the local liu-ti-tiao (六底吊), six-less-tiao, of 494 cash, the standard book rate exchange for which is 370 tiao to Huangp'ing Tls. 100. There are no bank-notes in circulation.

Kiaochow—(Shantung). (1911).

Before the year 1905 Shantung had no coinage of its own, but existed on the time-worn cash, supplemented later by the modern 10 cash piece from other provinces, which exchanged as high as 80 to $1. In 1905 the Tsinanfu Mint was established, and realised a profit of 30 per cent. as long as the output was kept in reasonable proportion to the demand. This continued till the end of 1906, when the exchange stood about 100 copper coins to the dollar. From May 1907 a gradual downward movement commenced, influenced by over-production and, especially, by the influx of similar coins from the Mints of other provinces, where the coins had sooner depreciated in value and thereby offered a good profit to the importer into Shantung. The people objected to the new coin, because its minting gradually absorbed, without replacing, the old 1 cash piece. Eventually there were amongst the copper coins circulating in the province 60 per cent. Shantung coined and 40 per cent. from other provinces, and by September 1907, the exchange stood at 115. A mistaken attempt by the government to remedy matters by forbidding the import and seizing outside coins further discredited them with the people, and in October of the same year they went down to 132, and have remained thereabouts ever since.

Tientsin—(Chihli). (1911).

In 1907 the Government bought back all the copper 10 cash pieces (tang-shih-ti-ta-ch'ien 當十的大錢), to be melted and transformed into new copper cents. The Ta Ching Bank was in charge of the operation, bought the cash by weight, and made, it is said, a handsome profit on the transaction. But the over-issue of the new copper cents soon depreciated their value by 30 or 40 per cent.; prices went up in proportion, and caused widespread dissatisfaction among the people. On February 14, 1908, an Edict ordered the Ministry of Finance to devote half a million taels to the relief of the Peking money market, copper coins were bought back until they had appreciated again to a certain standard, and the importation of outside coins to the capital was forbidden. The market price, which had ranged between 193 and 199 copper cents to the silver tael, fell to 163, and remained thereabout while the half million taels were being spent to keep it down. At the same time, in Tientsin and Paotingfu, it ranged from 190 to 200, with a light fall of 3 or 4 per cent. within a few days after the issue of the Edict. When the short distance and easy communication with Peking are considered, one may realise the severe repression that must have been necessary to prevent clandestine exchange, which tempted merchants, pedlars, etc., with the prospect of a profit of 10 to 20 per cent. in a few hours.

Chungking—(Szechuen). (1911).

Copper coins—cash and 1 cent pieces—have undergone a continual depreciation during the decade. In 1902 1,200 cash were equal to 1 tael, the present rate is 1,550 to 1,620. The exchange has thus reverted to the conditions prevailing 20 years ago. The reasons for this depreciation are said to be the increase of copper coins on the market by the introduction of 1 cent pieces and the scarcity of silver prevailing from 1905 to 1909. The subsequent recovery of the silver market failed to restore the former ratio of exchange between taels and copper coins, because the disappearance of opium greatly reduced the demand for the latter. Formerly, large quantities of 1 cent pieces and cash were sent up country every year to purchase the small lots of opium from individual farmers, but this need has now ceased. The ratio between silver and copper coins was also adversely affected by the importation of great quantities of the latter from Ichang. In Hupeh, copper coins had depreciated to an even greater extent, and junk-masters and merchants were not slow to avail themselves of this opportunity. They purchased copper coins at Ichang and smuggled them into Szechwan, where they resold them at a great profit. It took some time before the official heard of this illicit trade, which was at once prohibited, with the result that now only Szechwan copper cents are accepted in the province. The rate of exchange between copper cents and cash has always been 1 to 10.

(1921).

Copper Coins and Cash. Since the introduction of the Republican 50 cash and 100 cash brass pieces by the Chungking and Chengtu Mints the cash currency has depreciated greatly. In 1912 one tael of silver would exchange for 1,800 cash, in 1916 for 2,500 cash, and in 1921 for 3,030 cash. The old cash, having an intrinsic value greater than the face value, has practically disappeared, as a brisk trade sprang up in melting down this currency in spite of it being prohibited by the Government.

Wanhsien—(Szechuen). (1921).

The minted currency in use consists of four sorts of copper coins, 10, 20, 50 and 100 cash pieces.

Ichang—(Hupeh). (1911).

At the beginning of the decade the scarcity of copper cash was felt severely at Ichang, as elsewhere, and the exchange rate rose steadily from 1,282 cash = Hk. Tls. 1 at the end of 1901 to 1,123 cash at the end of 1903. The 5 cash and 10 cash copper coins issued by the Hupeh Mint in 1902 were eagerly taken up by the people, although the face value of these coins greatly exceeds their intrinsic value; but so great was the dearth of cash that, in spite of the floods of copper coins poured into the district, the demand far exceeded the supply for over two years, and little relief of the stringency became apparent till the end of 1904, when the rate had fallen to 1,237 cash. Heavy importations of copper cents during 1905 reduced the rate to Hk. Tls. 1 = 1,703 cash (in copper cents); and though there was a recovery to 1,613 cash per tael in the following year, the tendency to depreciation of the copper coins still continues, the rates during 1911, before the revolution, varying from 1,680 to 2,100 cash to the Haikwan tael. According to the well-known law that the inferior currency drives out the superior, the copper cents have almost completely supplanted the old-style cash, though, curiously enough, the bad cash were the first to disappear.

(1921).

In the Ichang district, as in many other parts of China, the poorer classes have suffered most from the continued debasement of the currency and the consequent increase in the cost of living. Official attempts to prevent Hupeh from being flooded with Szechwan brass and copper coins have met with only partial success, and large amounts have passed the provincial frontier surreptitiously. At the present time the Szechwan 50 cash piece is the most used coin in the Ichang district.

Shasi—(Hupeh). (1911).

The currency used in the Shasi district can hardly be called a satisfactory medium between buyer and seller, the farmers, and indeed, 90 per cent. of the population, favouring the copper cash. A carrier doing the marketing for distant villages may frequently be seen driving his donkey to market loaded with strings of cash, and returning with provisions less in weight than the purchasing medium. Even in peaceful years silver is scarce and expensive, and paper money is accepted with great caution, if accepted at all, anywhere out of the immediate neighbourhood of the issuing cash shop.

The following figures give the average exchange between cash and Hk. Tls. 1:—

	Cash.		*Cash.*
1902	1,200	1907	1,620
1903	1,170	1908	1,790
1904	1,200	1909	1,950
1905	1,420	1910	1,935
1906	1,620	1911	1,900

(1921).

The continual influx of the depreciated Szechwan copper coins, chiefly by junk, has had the effect of driving out the Hupeh copper coin and has led to a steady depreciation of the value of cash, as will be seen by the following figures giving the average exchange between cash and Hk. Tls. 1, during the last 10 years:—

	Cash.		*Cash.*
1912	1,890	1917	2,350
1913	2,060	1918	2,400
1914	2,010	1919	2,440
1915	2,080	1920	2,500
1916	2,250	1921	2,760

In 1912 the local authorities, in order to boost up the depreciated currency, issued a proclamation fixing the rate of the Hupeh dollar note at 1,200 cash, but this rate was only obtainable by the soldier at, so to speak, the point of the bayonet, and the value of cash steadily depreciated. In 1914 the market steadied, and the value of cash appreciated somewhat, but from then on the fall was persistent. In 1919 there was a marked increase in the influx of the depreciated Szechwan copper coins, and heavy shipments of Hupeh copper coins were made to Hankow. On the 23rd June 1920, with a view to putting a stop to this speculative business, an embargo was placed by the local authorities on the export of copper coins, and in 1921 an official proclamation by the Ministry of Finance was issued, making it an offence to transport copper coins to the value of over 50 tiao except under huchao.

Hankow—(Hupeh). (1911).

But copper has been the crux of the situation. China is usually described as a silver standard country, but its real standard is copper. It was found that the intrinsic value of cash was greater than the face value, especially in the older varieties. A brisk trade sprang up in melting them down, which all the efforts of the government failed to stop. So cash rose to a considerable premium as compared to silver, and upset buying and selling of all descriptions, as whatever the amount of the transaction, the base of it is regulated by the cash value, the price of the catty regulating that of the larger amount.

The necessity for more copper currency was obvious, and the remedy was equally obvious to the officials, as the minting of tokens of a face value of 10 cash promised large profits. They would not listen to advice not to depreciate the coinage by flooding the market with tokens which would quickly be at a discount. A Mint was opened in 1902, and the stamping machines were working day and night in 1903, until, in 1904, exchange, which had ruled at about 1,050 cash per tael, varied from 1,075 to 1,257 cash. The copper imported for the Mints was: in 1901, nil; in 1902, 6,860 piculs; in 1903, 36,870 piculs; and in 1904, 103,670 piculs. A large quantity of this was re-exported in the following years, the upset to business caused by such big deals in copper having a harmful effect on trade. The outturn of the Mint was kept secret; but it was calculated that at least 70,000 piculs were converted into 10 cash pieces in 1904. Each picul produced 8,000 coins of almost pure copper, which works out to 560 million pieces for 1904. In addition, 10,699 piculs of discs, ready for stamping, were imported to feed the machines; some of these discs contained a very large percentage of brass. The output continued in 1905, the result being that the cash value became an unknown quantity, and much loss to business men and the man in the street resulted. In 1911 the rate was 1,800 cash per tael. In 1909 the Imperial Government stopped the minting of such coins—too late to remedy the evil, as the province was flooded with the tokens.

(1921).

Besides the subsidiary silver coins, there is the currency of the toiling classes—the cash coinage. Since 1916 this coinage has undergone a serious modification, firstly owing to its conversion into 10 cash pieces (copper cents) by the provincial government Mints, and secondly owing to its having been clandestinely melted into brass ingots in great quantities and exported abroad. Thus the familiar cash, dear to the people, has practically disappeared from this neighbourhood; to such an extent is this true that as early as 1917 the dollar exchanged with considerable fluctuation for about 1,400 cash, but was payable only in coppers—140 to the dollar. These coppers in denominations of 10 and 20 cash have since been minted as a source of revenue in such quantities as to considerably increase the ratio of depreciation.

The following comparative table of average exchanges shows the depreciation of the copper coinage during the decade compared with the silver dollar:—

	Cash.		*Cash.*
1912	1,309	1917	1,400
1913	1,304	1918	1,493
1914	1,388	1919	1,420
1915	1,404	1920	1,571
1916	1,409	1921	1,612

Hankow, being situated in proximity to an active provincial Mint, has suffered more from the depreciated copper currency than other towns, and the lower classes were the most heavily hit. In fact, a large proportion of the people are paid, and the farmers sell their produce to middlemen on the markets, in coppers; and, as wages always rise much more slowly than goods and very seldom to the same extent, this unsound currency brings loss on all wage-earners and profits only the cash shops, who speculate on the vagaries of exchange. In a country like China, with the majority of the people poor even in good years, a depreciated copper currency necessarily tends to aggravate the struggle for existence and must result in a reduction of their purchasing power.

A probably unique feature of the Chinese copper currency is the fact that there is no legal ratio between cash and dollar and cash and tael, the exchange rate being determined as is the case with goods by supply and demand between copper and silver. Besides, the copper coin is not a token coin, and the amount of pure copper it contains is different from the amount contained in 10 brass cash, although it is meant to represent 10 cash. These differences in weight and fineness produce fluctuations in exchange rates also between the brass cash and the copper coin. And so it happens that the silver, copper, and brass currencies have no connexion between each other, but go their own way, each following its up or down course, determined by demand and supply or other causes. This confusion arose from the fact that the government failed to take steps towards restricting the amount of copper coin to be used and the amount to be minted; nor were precautions taken to maintain a legal ratio by ordering state banks to exchange cash for copper coins and vice versa at rates fixed by law.

Yochow—(Hunan). (1911).

The ordinary medium of exchange in this district is the copper cent. The copper cash is comparatively scarce, and the tiao exists only in the form of 100 copper cents. The tiao notes which are issued by the Hunan and the Hupeh Government Banks, and are exchangeable for 100 copper cents, are very common; but the Chinese have always shown a preference for those originating from the sister province. Hupeh dollars, both in the form of Government Bank notes of one dollar each and of silver dollar coins, are much used in Hunan. These are known to have exchanged for as much as 140 copper cents to a dollar in 1908. During the revolution there was such a great demand for silver that a Hupeh or a Mexican dollar coin fetched as much as 150 copper cents. The lowest rate known is 78 copper cents to a dollar, in 1902.

(1921).

The copper cents remains the ordinary medium of exchange in the district, and copper cash, which were comparatively scarce in 1911, are now hardly seen. Cash notes of various denominations issued by various native banks and cash shops were, however, in circulation up to the end of 1918. These notes were not exchangeable for metal but only for other notes issued by the Hunan Provincial Bank (湖南銀行), which got into difficulties and closed. The loss and suffering in consequence to the people locally was very great.

Kiukiang—(Kiangsi). (1921).

Copper cash continued to fall throughout the decade and now stand at about 1,600 to the dollar. Cash, however, are now no longer minted and are rarely met with, the greater number having gone into the melting-pot. Their place has been taken by copper cents, two denominations of which are in circulation, the 10 cash and 20 cash piece. The former is accepted at par, but there is a small discount on the latter. Certains cash shops, each guaranteed by three firms of standing, are allowed to issue notes of 1,000 cash, and the Bank of China also issues notes of 100 cash and 500 cash. All these notes circulate freely and at par.

Wuhu—(Anhwei). (1911).

The provincial Mint at Anking, which had been closed and dismantled in 1899, was supplied with new machinery in 1902 and began the minting of copper cash and 5 cash and 10 cash pieces. The smaller coins were not minted for long, and for several years only 10 cash pieces were issued. In 1905, 240 millions were said to have been coined, and in that year they exchanged at an average of 95 to the Mexican dollar. The Mint was closed in June, 1907, after having apparently overflooded the market with 10 cash pieces, which in 1910 had an average exchange value of 137.7 per dollar. They were still cheaper in 1911, but the conditions of that year were abnormal.

It is a curious fact that Anhwei cents are very scarce in this town, nearly all those in circulation bearing the names of other provinces and Mints. The explanation appears to be that gambling in exchange rates between different localities tends to the shipment of local coins to other provinces, and vice versa.

Copper cash have been gradually disappearing from circulation, and are now only used for fractional amounts, having been replaced by the copper cents with the nominal value of 10 cash. So scarce are actual "cash" that some shops are issuing small bamboo slips of that nominal value for purposes of small change. These are only recognised by the shops which originally issued them. Market rates, however, are still quoted. The cash exchange has varied from 817 per Mexican dollar in 1904 to over 1,500 in 1911.

(1921).

The copper cash depreciated to such an extent that at one time in 1916 their intrinsic value became higher than their face value; and, while the poor classes suffered from the evils of a debased currency, a great quantity of the coins was either melted or exported. Repressive measures were adopted without much effect on smugglers and counterfeiters. In view of the necessity for more copper currency and also for the purposes of revenue the authorities flooded the market with copper cent pieces, which soon ceased to command their original value. The Anking Mint restarted operations in December, 1919, being capable of coining one cent copper pieces at the rate of one million a day. In 1920 13,800,000 copper cents were imported through the Maritime Customs, and by December 1921, the 10 cash pieces had an average exchange value of 157 per dollar, as compared with 126, the highest value during the decade. As foreign goods are bought with "big" money and retailed for "small" money, the present market exchange is harmful to both foreign merchants and native dealers.

Nanking—(Kiangsu). (1911).

A Mint was opened in the city in September, 1901, and closed in December, 1908. During its seven and a quarter years of activity it produced enormous numbers of copper cents—the amount turned out in 1908, its last working year, was 300 millions. It also coined 10 cents and 20 cents pieces in an almost equally lavish manner. In 1908 60 millions of these latter were turned out. The consequence of this unlimited output was that the old copper cash have practically disappeared.

Chinkiang—(Kiangsu). (1911).

In 1905 enormous quantities of copper cents were poured into the local market from Hangchow, Soochow, Nanking, Hankow, and other places, and the decision of the Peking authorities that after the end of the eighth moon these coins must not be sent out of the producing provinces—caused immense quantities to be rushed in to anticipate the prohibition. Nearly 400 millions of cents were passed through the Customs, in addition to unrecorded importations in native craft. Early in the year a Mint was established at Tsingkiangpu, for which were imported 339 millions of copper blanks and 5,059 piculs of copper ingots. This Mint, when in full work, had a capacity of one million cents a day. As was to be expected, the exchange value of copper cents fell rapidly from 84 to 104 to the dollar; and although the Mint was closed down, and in spite of the prohibition against importing from outside, exchange has never recovered, and stands now at 130 cents to the dollar. Copper cash naturally depreciated in value in the face of such conditions, and the fall was precipitated by want of demand. A more extended use of subsidiary silver coins, several years when crops have been ruined by floods, and especially the suppression of the cultivation of opium in the Suchow district, have all combined to reduce the demand for the humble cash, which is now exchanging at the rate of 1,883 to the Chinkiang tael, as against 1,200 in 1903.

Shanghai—(Kiangsu). (1911).

In dealing with this question the main fact to be borne in mind is that while China uses silver as its staple medium of exchange, yet such silver has practically never been actually coined and universally accepted at its face value throughout the country, while the true basic currency was the coined copper "cash." Owing to the lack of uniformity in the standard of these cash, their price in relation to the local unit of silver—the tael—has varied daily in all places. Since 1904 the provincial Mints have introduced a copper coin, known as a 10 cash piece; but the metal from which these were stamped soon depreciated from the original standard, and, in addition, the coin was largely over-issued, and consequently soon ceased to command its original value. These have now become practically the local currency for the people, only the units figure being payable in actual copper cash; but their value for Shanghai Tls. 10 has depreciated very seriously since their original issue. Whereas in 1905 the price per Shanghai Tls. 10 payable in 10 cash pieces, varied from 1,158 in January to 1,440 in December, during 1910 no less than 1,847 pieces, were required to equal the same amount.

Soochow—(Kiangsu). (1911).

It is not possible to ascertain the total output of the two local copper Mints, built in 1898 and 1904, and closed in 1906. But from 1902 copper coins, local and imported, have greatly declined in value. In 1902 88 coppers were worth $1, but sank until in 1911 $1 exchanged for 132 coppers. Good copper cash entirely disappeared, due to illegal melting down, and left a limited quantity of very questionable quality that was hardly enough to supplement the copper coins as a fractional auxiliary.

Hangchow—(Chekiang). (1911).

The exchange between the various currencies changes constantly, and may differ at the same time in various parts of this district. The exchange between taels and dollars is generally in sympathy with the Shanghai exchange. A dollar was worth 1,000 cash in 1901; the rate is now about 1,300 cash. The exchange between dollars and subsidiary silver coins has generally been, and is now, $1 = 11 10 cents pieces. The Hangchow Mints having flooded the province in 1905 with copper cents, these have very much depreciated in value. Originally issued at 90 to the dollar, they have fallen to 130 per dollar.

There were formerly three Mints in Hangchow, one silver Mint, where dollars and subsidiary coins were turned out from 1897 to 1903, when it was closed, and two copper Mints, for the coining of copper cents and 10 cash pieces, opened respectively in 1903 and 1905, and both closed in 1906.

Ningpo—(Chekiang). (1911).

The introduction of the 10 cash piece took place in 1904. Though not the first of China's modern coins, it is undoubtedly the most useful and popular. From the way it sprang immediately into favour, it is evident that it filled a long-felt want. Copper cash were rapidly supplanted by the new arrival, and have practically disappeared. These 10 cash pieces, however, owing to over-production, have been for some years at a discount. The following figures show the average value per Mexican dollar:—

	pieces		*pieces*
1905 . . .	95	1908 . . .	118
1906 . . .	111	1909 . . .	133
1907 . . .	107	1910 . . .	129

(1921).

The value of the copper cent, or 10 cash piece, remained fairly steady up to the year 1921, exchanging for 130–135 to the dollar. Early in the year, however, exchange was upset by the continuous influx from Shanghai of light-weight coins, and the importation of copper cents, except in negligible quantities was consequently prohibited. But this injunction failed to arrest the depreciation of the 10 cash piece, which now exchanges at 155 to the dollar.

Foochow—(Fukien). (1911).

The 10 cash pieces produced were in strong favour both locally and in other provinces, and were commonly exchanged on the market there at 13 cash or at the rate of 99–100 for a "chopped" dollar in Shanghai 92–95 of these 10 cash pieces, could be exchanged for a clean Mexican dollar, and, accordingly, there ensued a steady and profitable export to Shanghai. In 1905 two additional Mints were established, one at the Arms Factory, near the Upper Bridge, and the other at the Mamoi Arsenal, the result being that a combined total daily output was attained of two million copper 10 cash pieces. When the new Mints had been in operation but two months, the Central Government placed a ban on the extraprovincial export and limited the amount coined to 300,000 pieces per day. Thereupon the two new Mints were closed, and have since remained idle, and the city Mint, after experimenting with a two cash piece in 1907, 1908, and 1909, was also shut down in December, 1910.

For the information contained in the following paragraphs we are indebted to the *Chinese Economic Bulletin,* 1924 and 1925:

Depreciation of Copper Currency in Shansi.

During the first few years of the Republic, the Shansi market was entirely free from debased copper coins. The fractional currency of the province then consisted chiefly of brass cash. Later on, it is reported, forgers in Tsingtao collected brass cash from Shansi, melted them down, and sent them back in the form of debased coppers. From this illegal traffic the forgers made a rich haul, because, according to the market exchange rate, ten brass cash were equivalent to one copper, yet the intrinsic value of ten cash exceeded that of a copper several times. In order to stop the inflow of debased coppers, the authorities in 1919 opened a Mint in Taiyuan and began to mint coppers. At first the new copper coins did not depreciate to any marked extent, because large numbers of the coins found their way to the different districts of the province to take the place of the brass cash, which became scarce as the result of exportation by the above-mentioned forgers. Recently, the districts have been flooded with the new coins, whose exchange rate has dropped with remarkable rapidity. In 1919 and 1920, the copper exchange rate on the Taiyuan market was 150–160 coppers to the dollar. It remained at this point for a while and dropped very gradually. Even as late as January, 1924, the rate was a little over 200 coppers. During last year there was a sudden drop, which brought the rate to 260–270 coppers to the dollar by the end of the year. A further fall from 260–290 coppers was recorded in the first six months of the present year and depreciation still continues. By the beginning of August, a dollar exchanged for 293 coppers on the Taiyuan market, but a week after a dollar was good for 295 coppers. Copper notes also circulate in Taiyuan and other busy centers. The notes are issued by the Shansi Provincial Bank surcharged with the name of the place for which they are issued. Hence, they circulate only locally. The notes are of four different denominations; namely, 10, 20, 50 and 100 coppers. So far the notes are at par with the copper coins.

Copper currency in Shansi province has depreciated to one-third of its former value in the past ten or twelve years. In 1912 and 1913, the dollar exchange rate was equivalent to 1,000 cash or so, while coppers, being still scarce on the market, were at a premium of from 10 to 20 per cent.; that is, a dollar exchanged for only 90 or 100 coppers (The legal exchange rate is: 10 cash is equivalent to a copper; 1,100 cash is equivalent to 110 coppers). In the next few years, coppers were imported or smuggled into the province in large numbers, chiefly, it is alleged, by forgers, who forged the coppers by smelting the brass cash collected in Shantung and other provinces. This caused the copper exchange rate to drop to 140 coppers to the dollar in 1915 and brass cash gradually disappeared from circulation. The copper currency, however, continued to depreciate as more and more of the spurious and light-weight coppers were dumped on the Shansi market. In 1920–1921 the rate was 170–180 coppers to the dollar and in 1923, 200 coppers. The situation was aggravated by the minting of coppers by the Shansi provincial Mint. In 1919–1920 the Shansi authorities, being unable to stop the inflow of coppers into Shansi from other provinces, set up a Mint and minted coppers of their own. This hastened the depreciation of copper currency. The greatest drop in the copper exchange rate, however, happened last year. The rates recorded were: January (1924), 215–216 coppers; April, 247–248 coppers; August, 260–270 coppers; and December, 290 coppers.

The depreciation of copper currency hits the small traders very badly, because they sell their goods in cash or coppers. This class includes hawkers and peddlers. Most of the small shops now no longer sell their goods in cash or coppers but on the dollar cent basis. Shansi authorities may soon order the Shansi provincial Mint to stop the minting of coppers for the time being.

Dollar Exchange Rates in Hunan.

The following were the dollar exchange rates current in Changsha (Hunan) during 1924:

	Highest	*Lowest*	*Difference*
January	226 coppers	222 coppers	4 coppers
February	229 ”	224 ”	5 ”
March	238 ”	227 ”	11 ”
April	229 ”	227 ”	2 ”
May	239 ”	229 ”	10 ”
June	242 ”	233 ”	9 ”
July	249 ”	237 ”	12 ”
August	249 ”	239 ”	10 ”
September	263 ”	249 ”	14 ”
October	275 ”	262 ”	13 ”
November	287 ”	276 ”	11 ”
December	289 ”	275 ”	14 ”

Copper Coins and Notes in Chungking.

Copper coins in Chungking are issued by the Government Mint in Chengtu and the Copper Mint in Chungking in 10 and 20 cents denominations. Five cents pieces were formerly issued but have now become very scarce. One silver dollar is at present exchangeable for 255 20 cents copper coins, *i.e.*, 510 copper cents payable in 20 cents pieces, or for 408 10 cents copper coins, showing a greater depreciation of 20 cents pieces, than of 10 cents pieces. Copper notes on the Chungking market are issued by the Szechuan Government Exchange, the Chungking Municipal Council, and the Chungking Chamber of Commerce. They are in 1 cent, 2 cents, 2.5 cents, and 5 cents denominations. The 100 cents copper notes have all been redeemed by the Government Exchange. There are no special exchange shops for copper notes.

Currency in Kansu.

There are two kinds of subsidiary coins, copper and brass cash. The difference in intrinsic value between the coppers and the brass cash was recently so great as to tempt the provincial officials to melt cash coins and recast them into coppers. The profits were enormous. A tael in the spring of 1922 was equivalent to 2,200 or 2,300 cash and every 1,000 cash could be recast into 300 20 cash coppers. The officials turned the cash into coppers in great numbers and sometimes even granted or farmed out this right. Debased and under-weight coppers immediately flooded the market and inflation caused the copper currency to depreciate to an unprecedentedly low point—900 20 cash coppers to the tael.

Last summer the Kansu officials outlined a program for currency reorganisation. The currency notes were first redeemed at their market rate—40 per cent. of their face value. They were then replaced by a series of dollar notes issued by the Kansu provincial bank. The debased and underweight coppers are also being collected and destroyed. In their place, a new kind of copper coin, better stamped and higher in intrinsic value, is being issued.

Copper Currency in Hupeh Province.

A large number of one cent copper coins of the Hupeh Provincial Mint were melted in 1918, 1919, and subsequently re-cast into two cents copper pieces. One cent coppers have therefore become very scarce in Hupeh province. And owing to excessive minting, two cents coppers have depreciated to the present exchange rate of 56 coins and four cash for one dragon note of 1,000 cash or 1,000 one cent coppers, instead of the original rate of 50 two cents coppers. Outside the provincial boundary, *e.g.,* at Kiukiang, Anking, Wuhu, Nanking, and Chinkiang, they are 20 per cent. below par. In Tangyang (當陽), Kingmen (荆門), Yuanan (遠安), and other districts in western Hupeh, one cent coppers were abundant on the market in early Republican years, but were later driven out by debased coins from Szechwan, which in turn were replaced by still more debased cash from Ichang and neighborhood. These latter have depreciated far below nominal value, causing great inconvenience to the public.

In 1920 large quantities of copper coins of two cents denomination were smuggled from Szechwan into Ichang and Shasi, and widely distributed in central and western Hupeh. Daily quotations of Szechwan coins were fixed on the Ichang and the Shasi market. Later, Szechwan coins of five cents denomination were also introduced on the Hupeh market. Despite the proposal of the Provincial Assembly to prohibit this smuggling, large denomination Szechwan coppers of five cents and more recently 10 cents denomination, have circulated on the Hupeh market as far as Sinti (新堤) Light coins of two cents denomination have also been smuggled into the province from Hunan. Government prohibition has had very little effect on the smugglers. The Governor, however, has recently sent four delegates to Kingmen, Shasi, Ichang, Sinti, and Paotachow (寶塔州), to investigate the actual amount of Hunan coppers on the Hupeh market, prior to the enforcement of stricter measures for the prohibition of smuggling.

Wuchang Mint.

Since the commencement of operations in 1894, the mint has coined silver dollars chiefly on behalf of banks. The coinage of one cent coppers started in 1900. Definite arrangements were made in 1903 for one-third of the number of days in the month to be devoted to silver coinage, and the remaining number to copper coinage, and that copper pieces might be coined when the mine was short of silver bullion. In 1904, Ta Ching Dollars (大清銀幣) were coined. In 1906, copper coinage was suspended, owing to excessive issue. In May, 1916, one cent copper coins weighing 1.8 mace apiece, K'uping standard, were coined. In 1917, two cents copper pieces were coined with copper remelted by the Hupeh Government Exchange from cash, having a fineness of 99.3 per cent. The remelted copper was brittle and not fit for the addition of zinc. To make an alloy for coinage, 15 catties of cash were therefore added to every 100 catties of the remelted copper. Later in the same year, the addition of cash was increased to 25 catties per 100 catties of remelted copper, making a fineness of 90 per cent. These two cents copper coins weighed three mace apiece, K'uping standard. The moulds of the former Peiyang Mint, bearing a dragon on one face and the characters of Kwang Hsu Currency (光緒通寶), on the other, were still used. The weight, however, was reduced in September of the same year to 2.8 mace for a two cents piece and 1.6 mace for a one cent piece. In June, 1919, one cent copper coins were again increased in weight to 1.8 mace apiece. The daily output grew enormously until April, this year, when copper coinage was suspended, silver dollars stopped in 1920.

Following were exchange rates in Hankow between copper coins and silver from 1915 to 1924 exclusive:—

Year	100 coppers exchanged for silver		$1 exchanged for coppers	
	Highest	Lowest	Highest	Lowest
1915	Tls. 0.5190	Tls. 0.4900	144 copper cents	137 copper cents.
1916	0.5180	0.4660	149 " "	136 " "
1917	0.5500	0.5040	140 " "	130 " "
1918	0.5200	0.4900	142 " "	136 " "
1919	0.5160	0.4700	147 " "	138 " "
1920	0.4950	0.4410	152 " "	143 " "
1921	0.4690	0.4200	168 " "	150 " "
1922	0.3900	0.3270	212 " "	169 " "
1923	0.4360	0.3740	189 " "	162 " "
1924	0.3335	0.2635	269 " " and 3 cash	209 " " and 5 cash

Copper Depreciation in Shanghai.

Copper coins have been depreciating ever since 1917. In 1923, the exchange rate of a dollar in terms of coppers rose from 1,763 to 1,815, increasing about 52 coppers in a year. This increase, though insignificant in itself, did not affect the community to any noticeable extent because it was gradual and not abnormal. In 1924, however, the situation was aggravated. Violent fluctuations were registered several times, causing much distress and uneasiness. On January 1, this year, the rate was 2,050 coppers; six months later, it rose to 2,283 coppers; and, on October 1, it reached 2,465 coppers. The following reveals the various rates current in the last few years:—

Date	*Rate of One Shanghai Tael*	*Rate for One Dollar*
January 1, 1923	2,425	1,763
January 1, 1924	2,530	1,817
June 1, 1924	2,740	1,966
January 1, 1925	2,790	2,050
February 1, 1925	2,850	2,079
March 1, 1925	2,020	2,171
April 1, 1925	3,150	2,284
May 1, 1925	3,140	2,287
June 1, 1925	3,120	2,283
July 1, 1925	3,130	2,271
August 1, 1925	3,200	2,320
September 1, 1925	3,240	2,356
October 1, 1925	3,400	2,465

The heavy depreciation since the beginning of this year is understood to be largely attributable to excessive minting and the great influx of depreciated copper coins from Manchuria. A comparative study of the depreciation since 1917 is given hereunder:—

Date	*Shanghai Tael converted into Coppers*	*Percentage*
June 1, 1917	1,785	100. %
June 1, 1918	1,795	100.56%
June 3, 1919	1,832	102.63%
June 1, 1920	1,895	106.16%
June 1, 1921	2,000	112.04%
June 1, 1922	2,360	132.21%
June 1, 1923	2,505	140.33%
June 1, 1924	2,740	153.50%
January 2, 1925 . . .	2,790	156.30%
June 1, 1925	3,120	174.90%
October 1, 1925 . . .	3,400	190.47%

Thus coppers have depreciated by almost 100 per cent. since June 1, 1917. This abnormal drop has been accompanied by an increase in the cost of living. Generally speaking, what was sold for a copper in 1917 cannot be obtained at less than four to five coppers nowadays. The working classes are almost all paid on a copper basis; and the above factors have given rise to much labour unrest, as is testified in the number of strikes recorded from time to time in the *Bulletin.* But the increases in wages obtained as a result have not kept pace with the advance in prices.

Examination of the rate of exchange between the silver dollar and the copper coin during the past decade shows an especially marked depreciation since 1921. Until the middle of 1920, the dollar at Shanghai, to take an example, purchased around 135 coppers. Through extensive minting of a coin, the basic metal of which had a value considerably below the coin value, the market gradually became saturated, and the rate has now gone up to above 200. This state of things prevails all over the country. Depreciation became a natural development of the inability of the government to maintain a legal ratio between a cheaply manufactured subsidiary coin and the dollar of silver, which is the monetary basis.

Minting of the copper coin was begun in Kwangtung province in 1900. Its value was 10 cash, and it was intended to alleviate a shortage in this smaller and historic coin. The following year an Imperial edict ordered coastal and river provinces to follow the example set by Kwangtung. Figures of the total copper coinage to date are not obtainable, but from 1900 to December 31, 1917, the total of 10 cash pieces minted was 31,682,102,308 and in addition there were 20 cash pieces to the number of 386,292,308. The coin was supposed to contain 95 per cent. pure copper. As customarily minted, it contains 88.75 per cent. of copper, 8.80 per cent. of pewter and 2.45 per cent. of lead.

The following table gives exchange quotations at Shanghai between the copper and the silver dollar since 1912. The quotations are for the last day of the month:—

1912	June,	132.	1919	June,	135.5
	December,	123.		December,	136.
1913	June,	130.	1920	June,	138.
	December,	130.		December,	141.5
1914	June,	135.	1921	June,	150.3
	December,	139.		December,	154.6
1915	June,	139.	1922	June,	171.6
	December,	136.		December,	174.7
1916	June,	139.	1923	June,	178.4
	December,	127.		December,	181.6
1917	June,	131.	1924	June,	193.8
	December,	129.		December,	206.4
1918	June,	131.	1925	June,	—
	December,	132.9			

Comparative quotations given below show the trend in the exchange rate at Shanghai and at some other financial centers between December, 1918, and March 1, 1925:—

	December, 1918.	*February, 1921.*	*June, 1922.*	*March, 1925.*
Shanghai	132.57	143.70	171	217.00
Chefoo	134.70	145.70	175	247.40
Chinkiang	134.07	144.40	185	231.00
Hangchow	132.00	143.00	180	197.00
Hankow	138.47	151.50	182	264.00
Nanking	134.30	145.00	169	227.40
Ningpo	131.73	143.50	170	204.00
Soochow	132.55	143.00	177	210.00
Tientsin	137.82	148.40	176	280.00

APPENDIX VII.

Official Bank's Selling Rates for Telegraphic Transfer on London, as:—

Year	Highest	Lowest	Average	Year	Highest	Lowest	Average
1890	5/3⅛	4/2⅝	4/8⅞	1908	2/7	2/2⅜	2/4¾
1891	4/8½	4/2½	4/5½	1909	2/5¼	2/3½	2/3⅞
1892	4/2¾	3/8½	3/11⅝	1910	2/6⅜	2/3½	2/4$^{15}/_{16}$
1893	3/10⅜	3/1⅜	3/11⅝	1911	2/4	2/5⅞	2/4$^{15}/_{16}$
1894	3/1¾	2/7⅞	3/5⅞	1912	2/5$^{13}/_{16}$	2/10$^{7}/_{16}$	2/8⅝
1895	3/0⅞	2/8⅜	3/5⅞	1913	2/10$^{11}/_{16}$	2/6¾	2/8½
1896	3/1⅝	2/10⅝	2/10⅝	1914	2/7⅝	2/1⅞	2/5⅜
1897	2/11⅛	2/3¼	2/11⅞	1915	2/7¾	2/2¾	2/3⅞
1898	2/5⅜	2/8⅞	2/7$^{3}/_{16}$	1916	3/6½	2/6⅝	2/11$^{11}/_{16}$
1899	2/7	2/9⅛	2/8	1917	4/10½	3/3½	3/10⅜
1900	2/11¼	2/8	2/9⅝	1918	5/7	4/2½	4/8$^{11}/_{16}$
1901	2/10½	2/5	2/7¾	1919	7/10	4/6	5/7⅞
1902	2/6½	2/1¾	2/4	1920	9/3	3/11	6/1$^{7}/_{16}$
1903	2/7¼	2/1⅝	2/4½	1921	4/1½	2/11	3/6⅜
1904	2/8¾	2/3⅞	2/6½	1922	3/7½	3/0	3/4¼
1905	2/11	2/6⅛	2/8¾	1923	3/4	3/0	3/1½
1906	3/2	2/9½	2/11¾	1924	3/5¾	3/1¼	3/3$^{3}/_{16}$
1907	3/-	2/4⅝	2/8⅞	1925	3/3¼	3/0¼	3/1½

***N.B.*—Figures for the period from 1890–1918 have been compiled by Mr. H. F. Bell, while those from 1919 onwards are the author's compilation.**

Only the averages from 1919 onwards are real average rates, while the figures referring to previous years standing in the "average" column are merely the mean rate between highest and lowest.

GLOSSARY OF BANKING TERMS

CONTAINED IN THIS VOLUME AND NOT PREVIOUSLY DEFINED THERE.

ARBITRAGE is of Latin origin and is derived from the word "arbiter," meaning to estimate or to judge. It compares prices ruling in one market with those in another market in order to determine their difference with a view to benefiting thereby.

ARBITRATED RATES OF EXCHANGE are rates resultant from operations between two countries with a different monetary standard. By arbitrated rate of bullion is understood the relation between the quotations of gold or silver of a given fineness, as they exist at the same time in two different countries.

ASSAY means to test. An assay of bullion and metals in general is effected by chemical means.

BANK'S BUYING RATE is the quotation at which a bank stands ready to purchase foreign exchange against either local currency or the currency of a third country.

BANK DISCOUNT is interest taken in advance for the unexpired period of a written obligation. Discount rates are officially issued, and altered according to requirements by government banks, but discount transactions taking place in the market are merely guided by official quotations with which they do not always coincide.

BANK'S SELLING RATE is the price at which a bank offers to sell foreign currency,—either coin, cable transfer, sight or usuance drafts,—against local currency.

BANKER'S CREDIT is an authorisation of a bank in favor of an exporter to be drawn upon under certain clearly defined terms. Amount, usuance of drafts, time in force and other essentials are distinctly stipulated. If all the terms have been complied with, the bank undertakes to accept the draft or drafts and to pay its face value on due date to the holder in due course.

BAR GOLD see GOLD BARS.

BEAR is the name applied to a speculator in foreign exchange, stocks, bullion or merchandise, who anticipates a fall in one or more of these commodities, which he does not own. He therefore sells short for forward delivery, trusting to be able to buy at a lower price before settlement day; the eventual difference would represent his profit.

BILL OF EXCHANGE is an unconditional order made in writing by one party requesting another party to render payment to bearer or order, on a clearly stipulated future term, or at sight, of a certain amount of money. Such a document becomes a negociable instrument.

BIMETALLIC STANDARD denotes that a country has both gold and silver standard conjointly.

BROKER is a person who buys or sells on behalf of principals against a commission previously agreed upon.

BROKERAGE is the remuneration charged by brokers to their clients after having carried out their orders to buy or to sell on their behalf. The brokerage is usually a percentage on the total amount realised and is almost invariably stipulated beforehand.

BULL is the term for a speculator in shares, foreign exchange, bullion or merchandise, who expects a rise in any of these commodities. He thereupon buys for forward delivery, trusting to be able to sell out at a profit before the settlement day.

BULLION is the name for gold or silver in bars or in another distinct shape, except coins. Only if coins are shipped and/or sold by weight, instead of by count, they may also be termed bullion.

CABLE RATE is the quotation at which a bank is ready to transfer funds by telegram.

CANDAREEN is the one-hundredth part of a tael.

CHAIN RULE is a mechanical method of mathematics comparing two quantities depending on other known quantities. The grouping begins with a question on the left which leads to a series of equations following each other like the links of a chain. The typical condition is that the link on the right is followed by a link on the left calling for the same quantity; the last link must be of the same description as the link with which the chain was initiated.

Example:

? rupees	: 1 £
1 £	: 240 pence
18¼ pence	: 1 rupee

$$\frac{1 \times 240}{1 \times 18.25} = \mathit{13.15.}$$

CHEQUE is derived from *echecs,* chess. Originally it was spelled "check," in which form it is known to this day in the United States. In Europe the cheque was first employed about A.D. 1780, though it was used much before that time in China. Definition: a cheque is a bill of exchange payable at sight and drawn on a banking institution.

CHEQUE RATE is a term employed in connection with foreign exchanges, signifying the price at which a demand draft, or cheque drawn in a foreign currency, can be negociated.

COINAGE is the act of coining money from metals.

COMMISSION is the compensation charged by bankers (or others) for transactions carried through.

CREDITS is popularly used for "drafts drawn under bankers Letters of Credit."

CURRENCY this term was originally applied to the currency (the passing from hand to hand) of money. In modern times it denotes money itself, as fixed by law. There is metallic currency in vogue, as well as fiduciary (banknotes) currency.

CROSS-RATE is the quotation between two countries as viewed from a third country.

D/A denotes "documents deliverable against acceptance of a draft."

D/D stands for "demand draft." The term "draft" has no legal significance, but as it invariably is issued on a drawee, it partakes of the nature of either a cheque or a bill of exchange, payable on presentation.

DELIVERY as banking term for foreign exchange means the handing over of foreign against local currency, *i.e.,* the fulfilment of the terms of an exchange contract.

DEMONETISE means the withdrawal from circulation by law of coins and/or banknotes. Demonetised currency ceases to be legal tender.

DEPRECIATED CURRENCY means metal or paper currency circulating for less than its face value.

DISCOUNT is the sum deducted for the ready payment of a debt which is due at a future date. To discount a bill of exchange, due at a future date, means either to purchase or to sell a long bill at the present price, calculated at a clearly stipulated rate of discount.

DISCOUNTABLE refers to bills of exchange the drawee of which is of sufficiently good standing to permit its being discounted before maturity. While the standing of the acceptor forms the principal condition making a bill discountable, there are other factors which may prevent it, as for instance limitations as to negotiability, the currency, the domicile of the bill, the absence of a discount market, etc.

DOCUMENTARY BILL is a bill to which a set of shipping documents is appended, principally for the purpose of affording to the holder collateral security. These documents may be of a varied nature and comprise *inter alia* Bill of Lading, Invoice, Insurance Certificate, Weight Lists, Certificate of Origin, Consular Invoices, Health Certificate, etc.

D/P stands for "documents deliverable against payment of the draft."

DRAFT see D/D.

DRAWEE is the party mentioned in a bill of exchange to whom an order to pay is addressed.

DRAWER is the party who signs a bill of exchange as issuer, ordering a second party to render payment of a certain sum on a certain date.

DRAWING RATE is the quotation at which a bank will draw foreign currency; in other words, at the bank's selling rate.

EXCHANGE is used in various ways. It may mean trade in the sense of exchange of goods; or it may signify *Bourse,*—Stock Exchange. From the banker's point of view it is a synonym for the exchange of currencies,—foreign against local, or foreign against another kind of foreign currency.

FACE VALUE is the (nominal) amount appearing on the face of coins, banknotes, stocks and shares, etc.

FINENESS is the contents of pure metal in coins, bars or metallic amalgamations. The fineness is generally expressed in *per mille.*

FIRM OFFER is a definite offer, holding good for a clearly defined period.

FOREIGN EXCHANGES comprise all those transactions which have for their purpose the transfer of money from one country to another. When the foreign exchanges are favoring a country it means that specie will be about to be shipped to that country. Adverse foreign exchanges signify the necessity of exporting bullion abroad.

FORWARD PRICE is the quotation for delivery and payment at a future date.

FREE COINAGE is the privilege granted to the public to present standard metal to the mint for conversion there of current coins. Usually there is a charge made by the Mint for its services. Free coinage therefore does not denote that the money metal is converted into coin free of charge, but it signifies that it may be presented to the Mint without maximum limit.

FUTURE DELIVERY, when the term relates to foreign exchange, denotes a transaction in terms of which the seller agrees to deliver to the buyer a clearly stipulated sum of foreign currency at a designated future date at a price previously agreed upon.

GOLD BARS in the Occident are usually of a weight of 12½ kilos (400 ounces troy) and of a fineness of 0.996. About Gold Bars in China see Chapters III and IV.

GOLD BULLION is melted gold, refined and usually in the shape of bars. In the majority of cases an issuing bank's reserve will be held in part in gold bullion, refined to either tally with the country's legal standard, or else as near as possible 1000 fine.

GOLD EXCHANGE STANDARD is a system under which the local currency is convertible into the currency of a country which has the gold standard. The rate of exchange at which the conversion is effected is officially fixed and in normal times almost stationery.

GOLD MOVEMENTS are exports and/or imports of gold made with one of the following objects:—

(*a*) the payment of an indebtedness by one gold-using country to another; (*b*) the commercial movement of gold between one gold-using and non-gold-using country, or between two countries, both of which have not adopted the gold standard; (*c*) gold from the mining districts and also manufactured golden articles.

GOLD POINTS are the two limits beyond which the import and the export of gold between two countries with a gold standard begin to pay.

GOLD STANDARD means that the unit of the legalised currency in any form (be it silver or fiat money) into a fixed quantity of standard gold,—and also vice versa. The existence of a gold standard includes the free movement of gold in any shape to or from the country concerned.

GRESHAM'S LAW was created in the sixteenth century by Sir Thomas Gresham, who decreed: "If coins of the same metal, but of varying weight and quality circulate together at the same nominal value, the worse coins will tend to drive the better from circulation, but the better will never drive out the worse."

HEDGE is the counterpart of a prior speculation; as such it retains its speculative character but reduces the risk of the major speculation.

INCONVERTIBLE PAPER CURRENCY is represented by banknotes which cannot be exchanged for metal of the kind for which it calls; or even for a part of the face amount only.

INGOT is a bar or wedge of metal.

INTEREST is the service which money renders in its employment.

INTRINSIC VALUE. Strictly speaking the expression is not absolutely logical. The intrinsic value of a coin,—the value within itself,—is the market value of the metal contained in the coin.

Under certain conditions it may occur that in certain districts the metal contained in a coin is of no value at all, because it cannot be exchanged there for anything.

LEGAL TENDER is money in certain forms which is generally acceptable within the country as means of payment. Legal tender is money of such description which any person within the country is forced to accept in settlement of a liability; otherwise he will put himself in the wrong. The term of legal tender may be explained as an article which the law admits as valid for the discharge of a monetary obligation.

LETTER OF CREDIT is a document issued by a banker, authorising either another banker to negociate drafts drawn by a third party on the issuer; or authorising the party to whom it is addressed to draw on the issuing bank. Letters of Credit invariably contain stipulations as to the total amount, usuance of drafts, documents, validity, shipment of goods, etc., etc.

MACE is the tenth part of a tael.

MARGIN is a term employed in banking in various senses. It may mean the difference between the face amount of a loan and the value of the security. In foreign exchange it is used in the sense "margin of profit." Arbitragists refer to the difference between exchange quotations of the same denomination, as obtainable at one time in two different places, as "margin."

MARKET RATE is the price actually obtainable in the open market, as compared with official quotations. The term refers to shares, bonds, foreign currencies, discounts and commodities in general.

MATURITY means the date on which a bill of exchange becomes due for payment.

MINT the buildings where money is coined. The term is derived from the Latin word *Moneta,* a surname of Juno whose temple the Romans employed as a Mint.

MINT PAR is a figure expressing the number of the standard money units of one country which contain the same quantity of the identical precious metal as the standard money unit of the other country, provided both currency units contain the exact pure metal contents prescribed by law. There is no mint par between a gold-using country and another one with a silver standard,—or one with an inconvertible paper currency. The mint par between Great Britain and U.S.A., for example, is $4.8665 for 1 pound Sterling, which means that the latter contains exactly as many grains of pure gold as U.S. $4.8665. There exists, of course, also a mint par within a country in which two units of the same metal are in circulation. For instance, one can well speak of a mint par between the Shanghai sycee tael and the

Yuan Shih Kai dollar. The mint par between two countries with the same standard never varies, provided both countries maintain tl e same coinage laws.

MINT PRICE of gold is the quantity of gold coin which the Mint of a gold-standard country will pay per unit (kilogram, ounce), in return for gold bullion handed over to it for coinage. In determining the mint price the folowing factors come into consideration: the laws defining the standard of the monetary unit and the statutes establishing the system of free coinage, or fixing the coinage fees. There is no mint price for silver in gold-using countries.

MONEY is the standard by which the value of commodities is measured; is the article which is universally recognised as medium for their purchase and sale. The principal characteristic of money is that it is received without reliance upon the personal credit of the person offering it and that it is accepted without reference to an assay of its quality. There is standard money (gold) as well as representative money (fiat money).

NOMINAL means existing merely in name.

OPTION, when referring to foreign exchange, usually denotes the right to choose the day of delivery within the term originally agreed upon.

OVERBOUGHT, when relating to foreign exchange, means that one has bought more foreign currency than sold.

OVERSOLD, when relating to foreign exchange, denotes that sales of foreign currency exceed in volume the purchases of the identical currency, *i.e.*, there is an uncovered balance left open for future cover.

PAR OF EXCHANGE (see MINT PAR).

PARITY is the position between two rates of exchange at which the two record the same value-ratio. In a narrower sense money is at a parity whenever the actual value is maintaining itself exactly at its nominal value.

PREMIUM is a bounty on the basic price of any commodity as fixed by law or by the market. When the market value of stocks, shares, coins, etc., is higher than the nominal value, these commodities are said to be at a premium.

RATE OF EXCHANGE, the price of money current in one country expressed in the currency of another country.

REMEDIUM, (remedy) is the allowance made by law within which the national coinage is permitted to deviate from the prescribed standard—weight and fineness.

REMITTING RATE is the rate at which a bank can remit foreign currency, *i.e.,* the bank's buying quotation for foreign currency.

SEIGNIORAGE is the charge made by the Mint for coinage. In another meaning it is used to indicate the profit derived by the government from the production of subsidiary and token coins.

SETTLEMENT DAYS are the days fixed by the Exchanges, on which engagements in shares, bonds, foreign exchange and commodities are squared.

SPECIE is derived from the Latin word *specio,* to look. By it is meant visible metallic money, as distinguished from paper money.

SPOT denotes ready delivery.

STANDARD MONEY is the form of money with which all others are kept at a parity.

STANDARDING is the determination of the quantity of standard metal producible from the gross weight, according to its fineness, as per official assay.

T.T. stands for Telegraphic Transfer. It means that funds are remitted by cable.

THREE-CORNERED ARBITRAGE, also known as compound arbitrage. It refers to exchange between two countries produced by remittances through an intermediary country in any other than direct paper of that country.

TOKEN MONEY consists of subsidiary coins the intrinsic value of which is below the face value.

TOLERANCE (see REMEDIUM).

USUANCE is the period for which a bill of exchange is to run.

SUBJECT INDEX.

CORRIGENDA

Page 15, line 13 from top *for* \$20 *read* \$10.

Page 15, line 14 „ „ *for* \$10 *read* \$20.

Page 46, line 20 „ „ *for* "At a later stage will be found a complete transaction, etc." *read* "At a later stage will be found a complete translation, etc."

Page 70, line 5 from top *for* "During the first eight months, etc." *read* "During the entire year of 1925 shipments of gold bars from Shanghai to the United States amounted to only 4604 ounces, valued at U.S. \$100,171, as against 142,394 ounces, valued at U.S. \$3,844,238 during 1924."

Page 171, line 14 from bottom *for* "In the autumn of 1914, etc." *read* "In the Autumn of 1924, etc."

Page 271, line 14 from bottom *for* "100 Canton Taels, etc." *read* "100,000 Canton taels, etc."

Page 286, line 4 from top *for* "with the buyer of gold currency" *read* "with the buyer of foreign currency."

ADDENDA

Page 24 1925 . . . 3*s.*/5⅞*d.*

„ 159

	1925
	Pence
Highest	33 7/16
Lowest	31 1/16
Range	2⅜
Average	32⅛

Page 206 (*d*) *Import of bar silver into Shanghai.*

	1925
From U.S.A.	43,034 bars
„ *London*	12,033 „
Re-shipments	8,075 „